The Jews of Poland

The Jewish Publication Society of America

Philadelphia   5736 / 1976

The Jews of Poland

A Social and
Economic History
of the Jewish Community
in Poland from 1100 to 1800
by Bernard D. Weinryb

copyright © 1972 by
The Jewish Publication Society of America
All rights reserved
Second edition, 1976
ISBN 0–8276–0016–X
Library of Congress catalog card number 72–12178
Manufactured in the United States of America
The publication of this book
was made possible through the cooperation
of the Memorial Foundation for Jewish Culture

For Doris—
wife and co-worker

Preface

The first documented information on a Jewish community in Poland dates from the end of the twelfth century, though individual Jews may have been there earlier. Their number gradually increased for about three hundred years. By the end of the fifteenth century it had reached between ten and fifteen thousand, a more significant figure in those times than it would be today. Immigration and natural growth augmented their numbers manyfold in the next century and a half. During and after the catastrophe in the wake of the Chmielnicki cossack uprising in 1648, Jews from Poland began emigrating westward. They settled first in neighboring Silesia and Bohemia and in Germany. Some of them went as far as Amsterdam, Hamburg, and even London. In the subsequent centuries they moved farther westward—overseas to the Americas—and eastward, to Russia and some to Palestine.

Beginning with the middle of the seventeenth century and continuing for about a hundred years, emigration from Poland trickled slowly into Germany and Rumania, and spilled over into Russia and Hungary in the second half of the eighteenth century. Throughout the nineteenth century and up to the outbreak of World War II, East European Jewry—actually Polish Jews and their descendants—infused new blood into the small West European Jewish communities and "colonized" Great Britain, the United States, Canada, Argentina, Brazil, and other Latin American states, as well as South Africa and Palestine. By the middle of the twentieth century, when the world was recuperating from the Nazi holocaust, the descendants of Polish Jewry constituted the bulk of world Jewry, forming the backbone of the large Jewish communities in the United States and the USSR, the Jewish population of the newly founded State of Israel, and the Jewish settlements in Latin America, South Africa, and England. The Polish Jewish (or East European Jewish) religious and secular traditions, the cultural values and way of life—or rudiments and derivatives thereof —prevailed among most Ashkenazic Jews the world over. The small remnant in Poland after World War II, numbering a few score thousand, was further depleted mainly by emigration.

The beginnings, growth, gathering of strength, expansion, creation of cultural and ideological values and of a way of life, dispersion, suffering, catastrophe, and decline of Polish Jewry during these seven or eight centuries did not take place in a vacuum or in isolation. They occurred in the setting of the Polish land and the Polish state, home of the Poles and others of various ethnic and racial backgrounds. Two peoples rarely live side by side for long without experiencing some friction. In Poland, too, tensions, quarrels, assault, arbitrary interference by authorities and ruling groups, and other disturbances at times outweighed the support tendered the Jews by high-minded liberal groups or given them for political, pecuniary, or other reasons. These were the trends that formed the background for the internal cohesion, organizational strength, mutual help, hopes, and beliefs of Polish Jewry.

This book tells the story of Polish Jewry. It traces the growth of a group of Jews numbering perhaps no more than a few score people to a community of millions. It records their struggle for existence—sometimes for life itself—within the framework and at times *against* the framework of the sociopolitical environment of the country and of the world, and depicts their way of life, their dispersion and final decline, and the heritage they left behind.

Every historical situation is complex and fraught with contradictions, and the case of a minority such as the Jews is probably particularly complicated. Jewish history in Poland, like the history of any minority generally, is the outcome of two processes that sometimes run parallel and sometimes cross or conflict. One process is Poland's own development of her land and people, and her relations with the outer world. Expanding or shrinking, disintegrating or being reconstructed, struggling to subsist or living in abundance, at peace or at war, enjoying internal accord or suffering tensions, riddled by prejudice or strengthened by spiritual growth, the country formed the spatial-temporal background for the Jews and their development.

The second pertinent process is the internal Jewish development, the progression of the Jewish community based on a communal heritage and values, shared interests, beliefs, and commitments. The course of this development was of necessity influenced by the community's absorption and transformation of the environmental "signals" and its reactions both positive and negative, to external stimuli in accordance with its specific needs. This involved accommodating to the environment, yet attempting to preserve group cohesiveness; it meant absorbing values, behavior patterns, and techniques from the environment (either in their original form and content or through Judaization) and combining them with the Jewish heritage and the influences emanating from Jews in other countries. The result was a crisscrossing of ways, parallel developments and trends, as well as differences.

Decisive events in Polish history caused crises in Jewish life, too. But the Jews did not always react to them in the same way as did their neighbors. Experiences did not necessarily affect the Jews and Poles identically. There were almost always trends and developments in Jewish life that differed, at times a little, at other times a great deal, from those of the host country.

When a minority is new to a country it is not evenly distributed among all social classes and economic positions. Finding sources of livelihood already occupied and social positions established and monopolized, newcomers are forced to adapt themselves to infertile ground, to sources of income yet untapped or not fully developed. They may have recourse to their former experience and know-how or to their contacts abroad. For a considerable period they will engage in a limited number of socioeconomic pursuits, to which they will apply themselves with extra zeal.

The majority will tolerate the minority as long as its members do not infringe upon their own positions. But should changed conditions or population growth cause a real or imagined infringement, or should the infertile ground of the minority become fertile and more attractive, a struggle for space may ensue, and each group will do its utmost to gain the upper hand. The majority group may employ political force, discrimination, legal limitations, and sometimes even mob action. The minority tries to compete by offering better services, improved means of production, and innovations; or it may resort to persuasion. If all these fail, it is forced to fall back upon other infertile ground in an attempt to develop it.

Hence the socioeconomic life of a minority such as the Jews is often more restricted and one-sided than that of the other inhabitants of a country, but it may be more intense and more successful within the limited areas. Since members of such a minority are concentrated in certain sectors (in which they sometimes assume a dominant position) but are poorly represented in others, they appear to be different from the rest of the population. The narrower occupational range and the difference in social position and structure also contribute to development along distinctive lines, which often diverge from those of the majority. The tendency to turn inward toward one's own group is heightened. Thus in socioeconomic life, often in political and legal situations, and in the cultural-spiritual-religious sphere, the patterns of the minority are not identical with those of the majority.

The life pattern of the Jews in the Diaspora is conditioned not only by the natural and social environment of the country of residence, but also by their own social environment—by their heritage, skills, adaptability, and cohesiveness. As a minority they absorb elements of their environment, but they are also conditioned by the heritage of their own history, religion, and culture, as well as by the possibility of contacts with their places of origin and kindred Jewish groups. This leads to a distinctive Jewish existence, which in the case of Polish Jewry embodied elements of both Jewishness and Polishness. Jewish history in Poland thus deals with these two processes: Polish history and Jewish life, often with emphasis on the latter.

But there is also a third dimension to the history of the Jews in Poland, namely, their relations with the Jews in other countries. As an outgrowth of European Ashkenazic Jewry, Polish Jewry was at first guided by the mores of the parent group, especially because Polish Jewry was absorbing intellectual and other elements from Western Jewish communities. Later, Polish Jews influenced Jewish communities in other countries, while still being in turn affected by them. Contacts and interaction with these other communities continually created some feeling of unity and perpetuated the concept of Jewish peoplehood, of which Polish Jewry ultimately became a vital factor.

This tridimensional character of Polish Jewish history (Poland–Polish Jewry–world Jewry) inevitably increases the complexity of the historian's task. Writing history does not mean packing the narrative with wild guesses and speculation.

Although imagination is a valuable asset in reconstructing the past, it is useful only when tested by factual historical evidence. In attempting to re-create the past a historian must remain as near to life situations as possible; his primary responsibility is to consult source materials and to weigh their evidence accurately, while vigorously applying the critical method. Today this involves not only historical-mindedness— the employment of techniques of internal and external text criticism—but also an awareness of the achievements of psychological and sociological research during the last half century. In dealing with records he must be on guard against disguises, sublimation, rationalization, transference, projection, and displacement. He must also take into account that in time each society develops a ritualistic language, a traditional phraseology, which becomes part of ritual but has little or no actual meaning. He must realize, too, that the same word, or the same concept in most cases, means very different things when used by differently situated persons. This opens the way to a clearer understanding of the records. It is also helpful to realize that in every society there is a difference between ideas and conduct, between principle and practice. It is well to beware of clichés, and to note that while religious metaphors are often borrowed to express profane sentiments, simple actions and mundane expressions may sometimes bear witness to a religious or intellectual state of mind.

The author has tried to blend into one picture the very small and the very large. He has attempted to capture the special situation of each period, to convey some idea of how it must have felt to live at that time. He has attempted to understand actions and attitudes from within, from the position of the various actors and groups in this life drama of coexistence. For this purpose it became necessary to concentrate somewhat on analysis of stresses and strains, to avoid undue parochialism, and to set the story in a broader context by combining the "inside" with the "outside." He hopes thus to have achieved some relative objectivity and to have dispelled certain myths.

It would be unfair to take the spoken or written word—the main sources of historical writings—at face value. For the historian the important things should be what people did and why, so that we may appreciate their thoughts and reasons.

This leads to another point. Written history often relies on extreme examples or on verbal pronouncements, or it deals only with certain selected details ("There is no truth except in details," averred the French historian Fustel de Coulanges). But neither extreme cases nor details alone can ascertain how representative the facts are or uncover the meaning of verbal statements of vital importance for the historian. The facts of history, being mostly fragmentary, elusive, and subjective, cannot be dealt with in isolation. They have to be seen in totality, in their relatedness and correspondence. Only a "macrohistory" that deals with total pictures instead of with small parts of the picture can help us avoid the fallacies caused by fragmentation. Such an approach often enables us to differentiate between practice and preaching, between deed and idea, action and thought, and to distinguish the essential from the accidental, the salient practice of many from the prohibitions imposed by state, church, or other institutions. Life in the past was more vivid and diversified than is indicated by the rules of conduct that were written down. The attempt made here to forgo the fragmentation of history in favor of macrohistory seems to open up some new vistas of historical understanding.

One of the main purposes of this book is to humanize Jewish history in Poland. The author sees the Jews not in terms of black or white, saints or sinners, angels or devils, but rather as human beings acting and reacting humanly to the exigencies of life with courage, high ideals, beliefs, and sacrifices on the one hand, and with weakness, frailty, passions, ambitions, and digressions on the other.

This preface would not be complete without some technical statements. Synthetic comprehensive historical works are usually based on available monographs and studies rather than on original research in primary sources. While working on this project the author made the discovery that in this field many sources had been misquoted or misinterpreted. For this reason it seemed imperative to refer to primary source materials wherever possible. (The outcome of one such search is related in the little book *Beginnings of East European Jewry*, 1962.) But in some instances it was technically impossible to do this, and in others the sources had been destroyed in World War II. Every effort was made to utilize the accessible sources, but reluctantly the author had to rely also on secondary accounts in many cases. At times he had even to quote an author who in other instances has proved to be inaccurate. Such quotations have been used mostly when the "fact" appeared to be a historical probability. The situation improves as the narrative becomes fuller and approaches the modern period, and the necessity of relying on other authors' writings diminishes. Here a great part of the findings are based on the writer's original research, which has continued for more than a quarter of a century, some of it published in earlier studies and papers.

The result—this book—may not always agree with my predecessors' interpretations or evaluations of a source, but in most such cases I have tried to avoid filling the recital with unnecessary polemics, preferring to present my own version. Only in the case of an entirely incorrect quotation or a major problem has a comment been made, usually in a note. Limited space necessitated sparing use of notes and titles listed in the Bibliography. I have avoided bibliographical excursus, particularly where listings would simply repeat what is already noted in other publications.

In the course of a long period of research and work in libraries and archives in Breslau, Berlin, Warsaw, Jerusalem, New York, and elsewhere, I was fortunate in receiving a great deal of friendly help and cooperation. A list of all who have come to my aid would be too cumbersome and might cause unpleasantness for some in Eastern Europe. Suffice it here to mention only the Columbia University and the Jewish Theological Seminary libraries in New York City, the Hebrew Union College Library in Cincinnati, Harvard University Library, and the libraries of the Dropsie University of Philadelphia and Yeshiva University of New York City. Some of these libraries waived official requirements in placing rare materials for prolonged times at my disposal.

I am also indebted to the Social Science Research Council for traveling grants and a Faculty Fellowship, the Lucius Littauer Foundation, the Kohut Foundation Fund, and the Mina and Louis Epstein Fund of the American Academy for Jewish Research for research grants. The Conference on Jewish Claims against Germany —now the Memorial Foundation for Jewish Culture—contributed toward the printing costs. To all these, and others not named here, I offer my sincere thanks.

Volume 2, *The Jews of Poland: Economic Life and Society,* is now being prepared for publication.

Contents

Tables

The Jews of Poland

Introduction: The Background

Eastern Europe is a term that came to designate a huge area of over three million square miles stretching approximately from the Elbe or Oder rivers and the Carpathian Mountains in the west to the Ural Mountains (where Asia begins) in the east, and from the Baltic Sea in the north to the Black Sea in the south.[1] Throughout prehistoric and early historic centuries many racial and ethnic groups from the East (Asia) and, in part, from the West tried to force their way in various directions through this area. Others came from the south through the Balkans and Black Sea shores. All these peoples—the Scythians, Sarmatians, Greeks, Goths, Alans, Huns, Avars, Antes, the Slavic tribes, Balts, Ugro-Finns, Bulgars, Khazars, Tatars, and others—invaded territories simultaneously or at different times, formed political structures, and either organized whole regions or colonized certain areas (like the Greek colonies on the northern Black Sea shores), only to disintegrate or be driven out by new invaders. Still others came later as colonizers or immigrants—Germans, Valons, Italians, Jews, and Armenians.

Most of the many races and groups that passed through or lived in the East European area either left remnants behind when they moved away or themselves settled there permanently. Some of them became dominant in the region during the first millennium c.e. Various Slavic tribes concentrated in the west, the east, and the southeast. Around the tenth century c.e. western and eastern Slavic tribes formed Czech, Polish, and Russian states, respectively, in the western parts of Eastern Europe and in the southern and central regions. Poland and Russia evolved from these states. In the northwest, meanwhile, the Lithuanians organized a political structure of their own.

Poland

Throughout most of the country's thousand-year history Poland has remained a vague concept geographically and ethnographically. Apparently derived from the name of the tribe Polanie (field-dwellers, from the Slavic *pole*, which means field), the name Poland was first used to designate western Slavic tribes living in the western parts of Eastern Europe, roughly between the basins of two rivers, the Oder and the Vistula, and bounded on the south by the ridges of the Carpathian Mountains. With the passing centuries other tribes and groups were absorbed, while part of the original population was lost. At times the region formed a polyglot, multinational state. These and other changes paralleled the shifting political boundaries of the periods in question: "In the course of its history Poland has taken a large number of different forms. Almost every century has seen its territory modified and the political lines that bounded it changed."[2]

Located in east-central Europe, Poland was hemmed in by sometimes flourishing and sometimes declining neighbors. The German states (or German Empire) lay to the west, the Lithuanian tribes to the northeast, and to the east and southeast were the eastern Slavs, founders of the Russian state. As a result of both external and internal pressures and counterpressures, Poland underwent alternate processes of expansion and contraction—sometimes to the west and sometimes to the east or to the north, the Baltic Sea region, or the southeast, the Ukraine.

Beginning with the second half of the tenth century the Polish Piast dynasty attempted to consolidate the new state. This led to the coronation in 1025 of Boleslas the Brave (in Polish, Boleslaw Chrobry), 992–1025. Subsequent dissension among his sons reversed the trend. Separatist tendencies resulted in a division of the country into small duchies (among them Silesia in the west, Great Poland in the north, Little Poland in the south, and Mazovia in the east), some of which were in time further subdivided into petty principalities. Poland was not consolidated into a large state until the second half of the fourteenth century (except for the semi-independent duchies of Mazovia and Silesia). The last ruler of the Piast dynasty, Casimir III, later known as Casimir the Great (1333–70), built up a united state.

Meanwhile, the strength of the western neighbors had increased and they absorbed some adjacent Polish lands (in the fourteenth century most of Silesia came under Bohemian-German sovereignty); this resulted in the Poles' pressing in the opposite direction, toward the east and southeast. This became pronounced after the union with Lithuania in 1386, a loose personal union sharing the same ruler which was formalized in 1569.

After the Mongol invasion in the thirteenth century, Lithuania had absorbed western and southern Russian lands. When Lithuania amalgamated with Poland in 1569 a large united state was formed, embracing Poland, Lithuania, and Ruthenia (the Ukraine, meaning "borderlands"); this expanded farther eastward and absorbed some Russian territories. At the beginning of the seventeenth century an attempt was even made to turn the Moscow state into a Polish satellite. As the Muscovite Russian state began to gain strength and expand, it exerted increasing pressure upon eastern Poland until, following the cossack uprising in the mid-seventeenth century, a part of the Ukraine went to Russia. Somewhat more than a century later, in 1772, Poland lost some of its territory to its eastern and western neighbors (the first partition by Russia, Prussia, and Austria), and less than twenty-five years after that was deprived of all independence when it was partitioned by the same neighbors in 1793 and 1795.

After more than a century under the domination of the three states—with some parts enjoying a certain autonomy at times or brief periods of semi-independent statehood—following World War I Poland was restored as an independent state, regaining most of its historical territory. After again being invaded by both neighbors —Nazi Germany and Soviet Russia—during World War II it was reconstituted after the war as a state falling within the Eastern (that is, the Russian) sphere of influence and was shifted geographically westward. The eastern provinces, comprising some 69,856 square miles, went to Russia, and Poland was compensated for this loss by the decisions of the Yalta and Potsdam conferences (1945) to give her territory taken from Germany (Silesia, Pomerania, and parts of eastern Prussia). While the final determination of Poland's western frontiers was left to a future peace conference (which so far has not materialized), the former German territories up to the Oder-Western Neisse line—about forty thousand square miles—remained under the administration of the Polish state. More recently, in 1970, the West German treaties with Poland and Soviet Russia recognized Poland's western borders. These treaties were ratified in May 1972. Meanwhile, Poland had resettled this area with Poles repatriated from the eastern parts after it was emptied of German population, who left voluntarily or were evicted.

For most of these centuries the shifting borders and other factors were causing changes in Poland's ethnic structure. Colonization by Germans in the thirteenth and fourteenth centuries gave the cities a German character, at least for a while. The united kingdom of Casimir the Great in the fourteenth century, and the Polish-Lithuanian united empire of the subsequent centuries harbored an ethnically polyglot population. It comprised Poles, Lithuanians, Ukrainians, Armenians, Tatars, Germans, and Jews, as well as some Frenchmen and Italians.

In the century and a half of foreign rule on Polish lands, Germans and Russians settled in the western and eastern parts respectively, partly as a result of a deliberate policy of colonization and depolonization on the part of the ruling states. In the reconstituted post-World War I Poland, about one-third of the population was ethnically of non-Polish origin. In the course of World War II and the postwar years Poland became largely monolithic ethnically. Extermination of the Jews by the Nazis, the ceding of eastern Poland to Russia, the expulsion of the Germans from the newly acquired western parts, and population exchanges left only a very small segment of minorities in the country (about 1.5 percent in 1963, compared with 31.1 percent in 1931).

Geography and Economics

Geographically, Poland was originally mostly a large plain comprising marshlands and meadows; a large part of it was covered by forests and crisscrossed by rivers, most of them navigable. The roads that existed were passable only part of the year. Winter snowstorms, fall rains, melting ice and snow, and the swollen rivers in the spring turned many roads into traps for wheeled wagons and their passengers. The only mountains, the Carpathian, were on the western and southern fringes, and Poland had only occasional access to the sea (the Baltic and to some extent the Black Sea) in the course of her history.

Situated on a plain, the country was exposed to enemy attacks and raids, but by the same token it was in a favorable position to stage its own raids into the territory of a weaker neighbor. The abundance of soil, water, woods, and their products determined the direction of the country's economy: trade in agricultural products —grain, cattle, fish, fur, linen, timber—some of which were exported. Some of these products were reprocessed by craftsmen, both for local use and for limited export. Among these were tanners and furriers, brewers and meadmakers, mill and sawmill workers. Ashes, potash, tar, charcoal, and shingles were produced in the forests. Of the mining products, rock salt from the mines of Wieliczka and Bochnia and the saline springs in Red Russia should be mentioned. Salt played an important role in the Middle Ages and early modern times, both as a commodity on the local market and for export. Other products, produced mostly on a small scale, were lead, silver, iron, glass, and metalware.

On the other hand a certain isolation and backwardness resulted from Poland's geography. She lacked communications, and had little contact with world trade routes. During the Middle Ages an indirect route or two ran through the south to some of the markets in the Orient. In the west a road from Hungary through Poland formed a link with German markets. A sea route through the Baltic was opened, used mainly after the second half of the fifteenth century. These routes afforded opportunities to export agricultural goods, import manufactured ones, and engage in some transit trade. This even led to periods of prosperity. But these conditions did not become a vital factor in inducing sustained economic growth. The concentration of the main international trade routes, first in the Mediterranean and later (after the sixteenth century) in the Atlantic states, left an inland—at least in relation to these routes and seas—country such as Poland little chance for economic growth. Increased industrial production had to await the nineteenth century, when a huge hinterland market in Russia served as one incentive for the development of the Polish textile industry.

Social Structure

Poland's sociopolitical structure passed through stages resembling, but not entirely identical with, those experienced by some other European states. In Western Europe, either concurrently with feudal formations or after them, self-governing cities and towns arose, with their artisans' guilds, merchant associations, and patriciates, some of which became city-states. In many of them, and in other small states, power was later concentrated in the hands of more or less absolute rulers or oligarchies. Commercial and industrial developments resulted in economic growth and further stratification of society.

The trends in Poland, however, differed in some respects from those in the rest of Europe. Poland did not attain the stage of consolidation into an absolute state. The death in 1370 of Casimir the Great, the last male in the Piast line, began a series of developments that made the throne dependent, first on agreements with the nobility and later on the nobility's election of a king. Thus the king became dependent upon the nobility, the ruling elite. In an effort to counteract their weakening position, some kings embarked on political, dynastic, or economic ventures of their own. These were not always in the country's best interests.

Nobility

The nobility comprised several segments: the large landowners (the magnates), the middle knighthood, and the minor gentry (the *szlachta* or squires). An early aim of the nobility was to free their estates from the rule of the judicial, administrative, and fiscal authority of the state by a legal form that became known as immunity (a sort of independence from the king or prince). Beginning with the fourteenth century, as each successive dynasty expired, or even upon the death of a king, the next ruler was obliged to pander to the nobility to insure their support. Starting in 1374 the nobility received one charter after another exempting them from most taxes, promising them positions, establishing a parliament of nobles *(sejm),* and limiting the king's right to introduce new legislation *(nihil novi,* 1505).

Thus the nobility became the state's major force. The king was assigned a secondary role. In practice he lost his power to the rich magnates—who built up for themselves virtually independent economic sovereignties and semistates and often maintained private armies—as well as to the lower nobility, whose support he needed both in war and in peace. The magnates and the *szlachta* both placed private, local, and regional interests before national loyalties. In the seventeenth and eighteenth centuries this hampered development of an effective system of central political institutions.

This fragmentation of power meant that the pressure of city burghers for more and more monopolistic privileges and the efforts of the nobility to maintain the privileged status of agriculture stifled any possibility of economic development; this in a country that needed changes in order to keep up with the shifting of world trade routes farther west to European countries located on the Atlantic and with the fluctuation in the trade in Poland's agricultural goods for the European market. Nor could this weak central government reorganize and modernize the state and the army for defense against the two powers rising on either side of Poland: Brandenburg-Prussia and Russia. Such circumstances contributed to the country's final downfall.

Church

Besides the nobility, the Catholic Church, too, became a strong, influential power in the country. Originally transplanted from Germany, the church evolved into a national Polish institution, fostering polonization, Polish culture, and other patriotic causes. As an institution it had received privileges from the princes in the centuries of Polish particularism and continued to be favored by the kings. The bishops, princes of the church, shared the privileged position of the nobility, from which they usually originated. They drew further strength from the fact that during the Middle Ages and even later some of them held the highest positions in the state. The lower clergy played its part by exerting a great influence on the masses. They fostered the people's aims, at times supporting their causes in a frenzy of religious or nationalist fervor, or both; they cultivated religious and group chauvinism, which occasionally turned into xenophobia leading to attacks upon "heretics": non-Catholics or non-Poles, and Jews.

A residue of the church's strength in Poland has lasted right up to the present day. During the century or so of political subjugation, the Polish Church served as a stronghold of Polonism and of conservative and ethnocentric nationalism. The same is true for the interwar years. In Communist dominated post-World War II Poland, as well, the church has remained an influential power with which even the Communist party leaders have had to reckon.

Cities

Beginning with the thirteenth century, the existing Polish cities underwent changes, and some new ones were founded in the course of German colonization. From then on the cities were mostly based on German law (called also Magdeburg Law), by which they gained autonomy, and the princes' power over them was considerably weakened. Other paraphernalia of the city-system were also either transferred from the West or emulated in Poland. They included such features as exclusiveness, the principle of acquired rights, organization in guilds and merchant associations, and stratification. The result was cleavages between the patriciate and the rich merchants who constituted the city government, on one hand, and on the other, the shopkeepers and artisans, who, although they too were entitled to citizenship rights (cives), for the most part played second fiddle. The third and lowest group consisted of workers and domestics, people without permanent employment, the plebes (mob), who had no citizenship rights at all (they were regarded as dwellers, incolae) but usually supported the middle group in its struggle against the patricians.

In Poland this struggle had a special angle: ethnic, religious, and nationalist issues were superimposed upon or connected with the social stratification. The patricians were originally mainly Germans (the middle group was partially German) and the plebes were predominantly Polish. The ensuing ethnic-national tensions, the relatively late organization of the guilds and merchant associations, and the strong political position of the antagonistic Polish nobility contributed to the failure of the cities to become a powerful factor in the state. Only in Pomerania and Silesia, where the German element had a dominant position, did the city population early achieve considerable development, and there they played a political role.[3]

The Peasants

The peasants constituted the bulk of the population in medieval Poland, about 70 percent or more. Originally some of them may have been freemen and some unfree (war prisoners and people unable to pay their debts), but in time most peasants became tenants of the lord, who was regarded as the owner of the land, as in the feudal system of Western Europe. With the German colonization, beginning in the second half of the thirteenth century, new settlements grew up with a different legal status, and older ones converted to the new system. This brought a change in the peasants' situation. Generally a new settler received a portion of land (168–242 hectares), in return for which (after a few "free years") he was obliged to pay a certain annual sum in cash and the rest in gifts (eggs, chickens, cheese, and the like) for holidays or other occasions. Such a peasant was regarded as a freeman with the right to move away. In the villages settled on the basis of German law the peasants gained a certain autonomy, with a council presided over by the bailiff. This council served as a court of first instance for the peasants.

With the growth of grain export in the fifteenth century a considerable number of estates began to be transformed into a manorial system, producing grain and other agricultural products for the market. The tenancy system, based on rents or some labor, or both, was changed into a system of servitude, of serf labor amounting to two or three days a week, as well as the duty of transporting grain to market, and other services. The peasants finally lost legal protection in 1518, when the king ceased to consider their complaints against the lords. The peasants now remained virtually at the mercy of the lords, who decided on the levies to be imposed upon them in the form of services and the use of monopolies and held jurisdiction over them. The lords often misused their privileges to exploit the peasants subject to their whims.

This abuse was only slightly tempered by the tenets of customary law, a nominal peasants' self-government consisting of a nominated bailiff and elected aldermen. The Polish peasant remained a serf, limited in his right of movement until the 1860s.

The Jews

This was the geographic and sociopolitical framework to which Jewish life in Poland had to adapt. Immigrating as individuals and in tiny groups (some in the twelfth century but mainly in the thirteenth century and later) during the epoch of Polish particularism, the Jews at first settled in the west (Silesia, Pomerania, Great and Little Poland) under the protection of the princes. At first they apparently formed a few isolated islands. The consolidation of the Polish state in the fourteenth century brought some uniformity into the Jewish situation, accompanied apparently by new immigration. But their total number was still very small, amounting possibly to a few thousand persons or less* (out of a total estimated population of 1¼–2

---

*As a parallel it should be mentioned that at the beginning of the nineteenth century, 150 years after the start of Jewish settlement in America, there were only about twenty-five hundred Jews in the United States.

million). In the following centuries of consolidation and growth of the Polish state, its expansion toward the east was accompanied by an increase in Jewish population, though this increase was slow at first.

In some respects the kings favored the Jews. For economic and other reasons they granted Jews rights (privileges) for settlement and economic activity. They also gave them certain autonomous rights that were similar to the ones they had in the West (and like those of another minority in Poland—the Armenians). As the power of the kings decreased, the Jews became more vulnerable to political and even physical attack by their main adversaries in the older settlements, the large royal cities. The burghers and artisans succeeded in partially ousting them, or at least limiting their activities.

But there was another side to the change in the power relations. The rise of the church and the nobility, particularly the latter, signified a new opportunity for the Jews. In their attempt to build up their own estates and enlarge their incomes, noblemen and some bishops rented to Jews houses they owned near or even inside the cities, the strongholds of the burghers, or else they founded new cities and towns that they opened to Jews; in later centuries they encouraged the Jews to settle in their villages.

Living in the villages as innkeepers and as managers of the lords' estates and collectors of revenues, the Jews came into close contact with the most numerous and most exploited sector of the Polish population—the peasants. The Jew became the middleman between the lord and the peasant, partly as a handmaid of the former, partly fulfilling some functions for the latter (selling to him and buying from him). In time the Jews became entrenched in the villages (mostly in the southeastern areas) and to some extent became identified by the peasant with the exploiter—the landlord—while at the same time culturally they were growing somewhat nearer to the peasants. Both these developments were bound to have repercussions in subsequent centuries.

Neither the nobles nor the churchmen were essentially pro-Jewish; their activities and attitudes took various directions. The church's anti-Jewish tendencies and policies, fostered by its numerous organizations, may often have outweighed the advantages church leaders offered the Jews. But in the case of the nobility, the occasional excess by an eccentric nobleman in mistreating a Jew (after 1539 Jews living in villages or towns belonging to a nobleman—or the church—were also under their jurisdiction) was several times counterbalanced by the opportunities for settlement and economic favors they offered to the Jews. This was especially true during the epoch of intensified eastward expansion of the Polish state, when many magnates acquired very large estates. These and other opportunities enabled the tiny Jewish groups of the fifteenth century to grow, through natural increase and immigration, during the following century and a half, to expand to new areas, and to entrench themselves in economic and status-raising positions in the country. As the Jewish population reached the "take-off period"—to use a modern economic term signifying a stage when enough resources are available for the beginning of continuous development—growth became to some extent self-sustained, and the expansion of the Jewish population continued even during the century or so of Poland's decline. On the eve of the Polish partitions some three-quarters of a million Jews lived in Poland and Lithuania, constituting about 10 percent of the country's total population. At that time Polish Jewry comprised the largest single group in world Jewry.

The Actual Jew and the Theological Jew

Several factors favored Polish Jewry's increasing numbers and importance even prior to the seventeenth and eighteenth centuries, when West European Jews also began to develop. In economically backward Poland the Jews, being an urban element, were able to make themselves useful economically and organizationally.

During the Middle Ages the great power of the monarchs in some West European countries (England and France) contributed to the wholesale expulsion of Jews from their land. In others (such as Germany) the strength of the cities helped get some Jewish groups expelled while those who could remain, mostly temporarily, were humiliated.

In Poland royal power may have been too weak to afford Jews full protection, but by the same token it was incapable of fully enforcing whatever anti-Jewish regulations were introduced. The burghers of the royal cities in Poland tried to apply the Western principle of acquired rights by supplementing the limitations imposed by nature with such manmade restrictive practices as monopolizing sources of income through guilds and merchant associations. But these associations, coming late to Poland, were not strong enough to exclude Jews completely from the cities. At the same time hundreds and thousands of noblemen had opened their doors to Jews in towns and villages. Here both the commercial background and the organizational talents of the Jews enabled them to engage in gainful activity. Trade, moneylending, tax and revenue farming, and estate leaseholding are usually the most profitable occupations in an agricultural country. Engaging in these occupations had made it possible for a number of Jews to become wealthy as early as the sixteenth century (and possibly earlier).

Unlike their counterparts in West European countries, the Jews in Poland did not confine themselves to lending money; even more often they borrowed it to support their enterprises. Being not only creditors of non-Jews but to a considerable degree also their debtors placed the Polish Jews in a different situation from those in the West. The European custom of canceling debts to Jews and even expelling those to whom one was indebted was hardly applicable here. Once the Jews and their kehilla (community) owed considerable amounts to non-Jews, the latter—nobles, churchmen, monasteries, and churches—were interested in their welfare and in keeping them in Poland. (Documentary evidence of this concern comes mainly from the eighteenth century, but one is justified in assuming that it also existed earlier.) This counterbalanced those who advocated Poland's following the West European pattern in her treatment of Jews.

One seems to be justified in assuming that lending large sums to Jews presupposes a degree of trust in the Jew's honesty on the part of the Christian lender—which amounts to discarding the cliché about Jewish dishonesty. This was reinforced in part from another direction. Individual Jews met with individual Poles—landowners or their estate managers—face to face in many cases where trust and honesty of the leaseholder or the revenue farmer was important. And in many cases the Poles apparently were not disappointed.

In short, the Polish-Jewish contact tended to be less of the theological Christian and the theological Jew relationship (burdened with all the age-old prejudices and preconceived ideas) than that of the actual Pole and the actual Jew—in other words, a more human relationship. This may have been at the root of the more favorable development of the Jewish group in Poland. Once established as a large group, Polish Jewry was able to endure even after the state collapsed.

The Jewish population continued to increase in Polish lands following the partitions, with the Jews partially adjusting themselves to the new states, even peopling the formerly *judenrein* Russia, forming "colonies" in Western Europe, and emigrating overseas. Their proportion in the total population in Poland remained at about 10 percent in the reconstituted Poland of the interwar years.

Parallel with population growth went the strengthening and multiplying of communities, and cultural and social maturation. During the fifteenth and even at the beginning of the sixteenth century not only was Polish Jewry small, but it also manifested the characteristics of a recently formed immigrant society and drew most of its spiritual and sociocultural sustenance from the West. For a century or so a Polish Jewish way of life developed, and local customs (minhag) gained prestige and became embodied in a cultural pattern, giving some distinctiveness to Polish Jewish culture. Promoted by second- and third-generation immigrants, the specific Polish Jewish pattern was further strengthened during the following centuries, absorbing new traits and changes.

Advancing in time beyond the scope of this book let us add that during the years of World War II and the German occupation, the Nazis turned Poland into a slaughterhouse for Jews (not only Polish Jews). Inaugurating their oppressive methods immediately after the occupation, the German authorities developed step by step various methods of annihilation, ranging from starvation to systematic transportation to camps in which the Jews were worked to death or gassed. At the end of the war only a small remnant of Polish Jews survived in the country or returned from Russia and from labor camps in Germany.

After World War II

In the new Poland following World War II, which was shifted geographically westward (and sociopolitically eastward), Polish Jews settled also in the western parts. Silesia and to some extent Pomerania eventually harbored about half the Jews in Poland. By an accident of history a great part of the Jewish survivors lived now in the western areas where the first Jewish settlements in Poland began some seven hundred to eight hundred years ago. However, their total number, though much larger than in the thirteenth and fourteenth centuries, was very small. It amounted only to some twenty-five or thirty thousand, or about one-tenth of one percent of the total population by 1967. This insignificant remnant was all that remained of Polish Jews in Poland after the decimation during the war and the postwar emigrations.

After the Israeli-Arab War of 1967 and Poland's siding with the Russian pro-Arab stand, new pressures upon Polish Jews resulted in a slow exodus that further reduced their number considerably. At the same time millions of former Polish Jews—and descendants of Polish Jews—are spread the world over: in Israel, the Americas, European countries, South Africa, and Oceania. These constitute the majority of world Jewry and the bulk of Ashkenazic Jewry today.

I

Beginnings: Middle Ages

1 *Immigration and Settlement*

The beginnings of Jewish settlement in Polish lands are buried in the dim past and are as obscure as most beginnings, including Poland's own. The early coming of Jews to Polish lands was not initiated by any official act of government or prince, nor was it a mass movement. The first arrivals seem to have been a few individuals or small groups who probably came for a variety of reasons, like oppression in other lands or the expectation of opportunity in the new country. Or they may have come in connection with trade or with the contemporary vogue among German colonists to settle in Poland. Possibly all these reasons, as well as others, were factors. But to a great extent Jewish settlement in Poland was apparently the counterpart of the German colonization of the country that began in the thirteenth century. Whatever may have been the reasons for immigration, there is no documentary evidence of its origins.

Legends

Three principal Jewish legends (and some auxiliary ones) exist about the early times. According to one story the Poles could not decide upon a successor to their prince, who had just died. They resolved that the first man to enter the town the next morning would become prince. It so happened that a Jew, Abraham Prochownik, was the first arrival, and he was duly proclaimed prince. He, however, persuaded the Poles to take one of their own people instead. Thus was the founder of the Piast dynasty, a mythical person in Polish history, made the Polish prince.

Another legend places the coming of the Jews to Poland at the end of the ninth century, at the time of the second semimythical Polish prince. At that time—so runs the legend—Jews in Germany were being persecuted; in 889 a delegation of five rabbis came from Germany to the Polish prince requesting the right to settle. After a council meeting lasting three days their request was granted. Another version has it that the prince offered them asylum in exchange for prayers to assure a timely rainfall. Thus, supposedly, the first large group of Jewish immigrants came from Germany in 894, and the prince subsequently granted Jews the rights of free immigration, communal autonomy, and protection.[1]

A third legend, still being handed down by word of mouth in the nineteenth and twentieth centuries, connects the beginning of Jewish settlement in Poland with the Spanish expulsion in 1492. According to this tale, when the Jews were expelled from Spain they wandered eastward. In the course of their long wanderings they rested, and said *"Poh lin,"* which in Hebrew means "Here, stay overnight." (Another version is that they found a note that dropped from the sky.) The country got its name in German, Hebrew, and Yiddish—Polen—from this word.[2]

Individual communities harbored traditions of their own. Thus a town in Galicia boasts that the prophet Jeremiah was buried there; Lublin, Poland, where Jews are known to have lived since the end of the fifteenth century, claims that a pupil of the Tanna R. Meir (second century c.e.) was buried in its cemetery. (This cemetery, however, is no older than the sixteenth century.)

One need go to no great lengths to "prove" that neither the prophet Jeremiah nor the sage of the second century c.e. was ever in Poland. But whether the central Polish Jewish legends conceal a core of fact is a moot point. Usually a myth or legend has to be continually recounted to remain alive. Its only source of perpetuity is the interest or meaning it has for each generation. The Polish Jewish legends in question are of recent origin and have no older traces. One of them shows indications of imitating a Spanish Jewish story first accounted for around 1500.[3] But even if such legends do embody a modicum of fact they can hardly concern "prehistoric" times. An analysis of the first legend will show that it could not have been created earlier than the late Middle Ages. The name Prochownik in the first story means gunpowder merchant or maker of gunpowder. This indicates that the legend cannot antedate the thirteenth or fourteenth century, when gunpowder first became known in Europe. The story of the five rabbis from Germany requesting refuge is apparently of still more recent origin. All five names are Sephardic.[4] This would seem to indicate that the story could have originated about the time of or after the expulsion of Jews from Spain (1492), when Sephardic Jews did come to Poland. The third legend mentions clearly the expulsion of Jews from Spain. There is no known record of any of these legends before the nineteenth century. The oldest known account is the one about the five rabbis, which dates from 1801,[5] though certain of its elements are mentioned at the end of the eighteenth century. All these stories are in the nature of etiological legends explaining existing situations or traditions, and were probably created in the eighteenth and nineteenth centuries* for apologetic and political reasons.[6]

---

*Until the eighteenth or nineteenth century Jews in Poland and in Europe generally were apparently unaware of the stories and legends connected with the early coming of Jews to Poland. David Gans (1541–1631), who had lived in Poland for a time, tells a number of stories in his *Zemach David* (1592) about Poland generally in the eighth and ninth and later centuries. But he does not begin to record anything about Jews until about the end of the fifteenth century. Jair Hayim Bachrach (c. 1639–1702), who was versed in a number of secular disciplines over and above rabbinic lore and who lived in many parts of Europe, did not hear anything about the existence of Jews in Poland before the fourteenth century. He states (responsum no. 1) that before the middle of the fourteenth century there was no known talmudic scholar in Poland "and possibly Jews had not yet settled there at all."

There are also some non-Jewish tales connected with Jews in Poland. A Polish chronicler, for instance, writing at the beginning of the twelfth century, tells of a Polish princess, Judith (died 1085), who ransomed Christian slaves from Jewish owners.[7] This and similar stories are hardly authentic, however, and are rather in the nature of didactic legends authored in much later times or simply "facts" copied from other regions, to be used for religious propaganda with no regard for chronology.

Theories and Speculations

There exists also a considerable body of theories and speculation (in some respects resembling the legends) about the origin of Polish Jewry—or of Jews in southern Russia, from which they could later have come to Poland. Each one dates the beginning of East European Jewry in a different era, ranging from almost biblical times to the eleventh or twelfth century C.E. These ideas have been propounded in historical writings since the end of the eighteenth and the beginning of the nineteenth century.

It would take us too far afield to trace the development and evolution of each of these hypotheses.[8] For our present purpose it will suffice to categorize and summarize them under several headings. They may be divided into two large groups:

1. *Northern Black Sea or southern Russian theories.* Most of these assume that the Black Sea–southern Russia area, where the early Russian state was formed in the ninth and tenth centuries, is where the Jews first settled in Slavic lands, and that they arrived either before, together with, or at the dawn of Slavic-Russian immigration. Theories range from the assumption that the Jews were descendants of early pre-Christian settlers in the Bosporus state (on the Black Sea), later augmented by conversion of the Khazars, to ideas about early immigrants from Palestine, Greece, Byzantium, and Persia, and Khazar descendants. Thus the Jews in Eastern Europe are assumed to be either Semitic, semi-Semitic, or completely non-Semitic in origin.

2. *Western theories.* These hypotheses regard the Jews in the Slavic countries as originating predominantly or solely in Western Europe.

Each of the two groups of hypotheses may, in turn, be subdivided into secondary hypotheses and theories.

The Black Sea–southern Russia theories fall into six categories:

a. Scythian theory: Around 600 B.C.E. Jews came directly from Palestine to Scythia, in the southeastern part of today's European Russia. Their numbers were later augmented both by new immigration and by proselytes.

b. Jews (the Ten Tribes) came from Babylonia and Persia to southern parts of modern Russia before the common era or in the first centuries C.E.

c. Jews came to the northern Black Sea region through Greece and Byzantium or from Palestine via Greece at the time of the Greco-Roman Bosporus kingdom or during the time of the Byzantine Empire, when oppression of Jews began there (seventh to tenth centuries C.E.).

d. In some way connected with the Black Sea theory is the Caucasus hypothesis. This assumes that Jews lived in the Caucasus after the destruction of the First Temple (sixth century B.C.E.) or even from the time of the exile of the Ten Tribes (the destruction of Samaria, 719 B.C.E.).

e. Khazar theory: The Khazars, and the ethnic Jews who lived in the Black Sea region from the first century B.C.E. or immigrated later, formed the backbone of Jewry in Eastern Europe. After the destruction of the Khazar state, they spread out to form nuclei of Jewish groups in the Slavic lands and Hungary. This Khazar theory has several nuances. Some regard the Jews as descendants of the Turkic Khazar tribes, while others think that they are descended from the Slavs, who were under the suzerainty of the Khazar state and thus became converted to Judaism (Gumplowicz). Still others relate East European Jews to both the Khazars and the ethnic Jews who lived in Khazaria.

f. Kenaan or Pan-Slav theory: This hypothesis, too, belongs to the Black Sea–southern Russia group, although it somewhat transcends the Black Sea geographic borders and has some connection with at least one of the Western theories. This hypothesis may be summarized as follows. Early Russian (or Polish) Jews, whatever their origin, were part and parcel of the local population, spoke the same Slavic language ("Kenaan" in Jewish sources), and followed the same customs. Later they were assimilated into the masses of German Jews who immigrated to the Slavic lands, adopting and modifying the German language into Yiddish and neglecting their older culture.

The Western theories may be divided into two groups:

a. Trade route hypothesis: An early trade route leading eastward passed through Slavic lands, particularly areas linked with the northern Black Sea shore. Jews participated in this trade and settled along the route at an early date.

b. Western persecution theory: Jews immigrated from the West, mainly from Germany and Bohemia, during the twelfth and thirteenth centuries, a period of persecution in Germany. Small settlements made up of Jews from the West may have originated earlier because of previous persecutions (Crusades) or because Jews made business trips eastward.

The division into different theories is not always so clearcut. These hypotheses and assumptions seldom stand alone. A few of them may be combined: sometimes one or more of the Black Sea–southern Russia theories are connected with the Western theories in a sort of compromise.[9]

Most of these theories, however, are no more than myths or speculation or wild guesses based on some vague or misunderstood references. The Khazar hypothesis has a certain dramatic background and was propounded as a result of large-scale falsifications in the nineteenth century.

The Khazars were a conglomerate of what appear to have been nomadic or seminomadic Turkic tribes from central Asia. From the sixth century c.e. or earlier, they lived in the territory between the northern Caucasus and the lower Volga River, in the southeastern part of European Russia. Spreading as far west as Kiev and conquering as they went, in the seventh century they succeeded in founding a strong state that served as a partial barrier against the northward advance of the Arabs, then at the crest of their expansion. Shortly before the middle of the eighth century (or perhaps later) the elite members of Khazar society, led by their king and his entourage, embraced Judaism; the rest of the Khazars, however, remained idolators or were converted eventually to Islam or Christianity.

The multiethnic and mutilingual Khazar empire flourished for two or three centuries, subjugating other tribes in its region and forcing some of its Slavic or Russian neighbors to pay tribute or tolls for the use of the commercial routes it controlled. In 965 (according to the *Russian Chronicle*) or thereabouts, the Kievan Russians overcame the Khazars, destroying their capital and other cities. Though Khazars may have stayed on in European Russia almost up to the time of the Mongol invasion in the thirteenth century, it seems that they never regained their old power —or so one judges from the obscurity that surrounds the remainder of their history. By about the eleventh century they were being hard pressed by the Cumans, another tribe of Ugro-Finnish or Turkish extraction.

The lack of information about the Khazars—we do not possess one word that comes indisputably from them—combined with certain accounts by Arab writers, many of whom were reporting events that happened long before their own time and who copied from each other, prepared the ground for all sorts of myths. Increasing the obscurity are Hebrew documents containing what is alleged to be an exchange of letters in the tenth century between Hasdai ibn Shapruth, a Hispanic Jewish dignitary, and one of the Khazars' Jewish kings, Joseph. Opinion about these letters ranges from the view that they are genuine to the judgment that they are complete forgeries; a well-founded surmise is that they are apocryphal or purely literary productions of the tenth century or later.

Still other legends were engendered by documents forged in the nineteenth century by a Russian Karaite named Abraham Firkovich (1785–1874). In the 1830s and 1840s Firkovich traveled through the Crimea and the Caucasus, combing cemeteries and synagogues for material on the Karaites; he also went to Palestine and Egypt, where he collected Hebrew manuscripts. The aim of all this was to convince the tsar's government that the Karaites had come to Russia before the time of Jesus and so could not have had a share in the responsibility for his crucifixion; thus they should, in contrast to other Jews, receive civic rights. Firkovich did, in fact, persuade the Russian government, but in so doing he left a long trail of forgeries behind him. He falsified the epitaphs on many gravestones and injected spurious passages into many old manuscripts in order to prove that Jews with Tatar names had lived in the Crimea in the first century B.C.E., that other Jews had come there from Persia, and that it was the Karaites who had converted the Khazars and thus founded the first Jewry in Russia. Firkovich also considerably extended the boundaries and inflated the importance of the Khazars' empire.

His "discoveries" led to a great controversy, with historians like Isaac Marcus Jost, Heinrich Graetz, and others accepting them as genuine, but many more rejecting them, including Moses Steinschneider, the German scholar Hermann Strack, and the Russian Jewish scholar A. Harkavy. Later even Professor D.A. Chwolson (1819–1911), who was instrumental in getting the tsarist government to buy the Firkovich collection for the library in Petersburg, had to admit that many documents were full of falsifications. He states: "I find myself in the situation of a lawyer who has to prove that not everything found in the house of a notorious thief is stolen goods." In the introduction to one edition of these documents Chwolson wrote:

> *Studying the gravestones and their inscriptions on the spot and comparing, over a period of many years, the copies . . . of these inscriptions [made by Firkovich], I came to the conclusion that Firkovich actually changed many dates and in this way transferred many inscriptions from the XVI and XVIII centuries to the X and XI. Everything which went through the hands of Firkovich is suspect.*

The efforts by some historians and writers to find in certain Polish toponyms (place-names) some indication of former Khazar or Jewish-Khazar settlements were in vain. It has been proven that these names have nothing to do with Khazars or Khazar tribes. They all have other meanings in Polish. Similarly, the rest of the hypotheses and speculations have little or no basis in reality[10] and lack any factual value for dealing with the early settlement of Jews in Poland. This end could better be reached by analysis of preserved source materials.

Early Documentary Mention

Historical facts and source material would seem to indicate that Jews appeared in Poland no earlier than the middle of the twelfth or beginning of the thirteenth century. Neither of two Jewish travelers of the second half of the twelfth century, Benjamin of Tudela, whose trips were taken between 1165 and 1173, or Petachya of Regensburg, who made his journeys between 1175 and 1190, says anything about Jewish communities in Eastern Europe.[11] Benjamin, whose itinerary is a source of information about the Jewish communities of his day in most parts of the world, does not mention the presence of Jews anywhere at all east of Prague. In the last chapter of his book, writing about Germany and her Jewish communities, he summarizes: "And in these cities many Jews are learned and rich." He goes on: "And after that [after Germany] there is Bohemia and the city called Prague, which is the beginning of the land Slavonia, which the Jews who live there [in Prague] call

Kanaan* because the people who live there sell their sons and daughters as slaves to all nations; these are the people of Russia and this is a large state from Prague to the city of Kiev." There follows a description of the winter cold in Russia, but no mention of Jews in that country. This is followed by a description of France and of Jews and the Jewish way of life there.

About a decade after Benjamin, Petachya of Regensburg traveled "from Prague in Bohemia to Poland, from Poland to Kiev in Russia, and from Russia . . . to Kadar [Crimea or land of Tatars] and . . . Khazaria." Of Jews in this whole region he says only: "And in the land Kadar there are no [rabbinite] Jews, only heretics [Karaites]." He goes on to relate how these Karaite Jews attributed their ignorance of non-Karaite Jewish teachings to the fact that their forefathers had not taught them. They said they had never heard of the Talmud. In other words, there were no rabbinic Jews in the entire neighborhood or region. This would be the only plausible explanation of why neither of these two travelers has anything to tell about Jews there. There were apparently no Jewish settlements in Poland-Russia at that time, even though an individual Jew may have been found here and there, mainly in the western parts.

Two documents from western Poland-Silesia—which until about the middle of the fourteenth century was a part of Poland—deal with Jews. One from about 1150 or 1200 mentions a Jew as owner or farmer of a village near Breslau (Wroclaw). Another document deals with two Jews (Joseph and Chaskel) in Sokolniki, a village near Breslau that was later incorporated into the city. If we are to assume that these documents are genuine or based on genuine ones (their authenticity may be doubtful) it will show that some Jews lived there before or around the end of the twelfth century. The oldest Jewish tombstone found in Breslau in 1917 is dated 1203. This and two or three other items of none too reliable origin seem to make up the entire "documentary heritage" up to the beginning of the thirteenth century. One may possibly also assume the existence of Jews in Poland at the end of the twelfth century from the report of the Polish chronicler Vincent Kadlubek, bishop of Cracow, who relates that Prince Mieszko III (1173–1209) imposed heavy fines on Christians caught molesting Jews. However, this statement may be a result of the chronicler's bias against Prince Mieszko, whom he may have intended to defile as a defender of Jews.[12]

This same period, the end of the twelfth and beginning of the thirteenth century, is the date of several hundred silver coins with Hebrew letters (bracteates, thin silver coins inscribed on one side only). Whatever their origin, these coins may bear witness to the existence of Jews in Poland. For our purpose it is immaterial whether

---

*In the Bible, Canaan was cursed by his grandfather Noah: "The lowest of slaves/Shall he be to his brothers" (Gen. 9:25). Benjamin, following suit, connects the name "Kenaan" for Slavic lands with slavery. This may have been his own explanation for an expression developed apparently in imitation of Latin documents which, from the ninth century on, used "Sclave" to mean both Slavonic people and people in the condition of servitude. In fact "Kenaan" in Hebrew of the Middle Ages seems to have been a generic name similar to the Arabic *as-saqaliba* (also *as-saqlab, Sasqlab;* Greek *Sklaboi*) applied to Slavic and also to non-Slavic (German and other) peoples.

they are regular coins made by Jewish minters for the princes, some sort of medals (as some Polish historians have believed), or, what is more likely, coins minted from their own silver by some Jews in the ducal or bishops' mints. In an age when minting was not centralized (in the thirteenth century Silesia alone had twenty-five mints) and depreciation of the currency was increasing, it was not unusual in Hungary, Poland, and elsewhere for an individual to receive permission to mint a certain amount of his own silver.[13]

Jewish sources confirm the existence of some Jews in Russia (Rus) or southern Poland or Galicia (both called Russia in Jewish sources) and Poland around the end of the twelfth century. Rabbi Eliezer ben Isaac from Bohemia (Prague) and Rabbi Isaac Durbalo from Germany or France visited Russia and possibly Poland at that time.

At this time—about the beginning of the thirteenth century—some Jewish settlements seem to have already been in existence. Correspondence between Rabbi Eliezer from Prague and the well-known Rabbi Jehuda Hachassid of Regensburg (died 1217)—in connection with the latter's objections to the custom among Eastern European Jews of giving the cantor gifts of food and the like at weddings and on holidays, instead of paying him a salary—indicates such a situation. The Prague rabbi points out that "in most places in Poland, Russia, and Hungary the Jews are unlearned because of poverty [or adversity] and they hire themselves whomever they find to serve as a cantor, a judge, and a teacher for their children, and they promise him all these [gifts]." Eliezer ben Isaac feared that without such gifts the cantor-teacher-judge would give up his position and then these Jews would remain "without Torah, without a judge, and without prayer."[14]

This correspondence indicates the presence of small Jewish groups or communities in Poland at the end of the twelfth or the beginning of the thirteenth century. They had probably only recently settled there and lacked any developed community organization. The newness and small size of the Jewish settlements can be deduced from the fact that neither of the two Jewish travelers of the third quarter of the twelfth century—Benjamin of Tudela and Petachya of Regensburg—even hinted at the existence of Jewish communities in the whole region, and from the situation described in Rabbi Eliezer's letter.

The thirteenth century, particularly the second half, is the date of the first real Jewish immigration to Poland. After the Mongol raid on Poland (1241) the earlier colonization trend from Western Europe gained importance. Known as the "German colonization," it involved mainly Germans but also included some Walloons, Flemings, and Dutch who settled in underdeveloped Polish areas, founding cities, towns, and villages. These new settlements were given a certain autonomy—the right to be administered in accordance with German law, or more particularly Magdeburg Law (the pattern evolved by the law court of Magdeburg). These waves of migration also brought in some Jews, and information about Jews in Poland increases during this period. Jews are mentioned in seven places in Silesia in the thirteenth century, two in Great Poland, and two in Pomerania. Other documents relate to a Jewish cemetery or the purchase of land for this purpose in Kalish in 1287. In Podolia, in southeastern Poland, a tombstone dated 1240 has been found, assuming the reading to be correct. It is possible, too, that the Jewish settlements in Cracow (Little Poland), Warsaw (Mazovia), and Vladimir in Volhynia were also founded in the thirteenth century.

In the thirteenth and the beginning of the fourteenth century Hebrew sources from the West mention a few Jews from Russia and Poland who came westward: an Itchaq from Russia, a pupil of Rabbi Jehuda Hachassid, and a pupil of Rabbi Asher ben Yechiel who came from Russia. If a name with "from Russia" or "from Poland" in it really signified that the bearer originated in that country (not simply that he traveled there) it could apparently serve as additional evidence for the existence of Jews in those regions in the thirteenth and fourteenth centuries.[15]

Be that as it may, a number of documents from the beginning of the second half of the thirteenth century deal with problems connected with settlement of Jews in different parts of Poland, which at that time was divided among a number of princes. This would seem to show that immigration and settlement were an issue which could not be ignored. Prince Boleslas the Chaste of Cracow (1243–79) granted a Cistercian monastery in Little Poland (1262) a privilege permitting the monks to settle people from different nationalities on their lands, with the exception of Jews. In western Pomerania (northern Poland) Duke Barnim I in December 1261 granted the Jews of Stettin and other parts of his country the right to live "according to the rights which the Jews of Magdeburg have."* Three years later the same duke expelled the Jews from another city (Greifswald) and forbade them to resettle there.[16] In the same year, 1264, Prince Boleslas the Pious of Kalish granted the Jews of his principality (Great Poland) a privilege or charter of Western origin, patterned upon the privileges granted by Frederick of Austria (1244), Bella IV of Hungary (1251), and King Ottokar II of Bohemia (1254). This served in turn as a pattern for privileges in other parts of Poland—in the Silesian principalities in 1295 and 1299. If the 1264 privilege is genuine,[17] as it seems to be, it signifies the beginning of a larger settlement of Jews in Poland. The privilege refers not only to individual Jews, but also to Jewish institutions—cemeteries and synagogues. The issuance of the privilege can be correlated with the other pieces of information we have mentioned that point to the existence of Jews in Poland during the thirteenth century.

It is also plausible that the rising interest of the Catholic Church in the problem of the Jews in Poland coincided with their increased settlement in the area. The church began at that time to act to separate Jews from non-Jews, restrict the number of synagogues, force Jews to wear special hats, and segregate them in specified

---

*The passage in the document may mean autonomy according to Magdeburg Law or simply the same rights as the Jews living in Magdeburg (the community there originated not later than the tenth century). The irony of the situation was that about two months earlier the ruler of the city, Archbishop Robert of Magdeburg, attacked the Jews during the Sukkoth holiday, imprisoned many of the wealthier ones, and forced them to pay him a huge ransom.

sections of the towns and cities (ghettos). Furthermore, the interest rate that Jews were permitted to charge was limited, and they were forbidden to farm tolls, hold office, or employ Christian help. Resolutions to this effect were passed at the Provincial Church Council in Breslau (having jurisdiction for the province of Gniezno, Great Poland) in February 1267, and at the synod in Ofen (Buda) in 1279, in which Polish and Hungarian churchmen participated and where the resolutions concerned both Jews and Muslims. Similar resolutions were passed at the church synod held in Łęczyca in Poland in 1285.[18]

Admittedly, most of these resolutions were patterned upon the ones passed at earlier European meetings of different church councils beginning in the sixth century, and were reemphasized at the Fourth Lateran Council in 1215 and in the synod in Vienna of May 1267 (for Austria and Bohemia). The fact that by the second half of the thirteenth century the Polish clergy had become interested (or their interest was aroused by the legates sent from Rome) in shielding Christians from contact with Jews and in limiting Jews with regard to settlement and occupations may indicate either that the Jewish impact was becoming stronger at that time or that it was new in Poland.

Certain externally unimportant differences in the texts of the resolutions of the synods in Breslau and Vienna in 1267, both conducted under the chairmanship of the same church dignitary, Cardinal Guido, may depict something of the specific situation in Poland. In the Polish resolutions there is a stronger tendency to separate the Jewish and Christian populations. The paragraph instituting ghettos "in order that the Christians should not be affected by the superstitions and bad morals of the Jews while living among them" is not found in the Vienna resolutions. On the other hand, the Vienna synod forbids the building of new synagogues entirely, whereas the one in Breslau sets a limitation of one synagogue in each place.[19] These two points may indicate that in Poland the immigration was really only beginning. The permission to build one synagogue per place was granted because in most parts of Poland synagogues were either nonexistent or few and far between, whereas the Vienna resolution, dealing with Austria and Bohemia, prohibited any new synagogues because a considerable number already existed in those countries.

The fourteenth century witnessed a sizable increase in Jewish settlements in Poland. In Silesia itself Jews are mentioned in thirty-two localities, compared with seven in the preceding century. Beyond the boundaries of Silesia, Cracow certainly had a Jewish community at that time, and we have information about the possible existence of Jewish communities in Poznań, Sandomierz (1367), and farther to the east in Lwów (1356), Brest Litovsk, and possibly also Warsaw. By the end of the century, we hear about Jewish cemeteries near Sandomierz and near Cracow.[20]

Court records preserved from the last quarter of the century tell of Jewish moneylenders, while others depict Jews as participating in local, intracity, and intraregional trade, and buying and selling houses. Some Jews are also mentioned in the role of toll farmers. We hear, too, of the first ritual murder accusation against Jews in

Poland (1347) and of persecution of Jews in some Polish places outside of Silesia during and after the Black Death (1347, 1349, and 1367).

On the other hand, this was the century of the granting and confirmation of the Jewish privileges by Casimir the Great (in 1334 and 1364) in Poland and in a number of cities farther to the east that were incorporated into the Polish state (1356, 1367, and again confirmed for Lwów by the king in 1367). There were also grants of privileges to Jews in three cities in Lithuania.

All in all, in the thirteenth century there were in Poland (outside of Silesia) four Jewish communities (or places where some Jews were found) and an additional five in the fourteenth century. Lithuania had two. The sum total of the Jewish population remained small, amounting perhaps to a maximum of a few thousand, but possibly only a few hundred, persons living among a total population of about a million or more. But these few formed the nucleus of Polish or East European Jewry, which was to be augmented in the following centuries by immigration mainly from Germany and Bohemia. The thirteenth and particularly the fourteenth centuries should be regarded as the time of real Jewish settlement in Poland; in the twelfth century only a few individuals or small groups may have existed there.

Where Did They Come From?

It will probably be impossible to say definitely where the hundreds or thousands of Jews in Poland in the thirteenth to fourteenth centuries came from. Lacking documentary evidence that could throw light on this problem one must turn elsewhere for some clues. An examination of the geographic distribution of the Jews in Europe and beyond at that time may be of some help. To the west of Poland—or of the Polish principalities—Jews lived in Bohemia and Germany-Austria.

To the east—in Kievan Russia—there were possibly Jews in the twelfth century, but they apparently disappeared with the Mongol invasions of the second quarter of the thirteenth century. There may also have been Jews in Volhynia in the thirteenth century, and there were Jews in the Genoese colony of Kaffa (Theodosia) on the Black Sea coast in the fourteenth century. There were considerable numbers of Jewish settlements west of Bohemia and Germany—England until 1290, France until 1395 and Spain; to the south there were settlements in Italy, Hungary, Greece, and Egypt; and in Asia—Palestine, Syria, Babylonia, Persia, and even India and China; there were some in Africa as well. Taking into account the hardships of travel in those days, it would appear that geographically one should look to Bohemia and Germany-Austria[21] as a main source of the immigration to Poland, with some individuals possibly coming also from Volhynia and Kaffa in the fourteenth century or from Italy.

These general considerations seem to be borne out by certain other indications. Let us consider the "geography of settlement." In a map of recorded factual information about Jews and Jewish communities in Poland, at the beginning Jews appear in the most westerly parts (Silesia, a little later Pomerania, western parts of Great and Little Poland) and move constantly toward the east. This spreading from the west toward the east was maintained during subsequent centuries. The direction of settlement may be seen as a clear general indication of the direction from which the immigrants came. This is also borne out by the first charters or privileges granted the Jewish settlers. As already mentioned, the Polish privileges are patterned upon the Austrian-Bohemian ones. If one takes at face value the introductory phrase of the charters, stating that they were granted (or approved) in accordance with the request of "our Jews" or of "the Jews in the country," the Jews may be taken to be coming from the West and asking for, or suggesting, Western-style privileges.[22]

That in the thirteenth century Polish princes took it for granted that Jewish settlers were coming from the West may also be concluded from the above-mentioned document forbidding the Cistercian order—from the West—to settle Jews and from the other document in west Pomerania (1261) granting Jews Magdeburg rights (or giving them the same rights as in Magdeburg).

In Silesia, which was Polish until about the middle of the fourteenth century, twenty-two Jewish tombstones were found dating from the thirteenth and fourteenth centuries. Both the names in the inscriptions (with one exception) and the texts seem to resemble the ones used by German Jewry. Similarly, the recorded names of over two hundred Jews in Silesia in the years 1330–60 are either the usual Hebrew ones common among Ashkenazic Jewry or of German Jewish origin, appearing either in German or translated into Slavic. Among sixty-six Jews in Breslau at that time who are designated with places of origin, most came from the immediate neighborhood, from Bohemia or Germany, with one from another part of Poland, and three from Russia (the term Russia may mean eastern Galicia–Red Russia–the Ukraine, or the Russian state). Recorded names of Jews in other parts of Poland in the fourteenth century and in Warsaw in the fifteenth are also either of German origin or are Slavic translations of German names.

Again, some remnants of a synagogue from the first half of the thirteenth century have been found in Breslau; they are of the same pattern as those of Regensburg, Worms, Erfurt, and Speyer. The synagogue of Kazimierz near Cracow of about a century later shows some resemblance to those of Prague and Worms. Another possible indication of the interdependence of Poland and Germany may be seen in the fact that the memory books of German Jewish communities of the same century record not only the suffering of the German Jewish communities, but also that of Jews in Cracow and Breslau and in five or six Jewish communities in Silesia.[23] Also, the above-mentioned correspondence between the Prague rabbi and Rabbi Jehuda Hachassid of Germany concerning the payment of the cantors, and other fragments of similar information indicate that in terms of religious customs East European Jewry followed the Franco-German pattern. Not only did Rabbi Jehuda Hachassid make the decision in this matter, but it appears that in Eastern Europe he was regarded as a final authority. The Prague rabbi closes his letter to Rabbi Jehuda Hachassid with these words: "Even if you now retreat from your decision, I am afraid that they heard your first words and the damage will have been done." Against a general background of particularistic trends and division of authority in Jewish immigrant communities throughout the ages, the attribution of some sort of absolute authority to a Western (German) rabbi would indicate the group's German origin.

More evidence of the German background of Polish Jews is preserved from the fourteenth and fifteenth centuries. The ritualistic tradition of Polish Jewry resembled that of French-German-Bohemian Jews. Abraham Klausner and Isaac Tyrnau (of the same period), in summarizing the liturgic customs of Ashkenazic Jewry in the fourteenth and fifteenth centuries, each include Polish Jews in their survey. In only two instances does Tyrnau note minor differences in Poland, but these are not peculiar to Poland alone. They are either characteristic of "'Moravia, Poland, and Bohemia" or of "Hungary, Moravia, and Poland." In other respects, too, Polish rituals resemble the German-Austrian and Bohemia-Moravian ones. Rabbi Israel Bruna (about 1460) mentions the customs of Austria-Poland-Saxony all together.[24] Other fragmentary information ranges from a declaration by a Jew in Breslau in 1435, which is written in German (with some "Jewish" changes) but in Hebrew script, to some German Jewish glosses in Warsaw documents of the fifteenth century, and a document in Cracow signed by the representatives of the Jewish community in 1485, which has a Hebrew, a German, and a German Jewish text. From the same century we have a statement by a German rabbi that "Poland, the state of Cracow, had for a long time been considered as a place of refuge for the expelled [Jews from Germany]."

All this information, though fragmentary, indicates that the bulk of Polish Jewry was of German-Bohemian origin in the thirteenth and fourteenth centuries, when Jewish settlement in Poland was founded, although a few individuals may have come from Italy or from the Genoese colony in Kaffa (Theodosia) on the Black Sea coast.[25]

Immigration and Jewish Population during the Fifteenth Century

More Jewish immigrants reached Poland during the fifteenth century, a time of frequent persecutions in Germany, Austria, Silesia, and Bohemia, and of expulsions from many cities and regions.[26]

The number of Jews in Germany at that time must have been small, since there were not many Jews in the whole of the West. Probably no more than twenty-five to fifty thousand Jews lived in the whole of Germany by the middle of the fifteenth century. But sizable groups of Jews were apparently streaming into Poland from Austria and Bohemia, as well as from Germany.

Again the evidence will be mostly indirect, but in this case it flows somewhat more steadily than for the preceding centuries. First, we find Jews—or documents about Jews—in more places in Poland itself and in the more easterly parts such as Galicia and Volhynia. Jews are also mentioned in Danzig (privilege of 1454) together with other newcomers: Lombards, Nurembergers, Scots, and English. Jews in Germany regarded Poland as a place of refuge and immigration, an attitude based apparently on what was known about the country at the time. Rabbi Meisterlin from Wiener Neustadt in Austria writes, in the first half of the fifteenth century, that Poland, "that state of Cracow and its environs, has for a long time been a refuge for the expellees [from Germany]." This is more or less repeated by another rabbi, Moses Mintz, of Landau, Wuerzburg, Bamberg, and Mayence, who himself had been expelled in 1461 and settled in Poland.

It seems that non-Jews in Germany, too, regarded Poland in the same way, for this point was made by a few Jew-baiters in their anti-Jewish pamphlets at the end of the fifteenth and the beginning of the sixteenth centuries.[27] These general statements may be corroborated by a number of facts, ranging from the names of Jews in Poland originating from place-names in Germany, to information about outstanding individuals or rabbis in Poland stemming from Germany, Bohemia, Hungary, or Silesia.*

What information we have on this migration is mostly indirect. Only in a few cases have we documentary evidence of the immigration itself. One is a document given (about 1434–44) by King Ladislas Jagiello to two Jews, Nehemias and Lazar from Regensburg (or Breslau), permitting them to settle in Poland with their families and other Jews. A similar grant was made in 1475 by Casimir IV to Jacob Anselmi of Venice, who apparently came from Kaffa at that time to settle in Poland with his family, and to other Jews from Kaffa, Italy, Spain, and Constantinople.

Beginning with the end of the fourteenth century and increasingly during the following century, among Jews in Poznań, Kalish, and Cracow we find names derived from places or lands in Germany or nearby countries (for instance, Ungar [Hungary], Frank [Franconia], Mintz [Mayence]). "The Polish-Ruthenian Jews," summarizes Schipper, "used at that time mostly names which were common in the upper German region (Bavaria, Austria) and in Silesia, Bohemia and Hungary." These names may serve as an indicator of the regions from which the Jews came.

In the middle of the fifteenth century the Fischel family from Nuremberg settled in Cracow and became one of the city's prominent families. At the end of the century we find in Poland the court Jew Abraham the Bohemian (formerly court Jew of the Bohemian-Hungarian king and the German emperor). At the same time a group of Bohemian Jews settled in Kazimierz near Cracow and in Cracow, where they organized a community of their own; this led to tensions between them and the older Cracow Jewish community.

Some of the better-known rabbis in Poland came from Germany. At the end of the fourteenth century and the beginning of the fifteenth we find in Cracow two who apparently came from Schweidnitz in Silesia. Around 1420 Rabbi Lipman Milhausen (or Yom Tov ben Solomon of Muehlhausen) came to Cracow from Prague. In the last quarter of the century there were in Cracow a Rabbi David Shprinz, formerly rabbi in Bamberg and Nuremberg, and Rabbi David Frank, also

*Silesia was at that time politically integrated into Bohemia and the German Reich.

from Nuremberg. In Poznań (Posen) we find, during the middle of the fifteenth century, a rabbi Moses Muriel who came from Halle, and Rabbi Pinchas, formerly of Wiener Neustadt in Austria. The above-mentioned Rabbi Moses Mintz, fleeing Germany, served as rabbi in Posnań for a number of years (1474–1508). In Brest Litovsk there was a rabbi hailing from Erfurt, Rabbi Yechiel Loria, the grandfather of the famous Polish rabbi Solomon Loria or Luria (c. 1510–73). The parents of another famous Polish rabbi, Rabbi Moses Isserles (c. 1520–72), came to Cracow from Germany in the last decade of the fifteenth century. At that same time the well-known rabbi Jacob Polak arrived from Prague to become rabbi of the Czech Jews in Cracow. Around this time, the Spanish Jew Isaac Hispanus came to Cracow and later became court physician to the Polish kings.

The settlement and number of Jews in Poland grew rapidly in the fifteenth century. In the fourteenth century there is documented proof that Jews lived in some nine or ten places (not including Silesia, which in that century became Bohemian-Austrian, or Pomerania, which the Teutonic knights occupied). By the fifteenth century, however, there were about 63 Jewish communities or places of Jewish domicile in Poland, including Volhynia, and two or three in Lithuania.* This growth and possible rooting in Poland seem also to be reflected in the fact that in the fifteenth century we find for the first time a few responsa of Western rabbis— Israel Bruna, Jacob Molin (died 1427), Joseph Kolon (1420–80), Israel Isserlein (1390–1460)—answering questions sent to them from Poland (see also chapter 5).

Number of Cities and Towns in Which Jews Are Mentioned during the 12th–16th Centuries[28]

Region	12th cent.	13th cent.	14th cent.	15th cent. Schipper count	15th cent. Feldman count	16th cent.
Silesia	4	7	32			
Great Poland		2	3	10	15	63
Little Poland			2	10	9	41
Mazovia				11	13	
Kujawy				5	4	
Red Russia			2	17	14	49
Podolia				3	3	4
Volhynia				3	3	22
Podlasie						7
Braclaw province						3
Lithuania			2			4
Pomerania		2		2	2	2
Kiev province						3
	4	11	41	61	63	198

*Jews were expelled from Lithuania in 1495 (a great part of them settled temporarily in Poland) but returned in 1503.

The accompanying table illustrates the history of Jewish settlement in the Polish lands, though it is admittedly somewhat inaccurate. Since it is based on an inventory of localities mentioned in various documents it may include some doubtful names, while some other places that may have harbored Jews long before they were mentioned in preserved records could have been overlooked. But it does give a graphic picture of the process of Jewish settlement in Poland. During the twelfth to the thirteenth centuries Jews are found only in a very few localities in western Poland, mainly in Silesia and in the thirteenth century in two places in neighboring Great Poland and two in Pomerania. The following century shows a considerable growth in Silesia with an overflow farther to the east. But nothing approaching a mass settlement can be observed until the fifteenth century. Silesia having been lost by Poland—by the middle of the preceding century it had become part of Austria-Bohemia—the other parts of Poland (for the most part western Great Poland and Little Poland, but also to some extent Red Russia [Galicia] absorbed many more Jews. Against nine localities in the fourteenth century, about sixty cities and towns in all of Poland were settled by Jews in the fifteenth century. And this was, as it were, in preparation for the coming large thrust of Jewish settlement, amounting to about two hundred localities mentioned during the sixteenth century. This will also be apparent in terms of Jewish population. Beginning possibly with a few score or a few hundred during the twelfth and thirteenth centuries, they may have increased to thousands by the fourteenth century, and reached even greater numbers in the next century.

There are a few estimates of the number of Jews in Poland by the end of the century, based on the amount of recorded taxes they paid. These estimates range from 10–11,000 to 17,400. (The last figure is definitely too high.) To these Jews of Poland proper should be added those who lived in Lithuania and Kiev. Altogether the number of Jews at the end of the fifteenth century would apparently have been between ten and fifteen thousand persons.

Today such numbers may appear negligible. In the Middle Ages, however, population figures in Europe were generally small. Large cities in Poland had populations of a few thousand or a little more. It should be remembered that the whole Jewish population in Germany in the first half of the fifteenth century amounted to between twenty-five and fifty thousand persons. During the second half of the century the Jewish population in Germany, Bohemia, and Silesia was considerably reduced through persecution, emigration, and expulsions. The ten or fifteen thousand Jews in Poland-Lithuania at that time (after the expulsion of Jews from Spain) may have made up one of the largest single concentrations of Jews in all of Western and central Europe.

2 *Legal and Political Situation*

A "privilege" or charter was a basic legal document used in the Middle Ages to confer special rights or protection on an individual or a group. In an era when no valid universal state law was applicable, special charters became necessary for groups (merchants, Jews), institutions (city, church, monastery), and individuals.

A charter or privilege either guaranteed protection or granted special rights, usually in return for duties performed or to be performed, or it established new legal status. The charters (of cities), as the Belgian historian Henri Pirenne pointed out, "were the product of special circumstances" and "limited themselves to fixing the principal outlines, to formulating some essential principles" around which there developed "a thick overgrowth of rights, usages, and unwritten privileges." The same applies to the Jewish privileges in Poland. The princes and kings granted group privileges, usually known as "general privileges," to Jews of a city or a region or the whole country, and individual privileges to specific persons.

The privilege Prince Boleslas the Pious of Great Poland and Kalish granted the Jews in 1264 served them as a legal basis throughout the Middle Ages and later. It was confirmed by Casimir the Great in 1364 for all of Poland and again in 1367 for the Jews "in Cracow, Sandomierz, and Lwów," as well as other Polish lands in an expanded version of the earlier charters. There exists also King Ladislas Jagiello's confirmation in 1387 of a nondescript statute from Casimir the Great for the Jews of Lwów and Red Russia, which contains provisions similar to the ones of 1367. But an undated document by Casimir the Great, which was confirmed by Casimir IV in 1453, amplifies Jewish autonomy and makes a few other changes. Virtually the same privilege given by Boleslas and Casimir the Great was issued for Lithuania by King Ladislas Jagiello of Poland, who was also grand duke of Lithuania; for Brest in 1388; and, with some changes, for Grodno in 1389. Beginning at that time most of the Polish kings confirmed the privileges, though they sometimes introduced a few changes.[1] The last Polish king, Stanislas August (1764–95), issued a compilation of all Jewish privileges in 1765, including a number of basic decrees concerning Jews issued in the sixteenth and seventeenth centuries.

As we have said, the content of the 1264 privilege strongly resembles the ones issued by Frederick of Austria (1244) as well as those of Bella IV of Hungary (1251) and Ottokar of Bohemia (1254), upon which it is based, and seems to have served as a sample for the Silesian ones subsequently issued by Prince Bolko I of Silesia (1295) and Prince Henry of Glogau (1299).

The Polish privilege or charter, like most of the others, exempted the Jews from the jurisdiction of the city, putting them under the prince or the king. The latter transferred his obligations to his lieutenant, the *wojewoda*,* or a special judge whom he appointed for this purpose. A "Jews' judge" *(judex Judaeorum)* was to adjudicate Jews "in the neighborhood of the synagogue or in some other place chosen by the Jews." Jews participated in the court as assessors to judge cases according to Jewish laws. The judge's jurisdiction extended to cases between Jew and non-Jew and to a limited extent between Jew and Jew. A Christian taking a Jew to court had to have both Jewish and Christian witnesses. A Christian who murdered a Jew suffered the usual penalty in addition to confiscation of his property by the prince, and a Christian wounding a Jew was penalized by a fine paid to the prince plus damages paid to the victim.

Other clauses in the privilege guaranteed Jews inviolability of person and property, with freedom to come and go. They forbade anyone to molest him on the roads or to demand higher tolls from him than those levied upon Christians. Penalties for vandalism in Jewish cemeteries or synagogues were specified.

The charters also protected certain other Jewish religious rights. The ones in 1264, 1334, and 1453 enjoined the non-Jewish debtor from forcing the Jewish creditor to accept money on the Sabbath, allowed ritual slaughter (shechita), and assured protection for Jewish funeral processions.

Another area covered by all the charters was early Jewish autonomy; touched upon in the first (1264) charter, it was further elaborated in the subsequent privileges (1367 and 1453), and fully developed in the sixteenth century. It was a principle of the Middle Ages that every man has the right to be judged according to his own laws. In accordance with this the Polish Jewish charters declared that in cases involving non-Jews and Jews, a Jewish defendant was to be judged by the Jews' judge according to Jewish law, and cases between Jews were to be decided in a Jewish court (court of Jewish aldermen).

In Warsaw (and Mazovia generally), which remained independent until the beginning of the sixteenth century, the legal situation of the Jews was similar to that of Poland proper, though with some differences.

Further regulations concerned the business relations between Christians and Jews and were mainly connected with lending money, either with or without pledges. There is a clause, like the one in the Hungarian-Bohemian privileges, prohibiting charges against Jews of using Christian blood for ritual purposes, asserting that the

---

* *Wojewoda* (*palatinus* or palatine), the king's administrator in a province (provincial governor) and also a military commander.

groundlessness of such accusations had been established by the papal bull (referring to the papal bull of Pope Innocent IV in 1247).

The Polish privilege, however, had a few other clauses. One of these permitted Jews to accept horses as pledges only by day (so as to avoid being charged with stealing); another forbade the mintmaster from having Jews arrested and accused of spreading false currency unless a representative of the king participated in the arrest. Jews were given the right to buy and sell any merchandise on the market, including bread and other foodstuffs, just like Christians; a Christian hearing a Jew call for help during the night was obligated to come to his assistance.* The Polish privilege, unlike its predecessors, fails to specify either the amount of fines or the highest permissible interest rate.

The undated version of the Boleslas-Casimir privilege that was confirmed in 1453 by Casimir IV (1447–92) contained a few changes. The most important were the clauses that invested Jewish elders with the authority to judge cases between Jews, making them influential in internal Jewish matters; the one granting permission to slaughter cattle according to Jewish ritual; and the one stipulating that a Jew cannot be brought before Christian ecclesiastical courts.†

Legal Status

According to the privileges, all rights emanated from the prince or king. He was both guardian and supreme judge of the Jews, having exclusive jurisdiction over them and protecting them from other segments of the population. In this their situation did not differ from that of other groups in Poland; "generally all lay estates and ethnic and religious factions in Poland were subject to the supreme jurisdiction of the king exercised either directly by him or indirectly through a deputy." In the case of the Jews this deputy was the palatine (in some places the *starosta*—county official) or the "Jews' judge" appointed by the latter. In the case of the Armenian minority (in Lwów) the Armenian bailiff was at first the king's deputy and later it was the city bailiff presiding in court together with Armenian elders.[2] In all cases the king's court served as the highest court of appeals.

The official legal status of Jews in Poland was apparently that of freemen "attached to the treasury,"[3] that is, dependent upon the king, as was the case in the West before the term *servi camerae* ("chamber serfs") appeared officially in 1236 in connection with the Jews of Austria. Around the time this term came into use in the West, Christian theologians and legal writers picked up the theological idea of "serfdom of Jewry" (*servitus Judaeorum*, because Jews rejected Jesus), a concept formulated in antiquity; this became a rationale for the "personal unfreedom" of Jews implied by chamber serfdom. It furnished the justification for the ruler to

---

*This resembles the obligation prevailing in European cities in the Middle Ages for a burgher to assist any other burgher calling for help.

†This stipulation was apparently intended to protect Jews from persecution by the church for alleged religious crimes such as ritual murder or profanation of the holy wafer of the mass, accusations that brought a great deal of suffering upon Jews in those times.

handle "his Jews" any way he liked, making them his "property" to pawn, rob, or expel, and empowering him to cancel debts owed to them.[4] In Poland the legal theory of *servitus Judaeorum* as a theoretical principle and the idea of chamber serfdom are not emphasized, nor does the term *servi camerae* appear.

Kings Ladislas Jagiello (1386–1434), Casimir IV (1447–92), and Alexander (1502–6) stated that they protected Jews because the principle of tolerance was in accordance with God's laws or because the king's tolerance should also be extended to Jews. There was no mention here or elsewhere of protection being given because the Jew belonged to the king.

At the end of the fourteenth century a theologian[5] pondered whether a Christian king had the right to expel Jews and Muslims or confiscate their possessions, and whether the pope could order him to do so. His reasoning led him to conclude that a king might exercise such a right only if the Jews so misbehaved as to endanger Christians. Neither this theologian nor other, more anti-Jewish writers in fifteenth-century Poland based their arguments on "Jewish serfdom." This concept does not even appear as a rationale when, in the sixteenth century, Jews were barred from some cities upon the insistence of the burghers (although a variety of other "reasons" were offered) or when, in the second half of the seventeenth century, Jews were threatened with expulsion from Poland. At one point the king commanded the Jews to pay a special levy in lieu of being expelled (1657) but no *servi camerae* rationalization was used. Some of the privileges granted by the kings to individual Jews (and non-Jews) appointed them as "servitors" or assigned them positions in "the circle of his servants,"[6] but this did not mean unfreedom. On the contrary, such "servitude" meant (for Jews and non-Jews alike) belonging to a privileged class that enjoyed a high legal status and exemption from all or most taxes and from any jurisdiction except that of the king, as well as other economic advantages.

In practice it was only in Silesia and Pomerania that the petty princes and city burghers—mostly Germans or Germanized Poles—emulated the German pattern of extortion and expulsion. In these localities Jews were "given to cities" and later expelled, and their property was confiscated.[7] (These regions became politically connected with Germany-Bohemia and the Teutonic order, respectively, in the fourteenth century.)

In Poland proper, however, which even at the end of the Middle Ages remained an underdeveloped, mainly agricultural country with a comparatively small, none too strong city population, the situation was different. The Polish kings generally did not expel Jews, annul the debts owed them, or confiscate their property. In the old Polish state the cities never achieved political importance. Unlike their German counterparts, the Polish cities did not attain full centralization nor did they form political units—city-states. In Poland the nobility achieved dominance and became an important factor in the fate of Jews. By the middle of the sixteenth century the nobles had acquired jurisdiction over Jews living on their estates. Like the kings, they may have favored the Jews for a number of reasons.

At any rate, expulsions with confiscation of property were rare. Jews were expelled from Lithuania in 1495 and returned in 1503, although Jews were banned from a number of cities. Nor were Jews "given away, sold, or mortgaged" to cities or to dignitaries, as they were in the West. The cases in which the king did temporarily give some taxes collected from Jews to a dignitary or an official for a limited time —in a few cases the grantee was a Jew—did not involve transference of power or jurisdiction over them to the grantee. In the one instance in which Jewish taxes were permanently given to a grantee (Inowroclaw in 1506) the document may make it appear that jurisdiction was also transferred, but in fact jurisdiction over these Jews remained with the king. The granting of Jewish taxes to a grantee was (including Inowroclaw) a fiscal transaction of a primitive nature in a country that lacked any organized treasury apparatus.[8] Instead of collecting the taxes from Jews and paying certain sums to the grantees, the king transferred the task of collection to the grantees, but this entailed no jurisdiction or rights over the Jews.

The official legal status of the Jews in Poland was that of freemen, apparently resembling that of the knights and gentry, and in certain respects that of the burghers. The privileges of the fourteenth century compare the Jews in Poland with noblemen in connection with the amount of fines to be paid by attackers in cases of bodily injury. Many of the kings' decrees in the sixteenth and seventeenth centuries emphasized that Jews, paying the same taxes as burghers, were entitled to the same rights, meaning equal residence, trade, and occupational rights.

In southern Poland,* too, "the Jews were free subjects of the grand duke [of Lithuania]. . . . In time the Jews came to resemble the burghers in terms of place of settlement and occupation, but in regard to personal rights they were more or less equal to the nobility."[9]

In decrees and some other official documents Jews are often referred to as either *Judaeis nostros* (meaning "our Jews" in a friendly sense, just as Armenians were called *Armenos nostros*), or they were called *infidus* (faithless) and *perfidus* (false) or nonbelievers (in Christ).†

It should be noted that while the mentioned status was prevalent, one cannot always generalize for the whole of Poland. The arbitrariness and decentralization of the Middle Ages created many exceptions. Mazovia in eastern Poland was, until 1526, independent or semi-independent and had some specific Jewish laws. In Kremenets in the south, which received the grant of Magdeburg Law in 1438, the *advocatus* or bailiff had jurisdiction not only over the burghers but also over Jews and Armenians, whereas in Luck and in Lwów, Jews and Armenians enjoyed au-

---

*By "southern Poland" we mean Rus (Red Russia or eastern Galicia), which became incorporated into Poland in the fourteenth century, Volhynia, which was under Lithuanian suzerainty (in 1569 it became an integral part of Poland), as well as Podolia and the Ukraine, also at first under Lithuanian suzerainty. Lithuania was in personal union with Poland from the end of the fourteenth century. This union became permanent in 1569. In the regions formerly under Lithuanian suzerainty rudiments of Lithuanian or Russian law existed for a time together with Polish law.

†A few documents concerning Jews are preserved in which both expressions are found—*Judaeis nostros* in the text and infidels or perfidious ones in the heading of the document. The latter seems to have been added by the official who later classified or arranged the documents.

tonomy from 1432.[10] In Lwów itself, beginning with the introduction of Magdeburg Law (1352), the bailiff also had jurisdiction over Tatars, Ruthenians, and Jews, whom he was obliged to adjudicate in accordance with the customs and laws of their respective group. Within a short time (by 1364 and 1367), the Jews of Lwów had been put on a par legally with the Jews in the rest of Poland. With all these and similar local differences there was a general pattern that, at least in theory, became applicable to the whole country.

Polish Jews seem to have regarded themselves as freemen on a par with the nobility. Rabbi Solomon Luria (sixteenth century) maintains that Jews with privileges (or residence rights)[11] are equal to the knights (he calls them *parashim*), so that the king has no right to take away their real property; even when Jews lack residence rights, the king is not entitled to seize money or other property. Such acts, if they occur, are to be regarded as arbitrary and therefore not binding upon the Jews (whenever they can help it). The context of Luria's statement shows that he is not just repeating the term *parashim* (Jews legally similar to the knights) used in the West a few centuries earlier, but is dealing with Polish situations and Polish noblemen (he speaks of "our noblemen"). For our purpose this shows that Luria, and apparently others too, regarded themselves theoretically as freemen "similar to the knights." Luria seems to consider that the privileges guarantee to the Jews freedom equal to that enjoyed by the gentry. A document in Mazovia (1457) says that Jews enjoyed the legal rights of noblemen *(jus nobilium)*. This is probably also what lies behind a Warsaw case in 1428, in which a Jew took a nobleman to court for calling him a dog.[12]

Similarly, Jews in Poland were not barred from carrying arms—which some historians connect with the development of the "unfreedom" of "chamber serfdom" in the West—nor were they generally subject to a degrading form of Jewish oath, which may have had some connection with the same development.

Not only did Jews in Poland wear swords and own other arms, which they used when necessary, but they were also at times ordered to do so. True, the Statute of Wiślica (1347) exempted Jews and burghers from the obligation of military service, but this did not disqualify the Jews from carrying arms or fighting in defense of the country or cities. When King Alexander allowed the Jews in Lithuania to return to their homes in 1503 (they had been expelled in 1495), he stipulated that they must supply one thousand riders in case of war. (This did not necessarily mean that they had to go to war themselves.) When Jews petitioned for release from this obligation in subsequent years, their rationale was that in the past they had not gone to war or sent out fighters, but there is no mention of their being forbidden to or excluded from doing so. In fact, they had participated in the defense of cities and towns, being for the most part obliged to do so, and not only in southern Poland. In Schweidnitz (Świdnica-Silesia) Jews were obliged to stand guard in 1328.

Though most of the information about Poland comes from the seventeenth century, it may show something about earlier centuries. In 1626 Jews in Luck received permission to rebuild their synagogue on the condition that it be a turreted fortress surmounted by cannons to be manned by Jews. Such fortress-synagogues existed also in Luboml (Volhynia), Shargrod (Podolia), Brody, Tarnopol, Żolkiew (Galicia), and possibly also in Lwów (the community outside the city walls). And in Rzeszów (Galicia), a private city belonging to a nobleman, all citizens, including Jews, were required to have a rifle, a certain amount of gunpowder, and cannonballs. Three commanders, one a burgher, one from the suburbs, and one a Jew, had to man the walls. (Later the duty of defense was transferred to the artisan guilds, including the Jewish artisan guild.) City officials frequently trained Jews in the use of firearms.

In actual fact, there were Jews in Poland using arms both alongside the burghers in defense of cities and also as individuals or in groups or as irregular forces (as at the time of the cossack uprisings in the middle of the seventeenth century and the Swedish invasion in 1655). At times Jews were even aggressors or members of a gang. A document from Lwów (1626) has been preserved which attests that "the Jews, according to the old customs, are participating in guarding and defending the city. . . . Throughout the whole period the Jewish guard has done its duty with arms, day and night . . . properly following the orders of the commanders."[13]

In the Middle Ages the right to take an oath as sole evidence, valid in court, was generally granted only to freemen. In Germany, where the Jew enjoyed this right, from the thirteenth century on various ways of degrading the Jew when he took the oath were instituted in legal practice. The "Jewish oath" *(more judaico)* contained derogatory expressions, and the procedure under which it was administered was insulting. The Jew taking the oath was obliged to stand on a swine's skin or barefoot on a three-legged stool. Should he falter he could be fined or the evidence invalidated. True, the prescription of the Polish privileges in connection with the oath was modeled on the pattern of the Austrian privilege (1244), but in Poland it was not superseded by insulting and degrading formulas and practices. During the Middle Ages the oath taken by a Jew in Poland had a simple formula—not very different from the one taken by a non-Jew. It had to be administered near the synagogue if the amount of money involved was small, and in the synagogue—sworn on the Torah or near the ark—for larger sums. When foreign influences caused different practices to become common in some Polish courts in the sixteenth century (in an attempt to misinterpret the words of the charters), Polish kings repeatedly (1551, 1553, 1576, 1580, 1585, 1593) forbade the illegal practice and the insulting form.[14]

All this seems to indicate clearly that the official status of the Jew in Poland was that of a freeman; this was not officially infringed upon by any concept of chamber serfdom and the rationales for servitude implied therein, or by any special procedure in taking the oath.[15] Also, the Jews' settlement rights in Poland, unlike those of the German Jews, were of a permanent nature rather than temporary (that is, they were not given for a limited number of years only).

Thus the Jews formed a legal group of freemen recognized by the princes, with self-government in internal matters and the right to be judged according to their own customary law. The medieval hierarchic concept of a society divided into "estates" and "orders," involving a multiplicity of jurisdictions, usually made various provisions for group differences, allowing each one (or most of them) a sort of autonomy in the use of its own law. (In Poland the Jews, the Armenians, the followers of the Greek Orthodox Church, and the Tatars enjoyed this right to varying degrees.)

Practice

This does not mean, however, that the legal status of the Jews and the generally favorable attitude of the kings, and the privileges they issued and confirmed, fully protected the Jews. What is true in law is not always true in fact. Legal enactments may reflect the legislator's wishes or programs, but not his will or ability to put them into practice. In the Middle Ages privileges and laws were even less likely to be put into effect than legislation in modern times. Before the spread of printing the texts of the documents were seldom available. The administration and the chancellery were poorly developed, and the procedure for presenting suits before the king or court and getting action on them was cumbersome, sometimes lasting for decades. Decisions and decrees remained unfulfilled.[16] During the Middle Ages and even later, the state (not only in Poland) lacked adequate machinery for implementing its laws and regulations, and for apprehending criminals, thieves, and other offenders. A "do-it-yourself" system prevailed. The best way to bring an offender to justice was for the victim to catch him (with the help of friends or hired personnel) and deliver him to the city or state authorities. In such circumstances many laws, decrees, and court decisions remained theoretical pronouncements.

Furthermore, most of the laws and decrees were the products of specific circumstances. They were issued for each case and perhaps were not always intended as permanent regulations. Acting under different pressures and with varied motives, kings sometimes issued contradictory decrees. The charters or privileges that the Jews regarded with a quasi-superstitious respect—as the burghers did their city charters—and the decrees in their favor, which were often obtained after a great deal of effort and possibly considerable expense, were frequently of relative or temporary value in practice.

This situation worked in two directions: imperfections and breaches of decrees and laws and violations of court decisions are found to be both pro- and anti-Jewish. The same sociocultural and political background that created a gap between the pro-Jewish privileges and decrees and their execution created a similar distance between the anti-Jewish laws and decrees and their execution. They, too, frequently stemmed from special circumstances and were put into practice either partially or not at all. Thus some of the disabilities and some of the privileges related to the Jews were only theoretical. All these charters, laws, and decrees became effective only if and when the king and his officials were willing and able to enforce them. And this depended upon a multiplicity of factors, principally the correlation of the impact of the other social forces in the country—the nobility, the clergy, the city burghers —and the influence of general trends both in the country and abroad.

Social Forces

As the state developed, the nobility—comparatively more numerous in Poland than in other countries—became more and more important in the government. At first the nobles achieved personal freedom and immunity from most taxes on their estates. Later they—or the regional dietines (local assemblies of nobles who elected representatives to the national diet) and the diet, which they dominated—controlled the state purse-strings, war and peace, legislation, and the election of the king. The wealthy and powerful filled the principal offices in the realm; they occupied seats in the senate, thereby virtually controlling the state machinery, while the gentry (lower nobility) aspired to some of these positions or otherwise tried to gain more voice in the affairs of the land. The attitudes of these two groups toward the Jews were in some ways dissimilar.

The big landowners settled Jews on their estates, founded cities and towns in which the Jews could settle, and became the protectors and overlords of "their" Jews. They employed Jews as toll farmers and estate managers, and frequently rented apartments and stores to Jews in houses they owned in the cities or near the cities. Since these properties (known as *jurydyki*) were free from city jurisdiction, these Jews were exempted from the jurisdiction and limitations imposed by the city. There were also those who, like the king, employed the Jews as moneylenders and bankers.

The lower nobility, *szlachta* or gentry, increasingly gained in importance from the fourteenth century on and became a vital factor after the statutes of 1454 and 1505. This class had a somewhat ambivalent attitude toward the Jews. On one hand, they sometimes needed to borrow from the Jews or otherwise utilize their services and by mortgaging their estates they were more likely than the wealthy landowners to be on the verge of losing them. Borrowing was mostly for consumption, with high interest rates prevailing. Since more often than not the debtor was unable to repay capital and interest, his resentment of his creditor was often given an anti-Jewish rationale. In the fifteenth century, when the gentry themselves turned to the export of agricultural products or took up toll farming, they regarded the Jews as competitors.

On the other hand, most of them shared the large landowners' opposition to the monopoly of the Christian merchant and artisan guilds and the high prices they charged. As consumers, the nobility as a whole was interested in low prices on ordinary and luxury goods. They also may have been anxious that the peasants not be overcharged for the few things they bought on the market, so they would have more cash available to pay rent to the landowner. Laws to control prices were passed (1423, 1454, 1465, 1496, 1503, 1504) and other laws were promulgated (1423) to break up the guilds. The nobles had nothing but disdain for both merchants and artisans, regarding them generally as cheats and rogues.

The same attitude may have colored the nobles' views of the Jews. Or they may have regarded the Jews as tools for breaking the monopoly of the city people, or at least as a source of cheaper wares. The nobles were also intent upon preventing the city burghers from becoming competitors in the export of agricultural products— trying to exclude them from foreign trade—or from becoming a political power for fear they might support the king's position and thereby diminish the nobles' status.[17] Some noblemen also needed loans from time to time, which they could procure from the Jews; or they were interested in the incomes from rents paid by Jews; or they entrusted them with the management of tolls or other enterprises of the estates.

The results were, therefore, varied and contradictory: there were attempts to curtail the Jews' activity in moneylending and mortgages on estates and in farming of tolls on one hand, and continued dealings with them individually and the foster-ing of their services on the other. Sometimes there was also support for them politically against the pressures of the city burghers. In 1423, for instance, the diet forbade Jews to lend money on estates or on promissory notes that could be made payable against the estates, and tried to exclude them from farming tolls and receiving other state incomes. (In one case in Lithuania in 1495 the indebtedness of the grand duke and the nobility to Jews may have served—as it did at different times in Western Europe—as one reason for the expulsion of the Jews and confisca-tion of their property.) At the same time most of the nobles continued business dealings with "their" Jews (and the courts continued to recognize, unlawfully, some promissory notes or the mortgages held by Jews), and in most cases officially or semiofficially protected and supported them.

Both the nobility and the king were also subject to another force active in Poland, namely, the church and clergy. Or at least they paid lip service to the ideas it promoted and propagated. The medieval Catholic Church was generally trying to keep Jews in a state of submission and inferiority. According to Christian doctrine, Jews were condemned to eternal servitude and punishment for their rejection and crucifixion of Christ. They were to remain scattered over the world, to live in servitude and submission as a bodily witness to the truth of the prophesies about Christ, while their conversion might be a prelude to the Last Judgment. The church was thus trying to degrade the Jews and keep them in an inferior social status, while at the same time making their existence harder in the hope that they would then choose to convert to Christianity.

In periods when the church was struggling to crush the heretics in its midst (the Waldenses in the thirteenth century, the Hussites in the fifteenth century, the Reformers in the sixteenth century) it usually also took more severe action against the Jewish "unbelievers." Individual clergymen and monks, as well as whole groups, combined their passion for the church with an emotional xenophobia or anti-Jewishness, or else viewed the rousing of such feelings as a calculated means for drawing people nearer to the church. Belonging to what we may term the interna-tional organization of the church, the clergy in Poland would have been more likely than other groups to be influenced by the anti-Jewish tendencies that developed in Western Europe in the late Middle Ages.

As early as the 1260s, when settlement of Jews had just begun in Poland, and three years after the Boleslas privilege was issued, the church was, as mentioned earlier, busily attempting to introduce its old ideas of separating the Jew from the non-Jew by putting him into a ghetto and distinguishing him by special attire. As we have seen, resolutions to this effect were passed at the synod held in Breslau in 1267 under the chairmanship—and probably by the initiative—of the papal legate, Cardinal Guido. The Jew was also required to pay the Catholic prelate a tax amounting approximately to the income the latter would have received had a Christian lived in the house the Jew occupied.[18] These resolutions were repeated at the synod held in Buda, Hungary, in 1279 with Polish church leaders participating, and again six years later at a synod in Lęczyca, Poland. On the latter occasion additional new prohibitions were placed on farming out tolls to Jews, and they were forbidden to administer tolls, mints, or public taxes.

These prescriptions set the pattern for the resolutions of the church synods and councils in Poland for the next few centuries, with new formulations or demands arising from time to time. Thus in Kalish in 1420 the demand was made that the king reduce "the oppression by the Jews," who charged high interest rates.

Admittedly, the synods' decisions were seldom enforced in Poland, less often even than in Western Europe. No really separate Jewish ghetto or Jew-badge was ever actually introduced in Poland. Although most cities and towns had a "Jewish street" *(vicus Judaeorum)*—just as some other groups, such as artisans, had a *vicus* of their own—there were usually some Jews who also owned houses beyond this boundary and some non-Jews whose residences were located on the Jewish street. Similarly, no special dress or other badge to distinguish Jews was ever enforced, despite some attempts by king or the *sejm* to give these laws legal backing (1370, 1386, 1423, 1454, 1538). Ideas concerning limitation of the interest rate or forbidding Jews to lend money on mortgages, emphasized in fifteenth-century Germany-Austria, found an echo in the Polish church council of Kalish (1420) and were incorporated in Polish legislation (the Statute of Warta in 1423, Piotrków in 1496).

The dignitaries of the organized church in Poland exerted considerable influence on state affairs as well as on the king. They sat in the state council—later the senate —and they filled high state positions. The clergy also understood how to foster certain groups' antipathies to the Jews, particularly the antagonism of the urban population. The higher church officials were, however, at the same time estate owners and managers of *jurydyki* (sections in and around cities free from city jurisdiction) where they quite often took in Jews, whose rentals formed an increasing source of revenue for the prelates, just as they did for the noblemen. Like the latter, the prelates employed Jews as managers and toll farmers or offered them shelter in their estate and city houses.

The fourth force in Poland, the burghers—the city dwellers—comprised several social strata. There were the rich merchants (the patricians) and the shopkeepers and artisans. The patricians usually controlled the city government; they owned houses and other real estate in the city and formed the ruling class, with the second group trying to gain some influence. Then there were the workers: the servants and others who had neither property nor citizenship rights, being only "inhabitants," and the mob *(vulgus).*

The first two groups, partially originating from Germany (at least those in the larger cities), transferred to Poland certain German attitudes toward the Jews. The shopkeepers and artisans particularly fostered the principle of acquired rights, with its monopolistic tendencies. They regarded the Jews as their competitors and attempted to use methods similar to those used in Germany to eliminate, or at least to control and subdue, them. The policy of medieval cities and towns has been described as "outspoken, consistent municipal egoism." Each city constituted a statelike unit that was exclusive and self-centered, reserving for itself all means of livelihood and trying to monopolize the economic life of the surrounding countryside for its citizens. By curtailing the middlemen between buyer and seller the city sought to assure its burghers a low cost of living. In an expanding economy there was the desire to grasp the lion's share of the profits; in a stationary or contracting period there was the need to keep what one had. The medieval theory of wealth was that riches and income are God-given, not produced. Hence an individual cannot extend his share in the market beyond a certain limit without impinging on the income or standard of living of other individuals.

In such a society competition was frowned upon as evil and as a "double crime" if the competitor was a "foreigner," that is, an outsider from another place or of another ethnic or religious group.

The prevalent climate of exclusiveness and egoism in the city tended to make any outsider appear menacing and to evoke the desire to exclude him or to curtail his activity. Most cities had staple rights. A stranger—even if he came from nearby or from the suburbs—was subjected to restrictions in trade, crafts, and settlement. As a merchant he could not pass through a city with his wares without staying there for at least a few days. He had to try to sell his merchandise to local merchants and not to consumers or to other "foreigners." As an artisan the stranger was barred from engaging in his craft or selling the goods produced. Nor was he allowed to settle without obtaining a permit from the city government.

The Jew was a double outsider—he did not belong to the in-group and he was of another religion—against whom more restrictive measures could be rationalized.

The situation remained more or less unchanged when cities, mostly in southern regions such as Lwów, harbored multiethnic and multireligious groups: Poles, some Germans, Ruthenians (Ukrainians), Armenians, Jews, and Tatars. The intensity of the struggle to monopolize the means of subsistence was only slightly diminished by the multiethnic and multireligious division. Nor was there any serious attempt among the minorities to cooperate in opposition to the dominant group (Poles, Germans, Catholics), despite the fact that Lwów was officially regarded as sheltering three "nations"—Poles, Ruthenians, and Armenians—each with some specific autonomous rights.

The climate of exclusiveness in the medieval city and the struggle for the means of subsistence tended to encourage each group to try to outdo the others in acquiring privileges and special rights for itself. Each group employed the religious-ethnic difference of the others as a weapon against them. Each defended its own privileges and its special status in a society based on monopoly and exclusiveness.[19]

The internal struggle in the Polish cities from the fourteenth century on between the "common people" (the lower strata of city dwellers and the mob) and the patricians, who constituted the ruling class, and tension between the rising Polish element and the established German group, only aggravated the situation. Some of the wealthy patricians who were least afraid of competition may not have been too ill-disposed toward certain individuals or groups of Jews, whereas the man in the street was often ready to oust his competitor the Jew by any means, including violence.

In those centuries the non-Jewish burgher, like the masses generally, the lower rungs of people in the Polish cities, lived in an almost uninterrupted state of fear, confusion, and anxiety resulting from repeated disasters such as epidemics, famines, attacks by the Tatars, or other warfare. Disaster and the threat of death may contribute to the rise of chiliastic movements, the practice of penitential exercises, and the advent of popular mysticism, but they also bring general demoralization, social breakdown, emotional disturbance, a sense of guilt, and the fear of loss of grace and of damnation. This state of excitation or overstimulation was conducive both to projection of the blame onto the "sinners," the Jews, making scapegoats of them, and to diversion of the parishioners' dissatisfaction with the church (for not being able to avert disaster) into concrete avenues.[20] At times frenzied eruptions of violence ensued. Fear of competition led to a struggle to expel the Jews or to limit their activities as toll and tax farmers, as merchants, traders, and to some extent as artisans. In the last third of the fifteenth century opposition to Jewish occupations and Jewish residence in the cities became intensified. This opposition had passed through various phases during the centuries of the old Polish state's existence.

All these frequently conflicting ideas and trends were interwoven with influences from abroad. Information that Jews were being expelled from certain parts of Germany or elsewhere, or were suffering persecution, had the effect of fanning the zeal of those who harbored anti-Jewish sentiments,*at the same time weakening the courage of those who were in one way or another inclined to defend the Jews.

Attitudes and Phenomena

The University of Cracow, founded in 1364 and revived in 1400 (located, incidentally, in the Jewish street and in houses that had been bought or requisitioned from Jews) became an intellectual center of Poland. Headed by the bishop of Cracow, the institution was run along the lines prevailing in similar institutions in Europe.

Here we find traces of anti-Jewish materials such as the writings of the convert

---

*Some historians assume that the expulsion of the Jews from Spain in 1492 had an impact on the decision to expel them from Lithuania in 1495.

Paulus de Santo Maria and similar anti-Jewish literature brought in from the West. Later, when printing was developed, anti-Jewish books and pamphlets were acquired by the university. These may have helped to form the minds of the students, the future churchmen. Some of the attitudes and sympathies can be gauged from marginal notes made by readers and copyists. On a manuscript telling the story of the 1385 pogrom against Jews in Prague there is a note saying: "I sing a song of praise to God the Almighty. Exterminate the Jews, Hallelujah." A fifteenth-century manuscript bears a note dated 1458: "The Jews are a misfortune for the Polish state, beginning from 1455 until their extermination";[21] and the city secretary comments in his official papers (1403) on how the king of Bohemia appraised Jewish possessions in order to confiscate them.

Admittedly other influences less inimical to Jews also came from abroad. Humanistic and Renaissance ideas came late to Poland and had a somewhat pacifying effect in some cases upon the views held about the Jews. Writers of the fifteenth century —the rector of the university, for instance, and a few others—who advocated modernization of the Polish state machinery and occasionally deplored clerical dominance, repeated the general clichés concerning the Jews, but to some extent their approach was more humane.

Humanism and the Renaissance also brought to Poland some Latin translations of the works of Maimonides, Ibn Ezra, and others which were introduced to the university library. Well-known humanists, too, found their way there and fostered the study of Greek and Hebrew. One of these, Filip Callimachos de Bounacorsi, from Italy, was influential at court, and more than once threw his weight on the side of the Jews. In 1495 he tried to dissuade the king from carrying out the expulsion from Cracow. The Cracow burghers, however, enlisted the help of the king's brother, Cardinal Frederick, to win the king over to their view.

The formative centuries of Jewish settlement in Poland were thus beset by the strains and conflicts engulfing Polish society, and were subject to the anxieties and confusion of those times: the stress of the often contradictory interests of the social forces and the impact of influences from abroad. Most of these things were unfavorable to the Jews. Jewish life was fraught with danger, catastrophes, and persecution to an even greater extent than that of the general population. They were also subject to some selective expulsions.

During the fourteenth and fifteenth centuries persecutions of Jews are known to have occurred in Poland (besides Silesia) at least nineteen times, ranging from local attacks to expulsion from a city or province. This would mean that on the average two or three persecutions took place during each generation.[22]

It should be noted that with the exception of two cases at the end of the fifteenth century, almost all the known cases of attacks and persecution occurred in a few west Polish centers (two or three in Warsaw). Further a list of the known "causes," or rather the rationales, for the persecutions will show that most of them were imitations of what was going on in the West. Four times a fire[23] was given as the justification, twice a blood libel, once or twice charges of desecration of the holy

Persecution of Jews in Poland in 14th–15th Centuries

Year	Place	Nature of Persecution	Circumstances or Rationale
1348–49	Cracow, Kalish, etc.		Black Death (similar accusations as in Germany)
1360	Cracow, etc.	burning	pestilence
1367	Poznań	pogrom	blood libel
1399	Poznań	rabbi and 13 Jews burned	profanation of holy wafer
1407	Cracow	pogrom	blood libel
1423	Cracow	attack	?
1434	Poznań	"	?
1445	Bochnia near Cracow	"	?
1447	Poznań	"	fire
1454–55	Cracow	pogrom	Capistrano agitates against nonbelievers and moneylenders
1455	Warsaw	expulsion	Capistrano agitates against nonbelievers and moneylenders
1463	Cracow, etc.	attack	Crusade
1464	Poznań	pogrom and partial expulsion	fire
1477	Cracow	attack	fire and/or epidemic
1483	Warsaw	expulsion	?
1494–95	Cracow	expulsion to Kazimierz	fire?
1495	Lithuania	expulsion	?
1498–1500	Lwów, Kazimierz-Cracow	attack	crusaders (against nonbelievers and Jews)
1498	Warsaw	expulsion	

wafer; twice the persecution was connected with Black Death and pestilence, twice with Capistrano's actions (see below), and twice with Crusades against the Turks —all of which were used as excuses for persecution of Jews in the West.*

All or most of these persecutions may, to be sure, have had a local "reason" and may have been instigated by the burghers of the cities in their anxiety to be rid of their competitors; or by the debtors of the Jews, who sought to cancel their debts in this way; or by local clergymen in connection with some upheaval or disaster; or by the plebes seeking a scapegoat to blame for their wretched situation. But the official motive was taken over from abroad or emulated prevalent foreign practice.

The pace of the struggle quickened in the second half of the fifteenth century, when the number of persecutions more than doubled, and was further accelerated

---

*The approach here (that influences came from the West) is not based on any idea of the existence of a stable national character of a group, in our case of one bent on persecution, in Germany. It maintains rather that human beings are likely to emulate others' behavior patterns and adopt their symbols and attitudes.

in the last two decades. The Polish cities, which since the preceding century had enjoyed prosperity partly resulting from trade with the West and the Levant, suffered a setback after the fall of Constantinople in 1453 and the conquest of the Balkans and the southern seaports by the Turks (Kaffa in 1475, Kilia and Akerman in 1484).

On the other hand, the burghers' organizations (artisans' guilds and merchants' associations) had meanwhile gained in importance, strengthening their activities and their propaganda against the Jews. The seemingly increased pace of Jewish immigration into Poland and the rising number of Jews turning to commerce during the second half of the century may have heightened the negative reaction to them.

By the end of the fifteenth century an open struggle between the non-Jewish merchants and artisans and the Jewish traders began. In 1485 the leaders of the Jewish community in Cracow appeared before the city council in Cracow and "acting of our own free will and without any compulsion" undertook to cease trading in any commodities except unredeemed pledges, and also to refrain—with some minor exceptions—from working as artisans. The "free will and without any compulsion" phrase was clearly only an official formula in a contract forced upon the Jews by the burghers, who could not get the state to ban Jews openly from trade and artisanship. In this period, too, such steps were taken against Jews in other places: in Warsaw the expulsion of 1483 was apparently an outcome of similar causes; in Lwów, Poznań, and Sandomierz pressure was exerted upon Jews, or upon the government, to limit Jewish trade. This culminated in part in expulsion of the Jews from Cracow to nearby Kazimierz in 1495, leaving them the right to tend their stores and businesses in Cracow itself. This struggle was destined to last for centuries.

Forms of Jewish Defense

The small groups of Jews in medieval Poland, sandwiched between the different strata of Polish society, each struggling for power and influence, had to rely greatly on their own initiative and tactics for survival and growth. These varied from incidental acts of physical defense against individual or group attackers to sustained attempts to fulfill needed functions for the king and the powerful, cultivation of friendly personal relations with them and their entourages, and the occasional use of bribes and protection. Casimir the Great (1333-70)* had a Jew, Leibka (or Levko) from Cracow for his court banker. Levko also became the manager of the state salt mines and the mint. After Casimir's death Levko continued his functions under King Louis of Hungary who became king of Poland (1370–84) and during the first years of the reign of Ladislas Jagiello (1386–1434). To another court Jew, Woloczko, the latter king also entrusted the function of *locator*, a special agent who colonized unsettled lands and founded a few villages.

*In the fifteenth century a Polish anti-Jewish historian created the myth of Casimir's Jewish mistress, Ester (or Esterka), on account of whom the king allegedly became friendly to Jews.

In the second half of the fifteenth century we find the well-to-do Fischel family in Cracow as court bankers of kings Casimir IV (1447–92), John Albrecht (1493–1501), and Alexander (1502–6). These and other Jews also acted as toll and tax farmers, which in those periods when the state lacked an organized revenue administration was the only means of bringing revenues into the treasury. Similar functions were filled by Jews for some of the powerful and influential members of the nobility or higher clergy. Through personal contact the king and the nobles came to know something of these Jews and in many cases learned to appreciate their usefulness; or else they simply felt the need for bankers, managers, and toll farmers.

This became more pronounced in the fifteenth century, when the income from the king's estates—a main item of revenue to the treasury—declined, and particularly in the second half of the century when, with the introduction of mercenary armies, the need for funds multiplied. These economic realities may have had an impact upon the king's policy concerning the Jews. Or at least they created a basis for building up good relations around the court and the manor, and served as a rationale for those non-Jews who were friendly to Jews. Nevertheless, they did not remain untouched by the anti-Jewish propaganda and the church's negative images of the Jew, and sometimes gave in to or paid lip service to these trends. This brought out many contradictions. Ladislas Jagiello, for instance, himself a convert to Christianity, did apparently try to persuade his court Jew to embrace "the true religion." When the latter refused, however, he ceased bothering him and continued to call him "our Jew." But one can hardly say which of the king's attitudes was the true one. Each may have been a result of special circumstances, pressures, influences, or political maneuvering. Thus we find the same king erecting a church and a monastery in Poznań on the site where the holy wafer was allegedly stolen by Jews (for which some of them were said to have been burned in 1399), and where some miracles had reputedly been observed. Similarly, this king issued the Statute of Warta (1423) forbidding Jews to lend money on mortgages or promissory notes—in accordance with the resolutions of the church council held in Kalish in 1420. However, in a safe-conduct document for a Jew he mentions his tolerance and his protection for the Jews against the dangers, persecutions, disdain, and humiliation they suffered from the Christians. And, in fact, after the 1407 attack upon Jews in Cracow, provoked in connection with a blood libel, the king held the city authorities responsible and demanded that nobody be allowed to leave until the transgressors had been caught, threatening the city with heavy fines. He took such vigorous action that the various groups in the city realized that, at least for some time, they had better comply with his demands.[24]

Casimir IV was a less zealous follower of the church than his father had been. In fact he tried to curtail its influence in the state. He was also impressed by the humanistic Renaissance trends coming from abroad, and confirmed the Jewish privileges in 1453. It was at this time that the Italian monk John Capistrano was seeking to strengthen the church by rousing the masses against heretics and non-believers and in this connection instigating persecutions and expulsions of Jews. In nearby Silesia many Jews suffered martyrs' deaths and the rest were expelled. The Jews in Poland thought that the confirmation of their privileges might help them if Capistrano were to arrive in Poland.Capistrano, as well as some Polish high church dignitaries, tried to persuade the king to withdraw his confirmation. At first the king was able to withstand their plea, but after Capistrano reached Poland, where he provoked a storm of anti-Jewish fury, the king was compelled to yield. The propaganda disseminated by the anti-Jewish churchmen, implying that the initial defeat suffered by the Polish forces in their war against the Teutonic order was "God's penalty" for having favored Jews, overwhelmed the gentry and they threatened to withdraw from the field.

The Statute of Nieszawa in 1454, which the gentry wrung from the king, limited his powers in several directions; it also contained a paragraph about cancellation of the confirmation of the Jewish privileges. Nevertheless, Casimir IV continued to protect the Jews.

Two years later (1456) the king indicated in an official document that he would not degrade the Jews by depriving them of his royal benevolence since "the principle of tolerance, which is in conformity with God's laws" obligated him to protect them. And he again confirmed most of the Jewish charters.

When a papal legate roused the population for a new Crusade against Turkey, and the crusaders united with the mob to organize a pogrom on Jews in Cracow (1463), the king fined the city council heavily, making the sum extra high to guarantee that peace would prevail. Similarly, in the same year he supported the Jews of Poznań when, having been charged with causing a fire, they were robbed and expelled. The king levied a fine and forced the city to readmit them.

Even King Alexander, who as grand duke of Lithuania had expelled the Jews from that country in 1495, apparently changed his tactics when he became king of Poland. In 1503 he allowed the Jews to return to Lithuania, and a year later he asserted that his treatment of the Jews befitted "kings and rulers who exercise tolerance not only in connection with those who believe in Christianity, but also with those who are followers of other religions."

These few examples would apparently justify the assumption—for lack of other reliable documentary materials—that behind the scenes Jews must have constantly conducted intensive defense and public relations activities, utilizing contacts with court circles and courtiers and friendly non-Jews, taking advantage of political circumstances (like the temporary absence from Cracow in 1453 of Cardinal Zbigniew Oleśnicki, to whom the king was opposed). From this the Jews may have appeared to be living in security and prosperity and exercising strong influence in the country. While some Polish writers created legends about the mythical powers of certain Jews (the above-mentioned Levko, according to a contemporary legend, allegedly used a charm ring to charm the king), others maintained that the Jews controlled the country. A newcomer from Alsace who became the Polish king's secretary wrote in 1516:

At this time the Jews are valued more and more highly; there is hardly a toll or tax which is not controlled by Jews or over which they do not strive to gain control. You would not find anybody among the great and mighty and the most important lords of the state who did not turn over management of his property to a Jew, who did not give to Jews power over Christians.

And a Polish chronicle of that time notes: "Even if the Polish diet would like to harm the Jews it would be unable to do so because the king, the lords, and the nobility are consistently on their side. No Polish nobleman can do without a Jew."[25] These statements, though undoubtedly exaggerated—they were written from an anti-Jewish viewpoint to complain about the power and important status achieved by Jews in a Christian country—reflect the image of the Jew in Polish society and may contain a nucleus of truth. They may give an inkling of the role that Jews, or at least some of them, played in the country.

Attitudes of Jews

Jews themselves, both within the country and abroad, looked upon Polish Jews as living in security. In an age when raids (by the Tatars and others) and wars were not infrequent, when disasters and epidemics occurred often, security was surely no more than a relative concept. This relatively secure feeling was apparently not greatly changed in the fifteenth century by occasional outbursts of mob violence or by an average of one persecution—mostly of a local nature—every eight or nine years. Each such episode may have been regarded by the Jews as just another of the frequent disasters of those years. Jews, or their financial elite, may have drawn inner strength from the important functions they fulfilled. When they acquired estates in payment of outstanding debts, they not only owned and managed them, but they also had jurisdiction over the peasants living there. Managers of mines and toll farmers usually exercised exclusive jurisdiction over an extensive staff, being themselves directly responsible only to the king. Such power was bound to give them a feeling of importance that may have seeped down to the other Jewish groups. Perhaps Jews exaggerated the actual value of the protection and the goodwill of their patrons, or their own power and importance, and looked upon the incidences of persecution as aberrations. But they seem to have regarded the charters and kings' decrees as substantial guarantees of their well-being. In many court cases between Jews and burghers, in complaints and appeals to the king and high officials, these documents served as a legal basis for their demands or defenses. And this fact (regardless of whether the case was won) made these documents appear trustworthy and important in the eyes of the Jews.

The following case from the sixteenth century may show something of these attitudes. Prince A. M. Kurbski (1530–98), commander in chief to Tsar Ivan IV of Moscovy (Russia), defected to Poland. There the Polish king gave him the town of Kowel in Volhynia. A conflict between his administrator and some Jews developed. One Saturday several Jews were arrested and jailed (in a dungeon full of water, according to the Jews' complaint), a number of Jewish stores were closed, and a considerable ransom was demanded. Jews from nearby Vladimir tried to force their release with the help of Polish officials and noblemen. The prince and his administrator, not being familiar with the situation in Poland or with the Jewish charters, refused even to give any reason for the arrest, maintaining that the Jews were the prince's property and at his mercy. In 1569 the Jews brought the case before the king in the *sejm*, and it was decided in favor of the Jews. The chancellor and speaker of the *sejm* intervened in their behalf, and they were released. The characteristic angle of the whole story is probably that Prince Kurbski (apparently when the case was before the king) wished to compromise and come to some agreement with the Jews, but the latter refused any compromise and insisted on their rights. The king's decree points out that the Jewish rights and privileges are to be fulfilled. It should be mentioned that in later years Prince Kurbski did business with Jews and borrowed various sums from them.[26]

Polish Jews considered themselves secure when they compared their own situation with that of the Jews in Silesia, Bohemia, and Germany, who suffered frequent persecution and periodic expulsions, and whose remnants kept seeking refuge in Poland. Even the formal official aspects of the Polish Jews' situation appeared more reliable. Unlike German-Bohemian Jews, who when readmitted usually received temporary residence rights, the Polish Jew received privileges that were permanent.

The formation of Jewish settlements in Poland and the crystallization of their legal and political situation was accomplished in an atmosphere of strain and stress, of hatred and violence, funneled in part through channels from abroad, and was aggravated by a generally harsh and explosive climate and the principle of exclusiveness of the medieval world, plus Christian-Jewish theological differences. These were counterbalanced by the partial support of kings and lords and by the Jews' own activity, enabling some of them to become wealthy and influential, which contributed to a general feeling of relative security.

Taxation

The available evidence seems to indicate that the Jew was not heavily taxed during the first few centuries of Jewish life in Poland (up to the end of the Middle Ages), and that the amount of taxes from Jews played no substantial part in the income of either state or king.[27]

The main sources of income for the state treasury and the king (the two were identical at that time) up to the last quarter of the fourteenth century were the king's estates, his salt and other mines, the mint, and various tolls. Taxes, mostly the land tax on estates, yielded only a small part (about 10 percent) of the revenue. By the end of the century the diminution of crown properties through sales and grants and the decline of the land tax paid on nobles' estates brought about some changes in the tax system. In the second half of the fifteenth century the noblemen and clergy paid a tax (12.5–25 percent) on the rents they collected from the peasants, and city people paid a property tax (4.16 percent). During the last half of the fifteenth century an excise tax was levied on beer and wine. One of the other taxes (called *stacyjne*) imposed upon city dwellers was a contribution toward the court's up-keep.[28] It originated from the general medieval king's or prince's "right of shelter": the obligation to furnish the lord and his entourage with lodging and subsistence during their stay in the city. Originally this was paid in kind;* later it was trans-formed into a money tax.

In some years there were also special levies for such specific purposes as war and other disasters. Cities collected a land or house tax from their own citizens, some special taxes for purposes of fortification of the walls, and a number of indirect taxes —for use of the scales, for instance, which were a city monopoly. In addition, landowners and peasants paid a tax to the church—the tithe.[29] There existed also a number of indirect taxes, tolls, and duties imposed on travelers and traders, on the roads, rivers, bridges, and so on.

Most of the Jewish privileges and decrees emphasize that Jewish merchants should pay tolls and other taxes at similar rates to non-Jews. A document of 1497 concerning the Lwów suburb stresses the fact that Jews and non-Jews pay identical taxes. In some places Jews were obliged (again, apparently in the same way as non-Jews) either to perform certain specific services for the king or his court, or to pay in lieu of so doing. The property tax rates paid by city dwellers to the king seem to have been doubled for Jews, at least during some years. In the fifteenth century, or some part of it, Jewish houseowners paid a yearly tax (*census annus*), which may have been a combination of a kind of head tax with the above-mentioned property tax or possibly with some other tax. Fragmentary figures covering a few years indicate that the larger communities, such as Poznań, Cracow, and Lwów, paid two hundred florins a year each and the smaller ones something between fifteen and forty florins a year. (Some historians assume that the payment was apportioned according to the number and type of the houses: large stone houses paid four florins, small wooden houses two florins each.)

In Mazovia and Warsaw, which until 1526 constituted semi-independent du-chies, the tax load of Jews was much higher than in the kingdom of Poland (Crown), in some years reaching exorbitant amounts.

Taxes were paid either by the individual Jew, by the community which was responsible for payment of this tax for all its members, or by a leading member who was assigned the duty of collecting it. For the end of the fifteenth century we have information about the jailing of Jewish elders in Lwów for arrears in tax payments. Sometimes the king would grant specific Jewish taxes from one place to a noble or high official for one year or more. A case is known in 1506 in which the Cracow annual Jewish tax was granted to a Jewish physician for life.

*Jews were earlier obliged to do this as well as to give food for the king's zoo (Cracow), take care of the mills (Lublin), or guard thieves and furnish the king with transportation (Lwów).

Sometimes the king temporarily relieved an individual or community from payment of the annual tax for one reason or another. On the other hand there were possibly (the source material is not very specific about them) some special taxes or gifts paid or given to the court on certain occasions (upon the renewal of privileges, for instance). It may also have been necessary to offer "gifts" to the high court officials. The charter of the fourteenth century enjoins officials not to demand payment from Jews, which hints that they were doing so. By the end of the fifteenth century—or possibly earlier—Jewish communities paid the *stacyjne* tax toward upkeep of the king's household (or possibly this label included all or most of the taxes Jews paid).*In 1475 the surburban Jewish community in Lwów (that city had two Jewish communities—one in the city and a separate one outside the city walls) paid collectively five marks in annual tax. Generally the loose contemporary use of terms to designate taxes precludes any accurate picture of taxation during the fifteenth century.

Jews, like others, paid tolls, court fines, and special emergency levies, but the sources do not indicate whether in practice these were at the same rate or higher than the ones non-Jews paid. It should also be mentioned that while special money for war purposes was levied from Jews, they were not obliged to furnish a contingent of fighters. By the fifteenth century, however, they may have participated in the city guard, as the Armenians did (mainly in southern Poland), although the extant information stems from the subsequent centuries.

Jewish property for which there were no legal heirs reverted to the king just as non-Jewish property did. Generally, unclaimed property reverted to the ruler during the Middle Ages. (From this are derived the state's present-day escheat rights in England and in most states of the U.S., according to which property and bank accounts whose rightful owner cannot be located belong to the state of his last known address.)

Jews, being under the protection of the king or princes, were officially free from taxation by the cities. But by the end of the fourteenth century (in Silesia as early as the thirteenth century) Jews in the larger cities—Cracow and Poznań (Posen)—paid to the cities land tax on their houses. In towns belonging to the nobility Jews were apparently taxed by the owners.

As early as 1267 and again at the beginning of the fifteenth century the church demanded that a Jew owning a house or land should pay the clergy a tax like the one a Christian would have to pay. But in fact it seems that these payments, if made at all, were no more than sporadic.

At the same time the Jews, like other people, paid the indirect taxes in the cities (for example, for use of the scales in the marketplace). Jews who took over land and estates from their non-Jewish debtors may have paid the tithe just as the former owners had done.[30]

---

*In the middle of the fifteenth century the Armenian community paid collectively a certain fixed amount for the king and apparently double the amount of city tax.

It is impossible to gain a realistic picture either of the tax burden borne by the Jew or of the ratio of its contribution to the treasury. The annual Jewish tax during the last half of the fifteenth century is estimated at nine hundred to a thousand florins. The *stacyjne* at the end of the century may have amounted to the same sum, or it may be that all taxes were lumped together under this term. For special emergency taxes some figures are reported from the end of the fifteenth century and the beginning of the sixteenth. In the former the levy was one florin (zloty) per householder and twelve grosz (two-fifths of a florin) per woman and child (amounting probably to several thousand florins). "Gifts" at the coronation of a new king or on other occasions may have totaled a few hundred florins or more at a time. But it is uncertain how much of this was paid prior to 1500. There may also have been other payments about which we do not know.[31] All in all these fragmentary figures seem to indicate that the tax load was not too heavy (with the exception of Warsaw from 1496 to 1503). They probably also show that taxes derived by the treasury from Jews generally covered only a tiny fraction of the king's state's budget.*

Some of the taxes that Jews paid in Poland during the sixteenth and seventeenth centuries may have been collected before that time, even though documentary evidence is lacking. Hence there is some indication that the individual Jew's tax load was heavier than it would appear from the above computation. A few documents from the end of the fifteenth and beginning of the sixteenth century deal with cases in which the king relieved certain individual Jews—usually as a sign of special consideration—from all taxes. Instead, he ordered them to pay an annual amount to the treasury.[32] This sum ranged from three zloty to as much as twenty zloty (or florins) in gold (gold currency was at that time 10–20 percent higher than the usual currency). If the "freeing from taxes" in these documents is not just a formula with no real meaning, this could indicate that the normal Jewish taxes per head of a household, at least of the richer class to which these grantees belonged, may have been far from low. And if this was so, taxation may, in fact, have been a greater burden for Jews than the few extant figures indicate.

---

*In the last quarter of the fourteenth century it amounted to some 200,000 ducats (or florins) annually, and it rose much higher during the fifteenth century with the expansion of the kingdom, the introduction of standing mercenary armies, and frequent wars.

3 Economic and Social Structure

The economic and occupational structure of the Jews in medieval Poland, as we piece it together from incidental fragmentary sources, was far from diversified. Lack of specialization, so typical of the Middle Ages, often led one individual to perform many varied economic functions, either consecutively or at the same time. Because of this fact and the inadequacy of the statistical data, our picture must remain a rather general one, affording little possibility of assessing the relative role in Jewish life of any specific occupation.

Jews in Poland in the formative centuries of the settlement were a small minority and a society of immigrants. As a minority, the economic choices open to its members were more limited than those available to the majority. Both economic and noneconomic factors play a role in evolving occupational distribution.[1] For example, newcomers cannot (or can to a slight extent only) penetrate the areas already occupied and monopolized by the majority. The immigrants' own occupational heritages also influence their choices. Modifications and changes come gradually as necessitated by the entirely new and different physical and social environment in the country of settlement.

This is observable in Poland in the differences between the western parts of the country and the southern regions. In such western parts as Silesia in the early days, and Cracow, Poznań, and others a little later, trade and artisanship at first played a small role, while moneylending was (at least for a time) a main occupation. The southern part, a less developed area, was a frontier region, and apparently afforded fewer possibilities for moneylending but more and better rewards for risk capital in trade, for the management of tolls, taxes, and estates, and greater opportunities in handicrafts. Two reasons for this situation were that here there were greater natural resources and fewer human obstacles; also, the lesser importance and slower organization of the non-Jewish artisan guilds resulted in weaker monopolistic tendencies, which left the Jews (and, incidentally, the Armenians) more elbow room. A Polish chronicle *(Maciej z Miechowa* or *Miechowita)*, printed in 1519–21, maintains: "In Russia [Rus, Red Russia] and Lithuania there are Jews who are not occupied as usurers . . . but are employed as craftsmen, agriculturists, often as overseers in collection of public tolls and taxes . . . pursue . . . medicine."[2] One is justified in assuming that this development predated the sixteenth century.

From the thirteenth century on, trade routes leading from the Black Sea coast and from the Crimean Italian colonies passed through parts of Podolia and Red Russia. Lwów (Lemberg) became a center of the oriental trade, where luxury wares and spices from the Orient were exchanged for European textiles and metal goods brought in from Silesia and Cracow. Italian merchants transported slaves from the Crimea through Lwów to the markets of Venice and Genoa in the fifteenth century. By the second half of the century transports of oxen and sheep were driven westward through Red Russia and Lwów. The latter was also a focal point for trade in furs, local beeswax, salt from the nearby mines, herring and other fish, wine, and a variety of commodities from different countries.

City autonomy (based on Magdeburg Law) came late to this southern region, and guilds were organized somewhat more slowly than in Poland proper. They were weaker here and the burghers were less influential, so that their policies of monopoly and exclusiveness had little chance of being strictly enforced. The whole southern region, the borderlands (called the Ukraine) was, from the fourteenth century on, subject to frequent invasions and attacks by Tatars, Moldavians (Rumanians), Turks, and warring Lithuanian princes.

The necessity for self-defense against such attacks imposed upon the burghers military obligations ranging from guarding the city walls to supplying field guards, and the obligation to "ride out armed on horseback against the foe together with the *palatinus*" (in Kiev, for instance). In these defensive measures the military commanders or other high officials of the king played the main role. In the wake of defense measures or otherwise, these officials assumed also other powers over the burghers and thus in practice reduced the latter's rights and influence, including their strength as adversaries of the Jews. This situation, plus the fact that Jews took part in the defense of some cities, was apparently the reason why Lwów, for instance, unlike several other Polish cities, refused to open its gates to those who attacked Jews, preferring to pay ransom—to the crusaders in 1463 and 1500 and to the cossack rebels in 1648. In terms of economic life this worked two ways: it was somewhat harder for the burghers to obtain approval for measures restricting Jews in their economic activities and easier for the Jews to circumvent such restrictions as were officially introduced.

In general the Jewish immigrants or refugees from Germany, Silesia, and Bohemia who came to Poland during the thirteenth to fifteenth centuries were an urban element, with a mainly commercial-financial background. This was a time when they were constantly losing ground in the West as traders and in part even as moneylenders, either being forced out of their economic positions by the city burghers or expelled. Immigrants to new countries usually try at first to make use of their former experience whenever possible by taking economic positions similar to the ones to which they had been accustomed. One may justifiably assume this to have been true of the Jews in Poland during the first centuries of their settlement. Such a trend is indicated by the privileges granted them in the thirteenth and fourteenth centuries and by documents of that period from Silesia, Great Poland, and Cracow. (These documents, however, by their very nature, being regulatory rather than descriptive and being imitations of the ones in the West, may have somewhat overemphasized moneylending and may therefore not be entirely representative of the actual situation.)[3]

In the medieval economy, with its lack of specialization, moneylending was not necessarily a separate livelihood; "the medieval banker was both moneylender and merchant."[4] He may have undertaken other functions, too, such as management of the prince's mint, supervision and collection of taxes and tolls, or management of estates acquired as a result of foreclosure.

We find in Poland a number of wealthy Jews who, either individually or in partnership with others, were engaged in all or most of these branches of business, often becoming creditors of the prince or king, occasionally even of a city.

Moneylending

In Polish Silesia, Jews appear early (thirteenth century) as lenders to private persons, to cities, and to princes. In the fourteenth century Levko, a wealthy Jew in Cracow, was loaning smaller amounts to nobles, burghers, and Polish kings (Casimir, Ludwig, Ladislas Jagiello), sometimes to the tune of thousands of florins. He served as manager of the king's salt mines (1368) and as co-manager of the mint; he owned a number of houses and lots in Cracow, dealt in real estate, and owned a brewery and other businesses. There were also others in Cracow engaged in substantial banking activities. In Poznań we find Levko's counterparts in two Jews, Aron Mishko and Jordan. In Lwów credit apparently played less of a role. Yet here, too, in the fifteenth century a Jewish moneylender, Woloczko (Wolf) was acting as tax farmer, the king's financial agent, and merchant. In 1423 the king appointed him as a *locator*—an agent administering settlement in new places. He founded and settled a few villages in which he served as bailiff.

In Luck (southern Poland) in the fourteenth century we find a Jew, Jacob Slomkowitz, who lent money to nobles, served as a tax farmer, had extensive business connections reaching as far as Cracow, where he owned some houses. In the second half of the fifteenth century a number of rich Jewish bankers—toll farmers—merchants prospered: the Fischels in Cracow or Kazimierz, who came from Germany at midcentury, Yosko (or Joseph) of Hrubieszów in southern Poland, and others. Each gained control of a variety of business enterprises, and each was, among other things, lending money or making large "down payments" to the king in anticipation of the latter's expected income from tolls and taxes.

Naturally, these leaders among the Jewish bankers and businessmen were not representative of all Jewish moneylender-businessmen in Poland of that period, some of whom were loaning even very small sums. The "banker of students" *(kampsor)* of the university in Cracow belonged to this last group. Casimir the Great appointed a Jew to this position in 1364, setting an upper limit on the interest rate. In 1400 another Jew was appointed to this position when the university was revived after a few decades of decline. In Warsaw—and in the less developed region of Mazovia generally—Jewish credit transactions were less frequent and involved smaller amounts. And of course fewer Jews were engaged in this occupation (during the fifteenth century ten names appear as lenders in Warsaw). Women are repeatedly found among the lenders, and in Poznań (1369, 1373) an *episcopus Judaeorum* (Jewish bishop), by which is to be understood a rabbi, a teacher, a board member, or some other functionary of the community, is mentioned as a lender.

The borrowers from these Jewish lenders ranged from kings, dukes, and cities (the latter mainly in Silesia), to higher and lower nobility, the clergy, city burghers, university students, and a scattering of peasants.

Obviously, the sums loaned and the conditions of credit varied considerably, ranging from thousands and tens of thousands of marks to as little as six or nine. In some cases the security offered for a loan was real estate, including whole villages or even cities; in others it was promissory notes. Small amounts were loaned either with or without a pledge. The interest rate apparently also varied considerably. In Poland generally loans secured on real estate brought 10–20 percent in the fourteenth century, but in the second half of the fifteenth century they paid no more than 8 percent and even less.[5] Loans without security carried higher interest. The privilege of 1347 permitted a Jew to demand an interest rate up to 54 percent (later increased to 108 percent), but for money loaned to students the maximum rate allowed was only 25 percent annually. In Warsaw rates ranged between 43 percent and 86 percent during the fifteenth century.

In practice the interest rate may have been lower or higher, depending on the credit rating of the borrower and the frequency with which the currency was depreciated. Depreciation of currency was a part of public finance in Europe during medieval times when no printing presses existed for the production of paper money and lack of revenue-collecting machinery made emergency taxing devices too cumbersome. Poland was no exception. (During the fourteenth century, for instance, the value of silver coins was reduced by half as a result of depreciation.) In years of increasing currency debasement moneylenders adjusted the interest rates in order to avoid losing money by depreciation.

High interest on loans, mostly unproductive ones, made repayment a serious problem. According to available records, if people were brought to court for payment of a loan of six marks and six years' interest or five marks and nine years' interest, that may have meant repayment of three or more times the original sum. There are also cases in which failure to repay the loan punctually caused the amount of the loan to be raised to up to five times the original sum. In some cases tardy borrowers were jailed, and on many occasions their real estate and villages were foreclosed and taken over by the Jewish lenders.[6]

The debtor's natural resentment of his creditor was increased when homeowners and landowners saw their properties foreclosed. Nobles and burghers—either because they were borrowers or because as lenders themselves they regarded Jews as competitors—struggled to oust the Jewish lenders, and were often assisted in their efforts by the church. This struggle became more intense around the middle of the fourteenth century, when new legislation made it possible for the creditor to seize real estate if the debtor did not pay punctually. (Earlier the debt had been automatically prolonged for one to three years or the property had remained in the hands of the creditor for usufruct only—until the income from the estate had paid up the debt.) Foreclosure then became a real danger, and debtors were of course anxious to avoid the loss of their estates and houses. At times they succeeded in persuading, or pressuring, the king to impose limitations upon loans on mortgages or promissory notes that could lead to foreclosures (privilege of 1347 for Little Poland; statutes of Warta in 1423, Nieszawe in 1454, Piotrków in 1496). The greater availability of non-Jewish credit may have had an impact upon the attitudes toward Jewish moneylenders.

In the fifteenth century moneylending by Jews met with opposition generally, not only in Poland. The tendencies of the Basel Ecumenical Council (1434) to forbid Jews to lend money for interest were an expression of the growing antagonism against Jewish lenders. During that century an attempt was made in Austria and Germany to eliminate Jews from moneylending for interest.

This general climate of opinion had an influence in Poland, too, even though in practice the intended impact of these restrictions was not always fully achieved. They were, to some extent, disregarded by the courts (particularly in the south). But these fifteenth-century limitations became either the cause of, or were otherwise connected with, a change in Jewish moneylending, even in Warsaw where the Polish statutes carried no weight. The rest of Mazovia seems to have been an exception because throughout the whole of the fifteenth century lending on real estate was allowed. In most of Poland Jewish moneylending declined after the first quarter of the fifteenth century—in Warsaw after the 1430s—and changed in character. Most loans were now given on pledges and involved smaller amounts.

There was also an observable shift in borrowers. The city burgher replaced the nobleman as the main borrower. In the south, however, the situation remained almost unchanged, with new Jewish bankers entering the scene. Although some new Jewish banking families still appeared in the second half of the century, the peak seems to have already passed. The number of loan entries in the books diminished further as more non-Jews became lenders from whom Jews, too, began borrowing. These non-Jews (businessmen, nobles, clergy) were often involved in lending large sums. This applies not only to some merchant princes in Cracow, who, besides their businesses were also engaged in banking on a considerable scale, but also to others. A computation of lending transactions in the Przemyśl region (Galicia or southeast Poland) in 1436–50 shows that Jewish "banking" operations accounted for only 0.2 percent of the total credit during those years. The main lenders and borrowers were the nobility, with city dwellers in second place. But some clergymen and even independent peasants were also lenders and borrowers.[7]

Although this less developed region, where apparently only a few Jews lived at that time, may not be representative for such cities as Cracow and Poznań, it may nevertheless indicate some realities. In Mazovia, too, there were Christian lenders. Generally, by the second half of the fifteenth century, the number of Jewish lenders seems to have been on the decline (for instance in Poznań and Cracow) as non-Jews partially took over this role.[8] At that time, cases are recorded in which the roles were reversed—Jews borrowed from non-Jews.[9] This may mean (if parallels from the sixteenth century may be applied to the fifteenth) that Jews were finding other types of enterprise (trade, leaseholding) more profitable or safer, and were using borrowed funds as well as their own for such purposes.[10]

In general, according to documentary evidence, the number of Jews involved in moneylending was small. The court books from the last quarter of the fourteenth century, in which entries about lending money were usually made, show about seventy Jewish creditors (fifty in Poznań and twenty in Cracow). In the first forty years of the fifteenth century four hundred such Jewish names appear,[11] with Warsaw accounting for about one hundred entries annually until the number declined at the end of the century, when only ten people were involved. Only a small part of the Jewish population seems to have been engaged in such activities, although the big bankers and lenders may have employed a number of assistants or agents.

Real Estate, Management of Village Estates, and Agriculture

Besides being actively engaged in buying and selling houses and lots, Jews also came to deal in real estate in connection with moneylending and eventual foreclosures. This also applied to village estates (only one case is known—the above-mentioned Woloczko from Lwów—to whom the king granted the right to be a *locator* [founder and administrator] of villages). In the sources and court books there is enough material, mostly from the fifteenth century on, to show that in a number of cases whole villages were foreclosed and passed into the possession of Jews, who, at least temporarily, administered them and derived revenue from them.* (In later centuries we also find Jews as leaseholders of estates.) This seems to have been mostly in southern Poland and Lithuania. In these regions some Jews also obtained the grand duke's permission to purchase villages or received such villages from him. In Mazovia we find some Jews selling cultivated land they had taken over earlier from

---

*The owner or lord of a village usually enjoyed the perquisites of local justice from the peasants. Such "servitude" on the part of Christians to a Jew was generally frowned upon in the framework of a medieval Christian society. Thus, unless a Jewish mortgagee coming into possession of a village estate could obtain special permission from the king to administer it himself, he had either to appoint a non-Jewish administrator or to sell the estate to a non-Jew. In southern Poland, however, the Jews mostly retained these estates and also owned non-Jewish slaves. In later centuries, as we shall see, certain Jews were exercising this function of local justice over Christians.

the non-Jewish debtors. When the Jews were expelled from Lithuania in 1495 the grand duke parceled out to non-Jews a number of formerly Jewish manorial possessions: estates, fishponds, mills, and houses. Later, upon their return, most of these estates were given back to the Jews.

It is unlikely, with perhaps minor exceptions, that Jewish estate owners cultivated the land with their own hands, any more than they caught the fish themselves. In the villages of the medieval feudal society, work on the land—including cattle raising, fishing, and similar occupations—was done by the peasant attached to the given land, in some cases by serfs with the owner or his representative serving as overseer or administrator. This also seems to have been the situation in villages owned or administered by Jews.

But in and around the towns it was different. Some of the urban population was usually actively engaged in agriculture, and there were agriculturists living in many urban settlements in Poland proper and still more in the eastern and southern borderlands. Jews there also owned land, pastures, and gardens (the privilege of 1389 to Grodno Jews mentions such Jewish possessions and pursuits). Their agricultural activities were, to a great extent, a sideline rather than a principal occupation.[12]

Like other groups in the cities, Jews for the most part lived on their own street. The medieval town was generally "divided into sectors in each of which there was some specialization in occupation or trade. In the Turkish Empire the sectors were characterized more by uniformity of faith or ethnic group . . . such voluntary segregation is commonly the act of a minority, whether a ruling minority (like the Turks in the Balkans) or not."[13] Some Christians, however, lived on the Jewish street, just as some Jews usually had houses in the non-Jewish sectors, acquired either through foreclosures resulting from moneylending or simply by purchase.

As lending money on mortgages and promissory notes decreased in the fifteenth century, there were fewer possibilities for Jews to obtain real estate, houses, and land when a debtor did not pay, although they were still occasionally able to do so.[14] The cities also instituted special proscriptions. In 1392 the city council of Cracow demanded that a Jew who purchased a house from a Christian sign a promise to resell it only to a Christian.[15] In Poznań we find a similar situation about half a century later (in 1449). This policy on the part of the city councils was intended to contain the spread of Jewish housing and thereby control the growth of the Jewish population.

On the other hand, the Jews in Lwów did not encounter difficulties in obtaining houses in this period. They could and did purchase houses located outside the Jewish street from burghers, nobles, and even princes of the church.[16]

Tax and Toll Farming

The medieval state, including the Polish state, had no regular revenue system, financial policy, or staffed revenue office. Revenues were inadequate, and levies were made in a haphazard manner: tolls were collected from merchants on the roads and at bridges and river crossings. As one author states: "They imposed new tolls on the slightest pretext but did not repeal them as the emergency passed." In Poland the number of toll stations and levies grew constantly with the development of roads and increasing traffic. At the beginning of the fourteenth century 250 toll stations existed, and later the number was increased as the states or the kings needed larger revenues. Private estate owners also often established toll stations of their own, collecting a fee for passage through their property.

The income from taxes and particularly tolls, as well as revenues from the mint or the mines, was farmed out in exchange for payment of a fixed annual sum to the treasury.[17] The tax farmers would collect as much as they could, often more than the official rates. Jews appear, either alone or in partnership with non-Jews, as farmers of some taxes and more often of tolls and others sources of income. In fact, the Jewish toll and revenue farmer was sometimes the first Jew to settle in a place. This seems to have been the case with a few Jewish lessees in Kiev at the end of the fifteenth century who became the founders of the renewed Jewish settlement there. This happened most often in the southern borderlands.[18] The ore mines, the salt mines, and often the mint were farmed out by princes and kings to entrepreneurs who paid a fixed sum annually and then usually took in a much higher amount.

As early as 1368, we find Levko of Cracow farming some state revenues and leaseholding the salt mines in Bochnia and Wieliczka. But the bulk of our information on Jews as tax and revenue farmers comes from the fifteenth century. Most of these Jews came from the southern parts of the country or were leasing taxes and custom duties, or revenues from mines located in the south.[19]

Tax, toll, and mine farming were complicated enterprises in those centuries. Each was a large-scale business and financial operation involving banking and credit and demanding commercial, financial, and organizational talent and policing activity. The "farmer" who paid in a lump sum did not always send the money to the treasury. He was a sort of financial agent for the king (or noble), whose creditors and beneficiaries he paid according to instructions; or he advanced larger sums to the king against future payments. Sometimes he also procured a variety of commodities for the court.

The toll stations and mines had to be manned by staffs of collectors, recorders, and enforcement officers. Despite the customary phrases in documents executed by the king, instructing the royal officials to help the leaseholder in his task, the latter was for the most part left to his own resources in enforcing collections. As a rule he was given absolute power and jurisdiction over his staff. The king's court alone could serve as a court of appeal against the leaseholder's decision. The numerous extant complaints about overcharging and the use of brutal force in the course of toll collecting—not necessarily by Jewish toll farmers—apparently attest to the "efficiency" of the enforcement staff.

The toll farmer had many opportunities to practice abuse. Rates were not always clearly fixed. The toll farmer and his employees had the right to search travelers' wagons and to confiscate the wares of anyone trying to avoid payment of tolls (by using side roads, and the like). Such confiscation was profitable, for 50 percent of the wares went to the toll farmer and the other 50 percent to the king. In 1627 the Lithuanian Community Council *(Vaad)* issued an ordinance forbidding the Jewish tax collectors to overcharge.

Those who thought they had been overcharged or had other complaints about the manner in which they were treated tended to regard this as Jewish oppression. Others, who would have liked to farm the tolls themselves, attempted to eliminate Jewish competition in this field by labeling it "Jewish oppression" or "Jewish dominance." The church fought this activity of the Jews, ostensibly for the reason that it placed Jews in administrative positions over Christians. The synod of 1267 in Breslau forbade the farming out of customs, revenues, and tolls to Jews. This proscription was repeated several times by the Wieluń-Kalish synod of 1420, and on several other occasions.

But in practice these restrictions were only partially enforced or else were valid for a brief period in western Poland only. Hence in 1516 an observer from Alsace (Decjusz) could remark, probably exaggerating to some extent: "There is almost no toll or tax that would not be under Jewish administration, or that the Jews would not attempt to get their hands on."[20] The struggle against Jewish tax and revenue farming took more concrete forms during the sixteenth century.

Trade

The privileges granted to Jews specified the right to travel around the country with merchandise and to pay the same tolls as non-Jews. This was also reiterated locally on several occasions (in 1226 in Rosenberg, Silesia; in 1327 in Nowy Sącz near Cracow). Some of the privileges (by Bolko I of Schweidnitz, Silesia; by Casimir III for Grodno in 1389) mention specifically the right to trade in commodities. Certain individual Jews obtained special grants to trade throughout the country and to be exempt from tolls. Moneylending and tax farming were not just concomitants of trade; they sometimes led directly to marketing—of unredeemed pledges and merchandise confiscated at toll stations.

Jews were also engaged in retail trade in other commodities—trade that the non-Jewish burghers tried to monopolize. Jewish butchers, for instance, were selling nonkosher (and possibly kosher) meat to non-Jews. Other wares, imported or local, their own or taken on consignment from both Jews and non-Jews, were sold by Jews in stores, stalls and houses, and possibly also peddled from door to door. Scarcity of source material for medieval times precludes a full depiction of this trade and its role in Jewish economic life during that period. One would seem to be justified in assuming that its volume was limited. In those times of nonspecialized economy, when people's needs were few, most of the commodity exchange in the towns may have been directly between the producer and the consumer, with the middleman creeping in only here and there. But we find that Jews were dealing in many types of merchandise: cattle, grain, honey, timber, horses, fur, textiles, and fish.

In the medieval town, with its "outspoken municipal egoism," the principle of acquired rights prevailed. The local merchant sought to monopolize all retail trade by trying to have all "foreigners" or strangers banned from engaging in it. Each artisans' guild followed suit for the items its members produced (except during fairs). For this reason Jews often took to international trade. They brought commodities such as spices, luxury goods, and animals from the East and southeast and manufactured goods from the West. This involved formidable risks to person and wares during the long drawn-out trips on robber-infested roads, and chances of having the goods confiscated by the various rulers and noblemen through whose domains they had to pass were great. But on the other hand it often yielded high profits.

Jews did not give up retail trade, however. We find Jews employed in retail trade in Silesia as early as the thirteenth century. For example, in Lwowek Śląski in 1249 they traded in minerals; in Klodzko they did so about 1300; in Breslau at the end of the thirteenth century there was retail trading in textiles (we learn this from a proscription forbidding it in the future). About a century later we find the burghers in Cracow complaining about being displaced by the Jews who "intrude" with their wares into the marketplace. In Warsaw in the first half or the middle of the fifteenth century Jews seem to have been doing retail business in a variety of wares, as well as serving as purveyors for the prince and some dignitaries.[21]

It was in this sphere of retail trade that the first blows were struck against Jews. We have already mentioned the city council of Breslau's 1301 proscription against the retail sale of textiles. In Warsaw the first limitation was apparently introduced in 1461. This period seems to have marked the beginning of an attack on Jewish trade—mainly retail—in Poland, which reached a peak in the last decades of the fifteenth century and spilled over into the following century. Either the growing Jewish immigration to Poland at that time, or a more definite shift of Jews toward trade, or a general decline in trade resulting from Turkish conquests led the non-Jewish burghers to take action to combat the "invasion." This resulted in a number of limitations and may also have furnished grounds for a few expulsions. In Warsaw, Jews (and other "strangers") were forbidden to participate in retail trade in 1483 and were expelled in the same year. An agreement made in 1485 between the Jewish community in Cracow and the city council has been preserved, in which the former undertake "out of goodwill and without any coercion" to abstain from trade and from selling anything but pledges. It is not known what sort of pressure made the Jews agree to resign from such business activity "without any coercion." But it is reasonable to assume that the expulsion of Jews from Cracow ten years later was the culmination of a struggle, perhaps a long-lasting one, between the city and the Jews, of which the agreement "without any coercion" was but a link in the chain. (The immediate cause of the expulsion was a big fire in 1494, followed by an attack upon the Jews.) In the same period (1488) legal limitations were also placed on Jewish trade in Lwów.

Foreign trade was more profitable and less controlled. A number of trade routes passed through Poland (especially after the thirteenth to fourteenth centuries): from the south (Hungary) to Cracow, and from there to the north and the Baltic Sea; from the Crimea (Genoese Kaffa colonies and others) to Volhynia and Red Russia (Luck, Lwòw), and thence to Cracow and Breslau and eventually farther west. In the fourteenth and especially the fifteenth centuries the Jews' share in this trade became more evident, especially the commerce from the colony of Kaffa, in the Crimea, to Lwów. Jews, Armenians, and some Greeks made business trips to the Crimea, and some of them also went to Constantinople after 1453.

In the fifteenth century a few Jews from Kaffa and Italy settled in Poland for commercial reasons and were joined by a few others from Constantinople and elsewhere. Most of this trade was concentrated around luxury wares from the Orient: spices, furs, cloth, wine, and sometimes slaves. Jews also dealt in cattle, oxen, horses, fish, grain, and timber.

In the fifteenth century Poznań became a center for trade and, to some extent, for export to Silesia and Germany. Jews, both local and from other parts of Poland (Kalish, Lwów, Cracow, Lęczyca), came there to sell such Polish commodities as horses, oxen, beeswax, linen, hides, and furs, and they bought Eastern and Western commodities (pepper, textiles, and the like) brought there from Breslau and German centers.

In the "northern trade"—through Baltic Sea ports—we find Jews from Lithuania and Volhynia in the fifteenth century after Danzig became a Polish possession. Earlier, Warsaw had been a center of this international trade from Lithuania. Jews, who were not permitted to enter Danzig until 1454, would come to Warsaw, whence they would conduct their business with merchants from the port city or with Warsaw businessmen (trading lumber, grain, cattle, horses, textiles, beeswax, furs, pepper, and silk). In later decades we find Brest Jews in Warsaw also doing business in partnership with local Jews.

Occasionally a Polish Jew went abroad. A few Jews from Kalish and other places came to Breslau in the fifteenth century. A Jew from Poland was found in Venice and another in Sicily (it is not clear whether the latter was there for business reasons).[22]

In wholesale trade, too, some limitations were placed upon foreigners, including Jews. The staple rights granted to most large cities prevented outsiders from passing through the city or its environs without staying there for a number of days or weeks and offering their commodities to the burghers and local merchants (not to other strangers). Other limitations on this kind of trade were also found in Polish cities. But here the prohibitions were far less effective than in retail trade. The Polish state had no commercial policy. Prohibitions were usually introduced under pressure from the burghers—often without any provision for executing these decrees. The city government was sometimes able to hinder Jewish commerce inside its walls, but it had no jurisdiction over Jews who traveled to other cities and towns, or even over those living in the suburbs or on the possessions of the nearby castle or lands of the noblemen.

The number of Jewish wholesale merchants in interurban and international trade, attending fairs, or traveling to outlying places and foreign countries must of necessity have been far from large in those times. Unavoidably long journeys, danger on the highways, great risks (of robbery and confiscation), and the necessity of traveling in caravans were limiting factors in this sort of trade. Only the wealthy had the means to risk such high stakes, which admittedly promised great profits. But connected with this limited number of entrepreneurs were many other Jews who took wares from them on consignment, bought and sold for them, or served as clerks, bookkeepers, and the like.

Crafts

Some Jews seem to have been active in crafts, but their number may have been insignificant. The 1389 privilege for Grodno mentions the right to work as artisans. It is reasonable to assume that some Jews were active in trades connected with Jewish religious traditions (tailors because of the religious proscription against mixing wool and linen, butchers to supply kosher meat, weavers of prayer shawls, and so on). On the other hand, one must realize that in the primitive way of life of those times many necessities (such as matza for Passover, bread for the Sabbath and for daily consumption) were prepared in the consumer's own home and needed no special craftsmen or only a part-time worker proficient in the craft.

The source material yields some information on butchers. The non-Jewish butchers' guild fought to limit the number and activity of Jews in that occupation. In Breslau, for instance, in 1315 the guild forced the Jews to agree that the non-Jewish butchers should designate the cattle to be slaughtered by Jews; the non-Jewish butchers would then sell the kosher meat to Jews, thus eliminating the Jewish butcher or reducing his function. In Kazimierz, near Cracow, a controversy among the butchers raged for some time. After a long struggle the butchers' guild compelled the Jews (1494) to agree to limit the number of Jewish butchers to four, with no right to employ assistants, and permitted them to slaughter and sell meat to Jews only.[23] In both these places the number of Jewish butchers was small (three in Breslau, four in Kazimierz), but Jewish butchers surely also existed in Poznań, Lwów, and other larger cities.

There is some indication that in Cracow, Jewish men and especially Jewish women were making and selling hats and collars, as well as other articles of clothing (in the sources these are called "poor" Jews). This may indicate that there were Jewish tailors and hatmakers producing for the market.

We know of the existence of Jewish tailors, blacksmiths, and shoemakers in Lwów. By the middle of the fifteenth century there was friction between these Jews and the artisans' guild, which was trying to eliminate nonmembers from the suburb. In 1458 a compromise provided for one Jewish tailor, one blacksmith, and two shoemakers "in addition to those Jewish shoemakers who have lived there a long time" to continue to ply their trades. From this one may assume that more than that number of Jewish tailors and blacksmiths existed. In Lwów there were also

Jewish tanners (we have information from 1460 and later), glaziers (1500), and other artisans.[24] In Warsaw at the end of the fifteenth century we find a furrier, a hatter, and two cord makers. There may have been Jewish tailors and furriers in Luck as early as the fifteenth century, although our information dates from 1539. Some Jews may also have been brewers and distillers, but these crafts were not yet widespread among Jews in those centuries. There may also have been a few Jews in certain other crafts, but the total number of Jewish artisans and their role in crafts in Poland during the Middle Ages was minimal, notwithstanding certain speculations to the contrary.[25]

There is little mention of Jewish artisans in either general or Jewish sources. Demand for their wares must have been very small in the semiprimitive Polish society of those centuries. Non-Jewish city craftsmen, organized into guilds, and the artisans in the villages and manors—some of whom remained only temporarily in the cities or simply came there to bring in their wares—were more than able to fill the demand.[26] The city guilds did their utmost to eliminate these village artisans or at least to reduce their competitiveness. The fact that we do not hear of opposition by the artisans' guilds to Jewish competition during these centuries (except for the butchers and some others in Lwów) may indicate that there were too few of them to create a clash. And when such a struggle did ensue, in the sixteenth and the first half of the seventeenth centuries, both the anti-Jewish writings of the time and the guilds tell of Jews having only recently learned their crafts and of non-Jews teaching them. (The guilds forbade their members to train Jews.)

Service Occupations and Professions

Wealthy Jews with extended business connections in banking, trade, or toll and tax farming apparently employed a considerable number of clerks and assistants, although the sources yield very scant information on this point. We hear something about an assistant to a Breslau Jew and of clerks and bookkeepers (four or five in Breslau),[27] and we know of the large staffs of the Jewish toll farmers over whom the latter had full jurisdiction. These staff members—secretaries, clerks, and collectors—were undoubtedly Jews, for some of the toll registers and many receipts were written in Yiddish or Hebrew. In fact, in 1671 the authorities issued an order forbidding receipts in these languages. We do not know, however, to which religious group the enforcement personnel—the guards—belonged.

Wealthy Jews employed Jewish domestic servants (in 1352 four are mentioned in Breslau), as well as non-Jewish servants.

In Cracow, Lwów, and Warsaw eleven Jewish physicians or "barber-doctors" are mentioned during the fifteenth century, one of them a woman, who may have been a midwife. Jewish midwives may also have been practicing in other places. An eye doctor and a midwife are mentioned as early as 1352 in Breslau. (Probably more Jewish physicians were practicing in Poland; the extant documents are of an incidental nature.)

It is interesting to note from the documents that some of the eleven physicians appear to have also been preparing and selling medicaments. One peculiarity of the physician's occupation—probably not just among Jewish doctors—is shown by a number of preserved contracts. The fees paid or agreed upon were subject to the physician's success. Should he fail, the patient was not obliged to pay; if he had already paid the physician had to refund the fee. In one case he was also obliged to refund the cost of the medicine.[28]

The rabbis, too, should be counted among the professionals, although until the end of the Middle Ages they probably did not receive any fixed salary. Their income came rather from payment for services rendered—as scribe, judge, performer of marriages, and possibly also as marriage broker. In the beginning the rabbis also acted as teachers and cantors. Apparently it was not until the fifteenth century that the rabbinate became divorced from the other functions—and then surely only in the larger cities. On the other hand, in many cases the rabbinate was probably not the incumbent's only means of making a living. He may have had other sources of income such as moneylending or other business. (This is documented for later centuries.)

Other professionals were the scribes (in 1352 one is mentioned in Breslau), the teachers (two or three in Breslau), the beadles* (one in Breslau), and apparently also the shochetim (ritual slaughterers). Wealthy Jews employed private teachers for their children.

All in all, the service occupations, including the professions, may have made up some 10–15 percent or less of the Jewish labor force of those times (estimate based on figures for Breslau in 1352). Most of the people working in these fields seem to have simultaneously fulfilled some other economic functions.

Structure

As we have said, it is impossible to undertake any reliable estimate of the occupational structure of Jews in medieval Poland. Both lack of specialization at that time and the fragmentary character of the source material preclude any such calculation. The situation in connection with the social structure is scarcely better. We know something about the existence of rich Jews—their activities left certain traces in records and court documents—and by implication we can learn about other Jews. But the information does not suffice to form any image of the relative importance of these groups in Jewish society. It was only in the sixteenth century that the problem of rich and poor occupied the minds of rabbis and Jewish authors in Poland. If the figures for Breslau around the middle of the fourteenth century are representative (Jews were resettled there after having been expelled a little earlier; apparently mainly taxpayers qualified for such resettlement) and if the preserved tax rolls are

---

*The beadle, or shamash, in those centuries (and later) may have meant the person who took care of the synagogue, and so on, or the one who did clerical work for the community and served as its contact with the outside world.

correct, about 15 percent of the Jewish population were earners of wages, salaries, and fees. The rest were independent owners of business enterprises. The same material also indicates that about 10 percent of the Jews were poor, and about 7 percent "very rich,"[29] thus placing about four-fifths of the Jewish population in the middle-income group, whatever this may have meant then.

4 Jewish Community Organization

By "community" one understands any group sharing the basic conditions of a common life. The term Jewish community, as used here, designates a group or society of Jews meeting life in a more or less similar way and evolving or maintaining a system of values and norms. The phrase also means an organization of Jews (kehilla) for the purpose of mutual assistance in life's exigencies and in the solution of its problems, for keeping alive their norms and values, stimulating the practice of their religion, and fulfilling needs in these and other areas.

This community organization, which the state usually invested with some authority, comprised two elements: (1) an internal Jewish framework based both on the varied needs of the group and on Jewish law, or derivatives thereof, and Jewish tradition; and (2) the legal framework of the state, imparting a certain autonomy to the kehilla and often making it a policing and tax collecting agency insofar as Jews were concerned. Without regard to which of these two elements came first in each locality—the internal or the external—in time the two became interwoven and institutionalized. They were transferred from country to country as the Jews migrated, becoming modified in the process of adaptation to the realities of life in new environments.

This Jewish communal organization and its institutions in Europe may have had some parallels in the ancient world, and the regulations it issued may or may not really have been based on the Talmud (or talmudic maxims interpreted to give traditional authority to the communal structure). But it was for the most part a product of the Middle Ages. It was based on or connected with the legal systems prevailing in medieval Europe, and it emulated "institutional and legal patterns developed by the non-Jewish nations."[1]

The corporate state structure of society in feudal Europe consisted of autonomous or semiautonomous estates or groups, each having a separate and different legal and jurisdictional system, courts, taxation scale, rights, privileges and obligations, and often also some separate police functions. Foreigners *(hospites)* had the right to be adjudicated according to their own laws. In Poland this fragmentation was multiplied several times by the introduction of a foreign system of autonomous cities (under the German or Magdeburg Law) with the German immigration of the thirteenth century, and with the evolution of a multinational state in the second half of the fourteenth century.

Towns and villages existed side by side, some ruled according to the new German law, others according to the usage of Polish law. With the fourteenth-century conquest of Red Russia (Galicia) and some other southern areas, whole regions of urban and village settlements based on Russian law were annexed, as well as some villages where Rumanians (Wallachs) settled and enjoyed autonomy on the basis of Rumanian law. Also in some southern cities—Lwów, for instance—the Russians (or Ruthenians) formed an autonomous community using Russian law. Other minorities, too, not concentrated in territories of their own, had the right to be judged according to their own laws. Among these were the Armenians and Tatars (Muslims). The latter came to Poland either as war prisoners or as settlers. Most of these nations, as they were called, enjoyed the right to form their own autonomous religious-cultural community organization with their own elected elders. The latter represented them outside the community, exercised some power over them, acted as judges or assessors in courts dealing with members of the group, and were responsible for the group's special taxes, which had to be paid to the authorities in a lump sum. The Armenians in Lwów (and later in other places) were subject to a court consisting of Armenian elders and a chairman known as the Armenian judge *(judex Armenorum)*. Sometimes he was an Armenian, but in later years the city bailiff filled this position.[2] The court functioned according to customs of Armenian law.*

The Jewish group and its community organization, the kehilla, became a component of this kaleidoscope of legal systems and autonomous structures. Like the other estates and ethnic and religious minorities, the Jews were adjudicated according to their own laws. Their elders, some of whom had to collect taxes from the individual Jews and pay them in a lump sum, enjoyed autonomous status with special rights, responsibilities, and power over members of the kehilla.

Jews generally enjoyed similar institutional autonomy during the Middle Ages and later in the Christian West as well as in the Muslim East (in the latter as part of the Millet System). In Poland, however, the many-sided system of legal and autonomous structures—not only in terms of estates but also of various legal systems and minority religious-cultural groups—apparently served as background for a broader development of Jewish community autonomy. In Poland the Jewish community organization, the kehilla, acquired wider prerogatives in the course of its historical development than in most other countries and built up a supercommunity: the *Vaadim*, the Four-Land Council, and the Lithuanian Community Council, which became apparently more important than similar superior councils elsewhere.

---

*For this purpose their law book *(Datastanagirk)* was translated—with some changes—into Polish and Latin and confirmed by the Polish king.

Historical Development

By the last centuries of the Middle Ages, when the Jewish settlement in Poland had taken form, Jews in the West (where the immigrants came from) already had a more or less stable kehilla system with elders, functionaries, rabbis, and procedures that had evolved over the course of several centuries.

Like the city generally, the kehilla comprised a mixture of universalism and particularism. On one hand, the general interests of the whole Jewish people, with its religious and ethical teachings and aspirations, were stressed; on the other, the self-interest of the local community and its members or leadership was emphasized. Membership in the kehilla, with its implied right of settlement and participation in the sources of income, was limited. In this way the kehilla, like the city generally, attempted to prevent newcomers from settling or, failing that, to charge them high "entrance fees." Often the kehilla also had the power to expel a member either with or without the ruler's approval. By the fifteenth century or earlier there were a number of places in which members had precedence over strangers, even with respect to reciting the mourners' *Kaddish* in the synagogue.

The taxpayers, that is the large taxpayers, were the important people. The leadership (parnasim, elders) were selected or nominated from among the most wealthy. These elected leaders sat in court as judges with or without the rabbis. They heard mainly financial cases, apportioned taxes, represented the community before the authorities, controlled the right of settlement, oversaw the economic as well as some other facets of life, and served as administrators of community property. The rabbinate became partly professionalized in Germany in the period following the Black Death (1349), but the rabbi may still have supplemented his income or even made his main living from other occupations. Authorization (semicha) gradually became a prerequisite for occupying the post. The rabbi dealt mainly with religious, moral, business, and family matters of the community. He sat in or presided over the Jewish court, occasionally represented the community vis-à-vis the authorities, and served at times as head of a yeshiva (academy for the study of talmudic lore); sometimes he also served as a parnas or leader of the kehilla.

The rabbi also assisted with problems of marriage and divorce, and had some control over ritual (kosher) food and drink and other religious matters. He had the right, often subject to the agreement of the lay leadership or the parnas, to penalize a member of the kehilla by fines or excommunication (herem) for transgressions or other reasons. The banning of a member (somewhat like the Christian excommunication) not only isolated the individual from the Jewish group, but could on occasion lead to confiscation of his property by the state or to even heavier penalties. The ban served as one of the most effective means of coercion in the hands of the rabbi or lay leadership or both. Ordinances and opinions of known and respected rabbi-scholars were often also accepted outside their own communities. Rabbis and lay leaders of a number of communities met at intervals in special synods and councils that issued ordinances concerning community matters. These regulations, together with those of the state, formalized the structure of the kehilla.[3]

Quite early, possibly from the twelfth century, a trend toward a hierarchical structure becomes observable in the communities. Leadership was concentrated in the hands of a small group of the wealthy and influential, whose handling of community affairs was at times arbitrary and dictatorial.[4]

The kehilla employed a number of officials in addition to the rabbi: a cantor (chazan—though the rabbi himself sometimes filled this position), one or more sextons (shamash) who fulfilled a variety of functions over and above taking care of the synagogue, a schoolteacher *(melamed dardeki)*, in many places also a bath attendant *(balan)*, and possibly a secretary, a slaughterer (shochet), and the like. The kehilla maintained such institutions as a synagogue (or several synagogues or prayer-houses or both), an abattoir for kosher slaughtering, a bathhouse (mikveh), a cemetery, occasionally a public bakery, a dance hall used mostly for weddings, a well, and a hospital. Their number and range apparently depended on the size and wealth of the given community.

Jews coming to Poland from Germany-Austria-Bohemia brought this communal heritage with them and undoubtedly sought to preserve it in the new settlements. Similarly, the state policy concerning the Jewish group (as reflected in the privileges) was based on Western models. Individual new immigrants and very small groups were at first able to achieve only limited copies of the Western kehilla organization with more primitive, less complicated institutions.

As already noted, the first factual mention of Jewish group life in Poland—the letter to Rabbi Jehuda Hachassid around 1200—gives the impression of a very small, uncomplicated unit. It was administered by an individual who taught the young, judged the adults, made decisions in ritual matters, and guided the prayers. This last duty probably meant serving as a cantor when necessary (which may have required a pleasant voice, as it did in later centuries), and above all simply being familiar with the order and ritual of prayer. Before printed prayer books became available this was a problem in all Jewish communities. The prayers had to be read aloud with the congregation repeating them or simply listening, since not everyone could afford to own a handwritten book, which was very expensive. Such a reader-teacher received certain gifts for his services, the group being too poor or too small to pay regular wages or a salary.

The early kehilla imposed hardly any settlement limitations *(herem hayishuv)* and exerted little control. There was no well-defined formal community board, and social differentiation between board members and other Jews appears to have been virtually nonexistent. Social stratification, institutionalization, and setting into a hierarchical system was to come later, with the growth of the Jewish population and the development of the kehilla institutions. This growth and expansion, as well as the increasing strength of the kehilla (which eventually exceeded the Western model), took several centuries.[5] Some nuclei, however, did apparently already exist in the Middle Ages, although the source material is not always explicit about this. The initial efforts went into building up or acquiring some institutional framework.

A cemetery may have been the first acquisition, although not every small community had one of its own; those that did not buried their dead in a neighboring place. Either at the same time or a little later came a synagogue. Some Jewish cemeteries are mentioned in the thirteenth century in Silesia (in Breslau in 1203 or 1248; in Schweidnitz before 1270; in Opava in 1281). Land was purchased in 1287 for a cemetery in Kalish, and there were others in the fourteenth century. Lwów's is officially recorded in 1414 but contained a gravestone dated 1378. Two are referred to in 1367 near Cracow and Sandomierz.

Synagogues are alluded to for the most part beginning with the fourteenth century. Breslau had three synagogues in 1349, one of which is described in 1352 as the old Jewish synagogue. Cracow had one in 1356 or earlier, Schweidnitz in 1330, Neisse in 1319, Poznań before 1367, and Kazimierz at the end of the fourteenth century.[6]

According to the Boleslas charter of 1264, and more specifically in fourteenth-century Polish privileges, there were provisions for the protection of Jewish institutions—synagogues and cemeteries—and grants giving Jews the right to be judged according to Jewish law. In Silesia and Mazovia (Warsaw)—the Polish western and eastern independent or semi-independent political units—Jews were subject to adjudication according to Jewish law. This was provided partially by the state and partially by the Jews themselves. According to the charter of the thirteenth century, jurisdiction over Jews was held by the prince in whose name the palatine or the appointed Jews' judge acted (in civil matters between Jews and Christians, in certain criminal matters between Jews, and in other matters between Jews if they requested intervention).

In the fourteenth century, according to the privileges, the internal Jewish court had jurisdiction over Jews in civil matters, while the king's jurisdiction, exercised by the palatine or his deputy or the Jews' judge sitting in court together with Jewish assessors, was concerned with mainly criminal or Jewish-Christian cases.

The above-mentioned information about the hiring of the cantor-judge-teacher at the beginning of the thirteenth century and the charters of 1264 and later presuppose some sort of community organization, loose as it may have been, even though the term is not mentioned. Somebody had to take care of hiring the cantor-teacher and someone had to negotiate or request the charters. The fourteenth-century privileges indicate more clearly the existence of Jewish community representatives to whom the privileges were granted. They certainly indicate the existence of community leaders, both as assessors of the court presided over by the Jews' judge* and as members of a purely Jewish court. The court of the Jews' judge

---

*The privileges of 1264 and those of the fourteenth century make Jews subject to jurisdiction by the prince or his palatine; the latter appoints a Jews' judge who sits in court, together with Jewish assessors. In Lwów (1356) for a while the city bailiff presided over the court with participation of Jewish assessors; later the arrangement of the privileges (a Jews' judge) became effective also for this region. Indicated in the privilege of 1334 and explicitly stated in that of 1367 is that disputes among Jews themselves are to be decided by Jewish elders *(antiquiores)*. Only when they did not want to or could not decide a matter was it transferred to the palatine or the Jews' judge. In Warsaw and Mazovia the order seems to have been reversed: the prince's court served as the first instance and the Jewish court as the second.

also had a Jewish *scolni* (belonging to the synagogue), a beadle, as one of it functionaries. The privilege of 1367 enjoins the Jews to obey their elders.

There are documents (from Breslau, Cracow, Poznań and Schweidnitz) which
contain allusions to a "Jewish bishop" *(episcopus Judaeorum)*, a term known in
Germany since the eleventh century, meaning a rabbi, a community leader, or a
teacher (in Warsaw), or a combination of all three, and possibly some additional
functions, in one person.[7] The task or tasks may have varied from place to place.
(In 1315 in Breslau, for instance, one and the same individual may have been rabbi,
ritual slaughterer, cantor, and teacher.) Beadles in Warsaw and Cracow are mentioned in the fifteenth century, as well as a teacher in Warsaw.

There are also other indications of the early existence of some sort of Jewish
community board, at least from the time when groups of Jews (not just a few
individuals) were settled in a place. Living as they did mostly in a Jewish street, with
some sort of extraterritorial status within the cities, they needed an organ to fulfill
certain municipal functions: to provide for the distribution of water—Cracow had
water pipes in the fourteenth century—for guards, and so on.

It may well be that the general outlines of the statute granted the Jews in
Schweidnitz (Świdnica, Silesia, at that time still an independent principality) in 1370
would be generally characteristic of Poland during the Middle Ages. The statute
foresees a board of the community organization consisting of four members to be
elected annually. This board, or the community as a whole, was to appoint a "Jewish
bishop," meaning a rabbi, "who would be a good and modest Jew and acceptable
to the whole community. In case he should cease to satisfy, the community might
discharge him after a year or two and the board of four would have the right either
to serve as judges themselves or to seek advice from another good and knowledgeable
Jew in order that justice should prevail among the rich as among the poor." Nobody
should refuse obedience to the board. All matters in the community should be
decided irrevocably by a majority. No foreign Jewish bishop should have jurisdiction
over native Jews.[8] The Jews in the other cities and towns of the principality (nine
are mentioned by name) are under the jurisdiction of the Jewish court in Schweidnitz and must pay their share of the local taxes.[9]

These simply expressed regulations show many of the elements of the later Jewish
community organization structure in Poland. (They may also have been applied
earlier in some measure in other parts of Poland.) But there was apparently not yet
any formally stabilized practice. This instability may have been the reason why the
Polish king experimented in the sixteenth century—with little success as we shall
see—with a number of organizational forms.

Growth and Institutionalization

With the rise of the Jewish population and its rooting in Polish soil its organizational framework, the kehilla, became more firmly established and institutionalized.
Stratification became clearer, and there was sharper division between leadership and

members; factions were formed, and internal social tensions arose. These trends apparently became more pronounced with increasing immigration and the ensuing differences and tensions between old-timers and newcomers. Be that as it may, by the fifteenth century (and possibly even in the fourteenth) the kehilla seems to have been functioning more fully and to have more nearly resembled the Western model. It was generally run by a regular board of four members (Breslau and Schweidnitz, Silesia, in the fourteenth century, Cracow in the second half of the fifteenth [we have documentation for 1465, 1469, 1485, and 1495], though Lwów had only three). The "Jewish bishop" or "Jewish doctor," as the rabbi is called in the sources, either participated in the board or presided over it, or he served as an employee. This varied in different places.[10] This board of four (or three) members either comprised the sole government of the community or was the executive body only, with a larger council of twelve or so members functioning by its side—the latter mainly in larger communities. To judge from the fragmentary information available, the board consisted mostly of the richest people in the community. In Cracow in 1465 we find the board consisting of three wealthy Jews—moneylenders or bankers—and one physician; in 1494 two of the four members were court bankers. In Lwów in 1492 the three board members included a banker or moneylender, a dealer in oxen, and a tax farmer.*

The function of the community organization in the fifteenth century seems to have been greatly expanded. Settlement—or citizenship—in the community was then beginning to be controlled. The *herem hayishuv*, the prerogative to grant and withdraw settlement rights, was being exercised by the community board, a fact that led to tensions and quarrels. (It is not clear whether the struggle between factions in Schweidnitz in 1370, in the wake of which the synagogue was closed for several weeks, was the result of such a situation or not.) Before 1460 we hear, for instance, that one who was forced to flee Pyzdry (in Great Poland) for fear of persecution by the authorities could settle—at least temporarily—in Poznań only after depositing a promissory note on a larger amount, apparently to guarantee that he would leave the community again or that he would pay an entrance fee. This led to litigation before the Jewish court. Nobody, it seems, could be admitted to settle in Cracow without the community council's approval. A case is recorded in 1477 in which the palatine's court, upon the demand of the community elders, passed a judgment expelling from Cracow two members of the Fischel family, who perhaps had arrived from Germany not much earlier. By the end of the century, with the arrival of new Jews from Bohemia and the resettlement of the Cracow Jews in Kazimierz, a bitter struggle between the factions began, which lasted about half a century and several times necessitated the intervention of the king (see chapter 5).

Similarly, the community became an important factor in taxation, apparently accounting for more than the small amounts needed for payment of state taxes. It

---

*Besides this Jewish kehilla within the city, Lwów had, in reality, another community in the suburb (or Old Lwów, existing from the time before the city walls and the new city were built in the fourteenth century). This was for the most part independent of the main kehilla.

is possible to gather from a responsum sent to Rabbi Israel Isserlein about a case in Poznań that the community evidently sought to collect considerable amounts from its members. Tensions and factional struggles are also found in other places. Poznań seems also to have been the site of sharp conflicts between rabbis (1455), a not-infrequent situation in Germany at that time.[11] In Poznań the conflict was connected with attempts by a new arrival to "create a place for himself."

With the broadening of the kehilla's functions in the fourteenth to fifteenth century it came into its own. Allowing for some differences according to place and time, the prerogatives of the community and its board included functions somewhat resembling those of the city council generally (though on a limited basis): representation of the Jewish group before the general society, collection of taxes, administration of Jewish institutions and of the Jewish street to some extent, jurisdiction over Jews (mainly in civil matters), control of admittance or nonadmittance of Jews to a specific community, and religious and educational matters (although the sources of the time scarcely mention them all).

Being the representative body of a minority living in an unfriendly environment, the Jewish community organization also had to fulfill some antidefamation and defense functions, ranging from requests to the king for protection, to court dealings with city councils or individual non-Jews, to public relations activities with influential personalities. All these functions were bound to expand considerably with the growth and consolidation of Polish Jewry in subsequent centuries.

5 The Medieval Polish Jew: A Composite Picture[1]

The Polish Jew of the Middle Ages was either an immigrant or an immigrant's son. He came from the West—Germany-Bohemia-Austria—bringing with him religious and other traditions, a way of life, customs, and probably also a vernacular (a German dialect or dialects that either already were or later became judaized—into Yiddish —by absorbing Hebrew and other elements).[2] In rare cases he may have been the bearer of a Germanized first name instead of or accompanying his Hebrew one. He may have had either a good, a rudimentary, or a total lack of knowledge of rabbinic Hebrew. He appears to have brought with him the model of, or the text for, charters to protect the Jewish minority in a Christian state; the ideas embodied in the privileges for Polish Jewry were patterned on these Western examples.

On arrival from the West the Jew settled first in the western parts of Poland and later either he himself or his sons moved slowly farther east. As former urbanites they settled in cities and towns.* In Lwów there were two sorts of Jewish settlers: those who took up residence within the city walls, and Jews who made their homes in the suburbs. Each group had its own separate community organization, judicature, and status. In the larger cities the Jew may have lived in either a brick or a wooden house, in a smaller city or town only in a wooden house or hut.

The Jewish immigrant moved from a more fully developed civilization to a less developed one. In those centuries the cities and towns in Poland were for the most part more primitive than their counterparts in Germany or Bohemia, even though, beginning with the German immigration of the thirteenth century, older and smaller Polish urban settlements were consolidated into larger ones, and people began to erect simple German-style buildings.

The layout of the cities in western Poland resembled those in eastern Germany. The marketplace with its stores and such important buildings as the town hall, church, and the town scales formed the center. From here narrow streets, often connected by side streets, ran toward the city walls or gates. Even in larger cities,

---

*There is no evidence of Jews living in villages and agricultural settlements in Poland during the Middle Ages. This was a later development (mainly during and after the sixteenth century).

such as the capital city of Cracow, not all the houses were built of brick or stone; some were of wood. In the parts of the country farther east most or all of the houses were constructed of wood. In Wilno, for instance, as late as the sixteenth century there were only wooden houses and huts, and many of the latter were dark with the thick smoke from an open fire without a chimney. In smaller towns people lived in divided wooden huts—one part for the owner and his family, another for the domestic animals. Some of the houses had small glassed hatches in the windows. By the end of the fifteenth century glass panes became available for large windows. Many houses had no toilets. Water pipes were installed in the large cities in the fourteenth to sixteenth centuries (in Cracow in the fourteenth century, in Lwów in 1407, in Lublin in 1535, in Wilno in the sixteenth century). Where there were no pipes the people had to rely on local wells and rivers for their water supply. The lack of available water accounts in part for the frequent disastrous fires in the cities. The water was brought into the houses either by water carriers or by members of the family.

The city was usually enclosed by a wall with gates, which were closed at sundown. The sealing off by walls set limits to the space available for expansion. Buildings were mostly set close together, streets were narrow, overcrowded, and unpaved. Only some of the main thoroughfares in the big cities were surfaced with wooden beams. In periods of heavy rains or in spring when the deep snow and ice melted, not only the roads but also the streets in the cities and towns turned to mud and were barely passable. There was no organized sewage disposal; rubbish and waste were either thrown out onto the streets in front of the houses or into the river. At best there were open drains in the streets through which dirty water flowed. Butchers' stalls, slaughterhouses, and breweries located in the center of the city, and fowl and domestic animals raised in the city only increased the waste and dirt, offering a breeding ground for the swarms of rats and mice that plagued the inhabitants. Epidemics resulted from these deplorably unhygienic conditions. The following description of conditions in Chester, England, in 1475 may generally apply to Poland:

> Butchers and poulterers were . . . careless [in] disposal of animal refuse; fishmongers and cooks and ordinary households were all guilty. . . . Women carrying entrails of animals from the butchers, carried them uncovered and threw them out near the gates to the public nuisance. . . . The private citizen was only too ready to dispose of dead dogs and cats by dropping them into the river or just over the town wall, or even by placing them in any open space. [3]

Households in the medieval Polish cities were plagued also by fleas and—during the summer—by flies. Winter brought still greater hazards: frequent blizzards and heavy frosts. Keeping warm by burning the firewood in the one stove of the house or huddling around the open fire of the hut for days and long nights taxed the energies and patience of many a city dweller.

Houses were very modestly furnished. In Wilno, for instance, in the sixteenth century the burghers still had almost no furniture. What was available during the Middle Ages consisted of benches running along the walls; in richer houses these were upholstered with various materials. In the center of the room stood a heavy table with simple heavy chairs. The well-to-do had also a mirror, usually a small round one. For lack of beds people slept on bare benches—in the wealthier homes, on covered ones. In the fifteenth century beds and bedding as well as clocks were introduced into the homes of the well-to-do and some of the middle class. Against the wall stood closets and all sorts of boxes, some of them fitted with iron clasps.

Food was cooked in earthenware pots and served in large bowls and platters of wood or tin. Knives, spoons, and forks were used seldom or not at all. (A foreign eyewitness tells how in 1484 the Polish king did not use any knife at meals, but broke the bread with his fingers.) Drinks were consumed from tin cups and goblets; glass cups were a rarity. Silver spoons and silver goblets were rare and were kept mostly for their value or as luxuries.

Jews in Poland during the Middle Ages were not segregated in special quarters because of any formal limitation. On the contrary, the privileges of the thirteenth to fifteenth centuries indicate that Jews could and should live anywhere among the rest of the people. They even proclaimed that non-Jews must come to the assistance of a Jewish neighbor calling for help upon being attacked during the night.

True, the church passed resolutions about segregation of the Jews, but this scarcely became legal practice. A Jewish street, however, often did exist in the medieval Polish city, in the same way as "wards" or "streets" based on other ethnic or occupational lines were the usual pattern in preindustrial cities. But Jewish residence was not limited to the Jewish street, nor were non-Jews excluded from living there (in Kazimierz-Cracow such segregation was introduced in 1532). In some places Jews, as mentioned, lived on the outskirts or in the suburbs. Lwów had an outlying Jewish settlement in addition to the Jewish quarter within the city, while Lublin's only Jewish settlement was beyond the city limits because of opposition to Jewish settlement within the city.

This Jewish street did not differ greatly from other streets. With the exception of Kazimierz, where Jews were herded following expulsion from Cracow in the last years of the fifteenth century, and possibly Poznań, the Jewish street during the Middle Ages was apparently not necessarily wider or narrower, cleaner or dirtier, roomier or more overcrowded than neighboring streets. (Only in later centuries did it sometimes become overcrowded.) But this Jewish street was evidently not among the most elegant either. In some cases the non-Jewish neighbors mentioned belonged to the lower rungs of society, being mainly artisans.*

The Jewish street usually ran either directly from the marketplace or from one

*In Silesian cities some non-Jews who lived in or near the Jewish street were of the category of outcasts in those years (the hangman or the flayer, for instance), which may show that these streets were located toward the periphery where the more unfortunate members of the city and the outcasts were usually harbored.

of the neighboring streets. The location of the Jewish street was at times set as far as possible from the church and some distance from the city square. The Jewish street was the site of the synagogue or synagogues, the Jewish public bath, and what was known in those centuries as the hospital (usually a place sheltering wayfarers as well as sick people), and possibly also other community buildings (dance hall and the like). The cemetery would be situated either at the end of the street or beyond the city gates.

In many cities and towns Jews owned gardens and meadows, located either near their houses or beyond the city gates. In Kazimierz Jews had their own marketplace (1488). By the end of the century, after the Jews of Cracow had been crowded into Kazimierz, "the Jewish city of Kazimierz," as it is called in the records, comprised a quadrangle with a few streets enclosed on one side by the city walls and on the other by a wall with three gates, leading to the non-Jewish city. Communication with the outside world—including Cracow, where Jews had their businesses—was possible only through one of these gates. Near the end of one street, not far from the city wall, stood the synagogue and nearby was a square where Jewish stores and stalls were located. At the other end of this square or street was a small Jewish cemetery.

After the Jews were expelled to Kazimierz in 1495, a new kind of Jewish street came into being in Cracow. It comprised a sort of bazaar with stores and stalls[4] but no homes. Jews went to Cracow to their businesses in the morning, returning home to Kazimierz for the night.

The houses in which they lived were, as mentioned, usually of wood and in some cases of brick or stone. The interior and contents were apparently either similar to or identical with those of the non-Jew. One description of the contents of a Jewish home in Warsaw in 1461 was preserved in a legal document prepared by the court. This gives factual information about contents and shows that in general the home contained objects not unlike those found in other houses. There were six tin bowls, seven tin cups, two kettles of which one was for water, two saucepans, three copper basins and a black basin, a saw, an iron stove and cupboard containing bedding and clothing. One featherbed was covered with fustian and the other one with Cologne cloth; two other featherbeds were covered with fur. Seven pillows, two purple covers, one green cover and one red, six towels, three bracelets or armlets, and three shirts (or nightgowns) were listed. Among the trinkets were a number of silver buckles. There were also two small barrels of wine and two tin dice for gambling. All this was estimated to be worth sixteen zloty. Also mentioned in other houses are a box in which to keep money, silver goblets, and a closet with drawers.[5]

Books

In some Jewish houses in Cracow—preserved fragmentary information tells of only a few cases—Jewish books were found. Around the middle of the fifteenth century documents from Breslau tell of a "box full of Jewish books" in one house, "a chest with Jewish books," "many small and large books," "eighteen Jewish books," and "one book, the Bible" in one of the houses, and four Jewish books in the butcher's house. Before 1490 a Poznań Jew is mentioned as possessing a few books. Thus the possession of books was apparently not too rare. This would also seem to be indicated by the fact that problems concerning the right to ownership of Hebrew books that had been bought by Jews from non-Jews (the latter having stolen them or taken them from the owners by force), were dealt with by rabbis in Germany and Austria.[6]

Further indication of the possession of books by Silesian Jews in the Middle Ages is furnished by a number of parchment fragments found in the bindings of some medieval manuscripts in the former library of the University in Breslau. The manuscripts came to the library from Breslau itself (ten items) and from neighboring places (about twenty items). The Hebrew fragments had been used as material with which to bind the Latin manuscripts. Assuming that the binding was made in Silesia itself and that the fragments came from Hebrew manuscripts that were left by— or taken from—Jews expelled from Silesia during the fourteenth or fifteenth century or earlier, they may serve as some indication of the kind of books most in use.

Of thirty-five fragments, nine are from Bible manuscripts (two from a Torah scroll and one from Psalms), six are Rashi commentary on the Bible, eight are Talmud and commentaries, three are midrash, eight are prayers and piyutim (mostly taken from machzor, a holiday prayer book).

In Warsaw some parchment fragments were found that had also been used for binding non-Jewish books. These parchments, originating from the fifteenth century (one from the sixteenth), contain fragments from the book of Jeremiah (with commentary or glosses in Yiddish and Hebrew), Deuteronomy, Exodus, and one fragment of a work, possibly Maimonides' *Sefer Hamitzvoth*, on the 613 commandments.[7]

It seems, however, that ownership of books (in manuscript form, of course) among Jews in Poland was limited. At least this could be deduced from a statement made by Rabbi Moses ben Jacob of Kiev, one of the few Polish Jewish authors of the Middle Ages. In the course of his lifetime he moved around to various parts of Poland, but he asserts that only in Kaffa, in the Crimea, where he arrived at the beginning of the sixteenth century, could he find the manuscripts needed for his study.

Clothing

Jews in the Western countries mostly wore clothes that distinguished them from non-Jews, possibly at first for religious reasons: as a barrier against the outside world. After the Fourth Lateran Council of 1215—in Germany from the second half of the thirteenth century—this may have resulted from a mandatory prescription.[8]

Beginning in 1267 the resolutions of the many church councils in Poland also ordered the Jews to wear distinctive clothing—at least hats—and at times the state required such identification. None of this seems to have been put into practice, or at least not for long. Burghers, church officials, and secular dignitaries complained on several occasions in the fifteenth century that Jews wore clothing indistinguishable from Christians. On the other hand, a rabbi of the sixteenth century deals with the problem of Jews who in certain situations were forced by fear to don clothing like that worn by Christians, which would indicate that there was ordinarily a distinction.[9]

Extant fragmentary materials give only a vague idea of the clothing worn by Jews. Miniatures on a thirteenth-century manuscript and on glass in a cathedral from the fourteenth century, as well as a picture from the fifteenth century (medieval painters usually used contemporary costumes rather than historical models) depict Jews in narrow round hats, or hats narrow at the top and wide at the bottom, or in round caps with or without fur. They are shown in short tunics over which a long sleeveless cape is worn; one man has no cloak, others are wearing long black cloaks with short sleeves and gold or silver trimming. Other fifteenth-century sources depict women's tunics as wide with open sleeves and trimmed with marten fur; men's black cloaks and brown tunics are trimmed with fur; a fur coat *(szuba)*, a silver belt, and a string of pearls are also mentioned as being worn by Jews.

At the beginning of the sixteenth century we find a Jew wearing a sheepskin coat with a leather belt. Another sixteenth-century source mentions—as clothing found on a murdered Jew—a *kolpak*, that is, a velvet hat, a shirt with bands, a gray coat with fur, a belt, phylacteries, and a sword.[10] The wearing of swords by Jews is also documented for the fifteenth and sixteenth centuries.

Food

Poor people in Poland lived mostly on cereals, black bread, vegetables, a few dairy products and eggs, and a little meat and fish. Wealthier people consumed white bread, dairy foods, a considerable amount of meat, fish, herring, groats, and groceries. The principal beverages were beer, mead, and occasionally wine. Jews apparently consumed more or less similar types of foods. But their meat was kosher, from ritually slaughtered animals. (There is information on Jewish butchers and the problems of selling the nonkosher parts to Christians.) Also one may surmise that they had white challah for the Sabbath, and that they ate kreplach and chremslach on holidays, bought fish on Fridays and matzoth for Passover. (All this is documented for Germany-Austria in the fourteenth and fifteenth centuries and for Poland much later.)

Immigrant Character

Immigration, the process of uprooting and transplanting, is usually an outcome of individual choice. The immigrant or refugee leaves his country with some hope of being able to improve his lot. Immigration presupposes some degree of selectivity. Immigrants, at least in the early stages of immigration, comprise the more adventurous, energetic, and optimistic types. Socially they are dissenters, young people from poor and underprivileged backgrounds, the uneducated or less learned—those on the lower rungs of society. The scholars and the well-established, the wealthy and the elite usually stay home at first, unless driven forth by a great emergency. They may follow later when settlements have passed their pioneering stage.

But in cases of forced emigration there is a difference. When people are driven out and obliged to leave a place or when they flee from fear, both rich and poor, learned and ignorant are to be found among the immigrants. The roles may even be reversed, with the wealthy, the well-established, the learned, and the other important individuals having a better chance to flee the old country and gain admission to the new one.* There does not, however, seem to have been any period of considerable mass immigration to Poland during the Middle Ages. Neither the general nor the Jewish sources indicate the existence of any such trend. With the possible exception of Bohemian Jews in Cracow at the end of the fifteenth century, Poland reveals no such "by-products" of immigration by larger groups from a specific country as the foundation of a closed community or congregation by people originating from a specific city or country (such as the Spanish exiles in Turkey).

Each type of immigrant will bring with him some experience, and many may also carry along some capital:

> *Immigrants do not usually arrive empty-handed, they bring with them their ideas, images, culture patterns and institutions. They try to implement their concepts so as to live in accordance with their own pattern and to create for themselves the kind of organizations to which they have been accustomed.*[11]

But the new environment and the new conditions often turn out to be different. This leads to conflicts and tensions, changes and modifications.

Another familiar trait among immigrants in a new country is the slackening of social control, of religious and ethical mores. With regard to economic and social behavior patterns, one finds some contradictory trends among immigrants: clinging to old ways and mores versus a readiness to change; hopelessness versus an unscrupulous urge for achievement. The individuals who fall into the latter group are usually endowed with considerable optimism, self-confidence, toughness, and adaptability. Concentration of skills in certain selected economic sectors combined with entrepreneurship and the use of risk capital may contribute to a rapid rise on the economic ladder for some, downfall into bankruptcy and poverty for others. One may venture to identify some of these characteristics among Polish Jews of the Middle Ages despite the paucity of the source material.

Jewish Religion

Polish Jews from the West brought to Poland the Ashkenazic (German) religious patterns, forms of prayer, and behavior norms. As we have already seen, German-

*The expellees from Spain in 1492 and the refugees from Nazi Germany in the 1930s are examples.

Austrian rabbis of the fourteenth and fifteenth centuries and Polish rabbis of the sixteenth century[12] emphasize time and again the relation of Polish Jews to the sphere of Ashkenazic religious culture. The cantor-teacher-judge of the twelfth to thirteenth centuries, as well as the first rabbis in Poland (fourteenth and mostly fifteenth centuries), came mainly from Germany-Austria-Bohemia-Silesia and undoubtedly followed the Ashkenazic trend and *nusach* (form of prayer). They brought also their books (manuscripts) and prayer books, but few of these survived to later days.[13] We can assume that the range of Jewish religious practices and rituals during the thirteenth to fifteenth centuries in Poland was similar to—if not necessarily entirely identical with—that of the countries from which the immigrants came. True, we have almost no factual information about religious practices in Poland of those centuries, but the assumption that Ashkenazic patterns were followed is based on several premises.

Traditional religious culture is usually repetitive rather than innovative. Rituals, institutions, and norms of behavior in traditional societies are generally of value only if they are taken from exemplary models, if they are imitations of sanctified patterns.[14] It is no different in Jewish tradition. But some small changes did take place. Something of what the rabbis of the sixteenth century (mainly Moses Isserles) codified as the Polish minhag (custom) had existed earlier. At any rate Moses Mintz from Bamberg, who became rabbi in Poznań in 1474, tells about finding there some customs for the wedding ceremony that were different from the ones he knew in Germany. He also noticed some slight differences in the procedure of granting a divorce.[15] Some other changes occurred, not perhaps in the norm so much as in the way the norm was construed in practice. Permissiveness usually prevails in new settlements, especially where little religious knowledge or learning finds its way in.

Learning

Correspondence with R. Jehuda Hachassid (at the end of twelfth or the beginning of the thirteenth century) maintains as we have seen that the contemporary settlements in Poland were too poor to have any "men learned in Torah." They would be unable to continue adhering to their religious tradition, since there was no one to guide them in prayer, instruct their children, or administer justice. They hired whoever they could find to fill this need. The same complaint that Polish Jews were not familiar enough with Jewish lore was reiterated more than two hundred years later by a Bohemian-German rabbi who was reluctant to ease a regulation since "they are not learned."[16] A responsum for Lwów (quoted below) about the killing of a Jew in the fifteenth century states that one of the murderers was illiterate and "could not read even one letter" of Hebrew.

In frontier regions, even as late as the sixteenth and seventeenth centuries, the existence of unlearned Jews unable to speak the Jewish vernacular or to "read even one letter in the Torah," is confirmed.[17] Little familiarity with Hebrew may also be indicated by some marginal notes made by Jews on court books in Warsaw

(1433–37). A Jew named Jacob[18] signed his name in Hebrew but made a number of mistakes,* although another writer (or writers) translated some Latin words into Hebrew more or less correctly. In fact, if one were to draw some conclusions about the entire Jewish community from the Karaites by analogy there would be an indication that study was not widespread in southern Poland. A statement about two Karaites—Jacob, a doctor from Luck, and Solomon ben Abraham from Kaffa, who came to Adrianople (Turkey) about 1450—emphasizes that in their own communities there was little study of the Torah.[19]

It is not until the second half of the fourteenth century that a few names of rabbis who were recognized as authorities appear in Silesia, (which was already connected with Bohemia). In Breslau or in Schweidnitz some sort of talmudic academy may have existed at that time. In Poland proper we first hear about some knowledgeable rabbis in the fifteenth century[20] and they are all newcomers, either refugees forced to flee from Germany and Bohemia or just immigrants. And one also hears in that century about a vagrant rabbi or pseudorabbi who was behaving in a way that other rabbis found reprehensible (living with two wives, for example) and issuing letters of divorce *(get)* without authorization or knowledge of the law.[21]

The entire Jewish literary heritage from medieval Polish Jews consists of a few Hebrew words on coins, a very limited number of Hebrew inscriptions on tombstones, and a statement written by a Polish-Silesian Jew (Yekutiel) in Yiddish or in German using Hebrew characters (1435). Also extant are a Hebrew document signed by the representatives of the Cracow community in 1485, in which they "agree to limit their economic activity," two Hebrew promissory notes, one Hebrew receipt, as well as one question sent to a Western rabbi in the fifteenth century. Answers to a few other questions have been preserved. There are also a few manuscripts (some published posthumously) written by Rabbi Moses ben Jacob of Kiev toward the end of the fifteenth century, the Hebrew and Yiddish notes on parchment in Warsaw already mentioned, and the manuscript fragments in Breslau.[22] In addition a few individuals from Poland-Russia may have gone to the West to study (or for other purposes) and may have participated there in rabbinical schools.[23]

Observance and Laxity

Lack of learning or limited learning must have had some influence upon behavior and observance. In a tradition-bound society conduct is controlled or induced by upholders of the tradition, by scholars and the clergy—both by actual control and by social control, by the example they set and the pattern they create. Where such traditional elite groups either do not exist or are very small (the letter to Rabbi Jehuda Hachassid quoted above—from about the beginning of the thirteenth century—seems to indicate that they were negligible) there is little possibility for control or meaningful example. This is especially so in an immigrant society, where permissiveness is generally more widespread. The breaking away from old moorings leads

---

* יכוב instead of יעקב.

to a weakening of established behavior patterns, while the new environment is not always conducive to strict adherence to all the old traditions. The result is not necessarily the disappearance of the old religious ways; instead, permissiveness pervades the old prescriptiveness.

Another trait often found in immigrant societies is the dominance of material values over spiritual ones. To a certain extent this seems to have been the situation among Jews in medieval Poland, although strict observance was no doubt the ideal and life was theoretically permeated with faith. A letter from Troki in Lithuania to Constantinople, written by the leader of the Karaite community in 1483, may be characteristic not only of the Karaites but may also apply to the rabbinite Jews (those who follow traditional Judaism based on the Talmud). The letter complains that

> *many communities in these regions are scattered and dispersed over the mountains without a shepherd looking after the flocks, refraining from understanding God's Torah but pursuing the imaginary [material] successes and regarding them as the essentials. . . . The crowds are arrogant toward the Torah, lax in religious observances . . . everyone does as he pleases.* [24]

Some extant fragments of information seem to confirm the existence of similar trends among rabbinite Jews.

The preserved question from the first half of the fifteenth century mentioned above (which seems to have come from Poznań, Poland) may indicate a trend toward transgressing religious law for the sake of material things. Abraham from Poland described to Rabbi Isserlein's father (first half of the fifteenth century) the following incident. At the time of a great fire in the city Jews carried their possessions through streets on Sabbath without an *eruv*,* put them in a cellar, excavated earth around it to cover up the door and window, and trampled the earth down—all things that a Jew should not do on the Sabbath. The question was what sort of penance should be required. [25]

There are other fragments of information that point in a similar direction. Moses Mintz, who came to Poland in 1474, was apparently reluctant to trust the Polish Jewish butchers in the matter of kosher meat. According to the testimony of Solomon Luria, Moses Mintz ate only meat that was prepared (the veins extracted) by his own trustworthy man. A mistrust of the average Jew in matters of kashruth was demonstrated again about half a century later. A resolution was passed by rabbis in southern Poland ("Russia") to regard any wine in the hands of Jews as "pagan wine . . . unless esteemed witnesses will testify to its being kosher." Suspicions voiced in connection with the reliability of ritual slaughterers also attest to this trend. No doubt a certain laxity in observance of Jewish religious laws was the basis for such suspicions on the part of some rabbis. Solomon Luria affirms that in his time (sixteenth century) the masses in many places drank any wine, having no regard as

---

*The establishment of a symbolical area within which carrying or walking on the Sabbath became permitted.

to whether or not it was kosher. And those who did not follow this trend were regarded as either haughty or foolish. Similarly, he tells of a slaughterer (shochet) who was ignorant of the rules for ritual slaughtering.[26]

Court books in Mazovia (1414) tell of a Jew drinking and gambling with dice with a non-Jew (probably at an inn). In Lithuania we find Jews eating and drinking together with non-Jews. In the same region Jews were using state courts instead of their own, and this does not seem to have been rare in other parts of Poland.

In Poland generally drunkenness as well as shooting craps and other games of chance were widespread, not only among the simple people but also among the Christian clergy; even the bishops indulged in them. In the local inns clergymen drank excessively and became intoxicated; they gambled and danced on Sundays as well as on weekdays, and were involved in sexual aberrations—marrying (in defiance of the prohibition of 1197) or keeping concubines despite the many local and general church prohibitions. Though such offenses seem to have been rarer among Jews, they did exist.[27]

Solomon Luria makes a special point of emphasizing some secularized or nonreligious ways of the Jews. He depicts girls dancing on holidays and says that one cannot stop them "because they will not listen." He also tells about cases of playing dice and of adultery.

We know also of a murder case in the fifteenth century. A question received from Lwów by a Western rabbi, Israel Bruna, tells of two Jews who killed a third Jew. One of the murderers used a knife, the other a piece of wood. The victim was himself "a complete ignoramus . . . who could not read even one letter . . . never put on philacteries"; and there was "no trace of Jewishness" in him. He began the fight by attempting to throw two pieces of wood at one of the assassins who was drunk. This murderer was later anxious to perform some act of penance, but the other killer was completely indifferent to the whole matter.[28]

Frontier Conditions

Immigrant character, frontier conditions, and environmental influences may have encouraged tendencies toward roughness, boldness, willingness to take risks, aggressiveness in business dealings, and even crime. Disputes and beatings among Jews occurred even in the synagogues in Lithuania and Poland. In Warsaw a Jew was accused in 1425 of breaking into a house and beating a Jewess; later he was also charged with stealing money; in 1433 the same individual was again denounced for beating another Jewess.

In the next few decades further cases were reported between Jews in the Warsaw courts: one accused the other of theft, but the case ended with withdrawal of the accusation. Other documents concern quarrels between a group of Jews from Brisk (Brest) in Warsaw and two local Jews, which landed the former in jail; a rich Jew in Warsaw who beat another Jew near the synagogue; a brawl between two families, with the women doing the main scrapping, in the course of which blood flowed.

The existence of some underworld elements among Jews is also attested. At the beginning of the sixteenth century "blind Aaron" was summoned to court in Lithuania and he hired a Christian driver with horse and buggy, and on the way there he attacked the driver and blinded him—" squeezed out his eyes" (perhaps it was a matter of self-defense). The Jewish community leaders refused to raise bail for him on the grounds that he was a drifter and a criminal. Other court records tell of Jews accused of being thieves but it is impossible to say whether the charges had any basis in reality. A few cases—assuming they were not the result of frame-ups—may show that the existence of underworld elements was not just a legend.

In 1455 a Jewish tax farmer in Lwów was accused of working with a gang of Jewish thieves and robbers and was heavily fined. Half a century later we hear of a band of Jewish robbers in western Poland who worked with non-Jews and assaulted both Jewish and non-Jewish merchants. Clashes with non-Jews were not necessarily confined to underworld elements. They were primarily attempts at self-defense, and seem to have occurred frequently. An individual Jew, being armed, would use his sword to defend himself against an attacker while traveling on the road. And groups of Jews or whole communities often defended themselves against an attack by the mob (as in Cracow in 1407 and 1494).

But there were also quarrels, beatings, and attacks between Jews and non-Jews, and Jews were sometimes the aggressors. A Jewish woman in Warsaw "insulted with words" and beat up a noblewoman in 1473, and did not even hesitate to offend the court that finally jailed her. And in another place in Mazovia court documents show Jews to have been the aggressors. The above-mentioned Levko, a rich Jew in Cracow, was accused of having attacked and beaten a Christian, for which he was locked up. A nobleman who had had too much to drink was on his way to his lodging in Lwów late one night during a Jewish holiday. Passing through the Jewish street he may possibly have behaved somewhat uncivilly. The Jews beat him up. Apparently he was injured and then thrown into the Jewish jail. An uproar ensued, with the nobility accusing Jews of having insulted one of their group. It ended with the king's granting Lwów Jews a safe-conduct document to protect them from the nobles' wrath.[29]

Such aggressive acts by Jews against non-Jews may attest either to a feeling of security on the part of Jews living among the none too friendly Christian majority, or to an aggressive mentality prone to take risks, or both. The Jews were at times so sure of themselves or took such risks that most attempts by non-Jews (chiefly church authorities) to curtail their activities were to little avail. A certain boldness on the part of wealthy Jews may have led in the same direction. As moneylenders they often foreclosed estates of the borrowers despite the latter's protest or attempts to organize resistance. In Silesia at the beginning of the fourteenth century a Jew, Solomon, served as a duke's courtmaster. Desiring to dislodge him from his position —ostensibly because a Jew should not hold office or a position of authority over Christians—the bishop resorted to having the threat of a ban against those Christians who obeyed orders issued by the Jew announced every Sunday in all churches. (The documents do not reveal whether this step was effective.) A nobleman who had some money difficulties with the banker Levko of Cracow sought help from the Pope Boniface IX. The latter asked the bishopric in Cracow to investigate the matter and eventually to forbid Christians, under pain of a ban, to deal with Levko. The complainant, and in the end the bishopric, too, lost the struggle. Years later the complainant's son had to settle the debt with Levko's heirs.[30]

Internal Tensions

Dissension between the various groups within an immigrant society seems to have occurred more often in some communities than in others (especially in Schweidnitz in the fourteenth century, Warsaw in the fifteenth, Kazimierz-Cracow at the end of the fifteenth and beginning of the sixteenth, Poznań in the fifteenth). The differences between the factions seem to have resulted at least in part from the varied origins of the community members. This would account for the instructions issued by the princes in Schweidnitz and Warsaw in connection with these quarrels. Such instructions forbade obedience to any orders issued by a "foreign" (outside) rabbi.

In Cracow such discord was known to exist between the indigenous and the immigrant groups.[31] Earlier, in 1477, an attempt had been made to expel from the city two immigrant brothers. In the same community (known as Kazimierz-Cracow following the expulsion from Cracow itself) there ensued a prolonged struggle between two factions: the older community made up of the small-town Kazimierz Jews, and the newcomers that were resettled there in 1495, who brought with them from the capital city of Cracow wealth, rank, and important connections.

The conflict was apparently accentuated by the increasingly important role Czech Jewish immigrants played in Cracow from the end of the fifteenth century and the fact that immigration from Bohemia continued for at least half a century. This immigration was primarily a result of persecutions, expulsions, and the insecure existence of Jews in Bohemia, but was also apparently connected with the Polish policy with regard to Bohemia. One of the Polish Jagiello line, Ladislas, was king of Bohemia, and his younger brother Sigismund, later king of Poland, had grown up at his brother's court in Bohemia. Thus individual Czech Jews could have established personal contacts with the king and high officials at the Polish court. We find here a man named Abraham Czech (or Bohemo), a former court Jew of the Czech king, who in Poland became the court Jew of Kings Alexander and Sigismund I. In 1518 the Polish king also granted individual privileges to settle in Poland to some Jews still in Bohemia (these are among the few extant permits for settlement of Jews), and took others and their possessions under his protection (1517) or generally allowed immigrants from Bohemia to remain in Poland (1542). Jewish Bohemian immigrants thus enjoyed a special status, and prior to the expulsion of 1495 they may possibly either have had their own community in Cracow or have dominated the Cracow Jewish kehilla. Jacob Polak, the founder of talmudic studies in Poland, came there some time before 1495 and apparently served as rabbi of the

Bohemian Jewish group, though the king's official appointment of him as rabbi is dated 1503.[32] He married the daughter of community leader Moses Fischel and soon took his place among the leaders, perhaps continuing to function as rabbi. In 1494 he spent some time in jail with other community leaders of Cracow.

The Cracow expellees, as epitomized by the Bohemian group, competed against the local Jews in Kazimierz and apparently sought to dominate the Jewish community and its institutions.

In the meantime, Rabbi Jacob Polak became involved in the problem of a divorce for his sister-in-law, in the course of which some German and Prague rabbis placed him under a ban. This aggravated his situation in the community, already undermined by the tensions between the indigenous Polish and the Czech Jews, and he had to flee. Upon his return to Poland about a year later, under a safe conduct from the king, he failed to regain his position as rabbi. A struggle between the Polish and the Czech groups for the rabbinate now came into the open. Rabbi Jacob Polak's mother-in-law, who had good connections with the court, succeeded in pushing through the candidacy of another son-in-law, the cabalist*Asher Lemel. The Czech Jews then elected a rabbi of their own, Rabbi Perez. The Bohemian group tried to impose Rabbi Perez on the whole community (apparently after 1516).

The king first sought a compromise: each group should have its own rabbi—the Bohemians, Rabbi Perez; the Poles, Rabbi Lemel—and they should share the synagogue. Every member was to be free to join either group. But this compromise did not work. The Polish Jews complained that the Czech group attempted to take from them the synagogue that they had erected before the Czechs' arrival. In November 1519 the king acknowledged the Polish Jews' rights to the synagogue, which he stipulated was to be used by the Czech Jews only with the former's permission. At the same time he prescribed that the leadership of the community organization, which in the "Jewish city of Kazimierz" also fulfilled the functions of a municipality, should be divided between the two groups. But this arrangement, like further decrees of the king and of the Cracow palatine along the same lines, were not very effective. The Polish Jews refused to give the Czech group the opportunity to participate in the government of the community-municipality or to offer them a lot on which to build a synagogue of their own.

This dissension was destined to plague Kazimierz-Cracow Jewry until the 1550s, even though after the deaths of both the Polish and the Czech rabbis, in the 1530s, the rabbinate was united in the person of Moses Fischel—a nephew of Rabbi Jacob Polak.[33]

Another sphere of tension was the apparent opposition to Sephardic Jews, who came to Poland in the last decades of the fifteenth century and in the years following the expulsion from Spain-Portugal, although the number of Spanish-Portuguese Jews in Poland was exceptionally small.

---

*A person who believes in the cabala, literally "tradition," an esoteric or mystic Jewish doctrine; a mystic.

This hostility was symbolized at the end of the fifteenth century by the problems encountered by a Jewish physician named Isaac (he was also called "Isaczek" and "Isaac Hispanus"). He served as physician to the king and high officials of the Polish court. The king exempted him from taxes and accorded him other privileges. But the Kazimierz-Cracow Jews were apparently biased against the man. Either as a reaction to the haughtiness generally ascribed to the Sephardic Jews in that period, or as a result of the differences in laws and customs on matrimony between Sephardic and Ashkenazic Jews, or simply because of differences in cultural background, the latter maintained that he was "of low origin" and were possibly trying to discredit his family. Dr. Isaac then went to the trouble of arranging for two Polish nobles, who were making a pilgrimage to the Holy Land, to get in touch with his sister and brother-in-law in Jerusalem. The latter certified that Isaac was a descendant of "the noble family of Abraham." On this basis the Polish king issued a document certifying that Isaac "descends from a noble Jewish family in Jerusalem" and forbidding the other Jews "to cause him any trouble" on account of his origins.[34] The preserved documents do not divulge how helpful the king's document actually was. Tension between Ashkenazim and Sephardim continued into the sixteenth century.

Jews and Christians: Converts

Everyday life and business relations brought Jews into contact with their neighbors, especially since the number of Jews was so small. Foodstuffs, animals for food and transport, wood for fuel and building, and many other necessities of life had to be bought from the Christian. The Jew sold his wares to the Christian, lent him money (or borrowed it), collected tolls and taxes from him. He traveled with him on the road—perhaps the only Jew among many non-Jews.[35] Sometimes Jews and non-Jews entered into partnerships.

The Jew also had many dealings, pleasant and unpleasant, with the Christian authorities: city council, high state officials, prince or king and their entourages. At times he served also as a court Jew, court banker, or "the king's servant" (meaning that he fulfilled important functions for the king). The Jew, appearing either in the general court or before the Jews' judge (*judex Judaeorum*), often had his deeds and debts entered in general court records.

These relations all required communication, and the Jew had to have some knowledge of the language of the country—Polish—and of the language of the documents—medieval Latin;* in southern Poland they also had to know Ruthenian (Ukrainian). On the other hand a few preserved official documents signed by Jews have an added Hebrew rendering or a German transcript in Hebrew letters, without which they apparently could not have understood the text well. One is justified in

*German, the language of the city authorities in many cities during most of the Middle Ages, was somewhat familiar to the Polish Jew through his vernacular, Yiddish, which at that time was closely related to German.

assuming that there were not many Jews familiar with the written form of the non-Jewish languages,[36] although most of them were apparently able to communicate orally with non-Jews.

This situation led also to some more intimate relationships. We have mentioned earlier that Jews—admittedly a small number—ate, drank, and even gambled (dice or craps) with non-Jews. We also find non-Jews guaranteeing Jewish debts and vice versa. There were also other types of friendships. We know of bishops, state, and city officials who defended Jews, of nobles who vouched for Jews or served as mediators in problems between Jews and non-Jews and even between Jew and Jew.[37] A few Jews who were versed in general knowledge may even have taken part in literary and philsophical discussions with non-Jewish intellectuals. Some information may indicate that in 1488–89 a Jew, Zul, joined in the literary discussions of a group known as Societas Vistulana, which existed around the king's court at that time.[38]

Permissiveness and day-to-day relations between Jews and non-Jews, as well as friendships between them, may have had an influence upon the conversion to Christianity of some individuals,* though their number was small as far as we know. And still greater was the impact of mutual contacts upon the relation of the convert to the Jewish community and vice versa.

Conversions were in part forced and in part voluntary. During attacks upon a Jewish community (Cracow in 1407, 1454, and 1463, for instance) it happened that some Jews converted from fear or because they were forced to do so by the attacking mob. In a Christian country such converts were generally obliged to remain Christians. There were laws forbidding their reconversion to Judaism. At the time of the expulsion from Lithuania (1495) a number of wealthy Jews—land and property owners and tax farmers, mainly from among those who had previously been assimilated with their neighbors—converted in Lithuania and in parts of southern Poland, which were under the domination of the Lithuanian state. Among the forced converts in Poland proper were the two children of a rich Cracow Jew named Smerlin, son of the first known "Jewish bishop" (community leader or rabbi of Cracow), who were in Cracow at the time of the attack in 1407. Their mother remained Jewish (the father appears to have been dead by that time). Another Jew, Samuel, converted in 1484 in Lwów. A few other converts, possibly voluntary, are mentioned in Cracow and elsewhere. Most of them appear to have been rather poor —one of them was a musician who became the king's trumpeter after his conversion in 1469. Other relatively poor Jews whom we find among the converted, apparently individually and of their own free will, are a butcher, Mikolaj (at the end of the fourteenth century), a tailor, Paul (before 1433), and a teacher (melamed?), Paul (before 1436).

But there were also converts of another kind. A man named Solomon-Jan, whose

---

*This may also have brought about the conversion of some Christians to Judaism (if these conversions do not belong in the category of anti-Semitic accusations). Some sources speak of "Judaization" of Christians, but it is not clear whether we deal here with real converts to Judaism or with dissenters from the organized Christian Church who were dubbed "Judaizers."

work on astronomy *Computus Judaicus* was preserved in the university library in Cracow,* is an example from the fourteenth century. Stefan Fischel, a member of the rich Jewish Fischel family from Cracow, converted at the end of the fifteenth century; his brother was a Jewish community leader in Cracow, and his niece was the wife of the famous rabbi Jacob Polak. Two of Stefan's sons were converted with him, but his wife and the other children remained Jewish.

A characteristic feature of the converts of those days was that they continued in their former "Jewish occupations" and maintained their good relationships with their Jewish relatives and other Jews.† The Smerlin children's mother, herself Jewish, made efforts after their conversion to transfer to them two houses she owned. Among the converts in Lithuania was Abraham Josefowicz, who was elevated to the nobility and later rose to a high post in the state, comparable to that of a minister of finance. But he kept up his toll farming and other businesses, and was of great help to his two Jewish brothers in their widespread business dealings. One of these Jewish brothers, Michael Josefowicz, served for a time as community leader of all Lithuanian Jewry, and the king elevated him to the rank of a noble even though he was a Jew.[39] Similar trends are found among a few individuals from lower strata. Conversely, about half a century later the case of a convert to Christianity who gave his property to his Jewish son is recorded.[40]

Kinship Groups

Whatever the actual relations between Jew and Christian may have been, and to whatever extent they may have lived side by side in practical life, definite barriers did separate them. These were fostered not only by differences in religion and belief —which were mutually exclusive—and by majority-minority tensions and animosities, but also by their images of each other.

For the Christian, the Jew was an infidel, a nonbeliever (this epithet is found in many medieval documents whenever a Jew is mentioned), which may or may not have had the connotation of a Christ-killer, but was surely a derogatory classification meant to stigmatize. Christian theology fostered the concept of the Jew doomed to eternal servitude, or of one that was inferior to the Christian and therefore unfit to occupy a position of supremacy over the latter. Social segregation from Jews was a postulate of the church.

Christianity and Christians also fostered a self-image of having been victimized for the sake of the cross—recalling the scriptural teachings and the early struggles of Christianity. A victim image implies an oppressor.[41] As a despiser of Christ and because of his inimical attitudes toward Christianity, the Jew came to be considered the oppressor. This contributed to accusations that he defiled the holy wafer so sacred to the Christians and killed Christian children for the purpose of taking their

---

*A reader of the manuscript added (1397?) the remark: "I am ashamed that this Jew knows so much."

†This trend is also found in countries outside of Poland at that time, as well as in Poland in the sixteenth and seventeenth centuries.

blood. These views could be bound up with generalizations about the Jew as an oppressor in practical life: Jews dispossessing Christian property owners or taking away the livelihood (by competition) from Christian artisans and businessmen.

The Jew paralleled these sentiments with ideas about the superiority of his own community, the chosenness of the Jews in comparison with the idolatry (paganism) of the others. Jews regarded themselves as distinct from other nations. Philosophically, God's election of Israel was held by some in the Middle Ages to be a result of the Jews' innate predisposition, which designated the Jewish nation as the future bearer of divine revelation.[42] In religious law the attitudes of talmudic norms and of halakha, which sought to create barriers between Jew and non-Jew, prevailed. It was generally thought that these laws of segregation from and nonfraternization with the gentiles applied also to Christians, although Jews realized the difference between the gentiles of antiquity and the Christians of medieval Europe. In practice many talmudic laws were rendered obsolete and some prescriptions for segregation dispensed with. But the principle remained.

To this image of the "theological" non-Jew and his differences from the Jew, one should add the image of the actual Christian neighbor and of the Christian ruler, which was mostly, or partially, that of an oppressor.[43] Unlike the Christians, the Jews did not have to transfer historical and theological images regarding the victim-oppressor relationship into the present. There was, as we have seen, some persecution of Jews in Poland during the Middle Ages, and possibly a number of individual skirmishes about which we know very little. In such a social climate the Jew tended to look inward rather than outward, drawing strength from group solidarity. The family was of paramount importance in his way of living. Most of the medieval Polish Jew's social life, his friendships, his social activities, and his whole mode of life were insular, despite the occasional gambling and drinking and fraternizing in other ways with non-Jews. The Jew married within the group, and his culture was largely a specialized one with which the non-Jew was unfamiliar. This in-group feeling was no doubt strengthened by the fact that the Jewish settlements were small and by the similarity of their internal cultural patterns. The group's cohesion remained intact despite squabbling among the members and the tensions arising from differences in origin, as well as competition[44] and social stratification within the Jewish community. The overriding idea was group distinctiveness, being different from the environment, though in practice some Jews may not have acknowledged this norm.

This separateness molded most of the characteristics of the Jews. They lived apart, concentrated in the Jewish street; they wore somewhat distinctive clothing—not necessarily that prescribed by the church, which had a derogatory implication; they gathered around the same institutions: the synagogue, the cemetery, the ritual bath, and the hospital; they married within the group; they were engaged in similar occupations; and, at least theoretically, they identified themselves with the same ideals and values. Their communications and interests were similar, as were their fears and hopes, despite socioeconomic stratification.

To a great degree this tightly knit grouping also determined the Jew's economic and social status. Solidarity and contacts played a considerable role in economic activity. The strength and structure of an enterprise, firm, or partnership were conditioned by group solidarity, which also may have helped in terms of development and seizing new opportunities. Jews went into partnership as moneylenders or merchants and toll farmers on a larger scale. (There were also some Jewish-Christian partnerships, but these seem to have been less frequent.) The employees in business enterprises and in toll and tax farming were Jews over whom the entrepreneur often exercised judicial rights.

Jews from different parts of the country may have formed partnerships or done business together, thus utilizing resources and opportunities to be found in widely separated places. An example is a rich Jew of Luck, Volhynia—Jacob Slomkowits—who had business contacts (apparently a partnership) with a Cracow Jew at the beginning of the fifteenth century. Later he married off his daughter who moved to Cracow, and a son moved to that same city.

Still more widespread was the identification of a family with an enterprise. Many family businesses or partnerships are mentioned, with the second or third generation often rising in importance and increasing their wealth. The three main moneylenders in Poznań at the end of the fourteenth century were working with wives, sons, or a son-in-law. The development of the family business of the well-to-do Cracow Jew Levko can be followed through three or four generations. His parents seem to have been people of some means who owned real estate. Levko himself apparently began as a dealer in real estate, branching out to become Cracow's leading Jewish banker, and he was also engaged in tax farming and other businesses. Upon his death in 1395 his wife and sons, some of whom were already involved, took over the business. Their business activities and those of their own sons can be traced through most of the fifteenth century.

Another such successful family business was that of the Fischels. Efraim Fischel came to Cracow some years before his death in 1485, and we are able to follow the development of four generations (with the exception of Stefan, who converted to Christianity), both in business and community leadership. Brothers and sons worked together, holding leading positions in the Jewish community, and some of them playing a role at the king's court. A second-generation Fischel converted to Christianity; a niece married the renowned rabbi Jacob Polak; and two brothers of the next generation suffered martyrs' deaths (in 1542 and 1551). In Silesia, too, we find partnerships among Jews, who were often relatives.[45]

Group solidarity may have facilitated the adjustment to external forces and enabled the Jews to cope somewhat more easily with the difficulties in the none too friendly environment, while the family enterprise provided for succession and offered additional motivation for dealing with problems encountered by aggressive business action.

As in economics, meeting fellow Jews in the marketplace in other walks of life may have had both a unifying and a dividing impact because of competition and other business problems. While in the synagogue, and outside after prayers on Saturdays and holidays, Jews in Poland apparently had a chance to engage in leisurely conversations, exchange general and Jewish news and opinions, and possibly also discuss the cantor's performance and criticize or praise his voice. Here public opinion was formed, community matters thrashed out, and rumors spread. Jews also visited each other on Saturdays and holidays and shared the joy or sorrow of such family occurrences as birth, marriage, sickness, and death.

Education, too, was introverted and insular, devoted exclusively to Jewish studies, even though some Jews were apparently versed in the language of the country and in the "office language" of the time: medieval Latin. Education took different forms: private teachers, community teacher (this seems to have been the situation at the beginning of the thirteenth century), and occasionally a yeshiva (talmudic academy) for adolescents and young men. There seems to have been a yeshiva in the fourteenth century in Schweidnitz, Silesia. At the turn of the fifteenth century Rabbi Jacob Polak was heading a yeshiva in Kazimierz-Cracow, and there may have been others in the second half of the fifteenth century, in Poznań, for instance, where learned rabbis—mostly immigrants from the West—lived. The attendance at such institutions of higher learning in Poland may have been extremely small, and the level of studies in the yeshiva not too high. But they were the forerunners of Torah study in Poland, for which the country became famous in subsequent centuries.

Women's Status

Ashkenazic (German) Jewry generally was somewhat ambivalent about its women. Biased male opinion branded them as frivolous and fickle in sexual matters. This being a man's world, the Jew daily thanked God "who hast not made me a woman." Only the man could be a full-fledged member of the Jewish community, and he alone was obliged to fulfill all the commandments of the Torah. Yet the family in Ashkenazic Jewish society was monogamous—mainly after the eleventh and twelfth centuries—and concubinage was almost nonexistent, whereas in Sephardic Jewry it was not unusual. Nevertheless the male was still all-important in Ashkenazic Jewry. *He* (or his father) negotiated a dowry, and *he* instigated divorce—although provisions against divorce unless the wife agreed to it were introduced.[46] His passions and primitive erotic drives were tempered or sublimated by religious requirements of perfection, chastity, and matrimonial fidelity, by emphasis on propagation as the main goal of matrimony, and by the avoidance of situations conducive to sexual "irregularities." Conversely, in order to protect the women, polygamy and compulsory divorce were forbidden,[47] and some attempts to insure women's property rights were made. There was also a noticeable tendency among rabbis to be somewhat lenient about freeing a deserted woman *(agunah)* so that she might remarry, although some of them insisted on strict adherence to the law.

In practice women shared the burden of making a living and in some cases were the main bearers of this burden. Individual women were lauded for outstanding learning, charitableness, or piety. They were also officially regarded as partners in property ownership.

A similar situation prevailed in Poland in the Middle Ages. Polish Jews followed the Ashkenazic traditions in matters pertaining to their women's status, just as they generally tended to do in many other spheres. At the end of the fifteenth century Rabbi Moses ben Jacob of Kiev—apparently the first Polish Jewish author—voiced the prevalent mistrust of women: "Just as it is impossible to find a white raven, so it is impossible to find a virtuous woman. . . . If there is no real adultery, there is something akin to it."

Later, Solomon Luria also seems to have been prejudiced against women, but at the same time he sought to protect them from abuse by the males,[48] even though he was opposed to forcing a husband to grant a divorce. Actually, in Poland we find extremes: husbands who beat their wives, and husbands whose wives played a role in business and even at the king's court. In Silesia and in Poland proper we find Jewish women as heads of households or businesses and as owners of houses. We find a number of widows of wealthy Jews becoming heads of firms, apparently having been active in business prior to their husbands' deaths.[49] Rachel (or Rashka), the mother-in-law of Rabbi Jacob Polak, was not only active in her husband's business but apparently also in community matters and at the king's court. There she was granted an honorary position and was the only Jewish person to receive the right to own a house in Cracow after the expulsion of Jews in 1495. Apparently her influence at court enhanced her standing in the Jewish community, where she succeeded in gaining support for her son-in-law (Rabbi Jacob Polak) in the fluctuations of his stormy career. She also knew how to advance the candidacy of another son-in-law (Rabbi Asher Lemel) as rabbi of the community in Kazimierz-Cracow.

Some other Jewish women, wives and widows of toll farmers, a physician, and businessmen, had connections in the court, from which they received various privileges and exemptions from taxes. Poor women, too, were active as street vendors or as producers of various articles of clothing. Rabbi Solomon Luria sums up the status of women in the sixteenth century: "Our women now conduct business in the house [and] represent the husband." Connected with the woman's standing in the world of business and affairs was her appearance in legal documents (receipts and contracts) on a par with her husband.[50]

The Image of the Idealized Jew

An ideal is defined as "a nonexistent situation . . . or behavior pattern which serves as an aim for the activity of a person or a group." It may serve as a source of energy or be a fantasy that compensates for the imperfection of reality. But "for the history of civilization the perennial dream of a sublime life has the value of a very important reality."[51] Though the ideals may very often be violated in practice, they provide society with a goal toward which to strive and a mirror for the beliefs and values that determine its direction and aims.

Jewish life and thought in the Middle Ages (like life in Europe generally) were saturated with ideas of faith, piety, and virtue, which were thought to be the essence of life. Although the image of the ideal Jew—as seen by contemporaries—does not always reflect day-to-day life, it does give us a clue to what the people regarded as a goal, what they aspired to, and what they dreamed of and strove to achieve. (As in other areas of Jewish life in Poland of those centuries, we are able, for lack of adequate sources, to sketch only a bare outline of the trends.[52])

It is customary to speak well of the dead and to inscribe laudatory epitaphs on headstones. Such praise may merely be empty phrases or it may depict the deceased's real qualities. Whichever it is, it conforms to an accepted ideal. The preserved headstones in Silesia will indicate that the ideal included piety, righteousness, honor, reliability, wealth, and continuous study of Torah.[53]

The few preserved responsa—actually, mainly answers from rabbis outside Poland, but they may help us to guess what the questions were—further indicate the ideals. A request for advice, an outline of a penance to be imposed on a murderer, the penalty for transgression of the Sabbath or for unseemly behavior in community quarrels—these clearly indicate that such negative conduct was regarded as a deviation from the ideal. For a clearer depiction of the ideal we may consider the case of Jekussiel, or Jekutiel, a Jew from Breslau who apparently enjoyed the protection of the Polish king. Practicing a common medieval form of extortion, the city of Breslau jailed him on the pretext that he was guilty of some sort of libel. He succeeded in escaping from jail, was recaptured, paid the city a larger sum, and was freed. He then complained to the Polish king, whereupon he was again thrown into jail, together with his mother, daughter, and brother, and in 1435 was forced to sign a document "of free will and without duress" stating that he was withdrawing his complaint to the king and would never repeat it. He seems to have been helped by some burghers (or city councilors) whom he bribed, and he had to swear under pain of ban, before Jews who acted as intermediaries, that he would not disclose these facts. Upon regaining his freedom he inquired of a German rabbi the extent to which this oath was binding.[54] The nature of this inquiry seems to indicate that despite all he had been through, Jekussiel was interested in the obligation to fulfill his oath. Another problem with which he was concerned was the extent of his moral responsibility for the death of one of his employees, whom he had sent somewhere and who was killed en route; he wondered how he could do penance, if it was necessary. Also concerned with repentance, as we have seen, were at least one of the murderers in Lwów and the Jews from an unnamed city (probably Poznań) who transgressed against the Sabbath in order to rescue their belongings from a fire.

We do not know whether Jekussiel followed the advice of the rabbi who decided that the oath "under ban" was binding, any more than we know whether the Jews who defiled the Sabbath fasted the forty days prescribed by the rabbi. Nor can we tell whether the man who killed the other Jew in Lwów really went through the whole very arduous gamut of penance plus the additional prescription imposed by the rabbi, Israel Bruna, to indemnify the dead man's family and, in accordance with the tradition of Jehuda Hachassid, "to wander from place to place for one year":

> *He shall attend synagogue services every day, especially on Mondays and Thurs-days. He shall enter the synagogue barefoot, and shall shackle himself with three iron chains, one on each hand with which he committed the transgression and one on his body. He shall wear these shackles during prayers. He shall be lashed publicly and loudly declare: "May it be known unto you, sirs, that I am a murderer and this is my atonement.". . . Upon leaving the synagogue, he shall prostrate himself on the threshold of the synagogue so that many persons may tread on him. He shall fast every day throughout the year, except on special days . . . [Sabbath, holidays and half-holidays] . . . He shall not sleep on pillows except on the Sabbath and holidays.*

All these ordeals were, or course, not easy to endure and we have no information about who, if anyone, actually went through with them. But the very fact that Jekussiel turned to the rabbi for advice, despite the oath's having been taken in a time of distress, and the fact that the others also sought to determine what they ought to do may indicate that the religious-moral tenets of the Jews were highly respected, at any rate by these particular individuals.

Heritage

Jews in Poland may have begun early to develop some customs of their own that differ slightly from those of Germany-Austria (Rabbi Moses Mintz reports such deviations in 1474 in connection with marriage and the marriage contract).[55] But in the main, Jewry in Poland during the Middle Ages was heir to the talmudic-halakhic Judaism developed by German (Ashkenazic) Jewry and to some extent emphasized the traditions emanating from the circle of Hassidim around Rabbi Jehuda Hachassid in the first half of the thirteenth century. Polish rabbis of the sixteenth to seventeenth century stressed this chain of tradition, and it is safe to assume that they followed the Jewish traditions of the fifteenth and earlier centuries. In fact, from the end of the twelfth century, when information about the existence of Jews in the country first appears in Jewish sources, until the end of the Middle Ages the fragments we have about spiritual contacts indicate a leaning toward Germany and the Jehuda Hachassid circle. As mentioned, our first information on a Jewish community in Poland (and Russia and Hungary) is connected with the name of Jehuda Hachassid. The few preserved responsa from Poland to German rabbis of the fifteenth century indicate the influence of followers of German Hassidim ("the Devout of Germany"). Some of the prescriptions for penance coming from there indicate the same trend. True, in Poland the "testaments of Rabbi Jehuda Hachassid seem to have been accepted to a small extent only,"[56] but nevertheless they apparently served as an ideal.

"The Devout of Germany" formulated a theory (if we may call it that) of a mystic relation to God, exhibiting some pantheistic and other leanings. They developed a system of penitence, apparently under Christian influence, "beginning with all sorts of fastings and leading, through various acts, frequently of a highly bizarre nature —of self-inflicted torture—to the supreme punishment of voluntary exile," as G. Scholem put it. This system is based on the medieval approach of severe retribution graded according to the severity of the sin.

Generally, in *Sefer Hassidim* by Rabbi Jehuda Hachassid the principle of reward and punishment—mostly in the afterlife—plays a big role. In stories and pronouncements the world and the afterlife are pictured as large "accounting houses" where good and bad deeds are properly recorded and evaluated and fitting rewards or punishment meted out, even to descendants generations later. It is as if the author or authors wish to convince the reader of the necessity for virtuous behavior with the help of the carrot-and-stick method of reward and retribution. In their pessimistic view of the world evil prevails, and "two thoughts plague the human being day and night: sex and money." So they formulated an ideal of human fairness, equality, and morality for selected individuals, an elite of "saints," transcending the official law and aiming for exaggeratedly ethical individual behavior.[57] These few "saints" may possibly have been intended to serve as good examples. Spiritual perfection and piety were regarded as the goals of human behavior in this world.

All this was overlaid with a symbolism linking things in terms of mysterious significance. The deeper significance of ordinary things, the sense that life is connected with the hidden meaning of the world, is symbolized among other things by the belief in the souls of the dead and their influence on the living, and the latter's obligation to labor for the salvation of these souls.

Without going into the problem of how far their moral ideals were influenced by the Christian environment and Christian monastic trends, it should be pointed out that this ideal of "the Devout of Germany" became a factor in Poland, even though here, as already mentioned, only a part of Rabbi Jehuda Hachassid's "testaments" were accepted.

Other Ideals

By the end of the fifteenth century some new Jewish ideals and goals may have come into Poland. Rabbi Jacob Polak, who settled in Cracow, became the founder of the pilpul school and a father of talmudic studies in that country.[58] At the same time some cabalistic trends, apparently from Sephardic sources, began to make their way into Polish Jewish communities. Moses ben Jacob of Kiev, who was born in Lithuania, studied in Constantinople and apparently there he picked up some cabalistic rudiments of Sephardic origin. Later in Poland—in Kiev, Luck, and other places—he may have spread them in some Jewish circles.[59] Then, too, the rabbi of the Polish Jewish community in Cracow at the end of the fifteenth century, Rabbi Asher Lemel, was known as a cabalist. Thus one is entitled to speculate that these various influences made up the image of the ideal Jew at that time. This image may have been a combination of the ideas of piety from the German Hassidim with the casuistic talmudic study of the West and cabalistic notions from the Sephardic school.

Despite all these spiritual, cabalistic-mystic, and idealistic trends and ideas of piety, Polish Jews of the Middle Ages (and later) apparently also maintained very practical approaches and attitudes. Their practicality may have been connected with their day-to-day roles in Polish society, either in a causal relationship or as a parallel development.

If these assumptions are correct, the ideal Jew may have represented the piety, virtue, moral, and social perfection of the German Hassidim, combined with acuity of talmudic study and pilpulistic and casuistic discussion and deliberation, interwoven with mysticism and symbolism. All of this was set against a background of practical activity, business affairs, and worldly interests, which had a moderating effect on the otherworldly trends. Thus as the Middle Ages waned the faint outlines of trends that were to pervade Polish Jewry in subsequent centuries may have already been just faintly perceptible among Polish Jews.

II

Growth, Rooting, and Expansion

6 Background, Jewish Population and Settlement

The three hundred years between the end of the fifteenth century and the partitions of Poland (in 1772, 1793, and 1795) mark an epoch in Polish history covering that country's expansion, the attainment of its peak in political, territorial, and economic growth, its subsequent decline, and its final disappearance as a state from the map of Europe.

During roughly the first half of this epoch, Poland was prospering despite the Turkish penetration to southern Europe, the stirrings in Moscovian Russia for expansion (in 1514 Smolensk was taken from Lithuania), and the pressures from the West exerted by Austria and the Teutonic order (which later became Prussia). True, the impact of the Turks' rising power at times somewhat canceled out the Austrian pressure, or even led to some cooperation between Poland and Austria (as, for instance, in the Polish-Austrian alliance of 1613 and the Polish kings' offers of support during some phases of the Thirty Years' War). Polish and Austrian cooperation culminated with the two forces defeating the Turks at Vienna in 1683.

On the other hand, the Reformation and the religious wars in central Europe weakened the Catholic Hapsburgs and contributed to the dissolution of the Teutonic order in northwestern Poland and its transformation to a secular duchy under Polish suzerainty. In the east the increasingly aggressive strength of Russia, combined with the constant threat of the Tatars from the southeast, contributed to the formation of a closer, more firmly established federation of Poland and Lithuania (the Union of Lublin in 1569), which until then had been only a dynastic union that was greatly plagued by tensions and frequent disruptions.

The union of 1569 made Poland and Lithuania into a multinational state, territorially the second largest in Europe and the sixth in population. It also enlarged the territory of Poland proper (the kingdom of Poland*) by the annexation of parts of Podlasie (the Bialystok region) and the Ukraine (the Volhynia and Kiev region), which until then had been linked with Lithuania. (Earlier, in 1466, western Prussia

*Polish terminology differentiates between *Korona* (Crown), meaning the kingdom of Poland, and the grand duchy of Lithuania.

or "Danzig-Pomerania," including the city of Danzig [Gdansk] and, in 1526 Mazovia, with Warsaw, had both been incorporated into Poland.) By the beginning of the seventeenth century, when internal dynastic problems developed in Moscovian Russia, Polish kings tried to subdue Russia and reduce it to a Polish satellite. The growth of Poland in the north, east, and southeast resulted in extended frontiers and brought the kingdom of Poland into direct contact with Sweden, Russia, and the Tatars, who were officially vassals of Turkey. This situation led to later repercussions.

Economically, after the middle of the fifteenth century Poland began to export agricultural and other raw products (grain, timber, potash, tar, livestock, hides, fur, salt, beeswax, and so on), becoming the granary of Western Europe. The concentration on agriculture was somewhat accelerated by rising prices for agricultural goods in Poland itself (in Cracow wheat prices increased fourfold), a result of both the world's growing demand for grain and the general inflation in Europe following the accumulation of silver and gold from Dutch, French, English, and Portuguese colonies.

The large market for grain and other agricultural products led to a transformation of the agricultural village: to a manorial system producing largely for the market and based on labor furnished by the peasants (serfs) in the form of servitude. The serfs became permanently bound to the soil and lost the legal protection of the king in 1518, after which their obligations to the landowners were constantly increased.

Internally, the Polish-Lithuanian state was polyglot, multinational, and multireligious. The union in 1569 brought together in one state Poles, Ukrainians, White Russians, Lithuanians, and a number of smaller minorities (Jews, Germans, Armenians, Tatars, and others), with ethnic Poles constituting only about two-fifths of the total.

Religious affiliation in Poland included Catholics, Greek Orthodox, Uniates or Greek Catholics (Byzantine rites and ceremonies coupled with acknowledgment of the pope's supremacy), Lutherans, Calvinists, Bohemian Brethren, Arians (anti-Trinitarians) in addition to Jews, adherents of the Armenian Church, and Muslims. The initial impact of the Reformation was a peaceful one, with both Catholics and Protestants holding high positions in the country.

The expansion toward the east, particularly after 1569, opened to Polish colonization large stretches of land in the Ukraine and some in White Russia. The magnates and particularly some lesser noblemen acquired large estates (latifundia) on which they founded many new villages, towns, and a few cities. They enticed peasants, Jews, Armenians, and some urban elements from the western parts of Poland or from abroad to settle in these places by granting them several years' exemption from corveé as well as other civic benefits.

Geography, time, politics, and internal social relations did not work in favor of the large Polish state, however. It was "squeezed in" between other nations gathering momentum for expansion—Prussia and Austria on the west, Russia on the east, and for a time Sweden on the north as well. In the south and southeast, Poland suffered from wars with Turkey or from constant attacks by the Tatars, who officially were vassals of Turkey; up to 1669 there had been 164 such attacks.

The epoch under consideration (sixteenth through eighteenth centuries) is the period in which European routes of world communication and trade shifted westward, toward the rising Atlantic states (first Spain, later France, the Netherlands, and England). This left Poland far behind economically and politically and meant that the cities in Poland were to some extent declining, a trend that was furthered by the country's emphasis on agriculture and by the attitudes and policies of the nobility, the elite of the agricultural sector. They opposed the urban guilds' and associations' monopolistic privileges and sought to weaken their position.

From the fourteenth century on, the nobility, the great lords and the gentry or *szlachta* (both those who owned villages and a great many serfs and the poorer ones who either owned a few serfs or tilled their holdings themselves) gained more and more political importance in the state. Having extracted greater privileges and rights from the kings and continually curtailed the latters' prerogatives, they succeeded in circumscribing the royal power still further in the sixteenth and seventeenth centuries. With the extinction of the Jagiellonian dynasty (1386–1572), the country became a "republic" ruled by the landed gentry in a parliament, called the *sejm*, with a king elected by the nobility to preside over it. Every new king was bound by new *pacta conventa*, the agreements by which he usually ceded certain powers to the nobles and assumed new burdens.

The parliament and the senate (restricted to bishops and a number of high officers of the state) appropriated more and more authority. The *sejm*, representing the gentry, became the main political force in the country. Eager to maintain their privileged status, the gentry and magnates thwarted, either by means of revolts as in 1606–7 or through the *sejm*, most of the attempts to strengthen the monarchy, form a regular standing army, or put through other reforms.

The squires conducted their *sejm* like some assemblies of the early Middle Ages: on the basis of a unanimous, not a majority, vote. The specific brand of Polish democracy based on the principle of a unanimous vote in the diet *(liberum veto)* led to many abuses either by outside powers or by Polish groups. By means of bribes and pressures one could induce an individual deputy to oppose certain bills and thus bring about the dissolution of the diet (after 1652, forty-eight out of fifty-five biennial sessions were dissolved in this way). This hindered the passage of resolutions and sabotaged the approval of budgets and levies, leaving the administration in a state of chaos and the country defenseless.

This situation plagued Poland during most of the seventeenth and eighteenth centuries. The void left by a lack of centralized power and effective government machinery enabled individual magnates to become semiautonomous rulers, maintaining armies of their own and conducting small wars, and encouraged groups of nobles to band together (forming "confederations") for various causes. Chaos and disorder reigned at times. Some kings themselves, often in competition with or imitation of the particularistic groups, outfitted private armies, led wars, and sponsored policies for reasons of their own prestige, with little regard for the effect upon the country at large. As a result Poland was often at war with one or more of her neighbors. Moreover, corruption and egotism became dominant factors in Polish life. This all took place at a time when both the neighbor on the east (Russia) and the one on the west (Prussia) were centralizing their government structures, modernizing their economies, and increasing their military strength. By the middle of the eighteenth century Russia and Austria had standing armies of about 300,000 each, Prussia had one of 200,000, and Poland only had some 12–16,000. The attempts to build up a mercenary army or to provide for a regular army (infantry) undertaken in Poland in the sixteenth century did not amount to much. The bill of 1524 to enroll cossacks in an army on the border steppes was halfheartedly put into effect, but it was done in a manner that contributed to a number of revolts later, the bloodiest in 1648.

The impact of all these social forces was aggravated by the divisions in religion, nationality, language, and social structure. Religious tolerance—of which the high point may have been the Confederation of 1573, signed by the lay members of the diet and guaranteeing absolute religious toleration of Protestant denominations—was not destined to be of lasting importance. Counter-Reformation had already brought the Jesuits to Poland (in 1564) and they opened schools and colleges, propagated intolerance, and precipitated Catholic reaction. As a result, Catholicism became a prerequisite for high offices in Poland and the former Lithuanian-Russian lands. Similarly, Protestants had only limited rights to be admitted to cities as burghers (Warsaw in 1580, Poznań in 1619, Cracow in 1627, Lublin in 1651) or to membership in the guilds.[1] Later, in the eighteenth century, non-Catholic noblemen lost some further part of their political rights.

On the lower levels of society mob riots and pogroms against Protestants were instigated in a number of cities from the end of the sixteenth century, and half a century later, in 1658, the Arians were expelled from Poland. In southern Poland religious tensions (Greek Orthodox versus Catholic) combined with social strife between the serfs (mostly Greek Orthodox) and the Polish gentry, between Ukrainians and Poles in the cities, and between the magnates and the lesser noblemen gave rise to a number of cossack* rebellions, of which the revolt led by Bogdan Chmielnicki in 1648 was the most violent. The cossack leaders were supported by the peasants and also to some extent by city people, and this gave the uprising a deeper significance. It precipitated a Twenty Years' War in Eastern Europe, with cossack

---

*Cossacks were paramilitary or military squads consisting mainly of Ukrainians but also including Poles, Germans, and other adventurers, who were originally organized for defense against attacks by the Tatars. (*Qazaq* is a word of Turkish origin meaning independent warrior.) They later had more stabilized military formations, but in peacetime engaged in agriculture, fishing, and so on, forming settlements of their own and identifying with the Ukrainian group. From the end of the sixteenth century some Polish military standing army groups were formed from among the cossacks.

(1648–55), Russian (1654–67), and Swedish (1655–60) invasions almost obliterating the Polish state.

The subsequent recovery and reconstruction (after 1667) did not lead to a change in the social and political order, but increased the weakness. Poland was finally reduced to a second-rate power in the Great Northern War (1701–21). Again in the eighteenth century the tensions and strife between the dominant Polish Catholics and the other religious-national groups (officially known as "the dissenters") became the bone of contention between Poland and her neighbors, and this gave Russia an ostensible reason for interfering in Polish affairs. This finally contributed to the Polish partitions.

Socially and economically, the destruction during the actual wars and their aftermath—oppression, plunder, and robbery—from Polish soldiers because they had not been paid (in 1661–63, 1666–67, 1696, and so on), as well as from the outbreaks of pestilence (in 1659–63, 1705–14 and other years) and famine (in 1656–59, 1662–63, 1714–15), led to a decline in population, the devastation of villages, and the deterioration of cities and towns.[2] Partial figures indicate that the population declined by one-third or more in some places or regions, and 10 to 15 percent of the villages were deserted. Considerable numbers of people were involved when, at the end of the Ukrainian-Russian-Polish wars (armistice of Andrusovo in 1667), a broad belt of White Russian and Ukrainian territory (Smolensk, Chernigov, Kiev, Poltava) went to Russia. It is estimated that by 1720 the Polish population was about six million.[3]

Devastation and population decline went hand in hand with a decrease in production of agricultural and artisan products and a reduction of trade. In both town and village this brought in its wake increased stratification, mounting pressures (taxation, social), and intensified conflict between the different groups. At the same time the power of the guilds in the cities declined somewhat as they were undermined by competition and shrinking employment opportunities. In time, particularly after the Great Northern War, the situation began to improve. The rate of population growth picked up. During half a century (1721–71) the population more than doubled, reaching about 12 million persons around the middle of the century. A revival of economic activity also began to be observable in both city and village.

Meanwhile, in the second half of the century lively public discussion developed, in the press and in the *sejm*, on the problems involved in effecting reforms in the monetary system and the treasury, in the city and its government, and in the situation and status of the peasantry. As a result, the cities acquired some degree of autonomy (in 1791), and minor concessions were made to the peasants and city dwellers (in 1768 and 1791). But politically Poland had earlier been reduced to a second-rate power, existing partly because of the tolerance of her neighbors—Russia, Prussia, and Austria—who had far outdistanced her politically and militarily. Thus Poland's downfall as a state (the partitions of 1772, 1793, and 1795) was already in the making.

The Jews

Jewish development and growth in Poland during these three centuries of the rise and decline of the Polish state runs parallel with the general tendencies to some extent, but it also shows some trends specifically its own. Its upward curve follows the rise of the country but does not fall abruptly with the latter's disintegration. It levels off or turns downward during one period but then partially recovers and begins to rise again.

In general these three centuries were an epoch of great growth for Polish Jewry, despite many setbacks. True, the Jews in Poland suffered along with the rest of the population—sometimes even more than they—from war, pestilence, hunger, destruction, attacks by soldiers and armed robbery, and invasion. As a minority group they were apt to be regarded with suspicion by any warring parties and were often treated as enemies by both. In time of upheaval and disorder a defenseless minority is more likely to fall prey to abuse and injustice than is the majority. Nevertheless, the Jewish group seems to have weathered the catastrophes of the middle of the seventeenth century somewhat better than the rest of the population. It was as if the Jews in that country had, during the preceding period, gathered the strength and vitality to enable them to survive disaster by adjusting to new conditions, taking advantage of chance situations, and making a persistent effort.

Like some other out-groups (in our times, for instance, the Chinese in southern Asia) the Jews in the cities, not having gained any monopoly to assure their share of the income pie, had been forced to develop some different attitudes and tactics from the majority. In Europe generally whenever calamity or economic decline struck the city in preindustrial times, many of the inhabitants returned to the countryside and reverted to their rural past to eke out a living in agrarian occupations. Having no such antecedents, the Jews either clung to the city and tried to evolve new procedures or else moved to rural or backward areas but took their "urban past" with them. They sought to introduce or to maintain some rudiments of urban economic life—the exchange of commodities and services and the use of certain skills, which sometimes involved experimentation, risks, and the utilization of chance possibilities.

As we have said, the rise of the nobility to a position of great influence on the policy and economy of the country, and the settlement methods they employed, (particularly in eastern Poland), created opportunities favorable to the Jews. True, the laws of 1539 and 1549 bestowing on the gentry jurisdiction over Jews living on their estates, thereby removing them to a great degree from royal protection, did open the way to some incidents of abuse and arbitrariness, but on the whole their relationship with the gentry was advantageous for the Jews. Consequently, it was not long before more than half of all Polish Jews were living on territories owned by the nobility and clergy, and more often than not Jews formed a larger percentage of the total population in such cities and towns and enjoyed greater freedom than in the royal cities.

The ten thousand or so Jews living in Poland at the end of fifteenth century were destined to increase during the next three centuries into a large community of hundreds of thousands and to become the backbone of European Jewry. The loose beginnings of community organization in the earlier period were transformed into a comprehensive community structure, although some status was lost in the second half of the eighteenth century. The weak religious-cultural tradition, mostly imported from the West, matured into a well-developed culture and way of life, and with the addition of some new patterns it took root in East European soil.

Another development of these centuries was the emergence of the village Jew as a significant component in the Jewish population and his consolidation as a pronounced type. Prior to that time a few individual Jews may have lived in rural settlements in Poland, but we have very little information about them. Their numbers and impact were minimal, and their "village identity" was often only temporary.

During the sixteenth to eighteenth centuries, however, conditions changed. With the great increase in Jewish population, the spread of Jewish settlements in Poland, and the movement eastward and southeastward, a type of village Jew, the *yishuvnik*, emerged to play a part both in internal Jewish life and in forming the attitudes of certain states (Poland, Prussia, Austria, Russia) toward the Jewish question generally in the eighteenth century.

The village Jews, for the most part isolated individuals within non-Jewish settlements, cut off from city and town life and spread thinly among the mostly illiterate local population, became involved with their non-Jewish neighbors. Living among Christians and sharing some of the joys and sorrows of their daily lives, the village Jew became somewhat estranged from the intellectualized, religious culture of the dominant city Jew. Illiteracy concerning Jewish religious literature, lack of knowledge of religious laws and practices, and some permissiveness in behavior patterns spread. Despite their ideal of remaining aloof as Jews, they found themselves becoming somehow immersed in the behavior patterns of the peasants around them. They could not avoid absorbing rudiments of the beliefs and superstitions of the surrounding Christian population. In outward appearance, in dress, in some ways of making a living, and partially in outlook, the village Jew became different from the city Jew and somewhat alienated from him. This helped to magnify the social differences between village and city Jews that had already developed because of the different status in Jewish society and its community organization.

The *yishuvnik* helped to foster a ferment of dissatisfaction and social protest within the Jewish community structure; later, in the nineteenth century, he served as a subject, sometimes a derided one, for Jewish literature (written in Yiddish and sometimes Hebrew).

On the other hand, the existence of a larger Jewish village population in the agricultural settlements, living in close contact with peasant-serfs and allegedly or actually exploiting them, gave government officials and landlords the excuse to make Jews the scapegoats for the peasantry's ills. From the eighteenth century on this partially biased attitude toward village Jews began to color the "Jewish problem" in Eastern Europe, and the states sought a solution by separating Jew from peasant, expelling the Jew from the village, or limiting his activities there, and other restrictions.

Population and Migration

The growth of the Jewish population in Poland stemmed from two sources: immigration, mainly during the first half of this period, and natural growth. Immigrants came principally from central Europe. (Few of the Sephardic Jews expelled from Spain in 1492 and from Portugal in 1497, and few of the Marranos [crypto-Jews] later, made their way to Poland. Of the ones that did, few remained there.)

From the south, too, from Kaffa in the Crimea, Turkey, the Balkans, and Italy some Sephardic Jews came to Poland. There was also an attempt to organize an entirely Jewish settlement consisting of Sephardic Jews in Zamość in the sixteenth century. But this attempt was not very successful, possibly for reasons beyond the control of the settlers. Some individual Sephardim who reached and settled on the Polish lands may later have left or been assimilated among the Polish Jewish population, but only a very small number of people were involved.

For the people from west central Europe, however, the situation seems to have been quite different. During the whole of the sixteenth century Jews in Germany, Austria, and Bohemia, were continually being expelled from cities and entire regions.[4] Some of these expellees apparently settled in Poland: the names of many Polish Jews indicate German extraction. During the first half of the sixteenth century Jews from Bohemia apparently gained entrance to Poland easily. As we have mentioned, direct and indirect contacts between Jews and King Sigismund I (1506–48) or his entourage apparently remained from the years when he lived at his brother's court in Bohemia or served as his viceroy in Silesia. We find that Sigismund protected some Bohemian Jews and their possessions against oppression in Bohemia, accorded them preferential treatment while allowing them to settle in Poland.[5]

In the seventeenth century, too, there was at least a trickle of immigration of Jews into Poland. Young people came to study in the yeshivot there, and some of them married and settled in the country.[6] Others were fleeing the impact of the Thirty Years' War (1618–48) in west central Europe. And in the same century Sephardic Jews attempted to organize a Jewish settlement of their own in Zamość, and a few dozen families actually did settle there. Some Jews came to Poland when they were expelled from Vienna in 1670. Others came for a variety of reasons.

Natural growth was another, and perhaps a principal, cause of the increase in population. Although mortality was high, epidemics took their toll, raids by Tatars and others destroyed life and property, and the sale of captives on the slave markets in the Middle East was not infrequent, nevertheless the population did increase.

There are reliable indications that despite the many scourges in Poland, the general population increase during these centuries was accompanied by an increase in the Jewish population. Pestilence may at times have taken a greater toll among the Jews since they were to a considerable extent concentrated in cities and towns, where epidemics probably were more severe. According to one theory, Jews, being predominantly city dwellers, early developed a greater immunity to epidemics than the non-Jews,[7] but there is no way of proving or disproving this and similar theories. On the other hand, in comparison with the non-Jewish population the Jews had a number of advantages demographically. Being free from military service they did not lose so many men of reproductive age in the recurrent wars. And unlike the Poles, young Jewish men and women were not entering the ranks of the celibate for religious convictions to become priests, monks, and nuns.

Not having any farming population, Jews did not follow the accepted European custom according to which secondborn and subsequent sons of farmers, as well as house servants, either had to forgo marriage or married late in life.

The principal factor governing population size in those centuries was the number of children surviving into adulthood, rather than the level of the birth rate. Fragmentary empirical information on Jews in Poland in that period seems to indicate that more children survived to adulthood in affluent families than in poor ones. There are some indications that the poorer families were small (some figures show that they had between 1.2 and 2.4 children per family). In contrast, a number of genealogies of business leaders, prominent rabbis, community leaders, and the like disclose that such people often had four, six, and sometimes even eight and nine children who reached adulthood.[8]

Among the many prevalent dangers menacing the infants' survival were hunger, filth, and the long cold winters, not to mention the various epidemics such as smallpox. Infants were breast-fed for a long time, and only wealthier families could afford to hire a wet-nurse whose duties (according to preserved contracts) included keeping the baby clean. The problems of adequate food and cleanliness continued to be acute even after the infant was weaned. Only the more affluent families could afford appropriate food, and they were the ones who were able to keep their houses warm, for this involved a relatively high expense. The number of children surviving among Polish Jews seems to have varied from one social level to another. One may speculate that the village *yishuvnik* may have had a better chance to raise a larger family, for even as poor as many of them were, they probably had enough healthful food from their own gardens—fresh vegetables and fruit—and milk and cheese. Firewood, too, was less costly in the countryside, where there were woods, than in the city. All this may have raised the survival chances of infants among village Jews.[9]

Whatever the reasons, natural growth among Jews seems to have been considerable. It contributed greatly to the transformation of the small group of Jews in Poland from about 10–12,000 persons in 1500 to some 80–100,000 at the end of the century, and about 150–170,000 half a century later. The loss suffered during the two decades that began with the cossack uprising of 1648 may have cut down the Jewish population by one quarter or so,[10] and the ensuing emigration to the

West, although not large, drained Polish Jewry of hundreds of people each year, possibly more.

This loss may have been balanced by a small immigration into Poland in the eighteenth century. Regenerative forces were also at work, and as early as the last quarter of the seventeenth century the number of Jews again began to rise. At any rate, it is from about then that we hear about Jews again settling in various towns and villages in eastern Poland, about an increase in the number of houses owned by them, and about more people in different towns.[11] By the middle of the eighteenth century the number of Jews in Poland reached over 500,000, or three times more than a century earlier.[12] A great part of Polish Jewry was now living in eastern Poland, in or near the regions in which they had been concentrated before the Chmielnicki uprising.

If preserved fragmentary information is at all reliable it could indicate that the growth in the post-Chmielnicki period was strong, even though the rate was a little slower than before.[13] At the time of the 1764 census the number of Jews in Poland amounted to over half a million and together with Lithuania they reached three-quarters of a million.[14]

Settlement

Before the end of the fifteenth century the Jews in Poland were concentrated mainly in the western parts of the country, living in some forty places (the number of functioning Jewish communities was smaller), with considerable numbers living in several big cities, for example Cracow, Poznań, and Lwów. Farther to the east and southeast Jews were found in only a limited number of settlements, aside from Lwów and a few other places in Red Russia (Galicia).

But beginning in the sixteenth century migration eastward was stimulated by several factors. There was the increasingly violent struggle of the burghers against the Jews in the western cities. This led to some local expulsions from cities (under the law of *de non tolerandis Judaeis*) and to limitations on the number of Jews or the parts of cities in which they could live. They were sometimes also subject to pogroms or other persecutions. The substantial population growth led to the need for new economic opportunities, and these were found more often than not in the eastern frontier regions.

In the less developed, mainly agricultural regions of the east, as in Lithuania, the Polish nobles and local nobility performed some of the functions of colonizers and town builders; sometimes, however, they simply exploited the labor force and resources of the villages. In this process of economic organization the Jewish element, partially or wholly urbanized, was useful as a source of managerial skills, tax and revenue farmers, innkeepers, traders, artisan-producers, moneylenders, agents, middlemen, and performers of dozens of other functions.[15] The stream of Jewish immigration and settlement thus moved from the westerly parts to those farther east, drawing in its wake some newcomers from abroad as well.

This eastward trend was interrupted, but not ended, by the events of the middle of the seventeenth century. People fled westward before the impact of the cossacks, the Tatars, and the Russian army. But no sooner did the attacks subside than some of the Jews returned, often only to be caught again by the invading bands and armies.[16] Heavier immigration from west to east Poland may have been delayed until the last decades of the century and the advent of a calmer period. Be that as it may, migration was also a fact of life in the eighteenth century. Around the second half of the century a rabbi states that Jews are constantly on the move.[17]

The further decline of the cities and the sources of income in western Poland, the stronger pressure exerted upon Jews by the burghers and the clergy, and the Jewish population explosion compelled them to "go east." There they could participate in the landlords' attempts to reconstruct their villages and towns or to found new ones. By the eighteenth century a large part of the Jewish population was settled in the eastern provinces. In 1764 only 29 percent of the Jews were living in western Poland, while 44 percent lived in the Ukrainian regions and 27 percent in the Lithuanian–White Russian parts. In other words, more than two-thirds of the Jews were settled in the eastern districts.

The distribution of Jews between urban settlements and villages shows a marked difference from region to region. Generally, in the extreme western, more highly developed provinces (Great Poland) the percentage of Jews in the rural villages was minimal, amounting to less than 2 percent. In the central and eastern provinces the percentage of village Jews varies from 19 percent (in eastern Galicia) to as high as 31 percent, 34 percent and 36 percent. In two provinces over half of the Jews were village Jews.[18] In other words, by the middle of the eighteenth century Polish Jews were concentrated predominantly in the eastern frontier regions, where they were, to a great degree, spread throughout the agricultural villages and nobility-owned small towns and cities, with a smaller part living in the larger royal cities.

Generally, Polish Jewry as a whole—if we take the fragmentary census of 1764 as a guide—was settled at the rate of about 70 percent in the towns and cities and less than one-third in the agricultural villages.* Each city or town in which Jews lived (there were 673 of them) absorbed only small groups for the most part. Almost one-third of all urban settlements contained a Jewish population of 100 or less; in about another third of the urban settlements the number of Jews amounted to 101–300. Between nine and twelve cities had a Jewish population of 2,000 persons or more each, with Brody in Galicia having 7,191 (8,600 after correction of the figure for omissions). Generally, about one-fifth (19 percent) of the city Jews lived in Jewish communities with 500 or more Jews each.

---

*A village in Eastern Europe (and in Europe generally) differs from its namesake in the United States. In the latter the village serves as a center (shopping, post office, administration, and so on) for the surrounding farm population, which lives spread out on the farms. In Europe the agricultural population lives in houses concentrated together in villages, with the fields lying beyond the dwelling area. The village in Europe is where the houses and buildings of the agricultural population are concentrated, while a neighboring town serves as the administrative center, shopping center, and so on.

The percentage of Jews in the total city population varied from city to city and region to region, ranging possibly from 8–10 to 33 percent. They formed a majority in a number of the cities and towns belonging to the nobility and the clergy. Because of the great number of such private urban settlements and the large proportion of Jews there, it seems that the total number of Jewish urban population equaled or even surpassed in size the total non-Jewish city population. In contrast with the urban population, the Jewish village population formed a small ratio of the total village population. By and large one or two Jewish families lived in a village, forming a negligible percentage of the total population of each village.

7 Legal Status, Theory and Practice

Growth and development of the Jewish population in Poland during the three centuries under review did not take place in a vacuum. They occurred within the framework of the country's laws and the enforcement of those laws or the lack of it; they were affected by the Jewish group's specific situation and the general conditions governing regulation of town and city life; and they were influenced by the fluctuations in the power relationships between the main social forces—the nobility, the kings, the church, and the townspeople.

In the period we are considering these phases were, in the main, neither identical with those of the preceding period nor did they constitute a complete break with the past. Similarly, these centuries were themselves not a unit of unchanging conditions, the sixteenth century, for instance, marking a time of growth for the Polish state and the eighteenth century being one of decline and attempted reconstruction. In each of these periods the Jews' status underwent some change both in theory and in practice.

As the kings' power waned, the other forces in the country exerted a stronger influence and had a greater impact, both negative and positive, upon the situation of the Jews. Then, too, privileges, laws, decrees, and court judgments were becoming less effective because of changes taking place in the state. The limits of law are the limits of enforcement, and the limits of enforcement are the limits of government and society. Many edicts were never executed.

Antisocial tendencies in society were increasing during this period. Frequent wars and the concomitant devastation, plunder, robbery by soldiers and brigands, as well as the internal religious-national and social struggles and tensions of the times, contributed toward the country's increasingly becoming a breeding ground for violence and disorder. And violence in turn breeds violence. With the decline of the state's power, individuals and groups were taking the law into their own hands rather than complying with the rules on the statute books.

With the systematic decline of the king's power and role, the nobility became more powerful both by law and in practice.

Nobility and Jews

The predominant role played by the nobles in Jewish life was the result of several ongoing processes. First, as we have mentioned, in 1539 and 1549 the king transferred to the nobles jurisdiction over Jews living on the nobles' private estates. This, combined with the nobles' colonization and founding of new settlements in the south and southeast, opened many possibilities for Jews to settle and earn a living on such private estates. The private regions owned by the nobility that developed in and around some royal cities *(jurydyki)* were free from jurisdiction by the cities and subject to the rule of their owners. In such regions Jews were able to settle and live without much regard to the burghers' attitudes toward them.

Thus two sorts of Jews (legally speaking) existed in Poland—"private" (nobility) Jews and "royal" Jews. Each group lived under largely separate legal and political conditions, although there was some official acknowledgment (mostly of scant practical value) that the king was overlord. The increase in the number of Jews in nobility-owned settlements may have been slow, but by the middle of the eighteenth century between one-half and three-fourths of all Polish Jews lived on such privately owned estates in both urban and rural settlements. One of the largest groups of Jews in a single urban settlement in Poland was located in the private city of Brody in 1764.

Generally, by the end of the seventeenth century the importance of the older Jewish cities—mainly royal cities—had declined economically and spiritually, and as community centers for the Jews. They began to be supplanted by new, mostly private cities belonging to the aristocracy. Lwów lost out to Żólkiew, Buczacz to Kolomyja and later Brody, Kaziemierz-Cracow to Pinczów and Lissa (Leszno), Poznań apparently to Swarzenz and Olkusz.

Legal conditions in such private urban settlements were usually more favorable than in the royal cities, affording Jews broader rights.[1] The landlords, concerned with the development of their estates and the income from them, were generally interested in the services that an urban commercial-artisan element like the Jews could provide. Thus Jews were often granted special privileges and somewhat broader rights, and some efforts were made to keep them in the towns. On the other hand, the few capricious or cruel lords had a virtually free hand to oppress their Jews at will (and also their non-Jews). For the "private" Jews the nobility, or more correctly each individual landowner, became to some extent both a main source of law and the main factor in its implementation, although courts and kings may sometimes have come to the aid of a Jew.

The landed aristocracy's influence on the Jews' situation also increased as a result of their growing role in the legislation of the country at large.

The diet *(sejm)* or parliament comprised three elements: the chamber of deputies, the senate, and the king. The chamber of deputies was made up of representatives of the gentry elected by local dietines (regional assemblies), and the senate consisted of high church dignitaries and high officials—also usually originating from the gentry and the clergy. The diet became the medium through which the nobles strengthened their legislative power. Self-interest, prejudice, foreign influences, and other factors led them, collectively and individually, to support legislation and practice that at times favored the Jews and at others discriminated against them. And this legislative power wielded by the nobility usually surpassed the king's own.

But there was no unanimous approach among the nobles toward the Jewish question. As evidenced by reports of the discussions in the diet,[2] some members asked that the Jews be expelled from Poland; others wanted to bar them from commerce; still others proposed they be granted complete freedom, praised their commercial activity, or otherwise defended them.

The Polish diet and the regional dietines, which on many issues formulated instructions to their delegates to the diet, shifted from pro- to anti-Jewish or vice versa, depending on time and circumstances. Nevertheless some specific patterns are discernible. A trend among the nobles in parliament to forbid Jews to farm state revenues and tolls is observable. This was based in great part on the poorer squires' desire to retain these sources of income for themselves. A secondary motive may also have been the prejudiced disinclination of the nobleman to have his wares and wagons checked by Jews—although he himself was generally free from tolls. (Many complaints to this effect are preserved in documents.)

Nobles in the diet and provincial dietines frequently voiced demands that the taxes paid by Jews be raised or that new ones be introduced. The district dietines in Poland had gradually become an arm of the state in levying and collecting taxes, and its members were interested in moving some of the tax burden onto the Jews. Propaganda concerning the "fabulous wealth" of the Jews or the latter's huge increase in numbers also occasionally made its impact. Similarly, in times of great religious agitation the nobility was apt to follow anti-Jewish trends, at least symbolically, even though they sometimes appeared in the *sejm* or at court just to defend Jews.

The 1505 prohibition barring Jews from becoming lessees of state revenues was later repeated many times by the diet. The 1538 diet in Piotrków passed a special set of resolutions to deal with Jews *(de Judaeus),* which, besides the mentioned prohibition, contains a general ban on trade in rural areas for everyone, including Jews. The *sejm* also denied Jews the right of free trade in the royal cities, making such rights dependent on the privileges granted a respective individual city and agreements made between the cities and the Jews. Another proscription required that Jews wear distinctive hats except when traveling, to distinguish them from the Christian population. These proscriptions were often renewed either separately or as a unit, and new ones were occasionally added (horse trading was prohibited in 1557, employment of Christian servants in 1565, the old law against lending money to Christians on mortgages was repeated in 1616, and so on).

The "agreements" signed by King Augustus II (1697–1733) at his coronation include his promise to forbid Jews to farm royal revenues and royal estates, as demanded by the nobility. The diet of 1703 forbade Jews to serve as clerks in customshouses, and the diet of 1768 again made the Jews' commercial rights in the cities dependent on an agreement with the city burghers.

In 1661 the diet annulled the royal permission to build a synagogue on a site located between two churches,[3] and in 1671 it approved the resolutions of the Poznań synod forbidding Jews to employ Christian servants or to appear on the streets on Sundays or Christian holidays at the time when religious services were being held in the churches. During the first half of the eighteenth century emphatic demands were heard at most sessions of the *sejm* that the poll tax paid by the Jews be increased, and that the Jewish communal institutions which collected this tax from them be abolished. These latter demands became law in 1764, at which time the Jews were also barred from trade in grain, cattle, and horses.

On the other hand, many resolutions by the diet were intended to free the Jews in various cities or regions from taxes while they recovered from fires or other calamities. Some granted them the rights of free trade and permission to live in cities. Others demanded the levying of heavy fines on anyone who attacked Jews (in 1678, 1680, and 1696). Similarly, in the time of interregnum in 1586 the senators and nobility of the provinces (voivodeships) of Cracow, Sandomierz, and Lublin took Jews under their protection. Sometimes in one session the *sejm* reached some decisions that were anti-Jewish and others that were pro-Jewish. For example, in 1690 the prohibition against Jews' farming state revenues was repeated, but at the same time the one demanding heavy fines from those who attacked Jews was also renewed.

The same inconsistency is also observable in the dietines. The dietine of Mazovia made mostly anti-Jewish demands, and in 1698 Kiev's required that the central and regional organs of Jewish autonomy be canceled and that Jews be forbidden to inherit from their parents the leasing of state revenues.

Dietines in "Russia" (east Galicia) also often opposed farming out road tolls to Jews and were resentful of Jewish competition with burghers in the cities. In 1761 they instructed their delegates to the *sejm* to request the closing of all Jewish printing shops and schools (haderim), the burning of all books in Hebrew and Yiddish, the prohibition of the use of any language except Polish and Latin in religious books and services, and the stipulation that Jewish religious services be controlled by two clergymen or representatives of the municipality to insure that the Jews did not use any anti-Christian expressions in their prayers.[4]

On the other hand, some of the resolutions were either wholly or partially pro-Jewish. Nobility delegates in Volhynia called for strict laws against attacks on Jews in 1623 and for freeing the Jews from taxes in 1662; those of Braclaw and Kiev in 1672 requested that Jews be freed from a part of their tax obligations. East Galician (in the language of the time "Russian") dietines again and again (in 1590, 1592, 1636, 1640, 1645, 1653, 1662, 1683, 1688, and 1689) demanded trade rights and the right of settlement for Jews in Lwów and other cities of the region and were opposed to high taxes for Jews. They spoke out against a bishop who prohibited the building of a synagogue in Przemyśl and against competition of the Armenians in Lwów with the Jews (1653). They opposed raising the Jewish poll tax, and they required the *sejm* to impose high fines on nobles who attacked Jews or used violently coercive methods to collect debts from Jews.

The same holds true for individual noblemen. The heads of counties *(starosta)*, who ruled the royal cities in the king's name, and the voivode (provincial governor) who, among other things, served as the official deputy of the king in matters concerning Jews, often defended Jews against both clergy and city people in economic and other matters;[5] sometimes, however, they either failed to fulfill their obligations in connection with the Jews or exploited them economically.

Polish Kings

The Polish kings had no overall or exclusively Polish economic policy. Kings and treasury accepted and approved the receipt of tolls, duties, taxes, and other revenues from businessmen and artisans with little regard to their ethnic or religious affiliations. This may explain statements found in decrees and other documents to the effect that since Jews (or Armenians, as the case may be) paid the same duties and taxes as the other city dwellers they were entitled to equal treatment.

On the private level most of the Polish kings after the end of the fifteenth century had their own Jewish court physicians, to whom they granted a variety of privileges. Some kings used the services of court Jews, either from abroad (Germany or Vienna) or from within Poland. Most of the kings had their favorite individual Jews on whom they conferred such honorary titles as "royal servant" (*servitor**), "royal factor" (broker), and in some cases "royal secretary" (1677). These Jews also gained all sorts of special privileges such as the freedom to live anywhere in the country, the right to own property, the right to practice various occupations or to engage in business, and exemption from any jurisdiction but that of the royal court.[6]

The kings often farmed out state revenues as well as those of their own private estates to Jews or appointed them main administrators of the tolls in a region or two despite the objections of the church synods and even against the resolutions passed by the *sejm*.[7] Some kings, such as Jan (John) Sobieski (1674–96), acquired reputations as befrienders of Jews among their contemporaries or even in later generations.

Most of the Polish kings confirmed the basic Jewish privileges, granted by Casimir the Great in the fourteenth century and others, and most of them also added new ones as the necessity arose. Over and above the general privileges, individual ones were also issued to many Jewish communities.

The basic privileges, as we know, generally provided for protection and security of life and property, freedom of worship, autonomous Jewish community institutions, and various degrees of freedom of settlement and occupational activity. But some of the old privileges were formulated in terms that were too general. Also, new

---

*The term *"servitor"* signified a high social and legal standing.

developments brought new problems for which provisions had to be made. New decrees thus became necessary to supplement or strengthen the old ones.

Thus privileges and decrees provide for equality with non-Jews in the payment of tolls (in 1515, 1518, 1527, 1532, 1550 [for Lublin], 1557, 1563, and 1635); for equal trade rights, including retail trade throughout the whole country, "because they pay the same taxes and carry the same burdens as non-Jews" (in 1532, 1564 [for Busk and Kolo], 1576 [Volhynia], 1578, 1580, 1646 [for Bar]); equal rights with the burghers in settlement, ownership of houses, and artisanship, or the cancellation of all limitations imposed by the cities upon Jews (in 1576, 1578, and 1633). Other decrees were intended to protect Jewish borrowers from violence on the part of the non-Jewish lender (in 1551, 1564, and 1576) or to free the Jewish community leaders from responsibility for individual bankrupt Jews (1635).

For the purpose of stemming attacks upon Jews in the cities, kings made city councils responsible for the safety of the Jews and threatened any attacker with the death penalty and confiscation of his possessions; city government and individual burghers were obliged to come to the aid of Jews and to defend them whenever they requested help (decrees in 1531, 1571, 1592, and 1633). Protection of Jews against the blood libel and the accusation of profanation of the holy wafer was the object of a number of decrees, which provided that such cases could be brought only before the highest court, to be tried in the presence of the king and the highest officials. No such case could be brought to court unless the accusations were based on the evidence of at least seven witnesses, three of them Jews (decrees in 1557, 1564, and 1566). Other decrees threatened the death penalty for those who falsely accused Jews of such crimes (1576). The kings also frequently relieved Jews, locally or regionally, from the payment of certain or all taxes when this was made necessary by a calamity such as fire or war; sometimes they issued to Jews moratoriums on the payment of debts.[8]

But like the prohibitory laws, these privileges, decrees, and orders were not always effective. Enactment of laws is not synonymous with enforcement, certainly not in a country where the rulers were unable to establish law and order. Besides, the whole system, or nonsystem, of granting separate privileges and rights to each group usually resulted in contradictions and inconsistencies. Often an exclusive right for one group conflicted with some of the rights of another group. These conflicts were compounded by the impact of the interests, biases, fears, beliefs, and emotions of the other social strata in the country.

For example, King Sigismund I (1508–48)—characterized as "a man of refinement and culture"[9]—issued a large number of decrees favoring Jews. He granted Lwów Jews the right to trade; Poznań Jews were permitted to live in the city and to own houses, and were given selective rights in trade (in 1515 and 1517); Belz Jews received the right to trade in almost every type of commodity in 1517. He put Polish Jews on a par with Christians in the payment of tolls (1527), issued a manifesto against violence on the part of the burghers (1531), and granted Jews the right to trade anywhere in the country on a par with Christians, since they paid the same taxes (1532). On many occasions he also either reduced or annulled Jewish taxes in several communities (in 1510, 1515, 1518, 1521, 1525, 1527, 1531, 1533, and 1537).

But during very nearly the same period, Jews' rights in commerce were limited (in Lwów, Cracow, Lublin, Poznań, Plock in 1521–23; Cracow and suburban Lwów in 1527), and the privilege of *de non tolerandis Judaeis* (exclusion of Jews) was granted to five or six cities and towns, including Warsaw in 1527.* Christians were forbidden to rent out houses to Jews and Jews to lease houses from Christians (Poznań, 1544; Cracow, Radziejów, 1546).

Sigismund Augustus (1548–72), who succeeded his father, Sigismund I, is regarded as a king who contributed to religious tolerance, was an enlightened patron of Renaissance humanism, and had considerable interests in literature. He issued decrees to protect Jewish debtors in 1551 and 1564, and decrees to guard against the blood libel in 1557, 1564, and 1566. He also gave special privileges (over and above the confirmation of the general Jewish privileges) to Jews in a number of cities and towns, granting them various rights to trade or equal rights with the burghers (in Kiev and Bochnia in 1555, Bar in 1556, Kolo and Busk in 1564)—the latter because "since they are burdened with the same state and city taxes they should have the same privileges as the others."

To Tyszowcy Jews he gave "all rights to own houses, land, and gardens, to trade including retail, and to engage in all kinds of occupations, since they pay all the same taxes as the non-Jews." For the sake of the Jews he decreed that market day was to be on a Tuesday or any other weekday, not on a Saturday. He also ordered Jews to pay the same tolls as non-Jews, and decreed that Cracow Jews benefit from the same privilege as Cracow burghers, paying only half tolls (1557). He freed Jews in some cities from paying tolls or taxes (in Luck in 1556, in Wiślica in 1557, in Vladimir in 1564), and he also refused to confirm a resolution by the *sejm* levying a special tax on Jewish wares (1564). But on the other hand, during his reign seven cities were ordered to be emptied of their Jews.

The same inconsistency characterizes the legislation of King Stephen Báthory (1575–86): equal rights for Jews and burghers, cancellation of all limitations on Jews in the cities, protection of Jews against attacks and blood libel (1576–78), coupled with removal of Jews from three or four cities and confirmation of craft guild statutes that provided for the exclusion of Jews.

These contradictory trends continued during the seventeenth century. On one

---

*Rationales for expelling Jews range from "The Christians who suffered from attacks by crusaders wish to reconstruct the city and are ready to pay the taxes of the Jews" (Miedzyrzecze in 1520) to "There are often thefts and other antisocial acts" (Warsaw in 1527) to simply "because of the pleading of the queen" (Samborz in 1542). One should hardly take such reasons for the decrees at face value, however. They may have been inserted later by a secretary or copyist, or they may simply have served as a rationale for issuing the decree, with no basis in reality.

hand kings tried to stem the rising anti-Jewish trends and the violence, which increased considerably in that era of wars, invasions, and their aftermath. On the other hand, the insecurities of the times made the kings more subject than ever to the impact of public opinion, pressure from various social strata, and resolutions by the *sejm*.[10] In addition, the issuance or confirmation of many privileges for non-Jewish artisans' guilds, with their monopolistic rights, often amounted to the legal exclusion of Jews and nonguild artisans generally from certain occupations, or from trade in the raw materials that artisans needed for their crafts.

Moreover, a Christian king's general mistrust of Jews sometimes led him to believe all kinds of rumors, and this in turn could bring calamity upon the Jews—especially when some pervasive anxiety or trend favored such a tendency. Thus the Turks' repeated military successes in Europe in the second quarter of the sixteenth century (the conquest of Belgrade in 1521, the invasion of Hungary in 1526, the occupation of Buda in 1541) brought rumors about the Jews' collusion with the Turks and their spying for them. Such implications contributed to the expulsion of Jews from Bohemia in 1541.

In Poland, King Sigismund I ordered the community leaders and rabbis of Cracow jailed in 1539. The reason given for this action was that a Turkish Jew who became a Muslim told the king that in Akerman he had seen many Poles who had turned Jewish; he alleged that they had requested the sultan to obtain the Polish king's permission to emigrate to Turkey. The same informer also told the king that a whole nest of such converts to Judaism existed in Lithuania. Two courtiers were dispatched to Lithuania to find the converts in 1540, but instead they began to oppress Jews, jailing some of them and instituting searches in the homes of others. This led to a lull in the commercial activities of the Jews. Pressure was then exerted on the king by Lithuanian noblemen, and the voivode and some other high personalities in Cracow interceded in behalf of the Jews; through the medium of Queen Bona this affair was brought to a close.[11]

The many contradictions and inconsistencies resulted in numerous long litigations in court, compromises, rescinding of decrees, and the search for new decrees and privileges needed by the parties in the courts. This had an inflationary impact on both the number and the value of the privileges, especially since most of the legislation favorable to Jews was pitted against the prevailing order of the cities.

Cities and Urban Regulations

The cities in Poland went through two distinct phases of development during the sixteenth to eighteenth centuries. First there was a period of growth, owing to large population increases in the existing cities as well as the founding of new ones. This was followed by a decline beginning with the cossack wars of 1648–67. Urban growth meant that the cities were striving for greater influence on the country and their opponents were attempting to control more strictly the monopoly they held in economic spheres.

The strivings of the burghers encountered opposition from the nobles, who were jealous of the riches acquired by many burghers. At the same time, as consumers the squires were concerned about the monopolistic tendencies of the burghers, and they tried to introduce price controls (in 1503, 1504, 1507, 1510, 1532, 1543, and 1565). But there was no straight line of opposition between the cities and the squires. Some of the burghers, having achieved great wealth, bought villages and estates, married off their daughters to noblemen, or in rarer cases were themselves made nobles.[12] This opened lines of communication between burgher and squire.

In the organization of the city itself the Polish urbanites had a ready model to follow—the structure of the city in the West.

The feudal order and the medieval economic system were characterized by the localism of the towns. Each town was concerned with the affairs of its own small group of burghers, and each group of burghers—the merchant guilds or the craft-guilds—cared, for the welfare of its own members, and defended their interests when these conflicted with the interests of other groups.

Each town's hand was against every other town. . . . Towns sought to protect or advance their interests in a variety of ways. In the first place, each tried to control the economic life of the surrounding countryside, to compel the villagers to sell their produce only to the town, to buy the things they needed only from it and . . . refrain from carrying on any manufactures which competed with those of the town. In the second place the stranger [one coming from outside the town] was subject to restrictions, whether he came to pass through, to trade, or to settle. If he was passing through with goods [if the town had staple rights] he might be obliged to offer them for sale for at least two or three days or to sell them to city merchants who then would carry them forward. If he came to trade he must not sell retail or deal with other foreigners except through a citizen broker. If he wished to settle, he must spend years—from ten to as many as twenty-five in Italy —before he could acquire the full rights that went with citizenship.

Within the towns businessmen and artisans were subject to a set of regulations and laws (formulated by the city council and the respective guilds, and laid down in privileges granted by the ruler) of an egalitarian character, so that any income would be fairly distributed among the members of each group.

Laws and regulations prohibited the individual from exercising the trade of his choice and regulated a person's staying in or leaving a specific place.

Set against a background of an inelastic market in a world of scarcity, limited production and demand, and a static income and wealth structure that was considered to be God-given, the system's primitive egalitarianism appeared to contemporaries to be a just method of assuring to everyone his share. This meant avoiding competition either from an outsider or between one member and another, and regarding any competition as a sort of robbery, as stealing another's share. Consequently, the regulatory practice of the medieval system, based on the principle of scarcity, became also the background of the period's ethos. A trader or artisan breaking the rules, or an outsider impinging upon someone's lawful livelihood, was not only considered a wrongdoer but also an immoral cheat and robber.[13]

In Western Europe the rise of the modern absolute state (sixteenth to seventeenth centuries), which tended to be intolerant of any authority but its own, weakened the role of the guilds and limited their power. In Poland, however, the medieval state continued to exist almost uninterruptedly until the end of the eighteenth century, and most of its economic ramifications also lasted until the demise of the Polish state. This meant that according to the prevailing custom and order Jews and other minorities, not being a part of the burghers' group, were not supposed to infringe on the latter's livelihood or to enjoy residence rights. Any privileges the rulers might grant them were thought to conflict with the monopolistic citizenry's rights. The Jews were not the only group against which efforts were made to put such excluding proscriptions into practice; many of the orders and prohibitions concerned other groups as well. Thus the *sejm* of 1562 refused settlement rights to "Italians, Scots and other foreigners . . . who are harming our cities."

Deeper Jewish penetration into the cities and city occupations occurred during the sixteenth and seventeenth centuries, when urbanization took great forward strides in Poland—new cities were founded and the older ones more than doubled their populations—and immigrants from abroad (Scots, Italians, Germans, and some Greeks and Netherlanders[14]) were absorbed. Jews were not the only ones to break the established system of the burghers, although since larger numbers of them were involved the opposition against them may at times have been somewhat stronger than against the others.

Meanwhile, in the growing cities class divisions became more pronounced. The rich and powerful became, as the cliché goes, richer and more powerful, and the poor grew poorer, with competition between these groups becoming more intense. Merchant associations and the various guilds tried to keep what they had and to acquire privileges and decrees protecting their own monopoly on exclusive production, sale, or purchase rights of certain wares or services. Specialization in production brought an increase in the number of separate guilds, and this heightened their monopolistic tendencies.* Each branch or subbranch became more and more an exclusive in-group that exerted every possible effort to exclude the out-group or the individuals who did not belong.

Such a situation fostered a considerable increase in tension between the various socioeconomic groups, with greater pressures and counterpressures among them and sharper struggles within their own groups, as well as against the various out-groups and outsiders.[15] In this fragmented premodern state the urban socioeconomic groups were busy chasing and obtaining all sorts of privileges both collectively and through individual guilds and associations. But little consistency was displayed, and in fact contradictory trends were often apparent.

*For instance, if members of a general guild (tailors) split up into specialized guilds (tailors, furriers, fur-hat makers), each one sought to monopolize his specific trade to the exclusion of the others (a tailor could no longer sew or sell a fur coat and vice versa).

As the Polish cities declined in the second half of the seventeenth century an effort was made to strengthen some of the monopolistic tendencies, even though the real importance of the urban classes was decreasing because of their waning economic strength—both absolutely and relatively.

Not only were trade, artisanship, and other urban occupations losing ground in the half-ruined cities, but the little that remained of them suffered from competition with "outsiders"—newcomers to the cities and newcomers to the occupations—whom the tightly knit, exclusive associations and guilds did not admit to membership. This made the struggle for a share in the pie even more severe and more violent, with both groups trying to extract more privileges and rights from the state or taking the law into their own hands, or both, in their attempts to achieve their ends. In this connection certain foreigners played a role—Germans for the most part—who apparently brought along with them a strong heritage regarding the traditional exclusiveness of the guilds and their rights. At any rate we find a considerable number of people with non-Polish names in Warsaw among those artisan leaders who stood in the forefront of the struggle against Jewish intrusion into their "exclusive rights."

The little man, the poorer storekeeper and the small artisan, suffered more (or thought he did) from the competition of the out-group. For this reason he was more aggressive in his opposition; he more readily took the law into his own hands, and he even blamed the city elders for being too softhearted toward the Jews.[16] He was joined by the mob, the disorganized low stratum, the *lumpenproletariat* in modern terminology, who in their anarchistic way made violence a way of life. This in turn often forced the municipality to make its demands more radical or condone the use of extreme measures.[17] This meant some intensification of the opposition to Jews and other minorities, mostly in terms of national or religious affiliation—Catholics versus Protestants and vice versa, or Catholics versus Armenians, Greek Orthodox, Tatars, and sometimes Italians or Scots. In this period political pressure became heavier at the same time that there was recourse to more severe and more violent nonpolitical means: attacks, pogroms, attempts to confiscate goods, and expulsion from a given city.

But, despite the apparent autonomy deriving from the so-called Magdeburg Law, the cities did not have arbitrary legal control over the Jews. Jews did not generally come under the city government's jurisdiction but rather under the king's (in the private cities mostly under the nobles'), and they were legally subject to king's privileges and the decisions of the *sejm*. Neither king nor nobility was consistently ready to support all the regulatory monopolistic tendencies of the city burghers. The nobles held trade and artisanship in contempt, were jealous of wealth acquired by some burghers, and as consumers were opposed to the monopolistic practices and regulations of the cities. Feeling the pinch of rising costs they legislated in the *sejm* to regulate prices and place ceilings on some commodities (in 1503, 1504, 1507, 1510, 1523, 1565, and so on). They were thus inclined to regard competition from the Jews favorably, and the Jewish "intruder" often found in theory—and even more in practice—a champion in the nobleman (either as estate owner or as the king's representative), and sometimes in the kings themselves and in some churchmen.

The Catholic Church

Sixteenth- to eighteenth-century Poland was no longer "that new Christian settlement"[18] whose new church needed careful protection. It had by then become a well-organized and wealthy institution wielding power and enjoying prestige. The church dignitaries assumed some quasi-legislative influence as the king's power waned, and they sought to enforce certain resolutions passed by the church synods. In this way the clergy obtained a decision from King Sigismund III (1587–1632) that the erection of new synagogues would need approval by the bishop of the respective region.

In the eighteenth century, during the reign of the weak Augustus III, some bishops grasped other legal powers and issued decrees (in Bar in 1717, in Przemyśl in 1743, in Rzeszów in 1746) forbidding Jews to leave their homes from the Thursday before Easter until after Easter, to work on Sundays and Christian holidays, or to employ Christian servants. In 1757 the bishop of Kamenets Podolski forced Jewish community leaders to participate in an official dispute with the Frankists, and later he confiscated some Talmud copies in Podolia and burned them at the stake. In a few other places (Brody, for one) bishops arranged official disputations or forced Jews to listen to Catholic preachers in the synagogue. On the whole, the church synods kept repeating the old proscriptions about Jews and passing resolutions about new ones. Thus the church synods in Gniezno in 1630 and Poznań in 1642 forbade Jewish barbers to shave Christians, said that Jewish physicians could not attend Christian patients, and tried to enforce a ban on Jewish trade by excommunicating any Christian who dealt with Jews. At the same time churchmen, some religious orders, and monks were poisoning the public mind with anti-Jewish propaganda and staging or engineering trials against Jews who were accused of ritual murder, profanation of the holy wafer, and sacrilege against the Christian religion.

Following the rise of the Counter-Reformation in Poland the Jesuit order there became active (1564), trying to use its colleges to train vigilantes and fighters for the faith. The religious tumult—manufactured violent attacks, beginning with the assault on the Calvinist meeting house in Cracow in 1574 and later attacks on private homes of Protestants—were to plague Poland for the subsequent two centuries, contributing greatly to the decline of Protestantism in the country. Of the same order were the court suits, staged at the instigation or pressure of clergy or friars, in which people were accused of blasphemy, sacrilege, and witchcraft. (According to one computation more than ten thousand court cases against witches were tried in Poland during the sixteenth and seventeenth centuries. The accused were subject to torture and macabre sentences such as "tearing out the blasphemous tongue" or burning at the stake.[19]

Mob action and tumult were methods that were also used against the "nonbelievers"—the Jews—at times instigated by clergymen, students, or city people, at times by the mobs on their own, stimulated by propaganda and public opinion, which in this period was nourished also by the printed word. With the development of printing and the increase in literacy, which was accompanied by a trend toward publication in the Polish language rather than in Latin, written attacks on Jews multiplied. During the seventeenth and eighteenth centuries a whole anti-Jewish literature developed, with some inevitable impact upon the attitudes toward Jews. Satires and caricatures of Jews were imported from Germany and translated into Polish. Pamphlets accusing Jews of cruelty, murder, and exploitation, some of them written by clergymen, were run off the press, helping to increase the anti-Jewish tendencies.

But the churchmen's attitude toward Jews did not follow a straight line. The church dignitaries were nobles, owners of landed estates or other sources of income, of houses and courts within and outside the cities. Like other nobles, they often leased these out to Jews, sold them their produce, or rented the houses to them. Sometimes this also happened with church property, especially with monasteries.

In some cases the monks had other reasons for their interest in the well-being of Jews, or rather of certain Jews or certain Jewish communities. Since the seventeenth century some monastic orders, having amassed large fortunes, had been lending money to individual Jews and Jewish communities against payment of interest. The loans were often long-term investments, the order or monastery being mainly interested in the regular receipt of an annual income. The interest rate on such long-term loans was usually lower than on regular loans. The time came when many pious Christians who had lent Jews money stipulated in their wills that upon their deaths certain sums should pass to a monastery or church, on the condition that the money be invested with a Jew or a Jewish community and earn an annuity for the institution.

The churchmen—bishops and archbishops—who had Jews as leaseholders on their estates or as tenants in their houses or who lent them money—churches and monasteries—tended to be interested in the well-being of their Jews despite the general anti-Jewish line. Sometimes they actually supported them or intervened in their behalf, although in some cases the business connections may have led to tensions or strife that could have been translated into anti-Jewish attitudes. But we find churchmen (Catholics and Uniates) who not only kept Jews on their lands and leased property to them, but who also went to court in their behalf or otherwise helped them. Sometimes churchmen defended "their" Jews (though not as often as the lay squires) or even Jews generally, intervening in their behalf or seeking to tone down somewhat the violent attacks upon them.[20]

Regional and Local Variations

There were also regional differences in local legislation and practices in Poland. Since the second half of the fifteenth century older Polish lands, or borderlands, had been incorporated into the Polish kingdom (parts of Silesia in 1454–56 and 1494, western Pomerania in the west in the fifteenth and sixteenth centuries, Mazovia and Warsaw in 1462, 1476, 1495, and 1526, and the Ukrainian regions after the Union of Lublin in 1569). Although these lands accepted Polish law either when they were incorporated or later, various regulations, usages, or traditions of their own remained in force.

This was also true in connection with the Jews. The Prussian-Pomeranian lands had traditionally been *judenrein* from the period of the Teutonic order's rule, and they attempted to remain so. Similarly, when Warsaw and Mazovia joined the Polish kingdom the former rulers' principle of *de non tolerandis Judaeis* was brought to the Polish kingdom, and the Polish king confirmed this prohibition against Jewish settlement (in Warsaw).

The situation in the Ukraine was more complicated. These parts of the former Russian principalities were joined to Lithuania in the fourteenth century by conquest. From then until the Union of Lublin in 1569 this region, united with Lithuania, was subject to the laws of that state. King Ladislas Jagiello adjusted the rights of the estates in Volhynia in 1432 to match those of Poland, and put the Jews of Luck on a par with the Jews of Cracow and Lwów. Nevertheless, until 1569 Jews in these regions were officially subject to the Lithuanian statutes of 1529 and 1566, which somewhat limited their rights as well as those of the Muslim Tatars. They could not appear in court as witnesses—mainly in cases dealing with real estate; own Christian slaves (slavery still existed in Lithuania in those centuries) or serfs; or hold debtors as hostages while they worked off their debts. There were other restrictions too.[21] The Polish kings who served simultaneously as dukes of Lithuania, Sigismund I in 1533 and Sigismund Augustus in 1564 and 1566, confirmed the older Lithuanian privileges to Jews, which strongly resembled those of the Jews in the Polish kingdom.

With the Union of Lublin in 1569 and the transfer of the Ukraine to the Polish kingdom proper, the Jews (or their representatives) swore allegiance to the Polish king and were put under the jurisdiction of the palatines, as in the Polish kingdom. In 1570 King Sigismund Augustus put the Jews of Luck and Vladimir on a par with the non-Jews by freeing them from almost all tolls in Lithuania and Poland. Then followed privileges and decrees (in 1576, 1578, and 1580) that gave the Jews in this region a legal status similar to that of Jews in the kingdom of Poland or of the burghers generally, granting them rights to trade anywhere and to sell retail, regulating the forms of dispensing justice and of the autonomous Jewish institutions. At the same time Jews were forbidden to work on most Christian holidays.

In terms of jurisdiction the Jews here had officially virtually the same status as in the kingdom of Poland: the Jewish defendant against a non-Jewish plaintiff was adjudicated by the palatine or the Jews' judge appointed by him in the presence of Jewish representatives. Cases of Jews against Jews were heard in the Jewish court.

Possibly even more here than in the kingdom of Poland there was a gap between what the privileges and decrees said and their translation into everyday life. Enforcement of any statute or law requires either a state the bulk of whose population has a sympathetic attitude, or a police state. Poland, especially in the southern frontier regions, was neither.

Noncompliance with the law seems to have been more usual here than in the older Polish lands, resulting in "illegal" practices that worked both for and against the Jews. In terms of judicature we find here that Jews sometimes agreed (freely or not?) to be adjudicated by the city court of Magdeburg Law (in Pereyaslavl in 1621), or that the county official or sheriff *(starosta)* could take Jews to the town court (in Vladimir in 1755). In the eighteenth century most instances of bishops who tried to assume legislative and police powers over Jews occurred in these southern regions.

On the other hand, most of the cases of noncompliance with the limitations imposed upon Jews in regard to farming tolls, state and other revenues, possessing Christian serfs, leasing and administering estates, and serving as overseers over Christians occurred in these regions too. Here Jews appear as leaseholders of large estates with hundreds or possibly thousands of serfs, of whole towns, and of town revenues farmed from town burghers themselves (Kowel in 1702 and others). Here, too, a considerable number of Jews lived in private cities, towns, and villages, and were subject to the jurisdiction, legislation, and protection of the noblemen owners, with all the inherent advantages and disadvantages.[22] And here too Jews continued to possess slaves during the seventeenth century, even forcing some of them to convert to Judaism.

In short, the legal and even more the practical situation of the Jews in the kingdom of Poland during the sixteenth to eighteenth centuries was far from following any straight line or pattern. It resembled rather a kaleidoscope whose combinations of design changed with period, region, and circumstances. The pattern was influenced by the interests, biases, fears, and beliefs of the social groups and subgroups in the country, by the impact of political and other forces, and, on the other hand, by the financial and actual position of the Jews themselves, their strength, their ingenuity in making friends and finding supporters, and in balancing one group against another.

Seen from today's perspective those variations and inconsistencies in the laws, and the discrepancy between law and practice, may seem senseless and chaotic, but people of those times apparently thought otherwise.

Anti-Semitism

The chaos insofar as Jews were concerned is often lumped under the all-embracing concept of anti-Semitism. The concept of anti-Semitism was coined in the 1870s to denote the racial character of Jew hatred. But it came to mean many facets of anti-Jewish sentiment, attitudes, beliefs, acts, policies, prejudices, as well as antipathy to Jews, denigration of their religion and culture, intolerance, discrimination, defamation, aggression, persecution, physical attacks, and other actions. Numerous studies of Jewish life and some general and specific books have labeled the trials and tribulations of Jewish life, or general historical events in their impact on Jewish groups in numberless countries and throughout the ages, under the general heading of anti-Semitism. This also applies to studies about Jewish life in Poland.

True, one can find in Poland through the centuries countless anti-Jewish trends and a great deal of opposition to the Jew. The Catholic was opposed to the Jew from a religious point of view. The city burgher and the artisan sought to exclude the Jew. But part of this and similar opposition to Jews could hardly be classified as blanket anti-Semitism. The concept anti-Semitism signifies a value judgment. We define and condemn anti-Semitism on moral grounds. But the opposition of the burgher or the artisans' guild member to the foreigner and the Jew in earlier ages was for the most part no more immoral, according to the opinion of those times, than is present-day opposition by union members to the employment of nonorganized labor. It became immoral (or anti-Semitic) when illegal means—extreme violence, staging blood libels, or expulsion—were employed to achieve the economic goals.

Thus to regard the inconsistencies of the laws and the manner of their execution in earlier ages as chaotic, and to look upon many of the anti-Jewish trends of those times as pure and simple anti-Semitism, would mean judging the past according to present-day values and concepts, rather than according to the very different ideas prevailing at that time. In reality, this would be misunderstanding or even falsifying the past. Instead, events should be studied in their historical context and interpreted within the context of the period in which they occurred. This would make the past intelligible to the present. And inconsistency and fragmentization was a part of the reality of those times.

A topical summary of the main problems and conditions will facilitate an interpretation of the period's significance.

Residence Rights

Residence rights were far from universal in medieval Europe with its fragmentation of authority and its caste system (estates). Unlike the modern nation-state, which guarantees every citizen residence rights, each prince, duke, estate-owner or city in the Middle Ages had the sovereign right to admit or exclude people. Becoming a subject or resident in such a tiny state meant acquiring protection and certain rights in connection with earning one's livelihood within that state, which were usually denied to the "foreigner," that is, anyone from a neighboring principality or locality. (Even today a foreigner needs a work permit in most parts of the world.)

Cities were usually separate entities. Each one (sometimes together with a tiny area surrounding it) constituted an independent or semi-independent administrative and economic unit officially run by and for its own members—the citizens. Only a citizen had the right to trade and to practice a craft (as limited by the usages and regulations governing his specific occupation). An outsider—even from a nearby urban or rural settlement or suburb—was a foreigner (in the language of the time a guest), whose rights were considerably curtailed. The burghers' general reluctance to share their city livelihood with anybody led to many limitations. This system was retained in most countries until the French Revolution and in Poland until the nineteenth century, with rudiments lasting even longer.

A basic requirement for citizenship in the Polish cities was adherence to the Catholic faith. With the rise of Protestantism in the sixteenth century, Protestants at first shared equal rights with Catholics; but in Polish Prussia, which was Protestant, it was the Catholics who suffered discrimination. Then as the Counter-Reformation gained strength in Poland discriminatory practices against the various Protestant denominations began to develop. These ranged from barring Protestants from city office to revoking their burgher rights and even to expulsion (a number of new private cities opened their doors to them).

The minorities, concentrated mainly in the borderlands (Red Russia or eastern Galicia, the Ukraine, Podolia)—Greek Orthodox, Catholics of the Greek rite (Uniates), and Armenians—were subject to a sort of second-class citizenship varying with place and time. Generally, cities tried to limit their numbers, their right to own houses, and the like.

Jews coming to Poland in the Middle Ages received residence rights from the princes and kings, which made them independent of the cities by exempting them from city jurisdiction and taxation and gave them a kind of extraterritorial status.

From the end of the fifteenth century the royal Polish cities became the scene of an ongoing struggle between the burghers and the Jews (and the Greek Orthodox and Armenians in the eastern provinces also). The burghers sought to reduce the number of Jews by limiting their residence rights or by expelling them from a city altogether (thereby diminishing their share in the city's livelihood). This was a many-faceted struggle that intensified with the growth of the Jewish population and either the rise and strengthening of the Christian population or the decline of the cities and of urban occupations. In the first instance the need to cut more slices from the pie and a sense of growing power led to a desire to oust the strangers. But as the city declined the urge to hold onto the remains predominated.

The legal means resorted to ranged from obtaining privileges and counter-privileges from the king and litigation in the courts, to "agreements" between city authorities and the Jewish community for the reduction or freezing of the area of settlement or the numbers permitted to live there. Or the city authorities might take the law into their own hands and make it impossible for Jews to acquire either houses or space for houses; or they might induce attacks and pogroms.

For their part, the Jews persistently disregarded legal limitations of numbers and space and availed themselves of the willingness of some high official—palatine or county steward *(starosta)*—who usually controlled the self-governing cities, to delay the execution of an order or court judgment almost ad infinitum.[23] In some instances Jews took up arms and actively defended their homes or streets. In other cases, with the help of the king and influential noblemen they succeeded in finding ways and means actually to extend the areas of their settlement legally.

In the large royal cities it became customary during the sixteenth century to negotiate and sign an agreement between the Jewish community and the city government (unlike earlier "agreements," which the Jews were forced to sign). Before the first agreement with Lwów the king prodded the city council to sign an accord with the Jews, arguing "the royal treasury will lose a lot from pauperization of the Jews, and it is obliged to see that they can make a living." When this proved fruitless, the Jews continued to transact business despite the limitations that had earlier been imposed on them and extended their area beyond the borders. This was accompanied by a legal struggle that passed all the instances of the various courts. By 1570 the case came to the *sejm*, which took a moderately pro-Jewish stand. Then the burghers began to negotiate and in 1581 signed the first agreement with the Jews. In this and subsequent agreements (in 1592, 1629, and 1635) the Jewish region was enlarged.

The same happened in Kazimierz-Cracow, where after prolonged badgering the first agreement between the Kazimierz Jews and the cities of Kazimierz and Stradom was signed in 1553, according to which "the Jewish city of Kazimierz" acquired land for expansion. And a similar thing happened in the second and third agreements (in 1583 and 1608) signed by both sides. (The conditions for free commercial activity were elaborated in further accords in 1609 and 1615.) In Poznań agreements (in 1550, confirmed in 1617 and 1697) gave Jews room to erect new houses.[24]

After the cities of western Pomerania were integrated into the Polish kingdom they continued to bar Jews. A score or more Polish royal cities, as well as a number of small towns and townlets owned for the most part by churchmen or religious institutions, were granted the privilege of *de non tolerandis Judaeis* during the sixteenth and seventeenth centuries. But Jews nevertheless found it possible to settle in or near a great many of these cities and towns, and in a few of them the anti-Jewish laws were not put into practice. In the main the score or so cities and towns (out of an estimated total of one thousand in Poland) that closed their doors to Jews were balanced by many scores of new cities and hundreds of urban settlements founded by estate owners that opened their doors to Jews or even invited them in. In western Poland some of these may have been urban settlements founded by or for Protestants. In other parts of the country these new cities and towns had few special characteristics, if any. When Jan Zamojski founded Zamość, which he dreamed of making an urban and cultural center, he gave Sephardic Jews a settlement privilege (1588). This privilege affirmed that the rights of the Jews were similar to those of other burghers: ownership of real estate and the right to sell it; freedom to leave the city; security of life and property in the whole of Poland; religious freedom: the right to build a synagogue, to own a ritual bath and a cemetery, and to maintain a Jewish school; the right to wear clothing similar to that of the non-Jews; and the right to bear arms. Freedom of economic activity was also granted with some minor limitations in trade and artisanship.

When Sigismund Grudzinski, the Kalish palatine, founded Swarzenz (later called Grzymalow) about ten miles from Poznań, he not only invited Jews to settle, but also gave them lots on which to build houses and even building material for a synagogue. Other nobles who founded urban settlements often invited Jews to settle and as an incentive freed them from taxes for a number of years. They generally gave Jewish settlers equal rights with non-Jews in economic matters (acquisition of land and houses, commerce, artisanship, production and sale of beverages, and so on) and in many instances also in some political matters—the right to participate in the election of aldermen and the mayor (in Bolechów, Kolomyja, Brody, Dubno, and other places.) In the seventeenth century the newly elected mayor of Bolechów "when taking the oath of office . . . [had] to declare that he would safeguard and defend the rights of Catholics, Greek Orthodox, and Jews."[25] In later years some of the landlords bowed to the church's demands and imposed certain discriminatory practices upon "their Jews," while others defied the church dignitiaries and their demands.[26] In addition about 25–30 percent of the total Jewish population found a place in the hundreds of rural settlements spread over the country.

The net result of these legal and extralegal struggles and developments was that the Jewish population of Poland—which multiplied about forty to fifty times in 250 years in Crown Poland, reaching about half a million by the middle of the eighteenth century—found relatively permanent homes in urban and rural settlements. In many of the large cities where their settlement had been most strenuously resisted for centuries they constituted a considerable proportion by the end of the eighteenth century: in Warsaw 8 percent; in Cracow 15 percent: in Poznań 25 percent; in many other towns large and small, mostly the private ones, they often formed a majority of the population, amounting in some cases to 80 or 90 percent. The absolute number of all Jews in the cities and towns apparently surpassed the total non-Jewish urban population in Poland by the second half of the eighteenth century.

Summarizing, one may say that Polish Jewry had *permanent* residence rights in the country during the sixteenth to eighteenth centuries—for the most part both de jure and de facto, although as non-Catholics they did not always enjoy the same rights as the majority group and probably had to guard their status more jealously than the majority. The recorded impressions of many travelers who visited Poland reinforce this, as do the many eighteenth-century documents—mostly from southern Poland—that designate the Jew as "citizen" or "burgher" before mentioning his name* (although the latter may also indicate mistaken interpretation of the terms).

Occupational Rights

In premodern cities occupational rights were to a great extent connected with citizenship and were deemed to be the monopoly of the burghers. Strangers or guests were usually barred from retail business, being permitted to engage in wholesale transactions only and to participate in fairs (at fairs guests were often also allowed

---

*In Polish, *obywatel* and *mieszczanin*. In some places such as Plock he is called *incola* (dweller), a designation usually reserved in Polish documents for Christian noncitizens. Complaints by burghers against Jewish settlements in cities that had the privilege of *de non tolerandis Judaeis* (Kamenets Podolski, for example) often point out that Jews had no permanent residence rights there.

to sell retail). They also were subject to the rules regarding staple rights of many cities, which obliged foreigners passing through a city or near it to remain for between three and fourteen days and to offer their commodities to the city merchants. Only if they failed to find buyers among the native merchants were they permitted to sell to other strangers or to take their wares away with them. About fifty of the larger cities in Poland had such staple privileges.

Citizenship was almost always a precondition for practicing a handicraft and often also for producing and selling hot beverages. As an urban element Jews were usually connected with trade and to some extent with handicrafts. They also participated in the production and sale of hot drinks, which belonged to the occupations connected with the leasing of revenues and taxes of the state, cities, and estate owners, in which Jews were active early in their history in Poland. Jews were also employed from an early date—either as a sideline or as a main occupation—in moneylending and banking.

Despite the general Jewish privileges of the Middle Ages that gave Jews occupational freedom in general terms, opposition to most Jewish economic activities arose early in Poland. As we have seen, it was moneylending and leasing of revenues and tolls that first aroused the antagonism of certain groups in Polish society and resulted in a number of legal curbs and prohibitions. At the end of the fifteenth century a struggle against Jewish economic activity in the cities began. The forced "agreement" between the city and the Jews in Cracow in 1485, according to which Jews undertook to refrain from any business except the sale of unredeemed pledges, was followed a few years later by limitations upon the trade of Jews in Lwów. This was further developed during the sixteenth century (in 1521 a few larger cities even attempted some sort of united front) with the growth of the Jewish urban population, and it lasted until the downfall of the Polish state. Efforts to limit or eliminate Jewish artisans also began early in Poland (when there were only a few of them in the country) and lasted until the partitions and later.

The intensity, forms, and results of this struggle against Jewish occupational rights depended greatly on the interests of the groups opposing the Jews, as well as on their power and influence, the socioeconomic and political circumstances of the time and place, and the persistence of the Jews and their ability to mobilize supporters.

Apparently the least spectacular and shortest fight was against Jewish moneylending (on mortgages on real estate). Changes in the money market, non-Jews turning to lending, and Jews becoming borrowers because of extended business operations largely minimized or annulled the problem of Jewish moneylending. But it was different for the other economic functions of the Jews.

Revenue and estate farming grew in proportion and volume with the development of the country in the sixteenth and seventeenth centuries and the expansion eastward and southward. Neither the state (treasury), nor the king and the private estate owners, nor even the cities had efficient methods for collecting the tolls and taxes or managing the revenues of the estates. The solution was to farm them out (in France this was done almost up to the French Revolution). Jews, having been urbanites for many generations, were apparently better able to organize the collection of incomes and properly utilize the possibilities than were many Poles. Solomon Maimon (1754–1800), who grew up in a family that for generations had been employed in estate and toll leasing, states (possibly he is exaggerating) that "they [the Jews] are also the only people [in Poland] who farm estates in towns and villages," and he cites the example of two brothers who leased all "the estates of Prince Radziwill and by means of greater industry as well as greater economy, they not only brought the estates into a better condition, but also enriched themselves in a short time."[27] Such a general"farmer" usually subleased individual sources of income, individual villages or inns, to other Jews.

As we have seen, during the Middle Ages some prohibitions were passed. From the beginning of the sixteenth century many resolutions by the *sejm* and regional dietines and the kings' decrees forbade the Jews to farm tolls and state revenues. The Jewish authorities, too—the Four-Land Council of Polish Jews—issued orders prohibiting the leasing of these sources of income (in 1580, 1676, and around 1720). In practice both government and Jewish prohibitions[28] had a limited impact in western Poland, where Jews played a minor role in this field in any case, fulfilling mostly the part of the sublessee.

In the southern parts of the country, the Ukraine, as well as in Red Russia or eastern Galicia and in Lithuania, Jews fulfilled a major function in leasing estates and all manner of revenues: royal, city, and private, both on their own and in partnership with non-Jews (Poles and Armenians) or as subleasers from non-Jewish general leasers. In this region they became a main factor in this field of activity, taking over many estates and urban settlements in leasehold and also filling functions of authority and power. Besides tax farming, Jews engaged in innkeeping and the sale of hot beverages.

A source from the mid-seventeenth century states: "Tax farming was the customary occupation of most Jews in the kingdom of Little Russia [the Ukraine] for they ruled in every part of Little Russia."[29] Travelers and other observers in the seventeenth and eighteenth centuries often pointed out that all the innkeepers in small urban settlements and villages were Jews. According to the partial 1764 census, tax farming, leasing of estates, innkeeping, and the sale of hard liquor in urban settlements amounted by the middle of the eighteenth century to 1.8 percent of the Jewish labor force in western Poland and 18 percent in the Ukraine; of the Jewish village population in the Polish kingdom as a whole (including the Ukraine) some 85–90 percent of the Jews were employed in these occupations.[30]

The two occupations from which the non-Jewish city dwellers tried hardest to bar Jews were commerce and artisanship. These pursuits had a tradition of merchant guilds and craft guilds whose functions were to maintain a monopoly of the local market for their respective members and to preserve a noncompetitive economic system. Trading by foreign merchants was severely restricted in the city except at fairs, nonmembers of the craft guilds were not permitted to practice their trades, and all forms of competition by outsiders were strictly forbidden. The two groups

—the merchants and artisans—formed the backbone of the city population and dominated it. The ruling elite usually comprised merchants, and the smaller businessmen and artisans sometimes participated in the municipal board or (mostly) served as a sort of "official opposition" to the city government. By means of open criticism, demands, and sometimes riots, they pressured the city government into taking a stricter line toward Jews and other minorities.

This struggle against the Jews, other religious or ethnic minorities, and outsiders continued in most of the royal cities and towns of Poland throughout the sixteenth to eighteenth centuries.

In southern Poland the cities attempted to impose limitations upon the Ruthenians and Armenians (in Lwów, for example) and almost everywhere upon the Jews —often simultaneously upon Jews and non-Jews, as in Lwów in the sixteenth century. The denial of occupational freedom had, as we have seen, further repercussions in the form of attempts to deny minorities residence rights or to expel them. The burghers conducted their fight on several planes, such as by seeking exclusive privileges for themselves from the king or the diet, or by limitations upon their opponents, or by causing Jews of a specific city to be treated as foreigners with trade rights limited to fairs and foreign wares. Or they took the law into their own hands, refusing to let Jewish merchants' wagons pass in or out (in Lwów also those of Armenians), resorting to imprisonment, confiscation of wares, violence—attacks[31] and pogroms, and sometimes blood libel and other fabricated accusations.

In all these attempts to limit or exclude Jews and other minorities from trade and crafts, as in the staged violence, it was the lower strata of the city, the small trader, the artisan, and the mob, who were in the forefront of the struggle. The urban elite, the wealthy merchants, were generally less apt to fear Jewish (or any other) competition. Besides, dealings in wholesale and foreign trade caused them to be less attuned to the notion of complete monopoly and control of the market. The merchant guilds could never achieve complete control in these fields. Foreigners were in one way or another permitted to attend fairs almost everywhere and to sell their wares wholesale at these fairs (less frequently retail, too). The lower strata—the small retailer, the street vendor, the craftsman—who were convinced of their "exclusive right" constantly encountered (or thought they did) the competition of the outsider. The craftsman also felt that the Jewish businessman was buying up all the raw materials or undermining his chances by bringing to the market the end product made outside the city. The anger engendered in the poor by Jewish competition served as a front for other grievances, such as their resentment of authority. The fury of their frustrations was often channeled into the Jewish problem. The small trader and the craftsman often exerted pressure upon the city council to be stricter toward the Jew or Armenian, charging the council with signing overly lenient agreements with the Jews or unduly favoring them* (this happened in Lwów and elsewhere).

---

*In Lwów the Ruthenians and Armenians also regarded the city's agreements with the Jews as discriminatory against themselves.

The outcome of it all was a series of prohibitions or limitations by king or diet, beginning in the sixteenth century, against Jewish trade and craftsmanship in different places, with exclusive privileges being granted to various craft guilds, along with another flow of privileges and decrees in favor of Jews. All this resulted in numerous endless lawsuits—a characteristic of feudal states generally. Again and again lawsuits followed each other; the law was scarcely enforced and violence against Jews recurred intermittently in some localities. But the decline of the cities after the second half of the seventeenth century, and the impoverishment of many burghers, cut down the political strength of the Polish city dweller and left a vacuum that Jews often succeeded in filling. Either with the support of the nobles or by their own energy and initiative they were often able to eke out a living, even when the non-Jewish burgher gave up because he was unwilling or unable to adjust himself to the loss of security and the rigidity of the guild system.

The fragmentary nature of the 1764 census with respect to the Jewish population —in many instances occupational figures are lacking—makes it hard to reach any reasonable estimate of the number of Jews occupied in commerce and artisanship. But later partial censuses indicate that both these fields played an important role in Jewish occupational structure in a number of cities and towns. General statements by Polish leaders, observations of travelers, and other indirect information place the Jews in the forefront of trade and artisanship. According to such information 75 percent or more of Polish exports and 10 percent of all imports were handled by Jews in the eighteenth century. In many small cities and towns most of the traders and artisans were Jews. Travelers often maintained that "all the traders are Jews" or that "Jews conquered all the trade."[32] Exaggerated though such generalizations may be, they do surely show a trend.

Justice and Judicature

Justice and judicature in this period, as in the Middle Ages, assumed a number of forms: cases of non-Jew versus Jew went to the Jews' judge, originally the palatine himself or his deputy (in Volhynia the *starosta*). Cases of Jew against Jew were heard by the Jewish court (court of dayanim or rabbis).

Beginning with the sixteenth century the court of the Jews' judge consisted either of a judge and a secretary appointed by the palatine, or of the deputy palatine and a secretary, or of the assistant palatine, a judge, and a secretary—all drawn from the nobility and appointed for the most part by the palatine. In some regions one of the appointees to this court was chosen from candidates proposed by the Jews. The court also included a public prosecutor (for cases that were of public interest) and a Jewish official, the beadle—who acted as the bailiff *(woźny)* and had other official duties—and, in principle, one or more Jewish assessors appointed by the Jewish community.

These courts convened in or near the synagogue, either at any time except during Jewish and Christian holidays or at specific times of the year (in Cracow after 1725, twice a year for a two-week session). The judges were paid by the case or received a salary (in Cracow in the eighteenth century the Jews' judge was paid fifteen hundred zloty annually and the secretary four hundred zloty). These were courts of the first instance[33] for cases of Christian versus Jew. But in practice some purely Jewish cases (Jew versus Jew) also came to these courts, sometimes as a court of the first instance and sometimes as a court of appeal against judgments of the Jewish court.

The Jewish court comprised a number of dayanim (judges), presided over by the rabbi. In large communities there were several sets of judges (usually three), each one consisting of at least three members and differing from each other in their range of competence. The first and lowest court had competence over cases involving small amounts of money and minor quarrels; the second group dealt with larger sums and more serious strife; the third and highest group of judges, presided over by the rabbi, had competence over cases involving large amounts of money, as well as religious and moral transgressions; in some communities they also judged criminal matters, mainly ones of a religious character.

The usual court of appeals for the court of the Jews' judge and the Jewish court was the personal court of the palatine,* with the royal court serving as the supreme court. Both these latter courts, however, were also empowered to serve as courts of the first instance in specific cases and circumstances.

After 1549 Jews living in cities, towns, or villages belonging to the nobility or the clergy were partially subject to the jurisdiction of the courts of the individual landowners, with all their various attitudes, practices, and whims. Some sort of pattern did develop, however, which grew out of customary law or adopted the forms evolved by the state. Thus in almost all private cities and towns, lawsuits between Jew and Jew were subject to the jurisdiction of the Jewish judges and the rabbi. These judges were either elected by the community and approved by the landowner or were appointed by him. The landowner also served in principle as a court of appeals from the Jewish court and as the only court in criminal matters. In all settlements—royal and "private"—lawsuits involving a Jew against a Christian had to be brought to the court to which the Christian defendant was subject (city court for burghers; district, castle, or chamberlain's court for nobles, and so on).

In practice, however, the system varied. The king had the power to exempt a Jew from all but his own personal jurisdiction; the *starosta*, as manager of royal estates and royal cities in the king's name, at times tried to put the Jews residing there under his own jurisdiction rather than that of the palatine. Cases having to do with city real estate came before the city court. In addition, in certain cases the parties had a choice of court to which they wished to be subject.

Officially the Jewish court and in part the court of the Jews' judge were supposed

*From the sixteenth century on there were cases in which the palatine agreed to forgo his right as judge of the second instance in favor of the Jewish court; he only continued to share in the income derived from fines.

to use Jewish law, and all other courts, Polish law. But in many cases the court of the Jews' judge applied Polish law too. On the other hand, Jewish parties, for the most part in the southern portions of the country, sometimes went to the general courts instead of to the Jewish court, despite the fact that the community leadership and the rabbis frowned upon such a practice. At the same time many court documents reveal that Jews in the private cities appeared in the general courts accompanied by nobles (secular or clergy) as plaintiffs or defendants.[34] This was apparently intended to strengthen the case and give it higher prestige in the courts. Hence the disparity, which has also been noted in other areas, between the laws as they were formulated and the manner in which they were observed, a disparity also evident in the matter of jurisdiction.

Religious Freedom

The religious freedom of non-Catholics in Poland, as in many other Catholic states before the French Revolution, was limited. As a multinational and multidenominational state since the fourteenth century, Poland did not follow the extreme principle of intolerance according to which the majority imposes its faith upon the minority (*Cuius regio eius religio:* He whose state it is, his is the religion). Poland adhered largely to another trend of the premodern state whereby members of minority groups had the right to follow their own religion and customs: autonomy. The Polish state generally gave minorities the right to organize as religious groups and to a certain extent protected their freedom to exercise their respective religions, even supervising their autonomous organizations. Meanwhile, Catholicism remained the state religion, all others being more or less tolerated. This left loopholes for discrimination and restriction in law and in practice.

The Jews in Poland were recognized as a religious group, with the right to an organizational structure of its own, and were promised protection for their religious customs and laws.

The first Polish privileges for Jews (thirteenth and fourteenth centuries) provide that Jews should not be forced to desecrate their Sabbath and holidays, "should not be forced to return pawns." This paragraph in the privileges dealing with the Sabbath has a heading "Jews should not be tried [in court] on holidays," which may be a later addition. Protection was also promised for synagogues, funeral processions, and cemeteries. The Jewish oath was recognized as valid proof in court proceedings and its form was prescribed. The Jewish method of slaughtering animals was acknowledged as permissible.

Protection of Sabbath and Holidays

The protection of the Jewish Sabbath and holidays from disturbance by non-Jews, formulated in a cryptic form in the earlier privileges, is elaborated in the later versions confirmed by the kings. The one confirmed by King Casimir IV in 1453 states clearly that anyone intruding upon a Jewish home on a Sabbath or holiday, "when the Jews do not dare to touch the money for the redemption of the pawn," would be punished "as a robber and a thief." Confirmations of the privileges in the sixteenth and seventeenth centuries forbid summoning Jews to the courts on Saturdays and holidays because of the inhibitions of the Jewish law (in 1571 and 1580 for Poznań and the edicts of 1576 and 1592 generally). Local ordinances, too, repeat these prescriptions (for instance that of the voivode of Cracow in 1659).

Apparently these prescriptions were generally more or less adhered to in practice, as confirmed both by the fact that there are no records of complaints or appeals by Jews protesting that they were forced to violate them, and by the information from the court of the Jews' judge. It should be added that kings and nobles who owned towns sometimes decreed that fairs and market days should not be held on a Saturday, or they prevailed upon the city people to add another market or fair day during the week for the sake of the Jews.

But the question of observing the Sabbath and holidays had another angle. Catholicism being the state religion, the church sought to make it mandatory for Jews to observe Sundays and Christian holidays. Church councils and city authorities often complained (in 1542, for example) that Jews "are working and trading publicly on Christian holidays." There are also complaints about Jews forcing or inducing their non-Jewish servants and employees to work on Sundays and holidays. Secular authorities (city, state, and nobles owning towns) attempted to introduce prohibitions against this. Thus the same edict of King Stephen Báthory of 1576 which states that "on holidays and the Sabbath they [the Jews] must not be tried" in court forbids them to work on Sundays and the main Christian holidays. Conversely, King John Casimir's 1661 privilege allowed Jews to transact business on Christian holidays.

Other decrees and agreements between Jews and city authorities allowed Jews to trade among themselves on Sundays and Christian holidays (but not with Christians) and generally at such fairs as were held on a holiday. The only limitation was that they had to avoid trading before mass had been celebrated in church and during the hours of services in the Christian churches. Similar compromises were also arranged in many of the private towns and cities.[35]

Ritual Slaughter

Ritual slaughter of animals (shechita), required by Jewish religious law, was generally recognized as essential for the Jews and therefore permitted. But ritual slaughter and observance of the Jewish religious laws connected with kashruth (food approved or fit for consumption by Jews) had a number of repercussions. Jews are forbidden to eat certain parts of the animal (terefa). Whole animals were sometimes found to be unsuitable because of a misstep in the slaughter ritual or because of conditions found inside the animal upon examination following slaughter. In consequence, the right to sell to non-Jews those parts or those animals that their religion apparently forbade Jews to consume became important.

But this met with opposition from two sources. Church authorities opposed such sales to Christians on the grounds that it would be degrading for Christians to consume Jews' castoffs. Christian butchers had practical reasons: to avoid competition by preventing Jewish butchers from selling meat to their prospective customers, especially since Jewish butchers could (and often did) slaughter more than the Jewish group needed so as to have meat to supply to the general population. Christian butchers therefore tried through their guilds to exclude Jews from the meat market,* or at least to minimize their impact by obtaining prohibitions against selling to non-Jews.[36]

In practice royal decrees and privileges (in 1453 and several times in the sixteenth century) gave Jews the right to slaughter according to Jewish ritual law and to sell to Christians any meat that "does not correspond to their purpose and desire,"[37] a right opposed by both the church and the Christian butchers. As early as 1267 the church synod in Breslau forbade Christians to purchase meat sold by Jews because their religion barred them from eating it, and about half a century later the city council of Breslau stopped Jews from selling any meat to Christians. Sporadic attempts to limit the right of Jews to sell meat to Christians were made in later centuries on various occasions. This was usually at the instigation of the butcher guilds desirous of excluding Jewish competitors. The agreement made in Breslau at the beginning of the fourteenth century between the butcher guild and the Jews —that Jewish slaughterers should use the guild's slaughterhouse to kill cattle delivered by the guild, which would then sell the permissible parts to the Jews[38]—may perhaps not have been imitated in later centuries. But Christian butchers often pressured for edicts limiting the number of Jewish butchers, or sought to achieve this end by violence or through "agreements" with Jewish communities. Thus in Cracow in 1494 it was "agreed" that Jews should have no more than four butchers. In 1562 the number was raised to eight but in 1622 again reduced to four. In fact, these limitations were not kept (by 1634 they had eighteen Jewish butchers). In Lwów the number was officially limited to eight in 1608, whereas there were actually many more—in 1610 possibly as many as seventy.

While Jews were seldom if ever troubled by a lack of kosher meat for their own consumption, at times they encountered the problem of selling the nonkosher parts to non-Jews. This was aggravated by the fact that Jewish butchers often served the general market under the pretext of selling this sort of meat to the Christian consumer—or so the Christian butchers and their guilds believed. Thus the whole

---

*In some places in medieval Germany they succeeded in completely eliminating the Jewish butcher by themselves supplying meat for Jews. The animals designed for Jews were slaughtered by a Jewish slaughterer—shochet—who also prepared the cuts and stamped them with a special seal to make them recognizable to Jewish customers. (This procedure also existed, apparently for other reasons, during the eighteenth century in New York City.)

matter was linked with the general struggle of the guilds to preserve their monopoly and in fact had little if anything to do with religion.

Synagogues and Cemeteries

Synagogues, Jewish cemeteries, and funeral processions were protected by the Jewish privileges (thirteenth and fourteenth centuries), which prescribed fines against anyone throwing stones at synagogues and invading or damaging a Jewish cemetery. In the confirmation of the privileges in 1453 these provisions were strengthened. In practice, however, they were not always observed. Violations seem to have increased after the second half of the sixteenth century with the strengthening of the Counter-Reformation in Poland. Sometimes when mobs (either organized by the Jesuits or of their own volition) fell upon the funeral processions of the anti-Trinitarians and attacked and often destroyed their meeting houses and churches, as well as those of other Protestant groups, some Jewish funeral processions and synagogues also suffered. In his 1633 confirmation of the privileges King Ladislas IV mentions that Jewish synagogues in various towns had been attacked. For this reason, the king forcefully forbade such acts and asked the governors to protect the synagogues and punish violators severely.[39] Nevertheless there were subsequent attacks on synagogues and Jewish funeral processions,[40] although apparently there were never systematic attacks such as were made against the anti-Trinitarians.

With regard to the synagogues, however, the church attempted (the church council of 1267 and others)—often successfully—to introduce limitations and prescriptions concerning the permissible number (in 1267: one synagogue to a place), the location (not near a church), and the size (smaller than a church) of synagogues. The church synod in Piotrków in 1542 wanted to limit the Jews to repairing old synagogues, with the building of new ones being forbidden. King Ladislas IV confirmed the right of the Jews to have synagogues built, but warned them to make sure to keep them smaller than the Christian churches. This made building a synagogue subject to permits from civil (king) or church (bishop) authorities, or both, with all the disadvantages attendant upon such a situation in a semifeudal state plagued by corruption, inefficiency, and disorder.

Sometimes a bishop would also regard his power to grant or deny such a permit as a means of attempting to extort certain concessions from the Jews.[41]

Political Rights

Polish society, like European society generally prior to the French Revolution, was largely based on privilege and tradition, with power vested in the rulers and the small groups of nobles and higher clergy. The vast majority of the people in the cities and the countryside were denied political privileges (rights) and the right to vote, except in the selection of a few petty local officers. The cities were self-governing but had very few political rights. City government was usually controlled by an oligarchy comprising a tiny elite group of rich merchants and professionals. The rest of the burghers—storekeepers, artisans, to say nothing of the lower strata—usually had little or no voice in city affairs.

Poland, unlike Germany, did not develop city-states to play some political role in running the larger national state. With few exceptions the cities would not send deputies to the sessions of the diet or district assemblies. The few larger cities such as Cracow, for instance, whose deputies were seated at the diet meetings, had hardly any voting rights (or did not exercise them).

After a prolonged struggle within the cities some permanent form of representation of the people was established in the city government. While subject to the city council, it also served at the same time as a sort of consultative body and exercised some control over the auditing of city finances.

Minorities—Armenians, Ruthenians, and Jews—were not generally regarded as full-fledged citizens of the cities and were not represented in the city government. They did have their own organizations, however, which for them took the place of or paralleled the city government.

The Ruthenian and Armenian "nations" in Lwów participated sporadically in the peoples' representation, which served, as we have mentioned, as a sort of consultative body alongside the city council. The Ruthenians were struggling for representation in the city council itself (besides having their own weak religious organization). They attained this goal legally in 1745 but had to wait a number of years longer for it to materialize. The Armenians in Lwów had their own organization, patterned to some extent on the city council. In certain other cities (Kamenets Podolski and Stanislawów), the Armenian "nation" had a city organization (city council, municipality, town hall) of its own paralleling the Polish municipality (or in Stanislawów the Polish-Ruthenian municipality).

Jews had no political rights in the royal cities, but like the Armenians and Ruthenians they had their own organization, the kehilla, which somewhat resembled the non-Jewish municipality (see below). In such Jewish towns as Kazimierz-Cracow and to some extent in places where Jewish streets existed, the kehilla served as a parallel institution to the general non-Jewish (for the most part Catholic) city government, fulfilling similar municipal and some political functions. In these and certain other places it fulfilled for the Jews economic and social roles, as well as religious ones, that were analogous to those of the city council for the general (Catholic) city. The Catholic municipality was the dominant one, but in many cases the representatives of the Jewish community or kehilla appeared in the company of the city representatives and acted in concert with them opposite a third party, as though they represented two parallel institutions. Documents addressed to the king or other authorities often speak in the name of the "city and the Jewish population," as if equating the two.

In many of the private cities and towns* Jews enjoyed some political rights, such

*Brody, Dubno, Dukla, Żabna, Zwenigorod, Bolechów.

as the right to vote in the elections for the mayor, the aldermen, and councilors. When taking the oath of office in Bolechów the newly elected mayor had to declare that he would defend equally the rights of the three national groups—the Catholics, the Ruthenians, and the Jews. In some other cities in the south, including the royal city of Luck, Jews had the right to send representatives to city council meetings at which reports were submitted and to participate in the discussion of the city finances. In a few towns where artisans participated in city government, Jewish artisans, too, were represented. These Jewish artisan representatives also sat in the municipal court on cases in which one party was a Jewish artisan.

While all this actually has little to do with civil rights and general suffrage as we have known it since the nineteenth century, to a limited degree it accorded the Jews in cities and towns political rights equal to those of the non-Jewish city dwellers and offered them the chance to take some part in local politics.

Another form of "political" activity exercised by Jews in Poland was through the medium of their shtadlan or syndic, who often worked together with representatives of the Jewish community. The syndic served as an advisor, defense lawyer, and lobbyist for larger Jewish communities and Jewish organizations (regional and country—Polish or Lithuanian—councils). At times he also represented individual Jews in dealings with the authorities, nobles, and clergy. Because of his knowledge of Polish and good contacts in government and other non-Jewish circles, he became a defender of the Jews and their intermediary in matters relating to the outside world.

Such syndics, who appear more frequently beginning with the seventeenth century, were prepared to draw upon various resources to defend Jewish interests vis-à-vis the state and the ruling elite. Their activity could be described as political in the sense of "efforts of groups [here the Jewish group] to gain authoritative political support for their objectives,"[42] rather than in terms of entering and participating in high office. This activity of the Jews through their representatives—the syndics and community leadership—may have had repercussions in the diffusion of political power, and not solely in matters relating to Jews. (In the eighteenth century some Poles accused the Jewish communities and their representatives of "interfering" in Polish political matters.)

In the Polish state, where most of the power was concentrated in the hands of the nobles as represented in the diet *(sejm)* and district assemblies (dietines), there was plenty of opportunity to influence the members—usually through advisors, lobbyists, and defenders. Gifts were the order of the day in most political matters in Poland. Prior to the election of each new Polish king the great European powers of that time used to spend considerable amounts trying to promote their candidate. Polish officials sought support for high office in the same way. A contemporary eighteenth-century observer relates that the commander in chief of the Polish army, with a view to gaining the favor of the gentry in political affairs, "sent people to Danzig and to the fair of Leipzig . . . to bring many articles, namely, clothes, materials, gold and silver watches, snuffboxes, and other valuables such as gold and jeweled rings" for presents to the nobles.

In such an environment the Jews took a similar attitude. Entries in the minute books of the Polish (and Lithuanian) Jewish Council (1681) cryptically mention "expenses for wages for the syndic [shtadlan] of the Four-Land Council in Warsaw, . . . expenses at the diet in Warsaw . . . and gifts to our lord the king and his nobles."[43]

On the local urban scene the voivode and other high officials regularly received gifts and salaries from the Jewish community for taking care of Jewish matters. A budget of the Jewish kehilla in Poznań 1637–38 has entries for sums paid to the palatine, the vice-palatine, the general, their secretaries, the city mayor, and others. That these gifts were made for services rendered becomes clear from another entry in the record book of the Poznań kehilla, dated 1639:

> *From ancient times it has been customary to give the general 200 zloty every year in order that he selects a mayor in accordance with our wishes—one whom we want—[the general had to confirm two mayors from a list of four candidates presented by the city council]. Now already a few times he failed to fulfill his promises. . . . This year he took one whom we did not want. . . . In the future the rule should be to withhold payment of the 200 zloty until after the selection of the mayor.*[44]

On the national scene the Jewish representatives were busy even before the diet sessions opened. Entries for 1623 in the extant minute book of Lithuanian Jewry (which is more comprehensive than that of the Polish council) mention the obligation of the principal Jewish communities "to watch that during the sessions of the district assemblies held before the diet . . . nothing new which could hurt us should be decided upon." Five years later the order was issued that four weeks before the session of the district assembly, the regional communal leaders should make sure that "the deputies to be elected [by the district assembly] should receive gifts and be asked to be benevolent in the diet." In those years and especially a little later the task of "being on the alert" at the sessions of the district assemblies, and of the diet in Warsaw, fell principally upon the shtadlan or syndic. In Warsaw, too, after the middle of the seventeenth century the Warsaw Committee (comprising representatives of the Polish Jewish council) met before each session of the *sejm* to see to it that no anti-Jewish legislation was passed. The committee also dealt with other important Polish Jewish matters.[45] A syndic's functions are set forth (in 1761 in Lithuania) as the representation, defense, and protection of the Jews at the local sessions of the law courts and "before the king and the dignitaries of the kingdom." He should be able "to stand before the king and the dignitaries and express himself [in Polish?] in a beautiful and flowery language." His remuneration was generally in the form of a tax immunity, a substantial salary, and an expense account for the time he had to be on duty at the law courts and district assembly sessions or before the *sejm*. Specific amounts varied, of course, with time and place. Some figures that have been preserved may indicate the relative importance of the syndic's position and the high expectations connected with his office. His salary was higher than the rabbi's,[46] and he also had recourse to other substantial income (by doing business on his own or being paid by private individuals for representing them). Generally the sums spent by the Jewish representatives at sessions of the diet seem to have been quite considerable.

It is probably inherent in the nature of such public relations work that some activities should remain unrecorded. But a few documents indicate some successes or show that Jewish representatives were able to order intervention in a certain direction[47] (relief from or reduction of taxes, changing attitudes of the king or diet deputies, or introducing resolutions in the diet—or "constitution"—on certain pro-Jewish points). One may surmise that in working with the nobles at the district assemblies, the syndics may sometimes have had some influence on the election (or nonelection) of a certain candidate to the diet, or have determined how he voted there. They may even have gone beyond the specific Jewish interests, in which case they were exercising some political power or using public relations methods to achieve certain goals in the political arena. One can see in this not the politics of the desirable but rather the politics of the possible. The relative success of such politics may be indirectly confirmed by a 1669 statement of the Braclaw regional nobles' assembly "that in practice Jews do not let any law materialize which is unfavorable to them,"[48] despite the gross exaggeration it contains.

Security of Life and Property

Prior to the rise of the modern state (eighteenth to nineteenth century) security of life and property was almost unknown. In the medieval world and for the most part up to and including the eighteenth century, men lived in continuous insecurity. Chronic wars, private wars between rivals, brigandage, violence, cruelty, aggressiveness, and the excitability of medieval man endangered the lives and property of most people much of the time. Protection of the individual by state and city authorities was weak and inadequate, law enforcement was rare, and the authorities were themselves generally ridden with superstition, persecution tendencies, and violence. Executions were cruel and public; extortion of confession by torture was the usual form of "justice." Harsh persecution of dissenters, charges of witchcraft, and the burning of witches were frequent occurrences.

The Huguenots in France, for instance, following the revocation of the Edict of Nantes in 1685 were subjected to fearful ordeals:

> While the soldiers quartered on the hapless Huguenots were forbidden to kill or to rape, they were allowed and encouraged to exert pressure by all means short of these extreme ones. They beat the men, tossed them in blankets, pulled out their hair, filled their houses with smoke, distended their bellies with water, kept them awake with maddening noises, and hung them up by the nose or by the toes; they stripped the women naked, and otherwise outraged their modesty.

In later years milder measures were adopted, but in 1732 these were followed by "a savage edict . . . which again revived the old methods of death, torture and the galleys."[49]

Accusations of witchcraft and the burning of witches after exacting confession by cruel torture were widespread in the whole of the Western world. Witches were violently persecuted in New England in the last decades of the seventeenth century, after which the persecutions began to peter out in the North American colonies. In England witchcraft accusations began to decline by the middle of the eighteenth century. The decline in Germany set in by the end of the seventeenth century but exceptions still took place sporadically, 1776 being the last date of a witch-hunt in Bavaria. In Poland in the course of about two centuries an estimated ten thousand witches were executed, the last two in 1793. People in Poland were also brought to court for "blasphemy" and "sacrilege"; some of them were sentenced to have "the blasphemous tongue torn out" or their hand burned.

In addition, any apparent security in Poland was made illusory by the perennial wars between neighboring nobles, the "small wars" organized by the magnates, raids by one noble and his entourage upon another—all over and above the frequent attacks of the Tatars beginning with the fifteenth century, the almost continuous wars of 1648–1717, and the attacks of the cossacks during those and subsequent decades.

Soldiers used force and torture to collect taxes from the peasants, and landowners treated their serfs cruelly. Highwaymen and robbers made many roads dangerous. In cities the walls afforded relative protection from attacks and pillage from outside. Nonetheless, military invasions, internal mob actions, and sometimes raids by nobles created many hazards to life and property there as well.

As we have seen, from the end of the sixteenth century on Poland was the site of much spontaneous or staged religious tumult: student and mob violence upon various Protestant groups, mainly the Arians, with destruction of life, property, and churches.

Being a minority, the Jews were in just as much danger as the others—possibly more. They may have suffered proportionally less from attacks by Tatars, for instance, since a larger proportion of Jews lived in walled cities that afforded some protection,* but perhaps they were more prone to individual or group attacks by the cossacks, pogroms, mob attacks, violence by Jesuit students, and blood libel and similar accusations. The toll among the Jews during the time of the cossack uprisings and subsequent invasions (1648–67) is variously estimated at between forty and a hundred thousand casualties, or 25–50 percent of the Jewish population in Poland. Most of the Poles in the region overrun by the cossacks were also killed. There are even some indications that at times the Poles were worse off than the Jews (the latter

---

*Estimates indicate that a peasant's house in a village in southern Poland had an "average life" of ten years before it was burned down or destroyed by the Tatars. Houses in the cities lasted much longer even though fires often devastated them.

could, for instance, be converted and join the cossacks, whereas Poles were not allowed to do so). But the total of the Polish victims in proportion to the Polish population was relatively smaller than that of the Jews. The same seems to have been true of the various attacks upon Jews in the eighteenth century by cossacks and other bands in southern Poland.

Assaults by robber bands roving the roads, the oppression suffered at the hands of Polish soldiers assigned to collect taxes, and the harsh treatment meted out to some innkeepers and other village Jews by the nobles—who sometimes imprisoned and even tortured them—may or may not have been more drastic when Jews were involved. They had some parallels in the situation of the general population, particularly the village population. But there was a difference between attacks by mobs and Jesuit students and the suffering caused by libels (although here, too, some parallels are to be found in similar measures taken in Poland against Protestant groups). The accompanying charts, incomplete though they may be, give some idea of these occurrences involving Jews.

Blood Libel, Charges of Profanation of the Holy Wafer, and Similar Accusations

1542 (or 1551)	Cracow		1663	Cracow (accusation of Calahore brothers of sacrilege)
1547	Rawa Mazowiecka (two Jews put to death)		1663	Poznań
1556	Sochaczew		1680	Tiktin
1561	Gombin		1689	Sluzk
1564	Sochaczew		1690	Sandomierz
1576	Gombin		1690	Near Lublin
1578	Lublin		1696	Poznań
1590	Szydlowiec		1698	Sandomierz
1595	Gostynin		1710	Biala
1597	Szydlowiec		1711	Leczno
1598	Pultusk			Mościsko
	Swiniarow		1711–13	Sandomierz
1600	Wyszegrod		1716	Dubno
1605	Sandomierz		1726	Lissa
	Bochnia		1728	Lwów (Reizes brothers)
1617	Sielec		1736–40	Poznań
1619	Sochaczew		1738	Gniezno
1620	Kalish		1747	Zaslaw
1624	Lęczyca		1748	Szepetówka
1630	Sandomierz			Dunajgrod
	Sochaczew		1753	Zitomir
1631	Cracow		1756	Jampol
1636	Lublin		1759	Stopnica—Przemyśl?
1637	Cracow		1760	Wojslawice
1638	Lwów		1763	Kalish
1639	Lęczyca		1769	Wojslawice
1653	Poznań		1779	Chrzanów
1656	Mohilev		1786	Lissa
1659	(attempt) Przemyśl		1787	Olkusz
	Rossieny			

Some Jews were also among the victims of witch-hunts. Several Jewish women were arrested and others even lynched.[50]

Pogroms, Attacks by Students and City People

1534	Plock	1638	Lwów suburb
1556	Plock	1639	Cracow
1557	Poznań	1640˜	Lwów
1557	Cracow	1641	Lwów
1560	Cracow	1642	Lwów
1570	Plock	1643	Lwów
1572	Lwów	1646	Lublin
1579	Plock		Przemyśl
1590	Plock	1656	Plock
1592	Lwów (attack on a	1660	Cracow
	Jewish funeral)	1662	Poznań
1598	Lwów		Cracow
1600	Lwów (suburb)	1663	Lwów*
1601	Lwów		Cracow
1613	Lwów		Poznań
1618	Lwów	1664	Cracow
	Poznań		Lwów
1621	Cracow		Wilno
1622	Cracow	1676	Lublin
1628	Cracow	1682	Cracow
	Przemyśl	1687	Poznań
	Lwów	1691	Wilno
1634	Lwów	1695	Poznań
1635	Wilno	1696	Poznań
1636	Lwów	1704	Krotoschin
1637	Brest Litovsk	1716	Poznań
	Cracow	1717	Poznań

These lists, each showing over fifty-odd persecutions of Jews in Poland during almost two centuries, are admittedly not exhaustive. A score or more could probably be added. This would bring the average up to two persecutions every three years. Western Poland, particularly its principal cities, was again and again the focus of recurrent persecutions. In the south such abuses were less frequent, except for Lwów, where they developed later, mainly around the middle of the seventeenth century. All in all forty-one cities and towns were involved in the persecutions listed above (out of over 600 cities and towns where Jews lived in Poland in 1764), some of them again and again. Poznań, Cracow, and Lwów together accounted for almost one-half of all the cases listed, while other places suffered only once or twice during the whole two centuries. One can thus see a connection between false accusations plus pogroms and the competitive struggle for livelihood between the burghers and the Jews. Except during the 1660s persecutions usually occurred in one place at a

*Attacks on individual Jews are recorded in Lwów in 1597, 1598, 1607, and 1765; Plock in 1553, 1560–65, 1582, 1584, 1601, 1648, 1655, and many others.

time but one may assume that the facts became known, perhaps even exaggerated, to Jews in other places through the grapevine or because communities were informed in connection with needed help.

Nearly every item on these lists represents a tale of terror, agony, and despair, of diabolical cruelty and violence, of torture and death, of victims burned alive, dismembered, and tormented by the hangman, of captives being held in underground waterlogged and vermin-infested dungeons, and of people attacked and maltreated by mobs.

This does not include either the cossack uprisings of the mid-seventeenth century, in which many Jewish communities perished, or the smaller-scale attacks of the eighteenth century. There were, too, many attacks on individuals or groups of a local nature about which we either lack information or such information as we have is scattered through many documents of individual communities and is difficult to obtain. Thus in the Plock archives there is mention of about forty mainly individual attacks on Jews (1500–1650).[51] The materials from Plock include notices of about twenty cases of Jews having attacked non-Jews and some forty incidents in which non-Jews assaulted Jews. There are also many documents (1683–1750) that record innumerable thefts, burglaries, and pilferings from Jews; their synagogues were broken into, and they were beaten and jailed without cause (in southern Poland). All this over and above the sufferings[52] during the sporadic forays during the eighteenth century. Most of the documents, however, deal with attacks on Jews and non-Jews alike.[53]

Our information on a great many cases of Jews being murdered in the south in the eighteenth century derives from court documents. The non-Jewish defendants were brought to court (or the document contains demands that they be brought to court), and some tell of their being found guilty, convicted, and executed. Some documents concern the sort of mixed Polish-Russian border commissions or courts set up in the Ukraine in the eighteenth century to deal with the extradition of attackers who fled across the border. There are many reports of nobles and clergy-landlords appearing in court or other offices and demanding that attackers of "their" Jews be punished; and their appearance probably helped to expedite action.

All this could indicate that crimes against Jewish life and property did not always go unpunished. This did not, of course, eliminate the threat to Jewish life and property or appreciably decrease the sufferings of the victims. They may have derived only scant consolation from the knowledge that non-Jews, too, were subject to the violence, lack of law and order, and anarchy and lawlessness that spread through Poland during the eighteenth century.

On the other hand, the perspective of history may sometimes make conditions appear far gloomier than they actually were for the generations living through them. For example, a historian of the next century gathering and summarizing all the information on violence now spread across the front pages of our daily newspapers —the muggings, murders, robberies, and vandalism reported every day—would be bound to form a distorted picture of our way of life and our sense of security. This also holds true for our own view of the past. People in past centuries saw the facts in the framework and context of their time and made what efforts they could to protect themselves, just as some try to do now when police protection proves inadequate.[54] Self-defense, armed or by other means, was not rare among Polish Jews of that time. In some cases they succeeded in repulsing the attacker, in others they failed. Means of self-protection ranged from the individual's use of arms, banding together on trips for mutual protection and defense against assault, and hiring guards, to attempts at "political self-defense" by means of influence and pressure exerted upon authorities, recourse to the courts, and other ways.[55] A few examples may depict the situation during that period. In Poznań at the end of 1687 the Jews defended themselves against attacks by students who joined artisans and riffraff in repeated raids on Jewish streets lasting three days. According to the chronicler, "it became a terrific war, army fighting army. . . . Every time they came to our street with drawn swords the Jews got the upper hand and drove them back, frightened, to the marketplace." In the fall of 1588, just before the Jewish New Year, an epidemic broke out in Cracow and spread to other parts of the country. The king with his court and high officials left the city. The leaders of the Jewish community and some of the wealthier Jews followed suit. On the eve of Rosh Hashanah some of the royal guards or others who had remained in town broke into a Jewish store to rob it. Jewish community officials who had not fled, together with some city officials, intervened and helped to nip the theft in the bud. One Jew from Kazimierz-Cracow writes: "We were worried that other guards [or soldiers] would do the same. . . . Those robbers were arrested and have been killed [executed?]; one is still in jail. The stolen goods will be returned."

From this and another letter we also learn that "they [the Jews] are supporting a large guard, namely, there are guards, Jewish guards being in the lead, and there are non-Jewish guards from Kazimierz" as well as official firemen from the city's fire department. The writers add that this was very expensive. One of them goes on to give assurance that there was now nothing more to fear. The tone of the letters is not panicky.[56]

Jews of those centuries also saw to it that non-Jewish offenders or murderers were brought to court. A rabbinic source from the middle of the seventeenth century states that if a man was murdered on the road his relatives[57] were duty bound to have the murderer brought to court. This means that he was to be sought out and thrown into jail. When the costs were exorbitant the community had to contribute toward them, otherwise "Jewish blood will be free for all." And the rabbi adds: "And so did we behave many times, and we arranged with the community leaders that they should place 'blood avengers' to persecute the murderers . . . and even in cases where they knew that nothing could be done [they tried to arrange a trial] in order that it should become known that Jewish blood is not free for all."[58]

These two cases—one in the sixteenth and one in the seventeenth century—seem to indicate that contemporaries did not regard their situation as hopeless, but tried to defend themselves in various ways, considering punishment of murderers as one means of increasing their own security.

8 Poland through the Eyes of Polish Jews

Posture of Polish Jewry

From the vantage point of today's ingrained ideas, equality before the law, freedom of movement, economic opportunity, and some security of person and property are taken for granted. By contrast, all the struggling (and achievement) of the Polish Jews in earlier centuries—for residence rights and occupational choice and their defenses against physical attack and mob riots—seem to have been one unbroken chain of suffering and deprivation (though the current curtailment of these and other freedoms in half or more of the world, the rising crime rate, delinquency, and rioting in this country as well as in Western Europe and Soviet Russia should give us some perspective). But to apply modern political, social, and legal concepts to past centuries—when circumstances were different and men had other attitudes and loyalties—is an unpardonable error. To make the past intelligible to the present one must interpret historical events in the context of the time and circumstances in which they took place. The significant question is how the people of those generations regarded their own situation rather than how we see it.

The only way to gain some perspective is to try to put ourselves in the shoes of the people of those times and imagine how they thought and acted. More concretely, we should inquire how Jews in Poland in the sixteenth through eighteenth centuries viewed the conditions under which they lived. Did they manifest a sense of helplessness and despondency under the impact of misery and violence? Did they sit back most of the time and bewail their lot, throwing up their hands in despair and idleness? The contrary seems to be true. Their lives seem to have been packed with adventure and activity, apparently to a far greater extent than those of the population at large. And this was not only because circumstances forced them to be active, for dire need and continuous suffering are not conducive to initiative, action, and achievement, or because Jews had acquired more rational approaches to life than other peoples, but mainly because this world of limitations and prescriptions and only relative security was their own world. In a precapitalistic society living in preindustrial cities, with their heterogeneity of groups and denominations, unequal rights, monopolistic tendencies in economic activity, and suppression of the middleman, the Jewish situation in Poland was apparently not regarded as very different from that of the other groups, with the possible exception of the Catholic elite. In an era when the residents of a city regarded people originating from outside the city walls as aliens, devoid of residence rights and with limited possibilities of making a living within the city, when minorities and occupational groups were usually localized in particular quarters or streets, when one Christian denomination regarded the others as heathens (the Catholics so regarded the Greek Orthodox), expelling them (the Huguenots in France and the Arians in Poland) or staging pogroms to destroy their churches (this was done to Protestants and Arians in Poland), the Jews' situation probably did not appear to them to be too abnormal.[1]

Jews in Poland must surely have realized that they were not the only victims of discrimination in the cities. The Protestants, too, were excluded as the Counter-Reformation grew, and neither the Ruthenians, the Armenians, or the Tatars (Muslims) enjoyed full citizenship or complete freedom of occupational activity in the cities. In fact, the great majority of Poles were themselves deprived of such advantages except in their own towns or cities. One may assume that because the "system" of those centuries was based on the principle of acquired rights for a small in-group, with widespread discrimination against the many out-groups, the Jews' responses were less negative to the order of things. In fact, the Jews used the same system themselves, not only in imitation of their environment but also, or mainly, because living in a similar world led them to evolve similar systems (although their environment may often have served as a model for them).

Monopolistic Tendencies

The spirit of monopoly and local exclusiveness was not confined to Christians vis-à-vis Jews. The Jews in most of Europe during the Middle Ages and later had "an elaborate system of trade protection . . . called the *herem hayishuv* . . . a prohibition against strangers taking up residence in an established community without formal permission, usually but not always, the unanimous consent of that community being required." This was based on or connected with the established right of residence (called *hezkat yishuv*) of those who already lived there.

For our purpose here it is irrelevant that certain rabbis (Jacob ben Meir Tam [1100–71], for instance) were opposed to residence limitations in the Jewish community or that others argued that these and other monopolistic prescriptions were not based on the Talmud but were either extratalmudic community regulations or were based on custom. In fact they existed in most European Jewish settlements except in the Ottoman Empire, apparently from the eleventh to twelfth century. The rabbis' discussions about the basis of these prescriptions were ex post facto, although they may have had some impact on later generations who used them as models.

In those early centuries the Jews followed these precepts in what they regarded as the natural order of things.[2] The Jewish commentator Rashi (Solomon ben Isaac [c. 1040–1105]) was so impregnated with the monopolistic trends of his times that he projected them back into early antiquity. In commenting on the expression "the merchant of the peoples" attributed by the prophet Ezekiel to Tyre (Ezekiel 27:3), Rashi assumes that the principle of the (limited) "rights of strangers" of the medieval city existed in the times of the prophet Ezekiel. He says: " . . . and it was the custom to forbid merchants who came from the south to do business with those of the north and one with the other but the townspeople bought from the one and sold to the other"—an arrangement that was part and parcel of the medieval city (or those that had staple rights, restrictions for out-of-city traders).[3]

Discrimination against "outsiders" in Jewish communities was not limited to residence rights and economic competition; it also touched matters of charity and in some places even the recitation of the mourners' *Kaddish* in the synagogue. With regard to charity the maxim prevailed that "the poor of your city have preference," already formulated in Talmud (Babli, Baba Mezia 71a) and practiced during the Middle Ages and early modern times. In many places the right to say *Kaddish* was denied a stranger when a local man had to recite the prayer.

In Poland the rabbis, too, wavered between seeking a talmudic basis for the right of the community (kehilla) to impose residence and other restrictions, and regarding them as customs or ordinances that nevertheless had binding force. A good many of them favored the latter approach. They also rationalized the need for such restrictions in various ways, ranging from fear of the non-Jews to prevention of "interference with one's livelihood."[4] In practice, Polish Jewry had an elaborate system of control over the monopoly in residence rights, occupations, marriage controls, credit, and often also travel and many other phases of life in those times. These were decreed and enforced by the local communities, the regional and other community councils, and the rabbis, sometimes helped by the non-Jewish authorities.[5]

The Jewish community granted citizenship to some upon payment of certain "entry money"[6] but denied it to others. In some cases Jews were expelled by the community organization or had their rights curtailed and their freedom of occupational activity limited. Jews also—either on their own or sometimes in combination with non-Jews—petitioned the state or city authorities to curtail the activities of foreign Jews and non-Jews.[7] An outside Jew without residence rights was not permitted to settle or transact business in the Jewish city of Kazimierz, and Jewish sections of Poznań, Lwów, and others, and no local Jew was allowed to rent him a house or "a corner" in which to remain for a while. Generally a foreigner was not supposed to stay in Cracow longer than three days. Jews without residence rights in a city were forbidden to marry there or even to have the betrothal document executed there (apparently for fear that they might remain there afterward).

The limitations upon non-Jews were somewhat more stringent. Being outsiders in the Jewish community they were subject to all the proscriptions applying to foreigners. Thus Jewish middlemen and agents were forbidden to put one non-Jewish businessman in contact with another or to bring a non-Jewish consumer into a non-Jewish store. Many warnings were issued to such agents against showing a non-Jew "how to do business" or divulging Jewish business secrets to him. (The latter was also forbidden to Jewish business people.) Jews who brought skins or fur into Lwów were only allowed to sell them to Jews.

Some of the general proscriptions were stricter when they concerned a non-Jew; for example, Jews were forbidden to rent a room to a non-Jew or a foreign Jew for business purposes (in Wlodawa in 1782). The Jew, however, could have procured one there during a fair, but the non-Jew couldn't. Non-Jews protested, and anti-Semitic writers railed against the proscription "not to do business with Christians."[8]

These and similar restrictions by the Jewish communities were not unlike limitations imposed by the cities generally. Another area controlled by the Jewish community was rents and leaseholds. This was called *hazakah* (right of occupation) and was arranged in order to avoid rising prices for rents and leaseholds and competitive bidding. In time the Jewish community gained control of these rents and leaseholds as monopolistic tendencies increased among the Jews.

Non-Jews were protesting against this "boycott" and control of the rents and leaseholds, and anti-Semitic writers were railing against the proscription which discriminated against Christians. There were attempts to forbid the practice of *hazakah*. The sporadic demands that Jews be forbidden the use of the *hazakah* principle led to some local proscriptions during the first decades of the eighteenth century and finally to a general prohibition in 1781.

One may speculate as to the effectiveness of the proscriptions by the non-Jewish burghers against the Jews or by the Jewish kehilla in those centuries in Poland. One may also try to explain the Jewish proscriptions against non-Jews as a reaction to those of the burghers. But for whatever reason, the fact remains that the monopolistic-exclusion principles were also an integral part of the Jewish way of life and could thus not be regarded as a constant anti-Semitic factor directed solely against themselves.

One may surmise therefore that in those centuries Jews in Poland would not have considered the monopolistic principles of the preindustrial city to be a constant anti-Jewish factor, directed solely against themselves. They tried—just as others did—either to attain a similiar privilege for themselves or to disregard or circumvent in practice the privileges of others.[9] Living in a world of harsh realities, of arbitrariness, violence, and self-interest, the Jews were themselves to some extent permeated with the violent tenor of life, and some of them used similar tactics. In an epoch and in a country where most of the time people were in danger of attacks by Tatars and Turks, of wars, soldiers, and robber gangs on the roads,[10] insecurity became the normal way of life, for people had never known anything different. One may say that just as people (Jews included) traveled the roads and journeyed to neighboring countries on business despite the danger of being killed on the highways, they also coped with the dangers in their own country. Apparently everyone was aware of the hazards but shrugged them off.

In any event, danger does not seem to have loomed large in the minds of the Jews of the sixteenth and seventeenth centuries. Preachers and other social critics in the second half of the sixteenth to the seventeenth century complained that the rich businessmen were constantly on the roads, but they saw the main trouble to be not the physical danger (although this too is mentioned) but that these travelers were prevented from studying Torah and neglected the education of their children.

In other words, Polish Jews of those centuries appear to have accepted the divisive and brutal world in which they lived. Only in times of catastrophe and great suffering did they voice complaints or think of themselves as unduly oppressed. Here too the Jewish belief in redemption may have proved a somewhat comforting factor. The idea of a future to be realized through divine intervention may have made suffering appear to be a prerequisite for the glory to come, although this messianism did not make fatalists of the Polish Jews.

Status

The definitions and concepts by which some historians characterize the Jewish position in Christian states generally—"precarious political standing," "right of residence not rooted in public law," "not being indigenous," "alien character," "lack of 'equal rights' "—are inapplicable to the realities of the Polish situation in medieval and early modern times. Only a very small percentage of the population in Poland—the nobility, in about 1600 estimated at less than 10 percent of the country's total population—had any aspiration to "rights." Less than half of this small group (the magnates and the wealthy landed gentry) had standing and influence in the country. The rest were known as "cottage squires" who for the most part worked the land themselves and whose political position was more or less dependent upon those in power—the king and the magnates.

The main body of the Polish population consisted of about 70 percent peasants and 20 percent city dwellers. The peasants were predominantly serfs bound to the soil; they were devoid of all or most freedoms (of movement, choice of occupation, and the like) and were obliged to render services to the landowners. The approximately one-fifth of the population comprising the city dwellers included both "citizens" and "dwellers" or "half-citizens" *(incola)*, comprising the lower classes. There were some differences between the royal cities and those privately owned by the nobles. Only persons admitted to citizenship had any voice or any claim to rights in the city of their domicile. Each city was an autonomous unit in which a citizen from any other city was regarded as an alien who had first to be admitted to citizenship or granted residence rights if he wanted to settle there permanently.

A main criterion was not "birthright" or nationality or being indigenous, but rather religion—adherence to the Catholic religion. In fact, in the southeastern cities (Lwów, for instance), where larger groups of indigenous non-Catholics and non-Poles resided (Russians or Ruthenians and Armenians), the "Polish group" embraced all Catholics (ethnic Poles, Germans, Italians, and others). In short, the greatest part of the city dwellers had to acquire residence rights through special grants from the rulers and powerful groups (charters from the king or nobles establishing a city or granting it Magdeburg Law, or grants of citizenship made to individuals by the city government).

A considerable part of the population of these cities had no citizens' rights at all. Non-Poles or non-Catholics who had lived in larger groups on the same spot for many centuries (the Ruthenians and Armenians in the south) had only their own brand of citizenship (autonomy), or as Polish historians put it,[11] they were "citizens under Russian and Armenian law respectively," their (limited) rights having been granted by the kings or owners of the cities.

Similarly, Jews in Poland were citizens or residents "under Jewish law" (Jewish autonomy) with their (limited) rights granted by the king or nobleman, or based on agreements with the cities, or both. In short, the status of almost all strata in Poland, including the Jews, was connected with political positions (their own or of other groups), which in turn depended on time and conjunction of power.

There was, however, another important factor: religion. The Catholic religion was the dividing line between "first-class citizens," if we may call them that (Catholics or Poles) and "second-class citizens" (Jews, Greek Orthodox, Armenians, Muslims, and, after the Counter-Reformation, Protestants). The Catholic Church pressed for separation from and degradation of the non-Catholic, particularly with regard to placing the latter on a lower status than the Catholic and forbidding him to exert power over a Catholic (for Jews this was rationalized as a punishment for their rejection of Christ). Various groups (burghers and some lower groups of the nobility) used these church attitudes as rationales for their more materialistic attempts to attain or retain monopolistic rights, by excluding or discriminating against the non-Catholic groups and, in certain areas, particularly against Jews. To some extent practical needs contributed toward turning the theological theories into facts.

But general comparisons of the status of Jews and non-Jews are likely to be exaggerated, with too much emphasis on theoretical positions and theology and not enough on the practices. A factual comparison, in contrast with a fictitious one, should take into account both theory and practice and weigh one against the other.

To begin with formalities, Jews in Poland (with the exception of the very few who had been ennobled) did not belong to the upper stratum of society. Nor were they counted among the unfree peasantry—the lowest stratum of serfs, constituting about two-thirds of the population. Still dealing with formalities, Jews in southeastern Poland (the parts incorporated into the Polish kingdom in 1569) were legally on a par with the nobles with regard to the amounts to be paid as indemnification for being wounded or killed.* According to some unconfirmed information this was also true in ethnic Poland during the early centuries.

If we go beyond formality and consider the prevailing practice the position of the Jew appears in a more favorable light. If he could not *be* a nobleman, he could *act*

---

*In medieval Europe—including Poland—the law set a certain price on the killing or wounding of an individual. The rate was set according to the social stratum to which the victim belonged (highest for noblemen, lowest for peasants).

like one—or in the place of one. Jewish lessees of the king's or nobles' villages and towns or of various taxes and other sources of revenue were accorded broad powers and status-bearing functions, often over large expanses populated by many people, not all of them peasants. To these Jews were transferred almost all the lord's powers, mostly including the perquisites of local justice.

The chronicler of the cossack massacres in 1648—Natan Hanover—tells of a man named Zachariah Sobilenki, a Jew "who was its [the town of Czyhirin's] governor and administrator. He was the nobleman's tax farmer, a customary occupation among Jews in the kingdom of Little Russia. For they ruled in every part of Little Russia [meaning the southeastern parts of Poland]." Perhaps Hanover may have exaggerated somewhat and Zachariah Sobilenki may even be a fictitious name. But the fact that the tax farmers had great power is also indicated in other sources.

A number of Jews actually did behave like nobles—conducting themselves haughtily, arrogantly, arbitrarily, dictatorially, and sometimes even recklessly. Their conduct may have ranged from that of the Jews in Lwów who, as we have seen, beat up a Polish nobleman who happened to pass through the Jewish section at night, apparently while drunk (1565) to that of a Jewish father and son, masked and disguised as Russian princes (this may possibly have happened on Purim), who injured or killed a non-Jew in Brest Litovsk; to that of a rich lessee of taxes in Lwów, Nachman Isakowicz, who (on the model of a Polish nobleman) made a foray with a number of other Jews onto the estate of a noble who had refused to pay his taxes and trampled his fields until he paid up. There are other such examples. In the first half of the seventeenth century the son of Nachman Isakowicz, Isaak Nachmanowicz, a lessee of estates, oppressed the peasants and used strict measures against those who complained to the authorities.

Another in the same category was King Jan Sobieski's (1674–96) court Jew, Bezalel ben Nathan, president of the Jewish kehilla in Zólkiew from 1689 (died 1696). His main occupation was tax and toll leasing (he called himself a "toll administrator" of the king) in southern Poland. He apparently behaved haughtily and rigidly in his "domain," the toll offices in Lwów, thereby provoking the ire of noblemen and churchmen. His case was brought before the Polish *sejm* in 1693, and many accusations were leveled against him—including the charge that he desecrated the Christian religion. Stories and satirical songs about him were circulated, some of which were reprinted abroad.

Another such case (eighteenth century) are the brothers Samuel and Gedalia of Krichev and Sluck in the north, who were lessees of Prince Radziwill. They acquired wide powers over the latter's estates, behaved arbitrarily against the clergy, smaller nobility, and peasants; they collected excessive dues and used the Radziwill soldiers to suppress the protests of those who suffered at their hands (their handling of matters with an iron fist is said to have been one of the reasons for the Vorshchilo uprising of the 1740s). According to Solomon Maimon these brothers had leased all the estates of Prince Radziwill and through hard work and thrift had not only improved the estates but also enriched themselves in a short time. They also treated the Jewish sublessees and innkeepers brutally, rousing them from idleness by flogging. They became known among Jews by "the name tyrants." (The Hassidic legend connected the names of these lessees with the Besht.)

A number of cases are also known in which a non-Jewish tax collector, a nobleman, or a court usher was simply afraid to enter the houses of prominent Jews on business, not wanting to risk being thrown out or beaten up. And there were Jewish riffraff who took revenge on noblemen who attacked Jews. Such boldness, which may have resulted from a feeling of security, was experienced not only by the individual Jew but also by the group or community organization. Already mentioned earlier was the case of Jews in Lwów who in 1616 refused to open the cellars of a house that had burned down for inspection by city authorities, arguing "we have our own offices" —meaning the kehilla. Many similar instances are known in which Polish Jewish communities or other groups refused to follow Polish court summonses or orders from other offices, and demands for payment of levies by regional offices were dealt with either passively (by doing nothing) or actively (by denying the validity of these demands).[12]

A more appropriate way to compare the status of Jew and non-Jew would be to consider conditions for Jews and non-Jewish city dwellers respectively (both being what we would now call generally middle class). We have seen that both Jew and non-Jew had either to acquire citizenship and residence rights in the city or be descended from one who had acquired them. Catholics had an advantage over non-Catholics in that only they could become full-fledged citizens of royal cities. But Jews could settle in private cities and exercise rights that were similar to or not too much dissimilar from those of Christians. In these cities the Jews were often called citizens, and to a degree they participated in elections to the city council and other offices.[13]

The generally lower status of Jews in the royal cities and in some private ones was in reality somewhat balanced by the existence of certain influential Jews who had access to the people in power, as well as by the practice developed in Poland during the sixteenth to eighteenth centuries of arranging agreements with cities[14] under which Jews were regarded somewhat as equal contrahents. The original idea of the agreements may have been to limit Jews in the cities. In practice it turned out that most prolongations of such an agreement—often arranged for ten years or so—led to enlargement of the Jewish sector or economic concessions (mostly owing to the support of the king or nobility), or both. The same also goes for the participation of the Jews in the city guard and their assumption of responsibilities in defense of city walls, particularly in the south.

The fact that kings granted some Jews, side by side with non-Jews, the honorary title of "king's servant," putting them under the direct jurisdiction of the court and exempting them from any other jurisdiction and most taxation or custom duties, must have given them some prestige.* Many preserved documents from the south-

---

*Bershadski assumes that a "king's servant" must have worn some sort of distinguishing emblem or symbol.

eastern region of Poland show Jewish names preceded by the title "sir" *(pan)*, just like non-Jewish ones, which may indicate some standing of the given Jews in the eyes of the scribe or grantor of the document.[15]

On the other hand, one should not overlook the fact that as a non-Catholic minority the Jews were on the whole regarded as inferiors (to say nothing of the occasional attacks upon them). Jews apparently also felt debased by a practice that developed in some cities: students of the Jesuit colleges and other schools would demand certain payments or gifts from Jews passing through. In some cases, as in Cracow, this was handled as a kind of tax having certain rates. The Jews complained about it to the rector of the university and heads of other institutions.[16]

But despite these shortcomings the non-Jews as well as the Jews themselves seem to have evaluated the Jewish position as one of some standing. Apparently one should not take at face value the constant complaints voiced by non-Jews about the high standing of Jews—these may be regarded as exaggerations. But we do have other, apparently more objective, statements. Cardinal Commendoni, who made two journeys in Poland during the second half of the sixteenth century, writes that many Jews lived in the (Polish) Ukraine, and, unlike Jews in other regions, they were not despised. On the contrary, they owned land, engaged in a large variety of occupations, and were well-off, highly respected people. Externally they did not differ from Christians: they were allowed to wear swords and bear arms and enjoyed rights similar to those of the rest of the people.

Jewish sources generally seem to indicate that many Jews regarded their status (either in theory or practice, or both) as a rather high one. It has already been mentioned that Solomon Luria—possibly having in mind the situation in the southeastern parts, where he functioned for some time as a rabbi—claimed that Jews who held charters (privileges) were on a level with the "knights" (nobles). Natan Hanover, like most of the other chroniclers of the 1648 catastrophe, depicts Polish Jews as having enjoyed high status and nostalgically recalls the "paradise lost." While nostalgia is generally likely to produce exaggerated images of the past, in this instance the rosy picture seems to have been partially authentic—or, more important for our present purpose, *the Jews of that time believed that it was.*

Over a century later the undertones of Ber of Bolechów's memoirs seem to reflect the view that in dealing with nobles, high state officials, or leaders of city councils, the Jew was more or less on an equal footing with them. In one instance he mentions in passing that the commander of the garrison in Lwów called him "My good sir," as he would an equal.

Wealthy Jews with good connections among those in power and, on the other hand, underworld elements believed in their own ability to take care of themselves, or to invoke the protection of the powerful. They frequently resorted to hard and brutal measures to achieve their ends—as did the nobles at one end of the scale and the non-Jewish underworld elements at the other. Many of them also often felt capable of finding their own way in the non-Jewish world without need of the protective arm of the Jewish community. Despite the disapproval of the rabbis and the communities, some Jews took their cases before non-Jewish courts. They were apparently sure that if they turned to non-Jewish authorities they would not encounter discrimination. The arrogance and self-assurance of such Jews is expressed well in a statement to a Jewish court made by a leaseholder of royal revenues, which is quoted in a responsum. The Jew declared: "I do not want to fulfill anything that Jews [Jewish court] decide. I wanted only to see if Jews will pronounce judgment over me or what manner of Jew would dare force me to be adjudicated by them."[17]

In short, the status of Jews in Poland was, or the Jews believed it was, like that of the other groups, determined in practice by their access to people in power and their ability to exploit it.

Views and Attitudes

The views and attitudes of Jews in those centuries concerning countries and non-Jews, as conveyed in verbal pronouncements, are not easy to determine. There were, of course, no pollsters in those times. What the Jews talked about among themselves remains unknown. (They used to gather outside the synagogue on the Sabbath and holy days after prayers and discuss everything under the sun.) Only through an oversight is an occasional sentence or two preserved that divulges an attitude on secular matters. Almost the entire written Jewish heritage has a religious veneer and deals with problems of religion, morals, and traditional views, or with the religious aspects of secular matters. This means that it is repetitive and uses mostly "models" rather than actual situations.[18]

Jewish tradition is bound up with the ideological concept of unbroken continuity since ancient times.[19] For this reason it has a tendency to repeat some old clichés with little information on actual views, and moreover what little there is, is inadvertently concealed. Rabbis may have qualified their legal statements according to time and place, but the phraseology was nonetheless repetitive. Their actual opinions were indicated by emphasis of one point and de-emphasis of another, by rationalization of an exception, by an inadvertent "heresy," or by a homiletic explanation.

Actions, too, often divulge attitudes. By doing some things and avoiding others, and by the way they do these things, human beings frequently betray their attitudes, their loves, their likes and dislikes. All this may explain the specific form of political views found in Jewish sources.

The first extant Jewish view on Jews in Poland comes, as mentioned, from a German rabbi Meisterlin in the 1440s, who mentions that the monk Capistrano was endangering the Jews "living under the Polish king in the kingdom of Cracow . . . which had for long served as a haven for the [Jewish] refugees."[20] We have to wait a century more for any record of the views of Polish Jews themselves. These originated with two of the most prestigious Polish rabbis of the sixteenth century, Solomon Luria (1510–73) and Moses Isserles (c. 1520–72). We have already spoken of Luria's opinion that Jews in Poland have settlement rights as free men "like the knights [noblemen]"; he praises the kings "who many times are kind to Jews and postpone for them the time of tax payment." Rabbi Moses Isserles of Cracow writes to a former student of his: "In this country [Poland] there is no fierce hatred of us as in Germany. May it so continue until the advent of the Messiah." He also says: "You will be better off in this country . . . you have here peace of mind." And in another context, when he is concerned about a feud between Jews (apparently in the 1550s), he points out that "this matter . . . may cause harm in Poland . . . where the king is well disposed towards our brethren. . . . Had not the Lord left us this land as a refuge, the fate of Israel would have been indeed unbearable. But by the grace of God, the king and his nobles are favorably disposed toward us."[21]

A colleague from Isserles's student days, Hayim ben Bezalel (1530-88), who studied in Poland and then left the country to become a rabbi in Friedberg, Germany, writes later how much better off the Jews are in Poland than in Germany: "It is known that, thank God, His people is in this land not despised and despoiled. Therefore a non-Jew coming to the Jewish street has respect for the public and is afraid to behave like a villain against Jews, while in Germany every Jew is wronged and oppressed the day long."[22]

The Polish rabbis mentioned earlier not only expressed approval of Poland but showed a positive attitude to that country in legal matters as well. Jews in galut (exile), eager to conduct themselves according to Jewish law, used the maxim "the law of the state is the law,"[23] in order to give, as it were, a "Jewish approval" to state legislation. However, this was understood to concern only general or original laws of kings and other legitimate rulers (not arbitrary decrees), and levies imposed on all inhabitants (not arbitrarily on a certain group or on individuals). In practice this did not really mean that the Jews could limit the ruler's power to legislate or to collect taxes. It amounted to recognition of the legal status within the Jewish community of a Jew who acquired property confiscated by the ruler from another Jew or one who became a lessee of taxes levied by the ruler. The recognition of the legality of the ruler's legislation or of his right to levy this or that tax as coming under the principle "the law of the state is the law" involved, as it were, recognition of his deeds and a positive attitude toward his rule.

In this connection we have a number of decisions by the two mentioned Polish rabbis of the sixteenth century. Solomon Luria accords such power not only with respect to original laws, but also "everything that the king innovated." He also extends the same rights to the noblemen in the affairs of their domains, and says they are entitled to any kind of levy even "if it is not fixed."

Moses Isserles goes still further. Under the principle of "the law of the state is the law" he accords recognition to a rabbi's appointment by the king and not by the Jewish community (it is possible that his own appointment as rabbi in Cracow came from the king) and acknowledges the "legality" of Jews' registering real estate deals and mortgages in the city records instead of the kehilla offices. (Concerning the latter he rationalizes that "if we should disqualify in these lands the non-Jewish laws concerning real estate the whole order will be ruined and no one's property will be secure."[24]) These legal opinions and legal arguments clearly show a positive view of Poland and her treatment of Jews.

Another sixteenth-century Polish Jewish source, the Karaite Isaac ben Abraham of Troki (1533–94), contrasted the situation in those countries where Jews suffered severe oppression and from which they were expelled (England, Spain, France) with conditions in those countries where Jews lived undisturbed, which apparently included Poland. He maintained that Christians were murdering Christians in England, Spain, and France (the Catholics were the victims in England, the Protestants in Spain and France) because God was punishing those countries for their oppression of Jews. In other countries in which Jews lived, the rulers "punish evildoers and those who would harm Jews, and strengthen the Jews with privileges that enable them to dwell in peace and security. The kings and nobles of these states—God give them peace—love good deeds and justice; therefore they do not do evil or harm the Jews living in their countries."[25] For this reason God sent peace among them.

The high regard in which Jews held Poland and her rulers apparently led to the creation of several legends. For instance, the minute books of the Jewish community in Kazimierz-Cracow tell of a fire that broke out in January 1595 in the royal castle (Wavel). The king, Sigismund III (1587–1632), we are told, refused to allow anybody but the Jews to extinguish the fire or to rescue his valuables.

And the king stood and looked on as the Jews exerted themselves and saw the conscientiousness with which they returned all the things rescued from or which were taken away during the fire . . . and this brought "a big peace" and the king's heart turned and he became a different person, to do good to his people Israel.[26]

King Sigismund III is characterized about half a century later by the chronicler of the 1648 cossack massacres, Natan Hanover, as one who "loved justice and loved Israel."

Most of the views presented here originated with the elite, the rabbis and the writers, but they are in some part relevant to the facts of life for other Jews who used general (non-Jewish) offices and general courts instead of the Jewish institutions. The mentioned rabbis' reactions were to some extent intended to provide a rationale for these actions and yet at the same time maintain the illusion that Jews followed Jewish law. In fact, we know of many examples of Jews' using general courts and offices to make contracts and to execute a variety of documents, or of their taking their cases to general courts.[27]

We hear of Jews spurning Jewish institutions in favor of non-Jewish ones. These incidents may range from instances where individual Jews—mostly wealthy ones—were seeking and obtaining special privileges that exempted them from the jurisdiction of the kehilla, to cases where whole groups preferred the general institution to the Jewish kehilla. A case in Kazimierz in 1608 may be characteristic. The kehilla and the city signed an agreement which among other things turned over some houses and lots to Jews for homes. The kehilla wanted to take over these properties and sell them to individual Jews. But the Jewish population protested vigorously and demanded the right for individual Jews to acquire them from the non-Jews (the city and probably also individual burghers). The leaders of the kehilla were forced to accede to their demand.[28] This would indicate that at least some Jews had confidence in the Polish court and in part also in the municipal offices, and believed that they would not encounter discrimination or derision there.

Trust in the Country

Trust in the stability of the country and its institutions and belief in their own relative security are apparently indicated by the very considerable scale upon which Jews in Poland functioned as entrepreneurs and businessmen. Uncertainty, extreme fear of what the future holds, or volatility of the sociopolitical atmosphere are not usually conducive to investments and large-scale operations—at least not to any that go much beyond the liquidity stage and the flexibility of short-term deals. Jews in Poland, however, were building tax farming, estate leasing, and commercial empires; erecting large houses to live in; and trying to amass (to some extent successfully) large fortunes to leave to their children.[29] Jewish sources relate: "Jews are building houses like the castles of the noblemen." "He is always building new enterprises and does not finish them during all his life." "He who tries to collect a big fortune does not do it only for himself but wants to leave it for his children." "There are those who inherit or leave inheritances, houses, wealth, gold chains."[30] Documentary evidence reveals that large fortunes were actually left by some Jews.

These attitudes of trust and confidence, possibly even pride, in Poland also come to the fore in a theoretical way in cryptic remarks made by rabbis and other Jewish authors of those times.* Some sixteenth- to seventeenth-century rabbis and preachers seem to have taken pride in the prosperity in Poland, stressing the opportunities open to Jews to rise on the economic ladder or the generally favorable attitude of the Polish creditor toward the Jewish debtor. Others, who criticize the drive to become rich among their contemporaries, depict them as self-made men making the most of their chances and optimistic about their own and the country's future.[31]

Some theories were voiced about the distinction that wealth brought. It was thought to prove God's grace toward the given individual or to be, as it were, remuneration for good deeds—which is to say that the rich are either elected by God or are pious and virtuous people. But the critics of society connected riches with a "love of the Diaspora" and a close relationship with non-Jews.[32] Both opinions show the high prestige achieved by wealth in Jewish society and are indicative of a positive attitude to the country and its rulers. (Good connections with the majority usually give prestige to minority peoples.)

The material opportunities afforded the Jews in Poland were not the only grounds

---

*The rabbis hardly expressed political views, but considered such views only as rationales for decisions in legal or ritual matters.

for their attitude toward the country. Jews generally valued their own way of life. Professor Maier Balaban, the late Jewish historian, formulated it this way:

> *Jews had their own objectives and aspirations, their institutions, courts, synagogues, schools, councils, their own taxation and means of implementation, their own* Weltanschauung, *their streets and towns, their rituals and ceremonies, their special rights recognized by the Polish government, their attire, their customs and behavior patterns, their guilds and associations, and their own language used at home and in community life.* [33]

The elite and the rabbis whose opinions have been preserved generally prized the self-government, the autonomy of the kehilla, and the regional and central councils that functioned in Poland. They considered the kehilla important for the Jewish group, both as an organization and because it helped them to maintain the Torah and its prescriptions.

Jews may also have regarded the overall organization of the community structure —the Four-Land Council—as a prestigious institution. At least this would seem to be indicated by Ber (Birkenthal) of Bolechów's words in the second half of the eighteenth century. According to him, the Four-Land Council was not only an institution to distribute the tax load among the Jewish communities and in which "great rabbis" drew up "regulations in accordance with the Jewish law," but it also afforded the Jews some status. "It was a small solace and a little honor, too, proving that Almighty God in His great pity and great lovingkindness had not deserted us." [34] In fact, in polemics Polish Jews argued that the Four-Land Council's eminence in Poland proved that God's promise, "the sceptre shall not depart from Judah" (Genesis 49:10), had been kept in the form of a political institution such as the Four-Land Council. This indicated that God's promise concerning the Messiah is also assured [35] of being kept.

The kehilla's tasks were held in such high esteem that they created a climate of adoration of the kehilla's leadership among at least certain groups of Jews. Some Jews looked upon these leaders as deserving of homage for having been "elected to high office by God." To others their power resembled or surpassed that of the Sanhedrin (high court) in the time of the Second Temple, or of the talmudic scholars, or the exilarch—all venerated personages among Jews in earlier ages. The good relationship of certain individuals with officials or important noblemen was both the cause and the effect of the prestige accorded these wealthy and influential community leaders. [36] From leadership of the local kehilla one might go on to become a delegate to and subsequently a leader of the regional Jewish Community Council and later of the Four-Land Council, the highest institution of Jewish autonomy. At each step one came into personal contact with more important officials and noblemen—at the top with the treasurer and deputy treasurer of the realm and certain other leaders of the state. In some cases these official contacts might also have led to close business relationships and consequently to "friendship in high places" with benefits for the leader himself and for the cause he was representing. Through the process of personalization the kehilla institutions acquired added value in the eyes of these leaders. The ultimate distinction for such a leader was to be presented to the king. Then he might become a court Jew and be honored with the title "servant of the king," or in rarer cases "secretary of the king." Either title opened for the appointee not only the likelihood of high honors but also a number of advantages in business affairs.

The rise of the Jewish community leader through the stages of the community hierarchy (and his increasing contacts with the influential officials and personalities) may have worked in two different ways on any given individual—but in our context both led to similar results. The most direct progression was the identification of the individual with the institution. The higher he rose on the ladder of prestige the more important to him the institution—the Jewish kehilla structure—became. But others abandoned ship in midstream, as it were. They (and some other Jews who attained wealth and prestige in different ways) used their contacts to free themselves from the Jewish kehilla—to obtain special privileges that exempted them from kehilla taxation and from kehilla adjudication. The trait common to both groups—those who identified with the kehilla and those who sought dispensation from it—was at least a certain trust in the outside world, in the Polish state and its leadership.

Appreciation and Identification

Jews in Poland, at least the rich and prosperous ones, the leadership of communities and councils and others, did not live in isolation. Having to be alert to both pro- and anti-Jewish trends in their environment and being able to share in the opportunities within the country, they apparently came to appreciate not only the objective possibilities, but also their chances of availing themselves of these. The wealthy Jewish merchant, the leaseholder of taxes and estates, the estate manager, and the importer came somehow to identify themselves with the country and its people.

Rabbis and preachers, possibly with a measure of exaggeration, pointed out that rich Jews were forgetting that they were in exile and were building permanent homes for themselves there. "The rich ones mostly live in peace and mix with non-Jews," wrote E. Luntschitz. Isaiah Hurwitz, writing sometime before 1623, was concerned about the manner in which such Jews regarded redemption: "A healthy and rich man," he argues, "does not need the redemption . . . what will it give him?" The rabbi advises such persons to think about past and possible future dangers so as not to appear hypocritical in saying prayers that express hope for redemption.[37] From the eighteenth century we again hear that Jewish businessmen and purveyors for the armies have widespread businesses, are grown powerful and haughty, and have little to do with Torah and the holy books. Another author relates that some Jews who deal with nobles often visit them dressed like non-Jews, fail to keep the Jewish dietary laws, and adopt the non-Jewish way of life. In his autobiography Maimon tells of a rich Jew who was leasing farms from the nobles: "This fellow was an ignoramus; [he] did not even understand the Jewish language; he used Russian."[38]

These rich and powerful Jews were also aware of the fact that wealth and power were "guarded," directly or indirectly, by the state, by the noblemen protectors, by the privileges and monopolistic rights granted to them either from without or from within (*hazakah* or right of occupation of the kehilla)—the latter itself made possible by the "outside" and protected by it. They began to look favorably on the non-Jewish world.

The poorer Jews, being generally excluded from the monopolies and lacking status, were of course not pleased about their exclusion. But their anger and opposition—which also found expression in the social criticism by some preachers—were turned against the seemingly immediate cause of their troubles, the Jewish elite groups, rather than against the outside world. On some occasions they even preferred protection by the authorities to protection by the Jews. Some rumblings of opposition may be detected in the seventeenth century, and active opposition by the lower groups to the kehilla hierarchy first appeared in a number of places in the second half of the eighteenth century (see below, chapter 12).

As in the preceding century, in the seventeenth we find a number of voices extolling the memory of the Polish kings. Ladislas IV (1632–48) is depicted as "pious" or as a "kind and benevolent king, who loved justice and loved Israel." Elsewhere he is characterized as "an upright king who is counted among the righteous who was always kind to Jews and kept his covenant with them." King John Casimir (c. 1648–68) is portrayed as "a just king, a God-fearing man, a friend of Israel."[39]

Some documentation also exists about Jews defending or rescuing Polish nobles. A Jewess saved the life of the Polish manager of a town when an assassin tried to kill him. In 1684 Jews joined the non-Jewish burghers of another town in beseeching raiders plundering the noble "to stop assaulting our lord." These episodes may also serve to indicate the Jewish attitude.[40]

In Catastrophic Times

The tribute to the Polish kings Ladislas IV and John Casimir was written during and after the catastrophe that befell the Jews and Poland with the cossack uprising of 1648 and the other tribulations, which lasted twenty years (see chapter 9). The Jewish writings of and about these catastrophic times, mainly the chronicles, clearly reveal identification with the Polish viewpoint—especially with that of the nobility —and a tendency to avoid or to minimize placing blame on the Poles for Jewish suffering. The Ukrainians, the cossacks, and to some extent also the Tatars are presented as "a contemptible nation," who are "lowly and vile." The traits attributed to them in the Jewish sources are not dissimilar from the ones in the Polish writings: they are "cruel, tricky, unreliable, cheats, contemptible, defiled, unclean, lowly peasants." There is also an observable tendency to make it seem that Polish commanders took special care of Jews and exerted special efforts to defend or to rescue them.

The chronicles and stories dealing with events of those years in which any sort of interpretation of the historical facts is given (such as Hanover's *Yeveyn metzulah* or Meir of Shebershin's *Zok Haitim*) are written from a pro-Polish viewpoint. When they report the miserable lot of the Ukrainian peasants, whose exploitation by the nobles contributed to the uprising, they do not seem to be condemning the Polish nobility and state. They tend to put almost all the blame on the Ukrainians. Reporting on the Polish-cossack wars, the chronicles (particularly in Hanover's *Yeveyn metzulah*, which is the most comprehensive) not only identify Jews with the Polish forces ("God was with us and with the king"), but are quite apologetic about Polish debacles, which are attributed to the slyness of Chmielnicki or to antiquated Polish practices.

For the most part nobles and Polish commanders are depicted as being concerned with the well-being of the Jews.

> *The nobles befriended the Jews exceedingly and became united with them . . . which contributed to the rescue of many. . . .*
>
> *Count Jeremy Wiśniowiecki was a friend of Israel . . . and with him escaped some five hundred Jews. . . . He carried them as on the wings of eagles until they were brought to their destination. . . .*
>
> *If danger lurked behind them he instructed them to proceed ahead and if the danger was in front, he went before them as a shield.*

Wiśniowiecki and another commander, Count Radziwill in Lithuania, are said to have undertaken campaigns solely for the purpose of avenging Jews. Against such a background the few reported cases (by Hanover) in which local Polish commanders or other Poles betrayed Jews (in Tulczyn) or refused to admit them into a fortress (Dubno), thus denying them protection from attack by cossacks, appear in these writings as aberrations from the general trend of Polish-Jewish cooperation. The report of the Tulczyn incident is an inexplicit description of the manner in which the Ukrainians broke their promise and later killed the Poles and the Polish commander, after having tortured him. "As they did so did God repay them, because they violated the pledge of the Jews. When the nobles heard of this, they were striken with remorse and henceforth supported the Jews."[41]

Such attitudes on the part of the Jews and their identification with the Poles are not specifically mid-seventeenth-century phenomena. About a hundred years later other cossacks, the *haidemaks*, renewed attacks in certain parts of the Ukraine. In Uman in 1768 many a Jew suffered a martyr's death.

The motif of a Polish general, Ksawery Branicki, who went out of his way to avenge the Jews killed in Uman and elsewhere reappears in Jewish sources. He is classified as a Hassid (pious man) who comforted the Jews and captured "many thousands" of *haidemaks* whom he had executed. We are not interested here in the measure of truth contained in this story (general sources ascribe the capturing of the few hundred—not thousands—of *haidemaks* to the Russian general Krechetnikov, while the Polish general Branicki merely decided their fate later). In our context it is interesting to point out that in the 1660s and the 1760s the Jewish chroniclers —mostly themselves refugees and survivors—and storytellers about the massacres identify with the Poles in the general analysis of the adversity. They also take pains to emphasize real or imagined special efforts by Polish commanders and leaders to defend Jews. A comparison with our times makes it clear that the attitude of those centuries is quite different from the stories told by refugees and survivors of the holocaust of 1939–45. In our time most writings by survivors of the Nazi massacres generally emphasize the collaboration of the various populations in occupied Eastern European countries with the Nazis in exterminating the Jews.* Historical comparisons across the centuries may be very tricky undertakings. The losses in our times were much greater both in terms of absolute and relative numbers. But one would seem justified in viewing these attempts of the seventeenth and eighteenth centuries as a result of pro-Polish attitudes of the times. This also seems likely from the valuational undertones of the nostalgia in looking back to Poland of the years before 1648.

Natan Hanover, writing some years after 1648, equates Jewish institutional life in Poland from before the catastrophe with that of Jerusalem before the destruction of the Second Temple. In terms of Jewish traditional values such a comparison denotes a high valuational approach. Hanover writes:

> *The Pillar of Justice was in the Kingdom of Poland as it was in Jerusalem before the destruction of the Temple. . . . For in every province there was a great Court. . . . If two important communities had a dispute between them, they would let themselves be judged by the heads of the Council of Four Lands. . . . The leaders of the Four Lands were like the Sanhedrin. . . . They had the authority to judge all Israel in the Kingdom of Poland . . . and to punish each man as they saw fit.*[42]

Another refugee, Moses Katz of Narol, later a rabbi in Metz, calls the country "Poland the admirable, devoted to Torah and high purposes."[43]

Valuation and Sympathetic Approach

The valuation and sympathetic approach to Poland seem to have persisted among Jews in the country until the state disappeared and or even later.

From a Polish Jewish cabalist, Heshel Zoref (died 1700), is preserved a vision about Poland that boils down to the statement that the Messiah will come first to Poland and Lithuania. About half a century later Jacob Frank (1726–91), the false

*Most of those published in countries belonging to the Russian bloc are exceptions. For political reasons the image there is being perpetuated of the respective native populations, particularly the Communists among them, making many special efforts in behalf of the Jews during the dark Nazi years.

Messiah who rose in the 1750s (see chapter 11), taught that Poland is the "chosen land": "It is the country that was promised to the patriarchs. Were I to be given all the countries of the world filled with jewels I would not leave Poland, since it is God's legacy and also the legacy of our fathers."[44]

According to the Hassidic stories[45] Israel Baal Shem Tov—Besht—(1700–60), the founder of Hassidism, seems to have had a positive attitude toward the non-Jewish population. He definitely opposed dealing dishonestly with non-Jews, regarding this as a cardinal sin. The clergymen in his stories are pictured as oppressing Jews, as is to some extent the *kommissar* of a town (the Christian manager who works on behalf of a landowner), whereas the nobleman owner appears for the most part as honest, not unkind, sometimes even pro-Jewish—although in one instance it is remarked that he behaves so only for his own benefit. On the other hand, the serf or peasant is usually characterized as likely to kill anybody, justifying his action "as non-Jews usually do" by rationalizing "the devil bit me."

Jacob Joseph of Polonnoe tells the story of a Jew who approached the landlord and attempted to outbid another Jew by offering to pay a higher rent for the leasehold. "The lord admonished the bidder: 'How did you dare to make your friend suffer?' "[46]

Pinchas of Koretz (c. 1726–91) seems to have trusted the Polish forces to stop the attacks of the cossacks (in 1768, at the time of the Gonta attacks) and opposed the idea that Jews should leave the Ukraine. He seems to have definitely belonged among those who had a positive attitude toward Poland. He expressed his opinion that Jews in Poland had an "easy galut," "easier than anywhere" (Germany and Turkey). He "protested" against Russian occupation of Poland and maintained that his prayers kept the Russians away.[47]

Some eighteenth-century Hassidic leaders may well have had stronger pro-Polish sympathies than the few stories would indicate. A residue of such feelings is found among subsequent generations of Hassidim.[48] The Hassidic leaders' attitude may have been connected, incidentally, with their realistic approach to "the now and the then," despite their mysticism and to some extent esoteric phraseology.

An anonymous Polish Jewish author, writing at the end of the seventeenth or the beginning of the eighteenth century, apparently gives the Poles "an attestation of fairness" by the statement that "it is well known that whenever a gentile [a Pole] knows that a Jew regards something as forbidden to him, he will never force the Jew to transgress his religious proscription" *(Taharot Hakodesh* [Amsterdam, 1733]).

Ber of Bolechów's memoirs generally show him to have been pro-Polish at certain times—both by the facts of which he writes and the manner in which he does so—even to the extent of stating that Polish officials were more inclined than the Jewish authorities to grant Jewish victims of a fire top rebates or postponement of payment of taxes, or that owners of towns and Polish officials helped Jews. His criticism of Poland concerns chiefly the dissolution of the Four-Land Council in 1764 and the lax utterances of the noble: "He talked in the hypocritical manner of the nobles."

Solomon Maimon, writing his autobiography in Prussia in the 1790s, a time and a place in which disdain for the deteriorating Polish state had developed, despite his criticism of the Polish landlord's intemperance admits that Poland has some virtues even while he depicts the negative aspects:

> *There is perhaps no country besides Poland where religious freedom and religious enmity are to be met with in equal degree. The Jews enjoy there a perfectly free exercise of their religion and all of their civil liberties; they have even a jurisdiction of their own. On the other hand, however, religious hatred goes so far that the name of Jew has become an abomination, and the abhorrence, which had taken root in barbarous times, continued to show its effects.*

It stands to reason that the pro-Polish sympathies of the Jews may have influenced their attitudes and actions during the Kościuszko uprising against the Russians in 1794–95. The Polish authorities' actions just prior to this uprising were not the sort to encourage Polish patriotism among Jews (in 1793 the Jews were about to be expelled from Warsaw). Nevertheless, Jews—apparently not necessarily the assimilated and polonized ones, whose number was minimal in those times—did play a role in the April 1794 insurrection against the Russian armies in Warsaw. Many sources confirm that groups of Jews helped the Polish forces in the insurrection, sometimes attacking Russian outposts on their own initiative and capturing cannons. Jews are also found to have participated substantially in the further stages of the Polish uprising in Warsaw and throughout the country. They manned a special Jewish regiment, joined militia outfits, furnished financial and material support such as uniforms and caps.[49]

Opinions, Attitudes, and Reality

The selected items in the foregoing pages cumulatively seem to point to a trend in at least part of Polish Jewish society. For our purpose the facts need not be proven true or false. We are not interested in the concrete facts themselves but rather in how the contemporaries viewed them. This does not imply either that the opinions, attitudes, and trends analyzed are deviations or that they constitute the norm. It is also not to be taken as indicating that the rabbis or the Jewish society, or both, of those centuries were either blind to their "real situation" or were so pro-Polish that they failed to see the drawbacks attendant upon living as a minority in that country. In fact, Hebrew sources do not overlook the tribulations of life in Poland generally or of life as a minority.

The rabbis mentioned above, as well as other rabbis and authors, will on occasion bewail the Jew's lot or point out that the Christians make false accusations (libels) against Jews, (mainly blood libel and accusations of desecration of the holy wafer). They also report attacks on the Jewish quarter against which Jews sometimes defended themselves and either succeeded in repulsing the attackers (in Poznań in 1688) or were overpowered by them (at Lwów in 1664, and others). Information on a considerable number of such cases (libels, attacks, and so on) is preserved in the form of entries in community records, dirges, or penitential prayers. These usually tell the story of an attack or murder, or an eventual rescue, depicting the torture and the burning at the stake of the accused, noting the latter's piety in dying as a martyr. Their tune is generally subdued and tearful, bewailing, complaining, asking God's help and compassion, or praying for deliverance from exile. There are also derogatory epithets for the adversaries (the attackers are "irresponsible," "feckless," "murderers," and the municipality that did not prevent the attack is "the wicked seat," those who believe in the wafer story are "fools"). There exist also a number of such items revealing angry undertones—God is asked to avenge the blood of the martyrs, or grievances are expressed against God's patience with the evildoers and oppressors.[50]

The Jews' difficulties and sufferings are also mentioned in some other writings. Almost all of them—including those alluded to earlier—use stereotyped images and older metaphors such as biblical verses to express their dismay or to depict the ordeals. In short, the authors of sixteenth- to eighteenth-century Poland did not gloss over the distress and suffering. In some cases they use harsh language about the tormentors; in others they spread rumors about impending dangers. Moreover, some of the authors manifest both pro and con opinions on Poland, depending upon the period or the case they deal with. Rabbi Joel Sirkis (1561–1640), for instance, deals with land ownership in connection with a Jewish ritual concerning willow twigs used for the Feast of Tabernacles. According to the Talmud these twigs should not come from stolen or confiscated land. Contrary to the eleventh-century approach, Rabbi Sirkis maintains that they may be taken from non-Jewish property, for "it should not be assumed that the non-Jews [in Poland] generally steal land from each other since an orderly legal procedure exists among them." But he adds that non-Jews may seize Jewish property, "as we see they bring false charges against us."[51] Even Solomon Luria who, as mentioned earlier, expressed favorable opinions about the king and the nobles and their handling of legal matters, occasionally finds non-Jews untrustworthy ("all their words are lies").

Thus it remains open to speculation which of these attitudes, the "good" one or the "bad" one, took precedence in the minds of the people of those times. (The pro-Polish view may have been motivated by the *need* to cultivate confidence in the country and its people for the sake of being able to continue to live there in relative tranquillity.)

But the oft-quoted Solomon Luria himself may offer an inkling of how Jews really saw their situation. He writes: "The Jews [Israel, in his words] in this time must not prosper too well in order to avoid becoming too proud, nor must they suffer too much punishment or they will vanish. All nations disappear, but the Jews prevail." He takes this statement from older sources but presents it so as to reflect his own times and views depicting the Jewish situation in Poland as neither ideal nor intolerable.

III

Events and Trends

Background

Life for the Jews in Poland developed within the framework of their social and political situation in the country and the changes taking place there. Fluctuating conditions, immigration, settlement and increasing numbers, physical assault and self-defense, competition, swings from prosperity to crisis and back, pressure or the lack of it—all these were the "normal" background of the struggle for existence.

Other, more drastic events often had a greater impact, either locally or regionally or even over the whole country. Among these were fires, epidemics, famines, wars and their aftermath, invasions, movement of military detachments pillaging and burning as they went back and forth, and raids, either by neighboring noblemen or (in the south) by Tatars or Turks. A statistical computation of such events (for instance, epidemics occurred in 1621–31, 1648, 1652–54, 1659, and 1660–62) may appear horrendous to a modern man who finds it hard to believe that people were able to endure so much. But these were not all such dreadful episodes and within the context of the time may not have been so unusual.

The late Dutch historian J. Huizinga depicts West European life around 1500:

Calamities and indigence were more afflicting than at present; it was more difficult to guard against them, and to find solace. Illness and health presented a more striking contrast; the cold and darkness of winter were more real evils. Honors and riches were relished with greater avidity and contrasted more vividly with surrounding misery.

In Poland, with a harsher climate than Western Europe's and untamed rivers that often overflowed their banks, all this may have been even more "afflicting." Living in such an environment may have meant that periodic epidemics, fires, and occasional famines were regarded simply as "normal calamities." In most cases Jews— apparently no less than other peoples—succeeded in rebuilding their houses in a relatively short time (in some cases the new houses were an improvement on the old ones). And not all epidemics gave rise to wholesale dying; some of them merely raised the death rate slightly. Nor did the movement of military detachments inevitably involve disaster and cruel oppression.[1]

In short these and other events varied in intensity and impact, and the people may have regarded them as a part of the exigencies of life to be feared and complained about when they occurred and rejoiced over when they passed easily or without much damage.

But there were also historical events that had a deeper and longer-lasting significance, deriving from the context in which they took place and the impact they exerted upon society. During the last two centuries of the existence of "Old Poland" (Poland before the partitions) certain historical events created for the Jews conditions transcending the normal. These were "the deluge" (as the mid-seventeenth-century catastrophes became known in Polish historiography), the attacks by the *haidemaks* (the cossacks, during the eighteenth century), and, in a different vein, the messianic trends of Sabbatai Zevi in the seventeenth century and Jacob Frank in the eighteenth, as well as Hassidism and the dawning Enlightenment (Haskalah) of the eighteenth century.

Both the material type of event, such as the catastrophes, and the spiritual trends as they developed in Poland were more or less consistent with the whole structure of the country and of Polish Jewry, despite their international significance in some instances. They also contributed to changes in Jewish life in Poland even though some of them had been transplanted in part from other countries.

9 The Catastrophe—
Cossack Uprising in 1648
and Its Aftermath

The Catastrophe

The cossacks (the name is of Turkish or Tatar origin and means "independent war adventurers") were apparently a by-product of the tension between the nomads of the southern Russian steppes and the inhabitants of the settled borderlands. We find them in the Moscow state (Russia) in the fifteenth century, comprising mainly Tatars in the service of the Russian state. In Poland the cossacks were mostly eastern Slavs and others who formed in part a sort of defense force against the Tatars.

Beginning with the fifteenth century, the newly founded khandom of the Crimean Tatars (descendants of the Mongols who had invaded the area in the thirteenth century) became a robber state whose hordes often raided the Ukraine,[2] devastated many places, and carried off both property and people. They used the latter as serfs, sold them as slaves, or held them for ransom. The Polish-Lithuanian state was unable to protect its borderland inhabitants completely from this menace. The sparsely settled population armed itself and created mobile squads whose members became known as cossacks.

By the middle of the sixteenth century the cossack warriors had organized themselves in the virtual no-man's-land on the lower Dnieper River and beyond the famous cataracts *("Zaporozhe")*. Among other things they were freebooters who occasionally raided the Crimea or Turkish possessions. Runaway serfs—mostly Ruthenian in origin—and adventurers of various nationalities, including some Jews, swelled the numbers of the cossacks.[3]

The Polish state soon began enlisting some of the cossacks to serve either in defense of the borderlands or as troops in its numerous wars. The cossacks drawn into service were granted the status of free warriors and enjoyed many privileges. The number of such "free" or registered cossacks varied in accordance with current needs, at times reaching significant proportions (forty thousand in 1621).

In due time a process of social stratification developed among the cossacks, whose leadership acquired—or aspired to—rights and privileges and wealth resembling those of the lower Polish nobility. On the other hand, registered cossacks who were dropped from the group (from the "register") were liable to revert to the status of serfs, subject to rule by the Polish nobility, that is, the landlords. This created tensions between the Polish state and the cossack community. Yet this situation tended to prevent development of too sharp a social gap between the "free" cossacks and the masses of Ukrainian peasant-serfs.

Another binding force between the two groups was the Greek Orthodox faith. They both sought to resist the pressure brought on them in Poland since 1596 to force them to become Uniates (who adhered to Greek Orthodox liturgy but recognized the authority of the pope). They upheld the purity of their religion, trying to defend the traditions and beliefs of their forefathers while regarding it as a symbol of their nationality and an expression of their freedom and independence. This religious or national antagonism (nationalism in those centuries was expressed in religious terms) had also a social angle, which made it more acute. The nobility and the magnates in the Ukraine, who owned most of the land and the villages, were Polish Catholics. As the overlords of the Ukrainian peasants they exploited them economically and forced them to carry a heavy burden of feudal dues and payments. This multiple split between the adversaries was apt to flare into active conflict at certain times, as happened more than once during the half-century preceding the uprising of 1648.

The Polish ruling class's apprehension concerning the possible growth of the cossacks' strength, plus changing attitudes toward the "free" cossacks, and the variety of positions taken by the local rulers, caused the Polish state to try to cut down the number of registered cossacks (in 1625 there were 6,000; in 1630, 8,000). These were some of the factors that contributed to several cossack rebellions (in 1592, 1595/96, 1625, 1630, 1635, and 1638). Such uprisings were easily suppressed by the Poles. But the insurrection by the Ukrainian forces that began in 1648 was destined to alter the whole history of the Ukraine and Poland and to precipitate a changed balance of power in all of Eastern and central Europe.

It was apparently set in motion by one cossack chieftain's reaction to wrongs he suffered at the hands of a Polish noble and high official. Bogdan Chmielnicki—a partly polonized man of means, whose father had served as a Polish official—had had some of his possessions confiscated and he was imprisoned. Chmielnicki fled at the end of 1647 and began to agitate for revolt. The cossack masses' dissatisfaction with the reduction in the official register and the looming threat of being again reduced to serfdom, as well as the religious, national, and economic tensions existing in the Ukraine between the Orthodox Ruthenians and the Catholic Polish overlords, helped to broaden the scope of the uprising. It evolved into a political struggle for freedom by the Ukrainians. Chmielnicki's alliance with the Tatar ruler and later with Russia gave the civil war international overtones.

In the beginning a few thousand registered cossacks went over to Chmielnicki, and he was soon able to muster an army that combined with the Tatar hordes to defeat the inadequate Polish forces sent against him. Ruthenian peasants, townsmen, some of the poorer Greek Orthodox gentry and clergy, some Poles (the Jewish chronicler Hanover says "some Polish lords") either joined the insurgents or formed detachments of their own. They traversed the country (May–June 1648) inflicting ruthless punishment upon nobles, Catholic clergy, Jews, and Uniates; they destroyed cities and towns in the Ukraine and spilled over into White Russia.[4] The accompanying Tatars looted, took many captives and left for home laden with booty. Amid this chaos Polish King Ladislas IV died. Chmielnicki then, for the most part, ceased his attacks. During the last months of the year Chmielnicki was again on the move. He defeated a Polish army, laid siege to Lwów, and reached Zamość in Poland proper in November, but returned home soon after.

The newly elected Polish king, John Casimir (1648–68), a brother of the deceased king, tried unsuccessfully to negotiate with Chmielnicki. The latter demanded full independence for the Ukraine. Later in 1649, when cossack-Tatar forces again struck at the Polish army, the Polish king managed to lure the Tatars into a separate peace (according to some sources he paid them a sizable sum), which forced Chmielnicki to a compromise. A peace or truce between the Poles and the cossacks was arranged in August 1649. Known as the Zborów Peace, it designated the voivodships (provinces) of Kiev, Tschernigov, and Braclaw as an autonomous cossack region. But there was reluctance on both sides to strive within their respective groups for acceptance of the truce. Each realized that some of the terms would not be acceptable in his own camp. Meanwhile, the cossacks, and particularly the local Ukrainians, blocked the return of the Polish nobles to some parts of the Ukraine.

Generally, however, the Zborów Peace brought a sort of pause in hostilities lasting about two years. Chmielnicki meanwhile entered into diplomatic relations with Russia. Then Chmielnicki and the Tatars again began to move against Poland. They were badly defeated (June 1651 near Beresteczko in Volhynia), and withdrew. The following September a peace was concluded but the Polish diet failed to ratify it. After almost two years of political meandering Chmielnicki and the Tatar khan were again in the field against the Poles by the end of 1653. The Tatars, however, concluded a separate peace with Poland in December 1653. Chmielnicki's negotiations with the Russian tsar to put an autonomous Ukraine under Russia's protection soon became a reality by virtue of an agreement signed in Pereyaslavl on January 18, 1654.

This launched a new war in which Russian and cossack forces marched together against Poland in the Ukraine and in the north in Byelorussia and Lithuania. By August 1655 the Russians and cossacks had captured Wilno (today Vilnius) and slaughtered several thousand of its inhabitants. Other cities such as Polock, Vitebsk, and Smolensk also fell into their hands. In the south a Russian army joined Chmielnicki in his new attacks against Poland. Cossack and Russian forces again laid siege to Lwów, captured Lublin, and reached the Vistula River (October–November 1655). This time the Tatars were on the Polish side. The pressure of the Tatar forces caused Chmielnicki to retreat.

Swedish Invasion

Meanwhile Charles X Gustavus of Sweden invaded west Poland. On September 8, 1655, he captured Warsaw and advanced toward Cracow. The Polish king fled to Silesia. Cracow fell on October 19. By the end of 1655 almost all of Poland except for Lwów and Gdansk was in the hands of the Swedes, Russians, and cossacks. Most of the Polish nobles had sworn allegiance to Charles, and the Polish state seemed doomed.

Requisitions, robbery, pillage, terrorism, and massacres by the Swedish army, and the rise of a Polish national spirit, provoked anti-Swedish riots and the organization of partisan skirmishes that culminated in an insurrection. The Polish king returned to Lwów at the end of 1655 and subsequently secured an armistice with Russia (where apprehension concerning the growth of Swedish strength was increasing). The war between Sweden and the Poles—with both their regular armies and (on the Polish side) Stephan Czarniecki's partisans participating—raged for the greater part of 1656.

By the middle of the year south Poland was virtually free from Swedes. Warsaw was retaken by the Poles and then lost again. By the end of 1656 the Swedish king negotiated a compact for the partition of Poland among Sweden, Brandenburg (Prussia), Transylvania, cossack Ukraine, and the Lithuanian magnate Boguslas Radziwill, who aspired to become the ruler of Lithuania. In 1657 this led to a new invasion of Poland by the Transylvanians and cossacks from the south and the Swedes from the north. George Rackoczy of Transylvania failed to take Lwów but captured Cracow.

Meanwhile, Sweden's back door became threatened by Denmark (which was allied with Poland), so that Charles Gustavus was forced to return to Sweden. Rackoczy was beaten as he rushed his forces to the aid of his homeland, which was being devastated by Polish troops. Cracow was retaken by the Austrian forces that came to assist Poland. The Polish-Swedish war was officially ended by the treaty of Oliva (near Gdansk) in 1660.

Cossack Ukraine

Soon after 1654, when cossack Ukraine became affiliated with Russia, the latter had made attempts to reduce cossack autonomy. Following the death of Bogdan Chmielnicki in 1657, pro-Polish tendencies increased among the cossack leadership, and this led to internal dissension. By the fall of 1658 the cossack leadership (or the influential sector of it) signed an agreement returning the Ukraine to Poland as an autonomous unit. The formerly dual state (ethnic Poland and Lithuania) became a threefold commonwealth (Poland, Lithuania, and Ruthenia), with special privileges for the Greek Orthodox religion in the "Ruthenian duchy."

Although the Moscow army invading the Ukraine was defeated by Polish-cossack-Tatar forces in July 1659, discord among the cossack chiefs continued. Russian attempts to regain the territory led to new Russian-Polish wars in 1660 and 1663, with the eastern Ukraine reverting to Russia as a protectorate (1659) and then back to Poland (1660).

Finally, in January 1667 the treaty of Andrusovo was signed between Russia and Poland. Under its terms the Ukraine was divided between Poland and Russia with the Dnieper River forming the border.

The twenty-year "deluge" (as the catastrophe is called in historiography) began with Bogdan Chmielnicki's 1648 uprising and came to an official end with the treaty of Andrusovo and the defeat of the Tatar-cossack forces that entered Poland in the summer of 1667.[5]

Devastation and Impoverishment

The wars and invasions, the concomitant outbreaks of epidemics (1659–63 and other years), famine (1655–56 and 1662–63), the plundering and murder committed by both foreign and Polish soldiers who retaliated against the populace when they were not paid, combined with the destruction wrought by the cossacks, Tatars, and Swedes, devastated city, town, and village. Incomplete figures show the depopulation of many villages and a decline of population in town and city (Warsaw, Poznań, and Cracow lost half their population), and even total destruction of many towns.[6]

The Jews and Cossack Uprisings

As mentioned, large numbers of Jews had settled in the Ukraine—including Volhynia and Podolia—during the sixteenth and seventeenth centuries. Between 1568 and 1648 Jewish population is estimated to have grown tenfold to twelvefold. A sizable number of these Jews, as we have mentioned, fulfilled economic functions as leaseholders of villages or whole towns as well as of inns, and as collectors of revenues for the nobility or the royal domain. Leaseholding was frequently associated with the exercise of certain powers, including jurisdiction over various sectors of the population. These activities and powers placed the Jews in the role of the Polish landlords, as it were, so that they often became de facto overlords in relation to the "lowly" (as the chronicler Hanover calls them) Ukrainians. In this way the Jew became identified with the Polish nobility—the Establishment, to use a modern concept—and was regarded as sharing responsibility for the real or imagined pressures exerted by this Establishment. Hanover, chronicler of the Chmielnicki uprising, may reflect the general climate of opinion when he relates: "[The Jew] was the nobleman's tax farmer, as was customary . . . of most Jews in the kingdom of Little Russia [Ukraine]. For they ruled in every part . . . a condition which aroused the jealousy of the peasants, and which was the cause of the massacres."

The Jews aroused no less resentment than the Polish overlords, possibly at times even more because of general anti-Jewish trends prevailing at various levels of Christian society in those times and because the peasant came into more contact with the leaseholder than with the landlord. The peasants, the "lowly" Ukrainians, who joined the cossack uprising, were the more extreme in terms of anti-Jewish and anti-Polish feelings and actions, and may have given an added impetus to the cossack atrocities and murders.

In fact, even before the 1648 revolt Jewish leaseholders were blamed for allegedly stimulating the spread of lawlessness. Contemporaries of the cossack revolt attribute it also to the extortionist practices of the Jews. Some memoir writers (the memoirs having been written or published later) mention also that the people hated the Jews because the latter were leaseholders of the Greek Orthodox churches. They allegedly held the keys to these church buildings and controlled their use. It is said that Jews demanded a fee for permitting the christening of a child, a wedding, and other church affairs. This theme appears again and again in Ukrainian folk songs and other material.

Actually, the churches may only rarely have been included in the leasehold of a village and thus controlled by a Jewish leaseholder. But the theme of control of the churches by Jews as a cause of the revolt and the cossacks' allegedly special mistreatment of Jews seems to have been generalized for purposes of anti-Jewish propaganda or as a justification for atrocities committed against Jews. Be that as it may, in an attempt to justify his 1648 revolt, Chmielnicki himself mentions "the wrongdoing, oppression and animosity of the Jews and Poles" but says nothing about religious matters. Not until much later is the motif of the churches having been in Jewish hands quoted in his name.[7]

This does not mean to say that a permanent animosity existed between the Ukrainians and Jews. In normal times relations between Jews and non-Jews seem to have been more or less amicable.

As related elsewhere in this book, the need for defense against the frequent attacks by the Tatars brought Jew and non-Jew together, officially—since both were obligated to take part in the self-defense—and also privately. This may be indicated by information from those regions about Christians "borrowing garments and jewelry from Jews to wear when attending church services on Christian holidays." Natan Hanover's references to "friendly Ukrainian neighbors" or to Ukrainians who "at first appear to the Jews as friends . . . [but] are deceitful and untrustworthy" may imply some sort of at least superficially good relationship. A complaint voiced by an estate owner that "the rebellious peasantry [of his estates] drew the Jews onto their side" may also denote that they were on good terms. Friendship between Jews and cossacks may also be deduced from Hanover's apparently fictitious story about the beginning of Chmielnicki's revolt. This story tells about two Jews who have the same last names: Zachariah Sobilenki and Jacob Sobilenki. The former is depicted as having informed upon Chmielnicki to the Polish authorities, causing him to be jailed, while the latter was his friend and advised him how to escape from jail.[8]

As mentioned, in dealing with a complaint the Polish ambassador pointed out to the Tatar khan that there were Jews among the cossacks. Some Jews had actively participated before 1648 in cossack detachments that went out either to loot or in defense.

A document dated 1620 forbids Jews and burghers in two cities to take part in cossack raids, and this may indicate that they had been doing so. A rabbinical source tells of a Jewish woman who demanded a divorce because of her husband's participation in cossack raids. A rabbinic responsum mentions a Jewish hero named Boruch, killed in 1611 near Moscow, who may have served in a cossack detachment. It should also be mentioned that the preserved cossack registers from 1619 to 1649 contain a number of Jewish names, which may have belonged either to Jews or to baptized Jews. One source (June 1648) tells that in some places attacked by cossacks "many Jews convert to Christianity and join the cossack forces." In general both before and after 1648 we find some baptized Jews in the Ukraine who rose to the rank of leader of cossack detachments, or became bishops in the Greek Orthodox Church. A story that is told about one commander of a cossack detachment, who, being a newly baptized Jew, intentionally stationed part of his troops near the Polish lines and later defected to the Poles, may also indicate that some baptized Jews served as cossack commanders—even though the facts of this particular story are not true (the commander mentioned there by name was not of Jewish origin[9]). Other information, too, seems to confirm the assumption about some closer relationship between cossack leaders and Jews at certain times.

In the 1590s the financial affairs and estate of a cossack leader were apparently managed by a Jew. And if one may believe a pastor from Stettin who accompanied a Swedish ambassador on a visit to the Ukraine in 1657 and had an audience with Chmielnicki, it would appear that the latter's treasurer was a (baptized?) Jew. Several decades after the end of the wars the cossack leadership in the Russian part of the Ukraine requested the Russian government to allow Jews to return to those parts, and they themselves used Jewish leaseholders on their estates.[10]

But any existing neighborly or personal relations between Jews and cossacks were cast aside by the force of the developments in times of upheaval. The spirit of revenge that forms the usual "popular sense of justice and sanctions the most rigorous penalties" was widespread among the lower classes of society. The primitive violence of the peasantry, as well as the general tenor of cruelty in those times, helped to turn the revolt into a war of extermination and atrocities against Poles and Jews.[11] The masses of the Ukrainian peasants and some of the townspeople regarded the revolt as a chance both to free themselves from the jurisdiction of their lords and to take revenge for real and imagined oppression by killing, looting, and destruction. Hanover depicts the Ukrainians as people "armed with clubs and scythes . . . inexperienced in warfare . . . [who fought] by loud and bitter shouting." This does not mean the regular cossack detachments, which were well trained, but the peasants and others who joined in. These Ukrainians, especially the villagers and their leaders, constituted the more radical and bloodthirsty wing in Chmielnicki's camp.

A recorded cossack attack on Jews seems to have occurred in the early 1620s. The cossack chieftain of the time, Borodawka, who had previously accused Jews of blaspheming Christianity, induced the cossacks to strike at the Jews in the Ukraine. During another cossack rebellion (Pawluk in 1637–38) the cossacks killed some Jews (two hundred according to Hanover) and Polish priests, and destroyed synagogues and churches. A decade later, in 1648, Chmielnicki is said to have ordered all Poles and Jews killed. When the cossack colonel Nebaba sent a detachment to take Gomel he ordered them to exterminate the townspeople down to the last one, as well as to burn the town.[12]

In practice the cossack revolt set in motion in April–May 1648, in which the Tatars participated and which swept the Ukraine for the better part of a year and was repeated in subsequent years, also embroiled other parts of Poland and Lithuania and brought death—often cruel death—and destruction to the Polish and Jewish urban populations. Some were taken prisoner and removed by the Tatars to their homeland or sold on the slave markets. Others survived by converting to the Greek Orthodox religion[13] or fled before the onrushing armies.

Most of the victims—Jews and Poles—suffered horrible deaths. Some of the stories told by contemporaries resemble the cruelties and horrors perpetrated by the Nazis in our own times. We hear of people being skinned alive; some commanders made a practice of this, afterward burning and destroying towns or parts of them. A letter written from Warsaw on August 2, 1648, tells of towns near Chernigov that capitulated to the cossacks, who subjected the Catholic nobles and the Jews to torture.

In the city of Mogila [?] they slaughtered 800 noblemen together with their wives and children as well as 700 Jews, also with wives and children. Some were cut into pieces, others were ordered to dig graves into which Jewish women and children were thrown and buried alive. Jews were given rifles and ordered to kill each other.[14]

The fact that some were buried alive is also confirmed in a Jewish source.

The Jewish chronicles have information to offer about the brutality and cruelty with which the Jews and Poles were killed.

Some were skinned alive and their flesh was thrown to the dogs; some had their hands and limbs chopped off and their bodies thrown on the highway to be trampled by wagons and crushed by horses; some had wounds inflicted upon them and were then thrown on the street to die a slow death . . . others were buried alive. The enemy slaughtered infants in their mothers' laps. They were sliced into pieces like fish. . . . The infants were hung on the breasts of their mothers. Some children were pierced with spears.

And about Zaslav it was written: "The Jews were led to the cemetery. . . . [They] entered the chapel on the cemetery and were killed there. Afterwards the building was set on fire. . . . The Catholic priests . . . were skinned alive while the dukes who had been interred for a long time were exhumed from their graves and tossed aside."[15]

We learn that again in 1655, when the Russian army and the cossacks captured

Lublin, they speared and tortured Jews or killed them some other way. As a result, "death and annihilation reigned" over the Jewish city. In White Russia, Russian and cossack forces did their share of killing and martyring the Jews. Other Jewish and non-Jewish sources tell of brutality and atrocities committed on Jews and Poles: women were raped, synagogues and churches were burned, cities and towns were destroyed.

When the Polish partisans under Stephan Czarniecki were clearing out the Swedes in western Poland they took "revenge" on many a Jewish community (and on Germans), whom they accused of collaboration with the enemy. The cruelty of these "Polish heroes" was essentially no less tyrannical than that of the cossacks and Russians.

In general, the murder of the population—Jews, nobles, Catholic and Uniate clergy (including nuns), Catholic and Uniate burghers—began immediately with the first moves of the Chmielnicki army in May 1648. The Tatar hordes, however, who several times came to Chmielnicki's aid in Poland, had no interest in exterminating the population and were seldom involved in such undertakings. Their main purpose was to gather as much booty as possible and to take prisoners, whom they would later either receive ransom for or sell on the slave market or employ as serfs. In fact, the agreement between Chmielnicki and the Tatar khan gave the Tatars the right to prisoners—Jews and Poles—and apparently it was binding on the cossacks to deliver such captives. Only ill or older prisoners were sometimes killed off by the Tatars. Hanover, with his flair for dramatization and exaggeration, may be depicting the real difference in the treatment of the Jews by Tatars and cossacks when he tells a story of how Jews from four communities went willingly over to the Tatars rather than fall into the hands of the cossacks.

> *They said: if we wait until the Ukrainians invade the city we will all either perish or we will be forced into baptism. . . . It is preferable that we fall captive to the Tatars. . . . This they did . . . some three thousand souls. . . . When the Tatars came into the city [the cantor] began to chant mournfully the prayer El maleh Rachamim [O God full of compassion]. . . . All the people burst into intensive weeping . . . the compassion of their captors was stirred. They consoled them with expressions of sympathy and said, "Do not despair. . . . There are ritual slaughterers among you, let them kill an abundance of sheep and oxen for your need and soon we will bring you to your bretheren in Constantinople to be ransomed."*

While Hanover estimates that there were three thousand Jews in this group, another source gives the numbers involved in two communities that went over to the Tatars as nine thousand persons.[16]

Regardless of the Tatars' real attitude toward the Jews, the Jews did not usually sit around in their homes awaiting their arrival, any more than they waited for the cossacks. Immediately following the first defeat of the Polish forces (May 16 and 26, 1648) Jews (and Poles) began a hurried flight—despite its being a holiday,

Shavuot (May 27)—northward and toward the fortified cities. "All of them took flight . . . unmindful of their gold and silver. They ran for their lives. . . . Whoever failed to escape or was unable to flee was killed." Such flight occurred again and again when the cossack forces advanced and approached the places where the refugees were. For a period of about two months after the first flight Hanover reports that "on that Sabbath . . . rows of horses and carts moved along three abreast, and for a stretch of seven miles . . . and [there were] innumerable pedestrians."

But fleeing did not always lead to safety. Many were overtaken on the way by the cossacks or peasants who had joined the cossacks. Others were caught in the cities where they gathered and perished there (Nemerow, Tulczyn, Narol, Polonnoe, Ostrog, Zaslav, Bar, and others). Sources tell of burghers in some of these cities who deceived the Jews, even though the latter were willing to fight the enemy out of the fortress. We are told of cossacks disguised as Poles being admitted to Nemerow and of a Polish commander in Tulczyn who tricked the Jews and delivered them to the cossacks. In Polonnoe the traitors were the Ukrainians who served in the Polish army, while in Bar the local Ukrainians let the cossacks in.

On the other hand, the Poles and the Jews collaborated in the defense of a number of fortified cities (Lwów, Żólkiew, Zamość, Brody), and the Poles refused to comply with Chmielnicki's demand that they deliver the Jews into his hands. And Poles and Jews together paid the demanded ransom money[17] (despite the Lwów burghers' bitter complaints to the *sejm* and bishop a year before [1647] that the Jews had "grabbed all the business").

During a lull in the military activities and the retreat of the cossacks southward, which came in late fall of 1648, and again after the Zborów Peace of 1649 some Jews returned to their homes—only to have to flee once again or to suffer death and martyrdom from new attacks by the cossacks. This was repeated in Lublin and in the northern parts, where cossacks and Russian army detachments killed Jews (Mogilev) or mistreated them, took them prisoner, or deported them to the interior Russian regions. Others again fled: some to Prussia, Amsterdam, and Hamburg, and some to Silesia and other places.[18]

Jews during the Swedish War

The Swedish armies demanded contributions, high excise taxes, and requisitions that affected the Jews as much as or more than the Christian population. But there is also some information about special mistreatment of the Jews by the Swedes. In Poznań the Swedish soldiers plundered the Jewish stores after they had occupied the city. In Kazimierz and Cracow both the Swedes and the Poles plundered Jewish stores. In several other places the Swedes killed the Jewish population. On the other hand, the Polish detachments and the partisan groups under General Stephan Czarniecki, who mistreated and murdered Jews, harassed the Swedes and reconquered many places from them.

It is difficult to say just how Jews in western Poland came to be regarded by Poles as traitors, since the Swedes did not handle them with kid gloves—unless one ventures the notion that Polish nobles who had gone over to the Swedes and sworn allegiance to them at the beginning of the Swedish war later needed a scapegoat to clear their own names. At any rate, as early as the beginning of 1656, when the king on his return to Poland was staying at the southern estate of the chief commander, Jerzy Lubomirski, he supposedly heard rumors that the Cracow Jews "showed the Swedes the weak spots of the Cracow fortifications and together with them stole the silver from the churches." On January 22, 1656, the king issued a document giving to the commander of the Polish army and the chancellor (state treasurer) the "Jewish city of Kazimierz" (Cracow), together with all the synagogues, houses, wares, valuables, and money left there by the Jews. Possessions of individual Jews who were accused of being traitors during the Swedish war were confiscated; in some cases these were returned after the owner had been cleared of the charges. A year later, when the expulsion from Poland of the anti-Trinitarians charged with treason was considered, ideas about expelling Jews were apparently rife. The same accusations also reached the ears of Czarniecki's partisans, who were fighting the Swedes. Catholic clergymen spread ideas about treacheries committed by Lutherans, anti-Trinitarians, and Jews. Some anti-Swedish propaganda writings of the time also contained anti-Jewish and anti-Trinitarian motifs. Some peasants maintained they had been told to kill Jews and Germans.

To some extent the attacks on Jews were the more extreme excesses of the soldiers in Czarniecki's detachments. Apparently having first allowed them certain "liberties" with the civil population, he was later unable to control their excesses either by orders or even by severe punishments (he complained about this situation in his letters to the king). Among the sectors of population attacked, the Germans and Jews were the hardest hit, the pretext being vengeance "for helping the Swedes." Whatever the context, the fact remains that a number of Jews were tortured or killed by the Czarniecki soldiers. According to one Jewish source 3,220 or 3,580 Jewish families (sixteen to twenty-one thousand Jews) were killed by Czarniecki's troops in twenty-seven to thirty cities and towns; many of these towns were burned down.[19] Other sources mention other towns (Gniezno, Pila [Schneidemühl], Pakość) where Jews were killed off, either by the Swedes or by the Poles.

Self-defense

Jews in southern Poland, as mentioned earlier, usually participated in the defense of the cities and towns. In same cases they were required to fulfill specific defense roles during the period of the cossack revolt. Both general and Jewish sources relate something about these efforts. According to information in the chronicles, Jews in Tulczyn defended themselves alongside the Poles. There were, we are told, two thousand Jewish fighters in Nemerow and "a number" of them in Polonnoe. Near Zaslav there were supposedly a few hundred Jewish fighters in the Polish army. It is also reported that a thousand Jews joined the Polish army near Beresteczko in 1651 while in Komarno, Lwów, Żólkiew and other places that the cossacks could not conquer Jews are reported to have participated very actively in the defense of the fortresses.

There exists also some information about Jews helping to defend Pinsk against the Russians and cossacks in 1655,[20] and a rumor about Jews having fought the Swedes together with the Polish armies near Sandomierz. When the Russian army laid siege to Vitebsk (this lasted fourteen weeks), non-Jewish neighbors affirmed later that the Jews stood guard, each having his own arms and each one doing his bit in defense against the assaults of the Russians. These fragmentary scraps of information can hardly be said to depict a quantitative participation by the Jews in the defense effort, and some may also be exaggerations, but they do indicate that such duties were undertaken. It appears also that the Poles valued the Jews' participation in the defense as a positive contribution. If Hanover is to be believed, some Polish commanders took Jewish detachments with them—or permitted such detachments to be formed—when they set out to take revenge on cossacks or Ukrainians. The role of Jews is clearly evinced by the fact that when the king feared that the cossacks were again about to move on Poland, he issued an order in May 1651 to prepare the defense of Cracow and decreed that the Jews should defend "their city, Kazimierz" themselves. In some cases the Jews may even have played a major role in defense. Thus we are told that in Bar a limited number of German mercenaries, together with the Jews and a few non-Jewish citizens, were a whole day "hitting the cossacks powerfully with the cannons."[21]

Losses

Loss of life and property among both the Jewish and the general population loomed large during these two decades of insurrection, invasions, and wars. Losses were caused by both invaders and attackers and, in part, also by Polish army units. Famine and epidemics, which swept either the whole or parts of the country during these years, contributed further to the havoc. Depopulation, burned-out towns and villages, desolation, hunger, and wholesale death were reported from many parts of Poland.

Jews, of course, suffered together with the whole land; in fact, they appear to have taken more than their share of the trouble. The attacks by the Czarniecki partisans upon Jews, on the pretext that the latter had been traitors at the time of the Swedish rule, is one example. The slaughter in the Ukraine may or may not have affected as many Poles as Jews, but the percentage of Jewish victims in the Jewish population (population estimates range from 170,000 to 480,000) seems to have been much higher than the comparable percentage of the non-Jewish victims in the total population (about ten million).

There is no way of comparing the ratio of Jewish and non-Jewish victims of the several epidemics[22] and famines. Lwów suffered an epidemic in 1651 and Cracow in 1652. According to a letter from Cracow requesting help, 1,250 Jews were supposedly dying every week in that city. Further information on deaths from hunger and epidemics comes from other places.[23]

In the matter of material losses we have a similar situation. Many sources—including official documents and the chronicles of those times—attest to the confiscations, robberies, and loss of Jewish wealth and property without, however, making it possible to gain any idea of the extent of such losses. If figures generally had little actual meaning before the age of statistics (some scholars classify them rather as "pictorial numbers" that are not approximates but rather "a part of a literary style" with no foundation in fact), then this applies also to figures appearing in both Jewish and non-Jewish sources dealing with "the deluge." Polish Jews at that time may have had a rather well-developed business mentality, so that figures connected with financial activities may have had more meaning for them that they did for non-Jews. In connection with population figures (and population losses), however, Jews may have been influenced more strongly than Christians by the biblical tradition (Samuel 24:1–16) that one should avoid counting people. And this may have helped make the numbers concerning people gross exaggerations.[24]

In general recent scholars dealing with the catastrophe of 1648–67 have attempted to take a more realistic approach and to be more critical of figures mentioned in the source materials. They consider them highly overstated and try to check them against reality. Thus it has been pointed out that the figure of hundreds of thousands (300,000 or 360,000) of cossacks and Ukrainians supposedly participating in the battles is an impossibility demographically, since the total population of all parts of the Ukraine involved in the revolt amounted to no more than one million. Others point out that figures given for those times (of Tatars, the Polish army, and so on) may be magnified as much as ten and more times.

Similarly, the Jewish chronicles of the period generally repeated various unverified rumors that filled the air at that time without having been able to check them or feeling the need to. Numbers meant little to these writers. (Hanover, for instance, confuses 1,800,000 with 18,000,000 and is somewhat inaccurate about dates.)

Thus the Hebrew chronicles tell of a Polish army of seventy thousand or eighty thousand fighting the cossacks in the fall of 1649, whereas the total Polish army generally amounted to between fourteen and eighteen thousand. Similarly, Hanover depicts the Polish army at the time of the battle near Beresteczko (August 1651) as being 680,000 strong (300,000 before Beresteczko and 300,000 reserves, plus 80,000 foreign mercenaries), whereas the total Polish army before Beresteczko amounted to only 33,000 men.[25]

Similar exaggerations could be found in the figures given in different chronicles for the number of victims. There is a wide discrepancy between one chronicle and another concerning many of the individual cities and towns, and most of the collateral sources give quite different figures.[26]

What we have said about the figures for individual localities also applies to the general quantitative information on Jewish losses. A summary of the figures for loss of life as reported in Jewish sources would appear as follows:

Yeveyn metzulah: killed, over 80,000; died in epidemics, 41,000 or 141,000; taken prisoner by the Tatars, over 20,000.

Petach Teshuva: destroyed, more than a thousand kehillot.

Megilat Eifa: killed, 100,000 during the first two years.

Zaar Bath Rabim: destroyed, 744 communities.

Tit ha-Yeveyn: destroyed, 140 (or 262) Jewish communities; killed, 670,000 (or 600,070?) householders and their wives and children.

This would amount to some 2,400,000–3,300,000 Jews,[27] an impossible figure for a Jewish population estimated to number between 170,000 and 480,000 persons. Menasseh ben Israel gives a figure of 180,000,[28] with 600,000 (sic) still remaining in Poland!

These figures are all grossly exaggerated, very much like the ones in the general sources, and those in *Tit ha-Yeveyn* are patently absurd. The fragmentary information of the period—and to a great extent information from subsequent years, including reports on recovery—clearly indicate that the catastrophe may not have been as great as has been assumed. In Kowel, a town in Volhynia, for instance, the sources declare that the Jews were killed by the cossacks and local Ukrainians in 1648 (one source has them drowned in the river). But when things had again quieted down Jews apparently began to return, or neighboring Jews came to settle there. Before long the Jewish population had considerably increased, so that the non-Jews requested—and received from the king (in 1670 and 1681)—a renewal of their older privileges prescribing certain limitations on settlement of Jews and the latter's obligation to participate in the guard and other activities. A generation later (1707) the Jewish population in Kowel had grown so large that it spread over most of the city and was to some extent crowding the non-Jews, constituting about two-thirds of the whole population.[29]

Pinsk in the north is apparently mentioned twice in *Tit ha-Yeveyn* (the second time as "Pinzach"). One entry gives the number of Jewish householders in Pinsk as 800 (3,200–4,000 persons) and the other as only 300 (1,200–1,500 persons) and "almost all were killed." The other two chronicles mention that most of the Jews succeeded in fleeing, leaving behind only a few "poor Jews" who were killed.[30]

In fact, Pinsk was conquered by the cossacks at the end of October 1648 and held by them for two weeks, and then in October 1655 again by the Russian and cossack forces, who remained there for a few days. Pinsk again came under cossack rule for five days in December 1659 and in the summer of 1660 for about two weeks. Some two years after the first occupation by the cossacks a court document (dated April 1650) notes that seventy-eight Jewish houses remained there and eighteen new ones were already being built. This would indicate that most of the Jews were back in town. In fact, some of them had fled earlier, others had converted to Christianity (later returning to Judaism), and some had been killed. The number of dead is placed at "a few dozen."[31]

Some eyewitnesses from other localities also belie reports of the large figures given in the chronicles for Narol and Lublin. One eyewitness speaks of "many Jews of

Narol" (survivors) who told him about a certain person who had been killed. This would mean there were many survivors. And with regard to Lublin, for which the number of Jews killed in 1655 is given in one place as 2,700 and in *Tit ha-Yeveyn* as 8–10,000 or 20,000, an eyewitness told the Jewish court that "there were killed a few hundred Jews on the first day"— after which the Jews made an agreement with the Russians and cossacks and no more killings occurred.[32]

Quite a few other documents concerning various places and regions in Poland either merely indicate the existence of a number of Jews, or depict a lively activity on their part, or note an active business and community life a few years after the catastrophe—a fact which surely testifies to considerable survival of life and property or speedy restoration, or both. On the other hand, the tax rolls of those years indicate a considerable decline in the number of houses ("hearths") as well as the existence of empty houses, and historians have taken this as a basis for their exaggerated ideas on the magnitude of the losses. But this may not be valid. First, many Jews and Poles had fled and did not return until some years later. Second, the term hearth *(dym)*, which supposedly indicates a house or dwelling, was not used exclusively in that sense. In the years after the catastrophe (1659 and 1662) "hearth" in Volhynia was not defined as "a house" but sometimes meant two, six, or many more houses—in one instance even three villages. It apparently designated a unit for taxation. At the same time some populated villages are listed as "deserted" in order to avoid taxation.[33]

Survival and Recovery

The exaggerations and inaccuracies with regard to figures we have noted may indicate that the combined total of losses was a good deal smaller than previously supposed. This would mean that the greater part of Polish Jewry survived the catastrophe, a fact confirmed indirectly by information from travelers and by government documents dealing with the granting of privileges, taxes, and Polish-Jewish relations.

A German, Ulrich Werdun (1632–80), who came to Poland in the company of a French government agent, traveled around the country between 1670 and 1672. Among other things his diary contains notes about Jews in different parts of Poland. According to these entries many Jews were at that time living in the Ukraine (or more exactly, Red Russia and Podolia), some of them as Christians. Of the twenty-three communities he describes or mentions, the only one he found empty was Narol —mentioned as having been destroyed by the cossacks. Some of the other cities that had suffered during the cossack wars are depicted as "having many Jews," "many Jews are rebuilding their houses" (which had been destroyed), "formerly many Jewish families lived there, now about 250," or "many Jews live there" (Zólkiew, Buczacz, Szarogrod, Lwów). In several other communities he found "many Jews," and his comments concerning the synagogues indicate that he found Jews there. Jews were also noted in a few villages.

About six years later another traveler "discovered" Jews in other cities and towns, including some that had suffered from the cossacks or Russians, or both (Nemerow, Lublin, Szczebrzesin, Brześć or Brest Litovsk). Traveling through much of Lithuania in the company of the Polish ambassador to Moscow, Bernhard Tanner found in that region a great many cities with a large number of Jews. In the villages Tanner saw Jewish innkeepers and pointed out that only Jews served in this capacity (he formulated, or else he heard from somebody, a theory that Polish nobles were reluctant to lease their inns to Poles since the latter liked to drink mead and vodka but did not like to settle their accounts). A generation later (1701) Nemerow is mentioned as a town that had earlier been destroyed but was at that time full of Jews.[34]

From 1669 and again at the beginning of the eighteenth century several other cities and towns showed large numbers of Jews or they reported the presence of newcomers or the growth of the population. Even though the figures may be exaggerated and the intervening half century may have seen a population increase, a large number of Jews must have remained in these and other places after the catastrophe (or those who had fled had returned) for their numbers to have increased as they did.[35]

The existence of considerable numbers of Jews in various cities and towns in the years following "the deluge" may also be deduced from the mass of documents concerning taxation of Jews (first about reducing the taxes because of the Jews' bad situation and later about payment), leaseholds to Jews, the granting or renewing of their privileges (or the privileges protecting non-Jews against "excessive" penetration by Jews), orders forbidding Jews to hire Christian servants, "agreements" between Jewish and non-Jewish city dwellers, and so on.[36] Of course there must have been considerable numbers of Jews to request all these privileges and orders, to hire Christian help, to make agreements with non-Jews, and to pay taxes.

Where did all these Jews come from? Some were Jews who had fled Poland and settled temporarily in the border regions (Silesia, Prussia, Moldavia, Hungary) part of whom later returned to Poland. (The few thousand or so who fled to far outlying countries and cities, such as Germany, Amsterdam, and other Western cities and countries, mostly settled there permanently.) Other Jews had survived the catastrophe by hiding in the woods or by moving northward or westward (whichever way seemed safer); or they found refuge on the estates of some nobleman or were sheltered by non-Jews—the number in the latter group may have been small.[*] The Jewish chronicles tell about Jewish women and children whom the cossacks refrained

---

[*] Writing today about the killings in the seventeenth century one must clearly distinguish between the Nazis, for whom *total* extermination of the Jews became a goal and a policy in the 1940–45 holocaust, and the seventeenth-century cossacks, who had no such policy. That was a period of frequent murder, violence, and brutal "revenge." The cossacks also originally wanted to bar Jews from their region. But they were not interested in or desirous of totally exterminating Jews from Europe or Poland. Nor did they possess the technical means to establish "death factories" like those of the Nazis. The cossacks were not racially oriented. This explains the high rate of survival in the seventeenth-century catastrophe as compared with the holocaust in the twentieth century.

from killing, and there is some information implying that Chmielnicki did not kill Jewish artisans, but there is no collateral evidence to prove this point. Both general and Jewish sources indicate that those who perished were to a degree the poor Jews who lacked the means (transportation) to flee. By implication this would seem to mean that people of substance fled and, in part, survived. Some of the prisoners taken by the Tatars may have been ransomed, either by their relatives or by Jewish communities in Poland.

The *pinkas* (minute book) of the Lithuanian Community Council shows clearly that thousands of refugees from the Ukraine were found there during those years and that there was some ransoming of prisoners. A considerable number of Jews survived the catastrophe through temporary conversion to Christianity. Hebrew chronicles mention this fact but apparently tend to minimize it. But non-Jewish sources tell more clearly about the baptism. A non-Jewish traveler, Hiltebrandt, who visited the Ukraine in 1657, points out that the surviving Jews—from the context he seems to mean many survivors—had converted to the Greek Orthodox faith.* All or most of those forced converts later returned to the Jewish faith (the Polish king gave them permission to do so as early as 1649), and they remained Jews. The Jewish prisoners taken by Moscovy during the war with Poland were for the most part released in accordance with the Andrusovo truce of 1667. And some of those who had converted came back illegally. Some Jewesses who had married Christians returned alone or with their children; in exceptional cases such women also illegally brought back their non-Jewish husbands, who became Jews.[37]

These survivors may have been numerous. The fragmentary information, however, affords very little possibility of forming a reliable estimate of the loss of life and wealth by the Jewish community in Poland during the critical two decades (1648-67). That a total of forty to fifty thousand persons perished (20–25 percent of the Jewish population in 1648) would appear to be a reasonable estimate. One should add to this some five to ten thousand Jews who fled Poland and settled abroad, or were ransomed by Turkish and Italian Jewish communities from the Tatars and did not return to Poland. Jews also seem to have rescued far more of their worldly possessions than older historians assumed (by hiding them or entrusting them to non-Jewish neighbors and friends, for instance). The few cases later brought to court may imply that in many more instances the Jews' possessions were returned to them without problems.

The relatively smaller decrease in Jewish population during the catastrophic years and the relatively small loss of property are also mirrored in and confirmed by information on Jewish commercial and other activity during these and subsequent years. The credit rating of the Jews and their community organization, the kehilla, among non-Jews both in Poland and abroad remained almost on the same level as before 1648. And this despite the fact that Jews in many regions had been reported

* The number of Jewish prisoners taken to Constantinople and other southern slave markets by the Tatars and whose ransoms were paid by Jews there cannot have been too large.

to be so poverty-stricken that authorities had relieved Jews of part of their tax obligations or granted them moratoriums on payment of their debts. A number of sources tell of loans granted by non-Jews to communities or to individual Jews, or concern gifts made by Christians to churches or monasteries on the condition that these funds be loaned to a Jewish community at the regular 8–10 percent interest rate (only one case is noted in which Vladimir Jews borrowed two hundred zloty at 20 percent in 1666).[38] Similarly, in 1659 the Jewish community in Luck was considered a reliable guarantor for a bail of ten thousand zloty—a large sum in those years. The Jewish community organizations of Great Poland (1668) and of Little Poland (1675) were able to borrow considerable amounts (4,000 and 7,976 Reichsthaler) in Breslau (now Wroclaw). In 1676, 1678, and 1680 the Polish Four-Land Council borrowed sizable sums from Christoph Bressler and George Miltens von Miltenberg, on which the interest does not seem to have been exorbitant. In Brody we find Jews (1661–66) both borrowing money from and lending it to non-Jews.[39]

This would imply that in the eyes of the non-Jews in Poland and abroad the decimation of the Jewish population did not seem too great and that the survivors were deemed to possess enough funds to cover subsequent repayment of such loans.

Similarly in the years of the catastrophe and soon after we note Jews participating in the fairs in Poland and abroad, purchasing wares worth considerable amounts either on credit or for cash. Thus some Jews from Kazimierz-Cracow, a city that was hard hit by the Swedish invasion in 1655–59, were in Breslau (Wroclaw) as early as 1659, and two of them there had goods worth 6,000 zloty. Another Cracow Jew whose houses had been destroyed and his stores looted during the Swedish war (he, together with some others, supposedly lost 700,000 zloty) was in Gdansk in 1660 purchasing commodities for 3,000 zloty. A few years later, in 1666, he was apparently again flourishing, for he was borrowing and lending sizable sums. Inspection of a Jewish store in Cracow in 1663 revealed a substantial stock of imported textiles.

Poznań was another city whose Jewish population suffered greatly from the 1657 plague and other calamities. Trying to stem an exodus from the city the Jewish community required bail or some other form of guarantee that those who left temporarily would return. The documents concerning these guarantees indicate that at least some of the people involved possessed substantial funds (if their guarantees were regarded as valid). Some of the individuals mentioned in these and other documents made business trips to the fairs in Gniezno (1649 and 1654) and Breslau (1657) to buy or sell commodities. From other localities, too, we hear of Jews in those times who were either in business, lending and borrowing money, or who purchased real estate or industrial enterprises (for instance, a brewery in Kraśnik in 1655).

In general we find Polish Jews traveling to fairs (Toruń, Breslau, Jaroslaw, and Lublin) as early as the 1650s, Cracow and Lwów Jews went to Frankfurt on the Oder and Toruń in 1658), while Jews from western Poland (Lissa, Kalish, Poznań) appear in Leipzig in 1650s–1660s, and their numbers increased after 1675. We hear also of a Jewish merchant in Cracow in 1669 who lost bills and promissory notes worth twenty-two thousand zloty in a fire (which would indicate either great wealth or ample credit). Other Cracow Jews were buying large quantities of furs and hides, for which they paid either in cash or with promissory notes (1664, 1667, 1668, 1671, 1674, and some even earlier). Polish Jews also again began to reach Gdansk for commercial purposes around 1660.

We also find Polish Jews paying for a permit to trade in Pomerania in 1663. Jews from Poznań and other parts of Great Poland, who since 1650 had paid two hundred Reichsthaler annually for seven years for trading rights in Brandenburg, succeeded in renewing these rights in 1660.[40]

All the foregoing would seem to show both that the population loss was not sufficiently high to impair greatly Jewish commercial activity and standing, and that despite the property losses some Jews still retained considerable funds and good credit standing so that they could immediately resume their business affairs and subsequently make a relatively swift recovery.

Such recovery may have been advanced by the virtually unbroken flow of documents from the king confirming the Jewish privileges and granting Jews permission to rebuild their houses, although here and there a sporadic limitation was also introduced or confirmed. Then, too, the orders sent out to cities and towns to protect Jews from mob attacks and to intervene in their behalf may have been of some help, despite the fact that these orders were not always carried out. But in the royal cities such orders may have served to soften the impact of the growing intensity of the burghers' struggle against Jewish trade.

In the privately owned cities and towns the owners (or at least a great many of them) were trying to help reconstruct the economic life, while in the smaller towns some of the non-Jewish residents were occupied as agriculturists (or had gone back to agriculture with the arrival of bad times), so that they scarcely interfered with Jewish commercial activity at all.

The moratoriums granted either to communities or to individual Jews, postponing payments of debts for a year or more, afforded further relief. Also either canceled or modified were the original orders for confiscation of Jewish property in Kazimierz-Cracow, as well as that of some individual Jews elsewhere who had been accused of treason at the time of the Swedish invasion.[41] At the same time the mass of documents of this kind, which were surely not granted without being requested by the people concerned, shows that many Jews had survived the catastrophe and were "alive and kicking."

Reaction, Attitudes, and Impact

At first the Jews of the Ukraine and Poland generally may not have been completely overwhelmed by events. They were, so to speak, inured to attack and capture by the Tatars. Nor was revolt by the cossacks a new phenomenon, the last before 1648 having occurred somewhat less than a decade earlier. For this reason plus the fact that they trusted the Polish forces, the Jews were apparently not initially too upset by what was happening. Hanover possibly mirrors the mood of his fellow Jews in telling metaphorically that when the Polish king and the nobles heard about the first moves of the Ukrainians in 1648 "they dismissed it as a joke, for they said: 'They will fall into our hands again as they did in their previous attempts.' "[42]

In fact, Jews who fled from the advancing cossack-Tatar forces began returning to their dwellings during each lull in the fighting, apparently believing that the worst must be over. When refugees from the Ukraine began to arrive in Lithuania the calamity was at first apparently again regarded as a temporary one. In 1649 the Lithuanian Community Council (Vaad) was mainly interested in ransoming the prisoners from Tatar hands and left the problem of support of the refugees to individual communities for the time being. A whole year passed before an attempt to tackle the problem was made. And it was two years before a more comprehensive arrangement was tried out by the Vaad.[43]

The cossacks and the Ukrainians, however, failed to fulfill the Jews' expectations that they would "fall into the hands" of the Poles; on the contrary, they defeated the latter time and again. Perhaps this contributed to the increased scorn and animosity toward the cossacks and Ukrainians that may have afforded the Jews an outlet for their disappointment. This, of course, added to the resentment caused by the massacres themselves, deepening the generally pro-Polish attitudes of the Jews. Contemporary Poles and Jews regarded Chmielnicki and the cossacks as traitors and rebels. Jewish sources of the time depict them also as cruel, tricky, unreliable, and unlearned in warfare, as soldiers who won by cheating. They are classified as contemptible, defiled, unclean lowly peasants, and dogs.[44]

Of course, such expressions denigrating, despising, and scorning the cossacks and Ukrainians, which are found in Jewish sources of the period dealing with the massacres of Jews,[45] had some relation to the generally pro-Polish orientation of the Jews and were also influenced by Polish opinion as a whole. But the emphasis on denigration and contempt for the Ukrainians may have fulfilled certain other functions at the same time. It helped to "explain" the catastrophe and thereby to minimize its psychological impact. Having placed the entire blame on the cossacks and Ukrainians (and partially the Tatars), Jewish survivors and refugees could not only look back nostalgically to their Polish past, but they could also avoid stirring up any widespread mistrust of Poles or Christians.[46] The way was left open for continued pro-Polish attitudes and trust in the Polish lords.

The Hebrew chronicles that report instances of Poles behaving treacherously toward the Jews emphasize, as a kind of counterbalance, some special efforts to rescue Jews from the cossacks. Though in Tulczyn they "betrayed" the Jews and in Dubno they refused them permission to enter the fortress, such duplicity was far outweighed by real or imagined cases of Poles helping and defending Jews. The Polish Commander Wiśniowiecki "loved the Jews," and when he withdrew his forces he took five hundred Jewish families along and transported them "in speed and safety." Another time he took a detachment to Nemerow "in order to revenge the Jews." Even the perfidy of the Tulczyn Poles turned out to be, as it were, beneficial. Not only were Poles also killed, but their fate as traitors supposedly taught the Poles in the rest of the country a lesson, so that they no longer trusted the cossacks and remained on the side of the Jews, a fact that helped Jews to survive.[47]

On the positive side, Jews in places that were not hit (or less severely hit) by the war tried in one way or another to help refugees fleeing before the cossacks. The Jews in Lithuania, as mentioned, were the first to come to their aid, beginning locally in their communities and later through the *Vaad*. As a start, the prohibition against foreigners settling in a kehilla and trading there was temporarily revoked. Responsibility for the poor was assigned to the kehillot, with a sort of quota denoting the number to be cared for by each kehilla. By 1652 the Lithuanian Community Council had undertaken to supervise a program in which the kehillot would look after two thousand needy refugees. Efforts were also made to help provide ransom money for those who had been taken prisoner.[48] Several communities within ethnic Poland (Cracow, Poznań, and others) absorbed some refugees, while world Jewry—Italy, Constantinople, Amsterdam, and Hamburg—contributed funds to ransom Jews from the Tatars, helped arriving refugees, and also sent money to some Polish communities.

From the religious angle Jews saw to it that those who had been baptized should be able to revert to Judaism—the king's order permitting this was apparently a result of their efforts. (According to Hanover, Jews took back by force the children who had been baptized.) They also made provisions for identification of people so as to avoid incestuous marriages. From the symbolic viewpoint an annual commemorative fast day was instituted: the twentieth of the Jewish month Sivan, the day Nemerow was taken by the cossacks; new or stricter and more elaborate rituals were arranged, and many prayers and dirges were composed (selichot and *El maleh Rachamim*, "O God full of compassion," recited for the dead).

The catastrophe's impact made itself felt in many directions. Besides the loss of population and wealth, a certain relaxation of social mores and discipline came about, and the violence connected with protracted war increased. The weakening of the Polish state led to some suffering and trouble for the Jews. The deterioration of the country's economy nurtured two contradictory trends. On one hand, the competition for what remained grew sharper, with non-Jews sometimes also resorting to noneconomic means to eliminate the Jew. In the decades after the catastrophe the increasing tension between Jews and non-Jews, and illegal acts perpetrated by non-Jews against Jews, were in one way or another connected with this economic struggle. On the other hand, in the nonethnically Polish regions—the Ukraine and Lithuania—Jews often enjoyed advantages over the other non-Poles because they were considered more trustworthy. (At other times the wish to reestablish law and order may have led Polish authorities to policies of appeasement of the Ukrainians, sometimes at the expense of the Jews).

The trend may be illustrated by a project introduced in the *sejm* in 1717 "to obliterate the Greek Orthodox and Uniate religions and the Russian nationality in the Russian regions" of Poland. One proposition put forward was that Jews should be encouraged to settle in the marketplaces of the cities and towns. In their customary efforts to concentrate all sources of income and profit in their own hands, it was argued they would drive the Russians (Ukrainians) from the towns.[49]

The catastrophe also had other consequences. The flight of some Polish Jews abroad during the war years (and the ransomed Polish Jews who remained abroad) precipitated an immigration trend destined in due course to become a leading migration movement westward and to some extent southward (to Moldavia). As usual in such cases, Polish Jews who settled in Germany, Prussia, Silesia, Moravia, and other countries brought over their relatives and served as rallying points for acquaintances and other Polish Jews who emigrated there.

Polish Jewish refugees discovered that Germany and other Western states were in need of Jewish religious intellectuals: rabbis, teachers, cantors, and the like. As a result, from the middle of the seventeenth century on a steady stream of such intellectuals and pseudointellectuals flowed to the Western states and partially also to the south.[50]

Beginning as a relatively small stream, this migratory movement carried some other individuals along with it from Poland to the West, thus opening the way for the future westward movement of East European Jewry which was destined in due time, after a century or more, to lead to large concentrations of East European Jews and their descendants in Western Europe and the Americas. For Poland itself this migration, small as it was at first, may have contributed (with other factors) to a decline in talmudic study, which becomes discernible from the seventeenth century on.

The uprooting of the Polish Jews during the years of the catastrophe apparently had another impact within Poland: the pace of internal migration quickened after the middle of the seventeenth century. First, the refugees were moving from place to place and from region to region. Following the wars they again set out—either to return to their old regions or to seek a permanent home elsewhere. Others moved from cities that were declining to ones that were rising, or to the towns and villages in the Ukraine which, though they had suffered in the wars, were being rebuilt.

Movement from place to place usually leads to a lowering of social norms and established behavior patterns and to slackening of communal life. Newcomers are usually not easily integrated into an existing social framework, and immigration actually becomes a factor in social stratification and division into classes. In seventeenth- to eighteenth-century Poland these processes had a firm basis in the legal code. As we have already seen, in Europe prior to the French Revolution both state and society differentiated legally and socially between the resident and the newcomer ("foreigner") in each settlement. The foreigner was usually barred from permanent settlement and from many means of earning a living. During the mid-seventeenth-century wars many Jewish communities made exceptions to the rules and admitted outsiders temporarily. In time, however, particularly when the wars were over, an effort was made to re-enforce the limiting laws against foreigners or the latter were required to pay large sums for the right to remain. The same was true in many cases of migration from place to place. Contemporaries complain that some refugees were looked down upon or were not welcomed in some places. Add to this the rapid Jewish population growth in the century after the catastrophe,[51] and it would appear plausible that there was disruption of the regulative practices of the communities.

All this created a good deal of tension between the various strata in the Jewish communities, and this found expression in internal quarrels and disruption of established community order.[52] As a result, the authority of the community organization and its leadership was seriously weakened.

Legacy

The treaty of Andrusovo in 1667 divided the Ukraine in two. The left bank of the Dnieper River (eastern Ukraine) went to Russia and the right bank (western Ukraine) remained with Poland. In the Russian part virtually no Jews remained except those who had been baptized plus a few hundred or thousands who were admitted from time to time (leaseholders and other business people)—only to be again expelled together with other Jews from Russia.[53]

In Polish Ukraine Jews could and did settle in large numbers, increasing during one century to three or more times the pre-1648 Jewish population. This Jewish population (along with Polish nobility and clergy) inherited a "legacy" from the Chmielnicki years in the form of attacks by cossack groups and peasants on a small scale and in a limited area. In the eighteenth century they were mostly known as *haidemaks*, meaning something like "rebels." The attacking groups were formed for the most part either because of inducement by and participation of some cossacks from the left bank—the Russian side—or because of ideas imported from there. Since the Polish forces in the Ukraine were inadequate, the hordes from across the border became a real menace. Moreover, events there—revolts and skirmishes of the cossacks—often spilled over to the Polish side.[54] In fact a large proportion of the *haidemak* detachments that roamed Poland came from the Russian side (60 percent among those who were caught at the end of 1768).[55] Such attacks (in 1702–4, 1708, and again in the 1730s and 1740s) ranged from beating up Jews on the roads, robbing them of their possessions, or killing them, to descending upon small, undefended towns and villages and either killing some of the Poles and Jews there—sometimes all who had not succeeded in fleeing—or taking them prisoner and selling them to the Tatars.[56] Although the cossack *haidemaks* of the eighteenth century pointed out their "legacy" from or their resemblance to the Chmielnicki rebels of 1648, defense of the Greek Orthodox faith and ideological motivation seem to have played a much smaller role among these groups.

The cossacks in both parts of the Ukraine had gone through a metamorphosis that resulted in virtual liquidation of their strength. The use of cossack detachments was canceled in Poland at the end of the seventeenth century. In Russia, Peter I destroyed the cossacks' center at the Dnieper cataracts in 1709 and expelled them from the region following betrayal by their leader (hetman) Mazepa, who had supported the Swedes against him. The cossacks were not allowed to return until 1734. In the Ukrainian folk songs and traditions concerning the *haidemaks* (though the songs and stories may be of later origin) one finds themes of their plundering Jews (and Poles) and murdering them by decapitation. And they are depicted as drunkards and rascals ready to rob not only Jews and Poles but Ukrainian peasants as well.[57] Sometimes the attackers—from either the Russian or the Polish side— were caught, brought to court, and given various sentences, mostly the death penalty.

Mixed Polish-Russian border courts functioned as clearinghouses of a sort for the Russian *haidemaks* or for Polish ones who fled across the border. The courts usually tried to find the transgressors; when they did, they condemned them to death or to penal servitude for life. It is impossible to say how many of the attackers were actually punished. It seems, however, that at least some of them were identified, caught, brought to court, and for the most part convicted.[58]

During the 1730s and 1740s *haidemak* detachments were increasingly active. In parts of the Kiev and Podolia regions many Jews were robbed and dozens killed. In the late 1760s the sporadic attacks again threatened to evolve into a larger-scale massacre. In this period Russia and Prussia forced the tottering Polish state to abolish the legal restrictions against "dissidents" (Greek Orthodox and Protestants). To counter this attempt a Confederacy of Patriotic Catholic Poles was organized in Bar in the Ukraine in 1768 for the defense of the Catholic religion. Russian troops moved into Polish Ukraine against the Confederates.

In the midst of this turmoil a *haidemak* group sought to renew the "tradition" of Chmielnicki. A cossack commander, Colonel Maksim Zhelezniak, falsified an order from Empress Catherine allegedly telling him to enter Poland "and to slaughter all the Poles and Jews, the detractors of our holy faith."[59] Heading a troop of a few hundred *haidemaks* and gathering some others around him, Zhelezniak raged through towns of the Kiev province and some other parts of the country killing Jews and Poles. Concomitantly three other *haidemak* leaders were pillaging and murdering in nearby regions. Jews and Poles fled seeking refuge in Bialocerkiew and Uman, both fortified cities in those times.

Uman was a private city belonging to the estate of a member of the Potocki family and had its own cossack guard detachment under the command of a Lieutenant Gonta. When it became known that Zhelezniak and his forces were on the way to Uman, the governor of the city made Gonta swear to remain loyal and sent him with his detachment against Zhelezniak. Gonta and his men, after some indecision while waiting in the steppe, betrayed his master and joined Zhelezniak. Their combined forces then marched upon the city. At first the Jews and Poles defended the city together, but then the governor, Mladanowski, made an agreement with the cossacks by which the Poles were promised immunity when the cossacks should enter the city. Once inside the city the *haidemaks* began by killing the Jews and later the Poles. Some cossacks penetrated into Balta, which at that time was under Turkish rule, and succeeded in killing some Polish Jews and Poles who had fled there.[60]

Before long Russian troops[61] and the Polish troops that remained faithful to the Polish king caught up with the cossack groups and arrested a number of *haidemaks*. Zhelezniak fled with his men but was later caught by the Russians. About nine hundred *haidemaks* were captured, of whom five hundred were brought to court. Some were sent to hard labor, others executed. The leaders were subjected to all sorts of torture.[62]

General and Jewish sources from 1768, like the ones dealing with the Chmielnicki massacres of a century earlier, depict the atrocities perpetrated by the cossack *haidemaks* and tell of their ruthlessness and depravity. Some of this reads like a copy of the earlier reports, but there is something new: reports now tell that the cossack chiefs punished by death any peasant or Greek Orthodox priest who hid a Jew. We are also told about forced baptism. Another variation here is that baptized Jews were made to kill their wives and children before being murdered themselves by the *haidemaks*.

As in the massacres of the 1640s, the sources apparently grossly exaggerate the number of victims. Thus the figures differ widely between one source and another. There are those who mention only small numbers of Jews killed, such as three hundred or five hundred. Others estimate three thousand in the synagogue alone and seven thousand all told. Still others gave much larger numbers. One source reports that thirty thousand died in Uman, another, that fifty to sixty thousand Jews were killed in Uman and three other communities. Another version is that in Uman eighteen thousand Jews and non-Jews perished.

The Jewish sources,[63] like those dealing with 1648, tend to minimize the psychological impact of the treacherous attitude of the Polish governor of Uman against the Jews. They describe how finally the Jews were avenged: the governor and the other Poles of Uman suffered the same fate as the Jews at the hands of the cossacks.

The motif of a Polish general going out of his way to avenge the Jews killed in Uman and elsewhere is also observable. Such a one was General Branicki (called in the source a Hassid, a pious man), who was prevailed upon by the Jews of Brody to help them. We are told that he comforted the Jews and set out to capture "many thousands" of cossacks, whom he executed.[64] In fact, as we have pointed out, General Branicki was scarcely involved in catching the *haidemaks*, but he was the person who decided the fate of those who were delivered to him by the Russian troops. In 1768 the Jews seem to have felt the same need as they had a century earlier to emphasize and exaggerate help received from the Poles as a means of satisfying their psychological need to feel secure by relying on the state forces and pro-Polish tendencies.

10 Messianism: The Sabbatai Zevi Upheaval and Its Impact

The Sabbatai Zevi messianic movement[1] of the seventeenth century did not originate and develop in Poland. In our present context we should really be interested only in the impact it had upon Polish Jewry and in its offshoot in Poland: Frankism in the eighteenth century. But to understand these developments it is necessary to review something of the general background. Writing in our age of disbelief it is also important to point out that in earlier ages myths were taken far more seriously than they are today and were regarded as "living facts" to be considered on a par with actual facts.

Messianism generally—the belief in the coming of a chiliastic leader who will perfect the world—is a phenomenon found in the context of supernatural beliefs throughout the centuries and not only among Jews.

This is not the place to go into the particulars of the problem of whether messianism was originally developed first among Jews or whether the hope for the solace of a future Golden Age is more universal in character.[2] The harsh realities of life, and man's yearning for a meaning to life, have caused generations of men from varied backgrounds to dream of a perfect future world and to cherish legends about a lost paradise—the Jews' lost Garden of Eden, Plato's tale of the lost Atlantis; and the Greco-Roman myth of an egalitarian state of nature. The Christian world, besides believing Christ to be the Messiah, also hoped for a Second Coming (after which a millennium, a messianic kingdom, would be established on earth). Eschatologies of world catastrophes and of world changes were repeatedly propounded: "Generation after generation was seized at least intermittently by a tense expectation of some sudden, miraculous event in which the world would be utterly transformed . . . [and] history would attain its fulfillment and justification."

Christian thought inherited from Judaism a tradition of prophetic pronouncements about messianic times (and the preceding upheavals and wars), which were later reinterpreted with infinite variations. These beliefs were strong in early Christianity but were discredited in the third and fourth centuries, when the physical kingdom of God became transformed into a spiritual one destined to enter the souls of the believers, and when the millennium began to be regarded (by Saint Augustine) as a mere continuation of human history. But though the church, by then organized, began to look upon chiliasm as a heresy and often fought it with sword and fire (burning at the stake), it endured in popular religion with infinite variations through the Middle Ages and early modern times, for the idea of the millennium appealed to many social strata.

The lore of the more popular eschatological fantasy was based on old Christian traditions, Jewish and other writings (Book of Daniel, Book of Revelation, the sibylline oracles), and social biases and preferences that varied at different times and in different places. But a number of general tendencies are discernible: "The Heavenly City is to appear on this earth . . . for the 'chosen people.' " A social struggle is imagined as uniquely important, "a cataclysm from which the world is to emerge totally transformed and redeemed."

Through many of these chiliastic upheavals ran the expectation of and belief in a leader, an "elect," a "prophet," the incarnation of a king, of Christ or a living God who would inspire by divine revelation: "On the strength of inspirations or revelations for which he claimed divine origin this leader would decree . . . a mission of vast dimensions and world-shaking importance."

The leaders of chiliasm were usually from society's bottom rungs—the lower clergy who left the parishes, monks who fled the monasteries, literate laymen, a hermit, an artisan, and once in a while a peasant. Such a leader, the elect of God, may sometimes have performed "miracles" and at other times may have appeared as a healer of the sick. We find leaders calling for repentance and their followers weeping and crying for forgiveness of their sins. Most of these leaders opposed the church and the clergy, declaring the sacraments invalid. Others "abolished" sin altogether, believing that by achieving perfection they had made sin impossible. Antinomianism—the idea that faith rather than the fulfillment of regulations is the essence of religion, bounding on anarchy—ensued. "Sin"—promiscuity and eroticism—became a symbol of spiritual emancipation. The Free Spirit movement flourished in the thirteenth and fourteenth centuries. Beghards in the fourteenth century practiced ritual nakedness and communal sexual orgies in Cologne in 1325. Parts of Taborite movement in Bohemia in the beginning of the sixteenth century regarded marriage as sin and practiced promiscuity and naked ritual dances. In the 1530s Anabaptists in Muenster (they called it "New Jerusalem") favored strict monogamy, but later they introduced forced polygamy. Ranters in Cromwell's England (mid-seventeenth century), pursuing total emancipation, came to self-deification ["every creature is God"], and believed that "sin can no longer exist"; since being bound to one woman is merely a result of the curse of Adam and Eve, erotic freedom was sanctioned, so they thought.

Some of the "Messiahs" abolished Sundays and fast days (Bockelson the "Messiah of the last days" in Muenster in the 1530s). Adepts of the Free Spirit considered themselves entitled to steal and rob. Others favored egalitarian communities and communal property (the Taborites in the fifteenth century, Hans Boehm in Niklashousen in 1470s, and others).

Most of these movements and trends favored—and their leaders practiced—violence, the killing of clergy and "sinners," terror, executions, armed revolt, the burning of property, and other irrational destructiveness. In many cases practical social conflicts and aspirations were endowed with a transcendental significance. In England during the sixteenth and seventeenth centuries millenarianism took a somewhat calmer form, concentrating generally on interpretation of the Scriptures and mathematical-mystical calculations of the year of Christ's Second Coming: 1588 or 1666. In its further development it somehow became identified simply with human progress. But a revolutionary streak persisted and came into the open during the revolutionary years of the mid-seventeenth century.

The Ranters of Cromwell's England followed variations of the doctrines of the Free Spirit: self-deification, anarchic eroticism, and, in part, abolition of private property and antinomianism ("God regardeth not the actions of the outward man, but of the heart"). Some groups concluded that there is no sin or that "to commit a sin" is in reality a great achievement ("Those are most perfect, and like to God and eternity, which do commit the greatest sins without least remorse or shame"). In practice there were leaders who impersonated Christ or God or claimed that God dwells in the flesh of men other than Christ. Among their followers were women who saw visions and proclaimed mystical revelations about them, as well as men and women who committed adultery or other "sins."[3]

In Christian chiliastic movements and sects the problems of "sin," both as committed—mainly in the sexual realm—and in the theoretical matter of "abolishing" it, are in great part connected with the duality and contradiction existing in Christian society. The church tried to formalize love, to contain the violent emotions of eroticism by sanctifying marriage and repressing other expressions. But in fact "sinful love" continued side by side with the sacrament, as expressed both in the license of the lower classes and in the crude sexual life of the higher classes. Rigid rules of behavior, with their implication of failure and the danger of condemnation, are apt to result in guilt feelings and fear—as well as self-hate because of failure to measure up to standards. Antinomianism—the "legalization," as it were, of permissiveness and sin or the transformation of these into virtues—not only created a chance to indulge some "forbidden" passions but may also have furthered emancipation from guilt feelings and self-hate. This may have served as one factor in attracting people to the given sect or movement.

In short, the Christian messianic movements of late medieval and early modern times contain the following motifs and tendencies (with all the variations between one element and another):

a belief in millenarianism—a desire to build the heavenly city of God on earth;
a rejection of the Establishment, of organized church and state;
antinomian ideas—emphasis on faith, not regulations;

a concern with sin and abolishment of sin, with ensuing forms of erotic freedom or erotic anarchy;

a belief in the leader as an elect;

self-deification; and

activism and violence coupled with some ideas on and attempts to achieve social justice.

Some of the motifs in Jewish messianic trends resembled those of Christian chiliasm, though the metaphors were taken from Jewish lore, and there were other differences.

Like Christian chiliasm, its Jewish counterpart (some would say the Jewish original), Jewish messianism in medieval times and later was not in harmony with the official Orthodox Jewish religion. Jewish prayers are permeated with themes of return to Palestine and redemption, and belief in the coming of the Messiah became one of the main articles of Jewish faith. Jewish lore furnished many fantasies about the hoped-for messianic age and the preceding cataclysm. But official Judaism for the most part disapproved of seeking to hasten the Messiah's coming or speculating about the year in which he would appear. The various imposters and false Messiahs who arose intermittently during the Middle Ages were generally decried officially.

Jewish messianic movements and ideas had a somewhat different history from Christian ones. Moreover, they underwent changes in the course of the almost two thousand years after Jews lost their independence. Of paramount importance to these movements was the idea of return to Palestine and the reconstruction of the national home, although some of them equated redemption of the Jews with redemption of the world at large, or with Palestine, so to speak, extending to other lands (one phantasmal promise was "Palestine is destined to spread out to all the countries of the world"). Besides Jewish national particularistic goals, the Messiah would materialize universal goals for all humanity. This is expressed in one of the High Holiday prayers: "Give glory, O Lord, to Thy people . . . joy to Thy land [Palestine], gladness to Thy city. . . . All wickedness shall be wholly consumed like smoke when Thou makest . . . arrogance pass away from the whole earth."[4]

All this is regarded as connected with Palestine. Being bound to a faraway country, Jewish chiliasts could hardly seek actively to build a "new Jerusalem" in any part of the country in which they lived. With the exception of some intermittent activism during, roughly, the first millennium C.E. (attempted revolts and other resorts to violence) Jewish messianism became more and more spiritual and passive. The Messiah may still have been regarded as a man of activity, a warrior who would redeem the Jews and punish their oppressors, but the idea developed of two Messiahs: the Messiah ben Joseph and the Messiah ben David, the warrior who would be killed and the redeemer, the true Messiah, as it were, or savior—who became a dominant figure in later centuries. As messianism became spiritualized and found expression in speculations about messianic times and the changes these times would bring, in dreams about the glory of the postmessianic era and fantasies about miraculous ways of reaching Palestine that left all activity to God, relatively passive measures such as prayer, expectation, fasting, cabalistic magic, and repentance were relied upon to bring the Messiah.

It was generally expected that God (or God's elect) would bring about the messianic age in some miraculous manner. Through the ages a massive lore about the messianic times evolved, ranging from opinions that the Messiah's coming would mean only that the Jews would regain political independence, to many ideas concerning the end of history, the resurrection of the dead, and cardinal changes in the world when God's kingdom is established.

Some mystics, either individuals or small groups, sometimes sought to speculate about the time of the Messiah's advent, but they were not supposed to divulge their knowledge to anyone else. But in times of peril and catastrophe, or for some other definite reason, the hope for redemption gained wider acknowledgment, in accordance with the belief that suffering is preparation for the Messiah's coming. The "day of wrath," the wars of Gog and Magog recounted in Jewish sources, and similar imagery of oppression were part and parcel of the fantasies about the coming of the Messiah.

Since Jewish messianism in the later centuries developed into a rather passive affair of meditation and speculation, its most active expression being fasting and repentance, it became mostly a matter of verbalized ideas and thought. Thus it became almost impossible to differentiate between metaphor and fact, or perhaps metaphors often became "facts" and wishful thinking, as it were, "involvement." This means that the question of how representative this or that idea or trend was remains a matter of conjecture and belief.

The expulsion of the Jews from Spain in 1492 was regarded as a great catastrophe and was followed by a number of messianic speculative attempts to compute the time of the Messiah's coming; mostly these were of a semipassive nature, some of them instigated by imposters. A generation or two later the mystics took over. At Safad in Palestine, Isaac Luria (1534–72), Hayim Vital (1543–1620), and other Jewish cabalists (mystics) formulated, or reformulated, the idea of exile as "a mystical theory of the path of redemption," regarding the exile of the Jews as a mission to uplift everything in the world. They produced an imagery in which "the old spirit of mystical contemplation is enriched by the new element of messianic fervor, with its apocalyptic dream of an end to the period of suffering and degradation."[5]

Some recent authors surmise that this reformulation of the ideas of Jewish mysticism—the Lurianic cabala—served to bring about the messianism of Sabbatai Zevi almost a century later, but for the most part they fail to prove this connection. (The existence of ideas says nothing about their impact; it is unclear how representative the adherents of the Lurianic cabala were. Also, Lurianic ideas were repudiated from the beginning by such leaders of the Sabbatai Zevi messianic movement as Nathan and, to some extent, Sabbatai himself.)

The messianism of Sabbatai Zevi (1626–76), which rose and fell in the course of a few years (1665 and 1666), concerned mainly Sephardic Jewry, especially those living mostly within the Ottoman Empire in southern Europe.

In general, the great majority of the imposters (false Messiahs) among Jews throughout the ages were Sephardic (from *Sepharad*, meaning Spain in Hebrew) or other oriental Jews. Before Sabbatai Zevi in the seventeenth century we find only about two or three Franco-Ashkenazic (from *Ashkenaz*, meaning Germany in Hebrew) pretenders.[6] Asher Lemlein, who operated (1502) in a predominantly Sephardic environment in Italy, was one of them. Besides Jacob Frank in the eighteenth century, one or two would-be Messiahs of Ashkenazic origin emerged as an aftermath of Sabbatai Zevi. These few Ashkenazim are found among dozens of known messianic pretenders in Jewish history.[7]

Sabbatai was apparently born into a Sephardic family in Smyrna (Izmir). Most of his contacts were in predominantly Sephardic and oriental Jewish communities (Smyrna-Izmir, Cairo, Salonika, Greece, to some extent Palestine, and Constantinople). His encounters with Ashkenazim do not seem to have been very advantageous for his cause. Sabbatai's "lieutenants," "prophets," "emissaries," and appointed "kings and princes" (Rosanes lists forty-one kings, Scholem, twenty-five) were also mainly Sephardim; the few Ashkenazim that were involved were born or lived in a Sephardic Jewish environment. Apparently the followers, too, were frequently if not exclusively of Sephardic origin. In Western Europe as well the Sephardim were much closer to the Sabbatai Zevi messianic movement than were the Ashkenazim.[8]

It would take us too far afield to investigate here the many differences between Sephardim and Ashkenazim that may have had a bearing on their respective attitudes toward false Messiahs. A few points should be mentioned, however. German (or French-German) Jews were latecomers to world Jewry, both quantitatively and qualitatively, and this may have contributed somewhat to the fact that Ashkenazic Jews did not have many "Messiahs." Sephardic Jewry indulged far more in messianic speculations than did Ashkenazic Jewry,[9] and it should be noted that in Sabbatai Zevi's time there were among the Sephardim many Marranos (crypto-Jews) and their children who had mostly lived—at least externally—as Christians in a Christian environment. Here the idea of the Messiah was kept alive both by the Christian spirit (belief in Jesus as the Messiah) and by the counterarguments denying the messiahship of Jesus and thereby strengthening belief in the expected arrival of the Jewish Messiah.

Because possession of Jewish books was fraught with great danger for the Marranos in Portugal or Spain, their knowledge of Hebrew disappeared and they used the same Latin translation of the Bible as the Christians. Those who wished to retain their Jewishness concentrated on the Old Testament. The essence of their Judaism centered mainly around a few doctrines, including the denial of Jesus' claim to have been the Messiah, which they highlighted to a greater extent than other Jews who could simply ignore him. This in turn placed the messianic hope of future restoration in special focus. Perhaps, too, the Marrano's desperate desire to uphold his crypto-Jewishness despite fear of the Inquisition led him to believe in the miraculous appearance of the Messiah as his only hope. Thus messianism may have become a main—sometimes the only—Jewish principle for many crypto-Jews.

This attitude of concentrating Judaism around one principle strengthened antinomian tendencies that existed among Spanish-Portuguese Jewry even before conversion. Isaac Abravanel and Solomon ibn Virga (both refugees from the Iberian peninsula themselves), writing a relatively short time after the expulsion from Spain, saw permissiveness among Spanish Jews—eating nonkosher food and having relations with non-Jewish women—as a main reason for the expulsion itself. Still earlier Joseph Albo had charged a part of Sephardic Jewry with denying the value of the commandments in favor of abstract faith. The Marranos who remained on the Iberian peninsula are said to have taught their children that many of the commandments, including the one forbidding them to follow Christianity, were mere intangibles. Such minimization of the value of the commandments was found in several forms among post-Marrano Jews. Those who were admitted into the secularized European culture were apt to revolt against the forms and ideas of traditional Judaism (Uriel da Costa was excommunicated by the rabbis in 1618; Baruch Spinoza was excommunicated in 1656; and still earlier a community leader of the Amsterdam kehilla, Dr. Abraham Farrar, had officially given philosophy precedence over the Talmud). Others may have needed to justify the antinomianism (or transgression against Jewish religious commandments) by transforming it into a virtue (thus becoming as it were, "predisposed" toward it).

Sephardic Jewry may have been further predisposed to such antinomian outbreaks because of the looser control of such Jewish religious patterns as, for instance, sexual behavior and eroticism—a sphere of considerable concern also among many Christian millenarists.[10]

Other widespread permissive patterns also existed among post-Marrano Jews. A glimpse into the minute book of the Sephardic kehilla in Hamburg in the seventeenth century, for instance, will yield some idea of these tendencies: some Jews shaved their beards, played cards, had close relationships with non-Jewish women, fought each other in the synagogue or street, bought meat from non-Jews, transacted business on the Sabbath, and the like.

Some of the former Marranos maintained their contacts with Portugal and Spain, drawing incomes from their property there, serving as agents of those countries in Holland, Hamburg, and elsewhere, and returning "home" temporarily for business purposes. This would apparently also indicate that some of these people did not mind living as Christians again, consuming nonkosher food, being deprived of prayer, and so on. This seems to be evinced by a resolution of the kehilla in Hamburg that one who traveled to Spain or Portugal should not be called to the Torah for two years after his return. Others, though already outside Portugal, postponed resumption of Judaism for economic reasons having to do with their possessions, or an inheritance, or on other grounds. Trips to Portugal-Spain were also made from Amsterdam.

Such contacts with and possible travel to Portugal-Spain may also mean that a number of post-Marrano Jews who had business contacts with the Iberian peninsula lived in Hamburg, Amsterdam, and other places *officially* as Christians, using Christian names (besides an "internal" Jewish name) and behaving in public as Christians for fear of the numerous spies and informers that the Inquisition maintained in places settled by former Marranos.

Among such groups antinomianism—with the problem of sin, which was often connected with messianism—was not abstract theory; it was designed to justify a certain practice and behavior pattern. Other groups reverting to Orthodox Judaism were plagued with problems pertaining to repentance for sins committed while they were living as Christians. On the other hand, the contrast between the high positions of power formerly held by some Marranos (plus their great wealth, prestigious social positions, and legal standing in the countries where they had lived) and the efforts in the new countries to limit their freedom (in Amsterdam by the clergy and guilds, in Hamburg by the mob, clergy, students, with limitations on possession of real estate there, and in Turkey mistreatment by local rulers, the Janissars, and so on[11]) may have inclined them to heed more attentively the promises of deliverance, of future glory and importance. In this way some of these Sephardim temporarily swelled the number of overt or covert "believers," thereby helping to create the impression of a sizable movement.

Technical reasons, too, contributed to this illusion. Sabbatianism is the only Jewish messianic movement about which many written traces have survived. Communications between countries were better developed in the seventeenth century than they had been in earlier ones; writing and publishing increased, and materials were more widely circulated; and certain non-Jewish chiliastic trends led non-Jews to become interested in Sabbatianism, and they wrote about it or sought and received information. Much of this material, which is considerable in bulk, has been preserved; some is genuine and some is doubtful, but historians usually tend to measure the significance of events by the volume of source material available.

Rise and Fall

Sabbatai Zevi was born in 1626 in Smyrna (Izmir), his father having come there from Greece. As a young man he became interested in Jewish mysticism—cabala—and sometime later, around 1648, he apparently began to believe that he was destined to be "the savior of the Jews."[12]

Judging by fragmentary information one can assume that by the age of twenty or so Sabbatai was suffering from some sort of mental disorder connected with sexual problems. Scholem assumes his illness to have been a manic-depressive psychosis with cyclic periods of elation and depression. To the people around him his behavior pattern appeared foolish or "sick." At first they paid scant attention to his beliefs and "revelations,"[13] but later he was expelled from Smyrna. He wandered about— to Salonika, some other Greek cities and towns, Constantinople, and back to Smyrna —for over a decade. In most places where he stopped he met some opposition to his strange behavior and his transgression of traditional mores or his messianic hopes, opposition that repeatedly forced him to leave or sometimes even resulted in his being expelled.

Along the way in Egypt in 1662 he befriended a wealthy, influential Jew, Raphael Joseph, in Cairo; this man was interested in cabala. Back in Jerusalem, Sabbatai seems to have estranged some by his queer behavior but also to have made a number of friends and acquaintances. In 1664 he again went to Cairo as a "messenger" to collect money for Jews in Jerusalem and apparently succeeded in bringing back a considerable sum. This may have encouraged him to express himself more openly about his messianic mission.

On the way back to Jerusalem he acquired a "prophet," Nathan of Gaza, a young man, apparently energetic and self-confident, who saw visions and heard "revelations" from angels designating Sabbatai as the Messiah. (According to Scholem, "Sabbatai Zevi came to him [to Nathan in Gaza] not as the Messiah . . . but seeking a cure for his psychosis . . . and was convinced by Nathan . . . of the authenticity of his messianic mission.") Nathan undertook "to make of him a messiah" by becoming his "prophet"—in reality his manager and public relations man. And before long (May–June 1665) Nathan began proclaiming that Sabbatai was the Messiah. He also falsified ("revealed to him") an apocalypse that had much earlier purportedly predicted Sabbatai's birth and adventures as a messiah.

Nathan soon convinced Sabbatai of his role, and Sabbatai began to play it in Gaza, attracting followers and believers. But when Sabbatai arrived in Jerusalem and apparently committed some antihalakhic acts, the traditional rabbis vehemently opposed him (though there were some who believed in him). They put him under a ban, tried to inform upon him to the Turkish authorities, and, according to some information, even wanted to kill him. But instead they expelled him from Jerusalem.

As Sabbatai again set out on his wanderings—to Safad, Damascus, and Smyrna—the religious climate had changed completely. Exaggerated information about the "Messiah," Nathan's propaganda disseminated by letters from Gaza, announced visions and proclamations from heaven, which set up a timetable for the Messiah's appearance. Magnified by varied rumors, stories, "information" on the marching of the forces of the Ten Tribes, and fabrications, this all made it possible for Sabbatai to find along the way "prophets" and "prophetesses" who cited his greatness, as well as groups of followers.

In Smyrna, which he reached around September–October 1665, Sabbatai seems to have remained inactive, perhaps in a deep depression, for some time. But by the beginning of December he "revealed" himself as the Messiah and gathered together a following made up mainly of common people,[14] with a sprinkling from the upper classes. He then began a series of activities that included some violence, such as breaking into a synagogue with his "guard" on a Saturday and disrupting and changing the procedure of the service in progress. He proclaimed himself to be the Messiah, parading in special "royal" attire, and introducing some outlandish ceremonies. He also dismissed the local rabbi and appointed instead one of his own followers. He appointed "kings," among whom he "divided the world." And he committed sacrilege involving, among other things, his relations with women.

Shortly afterwards he left for Constantinople, either to fulfill the proclaimed hopes that he would "take away the rule from the sultan" or because he was summoned by the Turkish authorities. He reached a Gallipoli port almost forty days after leaving Smyrna and was arrested either there or while still at sea and taken before the grand vizier. According to some reports he denied being a messiah and presented himself to the authorities as a Jerusalem rabbi collecting money for the poor. He was jailed but, possibly because of a large sum paid to the vizier, was later transferred to a Gallipoli fortress. There, a well-bribed jailer gave him a great deal of freedom and allowed people to visit him.

If we are to believe the various not very trustworthy accounts, Gallipoli became a central point for the believers, who came and went, paying their respects and bringing gifts to the "Messiah." Sabbatai lived there for the most part in a state of exultation. He broke a number of Jewish rituals (canceling the fasts of the seventeenth of Tamuz and the ninth of Av and turning them into holidays, arranging to celebrate the Sabbath on a weekday, and other things). He also—if we may believe some sources—behaved licentiously in erotic matters: he is said to have had between three and seventy young girls around him and to have indulged in homosexuality.

Another element, which came to the fore around the beginning of 1666, was the deification or self-deification of Sabbatai Zevi. He began to sign letters "I am your God Sabbatai Zevi." This led to an uproar among some Jerusalem rabbis. And again later he also indicated certain ideas on self-deification. Apparently some of his followers too deified him in later years.[15]

This situation did not last long—either because of a denunciation, possibly by Nehemia Hakohen, a cabalist from Poland who came to Turkey to visit Sabbatai but disagreed with him in the course of heated discussions about details in the process of redemption (see below); or because he may have been suspect to Turkish officials. Be that as it may, in September 1666 Sabbatai was taken to Adrianople, where the sultan's court was located at that time. Confronted, he again denied being a messiah and, apparently because he was faced with the choice between execution and conversion, finally renounced Judaism and adopted Islam. His name was changed to Mahmet Efendi, and he was granted a pension.

Sabbatai's conversion certainly may have resulted from simple fear for his life. His denial when accused of posing as a messiah and his assertion that others put him in that position against his will point to his fear of being executed. It was only later that the apostasy was turned into a mystery and a doctrine was evolved incorporating it into the Messiah's mission.

But one should not overlook the fact that Sabbatai may have been influenced by the duality in religious behavior that existed in the parts of the Ottoman Empire where he came from and through which he had traveled extensively (this over and above the duality to which the Marranos were accustomed). In the western and southwestern parts of the Turkish Empire there existed groups of crypto-Christians, people who publicly professed Islam but practiced Christianity in private. This is first mentioned in 1338 in Nicaea Anatolia and appeared later, during the fifteenth and sixteenth centuries, in Cyprus and the Balkans, lasting in part until the nine-teenth century. The Greek Orthodox Church viewed the crypto-Christians as "chil-dren of the church," although the Catholic Church did not. One may surmise that, being in danger of losing his life and having to act fast, Sabbatai may on the spur of the moment have pinned his hope on the relatively mild treatment accorded the crypto-Christians in Turkey (in contrast with the harsh lot of the crypto-Jews on the Iberian peninsula), hoping that this would enable him to continue being a Jew.

The double loyalty of the crypto-Christians in the Balkans was maintained to varying degrees, ranging from preservation of only minor parts of the Christian heritage to living a completely double life: attending church on Sunday and the mosque on Friday, having both a Christian and a Muslim name, marrying only among themselves and according to both Christian and Muslim rites, and having their children baptized and confirmed before the Muslim circumcision.[16] Sabbatai may have known about the situation of the crypto-Christians. His apparent familiarity with some Christian thought and terminology may indicate that the Christian world around him was not strange to him.

The scant reliable information on Sabbatai's conduct in the years following the conversion shows patterns of dual behavior somewhat resembling those practiced by the crypto-Christians, such as his continuing to use his former Hebrew names along with his Turkish one. Paralleling some of the converted Christian believers, Sabbatai is said to have kept near him in Gallipoli both a Torah scroll and a Koran, and to have prayed with his group first the Hebrew prayers and then the Muslim ones. He married his fourth wife in 1675 according to Jewish rites.[17] But whatever led Sabbatai to become an apostate, after a brief period of confusion he supposedly again experienced episodes of "illumination."

The majority of Sabbatai's followers reverted to the traditional Jewish belief, either upon hearing rumors of his apostasy or after confirming that it had taken place. But some of them did continue to congregate around him as he lived a double life: as a Jew and as a Muslim. Sometimes he appeared in a synagogue to pray. Other times he advocated propagation of the Muslim religion or even forced some in-dividuals to become Muslims.

Meanwhile, his lieutenants, including Nathan of Gaza and the former Marrano Abraham Miguel Cardozo, were trying to "theologize" the apostasy as they had previously done with Sabbatai's manias and depressions. They tried to explain it as a necessary step in the process of redemption and the idea of a "second coming" was conceived.[18] Some new dates for his revelation (1674, 1676) were formulated. The antinomian element seems by then to have become stronger.

In 1672 Sabbatai was arrested upon his arrival in Constantinople and later ex-pelled to the fortress Dulcigno (in Turkish, Ülgün) in Albania. Some information indicates that Jews bribed—or gave a gift to—Turkish officials to remove Sabbatai from places near larger Jewish settlements. In Dulcigno only a very few of his followers could come in contact with him. He died there in September 1676.

Impact

During Sabbatai's life—particularly in the years 1665–66—his messianism attracted many believers and followers, mainly among Sephardic Jews. The largest following was among Jews within the Ottoman Empire. At least in some cities here there were times when it became a sort of mass movement, in which the main participants were apparently from the lower rungs of Jewish society. It is said that in Smyrna about four hundred people converged around Sabbatai, and in Gallipoli more than four thousand (another source says four hundred). Among the learned and wealthy there seems to have been less enthusiasm for Sabbatai's messianism, although some of them did become ardent supporters and theoreticians of the movement. If, as reported, Sabbatai lived in luxury in Gallipoli—he is supposed to have used gold and silver utensils, and so on—such items were undoubtedly supplied by wealthy Jews.

Sephardic Jews in Egypt, Italy, and Palestine were somewhat less involved in the whole upheaval. But there, too, for a little while the overt opposition of the non-believers was slight.

In the West the Sephardim of Amsterdam and Hamburg were among the believers, with their community leadership pledging allegiance to the imposter and introducing a prayer in his honor. Amsterdam also sent him letters paying him homage. Two people left Amsterdam to visit Sabbatai[19]—it is uncertain whether as delegates or as private individuals—but instead remained in Italy. In Hamburg the kehilla considered sending a delegation to Sabbatai but refrained from doing so, apparently on account of opposition by a part of the community.

Our information on Hamburg includes authentic and objective reports. The minute books of the Hamburg (Sephardic) community have been preserved and were translated into German at the beginning of this century. (The original Portuguese copy has since disappeared.) The first entry in the minute book,[20] dated December 9, 1665, the seventh day of Hanukkah, reads:

> *Praise the Lord of the world for the news which came from the Levant, and conferred by those from Italy and other regions that He in His benevolence gave us a prophet in Palestine, the Haham R. Nathan Ashkenazi, and a King Messiah the Haham R. Sabbatai Zevi whom He has chosen to redeem his people from among the nations. . . . We believe in these news because of the many signs and portents—as we are informed—the prophet and king performed.*

The entry goes on to say that therefore all the prayers of the day, including the Hallel, were chanted to the melodies of Simchat Torah. Money was also collected and immediately distributed among the poor. The entry finishes with a wish that God might make the information true "and grant us our land."

By the end of December the community board was concerned about possible attacks by the non-Jewish mob because of the general information disseminated by non-Jews about the "Messiah," which in some places often had anti-Jewish overtones. The community leadership decided to ask the authorities to prevent publication of such pamphlets. They forbade Jews to talk to non-Jews about the Messiah and required them to turn over to the board, without showing them to anybody else, all letters they received in which news about the Messiah was mentioned.[21]

About two months later the community board (or a part of it) met with a few dozen members in a private house and "hastily without further reflection" decided to send two representatives to Constantinople "to bring homage to our king, Sabbatai Zevi." No sooner had the gathering left the house than opposition voices were raised, loudly complaining because they had not been given a chance to participate in the meeting. The board immediately had it announced in the synagogue on the evening of the same day that the resolution to send messengers to Sabbatai had no validity whatsoever, and invited all the members to a general assembly the following Sunday. But on Saturday the board already decided not to send any delegates to Constantinople and canceled the assembly called for the next day.[22] The opposition was apparently so strong that the "believers" were forced to retreat from their intention to send a delegation because the pro-Sabbatai board was afraid to face the general assembly.

The strength of the opposition (the "nonbelievers") is also made clear by the repeated warnings of the community board against the "troublemakers" who spoke disparagingly about Sabbatai, interfered in the synagogue when a prayer in his honor was being recited (*misheberach*), and had caused disturbances in the synagogue on the eve of Purim, when the parnasim had arranged a dance to celebrate the good news about the "Messiah."[23]

These and other entries in the minute book for the critical years (1665–66) reveal that the "believers," among whom were some of the leading members of the community, were apprehensive about the opposition, which seems (Sasportas and Scholem to the contrary) to have been quite considerable. For example, the Hamburg Sephardic community did not follow Sabbatai Zevi's order to abrogate the fast on the ninth day of Av and turn it into a holiday. In the main the minute book entries show that the faith of the believers was for the most part superficial, implying little commitment and having little meaning.

A true belief in Sabbatai Zevi as the Messiah should have at least minimized the fear or anxiety about the non-Jewish environment, but the contrary is true. We have already noted the anxiety generated among Jews by the fear that non-Jews would deride or oppress them because of the Messiah. A little later a book of sermons about the Messiah by Moses Gideon Abudiente was confiscated by the community board, which also attempted to prevent members from telling non-Jews anything about the Messiah. This anxiety undoubtedly resulted from the weak belief in and still weaker commitment to the Messiah.

Moreover, at the height of the Sabbatai Zevi upheaval, the community was interested in long-range plans connected with the security and settlement of the members in Hamburg. Hence the concern with ways and means to maintain the Jewish settlement in Glueckstadt (organized in 1618; then situated inside Denmark, a country friendly toward Jews), which had been regarded as a refuge for Hamburg Jews[24] whenever the authorities of that city might begin to oppress them. The community continued to take an interest in enlarging the synagogue in Hamburg, tried to sell the old houses, and made plans to enlarge the cemetery[25]—all of which evinces the lack of any real hope of an imminent move to Palestine. The rich (perhaps the richest) Jew, Isaac Senior Texeira, supposedly a faithful believer in Sabbatai Zevi, was at that very time so worried about the safety of his possessions, because of legal proceedings instituted by the Austrian emperor against his late father, that he officially transferred his belongings to somebody else. (Money for Palestine, too, in small, unimportant amounts was either sent by the community or given to the messengers from that country in a normal way.) Similarly, the dozens of entries dealing with support of the poor, business matters between members, medical services, and many other matters recorded in the minute book show no special involvement with or commitment to messianism or the Messiah.[26]

In brief, words, phrases, beliefs, and even some of the hopes touched the lives of the people—with certain minor exceptions—either only fleetingly or very superficially; but these never became internalized or caused them to change their ways.

We also find such little involvement in other places. In Amsterdam, despite all the expressed hopes for the Messiah, the rich people were not ready to finance passage to Palestine for the poor. Some did not even believe in the Messiah. This is pointed out in a Yiddish song that a man named Jacob Wolf Tausk or Toysk published in the summer of 1666 in Amsterdam. The song repeats many of the rumors about Sabbatai Zevi: that he went to the Turkish king asking for his crown, that after he was taken to jail the locked doors opened by themselves but Sabbatai did not want to leave the prison, and so on. But the two main themes seem to be the attempt to convince others—rich and poor alike—that they would soon leave for Palestine, thus encouraging them to make preparations for the journey; and to seek to assure himself and others that "the Messiah will come in this year," using an analogy with the deliverance from Egypt as "proof." This may indicate that people still needed such assurance.[27]

Discounting some exaggeration by contemporary non-Jews and by scholars of our own times,[28] believers attracted by Sabbatai Zevi and Nathan seem to have been few and far between in Germany, apart from Hamburg. Some German Jews believed in the "news" and rumors in circulation, while others did not. A booklet of instructions on how to repent was printed in Frankfurt on the Main. In Mayence we hear that in view of "the good news" thirteen Jews organized a group to meet with Rabbi Jair Hayim Bachrach for daily study. From a third place a Jew sent a few barrels with food and materials to his son in Hamburg to keep in readiness for him for the time when Jews would depart for Palestine (according to the memoirs of Glueckel of Hamelin written much later).

But in those years Jews in Germany were apparently less interested in leaving for Palestine than in remaining peacefully in Germany. They were mostly concerned about the rumors, exaggerations, and certain anti-Jewish pamphlets containing lies about the Jewish Messiah and the Jews, which were being spread in villages, towns, and cities. Because of these things non-Jews ceased paying their debts to Jews, attacked their persons, or broke windows in their houses. When the Jews sought the protection of the local rulers, the latter tried to dispel the rumors or to protect the Jews in other ways. Actual followers of Sabbatai Zevi seem to have been very few, even though some booklets concerning repentance were copied or published in Germany.

Repentance (teshuvah), an old Jewish principle, was often the only involvement and "activity," which may have temporarily been taken up by many. Repentance was traditionally regarded as a means of cleansing oneself of individual and group sins in the hope that this might help to hasten the Messiah's advent. Rabbis in those years supported in part the trend toward repentance for its own sake. But here, too, many cases appear to have been superficial. We hear of complaints that although people fasted and prayed they were not ready to alter their behavior or to "return the loot which had been taken."[29] This means that they were not prepared to give up part of their possessions for the sake of a belief in the Messiah.

Poland

Jews in Poland, like Jews in other countries, supported the belief in the Messiah's coming—at least with lip service—and officially regarded themselves as living in exile. They prayed for his coming and on occasion repeated the traditional "Next year in Jerusalem." Some among them also computed the date on which messianic times were expected to begin, or they studied, and in a few cases wrote, cabalistic works. A few extracted and repeated the speculation in the *Zohar* that the Messiah would appear in the year 408 (5408 of the Hebrew calendar or 1648 c.e.).

In every society, the Jewish not excepted, there is a gap between verbalized beliefs and actual behavior, which theoretically should result from emotional attachment to these beliefs and attempts to make them viable facts. The extent to which any value or trend—in this case the relationship to Palestine—played a role in the life of the people cannot be gauged from a ritualized repetition of certain phrases, formulas, or wishes alone. The verbal expressions of hope for the coming of the Messiah must be checked against the empirical data of attitudes and behavior. How deeply were the Jews actually involved in the hope of returning to Palestine? How did they act out their involvement? Conversely, what actual impact—not only verbalized—did this have on their life in the Diaspora? To what extent did the people behave differently in times of greater hope or greater stress? In what *active* ways did messianism find expression in the documentary heritage of the times?

Such questions are more easily asked than answered, for we lack direct sources other than the verbalized ones. One way to seek an answer is by checking the compatibility of the expressed beliefs with actual behavior. Actual involvement in messianism could be evinced by detachment from the galut, by a lack of concern for personal possessions in the Diaspora, for the dwelling place, the mode of life, the legal status, and the attitudes of the non-Jewish rulers there. No trace of such attitudes is to be found. Another way is to follow the changing attitudes toward Palestine and settlement there, which are revealed in rabbinic sources dealing with these matters in practical connections.

It appears that European rabbis from around 1000 c.e. either questioned the use of a symbolic relation of the individual Jew to Palestine for practical purposes or denied its validity. During the late medieval ages (twelfth to fifteenth centuries) rabbis wavered in their opinions between maintaining that to live in Palestine is meritorious and a husband may force his wife to follow him there, and denying both. Israel Isserlein (died in 1460) in replying to an inquiry expressed the opinion that it is a virtue to live in Palestine, but he did not overlook the realities of life there. Considering the difficult conditions in Palestine he thought that "each individual should judge his physical fitness and financial resources and then decide for himself to lead a God-fearing life and to keep His commandments."

Some Ashkenazic Jews actually did settle in Palestine, mainly in their old age, and others visited the Holy Land; but Isserlein's emphasis on the question of the possibilities for "a God-fearing life," sometimes extended to opportunities for Torah study, had some impact on the attitudes of Ashkenazic rabbis. Others thought that contributing to the tax load in the Diaspora was more important than settlement in Palestine; "piety and fulfilling of the commandments" in the galut took precedence over Palestine.[30]

A look at the Polish Jewish sources (sixteenth to seventeenth century) reveals the following picture. A few individuals settled in Palestine in their old age, and some arranged beforehand to have a modest income there; a few others may have gone there at a younger age. Polish Jewish communities provided some measure of support for Palestine, which was sent either through the "collector" for Palestine in Lwów or through other channels; and there were individuals who willed specific sums to the Palestine poor. These and similar actions may show some special relationship to Eretz Israel, but reflect little real preferential treatment of Palestine or involvement in the hope of early return. These gifts (both from individuals and communities) were mostly "for the poor of Palestine," with emphasis on the word "poor." This means that the rationale for giving was to a considerable degree the alleviation of poverty, the performance of a good deed, rather than helping build a Jewish country or supporting Palestine per se.*

Nor do the people of those times appear to have been ready to go the whole way and accord Palestine full preferential status, although the fact that Palestine's poor were granted "equal rights" with local poor (Jewish law requires that preference be given to the local poor) may reflect acknowledgment of a certain special attitude

---

*Perhaps we should not be accused of "presentism" (present-mindedness or judging the past by our own standards) if we recall that until the foundation of the State of Israel in 1948 many Jews in the Western countries regarded Palestine mainly as a haven for suffering and poor Jews of the world and supported this endeavor as a sort of charitable enterprise.

toward Palestine. The expressed opinion of Moses Isserles in the case of a sixteenth-century will indicates such an approach—that is, some special treatment on the part of the rabbis;[31] as he states in the opinion, though, he disagreed with Joseph Caro, who apparently advocated singling out this case.

Another sixteenth-century rabbi, Solomon Luria may typify the *practical* approach of Polish Jewry—or of Ashkenazic Jewry generally—toward settlement in Palestine during the centuries preceding modern Zionism. In quoting Rabbi Asher ben Yechiel (c. 1250–1327) Luria supported his opinion that living in the Diaspora should not be regarded as a sin, adding that living in Palestine is a "good deed." In another connection, Luria regarded it as a very serious transgression if a person who was on a temporary visit from Palestine persisted in conforming to the rituals practiced in that country, which differed somewhat from the rituals of Diaspora Jews. For example, when a certain Jew returned temporarily to Poland from Palestine and insisted on following Palestinian ritual, the rabbi expressed sharp disapproval and regarded the man's sudden death as God's just punishment for the grave sin. This seems to be very far removed from the view that life in Palestine had a special virtue or was particularly creditable or took precedence over religious behavior in the Diaspora.

Another contemporary, Samuel Edeles, points out in a (probably imaginary) dialogue with Christians that the Diaspora does not rank much lower than Palestine since the Jews there are able to fulfill most of God's commandments. This seems also to have been the opinion of Isaiah Hurewitz, even though he emphasized the holiness of Palestine and himself settled there. He repeatedly stressed the value of the galut and, as mentioned in an earlier chapter, stated that the rich do not need redemption from the galut. He sought to upgrade the Diaspora by saying that it is necessary, as it were, since it cleanses the Jews; that it is spreading holiness in the world; or that it will assure the continued existence of Palestine in the future. Others assigned to the synagogue in the Diaspora a role similar to that of Eretz Israel with regard to the ascent of the prayers to heaven. Another contemporary, Rabbi Mordekhai Yaffe, in commenting on a verse of the Bible (Isaiah 62:1) homiletically transforms the words "Zion" and "Jerusalem" from their physical meaning into "Jews marked by good deeds" and "God's people full of piety" respectively, probably intending to indicate that piety and good deeds take precedence.[32] Others admitted, openly or not so openly, that the usual praying for redemption was a formality only.[33] Later, in the eighteenth century, there is a strong trend in Hassidic thought favoring upgrading of the galut (see Appendix 4).

So much for theory. In practice some of the cases noted in seventeenth-century Jewish communities supply information about certain individuals who made financial arrangements for living in Palestine—in one such case the Lithuanian *Vaad* granted a former leader a sort of pension enabling him to move there. People also apparently traveled around Poland collecting money ostensibly for the purpose of settling in Palestine, but some of them remained in Poland.[34] Jewish communities and *Vaadim* (the overall community organizations) made arrangements for the collection of money for Palestine, sometimes helping a messenger from that country but at other times introducing strict controls over the movements of such messengers and threatening to confiscate their credentials if they stayed too long in Poland. An anti-Semitic pamphlet of 1618 accuses the Jews of sending money to Turkey—meaning, of course, Palestine. Even before 1648 the larger communities appointed a "collector" of these moneys and sent the money to Palestine through him, usually via Lwów. The *Vaadim* are known to have collected special funds for Palestine—mostly in response to some calamity in that country—and to have appointed overseers to take charge of these collections to which the communities were required to donate. But the many directives about seeing that the money reached its destination and was not used for local needs, and the documents evincing just this practice, may indicate the existence of laxity in this connection.

It is, of course, difficult to form any idea of the degree to which Polish Jewry supported Palestine from the few preserved fragments. One source (rather a general estimate) mentions a few thousand zloty a year sent to Palestine by Polish Jews for the years prior to 1648. The community budgets of Poznań for 1637/38 and 1645/46 seem to indicate that the community gave about three hundred zloty for the "poor of Palestine," which constituted about 1 percent of the expenses for 1637/38.[35]

At the same time, for the most part the Jews in Poland behaved mostly as though the Diaspora was their "natural" permanent habitat. As mentioned, rabbis complained that the Jews had no sense of the impermanence of life in the Diaspora. Rather, they built permanent homes in the "defiled" land; the wealthy ones lived in tranquillity, associated with non-Jews, and some amassed large fortunes for their children.[36] An anonymous author of the seventeenth or the beginning of the eighteenth century may perhaps have given the clearest picture of Polish Jewry's practical attitudes to the problems of the galut-Palestine and the Messiah when he wrote: "One should give thought to and hasten the coming of the prophet Elijah [the herald of the Messiah]. And until his coming, may God grant prosperity and success in all our work."[37] And their work mostly involved long-range plans. Polish Jews were concluding agreements and undertaking obligations that would cover many years, building up large-scale businesses, loaning or borrowing money on long terms, and attempting to gain "eternal" or long-range rights on certain revenues for which they competed with each other.

Joel Sirkis reported the case of a cantor who even refused to chant the traditional prayers and elegies about the destruction of the Temple on the ninth of Av—and this was many years before Sabbatai Zevi abrogated the fast of the ninth of Av. When asked for an explanation of his behavior the cantor replied that since he had not been present when the Temple was destroyed he bore no responsibility for its destruction. Provided this is not just a frame-up of the cantor by the rabbi, with whom he had apparently quarreled, it would indicate that there may have been Jews who did not consider exile a calamity.

In other words, there is enough evidence of a positive attitude toward the galut, both in theory and especially in practice. This attitude may not have been greatly upset by the sufferings during and after the Chmielnicki uprising and the Swedish invasion. As we have already seen, most of the Jewish chronicles and depictions of events in those troubled decades are permeated not only with nostalgia toward "Poland the precious"[38] but also to a great extent with an overriding idea of the general faultlessness of the Poles (Jews placed the blame for their troubles upon the Ukrainians and the "rascals"). They may have felt little psychological need to resort to mystic hopes, since they thought they could rely on the Polish king and nobility.

As mentioned in the preceding chapter, during the 1650s and later the Polish king had issued a number of decrees for the protection of the Jews (March 23, May 4, August 5, 1658; January 17, 1659; June 15, 1660; and others).[39] One may assume that in those years of war and destruction the royal decrees had even less practical value than in normal times. Nonetheless, the Jews made every effort to obtain these documents, which were seldom issued without strenuous perseverance on the part of those for whose protection they were designed. Unlike us, looking back from the vantage point of the present, the Jews of those times apparently saw some practical or psychological value in terms of security in such documents. A similar function may have been fulfilled by the endeavors on the part of the king and some noblemen and *starosta* to pass the decrees of the late 1650s and the 1660s against the ritual accusations and attacks on Jews in various places in Poland.[40] These privileges granted by the king, or the protection afforded by high officials and nobles, may have partially counteracted the activity against the Jews, or at least bolstered their morale by proving that "somebody cared." As mentioned, these years also produced a number of decrees freeing Jews from taxes and assessments for the army, or granting privileges to various groups of Jews.

The 1660s, the years of the rise and fall of the Sabbatai Zevi frenzy, mark both the beginning of a partial economic recovery for Jews in Poland and more frequent mob attacks on them. Extant Jewish community records in Poland for 1662–67 do not reflect particular alarm or anxiety among the Jews (except in 1664).[41] In fact, the majority of documents reflect long-range interests in the Diaspora instead, indicating the intention to remain in Poland, or they deal with problems concerning those who left Poland temporarily for other places in Europe and with their return to the country.

True, during or immediately after the Chmielnicki uprising of 1648 some writers pointed out that 1648 was to have been the year of the Messiah's coming but was instead a year of great trouble. But apparently this line of argument (or prayer) offers no real proof of true acute Messiah expectations. It may rather be a stereotyped response to calamity or a means of stressing the severity of the calamity by countering it with a real or imaginary hope of messianic times. This may also have grown out of the style of writing of those times. Many chronicles, descriptions of trouble, elegies or selichot, and the prayer *El maleh Rachamim*, ("O God full of compassion") penned in connection with a calamity, usually ended on a note of consolation or with a prayer for the coming of the Messiah and deliverance from the Diaspora, often also with a request that God take revenge on the adversaries.[42]

Mysticism and Cabala

Mysticism is defined as "a type of religion which puts the emphasis on immediate awareness of relations with God." There are also other, broader definitions of mysticism that make it a counterpart of philosophy, as it were, dealing with similar topics but with a different approach. Its main characteristics are feeling, intuitive vision, and emotional approach. "Jewish mysticism in its various forms"—according to Scholem—"represents an attempt to interpret the religious values of Judaism in terms of mystical values. It concentrates upon the idea of the living God who manifests Himself in the acts of Creation, Revelation and Redemption."[43]

The cabala, as Jewish mysticism became known, concerns itself with God and creation, good and evil, the mystic values of the letters of the Hebrew alphabet, life after death, speculations on the coming of the Messiah, demons and spirits, and the use of talismans and magic.

In the heritage of Polish Jewry one finds a few strains of mysticism. In the early days the teachings of Jehuda Hachassid ("the Devout") and his group came from the West in the twelfth to thirteenth centuries. These emphasized the themes of love (or fear) of God, God and Satan, paradise, resurrection, reward and punishment for the individual after death, resistance to temptation, strict justice, and spiritual perfection. A ritual of penance was formulated which involved numerous stages and prescribed a great variety of acts. Spiritual perfection, human fairness, and piety were regarded as goals for human behavior. Most of this was designed for select individuals.[44] A Lithuanian-Polish Jew, Moses ben Jacob of Kiev, wrote a cabalist book at the end of the fifteenth century. This work, which may be the first by a Jewish author in Eastern Europe generally, is full of "secrets" and was influenced by Nachmanides and the Sephardic strain of cabala, which the writer apparently picked up while in Constantinople. Its influence in Poland was minimal, however, since it remained in manuscript form for almost three centuries.[45]

During the sixteenth century the *Zohar* (first published in Mantua in 1558–60) became known in Poland, although it was not printed there until the beginning of the following century.[46] A few other cabalistic or semicabalistic works were printed in Poland as early as the end of the sixteenth century.[47]

But generally the Jewish printing shops in Lublin and Cracow (1547–1660) made little provision for cabalistic or mystic literature. Apparently no more than 10 percent of the nearly three hundred titles published would belong to this category. The printers concentrated mostly on prayer books, Talmud, rabbinic literature, responsa, and homiletic and similar works, over and above nearly one hundred titles in Yiddish. (Apparently the number of such "secular" works as Josipon, grammatical works like *Pirkey Eliyahu* by Eliyahu Bachur, a book about letter writing, and others equaled those on cabala.)

It goes without saying that the sparsity of cabalistic or mystic books printed in Poland cannot serve as conclusive proof that they were little in demand there; some could have been brought from abroad, although the preserved material on imported works indicates that these were in the category of prayer books and rabbinics. We have further indication of this from the eighteenth century. Incidental information on the number of books acquired or donated to the community of Lissa (Leszno, Jewish population in 1765: five to six thousand) after the fire in 1767 shows fifty-three titles, of which only one, *Shnei Luchot Habrith* by Isaiah Hurewitz, in two copies, could be counted as mystic literature. The rest consisted of the usual rabbinic literature (six copies of the Babylonian Talmud, four copies of *Tur Yoreh Dea*, and so on.)[48] This information—direct and inferred—showing the slow rate at which cabalistic media spread in Poland may be corroborated by the apparently negligible dissemination of the ideas themselves.[49] Moses Isserles and Samuel Edeles, the two sixteenth-century rabbis usually quoted, may simply have been exaggerating when they complained about the "many from among the common people" who rushed to study cabala or about those "who spend their time" with cabala.[50] They may have been reacting to a few copies of works brought to Poland from abroad. (Moses Isserles mentions three books by name, none of which was at that time printed in Poland.)

A generation or two later we hear the contrary. Isaiah Hurewitz asserts: "I saw those of the higher rungs in Jewish society [meaning cabalists] and their number is small. And most of the people are far from cabala. . . . Moreover, not only do they disclaim the cabala, but they maintain that nothing is true in the Torah save its literal meaning."[51]

The editor of the first Lurianic publication in Poland, *Tikkuney Shabbat* (published in Cracow in 1630 or 1609–12), which contains various liturgic parts for Fridays, mentions in his foreword that the Cracow rabbis who encouraged him to publish the book advised him to leave out the "internal secrets" (meaning real cabala), which apply only to a few individuals. Another one complains in 1643 that cabala is not studied in the same way as the Talmud.[52]

Polish Jewry's lack of great interest in cabala—both in printing and studying the books—may apparently be taken to indicate that such study was very far from being widespread and by no means involved many Polish Jews in specific cabalistic activity. Indeed, for the most part Polish Jews did not necessarily use the *Zohar* and similar writings for mystic speculations and ideas. They regarded them rather as a source of revealed lore *(torath hanigleh)*. For Moses Isserles the teachings of the *Zohar* were "revealed on Sinai," and he quotes them as laws with which he sometimes agrees and sometimes disagrees. For another rabbi, Benjamin Solnik, it is the next greatest book to the Talmud. And Joel Sirkis sees the cabala as the "source of the Torah and its core."[53] Other rabbis quoted cabalistic works as authorities in decisions in matters of law or ritual. Jehuda Loeb Puchowitzer wrote his *Divrey Hakhanim* in 1692 in order to make available the religious laws *(dinim)* found in the *Zohar*, the writings of Isaac Luria, and Hurewitz's *Shnei Luchot Habrith,* which a Jew "should know and fulfill."[54]

But even more characteristic of Polish mysticism is that when the esoteric Lurianic cabala (according to some, a main factor in the messianic Sabbatai Zevi upheaval) came to Poland it became eclectic, combining different cabalistic and semicabalistic approaches of varied ages and methods and replete with demonomania. This was facilitated both by the makeup of most of the Polish Jewish cabalists and the character of premodern Jewish thought. The cabalists in Poland were mostly preachers who usually based their deliberations on a conglomerate of different, at times contradictory, ideas and arguments. This was an outcome of the nature of traditional thought generally, which was usually associative rather than causative, with many internally unrelated elements packed together on the basis of mere external similarity. Professor Scholem has characterized the Polish cabala this way:

> *The elements are thrown together and the author does not discern the various contradictions between them. Lack of pure theoretical interest and an overwhelming homiletic interest . . . such an attitude is far from what should be called real Lurianic attitude. . . .*
>
> *The second line which singles out the writings of the leaders of the Polish Cabbalah of that generation [first half of the seventeenth century] is the strong attraction for them of the theory of evil ("Kelipah") and all matters connected with the world of devils and spirits. . . . What is surprising here is the degree to which they were fascinated with this field and the sharp personal grasp of evil ("Kelipoth"). Only in Poland . . . does one find Cabbalists who have no inclination to deepen their interest in the secrets and mysteries connected with God. . . . Nothing remained for them from all the teachings of Luria . . . save these elements which emphasize the individual struggle of each person against the evil spirits ("Kelipoth")—each one of the latter having a particular type and name. . . . A strange demonology has here been developed. . . . The need to "erase" a specific demon through a man's good deeds calls for the need to recognize its name and character . . . whole armies of evil spirits ("Kelipoth") appear here for the first time and around them is woven a kind of new mythology.[55]*

Scholem goes on to tell of some falsifications (which he calls "pseudo-epigraphic"), with other people's ideas being presented as though they had been Luria's.[56] This conglomerate was spread—insofar as it reached more than a few individuals—through the preachers, who used the materials for their sermons.[57] In other words, the Polish cabala of the pre-Sabbatai Zevi period consisted of a compilation—not necessarily a consistent one—of many pre-Lurianic and some Lurianic ideas, which had apparently little to do with messianism and redemption. We see also that the Lurianic idea of *tikkun,* which was supposed to mean "the world of messianic action,"[58] either did not exist among Polish cabalists or was submerged in a flood of concern with the satanical aspect of the world and "a strange demonology" of millions of evil spirits and devils filling the world. Additionally, any safeguards against the evil spirits—with their multiplicity of names, forms, and "causes," each created by a specific sin—were supposed to stem from the pious behavior of each individual Jew rather than community action or intervention by a messiah.

When the "revelation of the messiah [Sabbatai Zevi] came about," first in Gaza and later in Smyrna (Izmir) in the mid-1660s, Polish Jews had little to do with it. They were rarely found among the cronies of Sabbatai or Nathan, nor did they play any role in the developing drama.[59] Extant evidence shows only a few Polish Jews connected with the false Messiah, and most of these only marginally so. The preacher Berachya Beirach was "on his way to Palestine" when he went to see Sabbatai, but he died shortly thereafter. According to some information he sent a letter home to Cracow describing his visit. In 1666 a little book in Yiddish, *Tikkuney Teshuva me-eretz Hatzwi*, was published in Cracow, but this is not identical with the *Tikkuney Teshuva* that Nathan sent to several other cities. The content is collected from different earlier works. It may have been designed for repentance, which in that year was urged by believers in Sabbatai and by "doubting rabbis" (in order to transform possible belief in the false Messiah into "useful" penitence). The little book was printed with the approval (or on the initiative) of the Cracow rabbi Arye Loeb ben Zecharia Mendel.[60] If the unconfirmed information about Arye Loeb's being a follower of Sabbatai Zevi and even corresponding with Nathan of Gaza can be substantiated he may perhaps serve as a model for an uncommitted follower of Sabbatai.

We know for a fact that early in 1667 he and his son received from the Polish king the title of "servant of the king" (an honorary title that in Poland carried many privileges: freedom from most taxes and unlimited trading and similar rights). Since such titles were difficult to come by and it took considerable time and effort to acquire them, one may justifiably suppose that the rabbi had been involved in such endeavors during the years 1665–66. This would logically indicate that he was not much of a true believer in the false Messiah; or else even though a believer he nevertheless sought "insurance" elsewhere, which in reality means the same thing. In truth, almost all the speculations by scholars and other writers about the behavior and attitudes of Jews in Poland during the crucial years of the Sabbatai Zevi movement (1664–66) lack any factual foundation.[61]

Two rabbis from Lwów (the son and stepson of rabbi David Halevi, author of *Turey Zahav*, a commentary to *Shulchan Aruch*), traveled to Gallipoli to see Sabbatai Zevi. The trip was apparently undertaken for the purpose of investigating Sabbatai.[62] The two men (according to a Sabbatian source there were five) reached Gallipoli in the summer of 1666 a few days after the seventeenth of Tamuz, which Sabbatai had turned from a fast day into a holiday. Sabbatai apparently saw them at first only briefly, sending them on to one of his lieutenants in Constantinople, Abraham Yakhini, who was to prepare them in the "new belief." If one reads the sources about this visit carefully (much of the material is a combination of legend and fiction), one may form the following picture: Sabbatai or his managers or secretary sought strenuously to influence the two Polish rabbis. Preparations were made to impress them with Sabbatai's concern for Polish Jewry and his importance and influence. The rabbis, being held back from seeing Sabbatai, tried in the meantime to examine one of his "prophets," Moshe Saraval, concerning his leader. When they were finally admitted again to the presence of the "Messiah," Sabbatai was ready for them.

Entering the room they saw on Sabbatai's table a copy of *Zok Haitim,* a chronicle of the cossack massacres of 1648. He was dressed all in red, and the Torah he had with him was also covered in red. This symbolism of the 1648 massacres in Poland apparently made little impression on the two Polish guests—they were quite familiar with the events of 1648, which may no longer have seemed to them relevant. So Sabbatai tried to draw their attention to his "1648 exhibition," promising revenge on the oppressors of Polish Jews. He sang for them and sought to win them over by inquiring about their aged father. In the guise of being a healer Sabbatai sent the old man "medicine" and an item of clothing as a talisman. Sabbatai then tried to draw closer to them by singing a chapter from the psalter, which, we are told, usually enchanted onlookers or listeners. He also promised them some office in his "kingdom" to come and sent their father a letter in his own handwriting, again promising that "shortly I shall take vengeance for you." We are told that the two rabbis sent letters to Poland extolling the "Messiah" and that the letters made some impression there, but we do not know if it was really so.

This visit may have been Sabbatai's undoing if it is true, as reported, that he asked the two rabbis or their father to send to him Nehemia Hakohen, a Polish cabalist, a preacher or "prophet" from Poland. The latter arrived in Gallipoli about a month after the two rabbis had left. Nehemia seems to have come as a nonbeliever in Sabbatai. According to the stories, he and Sabbatai haggled for three days and nights (snatching a few hours' sleep now and then) about the procedure for the revelation of the Messiah. In accordance with traditional Jewish ideas Nehemia argued that before the appearance of the Messiah son of David—the real redeemer—another Messiah (son of Joseph) is supposed to appear and be killed. Non-Jewish sources mention that Nehemia himself claimed to have been the Messiah son of Joseph. Neither the many cabalistic writings that Sabbatai marshaled, nor the latter's assertion that a man called Abraham Zalman was the Messiah son of Joseph and had been killed during the Chmielnicki massacres, helped to convince Nehemia.

Fearing for his life, which he believed was endangered by Sabbatai's followers, Nehemia converted officially to the Muslim religion, informed the Turkish authorities of Sabbatai's activities, and left soon after for Poland. There he reverted to Judaism, denying that Sabbatai was the Messiah. (Nehemia is supposed to have told this story himself to Loeb ben Ozer in Amsterdam about thirty years later.) Nehemia's information to the Turkish authorities led to Sabbatai's being called before the sultan and his subsequent conversion.[63]

So far we have mentioned six Polish Jews (according to Sabbatian information there were nine) who became associated with Sabbatai's messianism. There may have been a few others. Of these six, Nehemia was apparently opposed to Sabbatai, the two rabbis from Poland were doubters, at least at first, and the rabbi of Cracow seems to have been only partially or not at all involved. This would leave two or three —adding the sons of Rabbi David would bring it to half a dozen or let's say a dozen or two (with the rest "thrown in for good measure")—full-fledged Sabbatians in Poland as of 1666. And this out of a Jewish population of one hundred thousand or more! These few individuals involved could scarcely have been representative of Polish Jewry.

To this one should add that a Cracow synagogue contains a handwritten haftorah collection with a dedicatory poem on the title page in which the Hebrew letters for Sabbatai are emphasized (enlarged). This might indicate that the writer or scribe was a Sabbatian.[64]

Reactions

In Poland, as in many another country, the reaction among the non-Jews to the news about the Jewish "Messiah" was varied though mainly unfriendly. A genuine Jewish Messiah would cast doubt on Jesus' role as a messiah. Those who heard about Sabbatai—mostly in a highly exaggerated form—reacted either by making fun of the whole matter and the Jews or by utilizing it for anti-Jewish propaganda or for attacks upon Jews. Examples of each of these types of reaction in Poland have been preserved, but we have no way of knowing how widespread they were.

A nobleman wrote an epigram about "the new Jewish Messiah" telling that his Jewish leaseholder stopped working the leased brewery because he was "relying on the country [Palestine], which is full of honey or wine." Later the Jew was unable to pay his rent.

Some others were eager to obtain information on the "Messiah" from Western Europe—some of the materials they received were preserved in Cracow and have for the most part an anti-Jewish overtone. The rank and file and the troublemakers used the "Messiah" incident in the spring of 1666 to stage pogroms, beat up Jews, or murder them. The Jews apparently requested protection from the authorities. A decree of May 5, 1666, from the Polish king says that for the second time licentious people were attempting to ruin the Polish Jews:

> Not long ago they spread news that the church authorities and the courts allegedly permitted oppression of Jews. Now . . . by disseminating the false news from foreign countries about some messiah, and trying to substantiate it in some places by means of printed sheets and pictures . . . they threaten the Jews with doom and oppression.

The king ordered that the Jews be protected and the pictures, prints, and writings be destroyed as falsifications.[65]

It all boils down to the fact that very few, possibly only a mere handful, Polish Jews were in any way identified with the false Messiah, and even these few not all positively. By no stretch of the imagination can any considerable part of Polish Jewry be thought to have been involved with the false Messiah, especially since, as mentioned earlier, the preserved Jewish and non-Jewish documents[66] give the impression of a stable, galut-oriented Jewish community. This does not mean to say that some Jews in Poland (outside of the handful) may not have been interested in the news about the "Messiah," or even have entertained for a while some abstract hope that the Messiah's coming might be imminent. In the seventeenth century Jews in Poland and other countries, as well as non-Jews, believed in all manner of rumors and tales connected with miracles and supernatural phenomena. And a messiah belonged in that category. Uncritical, passive belief in miracles is not identical with commitment to Sabbatai. What seems to be clear is that the bulk of Polish Jewry was scarcely involved in the messianism of those years, and Polish Jews were not active in the whole movement.

After the Conversion

The "Messiah" bubble burst for the most part in the Jewish communities following the conversion. Aside from apparently small pockets of believers and individuals here and there, the movement—insofar as it was a movement—disappeared.

This process varied from region to region. In the Sephardic communities in Turkey and Italy, where at least some Jews had followed Sabbatai's decree abrogating the fasts and instituting new holidays, the return was harder and the effects greater than in the Ashkenazic communities, which had never abrogated the fast of the ninth of Av. Italy, too, apparently began relatively early to make an end of Sabbatianism, if we take as characteristic a letter written in the name of Venice by Joseph Halevi of Livorno at the beginning of November 1666. In Egypt, Sabbatai and some of his followers were placed under ban about a month later. The anti-Sabbatians again became the leading force in the community of Amsterdam, while the leaders of the Sabbatians decreased to a small group. In Hamburg, Sasportas banned the Sabbatians almost immediately after conversion. What happened to Nathan may perhaps be typical of the fate of Sabbatianism in the years after the conversion. He was refused entry to Adrianopol in 1667, but in 1668 was permitted to enter Venice temporarily after he had signed a document repudiating his "prophecy." In those years he had to wander from place to place seeking shelter. After 1668 his influence apparently declined so much that the communities left him alone.[67]

A comparison of anti-Sabbatian and pro-Sabbatian sources may indicate a sharp decline in the number of believers in the decade or so after the conversion. Samuel Abohab of Venice maintains, as mentioned, that in "all Jewish communities" of Italy, and in many other countries of the world, the Jews repented and ceased to believe in Sabbatai Zevi. Following his conversion a Sabbatian apologist admits a great decline; he sees the number of remaining believers as very small, his only consolation being that "neutrals" were to be found among the nonbelievers.[68]

There remained some, apparently small, groups and a few individuals who tried to continue their activity, formulating theories about the "apostate Messiah" who expected to deliver the Jews (different dates were later set for his reappearance) and in some cases indulging in antinomian practices. Here and there an individual appeared as a "prophet" or in some other guise, claiming the title of Messiah. A more radical group was founded in 1683, a sect called Doenmeh (Turkish for "apostates"), whose members outwardly professed Islam. [69]

In Poland

In Poland there was apparently little to repent of in order to return to normality.[70] If penitence really had been practiced in some places during the preceding years this activity did not represent any inherent break in tradition. Traditional Jews were accustomed to penitence. The rabbis continually demanded teshuvah. Polish Jews practiced the harsher methods advocated by Jehuda Hachassid and his school (twelfth to thirteenth century in Germany). There is no shred of evidence that even when Sabbatai's "messianic mission" rose to its peak in 1665–66 Polish Jews (with the possible exception of a few individuals) abrogated the fast of the ninth of Av or introduced a special prayer in Sabbatai's honor. Some Jews may have had their expectations aroused by exaggerated "news" and propaganda disseminated at that time. But as we have said, this did not involve either commitment or activity. Nor do the many hundreds of varied community and state documents extant reveal any sign of tension in this direction. As if to point out the fallacy in assuming any confidence in the imminent arrival of God's kingdom the minute books of the communities and the responsa abound in materialistic concerns: fairs and business, competition, rights of settlement, problems of community organization, education and welfare, taxes, relations to Christian authorities, quarrels among rabbis and laymen, family affairs, and similar matters, in addition to religious and ritual subjects and many other mundane concerns, most of which deal mainly with a long-range future. The same is true of the non-Jewish archive documents.

From this overwhelming concern of the documents with such practical matters one is justified in concluding that these are the things that were relevant to the people of those times. Such things as belief in the messianism of Sabbatai Zevi either did not exist or were of little interest. The one exception in the documentary evidence is a ban that the Polish Four-Land Council in 1670 or 1672, or both, placed upon "the transgressors and blunderers who believe in Sabbatai Zevi."[71]

The ban in Poland may have been modeled on the ones in other countries (in Hamburg, for instance) or it may have had particular relevance for Podolia, which is specifically mentioned in the second ban. This may or may not indicate that there were some Sabbatians in Poland or Podolia in those years. (It has been suggested that because of the Polish-Turkish war, Polish Jews were eager to show the authorities in 1672 that they were not involved in anything stemming from Turkey.)

Thus those who may have still believed in Sabbatai were forced underground. Certainly there were Jews in Poland, though their number may have been negligible, who may have believed somewhat in the exaggerated stories about the Messiah or about the Ten Tribes, which were to come (or had come!) from the Sambation River, just as they believed stories of a supernatural character about the evil eye and the many ghosts, devils, and spirits supposedly filling the world.* A few individuals may have immersed themselves in cabalistic speculations becoming "prophets" and trying to perform miracles, predict the future, and function as "healers" *(baalei shem)*. But their outward behavior remained that of pious Jews generally: they studied, prayed, and fulfilled the requisite good deeds. Perhaps some did "see" visions and revelations, which they wrote down. And perhaps some had ideas and associative thoughts of a messianic character resembling Sabbatianism.

Such a one was Heshel Zoref (Goldsmith) from Wilno (1633–1700), who spent the last five years of his life in Cracow. During his lifetime nobody apparently recognized his belief in Sabbatai Zevi, and his writings, which remained in manuscript *(Sepher Hatzoref)*, were for a long time not acknowledged as having anything to do with Sabbatianism. Some of these writings supposedly later found their way into the hands of Israel Baal Shem Tov (Besht), who is said to have valued them highly. After Besht's death copies of the book were found in the possession of other Hassidic leaders. If we may believe the documents of the Sabbatians, Heshel Zoref had contact with some of their leaders and declared himself in accord with their ideology.[72]

There were also others who outwardly lived as traditional Jews but whose thoughts and writings contained rudiments of the ideology of Nathan of Gaza or other Sabbatians. Among these may probably be counted some who advocated such Sabbatian or near-Sabbatian ideas without perhaps realizing their heretical origin,[73] while others took their Sabbatianism underground for fear of persecution by Jewish authorities. A number of the latter were not recognized during their lifetimes, or even later, as having had anything to do with Sabbatian theory or thought. Research in cabala and Sabbatianism pursued during the last generation or so has discovered —sometimes only purported to have discovered—a number of such secret Sabbatians. They acted as individuals to some extent, though there may have been a loose group.

These groups often included people of disparate backgrounds who perhaps were not even aware of their differences. Thus the group that the preacher Jehuda Hachassid gathered for a journey to Palestine (in 1700, it is said to have comprised thirty-one families from Poland) included Hayim Malach, who apparently was a real Sabbatian. In 1691 he had lived in Italy, where he had connections with the moderate Sabbatians, and from 1692 to 1694 he lived in Adrianople and Salonika, where he was in contact with Samuel Primo (Sabbatai's secretary) and the radical group of Doenmeh (converted Sabbatians) led by Berachya. Returning to Poland he spread some of the radical ideas (in Żólkiew and elsewhere).

Upon the death of the leader, Jehuda Hachassid a few days after arrival in

---

*These beliefs and superstitions were for the most part of a rather passive nature, calling for no more than a special prayer, a talisman, a charm against the evil eye.

Palestine, Hayim Malach and his followers were expelled from the group, but they continued as a group and some of them joined the Doenmeh in Salonika. Again returning to Poland, in about 1705, Hayim continued to disseminate his Sabbatian propaganda, prophesying that Sabbatai would return in 1706. He contributed to the growth of some cells of the radical antinomian Sabbatians in Podolia, a few of whose members later appeared in Western Europe.

If we take literally the heresy-hunter Jacob Emden and those who follow his "conspiracy theory," most of Podolia and some other parts of Poland were supposedly infested by Sabbatians. But this is far from the truth. The listed names of the transgressors number a few dozen, some of whom were traveling abroad in Moravia, Bohemia, and Germany. More individuals may have been involved, but this is still a far cry from any sort of "movement." One seems justified in regarding the cells and groups of Sabbatians that were popping up at the end of the seventeenth and in the first half of the eighteenth century less as people united by a certain ideology (Sabbatianism) than as individuals united by the need to go underground or who were lumped together by their adversaries—the Establishment—who grouped them together so as to be better able to suppress them.

Most of those people—their number is very limited—seem to have belonged to the lower social strata of the Jewish religious intelligentsia: itinerant preachers who wandered from place to place, receiving no institutional fees but having to make do with a small gift from the kehilla or private alms or both; ordained or semiordained rabbis without rabbinical posts; "messengers" who came from Palestine to collect money for the needy in that country; scholars without a permanent occupation or position; an occasional cantor, healer, *baal shem* (miracle worker), peddler, and the like. Most of these individuals lacked status in the community and were controlled by the Establishment, which limited their activities.[74] In many instances these elements criticized the power-holders in the kehilla and the elite, the leadership and the wealthy, thus adding to existing tensions. By chance or by design some of them came in contact with Sabbatians or near-Sabbatians in countries outside of Poland and were influenced by their theories and behavior, or adopted certain of their external rituals and ideas—sometimes without actually becoming involved in Sabbatianism.

Generally this rudimentary real or fancied Sabbatianism in Jewish society of the post-Sabbatai Zevi decades apparently served two almost contradictory trends. For those who were on the fringe of Jewish society, who were alienated and estranged from that society, it may have furnished an ideological framework for self-identification. Whatever pride they were able to take in being "believers" helped them resist psychologically the power of the rich and the mighty. On the other hand, for the latter the identification "Sabbatianer" or "Shepsel" came to denote any rebel, anyone opposed to the elite, until "Sabbatianism" came to mean anything one disliked (in somewhat the same way that "Communist" is used today in some Western countries, or "American capitalist" in East European countries). In this way the ranks of the Sabbatians seemed to be swelled.

For some of these and others the ideology of the Sabbatianism or its nihilistic trend, which developed in the late seventeenth century—the antinomianism that either denied the existence of sin or claimed that sins against the Jewish law became virtues ("holiness of sin")—increased in importance. This approach, which is found also among some Christian millenarists, was either accepted or created by those who for one reason or another were "sinners" to begin with, particularly in sexual behavior.[75]

11 *Messianism's Aftereffect—Jacob Frank and Frankism*

Turbulence in the Eighteenth Century

The century following the short-lived Sabbatai Zevi messianism (1665–66) happened to be a period of rapid population growth for Polish Jewry. The number of Jews in Poland increased roughly three- or fourfold. It must have been a tremendous task for them to settle, find ways to make a living, and integrate into the framework of the existing Jewish organizational setup. The difficulties were further augmented because the country lay in ruins after two decades (1648–67) of uprisings, invasions, wars, famines, and epidemics. It was worst in the south where Jews resettled after having been victims of the cossack massacres or returned after having fled the region. Nor did the decades of the eighteenth century remain peaceful, which worsened the situation. *Haidemaks,* as we have seen, staged intermittent attacks in different places. Rerooting was made especially difficult by the fact that it had to be done individually by each person or family. There was no special agency to lighten the burden. This meant that competition between individuals became sharper and more intensive.

Such an epoch of resettlement and restructuring is always characterized by change accompanied by social and economic mobility. Upward and downward mobility are likely to create clusters of nouveaux riches and nouveaux pauvres, which in turn leads to social tension and alienation. The situation was aggravated in Poland by problems of settlement rights and payment of entry fees, which generally were handled by the elite, the kehilla leadership. Moreover, as we have seen, change and the processes of population growth, economic recovery, and mobility led to the rise of new towns and cities—mostly of the nobility-owned type—and the decline in importance of the older ones, the Jewish communities in the royal cities. At the end of the seventeenth century or the beginning of the eighteenth an author depicts the

> great hatred of today's aliens—the expellees from the Ukraine. . . . In time their Jewish friends [in the new places] will revolt and will become their foes and persecutors. . . . Those who can pay "ransom" to become citizens have a hope

... the rest must wander around ... remain at the bottom of the [social] ladder ... become wood cutters and water drawers, and the middlings are suspended in shame and there is no one to show compassion for them. [1]

The many shifts and changes tended to increase the numbers of the disaffected and the alienated: the lower strata of the religious "intelligentsia" such as itinerant preachers, rabbis without permanent positions, and others living on occasional earnings, on the one hand; and on the other, innkeepers and other village Jews whose positions were seized by competitors and people in the cities who had no specified means of existence (a sort of *lumpenproletariat* or lumpen middle class). In short, there existed people predisposed to become part of the silent or not-so-silent opposition. These circumstances may have given rise to the need to band together somehow or even organize around a common purpose, perhaps leading to a sort of sectarianism.

Such attitudes were apparently more prevalent in southern Poland, especially in Podolia. Having been conquered by Turkey in 1672 and later returned to Poland in 1699, Podolia was politically unstable. During the decades of Turkish rule some Jews apparently came in contact with radical Sabbatians in Turkey and may have picked up certain patterns from them.

In fact, in that period and the subsequent years the social controls of Jewish community life in the region were weakened, and the Jewish communities of Podolia were struggling to free themselves from the sovereignty of the Russian (Galician) *Vaad* (Council). The weaker social controls became, the more they were trangressed. The discrepancy between the unacceptable impulses and the normative realities of the Jewish world could then be reduced by rationalization or sublimation, making the biological drives respectable. In Poland in the period under review the formula "holiness of sin," which meant accepting sin or elevating its status, did not have to be invented. The theory may have been adopted from the radical groups in Turkey, where it had been developed earlier. [2] Since some of the radicals, the moderates, and those who were slanderously labeled Sabbatians could only practice deviant behavior underground, they were mostly lumped together by their adversaries. And, in fact, under pressure from the outside there may have been some cooperation between individuals despite their disparate attitudes; thus "cells" could have evolved.

There may also have been some other reasons why Podolia became a breeding place for Jewish sectarianism (Frankism and Hassidism). Patriarch Nikons's reforms of the Russian Greek Orthodox Church in Russia in 1654 led the Old Believers, who opposed the correction of the church books and other innovations, to dissociate themselves from the church (this was called *raskol*, schism). In due course the dissenters split into many sects and subsects. As time passed, some of these dissenters became radicals, rejecting church and state authorities and building up new ways of life, ranging from extreme asceticism to extreme lawlessness and depravity, or some combination of the two: Khlysty—flagellants, Skoptsy—self-emasculators, Molokane—milk drinkers, Dukhobortsy—spirit wrestlers, and others.

For the most part the Russian government mercilessly suppressed the dissenters, especially the radical groups, some of whom fled to Poland. In the eighteenth century a subgroup settled in Podolia that called itself Philipowcy* (tradition says it was founded in the seventeenth century by Danilo Philipov, who became "God of Zabaot"). We find among these and other sectarians a number of doctrines, traits, ideas, and behavior patterns of which rudiments are also present among the Frankists and Hassidim.

Because the Russian sects were forced underground our information on them is very fragmentary, somewhat general, and mostly based on oral recollections rather than on documentary materials. For this reason also it is often impossible to form any true idea of the time in which a particular pattern developed. Problems are also encountered in seeking a reasonable view of their origins. Moreover, satisfactory analysis of the parallels between Jewish and non-Jewish sects is difficult, providing little basis for an acceptable hypothesis about models and influences. But the fact that there are parallels, unless they are to be considered as general traits of sectarianism everywhere, indicates the possibility of some mutual copying.

Imitation was possible mainly in such places as the Ukraine generally and Podolia in particular,[3] where the Russian sectarians apparently settled extensively during the 1730s and formed a considerable part of the population in some places. Jews there lived for the most part in small towns and rural communities where a small group of separate individuals dwelt in close proximity to the other inhabitants. Thus the human contact (especially the economic contact apparently) between neighbors, the Jew and the non-Jew, was much closer than in the cities, where the living space was often separated by walls or streets. Thus there is a possibility that Jews were aware of developments among their neighbors and picked up some traits from them. Be that as it may, Jews appear to have known about the existence of some of these sectarians and to have had an inkling of their ideas[4] and some contact with them.

All these trends may have been influenced by the Jewish "heresy-hunt," if we may call it that, which developed in the eighteenth century.

Heresy-Hunt

As mentioned earlier, in the first years of the eighteenth century the problem of Hayim Malach's activity as a Sabbatian was raised through a 1705 letter from Jerusalem to the Polish Jewish Four-Land Council, and apparently also through letters from Constantinople to German and Polish communities.[5] Not long after this the heresy-hunt spread out to involve Jewish communities in many lands.

Nehemia Hayun was connected with these events. He was born in Sarajevo about 1650, studied in Hebron, served briefly as rabbi in Uskup, and led an adventurous existence in Turkey, Italy, Egypt, Palestine, and European countries. From Prague,

*See note 30.

where he lived in 1711–12, he traveled to Vienna, Nikolsburg, Prosnitz, Glogau, and Berlin—occasionally preaching in the Sabbatian mode.

In Berlin he succeeded in publishing his *Oz le-Elohim* in 1713, in which he sets forth a version of the post-Sabbatai Zevi Sabbatians' idea of a trinity: the hidden God (the First Cause or God of reason), the God of revelation(the God of religion or the God of Israel), and the Shekhina. The book was even approved by rabbis, who either did not read or did not understand the text. In Amsterdam he and a Sephardic rabbi, Rabbi Ayllon, who gave Hayun's book his approbation, were challenged by an Ashkenazic rabbi, Zevi Ashkenazi (father of Jacob Emden), who detected the heretical ideas in the book and started active opposition to the author. Although Rabbi Ashkenazi did not succeed in arousing the Sephardic or Ashkenazic communities in Amsterdam, he did contribute to stirring up communities elsewhere. Excommunications soon began to flow from Germany, Italy, Africa, and possibly also Poland.[6] At about the same time a few Sabbatians or persons accused of being Sabbatians were discovered in Poland (Moses Meir Kaminker of Żółkiew and others), possibly Moravia, and Germany. Bans were pronounced in many cities abroad as well as in Lwów and other places in Poland (1722–25) and were forwarded from one city to another. This created a climate of witch-hunting and suspicion.[7]

About a quarter of a century later a new controversy and heresy-hunt flared up within European Jewry also involving, to a great extent, the Jews of Poland. In Altona, Jacob Israel Emden (1697–1776), who had earlier begun to combat the Sabbatians, started a campaign in 1750 against Jonathan Eibeschitz (1690–1767), the newly appointed rabbi of the united community Altona-Hamburg-Wandsbeck. Emden maintained that Eibeschitz, who even prior to his appointment had been suspected of espousing Sabbatianism, must be a Sabbatian because the name Sabbatai appeared in a talisman he prepared. The Jewish community of Altona-Hamburg defended Eibeschitz against Emden. Many rabbis in Germany and beyond soon became involved in the controversy, taking sides and pronouncing bans against each other.[8]

Polish Jews began to take part in the dispute with the rabbi of Lublin (a former pupil of Eibeschitz's) placing a ban on Emden in 1751. Before long the Four-Land Council was embroiled in this controversy, with leaders dividing into pro-Emden and pro-Eibeschitz factions. The pro-Emden group enlisted the help of high Polish officials in an attempt to force the Lublin rabbi to withdraw his ban. After wrangling for a few years (the council was beset at that time with other internal problems too) the Four-Land Council decided in favor of Eibeschitz and in 1753 ordered Emden's anti-Eibeschitz pamphlets destroyed.

The controversy over the Emden-Eibeschitz struggle in and around the Polish Four-Land Council, with the two factions vying for support of the leadership and of the Polish authorities,[9] apparently intensified for Polish Jews the problems of Sabbatianism and the struggle against it, and may have increased their vigilance and alertness in this direction.

Either individual Sabbatians or cells of them seem to have lived in some places in Podolia and nearby. Some of these people may have had contacts with Berachya of the Doenmeh in Salonika. If we are to believe Ber Birkenthal (Ber of Bolechów), who wrote his memoirs some forty years later, there were Sabbatians in Nadwórna and Tysmenice who appeared to live like pious Jews but committed many sins in secret, including wife-swapping. The gap between these Jews and the genuinely pious seems, however, to have been narrow or even nonexistent. According to Ber himself, some of the secret Sabbatians came into close contact with pious Jews—two of them were guests in the house of Ber's father. Even Leib Krisa of Nadwórna, though apparently previously known as a sort of leader of a Sabbatian group and later as one of Frank's lieutenants (they converted to Christianity together), is depicted by Ber as one who mixed with other Jews (he came to Ber's house, where he read from the latter's *Zohar* set).

If we may believe Franciszek Antony Kobielski, the bishop of Luck, in his writings against the Jews, there were a number of Jewish women in Brody in 1752 accused of committing adultery (this was taken to mean that they belonged to the antinomian Sabbatians). The regional Russian (Galician) Jewish Community Council and the rabbis put a ban on the trangressors. Some of the husbands divorced their guilty wives while others complained to the nobleman owner of Brody, Stanislas Potocki. Potocki ordered the meeting of the regional council disbanded, the ban canceled, and the rabbis jailed. Potocki claimed that his investigation showed the accused Jews to be innocent.[10]

It is impossible—for lack of neutral evidence—to ascertain whether the rabbis in Brody really were overzealous with their accusations and ban. But they may well have been so in light of the climate of opinion created in connection with the Emden-Eibeschitz controversy. The same mood may also have contributed initially toward "inflation" of the Frankist heresy (though not necessarily toward creating it).

Frank and the Frankists

Jacob Frank was born about 1726, apparently in Korolówka, Podolia, a shtetel or small town (in 1765 it had a Jewish population of 183). Most of the biographical and autobiographical data are either intentionally falsified or otherwise incorrect.[11] It seems, however, that his father belonged to the lower classes (an innkeeper or small tax collector or bookbinder) despite Jacob's attempt to depict him as a rabbi. At the age of twelve Frank went to Bucharest, served for a while as a servant in the house of a Polish Jew, and then went to Constantinople and later to Salonika. There he came in close contact with the Berachya faction of the Doenmeh and apparently absorbed some of their beliefs. He is said to have studied the *Zohar* and other cabalistic works while he was there.[12] (The *Zohar* later became the Frankist group's holy book, for them a counterpart to the Talmud.)

Jacob Frank apparently combined in his own person the characteristics of a Turkish pasha and a Polish squire. Outwardly he imitated both. His headgear was seemingly copied from the Turkish, and his horses and carriage, with the accompanying footmen and riders, are said to have resembled those of the Polish nobles. Like the nobles he displayed material splendor and used rich utensils and other trappings (tradition ascribes gold and silver tableware to him). His idea of making his group into a militarily disciplined and trained unit, maintaining guards dressed like cavalry or the cossacks, and requiring everyone (even the girls) to undergo a sort of military training may have been motivated both by lust for power and the wish to parade as a Polish noble. The more important noblemen usually maintained their own guard or militia.

Totalitarianism and despotism of a sort were not unknown among the contemporary Christian sects in the Ukraine, but Frank seems to have carried them further than other leaders. Enormously egoistic, with strong erotic drives and a craving for power, he was intent upon enjoying life and emphasizing his despotic rule. (In Scholem's view "his greedy lust for power dominated him to the exclusion of any other motive.") He demanded absolute obedience of his followers and enforced it by means of penalties and even corporal punishments for the recalcitrant. He used sex as a drawing card to gain followers and himself indulged in it excessively.

His idea of settling Jews—or rather those who attached themselves to him—in a definite territorial unit may have been intended less as a solution for Jewish homelessness than as a means of providing a "kingdom" to satisfy his lust for power. (He is said to have pointed out that Sabbatai Zevi's role had been limited because he "did not taste the sweetness of power.")

Frank himself compensated in part with dreams and fabrications for the power he did not have in reality. He dreamed of becoming king of Poland with the aid of gold, and of helping the Austrian kaiser (the holy Roman emperor) wage his wars by a loan of 15–20 million ducats (a tremendous amount of money for those times) and an army that he would raise. He also invented stories about how in Turkey they wanted to give him "half an empire," many houses, about forty thousand horses with enough fodder for thirty years, and said that he possessed two treasures, one near the sea and the other near the Danube.[13]

Images

In general very little authentic information about Frank's background is available. A collection of his sayings, parables, prophecies, and explanations (*Księga Słów Pańskich* [Book of the Words of the Lord]) as well as a *Chronik*—both written or edited in later years by his followers—have survived. For the most part it is impossible to distinguish in these writings between fact and fancy, truth and outright lies (Frank indulged excessively in the latter), or to date any of the items. The images perpetuated by these works may or may not bear a relation to the actual facts. (This is also true of information obtained from anti-Frankist sources.) Perhaps the images evoked by these materials may reflect what the authors and editors saw, or wanted to see, in Frank rather than a true picture:

> (a) A man of little or no learning. He said: "I am a simple [unlearned] man"; "I was in your eyes an ordinary person without Torah and without learning"; "If learned people had been needed, a man of great learning would

have been sent to you [not I]." He claimed that he did not understand the parts of the *Zohar* he was quoting (but elsewhere he claims he explained it to the rabbi).[14]

(b) A person with little concern for learning and abnormal physical strength in his early years. He tells how as a child he did not want to study, tore up his books, criticized Jewish customs, and played pranks on his teachers. He ran around with non-Jewish boys, became a gang leader, and fought another gang; he led a group of thieves who fell upon a rich merchant and stole his wares. As a boy he had been known for his frivolity and recklessness, later he fought a notorious robber, and so on. His grandfather, too, had possessed enormous strength.

(c) A man with no regard in the past, for Jewish traditions and religious customs. In Turkey he is said to have openly desecrated the Sabbath and driven Jews out of a synagogue (in imitation of Sabbatai Zevi?).

(d) A healer, miracle worker, "prophet," seer of "visions," sorcerer.

(e) A leader (to some extent a military leader) who was fearless, holding the key to untold riches and happiness.

(f) A redeemer, a messiah (not to Palestine—he repudiated at least outwardly, the return to the Holy Land), a self-deifier, part of the Trinity.

(g) A man who propagated and practiced free love to excess, reformulated the theory of a "female Messiah" or female part of the Trinity, which was inherent in the "new Sabbatians" ideas on the Trinity, one part of which was the Shekhina.[15]

Some of these attributes apparently appealed to hundreds, possibly thousands, of Jews of the lower, less learned, classes in Podolia and neighboring regions. De-emphasis of study and learning and less strict fulfillment of the commandments *in practice* suited such groups of village Jews, innkeepers, revenue lessees, for close contacts with non-Jews were part of their daily routine.

The same may be said concerning the role of healer and miracle worker. A few similar themes appear in the Hassidic writings of that time—Hassidism developed in more or less the same period and region as Frankism. The function of healer was often attributed to the leader in the non-Jewish sects also. Frank's posing as a Polish squire and "playing soldiers," and even the ruthless discipline he imposed, may also have gone a long way toward impressing some Jews. The Jew regarded the Polish nobleman as a protector, more rarely as an oppressor. Intimacy with a noble carried prestige. Jewish moralists frequently complained about Jews' modeling their external behavior on that of the Polish nobility. As lessees or managers of noblemen's estates some Jews tried to imitate the mode of life of the owner, including his severity and authoritarianism. Also, as we have seen earlier, Polish Jews generally identified with the nobility.

In other words, most of Frank's real or attributed traits may have been approved of by some Jews, or were at least familiar to them. His innovations were the Messiah image and his self-deification, and the *official* sanction or advocacy of licentiousness (what was new was not casual illicit sexual aberrations caused by passions that could not always be absolutely curbed, but sexual depravity as a pattern). Also, the easy change from one religion to another—from Judaism to Islam and from that to Catholicism, with further attempts to convert to Greek Orthodox—was strange to Polish Jews, even though the eighteenth century shows increasing numbers of converts to Christianity. But the pressure of suppressed passions, the need for legalization of existing illicit relationships or promiscuity, or the rationalization of "the holiness of sin"—to lessen the burden of guilt feelings—may have done their part in turning individuals toward Frankism. It is said that guilt has a tendency to escalate. Some people, unable to acknowledge their guilt feelings, react with an impulse to do something still less acceptable. Another reaction may be the sublimation of the misdeed, and this may possibly be what we find here.

Assigning to a high place in the mythology the image of a female—based, among other things, on the *matronita:* the lady mentioned in the *Zohar* or the Shekhina —may have made licentiousness palatable to some Jews despite traces of opposition. They were apparently predisposed to accept change by the strong pressure exerted by the Orthodox Jews (the bans and exclusion from the group). Nevertheless, constant prodding, persuasion, and promises by Frank were still needed to persuade some hundreds of Jews to consider the idea of conversion to Catholicism: he undertook to make them rich, marry their children to nobles, and free them from internal Jewish quarrels and pressures.[16] If the extant materials are reliable, the initial idea in adopting Christianity was to organize a distinctive Jewish-Christian group, which may have appeared psychologically easier than to assimilate into the Polish Christian majority.

Perhaps the environment may also have been exerting some influence. As we have said, part of the actual behavior trends and attitudes of Frank and his close followers have some parallels among the Russian radical sects: the leader's authority becoming dictatorial and despotic, interpretation of visions by the leader according to his own fancy, his deification, his indulgence in sex orgies with women of his group, survival by evasion (the theory that it is permissible to profess any religion—Catholic, Greek Orthodox, Muslim—as long as one remains true to what one believes, was formulated by the first historical leader of the Doukhobors about 1750), sin needed for salvation or abrogation of everything holy and equalization in sin, lack of liturgy or fasts and rejection of the idea of redemption, opposition to the Establishment and abrogation of traditional sacred books, election of twelve apostles, existence of "spiritual sisters," and deification of women.[17]

Attitudes and Dreams

Frank had dreams (perhaps he really believed them) in which he saw himself as king of Poland; he blamed his followers for the fact that he never actually became a ruler in Poland. He envisioned himself as being able to help the holy Roman emperor with an army of thirty thousand men and a loan of millions of ducats, or even coming to the aid of the whole world. As we have noted, he liked above all "playing soldiers" and dreaming of armies. He wanted to teach Jews the military craft and to begin such instruction with the six-year-olds with a view to amassing an army of ten million Jews and one million other persons. Another favorite topic was his great wealth or treasure and his promises to enrich and glorify his followers. He also seems to have repeatedly pointed out that Jews, including his followers, came from lowly backgrounds and were therefore vile and contemptible.

Toward the end of his life Frank invented new stories about himself and his daughter Eva, claiming that they had royal blood. He took the name of Dobrucki or Dobrushki like one of his relatives because it sounded less Jewish, explaining that he had actually been born a crown prince. Eva, too, was supposedly not his natural daughter but a foster child given to him by a powerful ruler.[18]

These seem to have been the only constant themes. His other ideas and attitudes were rather a jumble of contradictions and inconsistencies.[19] For instance, he warned his followers not to mix with people of another nation and not to copulate or associate with their women, yet at other times he demanded that they mix and promised fathers that he would marry their children to spouses from the Polish nobility. On several occasions he demanded secrecy, advising his people to be evasive,[20] keep quiet, and avoid divulging their intentions or actions to others. Then again he pointed out that he always insisted that things be done openly to expose "the strange deeds" to the public view. Similarly, while reproaching his group for keeping up some of the Jewish customs he celebrated Hanukkah.[21]

Frank in Poland

He came—or returned—to Poland in December 1755. Later he claimed that in Turkey a prophet had come to him in a vision and induced or forced him to leave for Poland. He went first to Korolówka, his real or assumed birthplace and subsequently to Lwów. He lived there for a while with a group of followers in a house near the city gates. Among the tales concerning his stay in Lwów is one about a "Sabbatian" there who rode on horseback to the Lwów rabbi's house on Saturday morning flagrantly smoking his pipe. He was arrested—in another version, killed— by the Jews. (This story may in reality be a subsequent personification of the "sins" of the group.)

Frank left Lwów, supposedly in the company of fifteen followers, and made his way to Rohatyn, a small town where the Schorrs lived. They were among his first followers. From Rohatyn he went to a few other places, and by the end of January 1756 he reached Lanckrona, another small town in the same region. We are told that on the way Frank staged some orgiastic meeting in which, among others, two women of the Schorr family participated. The episode was repeated, becoming even more boisterous, in Lanckrona.

What really happened in the house where Jacob and his group stayed? Did the group actually dance around naked women (or a naked woman) kissing their breasts? And if so, how was it discovered? Various versions and stories about the incident exist. But it does seem certain that the rabbi of Lanckrona, or according to another version the Jewish lessee, sought help from the city official during the night of January 27. They forced their way into the house and arrested eight people, including Frank. The latter, being a foreign (Ottoman) subject, was freed the next morning. The local rabbi, and another rabbi made an investigation in Lanckrona and sent the findings to the regional Jewish Community Council.

Before long the regional rabbi of Satanow with two fellow rabbis formed a board of inquiry into the Lanckrona affair. About two dozen people, among them six women, appeared before the investigating board of rabbis (some had to be forced to do so) in the course of almost two weeks. They admitted committing many sins, great and small, ranging from smoking on Saturdays to "disavowal of the whole Torah," and there were frequent confessions of sexual depravity, adultery, and promiscuity. In many instances the sinners considered the sexual acts to have been a sort of religious rite or a "good deed" on the part of the women, who offered themselves only to the "worthy" ones. Most of the witnesses admitted having participated in all this depravity and sin; others spoke of the sinning they had seen with their own eyes or about which they had been told.[22]

It is, of course, impossible to distinguish truth from fancy or untruth in the confessions since the investigating court was far from impartial.[23] Be that as it may, the minutes of the investigation were brought before the regional Russian (Galician) Community Council, which placed a ban upon the participants and their supporters, forbidding Jews any contact with the sinners, including marriage to any of these families (their wives were declared "to be whores and their children bastards"). Some restrictions on the study of cabala and mysticism were also introduced. The ban was proclaimed in Brody and later, in the fall of 1756, was approved at the meeting of the Four-Land Council in Konstantinow. It seems to have been ordered repeated several times in a number of communities. To this end also a Hebrew pamphlet against the "Sabbatians" was published.[24] Such a ban excluded the offender from Jewish society and, by forbidding any relationship between him and the rest of the community, from most possibilities of earning a living.

Role of Polish Clergy

By the time these bans were proclaimed in the fall of 1756, the Frankist problem was about to take another turn. The bishop of Kamienec, to whose bishopric Lanckrona belonged, had shown an interest in the Lanckrona affair as early as the beginning of February.[25] He summoned the Jews and the Frankist group to his court so that he could adjudicate their differences. The Jews did not respond either to this summons or six or seven others that the bishop issued during 1756 and the first months of 1757. They considered the matter an internal Jewish problem in which non-Jewish authorities should not intervene.

On one occasion (March 23, 1757) the syndic (representative) of the regional Jewish Community Council of Podolia did declare his readiness to discuss the Lanckrona incident, but refused to deal with matters of creed and religion. The Frankist group, on the other hand, appeared before the bishop several times in 1756 and submitted to him, among other things, the principles of their antitalmudic creed,[26] trying thereby to set themselves up as a separate sect (of "contratalmudists" or antitalmudists). This may have given the bishop a pretext—assuming he needed one—to interfere in a religious controversy between two sects. The bishop sent his own investigative commission to Lanckrona (which failed to find the depravities the Jews complained about) and soon issued a document protecting the Frankists. Bishop Dembowski then took matters into his own hands. He fixed June 30, 1757, as a terminal date and demanded that the Jewish communities, particularly in Podolia, send rabbis and other representatives for a confrontation with the "Sabbatians" (or antitalmudists). He requested the nobles who owned the towns to induce the Jews to send their representatives. The latter comprised the rabbis and leaders from nine communities (nine rabbis and seventeen community leaders). Nineteen antitalmudists showed up, most of them from Podolia. Frank and some other non-Polish "Sabbatians" were absent. Only about four from each side participated in the actual debate.

The Disputation

Initially the antitalmudists may have expected such sundry advantages from a public debate with the Jews as achievement of autonomous status for their religious sect; improvement of their own situation by relieving the pressures exerted by the Jews; revenge on the Jews or protection from Polish clergy or the bishop of Kamienec, or both, in exchange for a rationale for anti-Jewish acts. It seems, however, that the Frankists did not yet seriously consider their own conversion to Christianity. But if we are to believe the later Frankist sources, Frank had already said: "I shall go together with twelve of my people to the Christian religion."

The bishop may at first have supported the antitalmudists (according to Ber Birkenthal, the bishop was the one who asked for the attack on the Talmud) for two reasons, namely, the Catholic Church's traditionally negative views on the Talmud (in the Christian world the Talmud was considered full of superstition, a symbol of Jewish separatism and obstinacy) and the intensification of the struggle between the impoverished Polish burghers and their Jewish competitors.[27] At the time of the first debate (June 1758) Bishop Dembowski does not yet seem to have been considering any sort of conversion, although this may not be entirely discounted. (The general missionary attitude of the Catholics toward the Jews in southern Poland of those times is illustrated by the efforts of a bishop in Brody little more than a decade earlier.)

At the time of this debate in Kamienec (June 20, 1757) the Lanckrona incident apparently no longer played any major role. The "independent" investigation by the bishop's official in Lanckrona was supposed to have shown him that the antitalmudists had committed no serious moral sins there.

The debate itself was based on the Frankists' nine principles, submitted in writing, together with motivations and sources, and of written answers by the representatives of the Jews. Both sides had the written materials translated into Polish with some assistance from non-Jews, since neither side was fully conversant with literary Polish. The live debate—insofar as such a debate took place—may have been conducted in a mixture of crude Polish-Ukrainian and possibly also some Yiddish (Balaban muses that they used Yiddish only), the languages Jews used in their daily lives to communicate with the surrounding populations.

The Frankists tried to base their nine principles on the Scriptures and other sources, emphasizing the negative character of the Talmud, the trinitarian nature of the godhead, and the incarnation of God in a human being. The Jews, for their part, attempted to correct their adversaries' misquotations or incorrect interpretations.

With some statements, such as those on the belief in one God and in the written Torah, the Jews could readily agree. Statements of a purely Christian character (on the Trinity, the incarnation of God in a human) the Jews left unanswered so as to avoid becoming involved in something that might resemble a Christian–anti-Christian dispute—especially in a Catholic country.

On October 17, 1757, the bishop's court announced its decision on the disputation: first, the Talmud, being a harmful book, should be burned; second, because the Jews were unable to produce valid proof of degenerate behavior by the antitalmudists on the night of January 27, 1756, in Lanckrona, the prosecutors were to be punished by flogging, and the community fined to pay damages.

In Poland decisions by ecclesiastical courts dealing with laymen could not be executed until they had been approved by a civil court. The city court of Kamienec approved the decision to burn the Talmud but not the fines or flogging.

The book-burning began in Podolia shortly thereafter, and it is said that in no time at all one thousand copies of single tractates went up in flames. Some Jews hid books or sent them to Turkey.

Jews who had access to high Polish officials lodged complaints in several places, among them the office of the papal nuncio in Warsaw. The latter promised to have the case reviewed in the capital. But Bishop Dembowski died suddenly. (Jews regarded his death as a punishment for his insistence on burning the Talmud; a number of legends about his unnatural death have been preserved.[28])

Playing at Conversion

With the bishop's death the antitalmudists lost their protector and had to withstand new pressures from the Jews. They are said to have been beaten in the streets by Jewish youngsters. Some of them fled to Turkey or to the Turkish borders. Beyond the Turkish borders lay (after late 1756 or early 1757) Frank's residence and his "court." Some of the Polish antitalmudists now found refuge there. But Polish Jews' warnings to the Jewish community in Constantinople, and possibly similar warnings through Emden and other European connections, alerted the Turkish Jewish communities to the danger to the Jewish religion inherent in the Frankist movement.

Frank and a group of his cronies apparently sought to avoid new persecution by converting to Islam, which gained them the protection of the Turkish authorities. But they were isolated in Turkey and would have liked to return to Poland. They approached the Polish king—perhaps with the support of some officials in Poland —who granted them a privilege (June 1758) promising protection to "the antitalmudists . . . who reject the Talmud . . . which is full of scorn and is damaging to church and fatherland . . ." and giving them the right to settle anywhere in Poland "and to complete the unfinished court case."[29]

In September 1758 the Frankists returned to Poland, followed by Frank himself in December. He established his court in Iwanye (near Kamieniec)—with all the trimmings including the "girls," or "sisters" as they were called. The others settled there and in a few nearby places. Frank adopted the role of a healer, magician, and leader. Some sex orgies (called "secret Sedarim") were arranged there.

In Iwanye, if we may believe Frank's later statements, he attempted to organize a new sect. Life at the "camp," as it became known, was based on communal principles, with one treasury for all run by Frank's lieutenant. Speaking in images and symbols Frank told his group: "I was chosen to effect the great transformation because I am a common man and thus will do everything properly. . . . I shall show you God and you will see my might and power. . . . God is good and is all-powerful but He acts through a human being"—apparently meaning himself. Frank also made other explicit statements at that time: "Up to now everything which has been done was for the sake of preserving the children of Israel, but now we no longer need either good deeds or prayers; we must listen and act." And a little later: "I sent a few people to Lwów . . . and ordered them to inform . . . that we are ready to convert."

Soon after that (February 1759) a delegation of Frankists of non-Polish origins appeared before Bishop Ladislas Alexander Lubienski of Lwów, requesting conversion to Catholicism and a disputation with the Jews for the purpose of revealing the latter's depravity "and their lust for Christian blood." The application was written (or translated) by one calling himself Malivda, a Polish nobleman named Antoni Kossakowsky, who had apparently earlier converted to the Greek Orthodox religion, later becoming a leader of a religious sect in Walachia (Philipowcy[30]) and finally reverting to Catholicism. Malivda remained the mouthpiece—in Polish—of the Frankists and wrote or translated their official materials up to the time of their conversion.

Bishop Lubienski, who had meanwhile left Lwów to become archbishop of Poland in Gniezno, had the Frankist application printed and distributed to many authorities, including the papal nuncio in Warsaw, who sent it on to the pope in

Rome with some comments of his own (among other things he mentions the readiness of fifteen thousand Jews to convert). But all these authorities (including the newly elected Pope Clement XIII), despite their elation over the possible conversion of many Jews, were sceptical and suspected insincere motivations. The pope asked for clarification and investigation.

Meanwhile, in May 1759 the Frankists—Leib Krisa and Elisha Shorr were their spokesmen—submitted a new application addressed to Archbishop Lubienski and the king, requesting right of settlement in certain towns and a disputation with the Jews in order to prove "that the wish to convert is not a result of their poverty but stems from their recognition of the value of Christianity." A little while later they submitted to the clergy in Lwów the conditions under which they would agree to become Catholics:

(a) The conversion should take place on the holiday of Epiphany, January 6, 1760 (in Lwów this was the beginning of a popular fair).
(b) They should be allowed to wear beards and earlocks.
(c) They could continue to wear Jewish clothing.
(d) They would be able to have double names—one Polish and one Jewish.
(e) They would be permitted to marry only among themselves.
(f) They would not eat pig's meat.
(g) They were to keep two rest days—Saturdays and Sundays.
(h) They would be allowed to continue study of *Zohar* and other cabalistic works.
(i) They undertook to prove from Talmud the truth of Christianity and the depravity of the Talmud itself, which should be burned.

These conditions—the only source for them are Ber Birkenthal's memoirs, written about thirty years later—may show that the Frankists still thought of forming a Christian-Jewish sect instead of submerging entirely among the Polish Catholics. They apparently also wanted to postpone the act of conversion for about a year.[31] The archbishop and possibly the pope, with their doubts and mistrust of the honesty of the Frankist intentions, apparently advocated swift conversion without any conditions, and they were not in favor of any public disputation. In Lwów, however, the clergy did arrange for the disputation, which began on July 17, 1759.

Disputation in Lwów

The disputation in Lwów was based on seven theses, which the Frankists submitted to the clergy in Lwów in their manifesto of May 25, 1759. The Frankists' representatives also promised on this occasion to convert to Christianity immediately after the end of the disputation.

Six of these theses dealt with Christ: the prophesies about the coming of the Messiah were fulfilled; the Messiah is the God who as man incarnate suffered for our salvation; since the coming of the real Messiah the sacrifices were abolished; the cross signifies the Trinity and is the Messiah's symbol; every human being should follow the Messiah, for this brings salvation; Christian baptism is the way to belief in the Messiah. The seventh thesis concerned the Talmud, holding that it teaches about the need for Christian blood and that anyone who believes in the Talmud is obliged to use such blood.

The six theses dealing with Christianity do not in reality refer to Jesus or Christ by name, but talk of "the Messiah." This fact was noted by a cardinal in Rome and the papal nuncio in Warsaw and revived their fears about a conspiracy on the part of the antitalmudists, or "Karaites" as they called them.

Whatever the reason for not mentioning Christ or Jesus by name, the Frankist theses in the Lwów disputation were more Christian and less Jewish than those in the preceding disputation in Kamienec or the points they submitted to the Lwów clergy. Balaban assumes (he says "seemingly") that the theses were formulated by clergymen in Lwów[32] and then given to the Frankists to be based by them on quotations from Talmud, *Zohar,* and other Jewish sources.

The debate was held in a large church in Lwów from which, according to Ber Birkenthal, all crosses and "idols" had been removed. Those Christian symbols that could not be taken away were covered with sheets ("so that Jews could keep their heads covered in church").

A procedure evolved in which the Frankists' statements and the Jews' replies, each prepared in advance, were read aloud in Polish (they were translations from Hebrew) and presented in writing to the other side. The oral discussions may have been partially included, or summarized in the written version, or for the most part simply omitted. The Jews usually submitted their answers some days after the reading and discussion of the given Frankist thesis.

The participants in this debate comprised some thirty to forty rabbis from southern Poland, ten or more Frankists—but not Frank himself, save during the last meeting—many Catholic churchmen, and many Jewish and non-Jewish onlookers who gained admission by purchasing a ticket.

The disputation opened on July 17, 1759, and was continued on July 20, 23, 30, and August 6. The first four themes—that the prophecies about the Messiah have all been fulfilled, that the Messiah is the real God who was incarnated in a human body for our redemption, that since the coming of the Messiah the sacrifices ceased, that the cross is connected with the Trinity and is the seal or symbol of the Messiah —were countered by the Jews with discussions and interpretations of biblical verses and talmudic sentences used. The rabbis realized that there was no one among the assembled Christians who understood enough Hebrew to be able to judge the value of either interpretation. Thus they could more or less limit themselves to a simple denial of the Frankist "proof" without going into a discussion of the thesis itself. On the two other themes (duty of the human being to follow the Messiah through the medium of Christian baptism) the rabbis remained silent, because these were questions concerning the basis of Christianity and they did not wish to become involved in a Jewish-Christian "dialogue."

The last theme was later scheduled to be debated on August 27. This point dealt with the Talmud and the alleged use of human blood by Jews ("the Talmud teaches the need for Christian blood and one who believes in Talmud is obliged to use blood"). Jews considered this a crucial question for them at that time. In the spring of the same year a blood libel accusation had been staged in Przemyśl—not far from Lwów—with the result that six Jews had been condemned to death. In Lwów the tension between Jew and non-Jew was heightened by the court's decision (in a case lasting several years) concerning Jews living outside the Jewish street. The Jews lost the case. An attack on Jewish stores and the resultant losses had developed in connection with this controversy. At that time a Polish Jew in Rome, Elyakum Zelig, was seeking to obtain a declaration by the pope against blood accusations. These events apparently contributed to the anxiety among the Lwów Jews. According to a letter from Poland written in the fall of 1759, during the disputation "darkness prevailed in almost all the towns of the [Lwów] region." In Lwów itself the Jews were provided with a guard of sixty soldiers, while in Lublin Jews spent considerable sums on security.

Ber Birkenthal, writing a few decades later, may be reflecting such anxiety even though he seemingly attributes it to other causes—causes that may not even have existed.[33] For whatever reason, Lwów Jews did try to counteract the intentions of the Frankists. According to Ber, they sent a delegation to a high-ranking clergyman named Wieniawski (Ber claimed that he was of higher rank than the monk Mikulski who was presiding over the disputation), but he would not receive them. Then, seeing Wieniawski on other private matters, Ber tried to influence him against the Frankists. Ber tells how he sought to persuade Wieniawski—and other clergymen present—that the Frankists were not sincere in wanting to become Christians. He told of their earlier conversion to the Muslim religion, their depravity in erotic matters, and their religious license; "and when the clergymen heard these things they examined us . . . for three hours." After this Wieniawski went to see the clergymen who were presiding over the debate and urged them to avoid allowing the Frankists to delay their conversion and to end the disputation quickly.

We cannot gauge the veracity of these memoirs, but the Jews do seem to have come in contact with Mikulski while he was in charge of the disputations (according to Ber, Mikulski himself suggested that the rabbi visit him) and to have gained his cooperation. It is mentioned, but this is not certain, that Mikulski was paid for his services; in another version he is said to have received the money but handed it over to the Frankists.

Jews and their community organization in Poland may have regarded the Frankist group as a threat to their existence. It was the first time in Polish Jewish history that a Jewish group openly opposed not only the Jewish Establishment but also the basic religious beliefs and practices and almost everything for which Jewry stood. Even more unusual, this opposing group turned to the outside world—the Catholic Church and the state—for support, being ready to betray the Jews. (Here and there individuals had behaved somewhat in this way throughout the centuries but being individuals they were, of course, less dangerous.)

The reality of a general threat apparently led to the sharp reaction by traditional Jewry toward Frank and his group. Jews in Poland, or some of their leaders, sought ways to eliminate the Frankists. One idea was to have the Christian Church authorities burn them at the stake as heretics. This suggestion is mentioned in a letter from Baruch ben David Yavan of Poland written as early as September 1757 (?), at the beginning of the Frank episode. Jacob Emden reprinted this letter and gave some details about the idea. Polish Jewish leaders asked Emden whether Jewish law justified their taking such action and also requested support of their plan through his good connections in Rome and elsewhere. Emden's reaction was positive in the matter of principle ("you will be blessed . . . if you will root out the evil from your midst"), but—he said in answering another inquiry—he doubted the practical possibility of doing so. He thought the costs of working through Rome would be exorbitant and that it would take a very long time to achieve the goal.[34] The attempt to expedite the conversion of the Frankists to Christianity was a second choice, possibly suggested by Emden.

Writing on October 23, 1759, Rabbi Abraham Hakohen of Zamość, a high official of the Four-Land Council, tells that at the Four-Land Council meeting at Konstantinow it was decided that "there is no other way" but to force the Frankists to convert. Two thousand ducats were allotted for this purpose "and thank God a few of them have already converted . . . we send to the nuncio in Warsaw . . . to separate them from the Jews." And in his imaginary discussion with the Frankists, Emden explains the phrase "separate from us." In another connection he thanks God "who separated us from the wicked."[35]

The tone and content of Ber's memoirs and his taking credit for his contribution in driving the Frankists toward conversion would also indicate that this became an approved Jewish tactic in those years. The aim was to instill suspicion regarding the true intentions of the Frankists in the minds of the Polish clergymen who ran the show, thereby inducing them to end the debate and force the Frankists to convert without delay.

The meeting of the disputants for presentation of the "Talmud–use of blood by Jews" theme of the Frankists was held on August 27, and Jacob Frank was present. The Jews were represented by the Lwów rabbi Hayim Cohen Rapport and two other rabbis; Ber Birkenthal, who knew Polish, attended at the rabbi's request.[36]

Jehuda Krisa (to become Krasinsky after conversion), who stated the Frankist accusations, began with an assurance that the Frankists were imparting the information not because they hated the Jews but because they loved their new religion. The "evidence" and "proof" of the use of blood by Jews consisted of a repetition of cases of blood libel mentioned in older anti-Jewish materials and an attempt to "prove" the use of blood from talmudic and other Jewish sources. Since no such sources exist, interpretations were invented. For instance, the recommendation in the *Shulchan Aruch* that red (*adom* in Hebrew) wine be used for the Seder was interpreted as *edom* (which contains the same Hebrew letters as *adom*), meaning Christian. When the "proofs" and the interpretations had been read aloud the meeting was adjourned. At the next session on September 10 the Jews were to give their answer.

But this first session in August had already been a sore disappointment to the Frankists. Such detailed casuistic interpretation of Hebrew sources could make little impression upon a Christian public not versed in Hebrew and knowing nothing of Jewish sources. The reaction against the Jews, for which the Frankists may have hoped, did not develop. The anxiety of the Jews seems also to have been unwarranted, though they still had to reply to the accusations.

Ber claims to have been the only Jew available on this occasion who knew Polish well. The syndic, a Jewish physician from Brody, having been educated abroad, was not sufficiently familiar with Polish, so the rabbi asked Ber Birkenthal to write the answers. He did so, apparently checking the style with a non-Jew. Using Christian sources Ber collected a number of statements by church fathers and Christians of various eras—including Hugo Grotius—attesting to the good character of the Jews. Similarly, positive non-Jewish opinions about the Talmud followed. In dealing with the specific quotations mentioned by the Frankists, Ber followed the rabbi's advice simply to deny some of the Frankist interpretations or their quotations from the text, since there was no impartial arbiter present who knew Hebrew well.

The answers were read aloud by Rabbi Rapport at the meeting on September 10, 1759. (According to Ber the chairman of the meeting, Mikulski, restrained the Frankists when they tried to disrupt the rabbi's speech.)

The verdict proclaimed the Frankists' right in connection with the first six theses, dealing with Christianity. (Nobody expected otherwise from a forum presided over by Catholic churchmen.) However, in connection with the seventh thesis—dealing with the Talmud and use of blood by Jews—which was the most sensitive for the Jews, there was no decision. The verdict was that since it was impossible to decide which side had the correct quotations and interpretations, the meeting would be adjourned and reconvened at some future date in the presence of two monks with a knowledge of Hebrew. No such meeting was ever called.

The end of the disputation was, for the most part, anticlimactic. The verdict neither approved nor denied the accusations against the Talmud and the Jews. The latter's fears of a possible burning of the Talmud, pogroms, or other attacks did not materialize. The Jews—to take Ber Birkenthal's story as an indication of the Jewish attitude—were satisfied that the Frankists (he says sixty of them) were forced to have their beards shaved and to be converted there and then, whereas "we left free and went through the main gates and we departed in peace. . . . I recognized the great miracle that God made in his compassion with the remnants of Israel."[37] This detail is apparently not correct; the conversion did not take place on the day of the disputation, but one week later.

Writing decades later Ber may have been confused about the details but he does depict the general situation: the feeling of relief among the Jews and their triumph over the Frankists.[38] This situation is also depicted by information and letters

Emden received from Poland soon after the conversion. They attest to a feeling among Jews in Poland that "God worked wonders for his people in Podolia." Stories were created about the non-Jews' changed attitude toward Jews, whom they began to hold in high esteem. Many non-Jews were reported to be converting to Judaism and details were given. (Forty Greek Orthodox people converted in Shklov, and two clergymen of the Kamieniec diocese fled to Turkey, where they converted to Judaism, assuming the names Abraham and Isaac.) Here again the particulars are apparently not true but the stories may reflect the optimistic climate among Jews resulting from the outcome of the disputation.[39]

The Frankists did not, at least at first, succeed in taking revenge on the Jews, nor did the clergy grant their preconditions for conversion. Once converted, they were more than ever subject to unilateral pressures by the clergy because they had lost their bargaining position.

Preparations for conversion had begun weeks before the end of the disputation, and the Frankists were instructed in Catholicism (if we may believe the clergymen, the Frankists took their studies seriously). The first group was converted about a week after the end of the disputation, and others followed. In their disappointment with the outcome of the disputation the Frankists may have sought other means of revenge—Ber Birkenthal reports the threat of "blood for blood," which Frankists made to the Lwów rabbi on the last day of the debate. Be that as it may, Frankists seem to have been involved, either directly or indirectly, in a blood libel that began in Wojslawice in the spring of 1760, in which six Jews were arrested and charged with killing a Christian child for religious purposes.[40]

Conversion and Aftermath

Once begun, conversion was continued at a comparatively rapid pace. In just over a year (September 1759 to November 1760) 514 Jews (156 men, 119 women, 239 children) were converted in Lwów. At the beginning of 1760, 15 Jews were converted in Warsaw, and in Kamieniec in 1755–60 about 30. This would amount to some 600 converts (assuming that there were also some in other places).[41]

Frank himself seems to have been converted first in Lwów and then again in Warsaw. He insisted on the Warsaw ceremony apparently in the hope that the king would serve as his godfather. For this purpose he went to Warsaw at the end of September 1759, accompanied by a small group of his supporters. On the way, just before the Frankists entered Lublin, Jews threw stones and dirt at them. A military detachment was sent to rescue them (the court later fined the Jewish ringleaders and the Jewish community in Lublin). In Warsaw, too, the Jews greeted the Frankists with stones and curses. Frank cited these incidents in requesting protection from the king.[42] At the same time he indicated his wish to be allowed to settle with his group on a specific territory. He is said to have refused offers by nobles to settle on their estates for fear that his people would become serfs. From the words of the papal nuncio in Warsaw it would appear that the suggested territory was in the south near the Turkish border. Subsequently, land in Lithuania close to the Russian border was proposed. But influential people, the nuncio among them, did not trust the Frankists sufficiently to have them "guarding" the Polish borders.

This mistrust deepened considerably following Frank's conversion on November 18, 1759. (Some of his followers converted in Warsaw either earlier or a few days later. Others came from Lwów to Warsaw and established a "camp" there.)

The close-knit association between Frank and his followers, the group's discipline, and the sight of Frank in his luxurious and oriental attire only strengthened the intrinsic suspicion of "new Christians." Some claim that an inside man betrayed Frank or that a Jew in Warsaw posed as a member of the group and later informed the clergy about Frank's conduct. Emden offers two versions. One is that a convert with whom Frank had quarreled betrayed him. The other version tells of a Jewish physician in Warsaw who converted with the Frankists solely for the purpose of being able to observe and denounce them. (He supposedly told the clergymen that the Frankists studied *Zohar* and sang Sabbatian songs.) In a letter from Poland it is mentioned that the parnas of the Four-Land Council was behind Frank's incarceration for life in Częstochowa.[43] Whatever truth there is to these rumors, the fact is that Lwów clergymen sent letters and reports to Warsaw also expressing mistrust. In Lwów one of the leading clergymen who had participated in the disputation had elicited from Frank's cronies a document in which in all innocence they described Frank's behavior, "prophecies," and attitudes. It was also brought to the attention of the papal nuncio that a group of fifty converts often gathered in Frank's house in Warsaw to sing Jewish songs and to worship him.

Frank was arrested on January 7, 1760, and a few weeks later he was brought before an ecclesiastical court for interrogation. The questions he was asked reveal the main charge and the chief reasons for distrust. Besides dealing with a few personal data, the questions were apparently concerned with two problems: his being a genuine believer in Christianity and his role as a leader of the group. The first group of questions concerned Frank's previous conversion to the Muslim religion, his function as a healer and prophet, his predictions of a messiah's coming, the question of why his followers called him "holy father," and his promise to bring in ten thousand converts. The second batch covered his unwillingness to permit his followers to disperse and his demand that they place their money in the communal treasury.

Frank denied some facts and evaded some questions. A few weeks later several of his followers were also brought before the court and questioned about Frank. They were told not to believe in Frank because he was a cheat and a swindler, but to become good honest Catholics.

By the end of February 1760 it was decided to separate Frank from his followers and for this purpose he was sent to Częstochowa,[44] where he was supposed to live in the old Polish fortress guarded by retired soldiers under the supervision of the clergy.

End of an Episode

The conversion of about six hundred Frankists and the banishment of Jacob Frank to Częstochowa actually ended Frankism for Polish Jewry. Frank and his "movement" were never more than a minor episode in Polish Jewish history. Their limited achievements may have been furthered by preconditions existing in Polish Jewish society: internal Jewish relations, hierarchical structure within the Jewish community, the gap between theory and practice, the need for change, and the existence of individual permissiveness. But, after all, the whole "movement" was localized in one region of southern Poland—Podolia and environs—and embraced only a small segment of the Jewish population there. Six hundred converts, and even assuming (without evidence) hundreds of followers who did not convert, constituted a minute group within a Jewish population in Poland of more than half a million, and only a tiny fraction of the Jewish population in Podolia itself (forty to fifty thousand Jews). Proportionately the whole affair would appear insignificant even during its peak years (1754–60).

Contemporary Jewry felt less threatened by the actual group than by the possible impact of their denunciations of Jewry upon the surrounding Christian majority. One expression of this fear was the public fast scheduled by the Jewish community in Lwów for the last day of the disputation. The Lwów rabbi, the chief representative of the Jews, is said to have donned a death shroud under his usual clothing, something Jews traditionally did in cases of extreme danger or distress. When such fears turned out to have been baseless, when the Frankist group was separated from the Jews by conversion and came under the domination of the Catholic authorities because of their suspect intentions, the entire episode shrank to one of marginal importance.

We have already seen that the Jews desired their separation. Jacob Emden, although not living in Poland, had been involved in the struggle with the Frankists and apparently expressed something of Polish Jewry's general sentiments when he exclaimed: "Thanks to God that He separated us from the wicked"[45] (meaning the Frankists or Sabbatians or both), and proceeds: "It was fulfilled in our days . . . in Poland [God's promise] 'and I will cut off the transgressors from you.' " A preacher from Poland, Perez ben Moses of Brody also mentions that the separation of the Frankists "was good for Jews."

Jews in Poland generally regarded Bishop Dembowski's death, the results of the disputation in Lwów, and the conversion of the Frankists as a sequence of miracles. They created a number of legends, which range from tales that the bishop was haunted by the Talmud tractates he had caused to be burned or that he was changed into a sorcerer after his death, to stories about Jews and non-Jews recognizing God's hand in protecting the Jews. As a result, some Christians, among them two clergymen who fled to Turkey, allegedly converted to Judaism and others were intending to do so. This was told by Jacob Emden in Germany on the basis of reports from Poland.[46] Another series of miracles and legends is contained in *Maaseh Nora be-Podolia*, which Emden published in 1769.

The contempt felt by many a believing Jew for the values, way of life, and practices of the converted Frankists, however, plus hatred of their leader, led to attempts to harm or dishonor them whenever a possibility presented itself. With the rise of the Russian influence in Poland in the mid-1760s, Frank began to talk about conversion to the Greek Orthodox religion ("to go to Esau" in his words) as a means of escaping from Częstochowa. When he sent messengers to Russia, Polish Jewish leaders attempted to thwart the plan. A letter written from Petersburg to Jacob Emden in 1768 says that one of the Polish Jewish leaders, Baruch ben David Yavan, appeared in Russia before the Polish representatives, the Russian high officials, and church officials to seek to discredit Frank's intentions. It is not possible to judge the validity of the claim in the Petersburg letter that Baruch ben David's efforts in Petersburg wrecked Frank's plans, but the fact remains that his delegates did return empty-handed.

It is interesting to note that according to this letter, Frank's representatives presented the Frankist group to the Russian authorities as a separate sect, desiring, among other things, to obtain a territory for settlement near the Turkish border and claiming that they had originally wanted to convert to the Greek Orthodox religion but had been forced to become Catholics. Frank wanted to exchange Catholicism for the Greek Orthodox religion[47] as a means of gaining his release from Częstochowa.

"Christian" Frankists

While he was in Częstochowa (1760–72) Frank and his group withdrew further from Jews and Judaism, despite their occasional use of phrases or ideas and symbols from Jewish sources. This radical estrangement from Judaism was not confined to sexual behavior, erotic orgies, and the theory of a female goddess or messiah, but spread also to general conduct (severe punishment for those who did not follow all his whims and the inhuman loyalty test or training in discipline consisting of standing on one's feet for three straight days) and the fostering of anti-Jewish attitudes.[48]

The dissociation, at least insofar as Frank was concerned, continued in the later stages in Brno (Brünn) and Offenbach. There he not only attended the Catholic services more or less regularly, but in the last years of his life (he died in 1791) he ceased to be Jacob Frank and assumed another name, claiming to be a king's son, or a squire, or a successor to a king. His daughter Eva "ceased to be his daughter" and became Frank's "foster daughter," entrusted to his care by the court of a mighty ruler.

It seems, however, that his radicalizing trends and his turning further and further from Jewish ways met with some resistance among his followers. His many complaints about their behavior and promises on his part found in the *Book of the Word of the Lord;* his grievances about their objections "that he had taken away their religion"; his claim that they were holding on to some Jewish commandments; his repeated assertions that "the Jews are the meanest among the nation," or "the most spiteful" in Poland and that "I took you away from the Jews in order that you should not follow in their ways"—all seem to be evidence of disagreements. There were also acts of disobedience as, for instance, when he ordered his followers to exchange wives. Other instances of disobedience seem to be indicated in a number of Frank's complaints.[49]

It was only during the first year in Częstochowa that Frank was more or less isolated. Gradually the regime of the fortress became more lenient—probably because the guards were bribed—so that his wife and some of his followers were able to come to live either with him or nearby. Częstochowa became for Frank a miniature of what Gallipoli was for Sabbatai Zevi. And the ideas he developed during this period were radically anti-Jewish. Not only did he want to bring his group into the Greek Orthodox faith, he also sent messengers to Moravia, Bohemia, and Podolia in 1768 (and again in 1772 to Bukowina) to proclaim to the Jews the need to convert. He took credit for having separated his followers from the Jews, whom he considered a quarrelsome and raucous nation.[50]

Meanwhile the first partition of Poland took place in 1772, followed by the conquest of Częstochowa by Russian troops. Frank was released at the beginning of 1773. After a brief abortive attempt to reestablish his leadership over the group in Warsaw—according to Kraushar the leaders there were no longer ready to submit to his authoritarianism—in 1773 he left with a small entourage for Brno (Brünn) in Moravia, where he established his "court." He remained there until 1788 when he again moved, this time to Offenbach. He died in 1791 and his "court" in Offenbach was maintained by his daughter Eva until her death in 1816.

Frank may have gone to Brno upon the urging of his Moravian followers, but when he left Poland his contact with the Polish group declined, even though some individual Polish Frankists may have visited Brno and Offenbach, respectively, and supported him with money.[51]

Frankist Remnants in Poland

The Frankists in Poland had to adjust to the reality of animosity on the part of the Jews and mistrust and unfriendliness in many of their new Catholic coreligionists (although some individuals helped them at times). This may have increased their nostalgia for the past. In fact, the official conversion of the Frankists does not seem to have made good Christians of them. They had not converted too willingly in the first place, even though we are told that before conversion they were eager to learn the essentials of that religion. Many wives left their Frankist husbands, taking their children with them. Their number must have been considerable because the Frankists, in their petition to the Polish king, asked him to see to it that their wives and children should be returned to them.[52]

The converts themselves apparently did not part easily with everything from their Jewish past. For one thing, many retained their Jewish names after conversion. The group in Warsaw, as mentioned, used to gather in Frank's apartment to sing Jewish songs, and they regarded him as a sort of Jewish or Jewish-Christian messiah. In time many of them apparently grew more accustomed to living as Christians officially or even in fact. Nevertheless, the survival of rudiments of their former Jewishness created a point of tension between them and Frank. The latter repeatedly reverted to this theme in his conversations and admonitions in Częstochowa and possibly even in Offenbach. We hear that he was chided for having deprived them of their faith, or that he rebuked them, saying, "You were Jews and remained Jews."[53] Frank also had to continue explaining and justifying their change of religion. He tried to overcome their nostalgia by depicting the great rewards in store for them, ranging from riches and happiness to achievement of high status and being loved by all the nations of the world. Another tactic was to portray Jews and Judaism as repulsive so as to create satisfaction in having left it.[54]

But there was no way back for those who remained in Poland (save perhaps for a few individuals), and in trying to adjust to their new role and to utilize the rights they had acquired they met with opposition on the part of some Polish groups. As early as 1764—in connection with the problem of granting nobility status to converts, not only Frankists—we hear a statement that "the number of converts grew lately, and, being sly by nature, they are rushing to achieve wealth, honor, the privileges of noblemen, public office, and other positions." Some non-Jews may have been reluctant to recognize the converts as Christians, or may have emphasized their separateness. (The census of 1764/65 listed seventy to eighty "contratalmudists" living in nine villages as innkeepers on the Zamojski estates.[55]

About a generation later we find a sort of campaign against the "new Christians," who were being accused of a number of sins: separateness, continuation in the "Jewish occupations" of innkeeping and small trade, competition against true Christians, and fraudulent practices. A Polish guild complained that the "neophytes of Frank deprive the burghers of the means of livelihood in every way . . . and that they send ready cash out of the country."[56] It was suggested that the converts be forbidden to engage in "Jewish occupations" and be diverted to agriculture, unskilled labor, and similar pursuits.

In fact, despite the earlier Frankists' declaration that "innkeeping was a crime" and the promise contained in the petition of 1759 to refrain and desist from innkeeping, the sale of beverages and "contributing to drunkenness and emaciation of Christian blood," many baptized Frankists did engage in these occupations. Increasing opportunities in the form of rights in the cities, and the originally favorable attitudes of some landowners, who turned over to them their inns after having expelled the former Jewish leaseholders, created auspicious situations for some converts. We also find them in other "Jewish occupations" (the Wolowskis, descendants of Frank's "prophet" Elisha Shorr from Rohatyn, made their money in the brewing business—another Jewish pursuit in the eighteenth century). Whether the "new Christians" held on to traditionally Jewish occupations or whether they acquired new positions, they met with opposition and hatred on the part of the Polish Christian population, although there were Poles who supported them.

This ambivalence showed up clearly during the Kościuszko uprising in Poland in 1794–95. On one hand, such second-generation converts and sons of converts as Jan Dembowski and Józef Czyński and others played significant roles in the uprising, reaching positions of command, while on the other hand, converts in Warsaw were accused of being anti-Polish spies and there was an attempt to stage a pogrom against them.

Since they did not constitute a large self-contained group and were deprived of access to the Jewish community, outside pressures apparently made them strive harder for assimilation and integration in the Polish population. This was especially true since integration could offer them certain advantages in their economic activities or enable them to play a role in Polish life. The changes in the makeup of the converted Frankists and their descendants no doubt influenced their attitudes toward Frank and his ideology. Their conduct may have ranged from covert or not-so-covert withdrawal from him, to apparently increasing alienation from Frankism and the ideas for which it stood.

We have mentioned that in 1773, when Frank came to Warsaw following his release from Częstochowa, he no longer found there a group prepared to submit to his whims and dictates. A few years later, in 1776, we hear about tension among the Frankists in Warsaw. The pilgrimages to Brno and Offenbach and the practice of sending money to those places gradually petered out, although some individuals may have continued these practices. By 1786 Frank's attempt to obtain money for his group from Warsaw met with partial failure. Fourteen years later Frank's son Roch returned empty-handed from seeking money in Warsaw. Still earlier we find converts or their children in Poland taking part in Polish cultural life.[57]

During the following decades and throughout the nineteenth century endogamous marriage declined among the descendants of the converted Frankists, although it was still practiced to some extent during the first half of the century. The Frankists became more and more polonized and played varied roles in Polish society, even though the latter did not always accept them wholeheartedly. Some outstanding Polish personalities were related to the descendants of the neophytes. It is not entirely certain whether or not the great Polish poet Adam Mickiewicz was such a descendant, but his wife, Celina Szymanowska, was a granddaughter of Elisha Shorr of Rohatyn. It may well be that some individuals retained for a long time certain rudiments of the former Frankist ritual.

Various fragments of information and opinions about the Frankists either confirm or deny the existence of separateness (remnants of endogamy, use of Jewish dishes,[58] influence of Jewish thought here and there). But it is hard to say how much fact there is in all this. The "facts" vary with the attitudes of the informant and the writer. Liberals and Jewish assimilationists tend to reduce the separateness, whereas anti-Jewish writers are apt to prolong the existence of the separateness of the Frankists. Some even do this as a warning to Polish society against the "Jewish danger" or "conspiracy." An irony of modern anti-Semitism that should be mentioned is that in the 1920s some Polish anti-Semites exploited Frank and his conversion so as to build up a case about the "perfidious" Jewish designs to destroy the Polish nation! On the other hand, some nationalist-minded Jews are sometimes ready to "discover the Jewish point" among the descendants of the Frankists. Most of this, however, seems to belong in the realm of fantasy rather than fact.[59]

12 *Hassidim and Hassidism*

The Hassidic[1] movement developed in the same region of Poland (Podolia and southern Volhynia) as Frankism, but it started a little earlier.[2] Israel Baal Shem Tov (literally, "Master of the Good Name"), the founder of the Hassidic movement, was born about 1700 either in the townlet of Okopy not far from Krolówka in Podolia, where Jacob Frank was born about 1726, or in a suburb of Kolomea in Galicia, also not far from that region. The early adherents of the two movements had fairly similar social origins. They belonged for the most part to the lower classes of the Jewish population. Among the Hassidim, however, the village Jew (innkeeper, leaseholder) and the itinerant preacher may have played a bigger role than they did among the Frankists. The number of Jewish artisans—in 1764 constituting about 25 percent of the Jewish population in Poland generally and 17.5 percent in Volhynia in city and town, but making up only 2–4.4 percent in the rural settlements —seems to have been negligible in both movements. In both Hassidism and Frankism we find de-emphasis of (in Frankism actual opposition to) Torah learning and study, with a preference for "Oral Torah" rather than Scripture and (in Hassidism especially during the first decades) cultivation of oral traditions, sayings, stories, and songs which were not written down until much later.[3] Since Frankism and Hassidism were both against the Jewish "Establishment" they were both critical of the existing religious and social order. Both were influenced by cabalistic ideas and images or at least by popular cabala and its phraseology, and, according to some writers and scholars, also by a residue of Sabbatianism. Both were also to some extent concerned with sin and the guilt feelings it aroused.

The two trends encountered opposition from institutional Judaism, and tradition-bound religious leaders placed bans on them both: on Frankism in 1756 and on Hassidism in 1772. But in each case the outcome was entirely different. The number of Frankists in Poland remained small, and they soon ceased to constitute a Jewish group (following their conversion to Catholicism); whereas Hassidism enjoyed considerable growth from the first and by the end of the eighteenth century had spread throughout Poland[4] and even found some response beyond that country.

The reasons for this divergence are many and varied. Frankism tried to solve the problem of sin by sublimating it and making it into a virtue, whereas Hassidism sought forgiveness through the zaddik's (leader's) "descent" and emendation by magic, and minimized the whole problem of sin.[5] In practice this meant the predominance of religious nihilism, hedonistic trends, and sexual freedom in the one, and the fostering of a sort of revivalist fervor and some traditional values in the other. (In Hassidism sexual frivolity was mainly limited to the occasional use of erotic expressions and images in the writings.) In the framework of a predominantly religious-traditional society Frankism may have meant revolution to the point of a complete break with the past. Hassidism, however, promoted a degree of reform, advocating or tolerating some permissiveness and deviations but in reality barely touching upon essentials.

Similarly antithetic were the tactics each employed: Frankists set the authority of the Catholic Church and the state against the Jewish Establishment, whereas Hassidim worked largely from within the Jewish community, using persuasion and discussion. Frankism, seeking apocalypse through a pseudo-Messiah, tended to create a crisis situation as soon as the dream met with tangible reality. Hassidism, on the other hand, at first followed the traditional Jewish approach of verbalized messianism with little or no substance, thereby avoiding conflict with actuality.[6] Frankism encountered a crisis situation almost immediately by defying official Judaism (and being banned) when the group was still very small. In direct contrast, Hassidism was fortunate in avoiding such a crisis for a generation or two, by which time the movement already had roots, commanded tens of thousands of adherents, and extended to many communities.

And last but not least, the difference in leadership inevitably made itself felt: on one hand there was a despot (Jacob Frank) out to build up a real or imagined "kingdom" of his own, subject to his whims, in which he would be able to fulfill his own drives (eroticism and lust for power) in imitation of Turkish pashas and Polish nobles; on the other there was a humble and compassionate[7] man (Besht) with dreams of a "kingdom of God" on earth or of man ascending to heaven.

All this contributed to Hassidism's development of a separate though parallel existence with official Judaism. Thus it was strong enough to withstand the pressures of organized Jewry when they came, while Frankism was nipped in the bud by these pressures.

Israel Besht (Israel Baal Shem Tov)

Israel Besht (c. 1700–60), the founder of Hassidism, is depicted in *Shivchey Habesht*,[8] which was published in 1815, more than half a century after his death, as having come from lowly origins. An orphan who continually ran away from the community school (Talmud Torah) because he did not want to study, he later became a teacher's assistant whose chief duty was to bring the pupils to school, a watchman or assistant beadle in the bet hamidrash, a teacher (melamed), and a hermit in the Carpathian Mountains, drawing a meager livelihood from digging loam and selling it in the town. Next he became an innkeeper; his wife ran the business while Besht was absorbed in his meditations. All this time he remained in abject poverty with a low status in society. Some change came about after he "revealed himself" at the age of thirty-six. He then moved to a town in Galicia (Tluste) where he became a teacher and apparently also a healer and exorcist.

From Itinerant Baal Shem to Sedentary Zaddik

The term *baal shem* was used in those centuries to designate a healer, quack doctor, miracle worker, or charmer.* These people treated their patients with folk remedies such as herbs, ointments, and salves, as well as incantations, prayers or study,[9] talismans, and similar "cures." Some of them also "expelled evil spirits" or served their clients with advice, predicted the future, or performed miracles.

Besides such local healers or exorcists, whose activity was limited to the towns and immediate neighborhoods in which they lived, there were others who became known throughout an entire region or the whole country. The first preserved references to such individuals by name are apparently from the seventeenth century. A Gedalia *baal shem* served as dayan (assistant rabbi) in Worms during the first quarter of the century (he died in 1622 or 1624). A Joel Baal Shem seems to have been known in Worms in the first half of the seventeenth century, and another of the same name was supposed to have been active in Poland at the time of the cossack uprising of 1648. An author by the name of Adam Baal Shem wrote two little storybooks published in the same century, and there are tales about an Eliyahu Baal Shem, a Joel Baal Shem of Zamość, and some others of the eighteenth century. Addition of the word *tov* (good) to the "title" *baal shem* (the acronym Besht means Master of the Good Name) may or may not indicate a "higher" position. At any rate the title "Besht" was already known in the seventeenth and eighteenth centuries before Israel Besht's time.[9a]

Israel Baal Shem Tov was active, at least for several years, as an itinerant healer. Traveling through the towns and particularly the villages of Podolia, eastern Galicia, and Volhynia he ministered to the needs of Jewish leaseholders, tax collectors, and innkeepers, and occasionally also tended a non-Jewish nobleman. He employed the familiar cures of the times: bloodletting, application of leeches, and possibly prayer. He also gave his clients talismans that he had prepared himself. Once in a while he was invited to visit a rich Jew and perform some magic or give advice. This information can be gleaned from various stories in the *Shivchey Habesht*. These stories may also indicate that, at least for a time, most of Besht's income was derived from such sources. One story tells how during one of his trips Besht wanted to return home but his servants or assistants told him: "You owe money and can't return now." Another relates that "he never kept money overnight. On the day of his arrival home he paid up his debts and spent the rest for charity."

* *Baal shem* means "master of [God's] name," with the help of which one accomplished healing and miracles.

We learn that when he reached Brody hardly anybody came to see him and he had no money, but afterwards when he "came to . . . [a small town] the people began to approach him asking for medicaments. In other places they came, too. Thus he brought home money." From time to time, however, Besht apparently also served as an itinerant shochet (religious slaughterer) in the villages, earning money when he needed it.[10]

Taken from the stories about Besht, this information may contain many rudiments of reality, though the legends formulated by his followers and admirers were no doubt intended to praise and sanctify Besht. Such stories continued to be told (at least in the form in which they have come down to us) years later, even after Hassidic leaders had shifted to a largely sedentary way of life. A more radical change in the life-style of the Hassidic leader, from itinerant wanderer to stay-at-home, seems to have taken place during the years 1760–72, when Ber of Mezeritch (Miedzyrzecze), Besht's successor, organized the Hassidic movement.[11] But a significant beginning already became discernible in the last ten to fifteen years of Besht's life.

Around the mid-1740s Besht settled permanently in Medzibozh, thus ceasing for the most part to be an itinerant healer. The stories about Besht again reflect the change. We hear about rabbis and others traveling to see him in Medzibozh, and about still others being persuaded to do so.[12] It seems that in certain Hassidic circles this change was regarded as a social upgrading: "When Besht came to Medzibozh he was not considered important in the eyes of the Hassidim . . . because of the name Baal Shem Tov by which he was called,"[13] indicating somehow that his importance came later. Some stories tell also how the wealthy, as well as other people in Medzibozh, at first refused to believe in Besht but were later convinced.[14]

Whatever these stories may indicate, the break with an itinerant existence and the permanent settlement were not complete, either for Besht himself or for the following generations of the zaddikim. Besht still sometimes journeyed to visit his Hassidim, just as some of the later Hassidic rabbis did. A few of them, like Nachum of Czernobyl, a disciple of Ber of Mezeritch, spent a great part of their lives in traveling.

The Image of Besht

As documentary evidence about Besht is nonexistent[15] we can do no more than conjure up some sort of image of him based on the legends and stories told by his pupils and followers (or adversaries). Though these must obviously be biased, they may nonetheless afford some idea of how Besht appeared to contemporaries and the subsequent generation or two.

In general these stories tell very little about Besht's personal life—his individual behavior patterns or attitudes. They depict rather an idealized Besht as a zaddik, a leader or one preparing for such leadership. At most we may glean some points about him that lie between individual personality and behavior, and public personality: for example, the information about his youth, his growing up, and his varied activities before he settled in Medzibozh, his marriage to the sister of Gershon of Kutov, his retreat to the mountains, his pretending to be illiterate and inferior and belonging to the lowest groups. Some of Besht's other characteristics (again somewhere between personal behavior and public image) are revealed in this way, too. For instance, having been told by his dying father while still a young child that "God is with you and therefore you should not fear anything," in his youth he once took a stick and killed a wild animal—in reality a sorcerer disguised as an animal—who wanted to prevent him from taking children to school.

Besht smoked a pipe, a popular habit among Jews in eighteenth-century Poland, liked horses, went to the ritual bath (mikveh) every day and sometimes more than once, when he practiced immersion in the mikveh as a magic ritual in preparation for such important tasks as performing a miracle or helping stave off calamities. (Sometimes when some such task was called for he asked that the mikveh be heated especially for him.) He slept little—it is said only two hours daily—and rose at midnight to chant the traditional midnight prayers for redemption of the Jews. He must have had a good voice, for in the synagogue he often led the worshipers in prayer.

Besht gave generously to charity of whatever funds he had or earned. He also was active in collecting and providing ransom money for poor people—mostly innkeepers—who were unable to pay their debts to the landowners. In his younger years he fasted many times each week. In other words, he practiced asceticism, which he later came to despise. He was apparently an accomplished storyteller, converting people to his ideas by way of a good tale. One Hassidic story tells how Besht converted Jacob Joseph, the rabbi of Szarogrod and later of Polonnoe. Besht arrived in Szarogrod early one summer morning; he

> stopped his wagon, called to the first man who came along . . . and began to tell him a story. . . . Another passerby stopped to hear . . . a third did the same. At last Besht had caused all the passersby, among whom was the sexton of the synagogue, to stop and listen to his tales. Now it was the custom of the [author of] Toledoth* to commence his morning prayers at eight o'clock in the summer, and the sexton had been on his way to open the doors of the synagogue at six-thirty as usual. When the Toledoth arrived at the synagogue that day he found it still locked. . . .
>
> The sexton finally left the circle of listeners and went to open the doors of the synagogue. When the Toledoth saw him, he was vexed and asked why the men who usually came each day for prayer were not there. Upon being told that a certain stranger was standing in the marketplace telling stories and that everyone was gathered around him, listening, the rabbi bristled with anger. . . . After the morning prayers the Toledoth ordered the sexton to bring the visiting storyteller to him, that

*Jacob Joseph wrote, among other things, a book *Toledoth Yaakov Josef.* In premodern times it was customary among Jews to call an author after the title of his book.

he might be flogged for interrupting communal prayers. . . . When he arrived the Toledoth *asked indignantly: "Art thou the one who interrupted the communal prayer?" He answered; "Rabbi, I am the one." The Baal Shem continued: "I request his eminence not to be angry with me. Let me tell him a story." Rabbi Jacob Joseph listened to the story and was deeply moved by it. He regained peace of mind and was no longer angry. . . . The Besht continued: "If his eminence would like I shall tell him another story." "Tell it to me," he replied. When the Besht had finished still a third story, the* Toledoth *entered into conversation with him and immediately "was joined" to him.*[16]

Besht appears to have been sociable, communicating with different types of people—non-Jews as well as Jews. We are told that Besht acted, at least for a time, as arbiter for a band of non-Jewish robbers (on the condition, apparently, that they wouldn't rob Jews), straightening out their internal quarrels and disagreements. When the Hassidic movement began to develop and Hassidic groups (minyanim, shtibel) or communities were organized, Besht tried to provide them with leadership or personnel (rabbi, slaughterer, and the like). Sometimes he accompanied the candidate to the assigned community and apparently stayed with him for a while in order to familiarize him with his duties and introduce him to the community.

On a more general level Besht defended Jews against criticism, and he was upset when a preacher criticized Jews in a sermon.

Legend is likely to idealize Besht in its eagerness to demonstrate his great learning and grasp of Jewish esoteric knowledge. According to legend, Besht was a highly learned Jewish scholar even before his revelation at the age of thirty-six. In *Shivchey Habesht* it is told that the wisdom of cabala came to him mainly from secret writings that a man named Rabbi Adam[17] found in a cave, and later had transferred to Israel Besht in accordance with advice from heaven. Before his revelation Besht pretended to be unlearned and studied only while others slept or when he was in seclusion and nobody could see him. But in truth he was always an eminent scholar. He is often given the title of rabbi[18] and is supposed to have sat on rabbinical courts and to have shown eminent scholars that he frequently was better versed in Torah than they.

Besht we are told, possessed extrasensory powers, reading people's unknown past and foretelling their future. He used these powers not only passively but also actively: to force thieves to return stolen goods or, more importantly, to intercede in heaven for individuals or communities. He is said to have accomplished a cure in one case, driven away the angel of death in another, revived a child, and warned a community of an attack. On the other hand, he purportedly rid people of demons and exorcised devils (dybbukim) from the bodies of the sick.

At first he was, as it were, "clumsy." In trying to establish contact with an angel he would cause a fire or a death. But he later became more adept. He had visions of the prophet Elijah. Besht—or his soul—was said to have risen to heaven and gone from chamber to chamber. He was helped in a "difficult case" by the Messiah. In other cases he received assistance from his "teacher," the ancient prophet Ahiya Hashiloni.

He also taught Torah in heaven and the listeners enjoyed it. His intervention in heaven helped to rescue Jews from a calamity, saved a city from the Tatars, and raised up prayers that had been locked out of heaven for fifty years. He promised to bring people to paradise and kept his promise. During prayers he became ecstatic to the point of shuddering or dancing around so much that objects in his vicinity shook. In certain situations of enthusiasm or contact with heaven his face radiated glowing light; divine fires were also visible around him.

Further Images of Besht

A well-known Polish author and rabbi (of Ostrog and later chief rabbi of the Ukraine and Podolia), who was not officially a Hassid himself, testifies: "Since becoming acquainted with my teacher and friend Rabbi Israel [Besht] I am convinced that his conduct was pure and holy, very pious. . . . [God's] secrets were open to him."[19]

Solomon Maimon (1754–1800) was almost a contemporary of Besht. About 1770 he stayed for a while at the "court" of Ber of Mezeritch, Besht's successor. Writing his memoirs after having lived in Germany for about two decades and having become an Enlightener and a secularist, he says Besht (by mistake he calls him Joel instead of Israel) "became very celebrated . . . on account of some lucky cures which he effected by means of his medical knowledge and his conjuring tricks and he gave out that this was done, not by natural means but solely through *Kabbala maasit* [practical cabala] and the use of sacred names. In this way he played a very successful game in Poland."

Another enlightened Polish Jew—Jacques Calmanson—repudiates Besht still more definitely: "The founder of Hassidism," he says, was "a fanatic rabbi who became known as a prophet exploiting the superstitions of the ignorant masses, who always seek miracles. He boasted that he could cure all illnesses through cabala. . . . The masses . . . flocked to him seeking to restore their health, but found only fraud."

Opponents (mitnagdim) of the Hassidim, writing in the 1790s, observe that Besht "despised God's Torah . . . through his heretic books. . . . He was empty without Torah. . . . They [Hassidim] said he knows something which he never saw," wrote Israel Leibel. Leibel also says, in a pamphlet he published 1799 in German: "Israel . . . aspired to power, but because he was lacking talmudic and other knowledge he had no hope of influencing others by his spiritual virtues. Therefore he chose another way—to conjure spirits. In order to attract the believers he behaved as a holy man and donned a mask of piety."

Other anti-Hassidic writings from the end of the eighteenth century repeat that "he did not belong to the learned class but kept himself as a prophet and seer and was somehow familiar with cures and use of the holy name." "Israel of Medshibozh

. . . was known as a *baal shem* [miracle worker] and not as a scholar. All the great men, with a few exceptions, despised him."[20]

Ambiguities in Hassidic Thought

The vagueness concerning Besht also pervades the accounts of his work, Hassidism, and its essence.[21] This is due not only to the makeup of the sources and the ideological divergence among the leaders, but also to the very nature of Hassidism and the Jewish religious culture generally.

Hassidism (we are mainly interested here in the beginnings spanning the development during the eighteenth century) was neither a philosophical, theosophical, cabalistic, or any other kind of *system*. For innumerable reasons it was, rather, discursive, epigrammatic, and more than a little inconsistent.

Traditional Jewish thought was, like medieval thought generally, mostly repetitive and associative. Hallowed old texts were used as authorities, and comparisons and similarities were based on verbal association, wordplay, allegory, and symbolism denoting some casual relationships. This meant that a later author might be using the old concepts and verbiage in a different sense, since almost any system of meaning varies from one historical period to another.

If Besht and his disciples were seeking ideas or affirmation of their own attitudes from old sources and cabalistic works they may have used existing terms and phraseology, making them mean what they wanted them to. Or if, as Scholem asserts, "no page of a Hassidic book can be understood without constant reference to the traditions . . . [of *Zohar* and Lurianic cabala]"[22] it is not to say that the Lurianic or Zoharic ideas, formulas, and terms used by Hassidism of necessity retained their original meaning. This is especially true because Hassidic writings—both the stories and what are known as the theoretical works—must suffer from the "translation complex."[23] The stories were told in Yiddish, and the Hebrew is a translation of this spoken Yiddish. The preserved "theoretical" Hassidic works consist mainly of transcribed "Oral Torah," which the zaddik "spoke" at mealtimes or on other occasions, and similar homilies. The zaddik's vernacular, too, was Yiddish and if he "spoke" the Torah in Hebrew-Aramaic he was greatly limited in his vocabulary and phraseology.

Thus he may have used stereotyped expressions without differentiating the subtlety of their exact meanings or, on the other hand, may have employed a vacillating terminology for one concept or idea especially since, as Scholem rightly points out, "Hasidic writers were not particularly creative in elaborating the theosophical points of Kabbalism."[24] One may say that they were not particularly interested in—or even capable of—developing these points.[25] Israel of Kozenitz claims that though he had read eight hundred cabalistic books before coming to his teacher, the Maggid of Mezeritch (Ber), he had really learned nothing from them, which may confirm the idea of the discrepancy between words and meaning.

Generally, some paradox and even contradiction is inherent in mystical writings, including those of the Hassidim. The mystic's language is "that of the emotionally moved artist who speaks in poetical pictures, in metaphors, figures of speech, large-spun comparisons, similes, analogies, myths, parables and allegories."[26] Metaphors, allegories, and parables are usually vague and nebulous and may be variously interpreted. This is particularly true of Hassidic writings, which consist mainly of homilies and sermons, a type of literature usually characterized by a lack of precision. A preacher will use an expression or term rather ad hoc, with little regard for its exact meaning.

Hassidic authors were aware of this situation and sought justifications for the divergent "explanations" of words in the Torah (almost every Hassidic homily proceeds from an expression in the Torah). Besht's extenuation is that "there is no word in the Torah that does not have two [different] meanings." Others claim defensively that the Torah's text is "relativistic," that "it was given to be exonerated according to the needs of the leaders of each epoch and that of each generation" or that "it was given without verbalization and therefore each one can verbalize and explain it according to his needs."[27]

The confusion about the meaning of the phraseology used may have been compounded by the fact that neither Besht nor Ber of Mezeritch and some of the other leaders wrote down their own words or deliberations for publication. This was done by pupils or a secretary (it was by no means a stenographic rendering!). And since publication usually came years after the death of the zaddik, it was impossible to verify the accuracy of the written version.

Besht's ideas are to be found in the stories told about him and in quotations by his disciples (Jacob Joseph incorporated in his writings over five hundred such quotations in Besht's name), and by his grandson. The story mentioned earlier of how Besht looked into a manuscript purportedly containing his sayings written down by someone other than himself, and exclaimed that there was not a single correct word of his, may indicate that those generations felt (or knew) that these were not exact reproductions. Apparently this sort of Hassidic publication of the eighteenth century is somewhat more accurately characterized by Shneur Zalman of Losna's (later Liady) description of another publication *(Zavaat Haribash*, 1793): "a collection [of Besht's] sayings which [others] collected who were unable to reproduce the correct language, but the content is true."[28] But since the given author was not quoted verbatim it is impossible to estimate the extent to which the terminology may have been changed.

The ambiguity of meaning may also have been either caused, or increased, primarily by the difference in backgrounds and setting between the cabalists and the Hassidim. The former comprised individuals or tiny groups who devoted their lives to study and the writing of esoteric works and ideas, often even refusing to make them public. The study and mystical exercise of the secrets of the cabala were performed in isolation, retreat, or secrecy. Abstract thought and symbolism were here abundant. Hassidim, however, were rather ordinary Jews with everyday problems, troubles, fears, and hopes. To reach them Hassidic leaders had to bring their ideas literally to the marketplace (as in the legend about Besht's telling stories in the market) and to meet both their needs and their capacity to understand. They made the cabalistic terms they used—intentionally or not—more concrete and actual, thereby often altering their meanings or implication. The doctrine, for instance, of "uplifting of the sparks" of divine life, which according to Lurianic cabala are scattered all over the world, in Hassidism came to mean (among other things) that since holy sparks were supposed to be everywhere there is no sphere of life devoid of significance. This transformed profane things into holy ones, and endowed material matters with religious value. For a Lurianic cabalist the phrase "uplifting of the sparks" had connoted a catastrophe, involving falling "sparks of light" from the divine realm into the lower depths, originated on the "other side," and it led to the entrenchment of demonic power. In Hassidism, however, the emphasis shifted from the catastrophic origin and the "other side" to the existence of sparks of divine light everywhere, inevitably endowing all activity with an essential spark of divinity.[29] There is a connection between the latter idea and the Hassidic attitudes toward reality and ways of expressing joy and other emotions.

Another source of inconsistency is the fact that Hassidism, while committed to Jewish religious tradition and most of what it stands for, appears to have concomitantly sanctioned nonreligious activities. The commandments and Torah were traditionally bound up with the imposition of numerous limitations. But Hassidim (Jacob Joseph of Polonnoe, for instance) assert "that the perfect man can perform the deepest meditations and acts of unification [with God] even through his most mundane actions such as eating, drinking, sexual intercourse, and business transactions."[30] Besht offered a different formulation of the same idea. They seem to be conferring religious sanction on nonreligious activities.

In short, ambiguity of doctrine and diversity of ideas, some of them hazy ones, are inherent in such a movement which, furthermore, inevitably varies with changing times (between the eighteenth and nineteenth centuries, for instance).

Between Tradition and Innovation

Despite the flexibility of Hassidic doctrine and practice and the vacillating terminology, it is possible to perceive certain basic essentials in the movement. Hassidism was, first and foremost, a Jewish religious pietist or revivalist trend, though Judaism was by no means unique in this respect. In Protestant Europe generally—England, Holland, Germany—publication of mystical works increased from the end of the seventeenth century. Some of them were concerned, parallel with "inner light," "inward divine illumination," and "religion of love," with opposition to the orthodox belief of eternal punishment and hell "as an emotional necessity for pious believers anxious to retain their faith in God and man."[31] And in the main, religious revivalism—the effort to enliven religious faith and make it relevant by new appeals and attitudes or practices—developed in a number of European countries during the seventeenth and eighteenth centuries, just as it did in the American colonies (the

"Great Awakening"). As though to limit the spread of the tendency toward secularism (Enlightenment), revivalism promoted a craving for a warm, emotional religion and also provided a response to the need for change (opposition to doctrinal formalism, to the established institutional framework). German pietists (theirs was known as a "religion of the heart"), the Quakers, founded by George Fox in England in the seventeenth century, the Moravian Brethren, John Wesley (1703–91) and his followers, the Methodists, as well as the itinerant preachers of the "Great Awakening" aroused emotional responses by protesting against rigidity and formalism and challenging established institutions. They appealed to the lower classes by the warmth they brought into religion, making it an intensely enthusiastic personal experience, and by their advocacy of social betterment. Fervent prayer and evangelical campaigns induced many to follow them.

Within Eastern Europe, including the region where Hassidism developed, another religious flare-up led to partially similar if not identical revivalist and anti-Establishment trends in the second half of the seventeenth century.

As mentioned, the *raskol* (schism) in the Greek Orthodox Church brought to life a variety of sects that denied the validity of the established church, believing it had become heretical and personified the antichrist. Some of these groups sought, with a new religious fervor, to save themselves (or the world) before the Second Coming (1669 and 1699).

As we saw in the preceding chapter, splinters of these varied sects settled in Podolia and the Polish Ukraine. The synod of the Uniates (Lwów, later Zamość) in 1720 manifested violent opposition to the Old Believers and their more bizarre sects. This may indicate that the sectarians were already numerous there. In the subsequent decades their numbers increased still further.[32]

Hassidism formed a corollary to non-Jewish revivalism—not necessarily influenced by the developments in the non-Jewish world but responding to similar (though not identical) situations, pressures, and needs of the Jews in Poland, or more precisely in Podolia-Volhynia. It was a Jewish religious movement that strove to make Jewish religion warm and emotional, abolish most formalism, and create "a religion of the heart" and a "religion of love," challenging some established institutions and justifying sectarianism.

On the surface Hassidism did not differ greatly from the non-Jewish religious revivalist trends. One can even find some parallels between Hassidism and some of the radical or mystical Russian Ukrainian sects. In addition to some minor bizarre behavior they show other trends in common with the Hassidim: de-emphasis or abrogation of and opposition to traditional sacred books and the traditional form of services; spiritualization of the faith; and development of new oral traditions with the help of legends, stories, and songs.

Among other themes and practices are to be found beliefs in the transmigration of souls, the immanence of God and His presence everywhere, individual salvation, union with God through prayer; the idea that sin is needed for salvation; confidence rooted in the certainty of divine companionship; ecstasy during worship; the wearing of long white robes or shirts with wide sleeves and broad girdles at gatherings for worship; ritual dancing, leaping, whirling, singing, with some persons turning somer-saults. Moreover, they gathered together for ritual meals and believed in mutual support—unity personified by the leaders. The leader was elite; he was regarded as a sort of prophet whose visions were valued; his charisma was regarded as hereditary. Finally, they admonished against self-esteem and demanded that one minimize the self (self-abnegation).[33]

The parallels in thought and theme between Hassidism[34] and the Christian sects may or may not indicate that either one influenced[35] the other. At least some imitations, for the most part in external matters, may not be excluded.

But in fact, there are certain fundamental differences arising out of the Jews' specific situation and religious background. Whereas Christian revivalists relied heavily on mass preaching, Hassidim and their leaders resorted largely to individual conversations and persuasion, storytelling, and similar more individualized methods of gaining attention. Christian revivalists painted the dangers of hell and damnation in lurid colors, and some of the Russian-Ukrainian sectarians sought salvation through such extreme means as mortification, self-immolation, and castration. The Hassidim were reacting negatively to the seventeenth- to eighteenth-century Jewish musar (moral) literature and preaching, and the latter's emphasis on hell, a multitude of demons, and horrors; they turned, so to speak, in the opposite direction.[36] They minimized the threat of hell and the devil by silence, and instead emphasized love of God and His immanence or omnipresence throughout the universe.

This meant above all absolute faith in God and His rule. Based on older Jewish sources, including cabalistic dicta, this idea became a cornerstone in Hassidic thought. The saying of the *Zohar* that "there is no place vacant from Him" became an important pseudopantheistic principle in most varieties of Hassidism. If God permeates every activity and every event and is a vital force, life is not to be divided into areas of good and bad.

A number of other principles and approaches are connected with this attitude. If God is everywhere and present in everything, then the demarcation between holy and secular is bound to disappear, or at least be minimized. Each object in the world and each activity carries within itself "divine sparks" contributing to its vitality and life. Thus one can serve God not only by good deeds and prayers, but also in everyday matters: eating, drinking, storytelling, and earning a living.[37] There is a Hassidic story about one Hassidic saint who maintained: "I did not go to the Maggid of Mezeritch to learn Torah from him but to watch him tie his bootlaces," that is, to observe his mundane activities.

Early Hassidism embodied another comparable notion, namely, if the Deity is the sole agent in the world, then He is also the sole agent in human actions. The good deeds of human beings come from God's power; prayers, study, and other acts of worship are, as it were, performed by the Shekhina, with man serving as vehicle or instrument.[38] This manifested itself in the furthering of some quietist elements, with their attendant ideas of passivity and demands for self-annihilation. Withdrawal of the human ego from consciousness, they thought, leads to the entry of the divine ego. Self-abasement was for the most part regarded as a means of avoiding vanity or the ill judgment of others and of restraining pride. It did not mean, in this case, either theoretically or in practice, the attainment of complete passivity or destruction of the personality and its responsibility, which sometimes led to abominable license among extremist mystics in Christianity.[39]

The views on vice and the "evil spirit" followed a similar course. It was hard to reconcile the idea of a good, all-loving and all-forgiving God with the existence of evil and the necessity for rewards and punishments and hell. In Hassidism—unlike older Jewish views, including that of cabala—evil was not a primeval, demonic force standing in opposition to the divine forces. It had no independent existence but was rather a distortion of goodness, or was regarded as "a chair (a step) to the good" or a requirement for doing good.[40] It could thus be emended into goodness. The normative parts of Hassidic thought seldom mention punishment for nonfulfillment of commandments and, one might say, they "forget" about hell.

It would apparently be too simplistic to regard Hassidism as a monistic world outlook. The doctrine has many variations, which are not infrequently contradictory. Moreover, pre-Hassidic Jewish thought (which nurtured Hassidism), combined with the realities of life, tended to develop themes of numerous dualisms: God and man, heaven and earth, spirit and matter, soul and body, virtue and sin, good and bad instincts, love for and fear of God. Though some effort was made to adjust these and other discrepancies, they could not always be reconciled.[41] Comprising body and soul, possessed of good and bad instincts, man should "extinguish" himself in his prayers so as to cleave to God or (according to those who see divine elements in the body) to reelevate the latter to its former high position or "change matter into form [spirit]." Evil, sin, "bad instincts" *(yeytzer hara)* were all—though each in a different way—seen as containing divine elements that could and should change everything into holiness or should (in various ways) be emended. Another attitude was that since everything comes from God and nothing is possible outside of Him, divine elements are, as it were, found in sin itself, or that the Shekhina clothes itself in sin. Otherwise the sinner could not commit the sin, "since only God gives the strength to do it."[42]

Innovative was the appearance of the leader popularly known as the Hassidic *rebbe* (the zaddik), who in contradistinction to the ordinary rabbi with his prescribed Torah learning, his dependence upon appointment, his duties and systematic behavior, was elite, a chosen one (perhaps self-chosen), whose strength lay in his popularity with the group, his charisma, religious personality, and often also his ability to originate his own specific behavior pattern.

The zaddik, the saint or illuminate, the elite plays a vital role in Hassidic theory and practice. The elect, who can (and does) reach high positions in the divine order, becomes a special sort of leader.[43] He is someone who has access, as it were, to the high spheres, who can raise the prayers of his generation to heaven and thus emendate their sins. His role as an intermediary is two-way. At the same time that he represents the people in heaven, as it were, he brings to them the bounty of life from heaven, "makes the spirit of the Lord reach them." He thus brings into contact the spiritual world on high and the material world below with its ordinary human beings, and draws heaven's attention to their needs.[44]

The zaddik thus becomes an intermediary between the community he leads, or its individual members, and the Divine. In the beginning of Hassidism the zaddik's leadership was conceived of as a mainly spiritual one; his functions included mystical powers of elevation of the community or its individuals, or both, through his cleaving to God. Later, mainly beginning with "the third generation" (disciples of the Great Maggid), the zaddik was visualized for the most part as representing "the whole generation," somewhat as Moses did. The whole world was created for the zaddik, who brings the people abundance and prosperity; he is able, as it were, to cause God to change His mind; he can also perform miracles. Going a step further, the zaddik, besides becoming the provider for his followers of spiritual possibilities for "raising" their prayers or performing a supernatural miracle, also furnishes the opportunity for them to satisfy their main material needs: to acquire "children, life, and liveli-hood."[45] This trend, heavily stressed by Elimelekh of Lizhajsk and some of his pupils, served, among other things, as additional emphasis on the zaddik's justifica-tion of his "right" to accept, or demand, funds from his Hassidim. This tendency was, however, already indicated earlier.[46]

The views on the zaddik's role also have some connection with his function as a "defender" of Jews vis-à-vis God and with his love of the Jewish people. Besht, according to legend, intervened in heaven for individuals or for the Jewish commu-nity. We also hear that he could not stand to listen to anyone criticizing the Jews' behavior. In general, Besht counted "love of Jews" as one of the three principles on which he based his new ways.[47]

Levi Yitzhak of Berdiczew (1740–1810) is known in the Hassidic story to have been a "defender of Israel" vis-à-vis heaven and an *ohev Yisrael* (a lover of Jews). He himself maintained: "Each one has to see to it that he loves fully every one of the Jews. . . . Each one should always defend Jews . . . and is not allowed to do otherwise, and only the zaddik who admonishes the people in a positive way can become a leader." A number of other Hassidic leaders followed suit, each expressing his "love of Jews" differently. They either simply forbade speaking ill about any Jew or made it a mitzva (commandment) to love Jews, or established love of Jews as a test of righteousness, and attempted to reinterpret the chastisement of the prophet Isaiah (1:2–4) in a positive way (making his words mean praise rather than rebuke[48]).

Doctrine and Practice

Doctrine is often a stereotyped mode of thought and behavior or "a more or less unified system of a normative character."[49] The elements of the Hassidic doctrine[50] were hardly new. These elements, as mentioned above, are found in older Jewish sources—cabalistic, popular cabalistic, and noncabalistic[51]—and were repeated in many non-Hassidic writings. Hassidism, however, sometimes altered their meaning and direction, or gave them a new emphasis. This generally helped to reduce the stringency of some of the general Jewish religious demands. To some extent ecstasy replaced rigorous practices or the latter were de-emphasized. This is not to say that Hassidism intended to denigrate religious practice and attitudes. On the contrary, as a revivalist trend it attempted to add vigor and relevance to Jewish religion by introducing enthusiasm and timeliness. But in doing so the leaders de-emphasized some of the older values, which in any case had been somewhat neglected in practice or had fallen into partial disuse, while some new values were moved into the foreground. In this way a new view of the world (cosmography) was created, placing the Jew in a new position.[52]

The older idea of (Jewish) man being placed on this horrible earth in order to fulfill God's precepts was, as it were, reversed. God in heaven needs the Jew ("there is no king without a nation"). Man can even control heavenly matters. Man, or rather the Jew, thus became a cocreator of the world, as it were. The zaddik can change God's will. As man assumed this new role it may have seemed inappropriate to emphasize the distinction between paradise and hell, the traditional ideas of reward and punishment, with emphasis on the latter. Man can elevate himself to heaven. In contrast with older Jewish ideas, punishment for and the dire results of failure to fulfill the precepts or for sinning are rarely mentioned in early Hassidic writings.[53]

Sin itself is also minimized or spiritualized for the most part. Thus we are told that should one happen to look at a beautiful woman (generally regarded in Jewish religious literature as a sin of the first magnitude) one has only to remember that her beauty comes from God, thereby transforming the transgression into praise of God. Sin becomes spiritualized into thought ("wayward thoughts"), which a man can rid himself of through some sort of special devotion, by rejecting it, or through his connection with the zaddik. Evil, usually emphasized in Jewish and some other religions, is seen as a step toward goodness; profane matters become endowed with holiness ("holy sparks"), and fulfillment of worldly needs assumes certain religious significance.[54] Among the ideas advanced was that some sin or sinners are necessary in order, as it were, to have something about which to pray.[55]

As a result, Hassidism's view of the world became a primarily optimistic one. In contrast with the older Jewish world picture of man alone and helpless in a universe swarming with all manner of demons, evil spirits, and angels of destruction, Hassidic writings depict him as a happy creature, confident in God, inhabiting a universe abounding in tranquillity, security, and joy, possessing a blissful confidence rooted in the certainty of divine companionship.

World Outlook of Musar (Moral) Literature (17–18th cent.)[56]	World Outlook of Hassidism

The world is full of sin and sinners. Jews do not observe the Sabbath properly, do not study Torah; they commit many transgressions, charge interest, etc. Manifold punishments await the sinners for each transgression. The penalties range from burning in hell through every sort of physical and mental suffering to falling victim to the millions of demons and evil spirits that inhabit the world. ("It is known the world is full of ... evil spirits born of the people's sins.") Man is constantly imperiled by these hordes, particularly during the night or when they take over a certain place ("as in Poznań in the 1680s"). They, as well as the spirits of the wicked, the ghosts, and Satan himself, are constantly waiting to attack people for the slightest transgression. To be more or less secure one must, in addition to using certain magical defenses, fulfill all the precepts and avoid all transgressions; one must study and pray most of the time, talk very little, and care little or nothing for secular matters; one should do penance and weep all the time, fast, roll in the snow, and mortify oneself. Required fast days range between forty and eighty-four and more, depending on the type of transgression.

God dwells in the world, and the universe is full of His goodness and glory. The human (Jew) should realize that the Shekhina is with him. There is no absolute evil and no absolute sin.

The *yeytzer hara* (evil spirit) attempts to deceive man into believing that he is a great sinner. In truth, man need not be too particular in these matters. Man has nothing to fear. God wants to have him near, and the zaddik helps him in many directions. It is sufficient if man fulfills one good deed (mitzva).

Secular matters have a deeper significance, and small talk an important function. Man should neither fast nor weep; he should not mortify himself, but should rather serve God in joy. Such human functions as eating and drinking contribute to joy of the soul; making a living, working for material gain, has positive sides.

Pre-Hassidic popular literature, both oral and written homilies, usually associated immoral thought with the immoral act, lust with adultery. Hassidic teaching reversed the trend: immoral acts became identified as "strange (or evil) thoughts" or as fantasy.[57] The changed ideas about fulfilling the precepts, about sin and penance, can also be illustrated by the following. In the second half of the sixteenth century a little book was published in Poland containing a catalog of personal sins *(Brit Abraham)*. It listed "minor sins," which, according to the author, people commit inadvertently. These are not mentioned in the confessions contained in the High Holiday prayers. In the reprinting of this little book sins sometimes began to "grow" and multiply. One such reprint of the catalog of personal sins that appeared more than a century later (in *Taharot Hakodesh*) contains an amplification of the sins both qualitatively and quantitatively. The original little book of a few pages now becomes a big "confessional" expanded to seventy pages, with repeated emphasis on the severity of the sins and the necessity for penance.[58]

This preoccupation with great and small sins in the pre-Hassidic period stands in contrast with such Hassidic ideas as: "God knew before he gave the Torah that Jews will not fulfill it. . . . We should not be punished because of this" (Pinchas Shapira of Korzec) or "God, I can assure you that chastisement and suffering will not make the Jews repent. So why torment them for nothing . . . please be good to all Jews" (Arye Leib of Shpola).[59]

In place of detailed descriptions and terrifying images of sins and their results, which overstimulate the fear of transgression and of hell and create guilt feelings, Hassidism offered a deflation of sin and evil. Instead of a punitive religion with nightmarish ordeals of penance (which, among other things, serve to reinforce inner guilt feelings[60]) the Hassidic Jew received assurance of God's goodness, of His need of the Jew and His desire to be served in joy. The feeling of being alone and helpless in a hostile world teeming with all sorts of demons, which had been a source of human anxiety, was replaced in Hassidism by one of being close to a loving God (communion with God) ready to forgive shortcomings, and of being protected by the rabbi (zaddik), the connecting link between heaven and earth.

With this change in tenor Hassidism gained acceptance among individuals and some groups.[61] The new religious ecstasy and revivalism also put fresh life into the faith for many a Jew, giving him a raison d'être and courage to face the exigencies of the times. In addition, these worldly and life-affirming tenets supplanted to a considerable extent the focus on the afterlife and the ascetic demands of traditional Jewish preaching and writing of those centuries.

Perhaps it was the practices of Hassidism even more than its doctrine that made it acceptable. For in Hassidism, as in many another movement, a difference developed rapidly between teachings and practice.

Among other things doctrine taught, for instance, that one need not be too particular about fulfilling the commandments, that it is sufficient to fulfill just one precept, and that Torah study is none too important. It offered assurance of the deeper significance of secular things: physical joy is a precondition for spiritual joy, and the leader, the zaddik, has the power to intercede in heaven for all his congregants' needs. In this atmosphere human frailty and man's general tendency to laxity did not necessarily lead to disgrace.[62] For example Besht's precept that one must rise at midnight or at least before sunrise for the early morning prayers may in practice have gone unheeded as the prayers were postponed at will. This is especially true since Hassidism considered prayers somewhat dependent on the proper mood for achieving communion with God and thus had an excuse for postponement.

Permissiveness, which had existed in practice to some extent even earlier among some Polish Jews, particularly apparently in the southern frontier regions of Volhynia-Podolia, could now find justification or toleration in Hassidic teachings on laxity in observance of the precepts. The permissible or required joy opened the door to natural human cheerfulness and exuberance, which led at times to some excesses.[63] Warnings that "one should not consider himself wicked" or "not to consider himself as nothing" but should rather develop self-esteem grew out of a practice far removed from the earlier demands for piety and served to sanction further disregard of doctrine.[64] The same may be said of the endowment of all profane things with a certain holiness (because of the "holy sparks" they contain), and especially the conferring of high prestige upon the business of making a living and making money by the rationalization that the goal was to use one's earnings for good deeds: for charity, raising a family, marrying off the children, and so on. In some cases Hassidic leaders reasoned that affluence affords peace of mind, which enables a man to serve God better. Even the zaddik needs to be prosperous if he is to fulfill the precepts and be able to study (Elimelekh of Lizhajsk). It is also said that Besht condoned some irregularities in business matters because the proceeds were being used for good purposes.[65] Besht and many of the zaddikim of the following generation opposed criticism of the Jews, demanding "love for Jews" and "defending" their practices, thereby boosting the Jewish man's ego.

In short, Hassidic doctrine made religion enthusiastic and meaningful by emphasizing a new kind of piety. It substituted a religion of love for a religion of fear, brought a merciful and compassionate God (not a jealous and vindictive one) down to earth, and raised man to heaven. It offered man a new, optimistic world outlook and, by de-emphasis of sin and hell, freed him from or eased his guilt feelings. Practice went further than doctrine and opened the way to increasing permissiveness. Both teaching and practice condoned many of man's failings, and a number of formerly despised activities gained dignity.

Practice is also found to differ from theory in other matters. Hassidism shows a tendency to spiritualize a number of things, and to remove their material content (Palestine, galut, some of the commandments and rituals). But Hassidism as a whole and Hassidim as individuals, unlike some non-Jewish quietist groups, did not turn into meditating, passive beings. Both the movement and individual Hassidim developed quite a bit of activism, both in terms of organizational talent (organization of the movement and fostering its growth) and in business acumen—many Hassidim becoming successful and rich entrepreneurs. The stereotype of idleness connected with being a Hassid was projected first by the mitnagdim and later by the Enlighteners in their struggle with Hassidism. But this was based on a rather small minority and mostly in later periods. In reality the majority of Hassidim were, or became, very active human beings—helped in part by the optimism brought into their lives by Hassidism (despite the theory of relying on *bitachon*—God's providence—only).

As in some other sects living in the region of southern Poland, including those of the Greek Orthodox Church, a gap developed between thought and practice. In Hassidism too (and not necessarily through imitation of other sects) once the group was on its own and less subject to an imposed discipline by the larger Jewish society, some of the more rigorous demands for abstinence and the more demanding practices partially fell into disuse, while some other practices that had earlier been frowned upon were now tolerated. In this way Hassidism shows tendencies toward reforming religious life without having to do it expressly. In other words, some of the hardships of Orthodox Jewish religious observance were, in fact, tempered without any official diminution of an individual's piety or Orthodox faith. Hassidism could thus become a reform religion without being forced to take upon itself the onus of a revolutionary trend or to bring about an official breach with Jewish piety and tradition.[66] (In later years Hassidism could, and did, easily emphasize its "traditional" aspects rather than the changes it wrought.)

At the same time the new leader, the charismatic zaddik, became an intermediary between man and God, an "address" to which the Hassid might turn in need and in joy, and a center for a new community, a separate unit, where man could find friendship and freedom from loneliness and alienation.[67]

There were also other advantages for the Jew who joined the Hassidic group. In the leader he found also a faith healer, sometimes an advisor in business and other matters, and a medium to bring him, through magic, luck and abundance from heaven. The Jew of those times and later valued the Hassidic rabbi's wisdom or good luck. Some of them made the rabbi a silent partner in their businesses—assigning him a cut in the profits—in the belief that this would bring them prosperity. (The practice was widespread from the nineteenth century on and is documented, though sparsely, for the end of the eighteenth. One may assume that it existed earlier, too.)

Growth

Despite this apparently favorable climate, the group at first gained new members only slowly. In the stories about Besht we find traces of the struggle for recognition both of Besht and of the formation of a Hassidic group. He had to convince a host of different types of people to become his followers.[68] Jacob Joseph of Polonnoe tells of "the struggle waged by those who wished to pray in a separate minyan," and he propagandizes for a separate (Hassidic) congregation.[69] It is possible that the community of Medzibozh finally became a Hassidic community during Besht's lifetime. He also succeeded in organizing some other congregations (or communities) of a Hassidic character. We have already mentioned how Besht sponsored men from his group as rabbis or slaughterers for this or that community.*

Some indirect information may indicate the existence of such groups as early as the 1750s. Mentioned at that time by opponents of Hassidism is the existence of groups, or a special sect, whose members performed all sorts of gestures and motions (movements) during prayers,[70] surely meaning the Hassidim. At the time of Besht's death in 1760 there apparently existed a number of such Hassidic organizational

---

*"Congregation" means here a separate Hassidic unit (*shtibel* connotes room in Hassidic parlance) in a Jewish community (kehilla), while "Hassidic community" designates a whole territorial unit, a community—or its leadership—which became Hassidic.

units in southern Poland, with thousands of followers.[71] This none too large group was destined to grow considerably in subsequent decades.

During the years when Besht's successor, Ber of Mezeritch, was the leader of the group (1760–72) the Hassidic movement experienced considerable growth. Mezeritch and its region of Volhynia, where the Maggid Ber resided, was nearer to the Polish-Lithuanian parts than Podolia and hence more accessible to them. Rabbi Ber himself, unlike Besht, was a well-known talmudic scholar, and this enabled him to attract a number of talmudists to Hassidism.

In addition, he was apparently, despite his poor health, a good organizer and sent "agents" into different parts of the country. One story tells about two friends who became "missionaries" for Hassidism in those years. In *Shivchey Habesht* one such mission is mentioned; it was entrusted to Aaron of Karlin, a disciple of Rabbi Ber and the founder of Hassidism in Karlin. Though recruitment of adherents may not have been this mission's sole purpose, it did help in this respect too. If the details of the story are authentic, he also tried to arrange some religious matters concerning family life, and according to other information he became partially involved in local community affairs.

Solomon Maimon, a contemporary, reports that the aim of the Hassidic leaders to spread their movement "sought chiefly to attract the youth to itself" and tells about "a young man who had already been initiated into the society [of Hassidim] and who was traveling around," apparently on such a mission. Maimon states also that emissaries were "sent everywhere, whose duty it was to preach the new doctrine and procure adherents." Maimon depicts this missionary as a young man of great energy and devotion, who knew how to persuade or force the older members of the community to follow him: "In his look was something so . . . commanding that he ruled men. Whenever he came he . . . made new regulations [in the community]. . . . The elders of the congregation, for the most part old respectable men, . . . trembled before his face."[72]

Maimon wrote these lines years later when he was already taking a negative view of Hassidism. Thus he may be exaggerating, just as he does in his statement that Hassidism "almost acquired dominion over the whole nation." But he may also be revealing something of the tenor of the 1760s to 1770s and the general feeling that the movement was growing and spreading.

Among Rabbi Ber's disciples we find a number originating from different parts of the Ukraine, Galicia, and Lithuania, who later became famous leaders of the movement: Levi Yitzhak of Berdiczew, Nachum of Czernobyl, Zeev Wolf of Zhitomir, Elimelekh of Lizhajsk, Michael of Zloczow, Aaron of Karlin, Mendel of Vitebsk, Abraham of Kalisk, Shneur Zalman of Losna (later of Liady), and others. These and other men became Hassidic leaders in the Ukraine, in Galicia, and in White Russia–Lithuania. In central Poland, where Hassidism came a little later (in the 1780s) Israel of Kozenitz, Jacob Itzhak Horowitz of Lanzut, later Lublin, and Jacob Itzhak of Przysucha became active. New Hassidic congregations arose in new places, and some new customs were also introduced or sanctioned. Thus Rabbi Ber had advocated use of the prayer book arranged by Isaac Luria. Through this the Sephardic *nusach* (form of prayer) became standard for Hassidim.[73] Both the growth and the spread of the Hassidic circles to new regions and the changes they introduced began to alarm the established Jewish communities and leading personalities.

Under Attack

Hassidism was religiously mildly reformist, as mentioned, wavering in practice between tradition and innovation, allowing a degree of permissiveness, open to illiterates or semiliterates,[74] and attracting followers also by the feeling of brotherhood and togetherness. But it also had several other aspects.

Socially it was the expression of people discontented with the kehilla oligarchy and the prestigious classes in Jewish society. It was brought into being by the lumpen intelligentsia—itinerant preachers, rabbis without positions or with shaky ones, ritual slaughterers, and similar elements. And it was nourished by the existence of masses of village Jews, innkeepers, lessees, and other such groups disregarded by the ruling elite. The opposition by these dissatisfied groups found expression not only in sharp criticism of the existing order—this was not new in Jewish life; it had been spreading during the eighteenth century—but also in an attempt to create a counterculture (to use a modern concept). This counterculture was innovative mainly in the new selection of its values but not in essence. The values themselves were taken from the age-old Jewish religious-cultural treasures. In overemphasizing the "new" values the Hassidim had to de-emphasize the old.

All this—the antihierarchic tendencies, the "easing of the yoke" of the commandments by condoning permissiveness, the feeling of community and belonging and the respect it commanded—were either designed for or became in fact a means of drawing in disaffected people and creating new nuclei for brotherliness and group living.

But all these facets of Hassidism were liable to become divisive, too, both in theory and in practice and still more in abuses of practice.

There were, first of all, fringe elements of the Hassidim—apparently mainly young people—who became "radicals" and both drove the permissiveness too far and used excessive criticism and satirized the existing order. Natural joie de vivre and the loosening of the old controls made some try to enjoy life and seek to indulge in some secular pleasure. Besht's tenet that "one should not pay too much attention to the restrictive severities; they may be Satan's doing" *(Zavaat Haribash)* could be regarded as a universal principle of permissiveness in many areas. Traditional Judaism, however, was based rather on a method of avoiding formulating principles even when individual concrete instances had to be changed. This was in order to keep the continuity of the halakha (Jewish law) intact. The exuberance of some "radicals" with their dancing, skipping, and whirling in public—in the synagogues and elsewhere—could appear offensive to a society that officially preached asceticism, and the satirizing and sharp criticizing of some of the old-time scholars was taken personally by these scholars and their entourages.

The spread of Hassidism northward (to Lithuania and White Russia) and to the southwest of Poland (Galicia) made some of the established Jewish communities uneasy. The new customs, the emphasis on faith and de-emphasis of study and mitzvot (good deeds), and even more the abuses that some Hassidim (or would-be Hassidim) permitted themselves[75] were bound to call forth a reaction toward the new movement. And the separation of the Hassidic "congregations," or the founding of a sect, as mitnagdim called it, may have appeared threatening to existing authority, the Establishment.

Divisiveness is forbidden or despised in many societies and groups, and the Jewish community was no exception. For hundreds of years rabbis and leaders took the biblical admonition "do not cluster together"[76] as a rationale to combat division into bands or clusters. This led first to criticism and later to attacks and attempts to eliminate the "new heresy."

Criticism

Jewish religious civilization is based on old traditions and principles which, in theory, are valid forever; and like many another traditional society it is opposed to innovation and change. For this reason Hassidism had encountered some opposition and criticism almost from the very beginning; these were concerned less with ideological problems than with more or less external behavior patterns. Disapprobation appeared as early as the middle of the eighteenth century. The works of Solomon of Chelm, Moses of Satanow, and Simcha of Zalzitz bear traces of such critical attitudes. Israel of Zamość, Moses Mendelssohn's teacher who later returned to Poland (he died in 1772), was even harsher. Besides accusing certain Hassidim of ignorance, of donning white garments, of practicing excessively immersion in the ritual bath and ecstatic singing, of overeating and drinking, he also pointed out that they were destroying the Torah, were behaving hypocritically, and would resort to any means to collect large sums of money.[77] A few years later Yehuda Loeb Margaliot[78] repeats many of these criticisms, even using a few sentences verbatim from Israel of Zamość's *Nezed Hadema*.

Solomon Dubno, Moses Mendelssohn's co-worker in translating the Bible, who left Berlin and reached Wilno in 1781, wrote a private letter in 1789 expressing mild criticism. He reproached the Hassidim for their limitless self-glorification and denounced some of their leaders as drunkards, as well as indicating certain other failings. We find somewhat sharper criticism by Solomon Itzhaq Halperin, rabbi in Galicia and Podolia, in notes probably written in the 1770s to his father's work *Beth Yacob:* "In our generation . . . a malignant leprosy is flowering that causes them to throw away the Oral Torah . . . and snatch at cabalistic books. . . . Some of them don white cloaks . . . [they] idle around and spend their days smoking tobacco . . . appoint slaughterers who use sharp slaughtering knives." He goes on to tell about

having seen illiterate Hassidim.[79] Mildly critical, too, was Ber Birkenthal of Bolechów (1723–1805) who, apparently writing in the 1790s, regarded the Hassidic
leaders as the successors to the *baalei shem*. He treated them hospitably privately
and supported them materially. But he opposed the changes they introduced into
the service and their permissiveness with respect to fulfilling the precepts. He also
regretted the divisiveness they caused in Jewish life.[80]

Attacks

The same accusations played a considerable role in the attacks against Hassidism
that began in Lithuania in 1771–72 and lasted for more than three decades. But
in this more ferocious mitnagdim-Hassidim controversy there was harsher invective
both in the documents and in the theoretical writings, as well as in the conduct of
the struggle.

Hassidism came relatively late to Lithuania–White Russia. The first "congregation" was founded in Karlin (a suburb of Pinsk) around 1769, but antagonism
was aroused by the subsequent founding of a few other Hassidic groups (in Minsk,
Losna, Kalisk, and possibly also in Pinsk, Shklov, and Wilno). In addition it seems
that in that part of the country the external abuses by some Hassidim were particularly blatant. (Abraham of Kalisk and his group are said to have "joked pro-
fusely and scornfully about talmudic scholars and would turn somersaults which
were considered frivolous. Solomon Maimon mentions "violation of the laws of decency.")

Such a background may have had some impact upon the growing opposition to
Hassidism. But the violence of the attacks—accompanied by bans, jailings, beatings,
expulsions, denunciations, soliciting support from the gentile authorities for help
against one's adversaries, and possibly some killings—may indicate that this controversy had a much broader base. It should rather be considered in the "Wilno–
Lithuania context."[81] The ongoing social struggle and social unrest there undoubtedly nourished the mitnagdim-Hassidim controversy or may even have caused it. In
fact, during most of the period in which this controversy raged, each new episode
began in Wilno-Lithuania, even those which subsequently spread in a somewhat
milder form to communities beyond that region.

In Wilno there was strife for about thirty years between the community oligarchy
and the rabbi, Samuel ben Avigdor. The kehilla leadership sought to curtail the
rabbi's influence and importance, even to the point of removing him as head of the
Jewish court and thereby making it impossible for him to limit any wrongdoing of
that court or to defend a victim of injustice. The masses, including all kinds of
ordinary Jews, tended to support the rabbi—if only to help him restrict the kehilla
leadership's absolute power or to introduce reforms to eliminate the kehilla's abuse
of power. These "ordinary people," as they are called in the documents, artisans and
businessmen, organized themselves in the 1780s into a fighting opposition under

acknowledged leadership. They divulged to the authorities the illegal financial practices of the kehilla and denounced the leaders.

In Vitebsk, too, Jewish artisans rebelled against the kehilla, and in Minsk in 1777 they began to importune the kehilla leadership (the latter complained of having been beaten and injured). The rebels then raided the office of the kehilla, turned its books over to the authorities, and with the help of soldiers tried to remove the kehilla rulers and apparently refused to let them enter the synagogue. The two parties complained about each other to a variety of authorities. The artisans charged that the kehilla leaders seized control of the kehilla, discriminated against the artisans, and collected undue taxes to enrich themselves. This struggle continued for another couple of years, giving rise to sundry forms of oppression of the artisans against which they time and again sought help from the authorities.[82]

The rebels in Wilno, like the Hassidim or would-be Hassidim, were in conflict with the community oligarchy and its spiritual leaders; one such was Eliyahu Wilno, the gaon of Wilno, who despite his family relationship to the rabbi supported the community leadership. Thus in complaining to the authorities in 1786 the "representatives of the ordinary people in Wilno" attacked Eliyahu Wilno and criticized the community leadership for paying him (in the documents he is called *Eliasz Zalmanowicz*, "patriarch") twenty-eight zloty a week, besides renting him an apartment and buying him fish and other commodities, although he "is doing nothing, does not contribute one penny to the kehilla, and even fails to pay his head tax." They demanded that the kehilla be made responsible for these lost funds. Whether this antagonism to Eliyahu Wilno was a result of the existence of Hassidim among the "ordinary Jews," as some historians surmise, or whether both groups opposed him because of his unqualified support of the kehilla oligarchy,[83] this stand may signify that their attitudes and positions were similar.

It may follow that the oligarchy in Wilno undertook to smash the Hassidic groups, the weaker link in the opposition against whom religious-ideological arguments could be marshaled (with the help of Eliyahu Wilno), either as a means of weakening the opposition or as a warning. One could find synchronization or parallelism in the struggle of the community with the two divisive groups by comparison of the dates. The first attack on Hassidim in Wilno took place in 1772; at that same time the kehilla elections brought in a slate of the rabbi's adversaries to replace some of his followers who had been elected the year before and had introduced an atmosphere of reconciliation.

In the 1780s the Hassidim were violently attacked. In these years the kehilla's quarrel with the rabbi was renewed, becoming acute in 1783. Two years later the rabbi was fired and the ensuing strife between the kehilla oligarchy and the "ordinary people" grew increasingly bitter. But by 1790 the struggle between the kehilla and the rabbi was brought to a standstill by a compromise, and exhaustion led to a respite in the "ordinary people's" opposition. Hostility toward Hassidim, too, was somewhat muted for several years, save for some reverberations from the old animosities. The revival of the fight in 1796 and 1798 may have sprung from the old feud; it may have been stimulated as well by the 1798 attempt of Hassidic leaders to get control of the kehilla.

Turning back to the beginning of the controversy, the initial attacks upon the Hassidim seem to have arisen from a dispute between Hassidim and anti-Hassidim (later called "mitnagdim") in Shklov in the winter of 1771–72. According to a letter written later by Shneur Zalman of Losna, the Shklov mitnagdim then enlisted Eliyahu Wilno's assistance, and this gave the initial thrust to the ensuing struggle. Perhaps it was one of the reasons why the Jewish court in Wilno began to investigate the matter and to gather evidence.[84]

Not long after this the existence of a "sect" was discovered in Wilno (in reality apparently a small "congregation" or minyan of Karliner Hassidim), led by a preacher named Hayim and one named Isser. During hol hamoed (between the first and last days) of Passover 1772 the community leaders and the judges sat in court and decided to close down the Hassidic conventicle and to force the preacher to ask publicly in the synagogue for forgiveness from Eliyahu Wilno, about whom he had allegedly spoken derogatively. As a result the preacher lost his position and, after being variously disgraced in public, had to leave Wilno.

The other leader, Isser, fared still worse. Investigation by the community board disclosed the existence of some Hassidic writings in Wilno. Hearings brought to light varied information on real or imagined behavior of the Hassidic group. The rabbinical court decided to burn the Hassidic writings publicly; to see that the leader, Isser, publicly confessed the "sins" of the Hassidim at prayer time in the synagogue on the Sabbath, whereupon a ban of excommunication should be proclaimed upon him and his followers; and to inform the Lithuanian kehillot of the steps taken.

The culprit Isser was thrown into the state jail for about a week to await the day set for carrying out the judgment (Saturday). The community administration then added a whipping to his punishment[85]; this was administered to Isser on the Friday prior to the Saturday when the ban of excommunication was proclaimed.

Letters and calls promptly went out to the community of Brisk (Brześć) and to other communities describing the depravity of the Hassidim and requesting that they be persecuted and their prayerhouses closed. This led to excommunications from a few kehillot and the closing of "congregations" in Lithuania–White Russia, at least temporarily. "Men began"—writes Solomon Maimon—"to disturb their meetings and to persecute them everywhere."[86]

Not satisfied to confine their work to the northern region the Wilno anti-Hassidim lost no time in sending letters and "advice" to kehillot in other parts of Poland, setting forth the danger of Hassidism and asking that it be dealt with sternly. The letter that reached Brody caused a reaction similar to the one in Wilno. Excommunication was to be the penalty for changing the *nusach* (form) of prayers or for using the Isaac Luria siddur (prayer book), except in the case of some long-established pre-Hassidic pietists in Brody who were exempted from the prohibitions. Also forbidden were the wearing of white clothing by men on the Sabbath and holidays, and the use of the sharp shechita knives employed by the Hassidim.

In some other communities the two factions apparently waged a struggle. From Leszniew, near Brody, we hear about "quarrels, squabbles," and attacks on community leaders. This community proceeded to forbid separate Hassidic prayerhouses or changes in the form of the prayers, and limited the permissible number of "sectarians" to be invited at one time to semipublic meals, prohibiting them to dance or turn somersaults.[87]

In this way began the first confrontation between the Hassidim and the mitnagdim,[88] which spread from the north to some southern parts of the country.

The "crimes" of which the Hassidim were accused in 1772 were, in brief, the sin of refusing to study Torah; contempt for Oral Law; derision of scholars; organization of separatist congregations (self-segregation); changing the traditional forms of the prayers; shouting, dancing, and singing during prayers and turning somersaults; too much feasting and pleasure seeking; praying late—after the assigned hours; "behaving like madmen"; teaching disregard of religious transgressions; inducing young people to travel to the zaddik and to participate in feasts, thereby incurring heavy expenses; failing to put on tefillin during hol hamoed; smoking pipes; the leader's feeding large groups with money received from wealthy people in return for promises that their sins would be forgiven. In Brody there is also mention of praying from the Ari (Isaac Luria) prayer book, the use of sharpened knives for slaughtering, as well as the study of cabala. There may also be a hint that some people accused Hassidim of being Sabbatians or Frankists, but this is debatable.[89]

Some of the "crimes" attributed to the Hassidim had already been mentioned in the earlier criticisms. These and the rest were for the most part repeated again and again in the later attacks upon Hassidism, with the addition of new ones and some shift in emphasis.

The Hassidic leaders seem to have been startled by these attacks. A number of them gathered in Rowno for a conference with the Maggid. The mood at this gathering was one of considerable sorrow, and a decision was apparently made to lie low at least for a time.

Meanwhile, the first partition of Poland, which followed by a few months the ban proclamation, and the death of the Great Maggid at the end of 1772 seem to have had little if any impact upon the controversy surrounding Hassidim and Hassidism.

In the meantime the leading mitnagdim in Lithuanian–White Russian regions and elsewhere were collecting all kinds of evidence against the Hassidim. Eliyahu Wilno appears to have very firmly opposed them. Around 1775 he refused to see Mendel of Polock and Shneur Zalman of Losna, who came to Wilno seeking reconciliation. And an attempt to arrange a debate in Shklov between the Hassidic leaders and the mitnagdim also misfired. According to a letter written later by Shneur Zalman, the Hassidim were mistreated there: they were locked in a cellar then forced to flee. A few of the Hassidic leaders, as mentioned later, then left for Palestine. The persecution they had to withstand no doubt played at least some role in their resolve to leave their places in Lithuania–White Russia. Some of them (Menachem Mendel of Vitebsk and Abraham of Kalisk) wrote conciliatory letters from Palestine to Wilno and several other places, apologizing for certain extreme behavior ("much was done because of childishness"), and denied some of the accusations against the Hassidim. They maintained that informers and other evildoers caused Eliyahu Wilno to become so set against them.[90]

Before long a new issue arose which, combined with the fact that Hassidic groups again began to reappear on the scene and possibly also with the current phase of the struggle against the Wilno rabbi, Samuel ben Avigdor, resulted in renewed hostilities against Hassidim and Hassidism. In 1780 the book *Toledoth Yacov Josef* by Jacob Joseph of Polonnoe appeared in print. It contains a number of Hassidic ideas and theories, quotations from Besht, as well as sharp criticism of Establishment rabbis and talmudic scholars (sometimes called "Jewish devils" in the book). This was, in fact, the first Hassidic book to appear. It was published by the son and son-in-law of the then aging Jacob Joseph. The actual publication may have been a family affair. Some historians assume, however, that the publication of the book was intended as a reply to the ban and the 1772 attacks. Whatever the reason, the appearance of *Toledoth Yacov Josef* may have contributed to another, to some extent fiercer, reaction on the part of the mitnagdim. Wilno again became the center of the anti-Hassidic activity.

In the summer of 1781 the 1772 ban of excommunication was renewed in Wilno and was stiffened to cover not only Hassidic groups (congregations or minyan) but also individuals; there were also demands that the latter be expelled from Wilno and that house owners be forbidden to rent them dwelling space. As in 1772, the Wilno mitnagdim took upon themselves to induce other communities to persecute the Hassidim. The Wilno community dispatched a delegation and a letter to the community leaders and rabbis gathered at the fair in Zelve (near Grodno) for meetings, asking them to take action against the Hassidim. These leaders followed Wilno's example with the addition of a few new proscriptions. They now made it illegal for Hassidim to remain overnight in the cities and prohibited business relations or possible marriage arrangements with them. The main kehillot instructed the smaller ones to introduce similar prohibitions and demanded that no one should replace the Ashkenazic with the Sephardic form of prayer or travel to places where there were Hassidic groups or rabbis.[91]

In 1781, as in 1772, the excommunications and attacks upon Hassidism in Lithuania had repercussions in several other parts of the country, including Brody. This time they may also have had some influence on the situation in Cracow, where a small Hassidic group had just been formed by a rabbi, Kalman Epstein, a pupil of the Galician Hassidic leader Elimelekh of Lizhajsk. In those years Cracow was also the scene of its own controversy between the community leadership and the masses, whose representative appealed to the government for some control of the community's financial affairs and demanded strictly accurate computations of the leaders' exhorbitant expenses. It is not impossible that the hostility to the small group of Hassidim was in some way connected with this controversy. But whether or not that was so, the ban proclaimed in Cracow in 1785 was not dissimilar from the ones proclaimed earlier in Wilno and other places in Lithuania. It forbids private prayer places (minyan) or changes in the form of the traditional (Ashkenazic) prayers.[92] During the next few years there were some anti-Hassidic activities in and around White Russia (Shklov, Mohilev), with attempts to call Shneur Zalman as a defendant before a community council or similar body (the preserved evidence is not entirely clear).

During those years some individual Hassidic leaders were more rigorously persecuted, even to the point of being forced out of—or driven away from—their places of residence (Levi Yitzhak [later of Berditchev] had to leave Pinsk, and Shlomo of Karlin was driven from that town).

A third major attack upon Hassidism occurred in Lithuania, which came under Russian suzerainty when the Polish state ceased to exist with the third partition of Poland in 1795.

The struggle between the kehilla oligarchy and the rabbi Samuel ben Avigdor had, as we have seen, ended. The opposition of the masses was exhausted after years of hostilities. Perhaps Eliyahu Wilno may have mellowed a little since the end of the 1780s, or at least shown no interest in further oppression of the Hassidic movement. First, he remained silent for some time; and second, he may even have made some attempts to mollify certain Hassidim (possibly not the more important leaders) in Wilno. An undated letter written by a man named Israel ben Eliezer of Wilno to Zevi in Shelisht has been preserved, telling how before the previous Rosh Hashanah (Jewish New Year) Eliyahu Wilno:

> sent one of his faithful people to conciliate me and to ask forgiveness for what he had done to me. I replied several times to the emissary with annoyance. . . . Later I decided not to be so quarrelsome and said to the mentioned emissary that if they would cancel all the excommunications which a few years ago were thrown upon the known people I would forgive him. . . . R. Eliyahu then told the emissary: "I myself will cancel all the bans." Later he sent David, the assistant rabbi of our community, to me. . . . I wrote him a letter then telling, among other things, that it is well known how much scorn, insult, and injustice he has piled upon me and how much humiliation my children and I have suffered without my having done anything wrong. This is an irreparable injustice. . . . I will only consent . . . if it is publicly announced in all synagogues and bet hamidrash on Yom Kippur eve before the Kol Nidre prayer that all the bans are canceled. . . . He answered through the mentioned envoy that he himself would stand up with a minyan before Kol Nidre and cancel the excommunications. And he sent me an ethrog so very beautiful that I remained speechless.

The letter writer adds that many of his congregation knew and took great satisfaction in all this, though others were disturbed and tried to obtain a rebuttal but could no longer do so since the facts had become widely known. He cautions that care should be exercised to make certain that the letter did not fall into the hands of the "mitnagdim, the informers."[93]

Provided this letter is genuine it could indicate that Eliyahu Wilno sought to conciliate at least some of the Hassidim in Wilno. There is the possibility, of course, that the letter is merely a fabrication associated with the rumors the Hassidim were spreading about Eliyahu Wilno's having changed his mind. He denied these rumors in a letter dated 1796, which he sent to a number of nearby communities; this letter had a limited effect on the anti-Hassidic struggle.

By 1796, after the second and third partitions (1793 and 1795) had completed the division of Poland among three states, the Russian-dominated part, comprising Lithuania, White Russia, Volhynia, Podolia, and Kiev province, was separated from the sectors that went to Prussia and Austria. The Russian regime, now ruling a great part of the formerly Polish Jews, was different from that of Old Poland.

Unlike Poland, Russia had no tradition of dealing with Jews, because prior to 1772 there had scarcely been any Jews in the realm. Now Russia's treatment of the Jews was, from the beginning, "vacillating and contradictory, often reversing itself and moving simultaneously in different directions. . . . Officially the Jews were assured of equal treatment 'without distinction of religion or nationality' denying the validity of the old Polish discriminatory laws against the Jews. But under pressure, as a result of administrative practices later sanctioned by the central authorities" practice differed from theory. The kehilla only retained its jurisdictional powers for a short time. "In 1783 Jews were granted rights similar to those of the non-Jews . . . to elect and to be elected [to general city offices]. . . . The Kehilla on the other hand subsequently lost much of its power as a result of this ostensible equality" (1786, 1795, 1799).[94] This would mean that the Russian authorities were less likely to support the "absolute autonomy" of the kehilla board.

Personnel, too, underwent changes. The centuries-old pattern of the Polish voivode (governor), with jurisdiction over Jews and established ways and means for the latter to deal with him, was now replaced by newer types among the government officials. As a result such newer groups of individuals as the Hassidim were able to form contacts and gain a hearing. (At the end of the 1790s three Jews, all Hassidim, served as "factors"—whatever that means—with the Russian police in Wilno.) Thus the older Jewish representatives and their links with the authorities lost some of their prestige and practical value.

Though the number of Hassidim had grown (they had two or more groups in Wilno, probably to some extent working secretly) it was still small. Nevertheless, they now became somewhat bolder, at times almost aggressive. Some of them also apparently thought that in the changed situation the anti-Hassidim might even agree to a compromise. The Wilno Hassidic group invited Shneur Zalman to Wilno for a discussion with Eliyahu Wilno, but Shneur Zalman refused the invitation on the grounds that earlier attempts had misfired.

This changing configuration may have been a contributing factor to the unleashing of the final bitter attack on Hassidim and Hassidism in Wilno in the fall of 1797, immediately following Eliyahu Wilno's death. The kehilla board may have intended to use this[95] to bolster its declining position in the new situation. The facts are these:

the kehilla board of Wilno renewed the bans on the Hassidim, adding new and more stringent regulations (prescribing expulsion from Wilno for any Jew suspected of pro-Hassidic leanings, depriving him of his settlement rights, removing him from any office in the community administration or other institution, and closing all the minyanim of the Hassidim). A special Committee of Five with a secret prosecutor was appointed to enforce these regulations and empowered to make decisions in all such matters.

During the winter of 1797/98 certain steps were taken. The Hassidic minyan (quorum) functioning in the house of Meir ben Raphael, a sometime member of the kehilla board since 1791, was forced to close and go underground. When it was later discovered in another house the owner was beaten and persecuted. A number of Hassidim, including Meir ben Raphael, suffered material losses through prohibitions or attacks on their homes. But the handling of the "culprit," as well as his behavior, differed greatly in Meir ben Raphael's case from that of the "culprit" R. Isser in 1772. The former was not thrown into jail or beaten as Isser had been in 1772, nor was he required (or made) to beg forgiveness publicly in the synagogue. Instead he was called before a Jewish court (sometime in March 1798), where he first tried to offer all manner of excuses for his continued membership in the Hassidic group. Later he changed his statement, admitting that he "did not find the truth in our community, but there in the Hassidic group is the truth and therefore he desired to be with them." The court forbade him for the rest of his life to keep any minyan in his house or to behave like a Hassid in other respects, and asked him to repent of his "sins."

Shortly after, however, the whole mitnagdim-Hassidim controversy took another turn through the involvement of the Russian authorities. This started around March 1798 with a complaint to the Russian-Lithuanian governor by one of the Hassidim, Yehuda ben Eliyahu, whose house had been attacked earlier by the mitnagdim. The complaint alleged that the kehilla board was persecuting the Hassidim, putting them under ban, and forbidding them to sell hot beverages. It also charged the board with embezzling the tax money collected from Jews. Soon afterwards (May 1798) the Wilno Hassidim succeeded in denouncing the kahal. They were helped in this by a slaughterer in the nearby town of Widz. He furnished the authorities with a Russian translation of a call issued by the Wilno kehilla attempting to collect money from neighboring communities to pay for intercession in Petersburg in connection with threatened legislation against leaseholding by Jews in villages and the sale of beverages. This meant that the Wilno kehilla was meddling against the state. The Jewish leadership's recourse to state authorities against individual Jews or groups was certainly no innovation in Jewish community relations in 1798. Older rabbinic sources often emphasize that it is permissible for a community to involve such authority against recalcitrant people. As we have seen, about half a century earlier the authority of the nobleman owner of a town was used against a group of Frankists in Lanckrona. Later the Polish-Jewish leadership intended to utilize the antisectarian laws of the Catholic Church to have the Frankists burned at the stake as heretics. In fact, they did take advantage of connections with the Catholic Church authorities to speed up the conversion of the Frankists. During the thirty-year struggle between the kehilla and the rabbi Samuel ben Avigdor, both sides went to the authorities a dozen times or more. And now again, in the struggle developing between the mitnagdim and the Hassidim, each side used state authorities against the other. It began, as we have mentioned, with the jailing of the Hassidic leader Isser in the state jail in Wilno in 1772. Later the Minsk mitnagdim apparently used the authorities against the Hassidim there. Now the Hassidim in Wilno got a speedy response from Russian officialdom. The governor's office reacted to the complaint by issuing a decision (April 26, 1798) allowing the Hassidim to pray in their own "congregations," in accordance with their own customs (as postulated by the law), and forbade the community leadership to inflict humiliating corporal punishment or bans "which would destroy social relations or interfere with commerce and industry." The community was also ordered to refrain from collecting exorbitant taxes and was denied the right to try civil or capital cases. The above-mentioned Russian translation supplied by the slaughterer in Widz prompted the Lithuanian governor's office to adopt a resolution on August 20, 1798, dismissing the Wilno community board (though the governors never signed the order). The community board then submitted a protest against the earlier order of April 26, 1798, but to no avail. They thereupon apparently decided to denounce the Hassidic leader, Shneur Zalman, before the highest authority: the tsar.

A denunciation signed by a man named Hirsh son of David (Davidovich) of Wilno—apparently an alias—was dispatched to the Russian chief state attorney in Petersburg (now Leningrad) incriminating Shneur Zalman for actions detrimental to the state.[96] This denunciation resulted in the arrest, in October 1798, of Shneur Zalman and twenty-two Hassidim from Wilno and elsewhere. After a thorough investigation by the Russian authorities, most of those arrested were released. Only Shneur Zalman and seven others were sent to Petersburg in chains, but when they got as far as Riga the seven were also released. Shneur Zalman was the only one to reach Petersburg under police guard. He was jailed for about two months, released at the end of November 1798, and returned home. The governor of White Russia then issued an order (December 15, 1798) that the rabbi and his followers were to be left alone.[97]

In Wilno, meanwhile, the Hassidim and the mitnagdim were each endeavoring to prejudice the Russian Lithuanian authorities against the other. The Hassidim presented a complaint to the governor denouncing the kehilla for falsifying the number of Jews during the 1795 census, so as to reduce the head taxes payable to the government, and then using the money for other purposes. The governor-general responded by ordering that the books be checked and the members of the Jewish courts and the leaders of the community dismissed. Next, officials and police, assisted by Hassidim, began trying to track down the authentic books.

The former kehilla board was replaced in 1799 by a newly elected one consisting of Hassidim and headed by Meir ben Raphael. Thus began the Hassidim's reign over the kehilla during which they, in turn, sometimes resorted to force and collusion with government officials to suppress the mitnagdim. Numerous investigations were conducted as a result of complaints and denunciations by one side or the other. In January 1800 the civil governor of Lithuania, Ivan Friesel, responded to an application by the former mitnagdim leaders to the tsar "about annihilating the sect of the Karliner [Hassidim] and allowing the kahal to deal with civil matters": Friesel informed them that the tsar ordered that the Hassidic group was to be tolerated and that the kehilla was to deal exclusively with Jewish religious affairs.

In this atmosphere of defeat for the mitnagdim Shneur Zalman of Losna was again denounced, this time by Rabbi Avigdor ben Hayim of Pinsk. Early in the same year (1800) he submitted a long document written in Hebrew. He had been ousted from his rabbinate in Pinsk through the Hassidim there, and he may now have been in collusion with the Wilno mitnagdim. The rabbi's application (or denunciation), sent to the tsar, consists of two parts: the first comprises bitter accusation of Hassidism, and the second demands indemnification for his great losses in Pinsk, for which the Hassidim were to blame. Rabbi Avigdor tried to connect Hassidism with Sabbatai Zevi and the Frankists and, by quoting certain passages from Besht's writings that allegedly contain teachings contrary to rabbinic law and Christian morality, insinuated that they were inimical to an orderly state or ruler.

It so happened that in 1800 the Russian writer and senator, Gabriel Derzhavin (1743–1816), was sent to White Russia to investigate the situation of the peasants. Derzhavin saw Shneur Zalman in Losna and depicted him and the Hassidim unfavorably in his report (apparently repeating some of the views he heard from the mitnagdim). Shneur Zalman, writes Derzhavin, is known in Byelorussia (White Russia) as one who settles disputes among Jews.

The Hassidim believe in this hypocrite whom they consider to be their patriarch. The Hassidim are sectarians, or schismatics. The Hassidim seduce the children of the well-to-do to hand over to their leader the gold and silver to send to Palestine for charity purposes, to keep the money till the Messiah will come, as the Jews wait for him every day and believe that he will build up their temple.

It is doubtful that this report by Derzhavin had any impact upon Shneur Zalman's arrest. (Derzhavin submitted his report on October 26, and the order to arrest Shneur Zalman and send him to Petersburg was issued on October 30—one could hardly expect Russian bureaucracy to work so fast.)

The problem of his arrest at that moment is also puzzling from another viewpoint. The chief state attorney in Petersburg, who ordered the arrest, must have been in possession of two very favorable statements from the military governor of Lithuania, General Michael Kutuzov,[98] who had previously been asked to investigate Rabbi Avigdor's complaint about "the Sabbatai Zevi sect." After a dispatch of July 12 in which he pointed out that Rabbi Avigdor's complaints lacked any legal basis, General Kutuzov forwarded a broader statement on July 30, in which he declared that there was no longer any such thing in Lithuania as what Rabbi Avigdor called the Sabbatai Zevi sect, and assuming that it probably meant the Hassidim. The general proceeds to tell the story of Shneur Zalman's first arrest and says that the tsar "found nothing in the behavior of this Jewish Hassidic group harmful either to the state and its morals, or likely to disturb the public peace." Therefore, continues the general, the tsar ordered that he be freed. He then describes the persecution of the Hassidim caused by Eliyahu Wilno and his followers, and ends by saying that "there is nothing in this sect to endanger the state or the Jewish community, unless one objects to the fact that they [Hassidim] eliminate some errors which have crept into the Jewish religion."[99]

Whatever the reason for his arrest, Shneur Zalman was freed after a few weeks (on November 17) but was asked to remain in Petersburg until the senate dealt with the case. By the end of March 1801, a few weeks after Alexander I became tsar, he was permitted to leave Petersburg and to return home. (The Habad [Lubawitch] movement still celebrates annually the dates on which the founder was freed by the Russian government.)

A little earlier (in August 1800) the court in Wilno had completed its investigation of the mitnagdim-Hassidim controversy and openly decried the earlier restrictions the kahal placed upon the Hassidim, pointing out that the April 1798 order of freedom for the Hassidim had worked well.

Both parties were apparently exhausted from the long struggle. After 1802 the two groups shared the leadership of the now weakened kehilla.

A few years later in the Statute of 1804 Jews were granted the right to organize a variety of religious groups, each permitted to maintain its own synagogues and rabbis. Thus Hassidism was legalized by implication.

Accusations and Images

During the thirty years of the mitnagdim-Hassidim confrontation countless accusations were aimed at Hassidism and the Hassidim, and negative images were drawn in Wilno and Brody and elsewhere. Most of these were repeated by the many critics, who sometimes used identical words or sentences, giving the impression that they simply copied from each other.

As already mentioned, at the beginning of the anti-Hassidic controversy (1772) the charges were failure to study Torah and holding such study in contempt, self-segregation into separate "congregations," changing the traditional liturgy, ignoring the established hours for morning and afternoon prayers, hedonism (feasting and enjoyment), dancing and "behaving like madmen"; in the south (Brody) mention is also made of the use of sharpened shechita knives and the study of cabala. The Hassidic leaders were also censured for promising to help the wealthy escape punishment in hell for their religious transgressions in exchange for money (which was used by these leaders to feed anyone who came along).

In the following decades some of these "sins" were further elaborated on. Thus the charge of neglecting the study of Talmud became at times a charge of forbidding such study; or the Hassidim were censured for seeking to burn the old Torah and replace it with writings by Besht and others which contradict the holy Torah. On the other hand, we find also that the Hassidim and their leaders were disparaged for their alleged ignorance of Torah or even cabala, and their homilies were proclaimed to be based on misunderstandings or inadequate familiarity with the texts.

The liturgy-changing offense was variously developed. The "third meal" on the Sabbath, for instance, was considered unduly prolonged, with unimportant Sabbath hymns taking up considerable time while grace after the meal was hurriedly mumbled. The evening prayer ushering out the Sabbath was said to be recited frivolously. There were also intimations that the Hassidim or their leaders recited all or a part of their prayers in solitude without a minyan. The original 1772 complaint about the eccentric gestures and cries of Hassidim at prayer was extended to describe their leaping and hand-clapping and their ridiculous swaying to right and left or bowing down, "all in order to frighten and amaze the people and the women."

Such conduct on the part of the Hassidim was regarded by the mitnagdim as sinful either because it was clearly contrary to established tradition or because it failed to comply with current usage. It was condemned as divisive innovation (leading to "two Torahs" or to the foundation of a special sect), creating a new Torah or an entirely new religion. In his *Sepher Havikuach* (1798) Israel Leibel advised that the denunciations be put to use, and he actually presented the argument that because it was a new sect or a new religion the government should outlaw Hassidism. Internally, too, these points were utilized in some of the excommunications: in the prohibitions against doing business with Hassidim, against permitting them to stay overnight in a Jewish house, or in other ways regarding them as non-Jews.[100] Occasionally one finds also the accusation that Hassidim are idol worshipers. This is reported in the name of Eliyahu Wilno, the rationale being the Hassidim's deification of their leader by ascribing to him supernatural qualities.

Another serious depravity attributed to the Hassidim was their idea of raising "strange (sinful) thoughts" (or having them raised through the zaddik). Here the critics either misunderstood or deliberately distorted[101] the Hassidic idea that "raising strange (sinful) thoughts" leads to expressing sin in action, whereas in truth the meaning for Hassidim was the reverse: eliminating sin by spiritualization and the transforming of lust into "thoughts" rather than action. Similarly, the mitnagdim took literally the erotic images sometimes used in Hassidic writings (either for illustrative purposes or in the nature of Freudian slips).

There followed a plethora of accusations in areas not always purely religious. Mitnagdim had to explain away (negatively) the attraction of Hassidism and deny its claim to prophecy or clairvoyance. For this reason the prediction of future events by Hassidic leaders was seen by their critics as magic or sorcery (as in Eliyahu Wilno's description of Israel Besht) or as mere fake and deception.

The leaders were projected as fakers and hypocrites mainly concerned with amassing wealth. They allegedly tried to coerce anyone who failed to give of his own accord and threatened, if he refused altogether, to kill him. They were said to promise their followers all sorts of things and to advise them in business matters. They were supposed to overindulge in food and drink to the point of getting drunk, and to take money from poor Jews without doing anything in return.

The images sketched purported to show that the services Hassidic leaders performed for their followers—healing, driving out ghosts (dybbukim), assisting in retrieving lost property, helping barren women, foretelling the future, performing miracles, and others—were nothing more than lies and deceptions. Either the zaddik failed to help in any way or his assistant (gabbai) gathered the necessary information and imparted it to the rabbi. The latter then pretended to know everything through prophecy or "holy spirit."[102] These and other assistants made propaganda for the zaddik and promised the Hassidim all sorts of help, miraculous solutions of problems, God's favor, or the fulfillment of other needs, in this way attracting all manner of people. Such aides were variously depicted as semiliterates, idlers and loafers, or as loathsome and worthless. (Only during the 1790s and later do we hear of talmudic scholars joining in these activities.) The point was stressed that most of the people coming to the zaddik were young—in one place their average age was placed at about twenty. (This may have been so, or perhaps youth was stressed to indicate that Hassidim were mostly unimportant people with no standing in society.) These youngsters, having no money, allegedly stole from their parents or wives who, together with the children, were left at home alone during holidays "without food and without clothing." Hassidism thus was pictured as destroying orderly Jewish family life.

Parallel with statements that women disapproved of their husbands' pilgrimages to the zaddik, critics of Hassidism assigned a large role to women in drawing people to the zaddik and participating in his doings. In one depiction of a Jew in trouble who appealed to a zaddik, only to end up losing all his possessions, a woman was portrayed as having advised him to seek help from the zaddik in the first place. There are statements that women enticed their husbands to make pilgrimages to the zaddik or that more women than men traveled to him. We also hear that women participated in the festivities around the zaddik and drank as much as the men. There followed further descriptions of women in trouble traveling to the rabbi and losing their money. The theme of barren women seeking help from the zaddikim was elaborated, and they were said to have come dressed in finery and to have participated with the men in feasting and drinking. There are descriptions of how the zaddik examined the women's breasts and promised them they would be able to bear children; there are accounts of how such women stayed for long intervals at the zaddik's "court," where they committed adultery with Hassidim, returning home when they were pregnant to persuade the husbands that they were the fathers of the offspring. Critics warned husbands not to let frivolous women travel to the zaddik.

Another area of strong criticism of the Hassidim was their pride and their contempt for anyone not belonging to their group. "And they say that these [non-

Hassidim] are not Jews at all. . . . And since he is not a Jew one may kill him or take away his money." "They already permitted the killing or beating of mitnagdim or informing upon them." The latter is a statement by Israel Leibel, who purportedly suffered such beatings himself. Others quoted cases of Hassidim killing a mitnagid, stealing, or breaking an oath—purportedly claiming or indicating that they were not obliged to behave otherwise to "outsiders" (other Jews). In *Sepher Havikuach* Israel Leibel summarized the opinions about Hassidim: "In the whole sect [Hassidim] there is no decent person. The bad ones are robbers and murderers. Everything they say is false. Some are adulterers, some bankrupts, some informers . . . or they falsify promissory notes."

These descriptions give an idea of how the mitnagdim saw Hassidism and Hassidim,[103] and the sort of image of them they wanted to present. There is no saying how much truth there is in all these accusations—especially since premodern authors often copied from each other and authors writing in rabbinic Hebrew "re-used" phrases, expressions, statements, and metaphors with little regard for the extent to which these corresponded with reality.

Reaction and Defense

The Hassidic group, including its leader, Rabbi Ber, felt menaced by the attacks of 1772 and by the bans. In Rowno (Volhynia), where Rabbi Ber lived at that time, a number of his disciples gathered for a "conference" in the summer of 1772. Among those present were Mendel of Vitebsk, then leader of the Hassidic group in Minsk, and Schneur Zalman of Losna. The atmosphere seems, if we may believe the legendary and near-legendary information, to have wavered between "revolutionary" and conservative trends, with the latter prevailing. It is said that the maggid opposed a counterban, which the young Hassidic leaders wanted to—or did— pronounce against those who put up the Wilno-Brody bans. According to one of Shneur Zalman's later letters, Abraham of Kalisk was afraid to appear at the meeting with Rabbi Ber and asked the others (Menachem Mendel of Vitebsk and Shneur Zalman) to intercede on his behalf with the Great Maggid. After the latter agreed to see Abraham, writes Shneur Zalman, "I went . . . to call him [Abraham] and entered together with him . . . the room of our great rabbi and I saw and heard how he [Ber] talked with him in harsh words about their bad behavior . . . of making fun of talmudic scholars . . . heaping scorn upon them in lawlessness and with great frivolity."[104] The Maggid was able to subdue the more extreme young hotheads a little. In other words, there was an attempt to mitigate the extremism among the Hassidic group, apparently in the hope of achieving some kind of reconciliation with the mitnagdim.

The conciliatory tendency seems to have prevailed, at least officially,[105] among those disciples of the Great Maggid who became leaders of the movement in various parts of the country after the latter's death at the end of 1772.

In practice the Hassidic leaders in Lithuania–White Russia sought to achieve a reconciliation with their archopponent Eliyahu Wilno and others. Menachem Mendel of Vitebsk went to Wilno in 1771, and again in the company of Shneur Zalman of Losna around 1775, in order to talk to the gaon and seek to pacify him, with some intermediaries making an effort to bring the two sides together. Eliyahu Wilno, however, refused to see them. In a letter written a few years later Menachem Mendel blamed the lack of success in coming to terms upon "informers who separate those who belong together." Both Menachem Mendel and Shneur Zalman, as already mentioned, also attempted to arrange or participate in a debate with mitnagdim in Shklov, but the latter responded by resorting to violence. (The information about the incident is, however, one-sided.) In later years Menachem Mendel and Shneur Zalman mostly advocated pacification of the mitnagdim or greater moderation in the struggle with them.

In fact, the emigration to Palestine of the Hassidic group headed by Menachem Mendel in 1777, and the establishment there of a Hassidic center designed to serve for Lithuania–White Russia as well, may have been motivated, among other things, by a wish to minimize direct friction with Eliyahu Wilno and his followers. In any case, Menachem Mendel, writing to his friends and followers at home, repeated the wish for peace with the mitnagdim, apologized for past extremist acts by Hassidim, attributing them to youthfulness and lack of knowledge of the youngsters "whom I drove out." Seeking peace he stated: "We forgive all those who troubled us."

Shneur Zalman, who became the leader of Hassidism in Lithuania–White Russia and founder of the Habad movement, repeatedly advocated conciliatory tendencies and was for the most part opposed to use of extreme means by Hassidim. Upon returning from jail in Petersburg, Shneur Zalman twice asked his followers to refrain from taking revenge on their adversaries, for he was opposed to any such action. He had also asked his followers not to react against the mitnagdim for having burned Besht's work, *Zavaat Haribash* (c. 1798). In later years he visited some mitnagdic rabbis in different places, trying personally to persuade them that Hassidism was far from heretical.

Elimelekh of Lizhajsk seems to have been careful to avoid coming out strongly against the mitnagdim. This appears in a letter from Elimelekh's son, apparently written in his father's behalf, in connection with the attacks upon Levi Yitzhak, at that time apparently in Pinsk (in the first half of the 1780s). First he tried to minimize the importance of the attack by quoting parallels that occurred with the patriarch Abraham and with Isaac Luria, and by statements that God brings trials upon the zaddik in order to raise him higher, "so will He also reward . . . [those] who have opponents rising against them with falsehoods and quarrels. . . . There may exist a great man who is great in Torah . . . and feuds possibly because he committed a sin and forgot to repent." This might indicate an attempt to minimize the whole matter. Elimelekh of Lizhajsk himself, at the end of his *Noam Elimelech*, deals with the mitnagdim-Hassidim confrontation in somewhat muffled tones: "We see how quarrelsome people attack zaddikim and speak about them with conceit and contempt," maintaining they do it for the glory of God. He goes on to allude to those adversaries who do not live in peace among themselves, suggesting their intentions may therefore be questionable.[106]

Parallel with the efforts to temper the language used against the adversaries went a few changes in doctrine. Among the Hassidic leaders who rose after the Great Maggid's death the antirabbinic ideas were somewhat muted. In their writings study of the Torah was often emphasized as worthwhile. (This may also have resulted from the fact that these leaders were to a great extent themselves known talmudists.) Thus Elimelekh of Lizhajsk (Galicia) pointed out that "Torah guards us," the main thing is Torah and prayer, a man should study Torah, Talmud, and so on. His prescriptions for behavior began: "At first a man should study Talmud, Rashi, Commentaries . . . and later Codes."

A similar or even stronger predilection for Torah was shown by Shneur Zalman of Losna (later of Liady), who warned against neglecting the prescription to study Torah containing the wisdom of God, which equals all the other commandments put together. Torah study should even take precedence over all the other commandments, since through grasping the laws of the Talmud and Codes "virtual oneness and unity with God can be achieved."[107] The lightheartedness with which Besht and his disciples regarded sin also seems to have been modified. Elimelekh of Lizhajsk and Shneur Zalman of Losna would appear to have been more concerned than their Hassidic predecessors with sin, evil, and penance. Shneur Zalman dwelt at length on evil and sin, seeing evil in mundane affairs. He also formulated a new doctrine which, while based in part on Besht's and Ber of Mezeritch's ideas, gave them a new turn and meaning. Differing from the earlier ones, mostly based on belief and emotion, Schneur Zalman's theory, called Habad,[108] was popularly understood to be based on intellect (*Tanya*, published at the end of 1796). The dualism of good and evil is here given greater prominence than in Besht's Hassidism. Leaning on the cabalist Hayim Vital, *Tanya* formulated the roles of two souls in the Jew: from one—the animal soul—stem the evil characteristics, while the other soul—the divine, possessed only by Jews—is the source of good. There is emphasis on Torah and the mitzvot (all 613, including the rabbinic injunctions), on an afterlife, on hell and repentance. Joy no longer meant material joy, but was limited to the soul. "One should rather view his body with scorn and find joy in the soul alone."[109]

There were other departures from earlier Hassidic doctrine and practice, sometimes rationalized apologetically as necessary because of "the current generation's weakness." A simplified method of kavvanah was introduced. Some thought that drinking must be curtailed (Elimelekh of Lizhajsk). "The uplifting of wayward (strange) thoughts," against which the mitnagdim were raging, underwent changes. In the 1770s some revisions were made. Shneur Zalman asserted in his *Tanya* that one should simply "remove them from his mind and further strengthen the power of concentration . . . . adopt an attitude as if he neither knows nor hears the thoughts which have befallen him." Elimelekh of Lizhajsk advises resorting to study of the Torah as a means of ridding oneself of "strange thoughts," or telling one's teacher or colleague about such thoughts, thereby breaking the power of the evil instinct.

He apparently also tried to mitigate the attack upon Hassidism's use of the Sephardic version of prayer by a reminder that it had been used earlier by certain individuals, that it was still (in his time) not designed for mass consumption, but rather for exceptional individuals (ascetics, those who never spoke an untruth, nondrinkers, and the like, and in the main any persons learned in Talmud, Tosafot, Rashi, and others) and for some of their followers.[110] In this way some of early Hassidism's "radical" ideas were eliminated or toned down.

By the end of the eighteenth century there were other Hassidic leaders who criticized the zaddikim for merely imitating externals (donning white garments, clapping their hands, and the like) or pursuing material goods, or failing to pray properly (Besht's grandsons Ephraim of Sadilkow and Baruch of Tulczyn, Zeev Wolf of Zhitomir), which may indicate such a turn toward tradition.

The active adversaries of Hassidism, however, were not interested in noting the subtle changes that Shneur Zalman, Elimelekh of Lizhajsk, and others introduced, nor could they discern the more conservative path that Hassidism was entering. In the heat of the struggle, and for the sake of a better argument, they attached greater importance to reiterating the old clichés of the more extreme Hassidic ideas and practices. The author of *Shever Poshim* (David of Makow) throws together all sorts of sins attributed to Hassidism, and not only does he fail to differentiate between the earlier writings (those of Jacob Joseph of Polonnoe) and those of Shneur Zalman, Elimelekh of Lizhajsk, and others, but he also presents the later ones as worse than the earlier ones. For example, he accuses the author of *Tanya* (Shneur Zalman) of "allowing the forbidden things," and the author of *Noam Elimelech* (Elimelekh of Lizhajsk) of going out of his way to scorn those who study Torah—all of which is incorrect.

The real change in tune was more correctly gauged by the extremist—or formerly extremist—Hassidim. Thus Abraham of Kalisk, head of the Hassidic group that went to Palestine in 1777, criticized Shneur Zalman in 1797 for his *Tanya*, maintaining that Shneur Zalman neglected Besht's emphasis on belief as opposed to fulfilling the precepts. The difference between the "new" and the "old" Hassidism seems to have been sensed by talmudic scholars and rabbis who, since the 1790s, had begun to join the movement, apparently in larger numbers (mitnagdim tell of this trend).

End of an Epoch

The mitnagdim's 1796–1800 attack on Hassidism was not only the last one connected with the Gaon's name, it also had a more limited impact than the preceding ones. It marked, in fact, the end of the epoch of large-scale mitnagdim-Hassidim confrontations. The division of the former Polish regions among three states—Russia, Prussia, and Austria—by 1795 to some extent cut the territorial continuity, while the new legal order introduced varying degrees of religious freedom. This meant official rights to belong to religious sects, which included Hassidic groups, and limitation of the kehilla's power to impose its regulations upon Jews. The latter involved either limiting the validity of the ban of excommunication upon Jews or forbidding it entirely. In Russian Poland the kehilla itself was dissolved in 1822. In fact, the last few acts of the Wilno mitnagdim (1798–1800) fall in the category of denunciation to the authorities rather than inter-Jewish activities. The attempt made in those years to elicit collaboration in anti-Hassidism by other formerly Polish territories outside of Lithuania found little response.

The preachers David of Makow and Israel of Slutzk (known also as Israel Leibel) apparently tried to carry this work to western or central Poland—the latter also to Galicia—without much success. In retrospect their efforts appear somewhat akin to tilting at windmills. In Warsaw—at that time under Prussian rule—two anti-Hassidic booklets appeared in 1798: *Zemir Aritzim* by David of Makow, and *Sepher Havikuach* by Israel of Slutzk.[111]

Israel Leibel had previously served as an anti-Hassidic preacher, having been induced to do so by Eliyahu Wilno's representative. *Sepher Havikuach* was commended by one of the leaders of this group. Following publication of his pamphlet, he traveled to Galicia and Vienna, preaching against Hassidism. According to some information, he was occasionally beaten up, and he met with various other difficulties, which the Hassidim were able to arrange with the help of some Austrian officials. In Vienna, Leibel succeeded in submitting a denunciation to the office dealing with Galicia (Galizische Hofkanzlei) and even managed to get an audience with Kaiser Franz. The result was an order forbidding public gatherings of the Hassidim. Israel Leibel apparently intended to form an anti-Hassidic "partnership" with the anti-Hassidic Enlighteners. For this purpose he had published in 1799 a German anti-Hassidic pamphlet[112] translated from Hebrew by one of the German-Jewish Enlighteners, in which, among other things, the immorality of the Hassidim is pointed out. After that, nothing further was heard of him.

The other anti-Hassidic preacher, David of Makow, who published his pamphlet *Zemir Aritzim*[113] about half a year after Israel Leibel's *Sepher Havikuach* came out, regarded himself as a disciple of Eliyahu Wilno and wanted to continue the latter's struggle against Hassidism. In his anonymously issued *Zemir Aritzim* (published in 1798, apparently in Warsaw) he attacks Besht and takes special notice of the then growing Hassidic movement in western Poland and its leaders: Jacob Itzhak Horowitz of Lanzut (later the "Seer of Lublin") and Israel of Kozenitz. He heaps contempt upon them and their followers, and satirizes their behavior and beliefs. Aware of the danger of fighting Hassidism, he nevertheless declares his willingness to suffer for the good deed of publicizing the "shameful" Hassidic deeds. For this purpose he (or his son) in later years collected materials and documents about Hassidim in a volume called *Shever Poshim*;[114] he no doubt wanted to publish it but it remained in manuscript with some copies being rewritten, circulated and, apparently, changed in the process.

David of Makow seems to have tried in later years to prevent his relatives from becoming Hassidim or to induce some rabbis to renew the ban of excommunication upon them. He also left a testament to his children (written in 1810 or 1814) in which he elucidates the depravities of the Hassidim, adding some new points to what he had said earlier. Unlike Israel Leibel, David of Makow had no illusions about coordinating anti-Hassidic activities with those of the Enlighteners. In *Zemir Aritzim* he complains about the increasing number of "epicureans and heretics" (maskilim).

But Israel Leibel, too, had soon become disenchanted with the Enlighteners. In the same year in which he published his anti-Hassidic German pamphlet he also put out an antimaskilic book in Hebrew.[115] There he not only condemns those who deny the existence of God and those who "deny a little and believe a little," but he also makes personal accusations against the Enlighteners. They boast, he says, that their ideas are based on "love for humanity," which the Torah demands. "But don't believe it. . . . They are full of hatred." If we are correct in assuming that Israel Leibel originally hoped to enlist Jewish Enlighteners in the struggle against Hassidim, we may surmise his disappointment when he discovered that the maskilim were in part heretics and nonbelievers. This may explain his disappearance from public view after 1799.

But whatever the reason, the anti-Hassidic fighters who wanted to take up Eliyahu Wilno's fallen standard were in those years of consolidation of "Hassidic power"[116] bound to fail; also, the mitnagdim-Hassidim confrontation had already passed its crest. A struggle with new means and arguments was now about to be taken up by the maskilim themselves, which lasted the greater part of the nineteenth century. At the same time Hassidism was undergoing changes leaning toward conservatism.

In the course of time changes occurred in the parts of the former Polish state that were incorporated into Russia, Prussia, and Austria. The semifeudal economic and social order was in the process of dissolution and with it also the erstwhile position of the Jews. The village Jew, the leaseholder and innkeeper, one of Hassidism's mainstays, and his way of life were undergoing a transformation, with many individuals being restricted, eliminated, or simply expelled from the villages. The Jewish Establishment, the kehilla, was losing its legal power or being eliminated (in 1822 in Congress Poland) and the Hassidim lost their target, so to speak. In truth, the Hassidim themselves, now becoming more urbanized than in the eighteenth century, became the backbone of many an urban community and in this way formed the new Establishment.[117] Their main adversary was becoming less and less the traditionalist—the mitnagid—and more and more the antitraditionalist (the Enlightener).

Similarly, the leaders, the Hassidic rabbis, no longer were semi-itinerant preachers and the "intelligentsia-proletariat," who were apt to be innovators, but became consolidated in "houses" and "dynasties" with their own "courts," traditions, and conservative trends. Thus the Hassidim began to aim not for more permissiveness but rather for maintenance of Jewish religious piety against the impact of the newer secular approaches.

This had already begun at the end of the eighteenth century in the Ukraine

(Nachman of Braclaw) and continued in Galicia and Congress Poland in the nineteenth century. In the latter period the few leaders who took Besht's ways seriously or wanted to persist in innovative ways (Jacob Itzhak of Przysucha and Simcha Bunem of Przysucha, for instance, during the first three decades of the nineteenth century) met mostly sharp opposition and even some persecution on the part of other Hassidic leaders.

Little by little Hassidism became largely a clerical-conservative group, divided into many "houses," but as a whole fighting the secular Enlighteners for the continutiy of a religious-traditional Judaism and traditional way of life. Some of the behavior patterns of the older Hassidim, which the mitnagdim originally fought with excommunication and other means, were to some extent continued by the newer "conservative" Hassidim. But they mostly became the outward marks of piety and religiosity and hence a part of religious-conservative Judaism's makeup in Poland. It may be an irony of history that the Hassidim, who in the eighteenth century had been accused of and persecuted for their neglect of and opposition to Torah study, later became the principal promoters of such study in Eastern Europe. They organized yeshivot and made the Hassidic *shtiblach* vital centers of Torah learning.

Appendix 1 Note on Polish Currency

The *mark* or *grzywna* (not actually minted, it served as "money of account"), originally contained 240 silver *denars*. Constant depreciation of the currency beginning with the eleventh century brought the mark (grzywna) to 1,400 denars *(bracteates)*. At the beginning of the fourteenth century the *grossus* (Polish, *grosz*) was introduced as a monetary unit. Forty-eight grosz constituted a mark or grzywna. Silver content of the grosz dropped by one half in the fifteenth century.

From the fourteenth century on, foreign gold coins were also in circulation: the *ducat* or *florin*, worth 14 grosz in 1325, 30 grosz in 1500. Silver *thalers* came into use in the sixteenth century. Since the end of the fifteenth century reckoning has been done in Polish florins or *zloty* worth 30 grosz. In subsequent centuries the real value of the monetary unit (zloty) fell considerably through depreciation of the silver content and almost constant inflation, while the content and value of the silver thaler and the gold florin were kept more or less constant.

Silver or Gold Content and Value of Polish Monetary Units

Grosz (silver content)	Silver Thaler (value)	Gold Ducat (3.4–3.5 gram gold)	Zloty*: 30 grosz (silver content)
15th cent. 0.77 gram	1500	1500 32 grosz	
end 16th cent. 0.60 "	1540 30 grosz	52 "	
	1551	60 " (2 zloty)	
	1600 37 "		1600 about 18.0 gram
1616 0.51 "			
1623 0.30 "			
	1650	180 " (6 ")	1650 8.15 "
	1673	360 " (12 ")	1663 3.36 "
	1702	540 " (18 ")	
	1776 240 "	502 " (16.75 ")	
	1786	540 " (18 ")	

*Beginning with the second half of the seventeenth century the purchasing power of the zloty fell by a half in one century.

Appendix 2 A Rabbi Tells of His Wanderings in the Wake of the Catastrophe (1648–1667)*

I am writing you, my beloved brother, all that has been buried in my heart since I was in your place about nine years ago. . . . You will surely have heard from our brother Israel that I was also driven away from Poland because of the war [apparently the Polish-Swedish war of 1655–60]. At that time I had my daughter with me, whom I married off by the sweat of my brow. I traveled from place to place and preached in almost all of Moravia and Austria . . . and collected only two hundred gulden . . . this was when I served as rabbi in Loschitz . . . and I gave this sum to my son-in-law as a dowry. . . . For the rest I took the talit from my head and the cloak off my shoulders and gave them as security. . . . Since I was robbed by the soldiers and nobody helped me. . . . During the last six years God gave me a modest living. . . . Then my stepdaughter came from Poland and asked me to return, so did my wife. . . . I went with them on foot and reached Hotziplotz near Zuelz in Silesia. There about forty rich, learned, and respectable Jewish householders were living— all from Poland. I preached for them on the Sabbath and the same Saturday evening they engaged me as their rabbi. I was there about two and one-half years, but remained penniless because of famine and the tremendous rise of food prices and I sold everything, pillows and bedcovers, in order to keep body and soul together. . . . Then came two messengers from nearby Lissa [Leszno] asking me to become their rabbi. . . . This was surely sent from heaven. . . . If we had stayed one month more in Hotziplotz we would certainly have died of hunger. . . . To this was added the panic and war with Turkey. . . . We fled naked and barefoot. [We ran away] during the month of Elul [September] into the fields, staying there about six weeks . . . [and] everything I had got lost. . . . It is impossible to describe all the troubles, the sadness, or the adventures which I have experienced. Because of this I aged tremendously and look like an old man of eighty. . . .

When I came here to Lissa I thought I'd be able to save up a little money. So

*This letter is found among J. Wagenseil's papers preserved at the Library of Leipzig. It was published in the original Hebrew by B. D. Weinryb, "From the Hebrew Correspondence of Johann Christian Wagenseil," *The Jewish Review* 2 (1944; Hebrew part): 119-21.

I did during the first and second years. And now I am like a rose among thistles who do to me like the bees, sting like scorpions, and their whispering is that of inciters and enticers. . . . The people who work against me are a bunch of illiterates out to humble a scholar . . . and their wives are still worse. . . .

Now advise me if I should come to Poland, sell my house and seats in the synagogue there and return with the money here to my daughters or remain there, or move to Germany. . . .

Appendix 3 Jewish Population in Old (Prepartition) Poland

Thomas Macaulay (1800–59), in the third chapter of his *History of England*, stated rightly that "one of the first objects of an inquirer who wishes to form a correct notion of the state of a community at a given time must be to ascertain of how many persons that community then consisted." Historians, however, only partially followed this advice. The general status of historical demography, and some evasion by historians of this subject, have served to deter other historians from dealing with population.[1] More recently, however, interest in demographic data seems to have been developing among historians. With the turn toward "quantitative history" and the current development of "cliometrics" (econometric history) in the field of economic history, increasing attempts are being made in the United States, England, and France to apply quantitative approaches to population data of the past.[2]

However, these trends barely touched Jewish historiography, if at all. In this field even less attention was paid to population than in general history, if one discounts certain "wild guesses" or "guesstimates," as the late Professor Wirth called them.[3] Among the possible reasons for this situation one may consider both the rarity of trained demographers tackling the problem of Jewish population and the lack of even partially reliable source materials. Unlike general data, Jewish sources contain very few, if any, of the sort of vital records found in churches and towns: listings of births, marriages, and deaths, for instance. There are, of course, no registers of Peter's pence payments by Jews since they did not contribute to the papacy.

Fewer tax rolls for Jews (or censuses for the purpose of taxation) are preserved than for the general population. The ones that *have* survived may be less reliable since taxes were usually imposed by an outside power and the taxpayers were apt to try to reduce their payments by cutting down their numbers (at the time of the 1764/65 census in Poland the Jews in some places may have hidden about one-fifth or more of the population). In addition, since Jews often paid the bulk of their taxes in a lump sum through the kehilla, the state possessed—or preserved—few tax registers of Jews. The internal Jewish sources—the kehilla books and registers—were, with minor exceptions, not greatly concerned with having or preserving regular tax lists. This makes Jewish historical statistics highly speculative, much more so than general historical statistics. Thus the field is opened to "dreams," prejudices, "nationalist" tendencies, or simply fictitious approaches.

Polish historical statistics generally present a number of difficulties to be overcome. Often territorial changes of the state, immigration waves from the West during the Middle Ages, and scarcity of population registers make it hard to estimate the size of the population. Even the availability of the Peter's pence registers for sizable parts of the country does not lighten the task much. There were variations in both the regulations and the practice of imposing and collecting this tax, in time as well as territorially. The registers do not always make it clear whether the tax was paid per householder (*dym*—hearth) or per person, and in the latter case what kind of person (age, sex). Nor do they show the kind and number of persons who were exempt. The authors dealing with this problem take different attitudes regarding the system and technique of exaction and the frequency of the Peter's pence collections in various provinces in Poland. Hence variations in the results of their computations.[4]

On Jews in Poland, as mentioned, still fewer materials exist. This makes any attempt at estimates more hazardous. Most historians—not excepting economic historians—generally keeping their eyes on the present, tend to exaggerate in their estimates of the past. As has been pointed out, "it seems to be psychologically hard to imagine that large cities of today . . . had in the past only tiny populations."[5] The same is true in connection with Jews.

The preserved materials for the fourteenth century consist, for the main part, of about two dozen tombstone inscriptions of Jews in Silesia (mainly Breslau) and lists of taxpayers and some others mentioned in connection with business deals or other transactions. Of these we find: in Breslau c. 1300–30: 13 names; 1330–60: 195 names. In smaller Silesian places the number is minuscule: in Goerlitz 1300–30: 6 names; 1330–60: 7 names; in Muensterberg 1300–30: 1 name. For 1330–60 we also have figures for eight other places: in Brieg 8 names are mentioned; in Neisse, 4; Schweidnitz, Neumarkt, Ohlau, 3 each; Liegnitz 2; and Trebnitz 1.

On the basis of these lists Brann estimates that in 1350–60 Breslau had some 130–140 Jewish family heads.[6] From parts of Poland lying to the east and south of Silesia a number of Jewish names are mentioned in the extant court books of the three large Jewish communities of Poland proper—Poznań, Cracow, and Lwów. Most of the preserved books date from the last quarter of the fourteenth century. They contain 73 Jewish names (20 in Cracow) in connection with moneylending and similar transactions. These figures tell very little about the number of Jews comprising the rest of the Jewish population even in those three cities, however, to say nothing of other parts of Poland. One author tried to compute the number of Jews in Cracow in the second half of the fourteenth century and came to the conclusion that there were a few hundred,[7] but his figures are of little value.

It is to Itzhak Schipper's credit that he made one of the first serious attempts to compute the number of Jews in Poland. Taking as a basis the annual taxes paid by

Jews presumably per house, he used a multiplier of 28–30 persons for stone houses (on which the tax was 4 zloty), and 15 for wooden houses (taxed at 2 zloty). The multiplier is based on some apparently incorrect information as to the average number of people to a house in the sixteenth to eighteenth centuries, assuming that this did not differ in the Middle Ages. Thus he found that the large communities of Poznań, Cracow, and Lwów had 1,400 Jews each in the fifteenth century. The smaller communities paid an average yearly tax amounting to about one-eighth of the sums paid by the large communities, according to which Schipper estimated an average of 175 persons, or 10,150 for these fifty-eight smaller communities. In light of these computations the Jewish city and town population would have amounted to some 14,700. To this he added a fifth, or about 3,000, for the Jewish village population (he estimated this by using the proportion of later centuries), and another one-third for the Jewry of Lithuania (again estimated according to a proportion in later centuries), and obtained a figure of some 18,000 for Poland proper and 6,000 for Lithuania, making a total of about 24,000.[8]

These figures have been generally accepted uncritically by Jewish historians, some of whom even rounded them out to a higher number.

But Schipper's figures have also been criticized as highly exaggerated. In truth, they do not provide even the basis of "very rough approximations," which historical demographers sometimes consider "sufficient in many historical contexts."[9] The amount of the annual taxes paid by the communities, especially the smaller ones, is highly speculative. The only extant information on the varied amounts paid in taxes around 1500 is for about five of the fifty-eight communities. Even assuming that this information on 8 percent of the communities is correct, it is hardly possible to draw conclusions about the other 92 percent. Nor do we know whether any clear relation existed between the tax and the number of houses (4 florins for a larger house, 2 florins for a smaller one), and it is dubious whether these were held to a more or less certain principle in all or most places. Also, in the main the multiplier for the number of people living in the houses appears to be entirely unrealistic. Available information shows that in the bigger cities (in later years) not all the Jewish houses were of stone, nor did they shelter anything like 28 persons. And far fewer than 14–15 persons lived in the houses in smaller cities.

In Poznań in 1619 the Jews lived in 128 buildings, of which only 46 (36 percent) were large stone houses with an average number of 16.5 occupants to a building (total Jewish population 2,122). Earlier, in 1590, the average number of people living in a building was only about 12.

In Lwów in 1550, 917 Jews lived in 82 buildings, which makes an average of about 11 per building. If we should use this multiplier of 11–12 persons per house—or the 16.5 figure—for the supposed 50 houses in each of the three cities at the end of the fifteenth century we will not find there more than 1,800 or 2,500 Jews, respectively.

A still larger discrepancy would appear between Schipper's projections of 14–15 persons per house in the smaller cities and the fragmented facts available. In Lublin 66 Jewish houses existed in 1564. Four years later, according to the lists of head tax,

350 Jews lived in the city, and in 1578 there were 500 Jews. This would make some 5.3 persons per house in 1564 and 7.6 in 1578 (assuming that the number of Jewish houses in Lublin did not increase during 1564–78). In the town of Parczew there were 60 persons in 10 Jewish houses in 1566. We also have lists of taxpayers from different places in the Ukraine and Podolia. In most cases both Jewish and non-Jewish houses are recorded. In some instances "houses" are also translated into "persons" (1565). We then see that each house sheltered 5–6 persons (Chmelnik: 5 houses with 29 persons; Sharabka: 5 houses with 25 persons; 1555, Hrubieszów: 5 houses 13 persons.[10] Polish historians, in fact, adopted this multiplier of 5–6 per house as a yardstick for measuring Jewish population in the sixteenth century. There is no reason to assume that fifty or a hundred years earlier many more Jews lived in each house. Using one of these multipliers—5, 6, or even 7.6—it would appear that the number of Jews living in the smaller towns fell somewhere between 4,176 and 5,290. This would give Poland proper (not counting Lithuania) something between 6,000 and 8,800 Jews (instead of Schipper's 18,000).[11] If we should add an unknown but very small number of village Jews, and an unknown number for Lithuania, it might bring the total number up to 10,000 or very slightly more.[12]

Population Growth

The roughly 10,000 Jews who lived in Poland at the end of the fifteenth century were destined to increase into a community of about three-quarters of a million or so in less than three centuries. The growth rate for the Jews was apparently higher than for the general population of the country.

Many Jewish and non-Jewish authors have dealt with the problem of real or imagined greater growth of Jewish population throughout the ages—not only in Poland—and have formulated some hypotheses about a lower mortality rate among Jews. The arguments vary. Some writers assume that Jews became selectively immune to devastating epidemics that swept medieval cities and, as urbanites, suffered less in modern times from sicknesses (TB and other diseases), which plagued village people who moved to the cities. Others hold that ritual prescriptions such as washing the hands, taking a ritual bath, and eating kosher food made their lives more hygienic so that more children survived into adulthood. Another argument is that the Jewish birth rate was higher because of early marriages.

There is actually no scientific way to prove or disprove these and similar assumptions. But one should not overlook the existence of indications that they are false. Jews in Poland and Germany used to flee the cities in time of an epidemic and remain in the country for the duration[13] (the community of Poznań even owned a special house outside the city for this purpose). Experience may have shown them that the city was less safe than the country at such times. Isaiah Hurewitz angrily complains that Jews who flee the city during other epidemics do not do so at the outbreak of smallpox. This, he charges, contributes to the extensive deaths among their children.[14] Thus Jews of those times appear to have considered it a relief to go to the country rather than staying in the cities. Incidental scraps of information seem to indicate that at least some Jews failed to adhere to state or city regulations about proper isolation of those who became ill of the plague: use of their clothing, or the ban on traveling from one place to another, and similar restrictions.

The idea that Jews were more immune to epidemics because of their cleanliness and diet seems to have been picked up from a fifteenth-century treatise (by a German physician in Paris), which may have had anti-Semitic overtones and may have been an attempt to explain—or apologize for—the attacks upon Jews during the big plague of the fourteenth century,[15] claiming that Jews die of the plague less than Christians. For this reason they were supposedly accused of bringing death to the Christians.

The assumptions that the Jews were cleaner also belong among generalizations that can scarcely be proven. Occasional non-Jewish and even Jewish sources sometimes seem to indicate the contrary. For instance, the Polish inspector assigned to survey the Jewish quarter in Poznań (1619) tells that among 128 houses there he found 54 of stone (46 large and 8 small) and 74 of wood. Describing the inhabitants he says: "In the spacious Jewish stone houses [*kamienicy*] in the city Jews are not crowded, but in the worst wooden houses a great many of them live together. This became clear during this revision. We found there the greatest congestion of people as well as the most dirt both in the houses and in the streets." Parallel Jewish sources from the same community in different years tell how garbage was left lying in the Jewish streets, and that the water pipes did not function, increasing the danger of contagion. It should be mentioned that the kahal's resolution to improve the conditions emphasizes fear of possible retribution on the part of the authorities for neglect rather than any inherent need for cleanliness.[16] Similarly, minor fragments found in Jewish sources (ritual literature and responsa) and also in non-Jewish ones indicate that Jews were hardly scrupulous about cleanliness in the streets and that even the ritual bath (mikveh) was sometimes less than immaculate. On the other hand, observing ritual kashruth laws may have had some impact on health, such as helping to avoid trichinosis.

The main reasons for greater Jewish population growth may however, have lain elsewhere. First, whereas many thousands of young Poles practiced celibacy (clergymen, nuns, monks), their Jewish counterparts were increasing the birth rate. The same is true of military service. In the recurring wars soldiers—usually in their reproductive years—often suffered even more from epidemics than from the enemy. These epidemics were the scourge of the armies at war, killing many more than the enemy did. (Of the 30,000-man Polish army at Vienna that went to relieve the Turkish siege in 1683, less than half returned.) Jewish youngsters did not generally serve in the army or go to the wars. Another factor making for a lower birth rate among non-Jews may have been the widely accepted custom in Europe for house servants, apprentices, journeymen, and secondborn and subsequent sons of farmers either to forgo marriage or to marry late. Jews, not having any farmer population, did not follow this custom, while the limitations in some communities on marriage for poorer people (see below) apparently concerned only those living in the largest cities. In other words, the reproductive potential may have been greater among Jews in Poland than among Poles because many thousands and tens of thousands of the latter's young people—mostly men but also some women—were denied this function either by self-imposed celibacy or by military service.[17] Early marriage may at times have contributed somewhat to a higher birth rate, although historians exaggerate the extent of child marriages among Jews in Poland in normal times.[18] One may also doubt the chances for the offspring of very young couples to survive the exigencies of growing up.

Generally, some fragmentary information seems to indicate that more children survived to adulthood in affluent families than in less affluent ones. A number of genealogies of business leaders, prominent rabbis, community leaders, and the like —generally belonging to the more affluent classes—show that such people often had four, six, sometimes even eight or nine children who reached adulthood, although there were also families with only two children. On the other hand, there are some indications that poorer families tended to be small ones. Thus a census of Polish Jewish innkeepers living in the Russian part of the Ukraine in 1736, who do not seem to have been affluent, shows a family size of a little less than 4.5 persons (less than 2.5 children). In Brody the 1764 census indicates that house owners had more children (more than one year old) per family than did tenants (house owners: adults 1,391, children 1,681, or an average of 1.2 children per adult; tenants: adults 1,782, children 1,113, or 0.6 children per adult).[19] It should also be added that overcrowding, which favors epidemics, was more prevalent among the poorer classes. We have already noted a Polish inspector's statement about the overcrowding in the poorer parts of the Jewish section of Poznań in 1619, as compared with the spacious living quarters of the wealthier ones, and his claim that in the poorer sections he found the insides of the houses dirty as well as the streets. The fact that the affluent class had spacious houses is also confirmed elsewhere.

During the sixteenth century and parts of the seventeenth some Jewish authors complained about the rich Jews who built large houses for themselves—like the non-Jews—or cautioned their own children (for instance Isaiah Hurewitz) not to build their houses too large.

The numbers of poorer people may have also been affected slightly by, among other things, the population policies of Polish Jewish communities, or some of them. Certain communities restricted the number of people with limited means who were allowed to marry. In the seventeenth century Poznań had a quota of six marriages per year for people with a dowry of 400 zloty or less. Domestic servants and other employees were forbidden to marry without the consent of two-thirds of the members of the kehilla administration. In Cracow the regulations of 1595 required a special marriage permit for girls with a dowry of less than 150 zloty.[20] Although the sextons were sometimes lax about enforcing these regulations, they may have helped to keep the birth rate down.

These indications of the gap between the children's survival rates in rich and in poor families could possibly be generalized if we take into account the conditions of the times. Among the many dangers menacing infants were hunger, filth, and the long cold winters, besides the various epidemics such as smallpox. Infants were breast-fed for a long time but only the wealthier families could afford to hire a wet-nurse, one of whose duties was to keep the baby clean (preserved regulations of communities mention contracts to feed and wash the baby). General literature of the seventeenth century depicts little children as gluttons, which may indicate that feeding was quite a problem. There is no reason to assume that conditions differed among the Jews. Adequate food and cleanliness continued to be problems even after the child was weaned, and only the affluent class could afford appropriate food such as fresh milk, meat, and vegetables, and a servant to do the necessary work. Keeping the house warm, too, was an expense which only affluent families could readily afford.[21] And the same holds true for a number of the other needs of a growing child, some of which were denied the children in poorer families, reducing their chance of survival.

In short, the number of children surviving among Polish Jews seems to have varied considerably from one social level to another. Also, in times of epidemics the survival was apparently greater in richer families than in poorer ones. It was mainly the richer people who left the cities. And the intensive care necessary for the sick was more within reach of those who could afford to pay the high cost.[22]

Empirical data about Jewish population growth may in part be deduced from general developments. Some rudimentary data may be found in certain tax rolls, censuses arranged for tax purposes, and information about houses settled by Jews. Thus development of larger Jewish settlement, the growth of commerce among Jews, and the expansion of Polish Jewish religious culture in the sixteenth and seventeenth centuries may indicate by implication Jewish population growth, since this was all connected with increasing numbers. The same trend is evinced by the information on expanding Jewish cities and Jewish streets, the building of larger or new synagogues, or the addition of lights to the existing synagogues.[23] These and similar points, however, hardly give any idea of quantitative data.

Something of this could be gauged, as mentioned, from some accounts of poll taxes and hearth taxes (podymne) and censuses arranged for purposes of collecting them, as well as from listings of the number of houses in Jewish hands (although these facts are not so clear-cut). The meaning of the concepts often changes with time; also, in practice matters were not handled according to the law. The poll tax was not always paid by everyone, and the average number of inhabitants of a "hearth" or house remains unclear.

A poll tax for Jews in Poland was introduced in 1549. It was prescribed that every Jew—with the exception of the very poor—pay one zloty annually. This prescription was repeated in 1570.[24] In connection with this poll tax censuses of Jews were supposed to have been arranged periodically; the law of 1549 prescribed a census as the first basis for the poll tax, but no materials on it have been preserved (if such a census generally took place at all). Aside from a few fragments there are no traces of other censuses, with the sole exception of the one in 1764.[25]

Some historians assume that at first the poll tax paid was not far from the actual number of Jews ("heads") in Lithuania and parts of Poland.[26] This may have some bearing with regard to the number of Jews in Lithuania, but the sums paid in Poland proper (1579: 10,000 zloty; 1581: 15,000 zloty) have apparently very little relationship to the actual number of Jews in that country in those years (who amounted to many more than 10–15,000). In other words, the implementation of the law was lax, and in many places only one zloty per family was in fact collected; also "head" came to mean different things (adults only, heads of families, and so on) at different times and in different places.

In addition, in those years Polish Jews were already paying this tax in a lump sum, not necessarily collected in equal amounts from each person or family. The poll tax became still further divorced from the actual number of Jews after 1591 when it was leased to the Three- (or Four-) Land Jewish Council (later, in Lithuania, to the Lithuanian Community Council) which, up to 1764, paid the Jewish poll tax annually in a lump sum after levying it on the communities—which again did not collect it in equal sums from all their members (such as one zloty per head or family). The lump sum paid did not, of course, remain constant but increased with the growth of the Jewish population, and also for other reasons, such as the decreasing value of the Polish monetary unit.

JEWISH POLL TAX IN POLAND

Year	Amount	
1591	20,000	zloty
1634	80,000	"
1656	70,000	"
1661	105,000	"
1673	105,000	"
1714	210,000	"
1726	220,000	"
1753	220,000	"

The increase in the amounts of the tax may generally be somehow indicative of population growth. In the discussions in the Polish parliament (sejm), which raised the amounts, rationales were heard about the growth of the Jewish population, but the members of the sejm had no real knowledge of the figures nor did these constitute the sole reason for raising the lump sums. Among the grounds for this raise were the constant depreciation of the monetary unit of Polish currency and the Polish treasury's growing need for funds.[27]

Another quantitative indication of the number of Jews is the counting of houses they owned ("hearths") or the tax rolls of taxes levied on such houses (podymne). But here, too, the quantitative value of a hearth in terms of the number of people involved remains unclear. Not only are the guesses and estimates of these numbers often exaggerated and contradictory, but the term hearth *(dym)* was not standard-ized and underwent some transformations with time. Thus in Volhynia in 1659, 1662, and other years hearth *(dym)* was not defined as a house but may have meant two, six, or some other number of houses. It apparently designated a unit of taxa-tion,[28] which may have meant different things at different times.

A computation of the Jewish population in the Ukraine shows that before the sixteenth century Jews lived (or are mentioned) in only two places. During the sixteenth century Jews settled in forty-nine localities and in the first half of seven-teenth century in sixty-four. Their numbers are given as follows:

YEAR	Nos.
1569[29]	4,000
1648	51,325
1765	131,865

These computations and estimates made by S. Ettinger on the basis of some tax rolls and listings of Jewish houses [30] are probably as nearly accurate as it is possible to be. The estimated growth from about 4,000 in 1569 to 51,325 in 1648, or about twelve times in eighty years, is, however, more illusory than real.

The Ukraine was divided into four voivodships. We do not have actual figures for the number of Jews living in two of these regions in the base year of 1569.

VOIVODSHIP	Nos. IN 1569	Nos. IN 1648
Volhynia	3,000	15,000
Podolia	750	4,000
Kiev	?	13,500
Braclaw	?	18,825
	Total	51,325

In other words, the rate of growth computed for both 1569 and 1648 would concern mainly two voivodships and will show an increase of five times in these eighty years.

This fivefold (or twelvefold?) gain in the course of some eighty years was not an outcome of natural growth alone. It was mainly a result of immigration of Jews from western and northern Poland into these southern parts of the country—a movement that ran parallel with the colonization of the region. Estimates indicate that popula-tion growth in the Ukraine generally was extremely rapid.[31]

Attempt at Quantitative Estimate of the Jewish Population in Poland

Although almost all population estimates for past centuries are brimful of "ifs," "ands," and "buts," such an attempt may give some idea of the population growth.

As scholars dealing with historical demography know, older population data are often very unsatisfactory. Nevertheless, they are frequently used because usually "the main interest centers not on the absolute numbers as such but on their relative importance" for comparison with other times and regions.[32] This is also true for data on Jews. Following this line of reasoning we may be able to discern some information useful for comparative purposes.

According to the figures of the 1764/65 census, 131,865 Jews lived in the four Ukrainian voivodships mentioned. The total number of Jews in ethnic Poland (Crown Poland) in that year is placed at 430,009.[33] Thus 30.7 percent of Polish Jewry (excluding Lithuania) lived in the Ukraine. Assuming that by 1648 the percentage was the same, this would indicate that about 170,000 Jews may have lived in the whole of Poland (again minus Lithuania) at that time.

These figures will, of course, hardly be accurate enough for detailed numerical value, and like other quantitative data of this kind they will be subject to a large margin of error. But they may indicate some trends, even though the rate of growth for 1648–1765 may have been more or less rapid in the rest of Poland than in the Ukraine,[34] since the latter was harder hit than the rest of Poland in the years of the Chmielnicki uprising and during the subsequent "deluge," as the troubles of 1648–67 came to be known. The growth had to make up for the greater losses, as it were. We must also realize that after the 1667 truce of Andrusovo between Poland and Russia, the nature of the growth changed and the rate of increase also had to offset the losses suffered during the "deluge" of 1648–67.

Before 1648 immigration of Jews to Poland, mainly from the West—Bohemia, Austria, Germany, but also from Italy and Turkey and some other regions—was an almost constant process. This migration lasted up to and including the time of the Thirty Years' War (1618–48). For a century after 1667 immigration of Jews to Poland was virtually nonexistent or at any rate very small. There was a slow trickle of Jewish emigration out of Poland to Germany and other Western countries.

The differences between the situation in the Ukraine and the rest of Poland may, of course, lessen the accuracy of detail of the figures in a computation based on comparative data from these two regions, but will perhaps not, after all, create too large a margin of error.

Losses during the "Deluge" and Recovery

Polish historians, as well as the Jewish ones, generally tended greatly to exaggerate the population and material losses during the years of the catastrophe (the "great losses" served as a rationale for the decline of the Polish state and that of the Jewish community). More recently Polish historians have tried to take a more realistic look at the materials. Figures for the participants in the wars were questioned on the basis of demographic data or documents, and it has been pointed out that the figures may be exaggerated as much as ten or more times.[35] This is also true of the Jewish chronicles of those times. The authors often reported unverified rumors and lacked any feeling for figures. N. Hanover, the author of *Yeveyn metzulah,* and other writers confuse figures (for Hanover 1,800,000 means 18,000,000), and they "increase" the size of the Polish army five to twenty times, that of the Tatars four to eight times.[36]

The same may be said for the figures mentioned in the chronicles for those killed or dead from epidemics. In fact, fragmented information on Jewish population and other aspects of Jewish life in the Ukraine in the early 1670s and 1680s belies these exaggerations. The existing fragmentary facts and figures about a number of places show that many Jews survived by hiding, others by temporary conversion to Christianity and later reversion to Judaism (the Polish king issued a decree allowing them to reconvert), or by temporarily settling in border regions (Silesia and elsewhere). A reasonable estimate would apparently be that the total loss of life did not exceed forty to fifty thousand people—despite the historians' far higher, exaggerated estimates. Such a figure would be high enough, representing a loss of 20–25 percent of the existing Jewish population of Poland-Lithuania on the eve of the Chmielnicki uprising.[37]

A Century of Population Growth

The century after 1667 seems to have been a time of considerable Jewish population growth. Circumstantial evidence depicts Jews in various communities multiplying rapidly and as relatively numerous in other places.[38] We have some detailed population figures for a few regions and localities. In Volhynia and Podolia the number of Jews increased approximately four to ten times between 1648 and 1764, and the number of places where Jews lived grew many times.

Jews in Volhynia and Podolia

	1648		1764–65*		
	no. of places	no. of Jews	no. of places urban	villages	no. of Jews
Volhynia	46	15,000	116	2,113	50,792–63,500
Podolia	18	4,000	51	503	38,384–47,700

In fifteen private towns of another region the number of Jews rose almost ten times from 1674 to 1764–65.

*R. Mahler, *Yidn in Zifern,* passim. The second figures for 1764 signify the corrected ones, which include children in their first year (otherwise not counted) and an estimated number who failed to register.

Number of Jews in Cities and Towns of Lublin Voivodship[*]

City	1661	1674	1764/5
Opole	—	38	324
Piaski	—	53	240
Konskowola	34	29	569
Bychawa	—	34	116
Baranow	—	10	170
Belżyce	—	96	514
Czemierniki	—	11	250
Bilgoraj	—	40	644
Lęczna	—	181	491
Kraśnik	114	52	921
Janow	50	—	390
Kurow	50	61	904
Markuszow	—	9	237
Modliborzyce	—	34	237
Zaklikow	25	—	203
Total	273	648	6,210

Though these detailed population figures are not all uniformly computed and may not be exactly accurate, they do show a trend—a relatively large growth, mainly in private (nobility owned) towns and cities. In fact, by 1765 two of the largest Jewish settlements in Poland were in two private cities: Brody in the south and Lissa (Leszno) in west-central Poland. Besides the growth of the older (pre-1670s) Jewish communities many new communities were settled by Jews.[39]

All in all, the 1765 census counted 430,009 Jews in the whole of Crown Poland, or 548,777 according to Dr. Mahler's corrections (for the infants up to one year old not included in the census and about 20 percent who were left out). This would mean that the estimated number of 170,000 persons for 1648 grew some three times in over a century, or, if we deduct from the 1648 figure the 20–25 percent estimated losses during the "deluge," we shall find a growth of about four times during the century from 1667 to 1765. That is growth of about 1.5–2 percent per annum.

Reconstructing a Birth and Death Rate

There are no data for a birth and death rate of Jews in Poland in those early years. The only records to survive are the entries in the *pinkas* of the Jewish burial society in Cracow for the years after 1543. On the basis of this document F. Wettstein constructed a list of averages of deaths among Jews in Cracow.

[*]Source: Tomasz Opas, *Biuletyn*, no. 67 (1968): 7, 12.

Years	Total Number	Annually
1543–1590	1,750	37–38
1590–1640	2,850	57
1640–1690	6,300	129
1690–1740	2,650	53
1740–1790	2,600	52

The variations between the years depend mainly on the health situation—in years of epidemics such as 1640–90 many more died—and possibly also on the varying size of the population (the latter is an unknown factor).

There is information that in 1578 Kazimierz (Cracow) had 2,060 Jews. Since the average number of deaths in those years was 37–38 annually this would mean about 2 percent a year. But this figure covers adults only. In Jewish communities deaths of infants and young children, usually up to the age of thirteen or fourteen, remained uncounted in olden times and were not entered in the registers of the burial societies. Since infant mortality was usually high, the number of deaths among the youngsters may have equaled that of the grown-ups. For Cracow, Wettstein found the kehilla's records of the deceased, including children, for the end of the eighteenth century. Here the total annual number of deaths is more than twice the number registered in the burial society's records for the same years.[40] Taking these facts as a guiding point it would appear that the total number of deaths in Cracow in 1578 was not 37–38, but about 74–76, or a little less than 4 percent annually. Thus an average annual birth rate of around 5.5–6 percent and a death rate of around 3.5–4 percent for about one hundred years gives a natural increase of about 2 percent per year, which would allow a population to grow some four times during this period. Such a model of 5.5–6 percent birth rate, 3.5–4 percent death rate, and about 2 percent net growth was found in some underdeveloped countries in Asia and Africa, including the Middle East, before the introduction there of antibiotics and other hygienic improvements during the last quarter of a century or so. It may have been near the reality among Jews in underdeveloped European countries two hundred years ago.[41] The attempt to apply such a model to Jews in Poland for the century from 1667–1765 does not imply that the years were all alike. It is rather meant as an average of fluctuations during the ninety-eight years.

Before concluding let us repeat that all data and computations presented—including Dr. Mahler's with the results of the 1764/1765 census and this writer's present study—are to some degree speculative. Their value is mainly not in detailed numerical accuracy but rather in depicting generally relative growth or decline. The implications can more often than not be corroborated by a varied assembly of nonquantitative data of growth of the Jewish population in Polish towns and cities and the foundation of new kehillot in the country.

Appendix 4 Aspects of Hassidic Doctrine

DEVEKUTH

Communion with God or *devekuth*—cleavage to God—became one of the central values in Hassidism. *"Devekuth,"* according to Gershom Scholem, "is a spiritual or contemplative act by which a man binds himself to the spiritual element inherent in the letters of the Torah or prayer"[1] (the letters being animated by the light of the En-Soph: the invisible or unknowable God).

The concept of *devekuth* was developed in the cabala and in older Jewish sources, but was more strongly emphasized in Hassidism and among the group around Besht, and to some extent it acquired a different meaning. It was also applied to secular matters.[2]

Cleavage to God may begin with prayer but it is also possible and desirable in other situations, for instance, while studying or even while performing certain secular tasks.

In the course of ecstatic prayer man ascends step by step and may spiritually reach (or his soul may do so) full cleavage with the Divine. "The purpose of Torah and all the mitzvot (commandments) is to 'cleave to Him' [Deuteronomy 10:20]."[3] It is also said that man's thought should always cleave to God.

As we shall see later, some trends in Hassidism advocated reducing Torah study in order to save time for practicing *devekuth*, or, as it were, unbroken contemplation, which is not easily achieved. Simple people who cannot achieve communion with God themselves should "cleave to the learned, which is like cleaving to God. . . . Through attachment to the scholars . . . the ignorant are bound up and united with their original essence and their root in the supernatural wisdom."[4]

There are two kinds of Devekuth. *One is that of the learned who cleaves to God directly and the other is that of common people who do not know how to cleave to the Lord directly. Therefore the Torah commands them "Thou shalt cleave unto Him" meaning to cleave to the learned [zaddik] which is like cleaving to God.*[5]

Some other variations are also mentioned. Thus in a letter written sometime after 1788 Abraham of Kalisk puts forward the idea that *devekuth* is a two-way process. A man in *devekuth* is, as it were, being repaid by God's providence. Averting one's thoughts from God results in a recession of divine providence. And so, since one is unprotected by God, *devekuth* itself could mean not only the individual's cleaving directly to God but also to the group to which he belongs. The individual may thus "have continuously the advantage of divine providence through his associates who are connected in *devekuth* with God." This apparently was an attempt to give *devekuth* a social basis and make the Hassidic group or community a vital factor.[6] It is, in fact, a modification of the original idea of cleavage. There were also some who modified it in other directions.

KAVVANAH, devotion or meditation during prayer (or during the fulfillment of other commandments) is an old Jewish religious demand. Lurianic cabala gave it some special meaning and a sort of magical flavor, making it an elaborate system of "highly specialized, technically focused acts" of contemplation. In Hassidism it came to mean something akin to *devekuth*. Besht himself made use of certain individual meditative practices and improvisations, or he either changed them into or confused them with *devekuth*, "attaching himself to the letters" of the words. In the post-Besht generations kavvanah seems to have met with some opposition and to have been modified by those for whom it connoted an emotional state of the worshiper. The modifications varied with each unit of prayer and concentrated on the literal meaning of the words or on the divine names. It is even recorded that Besht considered meditation (kavvanah) during prayer of far less value than prayer with enthusiasm (apparently meaning also with cleavage), and that Elimelekh of Lizhajsk gave up the entire system of kavvanoth, concentrating instead on the proper vocalization of the divine names.[7] On the other hand, Shneur Zalman of Liady was advocating some sort of kavvanah.[8]

Kavvanah and *devekuth* in Hassidism were closely connected with study and prayer, although they also touched upon other matters—even secular ones.

STUDY OF TORAH assumed a different meaning in Hassidism than in traditional Judaism. It was sometimes characterized as preparation for prayer, to which it must take second place.[9] The lower esteem study was held in is indicated by the statement that Besht achieved revelation by means of prayer, not of study.

In terms of subject matter Torah often meant musar (ethics) or *Shulchan Aruch* (Codes) to Hassidic leaders instead of Talmud. In their opposition to the Establishment and its values, among which Talmud study was of prime importance, Hassidim thought the main purpose of such study was to achieve prestige—and Hassidic doctrine was opposed to this.[10]

Besht's view of Torah study as *lishma*, meaning mainly "for the sake of the letter" (originally, for the sake of study, not for pecuniary or other reasons), for the purpose of unifying the magic qualities of the letters to their spiritual sources in heaven, divested study itself of much of its intellectual content. It became rather one means of contemplation—the other being prayer. The stories about Besht "saying," not studying, *Mishanayot, Zohar,* or *Eyn Yakov* may signify this change. Parallel with this, the emphasis on *devekuth,* the emotional contemplation and cleaving to God, connected with or becoming a main goal in study, could and did minimize actual study, so that knowledge of Torah decreased in value. (These approaches may in turn have been post-factum justifications of the little learning that existed among Hassidim of the eighteenth century.) Another later tradition attributed to Besht has it that "a man who recites Torah with love is deeply loved by God, who is not too strict with him so long as he says it correctly."[11] This seems further to emphasize the disregard of knowledge and intellectual understanding. It may have been a sort of justification by enthusiasm of a semiliterate who could not even read well. Other traditions add to the *lishma* also the meaning of study for the purpose of fulfilling the commandments or "for God's sake."

On the other hand, some Hassidic leaders (Mendel of Premyślan, for instance) considered that in the combination of Torah study with *devekuth,* (cleaving to God) the latter was the primary factor, with Torah study taking second place. From this comes the advice to refrain from too much study, which might interfere with thoughts about cleaving to God.[12] But most Hassidic literature of the post-Great Maggid period brims with the emphasis on Torah (often Torah and prayer). This becomes still clearer in the writings of the "third generation" *(Degel Machne Efraim; Noam Elimelech,* and of course, *Tanya).*

PRAYER, as mentioned earlier, is assigned a vital role in Hassidic doctrine.[13] Not only is it regarded at times as superior to Torah study but it is even considered divine. When a man prays "the Shekhina is speaking through his mouth"; or prayer is otherwise identified with the Shekhina.[14] The high esteem in which prayer was held is expressed in the following: "The human being himself does not realize that through his prayers he brings down abundance for all the world; also the angels profit from his prayer."[15]

Prayer was mostly looked upon as being more important than study: "The soul told the rabbi [Besht] that he became worthy of revelation of high [divine] matters not because of his study of much of Talmud and codes, but because of his prayers which he said always with great devotion [kavvanah]."[16] (In another connection his elevated position is seen as resulting from the "many immersions in the ritual bath."[17])

"WAYWARD THOUGHTS" or "sinful thoughts" or "alien thoughts" coming to one during prayer were regarded as disturbing the purpose of the prayers or even the prayers themselves. According to Buber, Hassidism viewed "alien thoughts" as being given off by the sparks of God's light, which yearn for liberation from the shells of evil. They come to us—in fantasy—as desires or temptations "acting in conjunction with evil spirits."[18] A tradition attributed to Besht claims that wayward thoughts can be emendated if one heeds the sparks of the Shekhina found within the sinful thought, thereby raising the wayward thoughts and purifying them. One should, however, make an effort to keep wayward thoughts out of one's prayers and at least see that the *Shema* is free from them.

Methods of freeing oneself from "alien thoughts" range from praying with enthusiasm, *devekuth*, reduction of oneself to nothingness, liberation (in fantasy) of the pure passion from its object, raising the sparks from their *kelipot*, (shells) or even simply trying to ignore them.[19] Another way is to transfer this task to the leader, the zaddik. In the last quarter of the eighteenth century or earlier attempts were made, or advocated, to revise the teachings and practices about "uplifting and restoring the wayward thoughts."[20]

Joy is another principle emphasized in Hassidism in connection with prayer, but it also has a place in other situations. To serve God in joy is an old Jewish precept found in the Bible (Deuteronomy 28:47) and repeated many times since, from Yehuda Halevi and Maimonides to the cabalists and some authors of musar literature in the sixteenth to eighteenth centuries.

In Hassidism sadness became identified with laziness in serving God or with ingratitude to God, and hence connected with evil; whereas joy indicated full belief and trust in God and his goodness.[21] "Crying is very bad because a man should serve God in joy . . . and he should always be joyful and should think and fully believe that the Shekhina is with him and guards him and that he is looking at the Creator and the Creator is looking at him."[22]

Similar ideas are emphasized by Jacob Joseph and other disciples of Besht, and by later generations. The soul is identified with joy.

In another connection it is claimed that without material joy the soul cannot experience spiritual joy. Praying in joy is preferred to study of the Torah. Some see joy as counteracting sin. For others joy while praying opens up all the doors to heaven, and rejoicing with a mitzva (good deed) keeps intact widom or the instinct to do good.[23]

For Shneur Zalman of Liady joy is a result of the recognition of God's greatness and omnipresence:

> *When one will deeply contemplate this, his heart will be gladdened and his soul will rejoice with joy and singing with all the heart and soul and might in the intensity of this faith which is tremendous . . . [and] he will doubly rejoice with the joy of the Lord and the tremendous gratification rendered to his blessed presence by virtue of his faith.*[24]

Exile and Redemption

Early Hassidim, like Jews in the Diaspora generally, regarded galut as a fact of life, despite varied speculations to the contrary. In the traditional view galut was seen as a state from which God would ultimately redeem the Jews, but for the most part no real impatience for such redemption was evident and there were few eschatological overtones. As mentioned earlier, Ashkenazic Jewry, at least after the fifteenth century, had the idea that Torah study and good deeds enhanced the standing of galut. The first Hassidim in the eighteenth century, not unlike some older authors, frequently sought a rationale for Diaspora life. Redemption, Palestine, and messianism were deemed important values denoting hopes that God would act. There was some speculation about the time of the Messiah's coming, and incidental trips or migration to Palestine were undertaken by a few individuals or groups. But little or no actuality for the immediate future was attached to any of this. And in the main, verbal expressions in favor of Palestine or wishing for redemption do not seem to imply commitment to concrete activity.

In any event, there is no feeling of dissociation from life in the Diaspora such as might indicate a real concern with and belief in the likelihood of imminent messianic times.[25] In fact, there were tendencies to assign important functions to galut or to empty the concepts of redemption, Palestine, and Zion of their concrete meanings and to spiritualize or equate them with functions in the Diaspora.

The writings of some preachers and authors of the period complain about "those who maintain that all the prayers about galut . . . and Zion and Jerusalem are in vain . . . since we were not answered" or say that "people do not believe that all Jews will fully repent [repentance supposedly being a prerequisite for redemption] so that they will not be redeemed." Others maintain "that in our time there is no shouting from the heart" and "our crying is not genuine" or "we are quiet and serene and our cries to God are barely audible," or "for how long . . . is nothing to be done to bring the Messiah?"[26]

If such statements reflect trends of those times (some are not dissimilar from complaints heard, for instance, two hundred years earlier) they would indicate a general background of disinterest or minimal interest in intensive messianism. Jacob Emden may be expressing some of the trends among Polish Jews—he regarded himself as their spokesman in relation to Frankists—when he emphasizes that Jews are not overanxious for redemption. In a hypothetical discussion with the Frankists he says: "About the coming of the Messiah . . . we do not wish to throw off the yoke of galut until God himself will have mercy on us."[27]

A couple of the stories about Besht himself may point either way. Two stories tell how Besht tried to go to Palestine: in one version he was turned back when he reached Constantinople, and in the other robbers led him to Palestine through "caves and tunnels," but he was forced to turn back en route. His brother-in-law, Gershon of Kutov, seems to have been disappointed with Besht's refusal to come to Palestine. In a letter dated 1748 he reproaches Besht: "I know your nature, that you must pray in your own minyan [synagogue] besides other matters,"[28] that is, Besht preferred his synagogue in galut to one in Palestine.

The letter that Besht wrote to Gershon of Kutov around 1750 or 1751, saying that he had seen the Messiah in heaven in 1747 and held a conversation with him, could be interpreted in two ways. Among other things the letter says that Besht asked the Messiah in his chambers in heaven: "When will you come?" and the answer was: "After your teachings have spread and become known in the world." Besht goes on to say that "he himself was very sad because of the long time" it would take until the coming of the Messiah. Some authors think this letter indicates that Besht took a messianic task upon himself; others, on the contrary, see Besht concentrating on individual salvation of the souls (mentioned in other parts of the letter) instead of group messianism, so that preparation for deliverance became a matter of prayers and meditation, not unlike the traditional procedure through the centuries. One should also realize that the letter may have been in part designed as propaganda for Besht's Hassidism by asserting that the latter must spread before the Messiah would come.[29] At the same time the letter contains a statement that could show that Besht was giving some thought to his own journey to Palestine: "God knows that I did not give up the idea of traveling to Palestine" (although this may be merely a meaningless expression).

As to other people settling in Palestine, Besht's attitude shifted, or so tradition tells us. When Jacob Joseph wanted to settle in Palestine, Besht asked his own brother-in-law there to befriend Jacob and to write "to the rich people to assign him a good subsistence." A few of Besht's followers actually did go to live in Palestine.

On the other hand, there were times when he actively opposed or at least did not favor emigration to Palestine. A story relates that Besht regarded *aliyah* as a sort of escapism or, worse, as induced by Satan. He is supposed to have several times forbidden Jacob Joseph to travel to that country: "Every time that you will feel a desire to travel to the Holy Land you should realize that your town is in trouble and Satan is confusing you so that you would not pray for your town [in the Diaspora]. So every time you feel a desire for the Holy Land pray for the town."[30] Another story tells how when Nachman of Horodenka wanted to journey to Palestine in 1764 he went to Besht's grave and came away filled with joy, saying that Besht had ordered him to go. If we take Rabbi Nachman's words literally it may appear that he had not expected Besht to allow him to travel to the Holy Land.

It is interesting to note that Hassidic sources relate that at least three of the first-generation leaders wanted to settle in Palestine but were held back against their wills. In addition to Besht himself and Jacob Joseph, something similar is also recounted about Pinchas Shapira of Korzec (c. 1725–91). He was prepared to go to Palestine in 1768 and had already hired wagons to transport him. But he suddenly fell ill and said to God: "Perhaps you do not want me to go to Palestine—then I will not go." Whereupon he immediately recovered. Perhaps these stories were supposed to symbolize the conflict between the traditional pro-Palestine yearning and the realities of life in galut.

In general, for Besht and some of his followers the concepts of galut, the Holy Land, and even the Messiah lost their actual meaning and underwent a process of further spiritualization. Galut came to signify not the physical exile but "the exile of the Shekhina in the *kelipa*" (evil spirit), or that of "the soul in the hands of the evil instinct" (*yeytzer hara)"*—its negative impact being that in exile one cannot "raise the holy sparks" to perfection. A variation on the same theme is that of galut being imposed on a Jew or Jews by other Jews. Or the claim that galut does not necessarily signify being subject to foreign rulers; it may rather involve the individual's surrender to his own bad drives and passions. In a similar vein are statements that galut incorporates great advantages or that redemption is being postponed for a good reason. The Holy Land (Eretz Israel or Zion) becomes identified with Torah study or the Shekhina, while failure to study or say one's prayers is equated with life in "foreign countries" or, in a word, galut. Pushing this reasoning or symbolism further, exile is sometimes elevated beyond the position of the old Jewish state: nowadays, during the time of galut, one can more easily achieve divine inspiration [ruah hakodesh] than at the time of the Temple.[31] This was the opinion expressed by Ber of Mezeritch, Elimelekh of Lizhajsk, and others.

In general, among Besht's disciples and the Hassidic leaders of the two subsequent generations we find very little interest in eschatological messianism, even though some phraseology or pious desires are retained. Galut had numerous meanings for Jacob Joseph of Polonnoe, who at one time (around 1750) thought of settling in Palestine, and he differentiates several sorts of galut: physical galut, in which one is subject to non-Jewish peoples; and spiritual galut, in which the soul is the captive of the evil instinct (yeytzer hara). Furthermore, physical galut is not exclusively a state of being held in captivity by the non-Jews. This is only one form of exile, and the easier one. A second, much harder kind is the "exile of the scholar" (talmid hakham) among the ignorant who despise him. A third sort of exile, the hardest of all, is that inflicted upon the pious scholar by the wicked scholars (the "Jewish devil" scholars).

Galut is a result of unwarranted hate among Jews, of conceit, of domination of one over the other, or of arrogance. Jacob Joseph felt galut could be counteracted by means of self-humiliation, elimination of impertinent people, and establishment of unity among Jews. Since the latter is normally impossible to achieve, God (or Elijah) should bring this peace. His writings also reveal rudiments of the Lurianic theory of kelipa (shell or evil spirit) and "holy sparks," the raising of which is called "deliverance." For this purpose, says Besht, "one should pray for his soul and his spirit, which are in exile with the yeytzer hara."[32] The ideas about exile and deliverance, which are repeated with some variation of these themes, are clearly far from any keen messianism[33]—especially since (again, in accordance with Besht) he stresses individual salvation. (Before praying for a general deliverance of the Jews one needs to pray for the personal deliverance of his own "soul.")

The Maggid of Mezeritch, far from encouraging messianism, instead seems to have emphasized the value of the galut. He pointed out "that to serve God in exile was easier and therefore more within the grasp of the devout than to serve him in Palestine." He also said that "holy inspiration [ruah hakodesh] is more readily attained today in galut than at the time of the Temple" in Palestine. Elsewhere Zion is often spiritualized to mean zaddik.[34] The Great Maggid—relates Shneur Zalman of Liady—also maintained that there are people (he said "souls") who especially need Palestine, and others who especially need the galut. This would mean that the two are equally important.[35]

Elimelekh of Lizhajsk agreed with Ber that ruah hakodesh is more easily attainable in galut. He also points out that in galut is holiness (although, in the main, true holiness will come only with the Messiah). He casts galut in an important role, and also spiritualizes Zion into the zaddik. A number of other Hassidic leaders point out "that wherever we fulfill God's will this is called redemption," that the quality of the Diaspora is equal to that of Palestine, that Zion connotes anywhere halakha is studied, and that Jerusalem is where there are full zaddikim.

The main trend among many Hassidic leaders of the few generations after Besht was to empty the concepts of Eretz Yisrael and Zion of their physical content. They sought to spiritualize the latter into a "heavenly" country ("Eretz Israel on high") and also into the zaddik ("Zion meaning the zaddik"). Or they embodied these ideas in their concept of galut ("all the synagogues possess the vitality of Eretz Yisrael") or tried to equalize the virtue of galut with that of Palestine even while admitting that Jews in the Diaspora were suffering.[36] Some of them even indicated opposition to praying for deliverance. Nachum of Czernobyl, who used many verbalizations of a messianic character, formulated the spiritualization of Palestine and the attribution of great worth to galut: "Even though a physical Eretz Israel exists, nevertheless its basis lies in the spiritual qualities and the vitality given it by the Creator. Even though we are in galut, nevertheless we possess the aspects of Eretz Yisrael. . . . All the synagogues . . . are invested by the Creator . . . with the life of Eretz Yisrael. . . . Praying there . . . one is in Eretz Yisrael."

Efraim of Sadilkow, Besht's grandson, shows very little messianic influence. He mentions having heard Besht claim that with some "help" (or "power") he would have been able to bring the Messiah. This statement may have been intentional propaganda, for the power to bring the Messiah was regarded as highly prestigious. In a couple of instances Rabbi Efraim expresses hope for the imminent coming of the messiah[37]—which may or may not mean the standard traditional hopes.

Ber of Mezeritch's disciples (Menachem Nachum of Czernobyl, Elimelekh of Lizhajsk, Shneur Zalman of Liady) call upon each Jew to develop his own soul as a part of the Messiah's soul, in order to contribute to his coming. They tell of the zaddik who could bring the Messiah, and they depict the "future messianic times" as the fulfillment of the Hassidic ideals.[38] This is neither more nor less than the traditional Jewish dream about the Messiah. The same is true of those who spiritualized Jerusalem, Zion into piety, or Torah study, and regarded the countries of galut as on a par with Eretz Israel as long as a man "fulfilled God's will there." Others saw galut as an "internal exile" with the individual immersed in sin and false desire, deliverance from which meant freeing oneself from all this.[39]

A few other zaddikim, for the most part at the very end of the eighteenth century, may have been slightly more interested in redemption and the Messiah,[40] although their involvement may not have gone much beyond the traditionally passive Messiah dream partially expressed in cabalistic terminology. It may well be that the letter Besht's nephew Yakir (the son of Gershon of Kutov) wrote in 1760 to his father-in-law in Brody reflects something of the ambivalence in this group's verbalization. This letter was in reply to his father-in-law's inquiry about moving from Poland to Palestine. In his salutation Yakir expresses the hope of "seeing him in Jerusalem when the Messiah will come." Taken at face value the words purport to indicate some hope for the speedy coming of the Messiah. But in the text of the letter Yakir advises him not to move to Palestine while he is young but to wait until he is seventy years old and has adequate funds to live on (which is in accordance with the old idea of settling in Palestine in one's old age).[41] Thus the wish expressed to see him "in Palestine when the Messiah will come" is no more than a standard phrase.

In practice, some new Hassidim did try to settle in Palestine during the second half of the eighteenth century or thereabouts, the frequency and extent of the trend depending both on personal preferences and varying situations. The first person from Hassidic circles that we know to have done so is Gershon of Kutov, Besht's brother-in-law, who settled in Hebron in 1747 and later moved to Jerusalem. (Gershon originally defied Besht but later became one of his followers.) A few of Besht's other supporters and sympathizers seem to have settled in Palestine either during his lifetime or in the 1760s after his death. The first larger group to make the journey was that of Nachman of Horodenka and Menachem Mendel of Premyślan and a few others in 1764, comprising fifteen adult males and fourteen women and children. Of the fifteen men some five or six or possibly more belonged to Besht's group.[42]

A larger immigration followed more than a decade later. As mentioned, in 1777 a group of Hassidim from Lithuania under the leadership of Menachem Mendel of Horodok (formerly of Vitebsk) and Abraham of Kalisk set out for Palestine.

These were the years following the first partition of Poland in 1772, when conditions were generally unsettled, especially for Jews. New borders were set, and parts of Poland came under new regimes with new laws and regulations. Austria and Prussia, having annexed parts of Poland as a result of this partition, were seeking to expel impoverished Jews, some of whom sought refuge in the Russian part. In the southern parts—the Ukraine—Jews were on the move too, trying among other things to migrate to the new southern Russian regions that Russia had won from Turkey (known as New Russia or Novorosiia). Some of those uprooted people joined the group of Hassidim (estimated at several dozen) who came from the northern parts now partially under Russian rule. They moved slowly southward toward the Black Sea, the trip taking about five or six months.[43] These people—denoted in the sources as "the poor"—may have been hoping to find support for their journey and other expenses.

The Hassidic group apparently comprised people of some means. The latters' emigration was motivated by the usual Jewish pro-Palestine attitudes and perhaps also by the pressures suffered in Lithuania in the wake of the 1772 ban upon Hassidim.

All in all about three hundred people reached Palestine, although one ship with eighty passengers sank, leaving only thirty survivors. The Hassidim constituted only a fraction of those who arrived in Palestine, but being people of means they assumed joint responsibility for the relatively large group that were poverty-stricken; they organized some immediate support as well as sending messengers abroad to bring in funds. As a result of this immigration, Jewish-Ashkenazic settlements, headed for the most part by the Hassidic leaders, grew up in Safad, Tiberias, and elsewhere. Some Hassidic rabbis also came to Palestine in the 1790s.[44]

The motives for these group and individual *aliyoth* were largely the traditional deference for the holiness of the land and the mitzva of living there or being buried there.[45] These were sometimes reinforced either by Hassidism's hope of contributing toward redemption or by special social and political circumstances.

The first of these motives is indicated both by the composition of the migrants (mostly persons of advanced age) and by the statements they made. The composition of the group that left for Palestine in 1764—fifteen men and fourteen women and children—reflects this, for the small number of children indicates a preponderance of people in advanced age groups. Menachem Mendel of Premyślan, on the other hand, rebukes his brother in Poland: "Until when will you stay abroad and listen to those who speak evil of the Holy Land?" But he admits that many think "that it is not good to stay in the [Holy Land] while one is alive."[46] Hassidic legend indicates also some belief that residing in Palestine might contribute to the coming of the Messiah.[47]

This sort of thinking about the "special quality" of Palestine, either for arousing God's compassion for his people or for some messianic purposes, may be indicated in letters written from Palestine to Poland by the leaders of the *aliya* of 1777. They express a desire "to pray for all Jews" so as to arouse compassion for them. One of these letter writers, Menachem Mendel of Horodok or Vitebsk, in a letter dated 1784, even seems to formulate a theory that "Jews are of a lower status than other peoples, and Palestine Jews are lower than Jews abroad"; he who raises them raises the Shekhina.[48] But these may have been ad hoc attitudes formulated largely to strengthen pleas for funds solicited for Palestine.

Abbreviations

Avodat Hagershuni	see Ashkenazi, Gershon, in Bibliography
AYZR	*Archiv Yugo-Zapadnoi Rossii*
Bach	see Joel b. Shmuel Sirkis, in Bibliography
Balaban, *Lwów*	M. Balaban. *Żydzi Lwowscy na przelomie XVI go i XVII wieku*. Lwów, 1906
Biuletyn	*Biuletyn Żydowskiego Instytutu Historycznego* (Warsaw)
Bleter	*Bleter far Geschichte* (Warsaw)
Chacham Zevi	see Ashkenazi, Tzevi b. Jacob, in Bibliography
ES	*Evreyskaya Starina*
Gelber, *Lvuv*	N.M. Gelber, ed. *Lvuv (Enziklopedia shel Galuyot*, vol. 4). Jerusalem–Tel Aviv, 1956
HS	YIVO *Historishe Shriften*
HUCA	*Hebrew Union College Annual*
HZK	Meir Balaban. *Historja Żydów w Krakowie*. Vols. 1 and 2. Cracow, 1931–36
IEN	*Istoriya Evreyskago Naroda*. Vols. 11 and 12. Moscow, 1915, 1921
JJLG	*Jahrbuch der Jüdisch-Literarischen Gesellschaft*
JJS	*Journal of Jewish Studies*
JQR	*The Jewish Quarterly Review*
JSS	*Jewish Social Studies*
KH	*Kwartalnik Historyczny*
KS	*Kiryath Sepher*
LY	Joseph b. Moses. *Leket Yosher*. Edited by J. Freiman. Berlin, 1903

Maggid devarov le-Yaakov   see Ber of Mezeritch, in Bibliography

Mahler, *Polin*   Raphael Mahler. *Toledot ha-yehudim ba-Polin.* Merchavia, Israel, 1946

Mahler, *Yidn in Zifern*   Raphael Mahler. *Yidn in amuliken Poilen in licht fun zifern.* Warsaw, 1958

MGWJ   *Monatschrift für Geschichte und Wissenschaft des Judentums*

MZ   *Miesięcznik Żydowski*

Or Haemeth   see Ber of Mezeritch, in Bibliography

PAAJR   *Proceedings of the American Academy for Jewish Research*

PK   Israel Isserlein. *Pesakim u-ketavim* (together with *Terumat Hadeshen*). Fürth, 1778

PML   S. Dubnow. *Pinkas Medinat Lita.* Berlin, 1925

PVAA   *Pinkas Vaad Arba Aratzot.* Edited by Israel Halperin. Jerusalem, 1945

REA   *Russko-Evreiski Arkhiv.* Vols. 1–3. Edited by S.A. Bershadski. Petersburg, 1882 et seq.

REJ   *Revue des Etudes Juives*

Rema   Rabbi Moses Isserles

RIN   *Regesty i nadpisi. Svod materialov dlya istorii evreev v Rossii.* Vols. 1–3

Ringelblum, *Warszawa*   see Ringelblum, *Żydzi w Warszawie*, in Bibliography

Sepher Shimush   see Jacob Emden, *Sepher Shimush*, in Bibliography

SH   R. Margalit, ed. *Sepher Hassidim.* Jerusalem, 1957

Shatzki, *Tach*   Jacob Shatzki. Introduction to *Yeveyn metzulah*, in *Gzeires Tach* YIVO. Wilno, 1938

Tanya   Shneur Zalman of Liady, *Liqqutei amarim.* Translated by Nissan Mindel. Brooklyn, 1962

TH   Israel Isserlein. *Sepher Terumat Hadeshen.* Fürth, 1778

Toledoth   Jacob Joseph. *Toledoth Yaakov Josef.* Warsaw, 1881

Weinryb, *Beginnings*   Bernard D. Weinryb. *The Beginnings of East-European Jewry in Legend and Historiography.* Leiden, 1962

Yeveyn metzulah see Hanover, N., in Bibliography

YS Solomon Luria, *Yam shel Shlomo*

ZNZ Yaakov Sasportas. *Zizit novel Zevi.* Edited by I. Tishbi. Jerusalem, 1954

ZPO *Żydzi w Polsce Odrodzonej*, Vol. 1, Warsaw, 1932

Żródla F. Kupfer and J. Lewicki. *Żródla Hebrajskie do dziejów słowian i niektórych innych ludów środkowej i wschodniej Europy.* Wroclaw–Warsaw, 1956

Notes*

Introduction

1 The term Eastern Europe, like many others used to designate such divisions, is an arbitrary one, and definitions vary greatly. See also the definition in Pounds, *Eastern Europe*, p. 1.
2 Wojciechowski, ed., *Poland's Place in Europe*, p. 9.
3 Bardach, *Historia*, 1: 122–25, 207–25.

Chapter 1

1 Sternberg, *Geschichte der Juden in Polen*, pp. 4 ff.; Dubnow, *History of the Jews in Russia and Poland*, 1: 40; J. Lelewel, *Polska Wieków Srednich*, 2.
2 *JJLG* 5 (1909): 147.
3 During the second half of the eighteenth century some Polish Jewish authors used the themes of Jews "providing" the country with rain and of Polish Jews having been admitted to Poland after negotiation with rulers, before that country had a king. "Our fathers told us . . . that it was known to all nations that God responds to Jews . . . to send rain. . . . The Spanish kings . . . when admitting Jews made a condition that they were obliged to pray for rain when necessary." Another story tells about Jews coming to Poland, negotiating with the rulers, bringing in immense treasures, and lending 30 million zloty (*Tel Orot* 68b; Braver, *Galitzia*, p. 203). The legend about Jews being invited to Spain to prevent drought and lack of water there is told by a refugee from Spain around the end of the fifteenth century (Abraham Sebah, *Zeror Hamor* [Venice, 1566], p. 105; *IEN* 12, part 1: 3). Solomon ibn Virga tells about Jews in Spain (Toledo and elsewhere) being asked to cause it to rain, which they do through their prayers. Other sources tell about the obligation of the Jews to bring rain in Spain, or of their being forced to do so. See *Sepher Shebet Yehuda* of Solomon ibn Virga, ed. Azriel Shohat (Jerusalem, 1947), pp. 142, 158; A. Neubauer, *Medieval Jewish Chronicles* (*Anecdota Oxoniensia*, vol. 1, part 4, Oxford, 1887), pp. 141–42; see also S. Bernstein, *HUCA* 19 (Hebrew part): 5. It seems that in the eighteenth century, when problems of the future status of Jews in Poland became acute, some of the older

*References that are abbreviated in the Notes will be found in full in the list of abbreviations or in the Selected Bibliography.

(not necessarily Polish) Jewish legends were combined to establish a basis for past rights. Polish historians attempt at times to use legends for historical or pseudohistorical purposes of discovering the origins of Poles. See, for example, Kazimierz Slaski, *Watki Historyczne w podaniach o początkach Polski* [*Historical elements in the legends about the origins of Poland*] (Poznań, 1968). The Polish geographer Stefan Wojciechowski tries to argue on the basis of general considerations that Jews already lived in Lublin in the eleventh century and that their cemetery is much older than the sixteenth century. See his "Yidn in Lublin im sechzenten Jarhundert" (Yiddish), pp. 108–38.

4   Their names were Hiskiya Sephardi, Akiba Estremaduri, Immanuel Ascaloni, Natanel Barceloni, and Levi Baccari. According to the rendering by Lelewel, the first and third were from Palestine and the fourth from India.

5   *Phylacterium oder Argenton und Philo im Schosse der Wahren Glueckselligkeit* (Berlin, 1801), summarized in *Der Orient* 10 (1849): 143–44, 155–56, 159–60; see also Eisenstein, *Die Stellung,* p. 6.

6   See particulars, Weinryb, *Beginnings,* pp. 1–11. In 1868 a non-Jew (Smolka) used the story of the "Jewish king Abraham" to defend Jews in the Galician diet *(sejm)* and to demand equality for them. There is also another legend about a Jewish king in Poland (Saul Wohl, a son of the rabbi in Padua) in the second half of the sixteenth century, who allegedly was king for a day. In this case it could be ascertained that nomination by the king (in 1589) as his "servant," putting him under direct jurisdiction of the throne, apparently served as the basis for the legend (*see* Balaban, *Yidn in Poilen* pp. 17–38).

7   For the sources see Weinryb, *Beginnings,* pp. 51 ff.

8   A comprehensive study on this subject is found in ibid., pp. 11 ff. It also shows the fallacy of speculating about the existence of a Jewish community in Przemyśl in the eleventh century on the basis of a fragment of a responsum in which circumstance, date, and place-name are dubious, or of identifying the twelfth-century Hebrew place-name "Polia" with Poland, when the context shows clearly that it refers to Italy (Apulia or Pola or both on the Adriatic Sea opposite Venice) (pp. 20–21, 57–58). There, too, is to be found the source for what follows here, unless otherwise indicated.

9   The theories here are formulated on the basis of the approaches taken by most historians, summarized in part by Berlin, *Istoricheskiya,* pp. 52–58; J. Brutzkus, "Istoki Russkago Evreystva," *Evreyski Mir* (Paris, 1939), pp. 17 ff.; Balaban, "Kiedy i skąd przybyli Żydzi do Polski," pp. 1 ff.; F. Friedmann, "Der Onhoib fun dem Yidishn Yishuv in Mizrakh-Europa," *Yidisher Kemfer* 32, no. 900 (April 1951): 35–42; and others.

10   The place-names are Koziary, Kozary, Kozarki, Kozarcy, etc. and Kawiory. The latter is supposed to be a derivation from Kabaroi—the name of a Khazar tribe. See Moshe Altbauer, "Mechkaro shel Yitzhak Shiper al hayesod Hakuzri-Yehudi bamizrach Eropa," in *Sepher Yitzhak Shiper,* ed. S. Eidelberg (New York, 1967), pp. 47–58; idem in *Heaver* 8 (1961): 64. See Weinryb, *Beginnings,* passim, about the particulars; see there also the evaluation of some earlier notes supposedly mentioning Jews in Poland.

11   *Masaoth Benyamin,* ed. M.N. Adler (Oxford, 1907); *Sibbub Rabi Petachya* (London, 1858).

12   Aronius, nos. 360, 361, 364; 375, 408; these documents deal with gifts to church

institutions. About falsifications of documents attesting to gifts to churches and monasteries, including those in Breslau, see A. Malecki, *KH* 18 (1904): 1–15, 411–80, and especially 433 ff.; see also *MGWJ* 33: 545. See Brann, *Geschichte der Juden*, about a few places in Silesia; Rosenthal, "Najstarsze," p. 3. Still more doubtful is the attempt to identify a lost fragment of a headstone from Breslau as originating in 1174 (Israel Rabin, "Steine und Schicksale," *Breslauer Juedisches Gemeindeblatt*, no. 9 (1926), p. 126. The Rabbi Benjamin of Vladimir mentioned in 1171 in Cologne (Aronius, no. 304; A.M. Haberman, *Sepher Gezeroth Ashkenaz ve-Zorfath* [Jerusalem, 1954], p. 128; *Żródla*, pp. 271–72) may or may not have been from Vladimir in Volhynia (Aronius tries to identify it with Vallendar in Germany). Whatever place is meant, it surely does not show the existence of a Jewish community there as assumed in *Żródla*. See also L. Zunz, *Literaturgeschichte der synagogalen Poesie* (Berlin, 1865), p. 25.

13 Rutkowski, *Historia gospodarcza*, p. 28. Coins with Hebrew letters originated at this time also in Saxony (1180–1212) and in Wuerzburg (1207–1227); cf. Aronius, nos. 389, 425; *Responsa R. Meir ben R. Baruch me-Rothenberg* (Prague, 1608), no. 903; *Żródla*, pp. 38 ff.; Brann, *Geschichte der Juden*, p. 5; idem, *MGWJ* (1918): 97–107; Rosenthal, "Najstarsze." The bracteates have been found in a number of places and are in different collections. It seems that nobody has been able to examine and compare all of them. They have been identified as originating in the last two decades of the twelfth and during the thirteenth century. The Hebrew inscriptions are only partly legible, and only on some of them could meaningful words be identified, such as *beracha* = blessing, benediction, or *Meshko beracha* = blessing to Meshko, or *Meshko Krol polski* (Hebrew transliteration of Polish words) = Mieszko, Polish king. For particulars, see Gumowski, "Monety Hebraiskie za Piastów," pp. 1–44. Even as late as 1504 the Polish king, Alexander, allowed a Jewess (Rachel Fischel, mother-in-law of Rabbi Jacob Polak) to mint coins from her silver. The profits from this operation were to be applied to his debt to her (Schipper, *Wirtshaftsgeschichte*, p. 277).

14 *Or Zarua*, 4, Aboda Zara, no. 128; *Mahzor Vitri*, ed. Horwitz, no. 275, p. 243, introduction, p. 36; *Responsa Maharan me-Rotenberg*, no. 112; *Żródla*, pp. 159 ff. It should, however, be mentioned that the sources are preserved in a late manuscript only and may contain later insertions. Rabbi Jehuda Hachassid appears in this letter as a strict formalist with little regard for actual community practice, whereas otherwise his writings are regarded as being "at pains to make allowances for human weakness and to show every consideration for the conditions of life in the community" (G. Scholem).

15 For earlier centuries scarcely any such information exists. Rabbi Moses ben Jacob of Kiev in the twelfth century seems to have been from Bohemia and the much-quoted Hebrew author Rabbi Shmuel from Russia (twelfth century) is no more than a myth. See Weinryb, in *The Seventy-fifth Anniversary Volume of the Jewish Quarterly Review*, pp. 528–43; See also Huberbrand, "Żródla do historii Żydów," pp. 16–46.

16 Brann, *Geschichte der Juden*, passim. Balaban, *MZ* 1: 10; M.N. Litinski, *Sepher koroth Podolia ve-Kadmonioth Hayehudim sham* (Odessa, 1895), pp. 20–21; *Kodeks Wielopolski*, no. 574; *Kodeks dyplomatyczny Molopolski*, no. 60; Eisenstein, *Die Stellung*, p. 50; Aronius, nos. 678, 693, 674; Schipper—and with him also Eisenstein and others—in theorizing that the Cistercians' prohibition against settling Jews was

issued because the Jews were regarded as *servi camerae* and stood under the prince's jurisdiction is, at best, a speculation lacking any basis in fact. It was generally not uncommon at that time for princes to elucidate in their charters which groups should be settled.

17 The original text has not been preserved, but Casimir the Great of Poland, approving the Jewish privileges in Poland in 1334, signifies that he approves the Boleslas privilege of 1264. (The Casimir text and other privileges are extant in a collection made in 1506.)

18 Jakob of Liege (later Pope Urban IV) came as legate to Poland in 1248 and held a synod in Breslau. Another such synod met there in 1264. Cardinal Guido, who masterminded the synods in Breslau and Vienna in 1267, came to Silesia twice in the year, in February 1267 for the synod in Breslau and again in June to Ratibor (Silnicki, *Ustrój kościola,* pp. 312–13).

19 Aronius, nos. 724, 725. About the general attitudes of the church see Grayzel, *The Church and the Jews.* Recently an attempt has been made to infer the existence of a large Jewish population in Poland at that time from the fact that an undated and unsigned breve (attributed to Pope Clement IV) mentions five synagogues in one city. However, this piece is found in Marino de Ebulo's formular—prepared for use by scribes as models for writing documents and letters. Part of these "are taken from real documents, others are fictional" (F. Schillmann, *Die Formular-sammlung des Marinus von Eboli* [Rome, 1929], 1: 47, 49, 51, 298). This breve seems to belong to the latter category (*Analecta vaticana 1202–1366; Monumenta Polonia Vaticana,* vol. 3, [Cracow, 1914], no. 515; Adam Vetulani, "The Jews in Medieval Poland," *Jewish Journal of Sociology* 4 [1962]: 278, 288 ff.). Vetulani's further arguments about the synod of 1267, as well as his apologetics for the church's claim that segregation of Jews from Christians was meant to safeguard the Jews, which smacks of the Nazi arguments in the 1930s, are valueless.

20 "Kawiory"—from Hebrew *kever, kvorim.* The Jewish cemetery in Magdeburg is also referred to in the documents (c. 1300) as *kefer, keuer, keffer,* or *judenkever (MGWJ,* 1865, pp. 244–45); F. Pekosinski, *Kodeks dyplomatyczny Krakowa,* 1, no. 92; Schipper, *Wirtshaftsgeschichte,* p. 43; see also Altbauer in *Heavar* 8 (1961): 64.

21 Since the end of the thirteenth century German Jews had also been immigrating to Italy; see M. Shulwass, *YIVO Bleter* 36 (1950): 159 ff. From there they, as well as some Italian Jews, may have come to Poland. See also Matthias Mieses, *Die Yiddische Sprache* (Berlin-Vienna, 1924), though some of his "facts" seem to lack proof.

22 See M. Balaban, "Wen un fun wanen zenen di Yidn gekumen kein Poilen," *Bleter* 13 (1960): 21; however, the author's argument that the granting of privileges may indicate that the Jews came to Poland by invitation does not seem plausible.

23 Rosenthal, "Najstarsze," pp. 13, 26–27; A. Grotte, "Die Beeinflussung juedischer oestlicher Sakralkunst durch Prager Vorbilder," *Jahrb. d. Gesellschaft fuer Gesch. d. Juden in der Czechoslovakischen Republik* (1934), 6: 464; *HZK* 1: 72, 38; R. Wischnitzer, *YIVO Bleter* 29 (1947): 13 ff.; S. Salfeld, *Das Martyrelogium des Nuerenberger Memorbuches* (Berlin, 1898), pp. 69, 78, 83 ff., 282, 284, 268, 249, 99, 161, 273, 287, 153, 286; see also pp. 28, 163.

24 Isaac Tyrnau, *Sepher Haminhagim* (Riva di Trento, 1551, and many subsequent printings); L. Zunz, *Die Ritus des Synagogalen Gottesdienstes* (Berlin, 1859), pp. 73,

98 ff., 125, 135, 138 ff. On the other hand, Rabbi Moses Mintz, who came to Poznań from Germany in 1474, noted that marriage contracts and a few of the marriage ceremonies were somewhat different in Poland from those of the country from which he came (*Responsa of Moses Mintz* [Lwów, 1851], no. 109). Rabbi Isaac from Vienna (c. 1190–1260) mentions still earlier that the ritual "in the land of Kenaan" resembles that of the Rhine communities (*Or Zarua*, 2, no. 50). It is, however, uncertain what country he meant by Kenaan—it apparently meant Bohemia, not Poland.

25 Marian Malowist, *Kaffa-Kolonia Genueska na Krymie i problem Wschodni w latach 1453–1475* (Warsaw, 1947), p. 64. See also Bersohn, no. 393.

26 Freiburg 1401, 1424, 1435; Speyer 1405, 1435; Meissen 1411; Mayence 1420, 1438, 1462; Austria 1420/21, 1454, 1496; Saxony 1432; Gratz 1439; Augsburg 1440; Wuerzburg 1453, 1489; Erfurt 1458; Bamberg 1475, 1478; Mecklenburg 1492; Breslau and other Silesian cities 1453, 1454; Magdeburg 1492/93; Styria, Karintia 1496; Salzburg 1498; Wuerttemberg 1498; Nuremberg, Ulm, 1499; Glogau 1484, Bavaria 1450.

27 *JJLG* 4: 298 ff., 307, 317, 323; *Responsa Moses Mintz*, nos. 63–64, 177; *MZ* 1: 242; Myer S. Lew, *The Jews of Poland* (London, 1944), p. 17; Schipper, *Kulturgeschichte*, pp. 118–19, 257–58, 204, 182 ff.; idem, *Wirtshaftsgeschichte*, pp. 154 ff.; idem, *Toledoth ha-Kalkalah*, pp. 511 ff.

28 The table is based on the following materials: Rosenthal, "Najstarsze," pp. 3–27; Elazar Feldman, "Do statystyki Żydów w dawnej Polsce," *MZ* 3 (1933): 130–35; idem, "Di eltste yedies wegn yidn in poylishe shteyt in XIV–XVI Yurhundert," pp. 59–73; Aronius, nos. 678, 693, 674; Ettinger, "Helkam shel Hayehudim," pp. 116–18. Places of Jewish settlement in those centuries are also mentioned in Lewin, *Lissa*, p. 1; idem, *JJLG* 4 (1906): 298 ff.; 5 (1907): 2; Elizabeta Horn in *Biuletyn*, no. 40, pp. 5–6. Some of these may increase the totals in the table somewhat.

Chapter 2

1 The Boleslas privilege of 1264 has not been preserved. But the introduction to the privilege granted by Casimir the Great in 1334 claims that it is a confirmation of the one granted in 1264. Some Polish historians assert that the claim mentioned in the Casimir privilege is unjustified and regard the privilege of 1264 as a falsification. But this seems to have been disproved. The privileges were collected by J. Laski in 1506 *(Commune incliti regni Poloniae privilegim et indultum, etc.).* Some of the larger Jewish communities in Poland had copies of the privileges in their archives. In Poznań (Posen) the leaders of the community in 1793 submitted to the Prussian authorities copies of seven privileges, together with a German translation. A summary of the privileges confirmed by the last Polish kings, based on the earlier ones, was preserved by the Cracow Jewish community, which was also in possession of the earlier ones before they were destroyed during the Swedish invasion of 1655 (M. Schorr, "Krakovskii svod statutov i privilegii," *ES* 1, 1: 247–64; 1, 3: 76–100; 1, 4: 223–45; idem, "Zasadnicze prawa," pp. 191–99; Balaban in *ES* 2 (1910): 38–60, 161–91; Bloch, *Die General Privilegien;* see also Aronius, nos. 518, 147, 597, pp. 1–25; *REA* 1. The Karaites in Troki received (1441) the rights of the Magdeburg Law, which gave them similar autonomy to that of the burghers generally.

2 Balzer, *Sądownictwo Ormiańskie*, pp. 97, 112, 121, 139, 145.

3   It is only somehow indicated in clause 30, dealing with pawnbrokerage (taken from the Austrian-Bohemian privileges), which says: "A Christian who takes away his pledge from a Jew by force, or does violence in the latter's house, should be heavily punished as one who brings damage to our treasury" *(camera)*. Later, in the fourteenth century, this situation is more clearly indicated in the formulation of the privilege: "We reserve the Jews and their funds for the treasury" or "the Jews are our subjects and their funds should be held ready for our needs" (Bloch, *Die General Privilegien*, pp. 50, 58); see also Gumplowicz, *Prawodawstwo Polskie;* Schorr, *Rechstellung und innere Verfassung*, pp. 5 ff.; Bershadski, *Litovskie evrei*, pp. 173 ff.

4   Kisch, *The Jews*, pp. 146–68; Aronius, no. 496; see also S.W. Baron, "Plentitude of Apostolic Powers and Medieval 'Jewish Serfdom,'" *Sepher Yobel Layitzhaq Baer* (Jerusalem, 1961), pp. 102–24; idem, "Medieval Nationalism and Jewish Serfdom," *Studies and Essays in Honor of A. Neuman* (Leiden, 1962), pp. 17–48. Baron tries to connect the concept with the struggle between empire and papacy. See also Weinryb, *JSS* 35 (1963): 210–11.

5   Pawel of Brudzew Wlodkowicz (rector of the University of Cracow), *Tractatus de protestate papae et imperatoris infidilium*; see also Bartoszewicz, *Antysemityzm*, p. 11.

6   Bersohn, nos. 65, 250, 292, 300, 469, 525, and others; *REA* 3, no. 44 (the grantee was a convert to Christianity); see also Otto Stobbe, *Die Juden in Deutschland waehrend des Mittelalters in politischer, socialer und rechtlicher Beziehung* (Berlin, 1923), pp. 13 ff. about the use of a similar term in Germany with reference to certain officials.

7   See Brann, *Geschichte der Juden*, pp. 15 ff., 18 ff., 22 ff.; Rosenthal, "Najstarsze," passim; Aronius, no. 693.

8   Bersohn, nos. 3, 4, 9, 12, 13, 15, 23, 27, 28, 36, 40, 47. Similarly, tax and toll farmers had to double as "treasury officials," often paying the king's creditors or paying for delivery of goods to the court instead of directly to the treasury. *REA* 1, nos. 15, 17, 22, 28, 30, 103, 131, and others; L. Lewin, "Geschichte der Juden in Inowroclaw," *Zeitschrift der Historischen Gesellschaft für die Provinz Posen* 15 (1900): 91; Balaban, *ES* 2:58.

9   Berlin, *Istoricheskiya*, p. 184, and the documents quoted there.

10   *RIN* 1: 187, 186.

11   The Hebrew word *kiyumim* may mean either or both (*YS*, Babba Kama, ch. 6, par. 14). The case deals with the principle of *dina-demalkhuta dina* (the law of the kingdom is the law). This principle meant in practice that in cases where the rabbis did not recognize the state (king's) laws on account of their arbitrariness, the acquisition of such confiscated property by a Jew was also not recognized. Thus the rightful Jewish owner could demand its return from a fellow Jew through the Jewish court.

12   Trunk, *HS* 2:211; E. Ringelblum, in *Yinger Historiker* (1926), 1:76.

13   *REA* 1:62; Balaban, *Yidn in Poilen*, pp. 259–67. Jewish sources in Germany-Austria note a few incidents of participation of Jews in city defense there, but these seem to have been only exceptional cases. Generally, taking an oath as proof in court was a prerogative of freemen in the Middle Ages (Kisch, *The Jews*, p. 139).

14   Particulars and sources: Lewin, "The Protection of Jewish Religious Rights," pp. 11–15. The oath was taken by non-Jews in Poland either near the church or within the church on the cross (Bardach, *Historia*, 1:352).

15 The analysis here is made despite the opinions of many historians, too numerous to elucidate. Balaban seems to have felt the incongruity of the term *servi camerae* for the status of the Jews in Poland. He made a compromise: chamber serfdom existed in Poland, but in Lithuania this principle did not take root, although the Jew-privileges there had been modeled upon the Polish ones (*ES* 2:324).

16 Kutrzeba, "Stanowisko prawne," p. 100.

17 Bardach, *Historia,* 2:60.

18 The Fourth Lateran Council (1215) demanded that the Jews pay the tithe to the church. In Germany such demands were made but seldom enforced (cf., for instance, Aronius, no. 527); Grayzel, *The Church and the Jews,* pp. 36 ff. and passim.

19 It should be mentioned, however, that "mixed" cities often did defend their Jewish population against bodily attacks from outsiders. On several occasions—for instance during the late Crusades and the Chmielnicki uprising of 1648–49—Lwów and a few other cities refused to open the gates, preferring to pay a ransom to rescue their Jews (see below, chapters 8 and 9).

20 See William L. Langer, "The Next Assignment," *American Historical Review* 63, no. 2 (Jan. 1958): 298 ff.; Cohn, *The Pursuit of the Millennium;* Huizinga, *The Waning of the Middle Ages,* pp. 9 ff.; Bruno Bettelheim and Morris Janowitz, *Dynamics of Prejudice* (New York, 1950), pp. 33, 165, 174.

21 Cf. Schipper, *Kulturgeschichte,* pp. 90–92; *HZK* 1:30.

22 We did not include here the earlier persecutions of Jews in Silesia (the expulsion from Breslau in 1219 or 1226 and other attacks) because in the period covered by our tabulation—mid-fourteenth to fifteenth centuries—Silesia was largely no longer connected with Poland. There may have been persecution of Jews in Kalish (1368, 1383) but the information is scarcely trustworthy. Also, the listings in the table may not be strictly accurate; there may have been more or fewer occurrences. Thus, for instance, it is very questionable whether Jews were actually burned in Poznań in 1399 (Perles, *MGWJ* 13 [1864]: 286–88). Exact information is lacking, and what does exist is not always reliable. (A Silesian historian maintained that medieval chroniclers regarded famines, fires, and persecution of Jews as repetitive phenomena, which they reported in certain years without regard to whether they had really occurred or not; Brann, *Geschichte der Juden,* p. 7, note 2; cf. also ibid., p. 94.)

23 In the late Middle Ages the practice had developed of making a fire the cause for persecuting Jews, either on the charge of having started it or of not having helped to extinguish it. German rabbis from the thirteenth century and later were of the opinion that any fire was to be regarded as a direct danger to life and property of Jews in any locality (Isaac ben Moses from Vienna, *Or Zarua,* 2, no. 38; *Responsa Isserlein,* no. 58; *Mordecai zu Shabbat,* ch. 16, no. 393; *Tur Orach Chayin,* no. 334; cf. also Brann, *Geschichte der Juden,* p. 52, note 1).

24 The court proceedings lasted about two years and then apparently petered out without much action being taken (*HZK* 1:33–35).

25 Quoted in Ptaśnik, *Kultura,* p. 354; *Chronica Polonorum,* 1521, quoted in Schipper, *Kulturgeschichte,* pp. 116–17; see idem, *Toledoth ha-Kalkalah,* pp. 495–96.

26 Zhizń Kniazia, *A.M. Kurbskogo na Litve i na Volyni,* cited in S. Ettinger, *Zion* 20 (1955): 138–40; *RIN* 1, nos. 561, 564, 565, 626, 656, 682.

27 In the historical literature it is generally maintained that Jews paid very high taxes in

Poland during the Middle Ages. This assumption is based on an analogy with situations in later centuries or in other countries, or is based on an atypical case or two, not characteristic for Poland generally (Ringelblum, *Warszawa*, p. 23). There is nothing in the source material to substantiate such an assumption. Cf. also Baron, *A Social and Religious History*, 8:191 ff., about the small role of Jewish taxation in medieval Byzantium.

28   Full name, *stacyjne królewskie*—king's lodging.

29   Rutkowski, *Historia gospodarcza*, pp. 69–72; *Historia*, 1, part 1:537 ff.; 558 ff.

30   Schipper in *IEN*, pp. 107 ff., 301 ff.; idem, *Wirtschaftsgeschichte*, pp. 307 ff.; idem, in *ZPO* 1:201 ff.; Balaban, *ES* 2:55;Bardach, *Historia*, 1:308; Bersohn, nos. 3, 4, 9, 37, 396, 399.

31   A coronation tax was introduced in Poland only in the sixteenth century. In the course of litigation between some Polish nobles during the fourteenth and fifteenth centuries, mention is made of large sums allegedly paid by Jews (1373). Following the death of Casimir III the assistant chancellor was accused by another official of having squandered sixteen thousand marks which King Casimir had received from Jews. In 1428 a nobleman in Cracow was charged with appropriating for himself half a million florins —a tremendous amount for those times—which the Jews had delivered to the treasury (Eisenstein, p. 151). There is no information on the conduct of the cases; it is hard to say whether these accusations are pure myth based on rumors about the great wealth of the Jews, or contain some nucleus of truth—even though the actual amounts are gross exaggerations.

32   *REA* 3, nos. 36, 66, 78, 104, 130.

Chapter 3

1   B.D. Weinryb, "Prolegomena to an Economic History of the Jews in Germany in Modern Times," *Leo Baeck Institute Year Book* (1956), 1:294–95; Simon Kuznets, "Economic Structure and Life of the Jews," in *The Jews: Their History, Culture and Religion*, ed. L. Finkelstein, 3d ed. (New York, 1960), 2:1,600 ff.

2   Maciejowski, *Żydzi*, p. 50.

3   The privileges were patterned upon those in Austria-Bohemia and therefore may not reflect the situation in Poland. In addition, moneylending transactions apparently need more regulations and documentation than trade. The privilege of 1264 has thirteen paragraphs dealing with moneylending and one or two connected with trade. A similar emphasis on moneylending is observable in the privileges of the fourteenth century. The only exception is the one granted to the Jews in Grodno, Lithuania, in 1389. The emphasis in that case is also on trade, handicrafts, and agricultural pursuits (*see* Bershadski, *Litovskie evrei*, pp. 238 ff.; *REA* 1, no. 2). But the value of this (and other privileges that are normative in character) as a document mirroring reality may be greatly diminished if one takes into account the fact that only a year earlier Jews in Brest Litovsk, in Lithuania, received a privilege that is almost a copy of the other Polish privileges with the emphasis on moneylending. It is not altogether impossible that the clerks, writing documents in the formal office Latin rather than the more familiar vernacular, often simply copied from existing models (formularies) with little regard for the text's appropriateness to the specific circumstances.

4   An attempt to identify some recorded loans by Jews of the fourteenth century as being

credits granted by a seller to a buyer seems to be unfounded (Eisenstein, *Die Stellung,* pp. 127 ff.).

5   Rutkowski, *Historia gospodarcza,* p. 67; see also Brann, *Geschichte der Juden,* p. 37; Ringelblum, *Warszawa,* p. 93. In Western Europe in the fourteenth century interest ranged from 5–25 percent for commercial loans, 15–50 percent for loans to princes (sometimes 80 percent), and 15–173 percent for personal loans. In the following century interest on commercial and personal loans fell to 5–15 percent and 6–43½ percent, respectively, while on loans to princes it apparently remained high; Sidney Homer, *A History of Interest Rates* (New Brunswick, 1963), pp. 103, 110.

6   Eisenstein, *Die Stellung,* pp. 133, 134, 135 ff.; 141–42; Schipper, *Wirtschaftsgeschichte,* pp. 78 ff.; *HZK* 1:9 ff., 13ff.

7

	No. of Lenders	No. of Borrowers
Nobles	1,395	1,436
Christian city dwellers	117	16
Clergymen	38	16
Independent peasants	17	38
Jews	9	3

(M. Ungeheuer, *Stosunki kredytowe w ziemi przemyskiej w polowie XV w.* (Lwów, 1929), cited in Mark, *Di geschichte,* p. 277; see also *Historia,* 1, part 1:519 ff.).

8   *HZK* 1:13–25, 38–39; Schipper, *Toledoth ha-Kalkalah,* pp. 524–39; Ringelblum, *Warszawa,* pp. 11, 22 ff., 71–99, 36; Trunk in *HS* 2:218, 221 ff.; idem, *Shtudies,* p. 14; H.M. Gelber, "Letoldot Yehudei Hrubieshov," in *Pinkas Hrubieszov,* ed. Baruch Kaplinski (Tel Aviv, 1962), pp. 28–29; idem, in *Sepher Luck,* p. 22; idem, editor, *Lvuv, Encyclopedia shel Galuyot* 4 (Jerusalem–Tel Aviv, 1956): 26. Schipper, *Wirtshaftsgeschichte,* p. 68, contains a table of loans made by Jews to the city of Breslau during the first half of the fourteenth century.

9   Figures from Poznań indicate the appearance of some non-Jewish moneylenders, an increase in the number of Jewish moneylenders and bankers up to 1464, and a sharp decline after that—possibly also due to a fire that year which may have destroyed promissory notes (Leon Koczy, "Studja nad dziejami gospodarczemi Żydów Poznańskich przed polową w.XVII," *Kronika miasta Poznania* 12 (1933): 279–91.

10 Many a historian concludes from the fact that Jews turned debtors (in the sixteenth century) that they had become poorer, and therefore had to borrow. Jewish sources of the time indicate that this was connected with prosperity and the fact that they were developing larger enterprises.

11 See A. Eisenstein, *MZ,* no. 11 (1933); B. Mark, *Biuletyn,* nos. 9–10 (1954), p. 9; Ringelblum, *Warszawa,* pp. 72–92.

12 Bershadski, *Litovskie evrei,* pp. 246 ff., 255 ff.; Schipper, *Toledoth ha-Kalkalah,* pp. 501 ff.; J. Goldberg, *Stosunki agrarne w miastach ziemi Wieluńskiej w drugiej polowie XVII i XVIII w.* (Łódź, 1960); *REA* 1:28, 32, 36.

13 Pounds, *Eastern Europe,* p. 143.

14 In Silesia also some Jews were lending money on real estate, and others owned property, in the fourteenth to fifteenth centuries.

15 M. Guthertz in *Yedios fun Yidishen Historishen Institut in Poilen,* November 1951

(Warsaw); L. Landsberger in *Zeitschrift für die Geschichte der Juden in Deutschland* 5 (1892): 390–92; *HZK* 1:27–28.

16 Schipper, *Wirtschaftsgeschichte*, pp. 292–306.

17 Herbert Heaton, *Economic History of Europe* (New York, 1948), pp. 159, 46; *Historia*, 1, part 1:463; Bershadski, *Litovskie evrei*, pp. 245–46. See also a list of tax farmers in Schipper, *Toledoth ha-Kalkalah*, pp. 522–23.

18 See, for instance, *REA* 1, nos. 10, 11, 13, 14, 15, 17, 21, 22, 24, 44; *REA* 3, nos. 3–4, 30, 33, 16–19, 24, 26, 32, 34, 43, 56; Bersohn, nos. 386, 389, 390–94, 398, 402, 404, 405, 408, 416, 125, 430.

19 Schipper, *Toledoth ha-Kalkalah*, pp. 520–24. The table on pp. 222–23 contains over thirty names of such entrepreneurs (up to the year 1500). A few others are mentioned as leaseholders of mines.

20 Quoted in Ptaśnik, *Kultura*, p. 354; see also *REA* 3, nos. 3, 4.

21 Rosenthal, "Najstarsze," passim; *HZK* 1: 26; Ringelblum, *Warszawa*, p. 49.

22 D. Goldberg-Feldman in *Bleter* 1(1934): 51 ff. *Responsa Joseph Kolon*, no. 184.

23 Brann, *Geschichte der Juden*, p. 23; *HZK* 1:39. In the struggle to eliminate Jews from the retail sale of foodstuffs, particularly meat, noneconomic rationales were used. These range from the contention that the Jews might poison Christians (resolution of the Breslau church synod in 1267) to the assertion that Christians should not eat meat which Jews regard as unclean (nonkosher).

24 Gelber, ed., *Lvuv*, p. 30: Schipper, *Wirtschaftsgeschichte*, pp. 255–56.

25 Some historians maintain that there were many Jewish artisans in Poland in the Middle Ages. They rely on a Latin pamphlet allegedly written by Jews in 1539, which says that at that time the number of Jewish artisans in Poland was 9,600, three times as many as in business. But all the information concerning the pamphlet comes from Czacki, *Rozprawa*, and Czacki is hardly reliable. Besides, it is highly unlikely that Jews would counteract the violent assaults on Jewish trade and other economic activities with an "apology" claiming that there were almost no Polish artisans and only about 500 merchants (or storekeepers), whereas the Jews had 3,200 merchants and three times as many artisans. This argument might have fitted into a seventeenth-century Western or Italian climate of mercantilism, but not that of backward Poland at the beginning of the sixteenth century. One may even surmise that if such a pamphlet really existed, which is very doubtful, it was an anti-Jewish fabrication rather than a Jewish apologia (see *HZK* 1: 211, 124 ff., 135–36). Bershadski (*Litovskie evrei*, pp. 83 ff.) tries to prove that Czacki's information is incorrect. See, however, Schipper, *Toledoth ha-Kalkalah*, pp. 541–42; idem, *Wirtschaftsgeschichte*, pp. 232 ff.; see also Brann, *Geschichte der Juden*, p. 59; Ringelblum, *Warszawa*, pp. 102 ff.; Mark in *Biuletyn*, nos. 9–10 (1954), pp. 5 ff.

26 See Henryk Samsonowicz, *Rzemioslo wiejskie w Polsce XIV–XVI w.* (Warsaw, 1954); *AYZR* 7, part 1, pp. 171; part 2, p.34.

27 Brann, *Geschichte der Juden*, passim.

28 Ringelblum, *Warszawa*, pp. 102–3.

29 Brann, *Geschichte der Juden*, pp. 37, 59 ff.

Chapter 4

1   See Baron, *The Jewish Community*, 1:22, 31 ff.; L. Finkelstein, *Jewish Self-government in the Middle Ages* (1924); Weinryb, *Texts*, pp. 4 ff.; Y.F. Baer, "Kavey yesod bahitpatchutah hahistorith shel hayahaduth bimey habeynayim," *Moznayim* 23 (1947): 304, 306; idem, *Zion* 15 (1950): 1–41.

2   Baechtold, *Süedwestrussland*, pp. 25 ff., 55 ff., and passim; Balzer, *Sądownictwo Ormiańskie;* idem, *Statut Ormianski w zatwierdzeniu Zygmunta I* [c. 1519] (Lwów, 1910).

3   Rabinowitz, *The Herem Hayishub*, pp. 15 ff.; H.J. Zimmels, *Beitraege zur Geschichte der Juden in Deutschland im 13. Jahrhundert insbesondere auf Grund d. Gutachten des R. Meir . . . Rothenburg* (Vienna, 1926), pp. 37 ff., 98 ff.; Baron, *The Jewish Community*, 2:4 ff.; Shlomo Eidelberg, *Jewish Life in Austria in the XVth Century* (Philadelphia, 1962), pp. 61 ff. and passim; M. Frank, *Kehiloth Ashkenaz u-batey dinahem* (Tel Aviv, 1937); *Responsa Moses Mintz*, no. 80; see also Baron, *PAAJR* 12 (1942): 34 ff.

4   See *Responsa J. Weil* (Cremona, 1557; Kapost, 1835), nos. 73, 173, 214; *PK*, nos. 214, 175, 174, 252, 253; A. Aptowitzer, *Introductio ad Sefer Rabiah* (Jerusalem, 1938), p. 454; *Responsa Israel Bruna* (Jerusalem, 1960), nos. 86, 87; *Responsa Joseph Kolon*, no. 170. See also Ben-Sason, *Zion* 27 (1962): 166–98; *SH*, nos. 1340, 1343–46.

5   Most of the writings dealing with Jewish community organization in Poland concentrate on the later centuries, beginning with the sixteenth century, for which enough sources—general and Jewish—are available to give a complete picture. By implication if not explicitly historians indicate that the same situation existed, or must have existed, earlier. This writer does not believe that this approach is proper methodologically. Before the fifteenth to sixteenth centuries the organizational form was apparently uncomplicated and barely established.

6   Rosenthal, "Najstarsze," pp. 14–15; Brann, *Geschichte der Juden*, pp. 31–32; *HZK* 1:6; M. Balaban, *Zabytki historyczne Żydów w Polsce* (Pisma Instytutu Nauk Judaistycznych w Warsawie) (Warsaw, 1929), pp. 48–49; Gelber, *Lvuv*, pp. 29, 345. The privileges (the Boleslas privilege of 1264 and those of the fourteenth century) speak of Jewish cemeteries and synagogues, but it is not clear whether they mean already existent ones or future ones.

7   Rosenthal, "Najstarsze," passim; Brann, *Geschichte der Juden*, pp. 32, 34 ff., 58–60, 70, 89; *HZK* 1:4 ff., 16 ff.

8   In Warsaw, too, the prince (1469) forbade the Jews to seek advice from foreign Jewish authorities. These restrictions may have been intended to avoid quarrels and controversies (in Schweidnitz the statute followed a prolonged internal struggle). Or they may have been in imitation of a general trend in Poland opposing dependence upon foreigners (in 1356 in Poland the burghers were forbidden to apply to the Magdeburg court for decisions).

9   Brann, *Geschichte der Juden*, pp. 70–72.

10 Ibid., pp. 89 ff., 70 ff.; *HZK* 1: 40 ff., 47, 230 ff.; Ringelblum, *Warszawa*, pp. 108 ff.; see also Schipper, *Kulturgeschichte*, pp. 128 ff.; idem, *YIVO Bleter* 5 (1933): 62 ff.

11 *PK*, nos. 73, 144, 126–28; *HZK* 1:70 ff.; *Responsa Israel Bruna*, no. 253 (254); *Responsa Jacob Weil*, no. 155; P. Bloch, *MGWJ*, 1903, pp. 348–49.

Chapter 5

1 This attempt to draw a composite picture of the Polish Jew is based on Max Weber's approach of an "ideal-type" picture. It contains a configuration of the characteristics most often observed in specimens of the group; not all characteristics need to be present in any one example. It is impossible, of course, to recapture fully the factual and emotional climate of that period, but we may reconstruct some of the general lines. The material for this chapter is drawn from a variety of sources, non-Jewish as well as Jewish, some originating in countries outside of Poland. Jewish source material about Poland prior to the end of the fifteenth century is hardly available. In some cases information from the sixteenth century is relied upon (when it is believed that a more or less similar situation existed earlier).

2 There exists a "Slavic school" that maintains that Jews in Poland and other Slavic countries originally spoke Polish or some other Slavic language. This school seems to have begun with Abraham Eliyahu Harkavy's Russian study "Ob jazyke evreev zhivshich v drevnee vremya na Rusi i o slovyanskich slovakh vstrechayemykh u evreyskikh pisateley," in *Trudy Vostochnago otdeleniya imperatorskago Russkago arkheologicheskago obshchestva* 14 (1865), which was reworked into a little Hebrew book *Hayehudim u-Sefat Haslavim* (1867). He was followed by a number of others (Bershadski, *Litovskie evrei;* R. Centnerszowa, *O jezyku Żydów w Polsce na Litwie i Rusi* [Warsaw, 1907]; Ben-Zion Rubinstein, *Di antshtayung un antviklung fun der yidisher Shprach* [Warsaw, 1922]; and others). Simon Dubnow refuted this contention for the sixteenth century in "Razgovornyi yazyk i narodnaya literatura polsko-litovskich evreyev v XVI i pervoy polovine XVII v," *ES* 1 (1909): 7–40. See also Moshe Altbauer, "Sh. Dubnov al leshon hadibur shel Yehuday mizrach Eropa," *Heavar*, ḥoveret S. Dubnov, 1961, pp. 60–64. One could now add some proof for the fifteenth century. In Warsaw a fifteenth-century translation into Yiddish of a few verses of Jeremiah has been preserved.

  Generally the fact that some Jews knew or spoke Russian or Polish is no proof of the existence of a Jewish Slavic vernacular. Nor is the existence of any such vernacular proven by certain Slavic glosses in Hebrew writings, or by Slavic names borne by Jews. Slavic glosses were also used in the later centuries when we know for sure that the Jews spoke Yiddish, and the Slavic names are not internal Jewish ones but those that non-Jewish scribes used sometimes when translating Hebrew or Yiddish names into Slavic. See now about the whole problem, Moshe Altbauer, *Achievements and Tasks in the Field of Jewish-Slavic Language Contact, Studies* (Paper delivered to the International Conference on "Jews and Slavs" held at the University of Los Angeles in March 1972) (Jerusalem, 1972).

3 G.S. Salisbury, *Street Life in Medieval England.* 2d ed. (Oxford, 1948), pp. 77, 90 ff.; see also *Historia*, 1, part 2:164.

4 *Historia*, 1, part 1: 398 ff., 530 ff.; Ptaśnik, *Miasta*, pp. 455 ff., 463, 470, 484 ff., 492–93; *HZK* 1:67, 69, 72, 96; *KH* 29 (1925): 336.

5 Ringelblum, *Warszawa*, pp. 135–37; Schipper, *Kulturgeschichte*, p. 214.

6 Brann, *Geschichte der Juden*, p. 114, note 3; *PK* nos. 69, 144.

7 B.D. Weinryb, "Kitei Kitvey Yad Ivriyim shel Yehuday Shlezya basof yemei habanayim," *KS* 14 (1937): 112–17; Ringelblum, *Warszawa*, pp. 123–26. It should be

pointed out that among all the fragments found there are only one or two from a daily prayer book.

8   Rabbi Jehuda Hachassid and Rabbi Eliezer ben Joel Halevi (twelfth to thirteenth century) imply that when traveling, Jews donned non-Jewish attire so that they would not be recognized. This indicates that at home they wore some sort of Jewish dress (Aptowitzer, *Introductio ad Sefer Rabiah*, pp. 450–51; *SH*, pp. 202–5, 240; Kisch, *The Jews*, pp. 295–99).

9   Schipper (*Kulturgeschichte*, pp. 221–22) quotes from a manuscript of a document given by the king to Jews in 1534, granting them the right to wear "usual clothing as until now" and not to be forced to wear any kind of special distinctive clothes. See also *HZK* 1: 87. If this document is genuine and Schipper quotes it properly, it will show that during the Middle Ages there was in Poland no "Jewish hat," etc.

10   F. Kopera, *Średniowieczne malarstwo w Polsce* (Cracow, 1925), pp. 5, 7, 9, 195, 198 cited in Schipper, *Kulturgeschichte*, pp. 215–18; Jacob b. Yichaq Halevi Polak, *Vayakum Eduth Bayaakov; HZK* 1: 85–86; Ringelblum, *Warszawa*, p. 137 (here and later some sixteenth-century materials are used in matters in which it seems safe to assume that they had hardly changed since the preceding century).

11   See also B.D. Weinryb in *PAJHS* 46 (March 1957): 378, 391.

12   See also *Darkey Moshe*, Yoreh Dea, 23, 4.

13   In Kazimierz there remained an illustrated manuscript of the Bible, written in the fourteenth century for a Regensburg community leader. This later came to Tyrnau near Pressburg and in 1494 to Cracow (*HZK* 1: 84).

14   See Eliade, *Cosmos and History*, pp. viii, 21, 28, 34.

15   *Responsa Moses Mintz*, nos. 109, 124.

16   *Mahzor Vitri*, p. 243; *Responsa Israel Bruna* (Stettin, 1860), no. 55. This is written to Cracow, but he mentions that in Poznań there are learned men (ibid., nos. 26, 50).

17   *Responsa Gevuroth Anashim* of Meir Katz (Sudzilkov, 1819), p. 26; *Responsa Benjamin Solnik*, no. 62.

18   Ringelblum in YIVO *Philological Series* 1 (1926): 334–35. It should be mentioned, however, that the toponym Russia used in those centuries may also mean countries or localities other than Russia in Eastern Europe; see Weinryb, "The Myth of Samuel of Russia," pp. 528–43.

19   Mann, *Texts and Studies*, 2: 707.

20   In 1420 (or thereabouts) Rabbi Yom Tov Lipmann Muehlhausen may have resided for a while in Cracow; possibly he wrote one of his works there. (He apparently came there as a refugee from Bohemia.) The period of his residence in Cracow must have been very short; at any rate he had no known impact upon the Jews in Cracow. See also Jehuda Kaufman, *R. Yom Tov Lipman Milhausen* [Hebrew](New York, 1927). By the middle of the century Poznań had a rabbi who originally came from Germany or Silesia.

21   His activity as described reminds one of the "reverends" of nineteenth-century America. The material is related in *Responsa Jacob Weil* (Hanau, 1680), nos. 85, 128; *PK*, no. 255; Brann, *Geschichte der Juden*, p. xlv. Rabbi Israel Isserlein, however, states there generally that "many are authorized [to judge] but only a few know [the law]."

22   The Cracow Hebrew document was preserved in Cracow archives together with a Latin translation. The Hebrew text was published by Wettstein, *Mipinkasey*, pp. i–ii,

reproduced in I. Halperin, ed., *Beth Yisrael Bapolin* 1 (1948): 16. On Rabbi Moses ben Jacob of Kiev, see Berlin, *Istoricheskiya*, pp. 192 ff.; Mann, *Texts and Studies*, 2: 700 ff. Rabbi Moses Mintz (rabbi in Posen from 1474–1508) left responsa, but they originate mostly from the time when he was rabbi in Germany. Only two concern Poland. The preserved question in *LY* is by Abraham from Poland. He was either a native of Poland or an immigrant. The responsa are found in *TH* and *Responsa Israel Bruna*.

23   An Isaac from Russia or Poland, and a Mordechai from Poland are mentioned in a commentary to the Bible, written about the middle of the thirteenth century in Bohemia or Germany, as having transmitted certain traditions to the author. A Moses from Kiev is supposed to have heard some halakhic decision from Rabenu Tam (died 1171). These may have been either young people from Poland (Russia?) who went to the West to study or emigrants from Poland to the West, or even Western travelers to Poland or Russia—people who traveled to a certain country were sometimes nicknamed or called by the name of that country. For the second half of the fourteenth century we know positively that a young man from Russia or Red Russia (Asher ben Sinai) came to Toledo for the purpose of studying with Rabbi Asher ben Yechiel (died 1397). But from the deliberation of the case in connection with a deserted woman *(agunah)* this seems to have been an exceptional case. To this group may also belong Judah Obernik, a student of Rabbi Israel Isserlein who became rabbi in Italy; (*Kerem Chemed* 7: 68–71; Zunz, *Zu Gesch. und Literatur*, 80; *Sepher Hayashar le-Rabenu Tam*, par. 552; A. Epstein, *MGWJ* 40: 134; 13: 387; Berlin, *Istoricheskiya*, pp. 171–74; *Kelaley Harosh*, par. 51, 11; see also *Responsa Joseph Kolon* (Sudzilkow, 1834), no. 184. It should be mentioned, however, that the toponym Russia used in those centuries may mean also other countries or localities than Russia in Eastern Europe (see Weinryb, "The Myth of Samuel of Russia," pp. 528–43).

24   Mann, *Texts and Studies*, 2: 698–99, 1140–41, 1143, 1147. The information about learned Jews and Karaites in Kiev in a letter dated 1481 from Constantinople, which reads: "[I was told] about the rabbinite and Karaite communities in Kiev who are learned" may be a result of the custom in those days of complimenting the addressee; or it may be based on hearsay (ibid., 1173; see also Berlin, *Istoricheskiya*, pp. 173, 190).

25   *LY* 1: 62–63; *PK* 60.

26   Rabbi Solomon Luria tells about Moses Mintz; see also *YS* Hulin, ch. 1, par. 36, 39, 6.

27   The book, *Shoshan Sodoth*, by Moses of Kiev, was published posthumously (Koretz, 1784). The passage containing this information is on pp. 67, 2 ff. In rabbinic literature of the fifteenth century there is a good deal about Jews in Germany-Austria gambling (dice and cards), stealing, and indulging in sexual license; *TH* 209, 267, 315; *PK* 29, 192, etc.; *Sam Hayim* of Abraham Ashkenazi, quoted in Zinberg in YIVO *Filologishe Shriften* 3: 179–80.

28   *Responsa Israel Bruna*, nos. 265, 264, 266. The one murderer who did not seek penance lost his citizen's rights in the Jewish community—he was declared unfit to be a witness and for some other functions. Transferring a transgressor or killer to general non-Jewish justice might have caused undue trouble or even danger—non-Jewish crowds tended to gather at a hanging and could attack Jews; or the culprit might be persuaded to convert to Christianity and become an informer against Jews.

Such a one was thus usually left alone except that his rights in the kehilla were limited. In some cases, however, he was put to death—either directly or by being turned over to the authorities. The contention that these responsa concern Loewenberg in Silesia (Brann, p. lxi) rather than Lemberg in southern Poland is invalidated by the fact that they emphasize the connection of Lemberg with Poznań. Rabbi Israel Bruna even suggests that the "learned of Posen" have the right to increase or decrease the penance that he prescribes. By the fifteenth century Silesia was part and parcel of Bohemia, and Polish communities such as Posen (Poznań) had no jurisdiction over it.

29 Ringelblum, *Warszawa*, pp. 117 ff., 133; Trunk, *Shtudies*, p. 221; Bershadski, *Litovskie evrei*, pp. 362 ff.; Schipper, *Kulturgeschichte*, pp. 235–36; Warschauer, *Stadtbuch von Posen* (Posen, 1892), pp. 333–39; Ptaśnik, *Kultura*, pp. 266 ff.; *REA* 3, nos. 115–19.

30 Brann, *Geschichte der Juden*, p. 22; *HZK* 1: 20, 44–52.

31 About quarrels in Breslau in the fifteenth century, see *Responsa Jacob Weil*, no. 146; see also *Responsa Israel Bruna*, no. 253.

32 *HZK* 1: 66 ff. In Jewish sources his rabbinical post is not mentioned; he appears there only as head of a yeshivah.

33 *HZK* 1: 67 ff., 101–12; *REA* 3, nos. 64, 81, 104, 98, 109, 121, 122, 147–48; Bersohn, nos. 450, 451, 455, 454, 492, 505.

34 *REA* 3, nos. 54, 61, 67; Bersohn, nos. 411, 412, 413; *HZK* 1: 82 ff. See Zimmels, *Ashkenazim and Sephardim*, pp. 282, 160 ff., about the claim of the Sephardim to be descendants of the nobility of Jerusalem and the differences in their matrimonial customs.

35 *Responsa Solomon Luria*, no. 94; idem, *YS* Hulin, ch. 8, 22.

36 This would explain the glosses on the mentioned fifteenth-century fragments of documents in Warsaw, which translate (or transliterate) into Hebrew names and expressions.

37 Trunk, *HS* 2:218–19; Ringelblum, *Warszawa*, pp. 130–31.

38 *HZK* 1: 81.

39 *HZK* 1: 87–92; Bershadski, *Litovskie evrei*, pp. 358 ff., 366, 368, 375, 381, 395 ff., 397 ff., 411 ff.; *REA* 3, no. 44; 1, nos. 185, 242, 195, 255, 290; 2, nos. 229, 277, and passim.

40 *RIN* 1, no. 641.

41 See Bernard E. Olson, *Faith and Prejudice* (1963), pp. 122 ff., 164 ff., about the residues of this concept even today.

42 Formulated clearly by Yehuda Halevi in the twelfth century. See also Katz, *Exclusiveness and Tolerance*, pp. 13–14.

43 Rabbi Solomon Luria, for instance, emphasizes the danger from non-Jews to which Jews in certain situations were exposed: *YS* Babba Kama, chs. 6, 26; 8, 59; 10, 21, 23; see also ibid., 8, 65. German rabbis in the fifteenth century were apparently struggling with the inconsistency between the facts of human relations between Jew and non-Jew and the halakhic tradition, whereas in Poland the rabbis seem to have been stricter (see *Responsa Israel Bruna*, nos. 52, 112, 202; *YS* Babba Kama, 8: 48, 4: 18, 10: 19; see also Jacob Katz, *Massorah Umashber* (Jerusalem, 1958), pp. 28 ff.

44 See also Brann, *Geschichte der Juden*, p. 57, note 1; *Responsa Solomon Luria*, nos. 11, 12.

45 Particulars are found in *HZK* 1:19–23, 68 ff.; Schipper, *Wirtschaftsgeschichte*, pp. 114 ff., 117, 187, and passim; Brann, *Geschichte der Juden*, pp. xvi, xxviii, xxix.

46 See Zeev W. Falk, *Nisuim u-Gerushin. Tikunim badiney hamishpacha bi-Yahadut Ashkenaz ve-Zorfat* (Jerusalem, 1961), pp. 18–31, 98 ff.

47 *SH*, nos. 44–45, 49, 69–70, 798, 1093–1100, 1102–7, 1110–11, 1131–32, 1134, 1136, 1141. Sephardic (Spanish-Portuguese) Jewry resorted to concubinage and the keeping of prostitutes. Sephardic Jewry also practiced polygamy and were more lenient about compulsory divorce. See Zimmels, *Ashkenazim and Sephardim*, pp. 166 ff., 254 ff., 257 ff. In Polish non-Jewish society of the fifteenth century we find complaints about harlots and adultery and defense of prostitution as the lesser evil. See Ptaśnik, *Kultura*, pp. 417–18.

48 *YS* and *Responsa Solomon Luria*, nos. 14, 24, 25, 32, 41, 45, 55, 69, 99.

49 For example, the wife and daughter of Levko of Cracow. See Brann, *Geschichte der Juden*, pp. xvi, xviii-xx, xxv-xxvii, xxix, xxxi, xxiv; *HZK* 1: 15, 21, 59, 106 ff., 110; *REA* 3, no. 122.

50 *Responsa Solomon Luria*, no. 99; Brann, *Geschichte der Juden*, pp. lxix-lxx.

51 Huizinga, *The Waning of the Middle Ages*, p. 94; see also pp. 77, 67.

52 We use here the extant headstones found in cemeteries, mainly in Silesia, a few existing Hebrew documents and responsa of Western rabbis, the *Sepher Hassidim* of the group around Rabbi Jehuda Hachassid (assuming that he, both directly and through his disciples, had an influence on Polish Jewry), and the few existing books written in the fifteenth century.

53 "Studied Torah day and night" is the phrase that appears.

54 Brann, *Geschichte der Juden*, pp. 102–4, lxviii-lxix; *Responsa Jacob Weil*, no. 53; see also no. 125 (Brann assumes that the question concerns the documents signed by Jekutiel [or Jekussiel], but the responsum seems to indicate otherwise). It is not impossible that this Jekussiel was identical with the "Kussel from Kalish" who brought a debtor to court in Silesia for nonpayment of a promissory note; Kisch, *The Jews*, pp. 229, 249, 258, 493.

55 *Responsa Moses Mintz*, no. 109, end; see also no. 114.

56 Rabbi Moses Mintz, rabbi in Poznań after 1474, points out (responsum no. 79) that "most of the testaments of Rabbi Jehuda Hachassid that did not spread are void." He may have meant Poland. See also Ben-Sason, *Hagut*, p. 12; *SH*, p. 28; *TH*, no. 131.

57 *SH*, nos. 2, 10, 21, 38, 29–32, 39, 43, 63, 138, 1292, 1300–1, 44–47, 49, 50, 51, 53, 55, 57–59, 61, 64, 69–71, 74, 78, 80, 83, 86–7, 89, 92–98, 102–3, 105–6, 118–19, 123, 136, 138, 151, 331, 335, 424, 555, 591, 879, 861, 984, 986, 978–80, 987, 1979, 1049, and many others. See also Y.F. Baer, "The Religious-Social Theory of 'Sepher Hassidim,' " *Zion* 3 (1937): 1–50; Scholem, *Major Trends*, pp. 80–118. These writings have been utilized here, but the overly idealistic approaches of the authors disregarded.

58 Study of Talmud was also emphasized by Rabbi Jehuda Hachassid, *SH*, no. 774.

59 Also among the manuscripts he left is a cabalistic work, *Shoshan Sodoth* (partly published posthumously in 1784).

Chapter 6

1 Janusz Tazbir, *Nietolerancja wyznaniowa i wygnanie Arian* (Warsaw, 1957).

2 Polish historiography generally regards the mid-seventeenth century catastrophe as a

turning point in Polish history, although some of the newer works emphasize that certain signs of decline were observable even before that. Jewish historiography has usually followed the same line of emphasis upon this as a catastrophe. Ukrainian as well as Russian historians of the last few decades have emphasized the value of the Chmielnicki revolt, with its goal of independence or else unity of the Ukraine with Russia, as a national revolutionary movement, and they are at pains to minimize the destruction and devastation that followed in the wake of this "progressive movement."

3   The figures used in this chapter are from *Historia*, 1, part 2: 616 ff. and passim unless otherwise indicated.

4   From Brandenburg, Berlin, and Frankfurt on the Oder in 1510 and 1573, Saxony in 1514, Erlangen in 1515, Bohemia in 1517, Regensburg in 1519, parts of Silesia in 1527, Bayreuth in 1528 and 1569, Ansbach in 1560–61, Brunswick in 1557 and 1590, and so on.

5   See Bersohn, nos. 450, 455, 454, 492, 505; *HZK* 1: 97–98.

6   C. Shmeruk, "Bachurim me-ashkenaz bi-yeshivoth Polin," *Sepher Yobel La-Yitzchak Baer* (Jerusalem, 1960), pp. 304–17, and the materials quoted there. However, his contention that these young people came with the intention of settling in Poland is rather farfetched. The few instances quoted are not sufficient for such a generalization. Occasional marriages and settlement were rather a result of, than a reason for, coming to study in Polish yeshivot.

7   Harry Lionel Shapiro, *The Jewish People: A Biological History* (Paris, 1960).

8   Particulars and documentation appear below, Appendix 3.

9   It is possible that the larger size of the family in the village than among the total Jewish population in the census of 1764 (3.5–4.7 against about 3.6 for the total) is at least in part a result of the higher survival rate in the village (see Mahler, *Yidn in Zifern*, pp. 33, 55).

10 Particulars about the figures and population trends are to be found in Appendix 3.

11 *RIN* 2, nos. 372, 984, 1365, 1498, 1469, 1337, 1197, 1185, 1563. V. Antonowich, *Monografiya po istorii Zapadnoy Rosii*, 1: 189; P. Mark in *Voskhod* 6 (1903): 17; see also Dinur, *Ba-mifneh ha-doroth*, pp. 112–14.

12 Population figures for the eighteenth century, unless otherwise indicated, are from Mahler, *Yidn in Zifern*.

13 See tables in Ettinger, *Zion* 21: 124.

14 The 1764 Polish census of the Jews is hardly comparable to any modern census. Not only are most population figures of the "prestatistical" era inaccurate, but the nature of this particular census may have further decreased its value. It was arranged for the specific purpose of collecting a higher amount of head tax from the Jews, and it would be natural for some Jews to be interested in making their numbers appear smaller so as to pay less tax. Information from certain places where a recheck has been made shows that a considerable number of "hidden" persons were found (up to 25 percent or even more). The census figure is therefore usually increased by an estimated 100–150,000 or more persons.

15 See also *Responsa Bach Hayeshanoth*, no. 76; *Responsa Mas'at Benyamin*, no. 107; *Responsa Zemach Zedek*, no. 88.

16 Hanover, *Yeveyn metzulah*, pp. 52, 70 ff. (English translation, pp. 95 ff.).

17 Meir Margaliot, *Meir Netivim* 1, no. 64.

18 The figures are according to Mahler's computations in *Yidn in Zifern*, pp. 49 ff. It should be mentioned that most of those percentages may be somewhat inaccurate since in many cases only parts of the registers of the census in the given province survived.

Chapter 7

1 Many Jewish historians, accepting the general trend of Polish historiography since the nineteenth century, which considered the decline of the older Polish state entirely the fault of the nobility, try to emphasize—usually out of all proportion—the arbitrariness of some landlords in their handling of Jews (as if to outweigh any favorable view of the nobility or as though they were ideologically opposed to the concept of nobility generally). But one cannot do otherwise than admit that in the private cities and towns the legal situation of the Jews was better than in the royal cities and "in a great number of private cities . . . existed Jewish equality on a par with other citizens, not only in economic matters but also in certain principles of political rights [participation in election of city officials]—for the first time in the history of Poland and to a certain degree in the whole of Europe." However, the historian "must" evaluate the transfer of jurisdiction over "private" Jews to the landowners in 1539 as a degradation of the Jews in the social hierarchy of Poland (see, for instance, Mahler, *Polin*, pp. 153, 156). The reality of the situation was usually different from what it was assumed by the "antinobility" historians to have been.

   Also, the Jews were not always subject to the arbitrary behavior of the landlords. At times they had recourse to the court (see *RIN* 2, no. 1836). In 1738 the court fined one estate owner who, contrary to a contract with an innkeeper, took apart the house designated for him. The court put the woman owner in jail for a week and ordered her to pay damages and to provide another house. The king and high officials sometimes took the side of the Jews (see the story above about Prince Kurbski and the Jews of Kowel).

2 For the sixteenth to seventeenth century; quoted in Czacki, *Rozprawa*, pp. 82, 96.

3 *RIN* 2, nos. 1474, 1131, 1132; *IEN*, 77, 78. *Volumina Legum* [law books], 4: 724, 959; 5: 77.

4 Mahler, *Polin*, p. 351. Fear that Jews might use anti-Christian expressions in their prayers may have been influenced by anti-Jewish agitation in Germany against the *Aleynu* prayer as containing anti-Christian phrases. It led to the Prussian order of August 28, 1703, demanding the elimination of some words from the prayer. Some anti-Jewish writings also dwelt on this point in later decades.

5 See also Ptaśnik, *Miasta* (1948), pp. 312 ff., 314.

6 Bersohn, nos. 250–53, 264, 269, 292, 300, 382, 385, 469, 528.

7 Bezalel from Żółkiew, the favored administrator of tolls of King Jan Sobieski, played a big role at the end of the seventeenth century, until attacks upon his methods and accusations of misapprehension of funds and his own haughty behavior against Christians brought his downfall in the 1690s, apparently after the king's death. See Balaban, *Yidn in Poilen*, pp. 59–68.

8 Bersohn, nos. 403, 423, 427, 436, 441, 457, 464, 478, 494, 497, 532, 541; *REA* 3:38, 46, 48–49, 68, 102, 168; Schorr, in *ZPO* 1:194.

9 Halecki, *Borderlands of Western Civilization*, p. 149.

10   Bersohn, nos. 146, 162, 164, 440–41, 446, 457, 461, 464, 470, 478–79, 483–84, 488, 494–95, 497, 504, 511, 514, 526, 532–33; *REA* 3, nos. 68, 92–93, 100, 102, 132, 135–36, 156, 170, 160–61, 163, 166, 175; *REA* 2:68, 116, 200; Trunk, *Plock*, 30 ff.

11   *HZK* 1:128–31; E. Zivier, "Juedische Bekehrungsversuche im XVI Jahrhundert," *Festschrift zum Siebzigsten Geburtstag Philipsons* (Leipzig, 1916), pp. 96–113; *RIN* 1, no. 396; see also W. Bohnstedt, *The Infidel Scourge of God: The Turkish Menace as Seen by German Pamphleteers of the Reformation Era* (Philadelphia, 1968). Queen Bona, from Italy, was known for her avarice. She advised the Cracow Jewish leaders to put up twenty thousand zloty in order to be freed from jail. There is no record of the bail having later been returned.

12   Ptaśnik, *Miasta* (1948), pp. 294 ff., 297 ff., 301 ff.

13   Heaton, *Economic History of Europe*, pp. 191 ff.; Abraham Edel, "Scarcity and Abundance in Ethical Theory," in *Freedom and Reason, Studies in Philosophy and Jewish Culture in Memory of Morris Raphael Cohen* (New York, 1951), p. 116.

14   *Historia*, 1, part 1:107; Ptaśnik, *Miasta* (1948), pp. 294 ff., 299 ff., and see also ibid. (1934), p. 177.

15   It is estimated that about a half of the city population consisted of the poor and underprivileged persons who had no citizenship rights (see *Historia*, 1, part 2: 496 ff.).

16   This happened in Lwów in 1577, 1581, 1602, and 1629.

17   This relationship and the attitude of the Jews may be represented to some extent by the following declaration by a Tykocin Jew in 1526: "If we Jews were obliged to use records confirmed by the city government, then the burghers who are hostile to the Jewish race could rob us of all our possessions" (quoted in Bershadski, *Litovskie evrei*, p. 416).

18   This expression was used by the church synod in Breslau (Wroclaw) in 1267 as a rationale for anti-Jewish resolutions.

19   *Historia*, 1, part 2: 799; Józef Putek, *Mroki Średniowieczne* (Warsaw, 1947), pp. 105 ff.

20   *RIN* 1, nos. 569, 571, 715–16, 588, 599, 607, 628, 635–36, 645–50; 2, nos. 1177, 1631; 3, nos. 2147, 2151–52.

21   *REA* 2, nos. 157, 158; 3, no. 244; 1, nos. 169, 337, p. 194. See also Z. Honig, "Di yurisdikzye iber yidn in Lite nuch der Lubliner unye," *YIVO Bleter* 14 (1939): 316–34.

22   *RIN* 2, no. 1357; 3, no. 2041; Bersohn, nos. 152, 224, 535, 192–93, 230, 233, 237; Ettinger, *Zion* 20: 128–37, 141 ff.

23   In Lublin, for instance, where the struggle lasted for about 135 years. Before the middle of the seventeenth century Jews lived for the most part in the suburb (near "the fortress"). Following the wars of 1648–60 and a fire that destroyed their region they moved into the city proper. The municipality immediately launched a violent anti-Jewish struggle, and the newly founded (Christian) "Merchants' Association" demanded their expulsion in 1692. Subsequent numerous court opinions, royal decrees, and special investigative commissions (in 1696, 1697, 1698, 1720, 1737, 1738, 1741, 1744, and 1761), with their pro- and anti-Jewish tendencies, resulted in most of the Jews being expelled after more than a century. A group of wealthy Jews remained, however, in the houses belonging to nobles and churchmen. The strife between the two groups continued. The king issued a decree of expulsion in 1780, but

when the city authorities attempted to carry it out, the *starosta* prevented them from doing so. It remained to the occupying Austrian forces of the city following the partition in 1795 to expel the Jews. Kamenets Podolski received the privilege of *de non tolerandis Judaeis* in 1598 and a royal decree expelling Jews in 1654. About a century passed before they were actually expelled in 1750—and still some of them remained.

24 Balaban, *Lwów*, pp. 403, 405 ff.; *HZK* 1: 189–208; Perles, *MGWJ*, 1864, p. 324.

25 J. Shatzki, *YIVO Bleter* 35 (1951); idem, *Pinkas Zamoshch*, 1957, pp. 22–26; Janina Morgensztern, "Uwagi o Żydach Sefardyjskich," *Biuletyn*, no. 38 (1961): 69–82; idem, "O osadnietwie Żydów w Zamościu na przelomie XVI i XVII w.," *Biuletyn*, nos. 43–44 (1962): 3–17; M. Wischnitzer, *The Memoirs of Ber of Bolechow* (London, 1922), pp. 2–3.

26 *RIN* 2, no. 1358; 3, no. 1876.

27 Maimon, *Autobiography*, p. 12 (although Maimon knows also of such inefficient leaseholders as his grandfather was [ibid., pp. 17 ff.]); see also I. Halperin, *Zion* 22 (1957): 56–67.

28 The Jewish prohibition is republished *PVAA*, nos. 1, 352. Similar ones were also imposed by the (Jewish) Lithuanian Community Council. It is not impossible that the prohibitions of the Jewish institutions were issued only pro forma, to satisfy a demand by the state. In any event, the Four-Land Council and many communities continued to handle tax farming (and tax farmers) as though this were a perfectly legal occupation (see *PVAA*, nos. 32, 192, 865, 996).

29 Hanover, *Yeveyn metzulah* (Hebrew), p. 25 (English), p. 36.

30 Figures from Mahler, *Yidn in Zifern*, pp. 101, 164.

31 Such attacks upon one who "transgressed" the rules of the guild were not confined to Poland. In the Middle Ages an English herring merchant, for instance, complained that because he sold his merchandise more cheaply the other merchants "assaulted him, beat him, ill treated him, and left him for dead" (quoted in Ephraim Lipson, *Economic History of England* (1929), 1: 246.

32 See particulars in N.M. Gelber in *HS* 1 (1929): 231, 252.

33 The preserved court books from Plock in the seventeenth century indicate that there the Jewish court, staffed by Jewish community elders and a non-Jewish notary, served as the court of the first instance, while the vice-palatine's court was the court of appeals. See Trunk, *Shtudies*, pp. 27–35.

34 Kutrzeba in *IEN*, pp. 233–242. *RIN* 2, nos. 1226–29, 1257, 1268, 1359, 1394, 1451, 1793, 1794, and many others.

35 Lewin, "The Protection of Jewish Religious Rights" (this source is also utilized for the following pages). Bloch, *Die General Privilegien*, pp. 102 ff.; Gumplowicz, *Prawodawstwo Polskie*, pp. 161 ff., 113, 103, 65; Bersohn, nos. 99, 138, 152, 306; Pazdro Doc. no. 8.; Schorr, *Żydzi w Przemyślu*, pp. 147–52, 107; idem, *ZPO* 1: 194–96; *RIN* 1: 944, 984; 2:1322, 1618; 3: 1917.

36 Similarly, at times Jewish bakers were forbidden to sell to non-Jews (in Plock in 1584 and 1649, for example). The tendency to limit the Jewish artisan to the Jewish customer (and the Jewish physician to the Jewish patient) was generally found in Christian Europe of the Middle Ages (see also Trunk, *Shtudies*, pp. 133–34).

37 Bloch, *Die General Privilegien;* Bersohn, no. 200; Schorr, *Organizacja*, pp. 81 ff.; idem, *Żydzi w Przemyślu*, p. 85; Balaban, *Lwów*, doc. no. 15.

38 Brann, *Geschichte der Juden*, pp. 12 ff., 23.

39 Bersohn, nos. 1–2; Gumplowicz, *Prawodawstwo Polskie,* pp. 167 ff.; Balaban, *Lwów,* doc. no. 85.

40 *RIN* 1:959.

41 Thus the bishop of Kamenets, in granting a permit to the Jews of Bar in 1717 to build a synagogue, demanded not only that the synagogue not be higher or richer than the local church, but also that Jews not employ Christian help, not sell food, arms, gunpowder, and other items to Turks or Tatars. Another Kamenets bishop, visiting the town of Husiatyn in 1741, closed up the synagogue that the Jews had built in place of an earlier one destroyed by fire, or ordered that it be removed and put a large fine on it. But the owner of the city, Michael Potocki, overruled the bishop's decree and ordered the Jews not to pay any fines. He informed the bishop "that he will not allow his Jews to be harmed" (*RIN* 2, nos. 1564–65; 3, no. 1876).

42 Fred Greene, *Dynamics of International Relations* (New York, 1964,) p. 6.

43 Ber of Bolechów, *Memoirs,* p. 67; Halperin, *PVAA,* no. 392; *PML,* pp. 284–89.

44 Weinryb, *Texts* (Hebrew part), pp. 54–59.

45 See Ignacy Schipper, "Komisja Warszawska," in *Sepher Hayobel Le-Mordecai Zeev Braude (Kitvey Hamakhon le-hokhmat Yisrael ba-Warshe,* 3–4) (Warsaw, 1931), pp. 1–11.

46 In Poznań (1638, 1644) his salary was higher than that of the rabbi. The general syndic of Polish Jewry had, of course, a higher salary than the one in Poznań (in 1674, 800 zloty against Poznań: in 1637/8, 300; in 1644, 600).

47 Isaac Lewin, "Udzial Żydów w wyborach Sejmowych w dawnej Polsce," *MZ,* 1932, and reprint; Halperin, *PVAA,* nos. 153, 173, 231, 236, 254, 257, 258, 342, 530, 621, 642; Weinryb, *Texts* (Hebrew part), pp. 57–61, 126 ff.; *MGWJ,* 1865, pp. 84 ff.; Schipper, "Komisja Warszawska"; Bersohn, nos. 268, 271, 283; see also Baron, *The Jewish Community,* 2:115–16.

48 *RIN* 1:1071.

49 Preserved Smith, *The Enlightenment, 1687–1776* (1962), 2:457, 473–74.

50 *RIN* 2, no. 1570; the lynching is recorded for Lithuania—with the king asking officials to defend Jews—but there were probably also similar cases in the kingdom of (Crown) Poland (see *RIN* 2, no. 1127).

51 Trunk, *Shtudies,* pp. 52–62; see also the entries in a minute book reprinted *HS* 2:581–82.

52 *RIN,* 1, nos. 561, 574, 592, 666, 706; 2, nos. 1221, 1226, 1227, 1228, 1229, 1238, 1257, 1267, 1268, 1344, 1359, 1388, 1394, 1451, 1631, 1748, 1753, 1764, 1770, 1776, 1780, 1786, 1788, 1790, 1791, 1792, 1793–94, 1807, 1812, 1819–21, 1831; 3, nos. 1862, 1892, 1898, 1934, 1943–48, 1961.

53 *RIN,* 1, nos. 571, 573, 640, 667, 683, 759; 2, nos. 1142, 1144, 1177, 1393; 3, no. 1952.

54 In some areas of New York City, for instance, "frightened and angry citizens have been banding together to protect themselves against criminal attacks." In the Crown Heights section of Brooklyn, Hassidic Jews began patrolling the area in radio cars. Tenants in Delano Village in northern Harlem and in buildings on Brent Park East and in some other regions were forming security teams and patrols to guard the buildings by the end of 1964; *New York Times,* December 15, 1964. Certain Jewish and non-Jewish groups repeated such attempts toward the end of the 1960s and beginning of the 1970s in New York and elsewhere.

55 Weinryb, *Texts,* pp. 40–41; Lewin, *Landessynode,* 1: 7.

56 Reprinted by Perles, "Geschichte der Juden in Posen," *MGWJ* 13 (1964): 457, and

in Israel Halperin, *Sepher Hagevura* (Tel Aviv, 1941), 1: 132. (A few other items about Poland are also reprinted there.) On Jewish self-defense in Poland see also M. Balaban, "Żydzi Polscy z bronią w reku w wieku XVI–XVIII," in *Album pamiatkowy ku czci Berka Joselewicza* (Warsaw, 1934), pp. 145–54; Weinryb, "Private Letters in Yiddish of 1588," pp. 64–67.

57 According to the existing law a "blood avenger" was entitled to demand punishment of his relative's murderer. (In past centuries—with differences from country to country —murder was not always prosecuted by the public prosecutor or state unless demanded by the relatives.)

58 *Responsa Zemach Zedek*, no. 111; see also *Sepher Hayovel le-Albek*, p. 269.

Chapter 8

1 Prof. J. Katz's appraisal (*Tradition and Crisis: Jewish Society at the End of the Middle Ages* [Glencoe, Ill., 1961], p. 15 ff.) of the specific legal status of the Jews, based on the fact that they were "deprived of any claim to residence without special pleading," is in part a transference of the modern nineteenth-century concepts to a "traditional" society. Regardless of what the case may have been in Germany, it has no relevance to Poland.

2 See Rabinowitz, *The Herem Hayishub*, pp. 10, 13, 90, 92, 121; Irving A. Agus, *Rabbi Meir of Rothenburg* (Philadelphia, 1947), 1: 57 ff., 119. Agus more recently speculates that "in order to improve their position vis-à-vis their powerful and fractious clients, the Jews *invented* [emphasis added] monopolistic practices of great strength and efficacy" which were later adopted by the non-Jewish burghers (Irving A. Agus, *Urban Civilization in Pre-Crusade Europe* [New York, 1965], 1:31).

3 See Bernard D. Weinryb, "Rashi against the Background of His Epoch," in *Rashi Anniversary Volume* of American Academy for Jewish Research (New York, 1941), pp. 39–46.

4 *Responsa Moses Isserles*, nos. 52, 73; idem, Rama to *Hoshen Mishpat*, 156, 7. Joseph Hakohen, *Responsa Sheerith Joseph*, no. 9. *Responsa Solomon Luria*, no. 36. Eliyakum Getz, *Eben Hashoham* 1, no. 28.

5 See M. Semiatitzki, "Hezkath hakehila ba-Polin," *Hamishpat Haibri* (Jerusalem, 1937), 5:199–253; Weinryb, *Texts*, passim; Z. Warhaftig, *He-chazakah ba-mishpat Haibri* (Jerusalem, 1964).

6 The Cracow Community Statute of 1595—the oldest preserved Jewish community statute from Poland—emphasizes the demand that a newcomer must pay more than old-timers since "his parents [ancestors] did not live here and did not contribute to the maintenance of the community."

7 Thus in 1569 the Jews and the Christian city councilors and burghers of Luck complained to the authorities that foreign merchants were entering the city and selling their wares at retail, as well as to each other (*RIN* 1, no. 569; see also nos. 666–67; 3, no. 2215).

8 Weinryb, *Texts* (Hebrew part), pp. 19–30, 87–91, 140–41, 222; Avron, *Pinkas*, nos. 27, 48, 83, 86, 113, 194, 219, 248, 337, 703, 716, 755, 941, 1002, 1113, 1943, 2004, 2101, 1473, 1630, 1809, 1838; M. Balaban, "Die Krakauer Juden Gemeindeordnung von 1595 und ihre Nachtraege," *JJLG* 10: 304, 312, 314, 329, 335, 346, 348, 353, 360; 11:89, 90–93, 99; idem, *Żydzi Lwowscy na przelomie XVIgo i XVII wieku* (Lwów

1906), p. 431; Buber, *Kirya nisgava*, pp. 81, 91, 112–113; Sebastian Miczyński, *Zwierciadlo Korony Polskiej* (Cracow, 1626); *PML* (Berlin, 1925), nos. 6–8, 46–47, 70, 73, 79, 83, 85, 87, 94, 104, 120–21, 123, 144, 172, 204, 217, 236, 249, 284, 293, 295, 301–2, 304, 404, 585, 600, 609, 642, 657, 661, 731, 746, 809; Lewin, *Geschichte der Juden in Lissa*, pp. 12–15.

9   See also *RIN* 1, no. 1519; 3, no. 2275. A speech by Stanislaw-Kazimir Bjenewski in the Polish *sejm* (1676) pointed out that "a law is not a law" and that all our troubles come because we don't follow the laws. The Braclaw regional dietine maintained (1661) that no law passed in Poland that is unfavorable to Jews can become effective in Poland; *AYZR* 2 (Kiev, 1888): viii; *RIN* 1, no. 1071. Many Jewish sources seem to indicate violations by Jews of ordinances and laws passed by the communities.

10 As mentioned earlier, the average life-span of a house in the countryside was ten years, since it was often burned down or destroyed by Tatars, invaders, or robbers.

11 Ptaśnik, *Miasta* (1934), p. 281 and passim.

12 Balaban, *Lwów*, pp. 14, 63 ff., 148 ff., 153, 190, 212, 473–77, 505; idem, *Yidn in Poilen*, pp. 41–42, 59–85; *RIN* 1, nos. 548, 666, 668, 695, 702, 713, 724, 760, 994; *RIN* 2, nos. 1351, 1389, 1765; *RIN* 3, nos. 1852, 1862, 1875, 1916; Maimon, *Autobiography*, pp. 11–12; Halperin, *Yehudim*, pp. 277–88 (and the bibliography); *Shivchey Habesht*, pp. 87–89; *HZK* 2:144–45; Elizabeta Horn in *Biuletyn*, no. 40 (1961), pp. 34–35. It should be mentioned that in 1792 (almost two hundred years after the confrontation in Cracow) Jews in a town in the Lublin region (Kazimierz on the Vistula, not to be confused with Kazimierz near Cracow) evinced an attitude similar to the one found in Cracow in 1616. In a conflict over use of the city scales the Jews announced to the non-Jewish citizens: "We are going to have our own scales. . . . We are not liable to your court and our kehilla means for us as much as the president [of the court]" (Wladyslaw Cwik in *Biuletyn*, no. 59 [1966], p. 33).

13 Ptaśnik, *Miasta* (1934), p. 246. In the Lublin region Jews also participated in the election of town officers. In a few royal towns they were officially called "citizens"; in one of them they were even sworn in as citizens (Wladyslaw Cwik in *Biuletyn*, no. 59 [1966], p. 33).

14 Cracow in 1553, Bar in 1556, Poznań in 1556, Przemyśl in 1568, Lwów in 1581 and 1592 (prolongation in 1602, 1616, and 1629), Plock in 1581, Pereyaslavl in 1623, and others.

15 *REA* 2, no. 229, and elsewhere.

16 These payments were called *kozubalec*, (which is supposed to mean "basket money"; Jews carrying baskets were taxed). In 1626 a somewhat satirical anti-Jewish pamphlet *Kozubales* mentions that these payments were connected with the execution of Christ by Jews (see *HZK* 1: 392–94; the pamphlet is reprinted in ibid.: 553–60). An anti-Semitic writer (Miczyński, *Zwierciadlo Korony Polskiej*) complains that "a holy and praiseworthy custom had now disappeared; previously boys and children seeing a Jew in town . . . threatened him with stones and mud, pulling his beard." Does this mean that the methods became more civil?

17 *Responsa Solomon Luria*, no. 4; Balaban, *Lwów*, pp. 44 ff., 63, 148 ff., 212.

18 Eliade, in *Cosmos and History*, elaborated on the general tendency of traditional societies to cling to transhistorical models and to deny concrete time and reality.

19 See also Katz, *Exclusiveness and Tolerance*, pp. 3 ff.

20 *Responsa Moses Mintz,* no. 63. The designation of the country as a haven for Jewish refugees can be seen as a positive view.

21 *YS* Baba Batra 10:21; *Responsa Rema,* nos. 95, 63.

22 Hayim ben Bezalel, *Vikuach mayim Hayim* (Amsterdam, 1712), Kelal 5, no. 4.

23 *Dina de-malkhuta dina,* formulated by Samuel, a leading Babylonian talmudic scholar of the third century.

24 *YS* Baba Batra 10:18, 21; *Responsa Rema,* no. 109.

25 *Hizzuq Emunah,* part 1, ch. 46. See the English translation (Isaac Troki, *Faith Strengthened,* trans. Moses Mocatt [New York, 1971]).

26 F. Wettstein, *Debarim Atikim,* p. 4. It seems that the entry in the minute book is from a later date. It neither begins with the usual "Today on . . ." nor does it have a passus at the end signifying the author (*sopher* = scribe) or date of entry.

27 *Responsa Rema,* nos. 108, 109, 93; *Responsa Bach,* no. 26, *Bach Hechadashot,* no. 42; *REA* 2, nos. 211–12.

28 *HZK* 1:197–98.

29 Only social critics were pointing out that all this was unstable. But these writers used traditional symbols, usually repetitive and perhaps having little to do with the realities of their times.

30 Isaiah Hurewitz, 1565–1630; Efraim Lunczyc, 1550–1619; Yedidya Gotlieb of the next generation (quotations in Ben-Sason, *Hagut,* pp. 116, 124, 127 ff.); *Yesh Nochlin,* p. 2b f.

31 See the many quotations (and interpretations) in Ben-Sason, *Hagut,* pp. 58 ff., 98 ff., 126–29; see also Ber of Bolechów, *Memoirs,* passim.

32 See the sources in Ben-Sason, *Hagut,* pp. 76, 81 ff., 84 ff., 91, 96.

33 Balaban, *Lwów,* p. xvii.

34 Ber of Bolechów, *Memoirs,* pp. 142–44.

35 As in a forced confrontation in Brody in the 1740s.

36 *Responsa Mas'at Benyamin,* no. 33; *Pney Yehoshua* (Amsterdam, 1615); Orach Hayim, no. 7; see also Ben-Sason, *Hagut,* pp. 142–43.

37 Hurewitz, *Schnei Luchot Habrith,* Messechet Tamid, p. 206a; Ben-Sason, *Hagut,* p. 91, note 5, 124; *Tarbiz* 29:305.

38 *Ohel Rachel,* p. 10; *Amunat Zadikim,* p. 29 (quoted in Holomshtok *Zeitschrift* 4:100); Maimon, *Autobiography,* p. 36.

39 *HZK* 1:227; Wettstein, *Dibrey Hefetz,* no. 2; Hanover, *Yeveyn metzulah* (Hebrew), pp. 21, 68, (English, pp. 30, 92); *Megilat Eifa,* 134.

40 *RIN* 2, nos. 1228, 1226.

41 Hanover, *Yeveyn metzulah,* pp. 49, 97, 50, 58, and passim.

42 Quotations are from the Mesch English translation, pp. 119–20, 110–15.

43 *Bakasha Niflaah,* published 1657. Gurland, *Lekorot* (Cracow, 1849), 3: 15–16.

44 Zoref's vision is reprinted in Kaidanower, *Kav Hayashar,* ch. 102 (Sulzbach edition, p. 108a). About Zoref, see Scholem, *Major Trends* (1967 ed.), pp. 332 ff.; *Kehilat Yofi* 2; Kraushar, *Frank i Frankiści,* 1: 308; A. Ashkoli in *Sinai* 12 (1943): 90–91.

45 Hassidic stories are highly questionable as a historical source for Hassidism. First, they were published late—*Shivchey Habesht* about half a century after the death of Israel Baal Shem Tov—Besht—and some others still later. They bear traces of later additions. Their historical reliability is still further weakened because certain images and

ideas show signs of imitating older sources (New Testament stories or stories connected with Isaac Luria, for example). Further doubt about the texts is aroused by the fact that their publication was intended—as Dinur points out—either to serve as propaganda for Hassidism generally or for a certain rabbi or his descendants. On the other hand, they comprise an important literary collection of materials on Hassidism that cannot be ignored. While no critical edition exists, many have utilized them either in the naive-nostalgic manner or by regarding them as true layers of original Hassidic thought (Buber), to which Scholem recently objected.

46   Jacob Joseph of Polonnoe, *Toledot Yaakov Joseph* (Warsaw, 1881), p. 39.

47   See Horodetski ed., *Shivchey Habesht*, pp. 109, 126, 39–40, 86–87, 91, 90, 100, 98; Abraham J. Heschel, "Reb Pinkhas Koritzer," *YIVO Bleter* 33 (1949): 39–47;

48   Some Hassidic leaders of the first half of the nineteenth century articulated their pro-Polish stand. One of them, Rabbi Shmuel Abba of Žichlin, expressed his idea (around 1831) that Jews should be grateful to the Poles because they had opened the doors to them. The political freedom of Poland should predate the coming of the Jewish Messiah. Another Hassidic rabbi, returning from a cure in Germany, asserted that the air there was defiling, while in Poland even "the trees in the woods wish to hear the Jewish prayers" *(Sepher Lahav Aysh* [Piotrkow, 1934], pp. 231, 238, quoted in N.M. Gelber, *Metzudah* 7 [London, 1954]: 229, 241; I.D. Beyt-Halevi, *Toledot Yehudey Kalish* [Tel Aviv, 1961], pp. 262–63).

One may apparently also see in the attempts of a number of Hassidic leaders of the second and third post-Besht generations (Israel Besht died in 1760) to spiritualize the ideas of exile and redemption as a positive attitude toward the country (Poland) of this exile. By placing the exile (galut) on a par with Palestine in their mystic scale of values, sometimes even higher than Palestine, they are also recognizing, as it were, that this exile—Poland—is regarded as important and highly estimated (see also Uffenheimer, *Hachasidut ka-mistika*, pp. 168–77, and below, chapter 12).

49   Ringelblum, *Żydzi w Powstaniu*, pp. 52 ff., and passim. In our case, the attitudes toward Poles and Poland as reflected in this literature may possibly afford us a truer reflection of the ideas of the eighteenth century. Orthodox Jews in Poland in the first quarter of the nineteenth century, from among whom the editors of the stories came, had not yet at that time developed any modern patriotic Polish ideas. The reported pro-Polish tendencies may rather be a leftover from the genuine old eighteenth-century tendencies.

50   Many of the items concerning Poland during the seventeenth to the eighteenth century are reprinted in Bernfeld, *Sepher ha-demaot*, 3: 94, 99–108, 164, 175, 190, 194–96, 198–203, 217–18, 220–30, 233, 237, 245.

51   *Teshuvot geonim batrai* (Żólkiew, 1795), no. 24.

Background and Chapter 9

1   Huizinga, *The Waning of the Middle Ages,* p. 9. A letter from Luck (1764) mentions fear of the Russian army detachments at the time of the interregnum created by the death of King Augustus III in October 1763: "But a few regiments already passed through our city, and thank God they did not harm us at all." There are also known cases of Prussian or Russian officers being billeted in Jewish houses while stationed in

Poland who later, in Germany, sought and found missing husbands of Jewish women in Poland (Mann, *Texts and Studies*, 2: 1335–36; *Keter Kehunah*, no. 76).

2   The name Ukraine (borderlands), originally a general designation for frontier regions of Ruthenia, gradually became a proper name designating a specific territory in southeastern Europe where wide steppes separated the permanent settlements from the Black Sea shores. This frontier region (Ukraine) was settled mainly by Ruthenians or "Little Russians." It was not until much later that the name Ukraine came to mean the whole southern part settled by the Ruthenians, who also became known as Ukrainians. On the rise of the cossacks, see also Guenther Stökel, *Die Entstehung des Kosakentums (Veroeffentlichungen des Osteuropa-Institutes*, München, no. 3) (Munich, 1953).

3   In 1601 the Polish ambassador to the Tatar khan pointed out that among the cossacks "are also found Turks, Tatars, Jews, Moscovites [Russians] and others" (Borovoy, "Natzionalno-osvoboditelnaya," p. 93).

4   Detachments consisting of peasants and newly joined city people and some of their commanders ("colonels"), such as Maksim Krzywonos, were more radical and more destructive than Chmielnicki himself—he sometimes had to give in to the extremists. This tension may have led to various rumors (July and September 1648) of internal quarrels and of a rebellion in the cossack camp, that the mob had killed Chmielnicki and made Krzywonos the supreme leader, or that Krzywonos was imprisoned by Chmielnicki; *Dokumenty*, pp. 97, 109 ff.; see also pp. 69 ff., 79 ff., 93 ff., 102; Shatzki *Tach*, p. 77; *RIN* 1: 901, 903. Also, at the time of negotiations for a peace in the fall of 1651 and after conclusion of the peace the mob and some of the minor chiefs tried to block it and plotted a sort of revolt. A few of them were executed by Chmielnicki. Ukrainian folk songs preserved some traces of these differences. *Dokumenty*, pp. 542–44, 618 ff., 640 ff., 644 ff.; and most of the Jewish chronicles *(Yeveyn metzulah, Tzok Haitim, Petach Teshuva)* indicate the greater violence of the peasants.

5   *Historia*, 1, part 2: 675–716; Halecki, *Borderlands of Western Civilization*, pp. 186–215; *The Cambridge History of Poland* (Cambridge, 1950), 1: 502–31.

6   *Historia*, 1, part 2: 618–52; *Polska w Okresie Drugiej wojny Pólnocnej 1655–1660*, vols. 1–2 (Warsaw, 1957); *Dokumenty*, passim.

7   *RIN* 1, nos. 877, 882, 883, 885, 888, 923; document no. 1 in *Dokumenty* (pp. 9–11) was not written before 1655 at the earliest. See also Shatzki, *Tach*, pp. 44–58.

8   Hanover, *Yeveyn metzulah*, pp. 25 ff.; *Responsa Mas'at Benyamin*, no. 86; *AYZR* 4, part 3 (Kiev, 1914): 570; Borovoy, "Natzionalno-osvoboditelnaya," p. 117.

9   *AYZR*, quoted in Ettinger, *Zion* 20: 149; Lipinski, *Z dziejów Ukrainy*, p. 373; Shatzki, *Tach*, pp. 12, 40–41; Borovoy, "Natzionalno-osvoboditelnaya," pp. 93, 117; *Bach Hayeshanot*, no. 57; *RIN* 1: 913, 973, 880.

10 *Zapiski naukovoho Tovaristva im. Sevchenko*, vols. 31–32, quoted in Ettinger, *Zion* 21: 126, note 70; Jacob, *Hiltebrandt's dreifache*, p. 96; Shatzki, *Tach*, p. 124; Borovoy, "Natzionalno-osvoboditelnaya," p. 103.

11 Polish military detachments destroyed some places. The Polish commander, N. Potocki, in his call to the cossacks to leave Chmielnicki (February 1648) and return to Poland, threatens that otherwise he will order their wives and children exterminated; and the voivode A. Kisel suggests a method of getting rid of the cossack problem by annihilating them and even blotting out the word cossack; *Dokumenty*, pp. 15, 22.

12 Berlin, *Istoricheskiya,* p. 188; *RIN* 1: 877; *Dokumenty,* p. 517; Hanover, *Yeveyn metzulah,* p. 22; *Responsa Pney Yehoshua* 2, no. 68; *Bach Hayeshanoth,* no. 47.

13 One source says that only Jews were permitted to be baptized as Greek Orthodox, while Poles were not accepted. Other sources indicate that ethnic Poles could also convert to the Greek Orthodox faith and survive (*RIN* 1, no. 880). Over a decade after the cossack uprising all foreigners and newly baptized persons—apparently including former Jews—were eliminated from the forces in cossack Ukraine (*RIN* 1, no. 973).

14 Quoted in Shatzki, *Tach,* p. 18; *RIN* 1, no. 901.

15 Hanover, *Yeveyn metzulah,* pp. 31–32, 52–53 (English trans., pp. 43, 70–71); *Zok Haitim* 2b, 3a, 8a, 8b; *RIN* 1, nos. 875, 877, 879, 901–3, 904; M. Balaban, *Die Judenstadt von Lublin* (Berlin, 1919), p. 48; *Responsa Amunath Shmuel,* no. 24.

16 Hanover, *Yeveyn metzulah,* p. 33; *Zaar bath rabim* (Lwów, 1906), p. 10; I. Halperin, "Shviya upedut bigzeyrat Ukraina," *Zion* 25: 20–22. Other sources mention hundreds of Jews killed in some of these communities (Gurland, *Lekorot ha-Gezeyrot al Yisrael,* 1: 14; *Tit ha-Yeveyn,* p. 9e).

17 Hanover, *Yeveyn metzulah,* pp. 37–44, 46 ff., 59, 64; *Megilat Eifa,* pp. 135 ff.; *Zok Haitim* 3ab, 4b, 5a, 7b, 8a, 9b; *Tit ha-Yeveyn,* pp. 417 ff., 422. Halperin (*Zion* 25: 23–27) expresses some doubts as to the correctness of information about the agreement of the Poles to deliver the Jews to the cossacks in Tulczyn; *Avodat Hagershuni* 1, nos. 36, 67, 106, 110; *Beth Yacob,* nos. 55, 104, 143; *Beth Hillel,* Eben Haezer, no. 7; *Zemach Zedek,* nos. 78, 88, 101, 113; *Eytan Haezrachi,* no. 22; *RIN* 1, nos. 900–1; see also *RIN* 1, nos. 884, 886–87, 889–91.

18 S. Dubnow in *Hapardes,* pp. 94–96, reprinted in Bernfeld, *Sepher ha-demaot,* 3: 187–190.

19 *HZK* 2: 4–18; Halperin, *Yehudim,* pp. 266–76; Adam Kersten, "Rola i udzial mass ludowych w walkach z najazdem Szwedzkim," *Polska* 1: 238; ibid., 263 ff., 270 ff., 276, 280; Adam Przyboś, "Stefan Czarniecki w latach 'Potopu,' " *Polska* 2: 160; Zofia Libiszowska, ibid., p. 497; Bernfeld, *Sepher ha-demaot,* 3: 191–203; *Tit ha-Yeveyn,* 426–27. General Czarniecki was the owner of Tiktin, which came to him in 1661. According to available information he and his heirs treated the Jewish inhabitants very well. It may well be that the atrocities and killing of the Jews was done in part against Czarniecki's will. See also L. Lewin, *Judenverfolgungen im Schwedisch-polnischen Kriege* (Posen, 1901); A.S. Hershberg, *Pinkos Bialystok* (New York, 1949) (Yiddish), 1: 39; Wladyslaw Rusinski, "Straty i zniszczenia w apoce wojny Szwedzkiej . . . ," *Polska* 2: 280 ff. Cracow Jews were also accused of telling the Swedes where a costly altar belonging to the church was hidden, and the court ordered them later to pay the church ten thousand zloty. They were paying installments on this amount for a long period. It took some time and effort to settle the problem of the "gift" of the "Jewish city of Kazimierz" which the king had made.

20 *RIN* 1, nos. 903, 961; *Zok Haitim* 3b, 9b; Hanover, *Yeveyn metzulah,* pp. 37, 63, 71, 80. From Lwów we have a 1626 document that confirms the considerable role Jews played in defense against the Tatars. Only about Narol does one chronicle report that the Jews wanted to flee, offering the rationale that they were not trained fighters. (*Zok Haitim* 8b); Nadav in *Zion* 31 (1966): 157; *PML,* no. 503.

21 *Dokumenty,* pp. 100, 407.

22 Harry I. Shapiro, *The Jewish People* (New York, 1960), p. 80; *New York Times*, Dec. 3, 1967, about ideas concerning causes of plagues.

23 Halperin in *Sepher Yobel la-Yitzchak Baer*, pp. 345, 347. According to the registration of the burial society in Cracow, eighteen hundred adults supposedly died in 1652, to which should be added 30–40 percent of the children, who were not usually registered; F. Wettstein, "Letoldot Yisrael Vachachamav Bapolin," *Haeshkol* 7 (Cracow, 1913): 195. A Polish source puts the whole number of the dead in Kazimierz-Cracow—apparently non-Jews and Jews combined—at 2, 578 in the spring and summer of 1652.

24 There are also indications that eyewitnesses in a catastrophic situation may be especially unreliable as far as figures are concerned. This phenomenon seems to appear in eyewitness evidence about the Nazi period in Europe. As one researcher puts it: "Witnesses who are educated will give an account of events but will not commit themselves by giving dates, while most of the uneducated witnesses will give exact dates most of which we know are incorrect. . . . Accounts given of the number of deportees, number of dead, etc. are nearly always unreliable"; K.Y. Ball-Kaduri, "Evidence of Witnesses, Its Value and Limitations," *Yad Vashem Studies* (Jerusalem, 1959), 3: 84. It may well be that "participant-observers" in any large catastrophe live through the event psychologically, as it were, "outside of time and outside of reality," and that therefore any figures that they remember tend to be unrealistic.

25 Zofia Libiszowska in *KH* 62, no. 3 (1955): 167; O. Górka, *Ogniem i mieczem a rzeczywistość historyczna* (Warsaw, 1934), p. 112; idem, "Nieznana kronika Tatarska lat 1644–50," *KH* 62, no. 3: 114, 118, 120; *Zok Haitim*, 7a, 10b; *Yeveyn metzulah*, pp. 54, 80 (the latter also repeats a highly exaggerated figure for the Chmielnicki army and the Tatars, putting the former at "a few hundred thousands" or at six hundred thousand and the latter at eighty thousand); Bohdan Baranowski, "Organizacja i sklad spoleczny wojska polskiego w polowie XVII w.," in *Polska* 2: 12–13, 16; also Hanover talks about eighty thousand Tatars, while their number is put at between ten and twenty thousand; *Polska* 2: 456; see also Zygmunt Abrahamowicz, *Historia Chana Islama Gereja III* (Warsaw, 1971).

26 *Killed*

Tulczyn: *YM (Yeveyn metzulah)* 1,500; *TH (Tit ha-Yeveyn)* about 6,000; *ME (Megilat Eifa)* about 3,000
Konstantin: *YM* 3,000; *TH* 6,000
Polonnoe: *YM* 10,000; *TH* 20,000; *ME* 10,000; *ZBR (Zaar bath rabim)* 15,000
Bar: *YM* 2,000; *TH* 15,000; *ME* 3,000
Narol: *ZH (Zok Haitim)* 10,000; *YM* 12,000; *TH* 20,000; *ZBR* 18,000
Ostrog: *YM* 600; *TH* 15,000 families (75,000 people); *ZBR* 7,000
Gomel: *RIN* 1: 884, 2,000; *TH* over 10,000; *ME* 1,500
Pinsk: *TH* 1,200–1,500 or 3,200–4,000

Died

Brody: *YM* 3,000; *TH* 6,400 householders (25–30,000 people)
Lwów: (died of hunger and in epidemics) *YM* 10,000; *ZBR* 6,000; *ME* a few thousand; *TH* 2,000–2,500 (?). According to non-Jewish information the total

number of Jewish and non-Jewish victims in Lwów amounted to 7,000 (Halperin in *Sepher Yobel Layitzhak F. Baer*, p. 338).
Most sources mention the figure 6,000 for Nemerow.

27 The number of persons per family is usually computed by Polish and Jewish historians at five. This figure is questioned on general considerations as not being a "reasonable figure . . . the man-wife-children unit being usually about 3.5." Figures for general and Jewish population in Polish cities in 1787–1802 indicate a family size of 3.5–4.2 (J.C. Russell, *Late Ancient and Medieval Population* [Philadelphia, 1958], p. 12; Henryk Grossman, in *Kwartalnik Statystyezny* 2, no. 1 [Warsaw, 1925], p. 19).

28 On the 600,000 Jews allegedly remaining in Poland, see Lucien Wolf, *Menasseh b. Israel's Mission to Oliver Cromwell* (London 1901), p. 87.

29 *RIN* 1: 899, 1109; 2: 1200, 1710.

30 *TH* 425, 424; *YM* 58; *ZH* 6a.

31 See N. Nadav, "Kehilath Pinsk batekufa shemigzeyroth Tach-Tat va-shalom andrusov," *Zion* 31 (1966): 154–55, 157, 171–72.

32 *Zemach Zedek*, nos. 103, 113. This eyewitness's statement may well have been correct. In fact, the city of Lublin did pay the Russians and the cossacks a large amount (reported as three hundred thousand zloty) in order to save the city. At any rate, five years later (1660) a Polish commission found fifty-six houses in Lublin, apparently with Jews, even though according to the latter they found there also about 250 lots of burned-out houses (*Polska* 2: 365; Balaban, *Die Judenstadt von Lublin*, pp. 45–49; D. Kaufmann, *MGWJ* 39 [1895]: 557 ff.). Some Jews seem to have done the same and paid a ransom, or others did it for them. This is confirmed by eyewitnesses.

There exists a rare contemporary tract about the devastation of Lublin by the Russians and cossacks: *Relation, oder aussführliche Beschreibung von der jämmerlichen und erbärmlichen Verstörung und Einäscherung so bey Eroberung der schönen Stadt Lublien von den Moscowitern und Cosacken barbarischer Weise verübet worden.* (N. p., 1656).

33 *RIN* 1, no. 947; Shatzki, *Tach*, pp. 86–87; Baranovich, *Magnatskoe*, pp. 13–16.

34 E. Liskie, "Ulryk Werdun i dziennik podróży jego po Polsce w latach 1670–1672," *Przewodnik Naukowy literacki*, vol. 4 (Lwów, 1876), quoted in Shatzki, *YIVO Bleter* 40 (1956): 212–14; *RIN* 2, nos. 1184, 1338.

35 See Dinur, *Ba-mifneh ha-doroth*, pp. 114–15. In 1669 the non-Jews of Pinsk complained that the Jews spread out, built, or bought many houses and stores, thus pushing out the non-Jews (*RIN* 2: 1498, 1563; see also 1251); *Akty Vilenskoy arkheografiches-koy Komisii* 29, nos. 14–15, 17; Nadav, "Kehilath Pinsk," pp. 182–83.

In Żólkiew the regulations of the community deal with such matters as that the synagogue had become too small for the increased population, taxes from the newcomers, or prohibitions against admitting newcomers for six or ten years (Buber, *Kirya nisgava*, pp. 92, 95, 98); on growth of population in the 1660s and 1670s, see Wurm, *Z dziejów*, p. 32.

36 *RIN* 1, nos. 908, 919, 927, 929, 936, 940, 944, 945, 960, 967, 1004, 1005, 1007, 1011, 1014, 1015–16, 1018–20, 1022, 1027, 1031, 1034, 1042, 1045, 1046, 1049, 1056, 1058, 1068, 1078, 1093, 1095, 1106; 2, no. 1202.

37 *Yeveyn metzulah*, p. 77; *Zok Haitim* 6b; *PML*, pp. 452, 454, 466, 484; *Beth Yacob*, introduction and nos. 55, 104, 143; Weinryb, *Texts*, p. 327; Shatzki, *Tach*, p. 123.

The fact that a rumor about Zamość's having been taken by the cossacks (which was not true) was accompanied by "information" that many Jews baptized and remained there may possibly indicate that baptism was not rare (*RIN* 1: 898); *RIN* 1, nos. 880, 887, 907–8, 927, 929, 936, 938–40, 943–44, 952, 954–55, 957–59, 960–62, 967, 972, 980–81, 983–84, 986, 988–90, 991, 994, 996, 999, 1000, 1001, 1004–5, 1007, 1011, 1013–15, 1018–20, 1022, 1027, 1032, 1033, 1034, 1038, 1042, 1043, 1049, 1056, 1059, 1068, 1070, 1073, 1076, 1078, 1080–82, 1093, 1095, 1097–98; *Beth Hillel, Eben Haezer*, no. 7; see also Wurm, *Z dziejów*, p. 109.

38 *PVAA*, nos. 205, 217; Weinryb, *Texts*, pp. 123, 350. Poznań and Cracow sent letters and messengers to Jews in other countries asking for help. Historians usually connected the high indebtedness of the Jewish communities with the catastrophe of 1648–67. This contention is disproved by the sources. Poznań was in trouble over high debts as early as 1593 and again in the 1630s and on the eve of the cossack uprising of 1648 (Weinryb, *Texts*, nos. 81, 82, 87, 93, 94b, 95). Cracow Jews borrowed money in 1642, before 1646, 1647, and earlier (*HZK* 2: 222, 223, 226). The indebtedness of the Lithuanian Community Council seems (if we assume that the fragmentary figures listed in *PML* give some real picture) to have been much less in 1655 and in 1667–76 than in 1647 (before the cossack revolt).

39 *RIN* 1, nos. 933, 974; Avron, *Pinkas*, nos. 1239, 1349; Weinryb, *Mechkarim*, pp. 29–30; Landsberg, *JJLG* 6: 257 ff., 267 ff.; *PVAA*, pp. 354, 364, 530; Gelber, *Brody*, p. 23.

40 Weinryb, *Texts*, nos. 19–28, 327; Avron, *Pinkas*, nos. 801, 806, 844, 853, 949, 959, 1043, 1047, 1206, 1224; *PVAA*, nos. 205, 214, 216, 218, 241, 250; Lewin, *Geschichte der Juden*, pp. 90–92; Janina Morgensztern, *Biuletyn*, no. 34, p. 88; *JJLG* 6: 268; *HZK* 2: 106 ff., 125.

41 Janina Morgensztern, "Regesty," *Biuletyn*, no. 58 (1966), nos. 15–18, 20–36, 41–46, 55, 57–58, 62, 88, 91, 93, 95–96, 113–15, 120–22, 127, 131–33, 192, 194–95, 216–18, 240, 245–46; idem, *Biuletyn* no. 67 (1968), nos. 1, 3–7, 10–13, 15, 19–20, 24–25, 28, 36, 45–48, 53, 56–58, 63, 70–72, 74, 80–86, 93, 134, 146, 156–57, 178, 181, 183, 186, 194, 196, 198, 200, 204–8, 210, 218, 235, 242–44.

42 Hanover, *Yeveyn metzulah*, p. 28.

43 *PML*, nos. 452, 454, 460, 463 ff., 480, 481; See also Sosis in *Zeitschrift* 2: 44 ff.

44 Hanover, *Yeveyn metzulah*, pp. 35 ff., 37, 54; *Megilat Eifa*, pp. 134, 136.

45 By comparison, the descriptions or elegies dealing with massacres of Jews by the Polish troops during and after the Swedish invasion (1655–60) contain very few, if any, such expressions of wrath and disdain of the Poles (see the materials published in Bernfeld, *Sepher ha-demaot*, 3: 90–206).

46 Compare this with the attitudes of Jewish survivors of the 1939–45 holocaust, who began to distrust Christian society generally: "Every cynical sigh [by Christians] of sympathy would only desecrate the holy shadows of our martyrs" (quoted in Peter Meyer, B.D. Weinryb et al., *The Jews in the Soviet Satellites*, p. 245. A report that Jewish authorities banned future settlement in the Ukraine is not borne out by the existing sources (see *RIN* 3, no. 2185; *PVAA*, pp. 79–80).

47 Elsewhere Hanover rationalizes the Jews' survival by claiming that they gathered intelligence about their "Greek Orthodox neighbors and friends" and were spying on them. They sent the information gathered in this way by special riders, and therefore

the Polish lords loved them and stood up for them *(Yeveyn metzulah,* pp. 35, 30, 43–44).

48 *PML,* nos. 460, 484–85.

49 *RIN* 2, no. 1568; see also Nadav, "Kehilath Pinsk," pp. 193 ff.

50 See also B.D. Weinryb, "Yehudey Polin," pp. 185 ff.

51 The Jewish population in Poland may have trebled or quadrupled during this century. Thomas R. Malthus maintains that after wars and epidemics population has a tendency to grow faster. The rapid rise of the birthrate in many countries following World War II may apparently serve as some proof of Malthus's hypothesis.

52 The number of entries in the minute books (*PML,* and others) dealing with quarrels and fights within the communities or among the leadership increases considerably in the second half of the seventeenth century. See also Dinur, *Ba-mifneh ha-doroth,* pp. 114 ff., about the eighteenth century.

53 Expulsions occurred in 1721, 1727, 1740, and 1742. Some of the baptized—and their children—attained high posts among the cossacks: father-in-law of the cossack chief (hetman) Orlik, brother-in-law of another hetman (Skoropadskij), colonels in the army, chief treasurer, and so on; *RIN* 2: 1425, 1455, 1617, 1642, 1647, 1652, 1658, 1680, 1690, 1698, 1702, 1729, 1741, 1772–74; 3: 1856, 1882, 1891, 1896, 1899–1900.

54 This happened in 1702–4, 1708, and other years; Baranovich, *Magnatskoe,* pp. 19 ff.; *RIN* 2, nos. 1373, 1374, 1390, 1430, 1439. In the Polish Ukraine cossack detachments connected with the Polish army were discontinued in 1699. Some, however, remained as guards on nobles' private estates.

55 Rawita-Gawronski, *Żydzi,* p. 221.

56 *RIN* 2, nos. 1366–67, 1371, 1374, 1378, 1384, 1390, 1401, 1428, 1430, 1439, 1495, 1501, 1748, 1753, 1764, 1770, 1776, 1780, 1790, 1794, 1812, 1816, 1819, 1826, 1831, 1837; 3, nos. 1936–37, 1942, 1947, 1986, 1989, 1992, 2014, 2045, 2049.

57 See also Rawita-Gawronski, *Żydzi,* pp. 184 ff., 248 ff.; Kirdan, *Ukrainskii Epos.*

58 *RIN* 2, nos. 1770, 1780, 1830, 1847; 3, nos. 1898, 1940, 1943, 1944, 1946–48, 1951, 1960, 1995–97, 1999, 2006, 2008, 2010, 2014, 2015, 2023, 2056, 2068, 2087–89, 2092, 2098.

59 RIN 3, nos. 2153, 2155.

60 RIN 3, nos. 2158–61, 2164–66, 2167; Rawita-Gawronski, *Żydzi,* pp. 226 ff.

61 The Russian state, unlike that of 1648, was interested in preventing events from getting out of hand. Also, contrary to the policy in connection with the Chmielnicki revolt, Russian border cities and fortresses were now ordered to give refuge to fleeing Jews, and we know of some cases in which this was actually done (RIN 3, nos. 2162–63).

62 Ksawery Branicki, to whom the captured *haidemaks* were turned over by the Russian commander, in his letter to the Polish king tells about the joy of the Polish landowners and the Jews that the *haidemaks* were caught, and their advice to "execute . . . burn . . . hang." Jewish sources give him credit as a defender of the Jews (having supposedly been induced by Jews from Brody to catch the *haidemaks*). According to other information Branicki and his troops were not involved in the apprehension of the *haidemaks,* but Branicki was the one to decide their fate (see RIN 3, no. 2178; Rawita-Gawronski, *Żydzi,* pp. 234–35).

63 Only a very few Jewish sources about the massacres of 1768 exist, and those that have

been preserved are of an entirely different character from the ones describing the events of 1648. For 1768 there are no chronicles or descriptions in Hebrew or similar documents. (Does this indicate that contemporaries of 1768 were much less shocked by the events or regarded them as less newsworthy than those of 1648? This would be quite understandable). The documentation consists mainly of a letter in Yiddish written in the summer of 1768, a prayer entered in the *pinkas* of the Jewish kehilla in Uman—surely not at the time of the killings, a "story" told anonymously in Yiddish, which was published fifteen years later in Fürth, Germany, as an addition to another book (1783) and a more extensive version published about half a century later in Sudzilkov in the Ukraine (in 1834 and 1838). A memoir, a few dirges, and a few notices are also preserved. A folk song in Yiddish preserved by word of mouth (recorded in the 1830s or 1840s) depicts the massacres of 1768 as worse than those of 1648, saying that during the Chmielnicki massacres Jews established an annual fast but that "today one should establish a fast day every week; there is more to cry for." These sources seem to be even less reliable than those of the 1640s.

64   One story has Gonta not only tricking the governor of Uman, but also the rabbi, whom he promised protection for the Jews. This may have some connection with a story told in a non-Jewish source that before Gonta left Uman to meet Zhelezniak he received a considerable number of gold pieces from the Jews, in exchange for which he promised to defend them (Rawita-Gawronski, *Żydzi,* p. 226); *RIN* 3, nos. 2161–65, 2168–69, 2171, 2173–74, 2178–79, 2180–82, 2185–86, 2191–95; S. Dubnow, "Der zweiter Churban fun ukraine," *HS* 1: 27–54, idem, *History of the Jews in Russia and Poland,* 1: 183–86; Gurland, *Lekorot,* pp. 6–8; idem, ibid., *Machberet Shlishit* (Cracow, 1889), pp. 28–35, 40. It is interesting to note that the Russian general, Krechetnikov, who with his detachment apprehended Gonta and other *haidemaks,* used Jews as scouts and spies for procuring information and for similar services while he was in Poland (*RIN* 3, no. 2196).

Chapter 10

1   Some writers show a tendency to label as "messianic movement" any information on a false Messiah or any expression of a Jewish messianic idea. This seems to constitute too loose a use of the word movement. A movement implies, among other things, a group activity, some sort of coordination among the followers, and is not to be equated with doctrines or ideas alone. Many incidents (actual or theoretical) of Jewish messianism are no more than ideas or expressions of hope, and have little to do with activity or movement. Titles using a phrase such as "Messianic Idea" (Joseph Klausner, *The Messianic Idea in Israel* [New York, 1955]; A.H. Silver, *The History of Messianic Speculation in Israel* [Boston, 1955]) are more appropriate than the word movements or *tenuoth* (Ashkoli, *Hatenuot Hameshichiot Bayisrael*). The Sabbatai Zevi "affair" may fall between "idea" or "speculation" and "movement." Actually, G. Scholem is concerned that there was so little activity in the Sabbatai Zevi "movement." His "apology" for it is Sabbatai's mental status of inactivity (see his *Sabbatai Zevi,* pp. 101, 571–72, 585). But the fact of little or no activity in many countries remains. About movements generally, see also Rudolf Heberle, *Social Movements* (New York, 1951) and C. Wendell King, *Social Movements in the United States* (New York, 1956). These publications concern the present day, but some of their definitions may also to some extent apply to earlier times.

2 See Y. Baer, "On the Problem of Eschatological Doctrine during the Period of the Second Temple," *Zion* 23–24 (1958–1959): 3–34, 141–65, on parallels in Jewish and Greek thought. It seems that the late A. Ashkoli (in his posthumous work mentioned in preceding note) also thought that messianism is a universal idea; this is clear from fragments of his introduction, which was not preserved.

3 Cohn, *The Pursuit of the Millennium*, pp. 30, 35–39, 45–47, 70, 78 ff., 83 ff., 107, 149 ff., 162, 190, 222, 229 ff., 231, 234, 237, 240 ff., 253, 273, 298 ff., 308, 321, 323, 325 ff., 331, 337 ff., 344, 351, 356, 360 (the quotations are from pp. xiii, 32, 308); Ernest Lee Tuveson, *Millennium and Utopia* (New York, 1964), pp. 47, 85 ff., 91 ff., 135 ff.

4 See also Klausner, *The Messianic Idea in Israel*, pp. 505–31; excerpts of texts in Ashkoli, *Hatenuot Hameshichiot Bayisrael*, passim.

5 Scholem, *Major Trends*, pp. 284, 287. Scholem, like some of the other "new-mystics" scholars (if we may call them that), regards cabala as an expression of the mood of the period; like them (in their "Zionist fervor"), he tends to interpret mystical speculations as actions in the direction of apocalyptic redemption and return to Palestine, and to stress all this out of proportion to reality. One is justified, however, in regarding most of these mystic fantasies of small groups as no more than an escape from reality with little actual impact.

6 See Cohen, *Messianic Postures*, p. 7 and passim.

7 This is not meant to imply that among the Ashkenzim there were no bookish speculations, no "forecasters" of the time of the Messiah's coming. But pretenders were very rare among Ashkenazim.

8 Contemporaries in both Amsterdam and Hamburg report that the letters about the Messiah were received by the "Portuguese" (Sephardic) communities and read in their synagogues. The Sephardim are depicted as leaders in the pro-Sabbatai trend, whereas the Ashkenazim were only followers or onlookers; Max Weinreich, "A Yidish Lied wegn Shabtai Zevi fun yur 1666," *Zeitschrift* 1: 167; *The Life of Glückel of Hamelin 1646–1724*, trans. Beth Zion Abrahams (New York, 1963), p. 45.

9 See the facts quoted by Cohen, *Messianic Postures*, p. 11; see also Ashkoli, *Hatenuot Hameshichiot Bayisrael*, vol. 1. It should be mentioned that in Amsterdam the Ashkenazim expressed doubts about the purity of the Sephardic families, denying that they were ritually true Jews and accusing some of them of disregard for the laws of the Torah (Ichaq Markon in *Ziyunim, Kovetz le-zikhro shel Y.N. Simchoni* [Berlin, 1929], p. 163).

10 Cases of adultery, extramarital intercourse, and relations with non-Jewish women are also found among Ashkenazic Jews, of course. But only among Spanish-Portuguese Jews do we find some who had official concubines and some communities that kept Jewish prostitutes (Zimmels, *Ashkenazim and Sephardim*, pp. 250–51); see Simcha Asaf, *Baohelei Yakov* (Jerusalem, 1943), pp. 158–60 and the sources quoted there.

11 *Responsa Bach* (Frankfurt on the Main, 1697[?]), no.5; Cecil Roth, *A History of the Marranos* (Philadelphia, 1941), p. 176 and passim; Jacob J. Petuchowski, *The Theology of Haham David Nieto* (New York, 1954), pp. 32–48; *JJLG* 5: 27 ff., 31, 38 ff.; 7: 162–63, 183, 188, 196–98, 204, 206, 231; 8: 231, 250, 253, 255, 260, 265–66, 279, 283–84; 10: 226, 232 ff., 253, 259, 270, 274, 288, 292; Asaf, *Baohelei Yakov*, pp. 147–50, 156–60, 167–69; Kellenbenz, *Sephardim*, pp. 31, 34 ff. 37 ff., 45 ff., 49, 52; Rosanes, *Divrei*, 3: 15 ff., 70 ff., 122, 192; 4: 6, 12. Abraham Senior Texeira was a very rich Jew (a former Marrano), banker and diplomatic representative of the queen

of Sweden, agent of Spain, and leader of the Jewish community in Hamburg. But when he died at the end of December 1665 his funeral cortege was attacked on its way to the Jewish cemetery and almost all the participants were mistreated. Earlier, he and his son, Isaac, were involved in a prolonged case brought against them by the emperor in Vienna, who, as head of the Catholic Church (the Holy Roman Empire), claimed all the Texeiras' wealth on the grounds that they were renegades from the Catholic religion (*JJLG* 11: 5–6).

12   There is a good deal of uncertainty about the biographical and other details of Sabbatai Zevi and his "movement," although we have many more sources regarding this messianism than about any other of the earlier false Messiahs. But these sources are hardly reliable. They consist of writings either by his followers (or former followers) or adversaries, reports and documents from a number of non-Jews who either saw in the Jewish "Messiah" a sensational occurrence and enlarged upon it, or were outright anti-Jewish. Almost all the communicators reported fables as facts, fabrications as occurrences, and fantasies as realities. In addition, they all exaggerated wildly and deliberately falsified the facts. Still others wrote half a century or more after the event (the memoirs of Glückel of Hamelin; those of Loeb b. Ozer, who also relates a good deal from hearsay; and so on). See also Scholem, *Sabbatai Zevi*, 1: 84, 92, 95, 121, and passim.

13   Scholem, *Sabbatai Zevi*, 1: 101–11.

14   A non-Jewish contemporary depicts them as fishermen, egg and fowl vendors, port workers, and servants.

15   Scholem, *Sabbatai Zevi*, 1: 290; 2: 719–20, 745–46, 786.

16   See Stavro Skendi, "Crypto Christianity in the Balkan Area under the Ottomans," *Slavic Review* 26 (1967): 227–46.

17   Scholem, *Sabbatai Zevi*, 1: 133, 173–79, 2: 618, 709, 730, 748–49, 761, 774. It should be mentioned that generally similar behavior is not always proof of influence or imitation; it may simply result from similar situations.

18   *ZNZ*, pp. 177–78; Scholem *Sabbatai Zevi*, 2: 586–87.

19   One of the two, Izaak Nahar, may have thought of returning to Portugal (on business or otherwise). In any event, his aunt had left him most of her wealth, specifying in her will that he was to receive it on the condition that he did not travel to Portugal. In 1666 he appears in Italy as a staunch believer in Sabbatai, whom he acclaims in his letters, but by the summer of 1667 he was already making efforts to obtain the rest of this inheritance (*JJLG* 8 [1911]: 279; 11: 34–39; see also Scholem, *Sabbatai Zevi*, 2: passim [see index]; *ZNZ*, pp. 24–25, 248, 250, 255).

20   In *Sabbatai Zevi* Scholem, who quotes this and other passages (1: 471 ff.), is none too exact in his translation and the remarks about them. Also, some of his interpretations are exaggerations—possibly because he takes things out of context. Thus Scholem precedes the first entry with the remark that the "community leaders recorded the following with *great solemnity*" (emphasis added). In fact, nothing is said about "solemnity," nor is the entry afforded any particular importance in the minute book; it is placed between two entries dealing with the standard decisions of the community to give support to a widow and to distribute wood to the poor during the winter, and is followed by similar entries, including one about payment for renovating the synagogue (*JJLG* 10 (1913): 292–93).

21   *JJLG* 10: 295. This anxiety, which was felt by the end of December 1665, was intensified by the mob attack a few days later upon the funeral of the rich community

leader Abraham Senior Texeira, mentioned above in note 11. The community petitioned the senate about it two weeks later. The dancing during the Feast of Esther
evening, celebrating the news about the Messiah, was interrupted, apparently by
Sabbatai's opponents; *JJLG* 11 (1916): 1–2; *ZNZ* 10, 47; Scholem, *Sabbatai Zevi*, 2:
473–74.

22 *JJLG*, 11: 5–6.

23 *JJLG*, 11: 9–10, 25, 29; see also p. 31; *ZNZ* 62, 132.

24 They decided to support Glückstadt financially "so that the community should always
be maintained to serve as a place of refuge in case, God forbid, conditions [in
Hamburg] should necessitate it." Glückstadt was, in those years, within the sphere of
the king of Denmark, who was at the time more liberal toward Jews; *JJLG* 11: 24–25,
27.

25 *JJLG* 11: 7, 52; B. Brilling, *YIVO Bleter* 5 (1933): 45. The passus in the announcement of the sale of the community house in order to "pay up the debts of the
community to be ready for the way on which we hope soon to leave with God's help"
and the one in the contract that says the community will pay a certain amount "if
the Messiah will come or not" do not necessarily indicate a real involvement in the
"Messiah business." They may be mere phraseology. In 1762, a century after the
mentioned passus had been added to the entry in Hamburg, the secretary of the Berlin
kehilla wrote in its minute book that the kehilla would repay the forty-five hundred
Reichsthaler it had borrowed from Halberstadt "in case the Messiah should come and
they should leave Berlin or else, God forbid, they would be expelled" (Joseph Meisl,
Protokolbuch der Juedischen Gemeinde Berlin [Jerusalem, 1962], p. 198, Hebrew
part). The passus about the coming of the Messiah seems in each instance (Hamburg
1666, Berlin 1762) to be no more than a phrase signifying "in the extreme case."

26 *JJLG* 11: 11, 15, 22, 52. Prof. Scholem's assumption that Sasportas intended to travel
to Italy and Jerusalem in the first months of 1666 because he was temporarily drawn
to the imposter may or may not have any validity as far as Sasportas is concerned. But
the kehilla's negative answer to his application for a grant of funds for this purpose
may show how little the board of the kehilla was *in fact* committed to messianism (or
that they knew that he was planning the trip for other reasons). They refused to
support his trip unless he took his family with him—the normal procedure in Hamburg
being that if a Jew left the city for good he received from the kehilla support for
traveling expenses (see *JJLG* 11:9; see also 10: 284–90).

27 "Ein schein nei lied fun Mashiach," reprinted by Max Weinreich, "A Yidish Lied
wegn Shabtai Zevi fun yur 1666," *Zeitschrift* 1 (Minsk, 1926): 159–72.

28 Thus Prof. Scholem tries to "show" that Rabbi Menachem Mendel ben Isaac, rabbi
in Frankfurt on the Main since 1664, must have been a supporter of Sabbatai because
in 1647 (sic), in appraising a cabalistic work he wrote: "Being before the coming of
our Messiah for whose coming we hope even when it will be delayed" (2: 456); but
this is nothing more than a paraphrase of the known principle of Maimonides.

29 In some places in the Ottoman Empire the Jews—or some of them—may really have
cut down or neglected their business matters, as related by none too reliable non-Jews
(Scholem, *Sabbatai Zevi*, 1: 294–95, 366–67, 374).

30 I. Isserlein, *Pesakim u-Ketavim*, no. 88; see also Zimmels, "Erez Israel," pp. 44–64;

Eidelberg, *Jewish Life in Austria*, pp. 100–4; see also the quotations in Shchepanski, *Eretz Yisrael*, 1: 31–32, 122, 134–36.

31 According to Jewish law the local poor should enjoy preferential treatment and should receive support before the poor of other countries or cities. The poor of Palestine were usually regarded—in the case of wills, gifts, and so on—as being on a par with the local poor. See also *Responsa Rema*, nos. 47–48, about a will. Neither Moses Isserles nor Joseph Caro argue here in terms of full preferential treatment for Palestine. Also, one should take into consideration that in the case under review the heirs tried to use a technicality in the will to avoid paying the willed amount for Palestine. In other words, in terms of practice—not rabbinical decisions—some people had no qualms about not paying willed sums to Palestine. A number of sixteenth- and seventeenth-century responsa have been preserved concerning legacies for Palestine, some of them from Poland. In many cases the heirs or the local community of the deceased refused to give up the money for Palestine or for the purpose designated in the will. In a number of cases of this sort the rabbis agreed with the heirs or the local community and decided that they had priority over "the poor of Jerusalem" (Kahane in *Sinai* 31 (1952): 15–43.

32 *YS* Yebamoth 6: 32; Hulin 8: 53; Edeles, *Hiddushey Agadoth*, Berakoth 8a, Erubin 10b; Hurewitz, *Shnei Luchot Habrith*, pp. 106a, 203a, 364a, 366a, 367a. Rabbi Yaffe's interpretation is quoted in Yehuda Rosenthal in *Sinai* 31 (1942): 332, note 126.

33 Hurewitz, *Shnei Luchot Habrith*, pp. 364a, 366a, 367a, 203a; *Yesod Joseph*, p. 49b; *Yesh Nochlin*, pp. 25b, 10a.

34 F. Wettstein, *Kadmoniot mi-Pinkasaoth Yeshanim*, 1892, p. 14; idem, *Mipinkesey*, pp. x, xiii; Weinryb, *Texts*, p. 50, nos, 138–39; *PML*, nos. 53, 286, 456, 462, 492, 523, 558; see also 808; *PVAA*, nos. 151, 200, 541, 657, 665, 870, 884; also p. 53, note 5.

35 Weinryb, *Texts*, p. 50, nos. 138–39; *PVAA*, nos. 172, 200. Counting only the expenditures for internal Jewish affairs (excluding taxes to the state and city and various payments to the authorities), the sum donated for Palestine in Poznań would be 3.5 percent. See also Israel Halperin, "Al yachasan shel hakehilot va-ha-vaadim be-Polin Laeretz Yisrael," *Zion* 1 (1936): 82–88.

36 Hurewitz, *Shnei Luchot Habrith*, p. 24g a; *Olloth Ephraim*, introduction.

37 *Taharot Hakodesh*, p. 29b.

38 This phrase was used by Moses Katz from Narol, later rabbi in Metz. See Gurland, *Lekorot*, 3: 15–16.

39 Cited in M. Balaban, "Sabataizm w Polsce," in *Ksiega Jubileuszowa ku czei Prof. Dr. Mojżesza Schorra* (Warsaw, 1935), pp. 57–59. Balaban quotes the decree of March 23 as "proof" that the later ones (sic) were of no practical help.

40 Ritual murder and similar accusations occurred in Różane, 1657 (two Jews suffered martyrs' deaths, 1659); Poznań, 1663 (outcome unknown); Cracow (Jews freed by court); Woina (?) (Jews freed); Cracow (Matatyahu Calahora burned); 1663–66, Ciechanow (stealing of the holy wafer; Jews bailed out by two noblemen); 1666, Mościska (inducement to steal from church: two Jews burned). Attacks on Jews took place in Lwów, 1664 (129 dead; loss estimated at 700,000 zloty); Cracow, 1664; Wilno, 1664 (attack on Jewish synagogue on Saturday: court sentenced attackers to death); Balaban, "Sabataizm," pp. 61–73; *HZK* 2: 24–31, 34. *RIN* 1, nos. 984, 987–988, 990, 996, 1005, 1026, 1031–32, 1034, 1043,–44, 1049.

41 Avron, *Pinkas*, nos. 936–1076 (no. 1062 mentions rising poverty as a rationale for cutting down on expenses); *PVAA*, nos. 241–67; *PML*, nos. 572–628; Lewin, *Landessynode*, pp. 91–92; Buber, *Kirya nisgava*, pp. 96–97.

42 See, for instance, Bernfeld, *Sepher ha-demaot*, 3: 89, 103, 108, 157, 161–62, 164, 168, 175–77, 184, 193–94, 196–99, 206, 217, 220, 232, 245, 247; *Tit ha-Yeveyn*, end; Gurland, *Lekorot*, 3 (1849): 27.

43 Frank Gaynor, ed., *Dictionary of Mysticism* (New York, 1953), p. 119; Scholem, *Major Trends*, p. 10; see Baumgardt, *Great Western Mystics*, pp. 6–7, 3–5.

44 Scholem, *Major Trends*, pp. 88–114.

45 *Shoshan Sodoth*, published in Koretz in 1784, contains parts of the work. Ben-Yacob (ed., *Otzar ha-Sepharim*) notes also an edition from Venice (1550) but this is questionable.

46 Published in Cracow, 1603; Lublin, 1623; many editions after 1750.

47 Meir ben Yechezkayl, *Abodath Hakodesh* (Cracow, 1577); *Sepher Hassidim* (Cracow, 1581); *Zavaat Rabbi Yehuda Hachassid*, 1583; *Sepher Mareh Kohen*, 1589; Moses Kordovaro, *Pardes Rimonim* (Cracow, 1592); Mordekhai Jaffe, *Lebush Eben Hayekara* (Lublin, 1595); *Zeror Hamor*, 1595; *Shaarey Gan Eden* (Lublin, 1597); *Tamim Yachdav*, 1592; Joseph Giktiliya, *Shaarey Orah*, 1600.

48 Lewin, *Geschichte der Juden*, p. 67, note 2.

49 Balaban, Scholem, and others assume that such a large study of cabala existed.

50 Isserles, *Torath haoleh*, part 3, ch. 4; Edeles, *Hiddushey Agadoth*, Hagigah 13a, quoted in Scholem, *Sabbatai Zevi*, 1: 61.

51 Hurewitz, *Shnei Luchot Habrith*, p. 41b.

52 Scholem, *Sabbatai Zevi*, 1: 62, note 2, 54, note 3; *KS* 26: 194. Scholem's "proof" about Poland being a center of cabala because S. Luzzatto in Italy mentions in 1638 that cabala "is accepted willingly . . . in Poland" needs to be backed up by real evidence that Luzzatto in Venice had firsthand knowledge of Polish Jews (Scholem, p. 60).

53 Isserles, *Torath Haoleh*, part 3, ch. 4; *Darkey Moshe*, Orach Hayim, 141, par. 2; 294, par. 2; Yoreh Dea, 115, par. 9; *Responsa Mas'at Benyamin*, no. 62; *Bach Hayeshanoth*, no. 5; some non-Polish rabbis also looked to the *Zohar* for rulings. Thus, for instance, Joseph Caro; see, H.J. Zimmels, "Rabbi Joseph Caro and His Attitude toward the Later Sephardi and Ashkenazi Schools," *Fourth World Congress of Jewish Studies, Papers* (1967), 1: 235–38; see also *YS* Hulin 8,6.

54 P. 3b. It should be mentioned that a German rabbi of Polish extraction, Zebi Hirsch ben Jacob Ashkenazi—and with him some others—took the *Zohar* as an authority in a decision affecting kosher-terefa *(Responsa Chachan Zevi*, nos. 74, 76; see also R. Margalioth, *Sinai* 29, nos. 11–12 [1951]: 381–85).

55 Scholem, *Sabbatai Zevi*, 1: 64.

56 This may be the meaning of the attitudes taken by two cabalists in the early 1660s, one of whom hails the spreading of the cabalist ideas and the other, a preacher, complains that too many "secrets" are being divulged in print (Jacob Temerles and Berachya Beirach); see quotations in Scholem, ibid., pp. 68–69.

57 Scholem, *Sabbatai Zevi*, 1: 62–64; idem, "Hatenua," pp. 37–38.

58 Scholem, *Major Trends*, p. 274; "The spread of Lurianic cabalism with its doctrine of *Tikkun*, of the restitution of cosmic harmony through the earthly medium of mystically elevated Judaism, could not but lead to an explosive manifestation of all those forces to which it owed its rise and success"; ibid., p. 287.

59   Scholem, *Sabbatai Zevi*, 1: 2, sees it as "strange that among the active people in Sabbatian propaganda one hardly finds Polish Jews."

60   Ibid., 2:495; idem, "Hatenua," p. 40, *HZK* 2:43, 48, 172.

61   The picture of Polish Jewish participation in the Sabbatai Zevi upheaval is, aside from general considerations, mainly based on four pieces of "documentary" evidence. All four would be thrown out of a court of law in about thirty seconds for lack of probative.

(a)   The statement that the Cracow rabbi Arye Loeb ben Zecharia Mendel copied the letters of Nathan the "prophet" and spread them among the scholars in Poland is supposedly taken from Dembitzer's *Klilat Yofi*, but this writer could not find it there (I used a 1960 offset reprint published in New York).

(b)   Sasportas's information that "through Poland" *(derech Polin)* writings reached Germany about Sabbatai's alleged success with the sultan (apparently the papers were sent via Poland and not by way of the sea because of a minor war in that region) becomes "from Poland" and is followed by an "analysis" of the alleged role of these stories in Poland itself.

(c)   The "facts" that Jews in Poland paraded in the streets with pictures of Sabbatai Zevi derive mainly from the mistaken injection of the word "Jews" in brackets into a translation of a decree by King John Casimir (dated May 5, 1666) against anti-Jewish baiters who spread false information on "some messiah" and disseminated falsified pictures and writings in order to attack Jews and rob them of their possessions. Thus through faulty translation "anti-Semites" became "Jews." (True, a bishop who issued an order a little later [on June 22, 1666] may, intentionally or not, have lumped Jews and non-Jews together, accusing Jews of "spreading writings and pictures with the help of people [non-Jews] from the gutter.") These charges may have been anti-Semitic, resembling in a way the twentieth-century anti-Semites' accusations that Jews make pogroms upon themselves. And the source for it all is an extremely anti-Jewish book published some sixty years later, when the writer could have altered the document or even fabricated it; Radlinski, *Prawda Chrzesciańska* [Lublin, 1728]; see also Balaban, *Letoldot,* pp. 30–31.

(d)   An anti-Semitic propaganda work, which repeats all the lies about Jews killing Christian children and using their blood, and "knows" (in 1669) that Sabbatai was defeated by a Turkish army of fifty thousand men, was skinned alive and the skin filled with straw, etc., is an "eyewitness" of Jews in Poland and "Russia" celebrating the coming of the Messiah and threatening the Christians with revenge, etc. etc. Joanikij Galyatovski's book *(The True Messiah, Jesus Christ, God's Son* [1669]), which belongs in the category of Christian anti-Jewish defamation literature, cannot, of course, serve as source material for facts on Jewish life. Even more important, he was physically unable to obtain any firsthand knowledge about Poland and Polish Jews. He lived in the part of the Ukraine that became *judenrein* and separated from Poland as a result of the Chmielnicki uprising of 1648. From 1654 until the truce of 1667 the war there precluded any contact between the two parts of the country. Galyatovski lived in Kiev from 1657 to 1665, when he moved farther east to another *judenrein* region. He was thus completely outside Poland and could not have seen or heard anything even approaching the truth about the behavior of Polish Jews during 1665–66 (Galyatovski, *Mesiya pravdivij Isus Christos syn Bozhii* [Kiev, 1669]; Albert M. Amman, *Abriss der Ostslavischen Kirchengeschichte* [Vienna, 1950], p. 352; see also Scholem, *Sabbatai Zevi*, 2: 493–502).

62   The available source, a manuscript of Loeb b. Ozer written almost half a century later, is only secondary, based on hearsay, and none too reliable; see Scholem, *Sabbatai Zevi*, 1: 300, note 2; 310, note 2; 2: 520, 535 about Loeb ben Ozer and about ZNZ and Emden, *Torath Hakanaut.*

63   ZNZ, pp. 76–79, 172, 174–75, 345–46; Emden, *Torath Hakanaut*, pp. 14 ff.; Scholem, *Sabbatai Zevi*, 2: 518–26; 554–63; idem, *Hatenua*, pp. 43 ff. Another Polish Jew, Abraham Kokish of Wilno, may have visited Sabbatai in Gallipoli, returning later via Amsterdam (Scholem, 2: 500).

64   It is also not impossible that by chance the scribe's name was Sabbatai. The year 1666 is not entirely clear. If so, this may have nothing to do with the "Messiah." Also a document was found in the archives of the Cracow community that some historians take to show that the writer was a Sabbatian. But this is a very doubtful document. The year is indicated, as is usual in rabbinic literature, by the numerical value of the letters of a sentence meaning in English "the redeemer, God's Messiah came" (or "come" in the sense of a plea). Balaban took it at first to mean 1660, later 1671 (the numerical value is actually 1650), arguing that the day of the week and of the month (Wednesday, the tenth of Cheshvan) is possible only in 1671. But this possibility exists during a number of years before 1671 (eight or ten times between 1638 and 1655) and after 1671. See M. Balaban, "Sabataizm," pp. 72, 80; *HZK* 2, picture following p. 48; Scholem, *Hatenua.*

65   Balaban, "Sabataizm," pp. 88–89. Anti-Semitic writings with a Messiah theme existed earlier in Poland, for instance, *Send Brief albo list od Żydów Polskich do mesjasza . . .* (1601); *Jericho nowe, w Którym się ukazuje o dowodzie mesjaszowem* (1615); see also Bartoszewicz, *Antysemityzm*, pp. 60–69, 72.

66   Scholem, *Sabbatai Zevi*, 2: 648, takes at face value the statement of Samuel Abohab of Venice that the "holy communities of Palestine, Turkey, Germany, Flanders, Poland and Russia . . . have burned [after Sabbatai's conversion] all their *pinkesim* and writings where Sabbatai was mentioned . . ." and assumes that a documentation existed but was intentionally destroyed. Thus, he argues, we have no evidence about the "facts." Of course such an assumption demands first of all evidence that Abohab did have firsthand knowledge of what was going on in Poland and in other countries. Moreover, if one is sure that Abohab's statement about the burning of the documents is reliable, one should also accept the main part of it—that "these communities repented" and gave up their Sabbatianism (the burning of the materials being a result of the repentance and the denial of the messianism of Sabbatai Zevi). In the meantime Scholem goes on to "prove" the contrary. See *Devar Shmuel*, p. 97a.

67   ZNZ, pp. 186–97; Scholem, *Sabbatai Zevi*, 2: 609, 637 ff.

68   *Devar Shmuel*, pp. 95–97b; Freiman, *Inyaney*, p. 44.

69   Sabbatai Raphael appeared in Amsterdam and Hamburg (1667), professing to be, among other things, a healer, and apparently found some followers among the Ashkenazim; Mordechai of Eisenstadt as a messiah in 1680. See Scholem, *Sabbatai Zevi*, 2: 586 ff.; ZNZ, pp. 272–89, 321–22.

70   Scholem points out that "few are the items of information from Poland" and wonders

why no trace of Sabbatianism was discovered there in community records. At the same time he admits that in Lithuania "Sabbatianism . . . disappeared more completely than in most other countries" (Scholem, *Sabbatai Zevi*, 2: 636; idem, *Major Trends*, p. 303; idem, *Hatenua*, p. 45.

71 *PVAA*, nos. 278, 939. The first ban was issued in conjunction with another one of an economic character. This may indicate that it was perhaps rather a formality.

72 Freiman, *Inyaney*, pp. 99–108; Scholem, *Hatenua*, pp. 49–52; idem, *Zion* 6: 91–92.

73 In premodern Jewish thought and writing eclecticism was widespread; an author picked up thoughts and passages from predecessors without much ado. It is possible that here, too, such processes were at work. If a seemingly Sabbatian author *(Hemdat Hayamim)* could integrate many parts and ideas of non-Sabbatians in his work, obviously a non-Sabbatian could do the same with Sabbatian passages (see Tishbi, *Netivey Amunah*, pp. 108–68).

74 See, for instance, *PML*, pp. 130, 596. The class consciousness of the Sabbatians, who belonged to a lower class, may also be gauged from their rather negative approach to wealthy people, for example, J. Tausk of Amsterdam. Nathan is said to have been antagonistic to wealthy people. Jehuda Hachassid identified the rich with the wicked in one of his sermons, *Zeitschrift* 1: 169–70. See Scholem, in *Sepher Dinaburg*, pp. 242, 255; Z. Rubashov, *Zion* 6:213.

75 Some of the stories about secret Sabbatians (at the end of seventeenth beginning of the eighteenth century) point out their erotic passion and depravity. Some of their writings abound in excessive erotic symbolism; Tishbi, *Netivey*, pp. 218–22.

Chapter 11

1 *Taharot Hakodesh*, part 2, p. 41a.

2 Scholem, *Major Trends*, p. 319; idem, "Mitzva habaah," pp. 370–71. Scholem sees in the "new Torah" the reason for sin. Using modern approaches of the behavioral sciences one is justified in reversing the order (sin leads to justification leads to "Torah of the higher world"); see also Scholem, *Hatenua*, pp. 54–55, about some books that appeared around 1700 in which rudiments of Sabbatianism may have been only subtly indicated.

3 Frederick C. Conybeare, *Russian Dissenters*, Harvard Theological Studies, vol. 10 (New York, 1969); Bolshakoff, *Russian Nonconformity;* Grass, *Die Russischen Sekten;* Woodcock and Avakumovic, *The Doukhobors;* Iryda Grek-Parisowa, "Niektóre wiadomości o Starowiernych zamieszkalych na terenie Polski," *Slavia Orientalis* 8, no. 4 (1959): 135–50; Wladyslaw A. Serczyk, *Gospodarstwo magnackie w województwie Podolskim w drugiej polowie XVIII w.* (Wroclaw, 1965), p. 24.

4 Jacob Frank chides his followers on one occasion with the words: "You were Jews and have remained Jews being lower than the Philipowcy." He apparently also alludes to the Philipowcy in another of his sayings (no. 2097). Then again Frank and his group used a former leader of such a dissident group as their defender, as their contact with the Polish clergy, and as a writer of documents in Polish for submission to the authorities. Kraushar assumes that Frank's contact with Malivda (Kossakowsky) stems from the time when Frank and a group of the Frankists lived in Turkey. Jews in Poland generally seem also to have had information on and possible contacts with the Philipowcy. Jacob Emden, whose information derives from the Polish Jewish leaders, tells

about the Philipowcy when, at the beginning of the 1760s, he extols the divine help for Polish Jews in getting rid of the Frankists. The facts he relates about some of the Philipowcy converting to Judaism may have been incorrect; his informers apparently confused the opposition of the non-Jewish sectarians to the official church with their inclination toward Judaism (Kraushar, *Frank i Frankiści*, 2:45; 1 [Hebrew]: 124–26, 246; Emden, *Sepher Shimush*, p. 84b).

About Hassidim and the sectarians there is only indirect information. Besht is reported by his grandson to have said that the songs (Lieder) of the non-Jews (apparently meaning the sectarians, in whose ceremonies and ritual songs played a big role) refer to awe and love spreading from heaven down to the earth. A story tells how Besht asked one of his followers, the rabbi Meir Margaliot, to leave his seven-year-old son with him for a while. The boy had a good voice and sang very well. Passing through a village one Sunday on a Christian holiday Besht and the youngster entered an inn where peasants were dancing to music played by an old Christian. Besht ordered drinks for the peasants and asked the little boy to sing for them. Again in Medzhibozh the boy sang before Christians, surpassing the singing of the Christian women *(Degel Machne Efraim* quoted in Raphael, *Sepher ha-Hasidut*, p. 42; Kahane, *R. Yisrael Besht*, pp. 88–89). For our present purpose it is really irrelevant whether or not the story or the quotation is really from Besht. They were told by his followers, which may serve as some indication of these Jewish–non-Jewish (sectarian) contacts.

5 Emden, *Torath Hakanaut*, pp. 27–28; *PVAA*, no. 542.

6 Scholem, *Major Trends*, pp. 321–24; Petuchowski, *The Theology of Haham David Nieto*, pp. 114–18; *PVAA*, no. 557; Emden, *Torath Hakanaut*, pp. 71–72; J. Sonne in *Kobez al Yad*, n.s. 2 (1938): 157–96. Hayun died in exile in Africa.

7 *PVAA*, nos. 542, 939 and p. 496; Emden, *Torath Hakanaut*, pp. 57–95; Freiman, *Inyaney*, pp. 117–36; Balaban, *Letoldoth*, pp. 60–67; Scholem, *Hatenua*, pp. 58–64. The ban of 1725 in Amsterdam mentions a ban of the Polish Four-Land Council and "the expulsion" of the Sabbatians from Poland. Balaban dates the Polish ban in 1722, Halperin in 1672.

8 Emden was by no means an objective judge of Eibeschitz. According to some information, Emden himself aspired to become the rabbi of the Altona community (his father served in this capacity for a while). In addition, Eibeschitz had become involved some thirty years earlier, when Emden's father was caught in the Hayun controversy, which contributed to his losing the position of rabbi. At that time Eibeschitz, still a very young man, sharply attacked Emden's father (preserved handwritten marginal notes by Emden on Eibeschitz deliberations are extremely anti-Eibeschitz). See R. Margalioth, *Sinai* 14, nos. 11–12 (1951): 379–88.

9 Balaban, *Letoldoth*, pp. 72–80; Emden, *Sefat Emeth;* Eibeschitz, *Luchot Ha-Edut* (Lwów, 1857); M.J. Cohen, *Jacob Emden, A Man of Controversy* (1937); Scholem, *KS* 16 (1939–40): 320–38; M.A. Perlmuter, *R. Jonathan Eibeschitz vayachso el hashabtaut* (Tel Aviv, 1947); *PVAA*, nos. 667–75, 679–81, 685–89, 692–95, 697–99, 717, 719, 722–26, 733–37, 740–43, 751–53, 755, 760; see also Yitzhak Werfel, *Rishonim va-achronim* (Tel Aviv, 1957), pp. 227–43,

10 Gelber, *Brody*, pp. 106–7; Braver, *Galitzia*, pp. 211–13.

11 We have to rely mostly on Frank's statements, and he changed these often (once he said he was born in Berżanka, another time in Krolówka, and still another time he said

he "hailed from Smyrna"). See Kraushar, *Frank i Frankiści*, vols. 1 and 2; see the first volume translated into Hebrew by Nahum Sokolow under the title *Frank va-aydato* (Warsaw, 1896), 1:47–48; Rabinowicz, "Jacob Frank in Brno," p. 429; see also ibid., pp. 430, 437, his statement about his possessions in Poland and Smyrna, which was untrue; see also Balaban, *Letoldoth*, pp. 69, 109.

12 According to some Frankist folklore Berachya made Jacob his heir before he died, which is an apparent impossibility since Berachya died about 1740, when Jacob was still an unknown fourteen-year-old boy. Frank is supposed to have come to Salonika in 1752. But indirectly he absorbed later many of Berachya's attitudes; see also Braver, *Galitzia*, p. 214.

13 Kraushar, *Frank i Frankiści*, 1: 245–46; 2: 13, 36, 66 ff., 97. Kraushar reprinted parts of Frank's *Book of the Words of the Lord*, marking them with numbers. These numbers are indicated when quoted. See also Rabinowicz, "Jacob Frank in Brno," passim.

14 Kraushar, *Frank i Frankiści*, 1: 49, 381, 385; 2:39, nos. 103, 140, 406, 1157, 1239 (the sayings are numbered by Kraushar in the reprint).

15 Some years ago a physician tried to depict Frank as a pathological type and to define his sickness as paranoia, erothomania, and mythomania (Z. Bychowski, in *Hatekufa* 14–15 [1922]: 703–20); see also no. 1506, Kraushar. In some Christian sects that were active in the Ukraine and Russia in the eighteenth century women were given a high standing, to the point of a kind of deification. Stories and testimonies about communal sexual orgies and free love (not dissimilar to those told about the Frankists) are also extant. See Grass, *Die Russischen Sekten*, 1: 18, 35, 81 ff., 434–46, 448–84; Woodcock and Avakumovic, *The Doukhobors*, pp. 69–79.

16 This was apparently no easy task for Frank. After the conversion some of the former Jews blamed him for having "taken away their faith" (nos. 1762, 1833, 1871, 2151).

17 Grass, *Die Russischen Sekten*, 1: 318, 434, 494, 612, 660, 675, 683–84, 687–88; Bolshakoff, *Russian Nonconformity*, pp. 72, 85–86, 91; Woodcock and Avakumovic, *The Doukhobors*, pp. 19, 20–22, 27, 29, 42, 56.

18 Kraushar, *Frank i Frankiści*, 1: 245–46, 421; 2: 11, 13, 36, 40, 66 ff., 68, 78, 97, 114–16, 233, nos. 885, 116, 1126, 1144, 1158, 1161, 1167, 1246, 1252, 1263, 1356, 1369, 1543, 1751, 1816, 1856, 2078.

19 Scholem's attempt to formulate Frank's "theology" is more speculative than factual, and not only because the quotations are too selective. Most of the two dozen quotations from Frank presented there are either incorrectly translated from Polish or taken out of context (see Scholem, "Mitzva habaah," pp. 383–85.

20 As a parallel it should be mentioned that a contemporary leader of the Doukhobors (Silvan Kolesnikov, c. 1750–75) advocated evasion for his followers (Woodcock and Avakumovic, *The Doukhobors*, p. 27).

21 Kraushar, *Frank i Frankiści*, 1: 420–21, 425, 387; 2: 77, 68–70, nos. 883, 889, 1013, 159, 1312, 1446, 2043.

22 Emden, *Sepher Shimush*, pp. 5a–7a.

23 Jewish courts in Poland seem sometimes to have resorted to beating in order to force confessions. Frankist sources, unreliable as they are, have it that recalcitrants that were caught were paraded through the streets with ropes around their necks, and so on;

Kraushar, *Frank i Frankiści* (Hebrew edition), 1: 73. See also Balaban, *Letoldoth*, pp. 114–20.

24 The pamphlet, *Herev pifiot*, was republished by N. Sokolow in his Hebrew translation of the first volume of Kraushar (pp. 77–81). See also Balaban, *Letoldoth*, pp. 110–28; Emden, *Sepher Shimush*, p. 7b. Ber Birkenthal tells another version of the Lanckrona incident (Braver, *Galitzia*, pp. 214 ff.).

25 According to the memoirs of Ber Birkenthal, the initiative came from the "Sabbatians," who turned to the bishop and told him about their antitalmudic views and approach to Christianity and asked for help in becoming a (recognized?) community independent of the Jewish rabbis and community leaders. But Balaban argues that the bishop's interest in the matter came before he decided that he meant to convert them (Braver, *Galitzia*, p. 217; Balaban, *Letoldoth*, p. 134).

26 That is, belief in God's commands as elucidated in the Torah; belief that the Talmud, being a commentary to the Torah, contains falsehoods and misrepresentations; belief in one God having three equal forms; belief in God incarnate in human form; belief that Jerusalem will not be rebuilt; the idea that Jewish belief in the coming of a messiah is in vain; belief that God himself will appear to clear the world of sin. See also Emden, *Sepher Shimush*, pp. 31a–70a.

27 This economic strife was accompanied by the printing of a host of anti-Jewish publications in which the alleged malice of the Jews and their use of Christian blood, and the depravity of the Talmud were main themes. Radlinski, *Prawda chrzescianska od nieprzyjaciela swego zezrnana t. j. traktat rabi Samuela . . .* (Lublin, 1732); Franciszek Neugeboren, *Zwierciadlo nedznych Żydów z ich wlasnych skryptów* (Wilno, 1732, 1735); Jan Bryktas, *Arcanum pertidiae judaicae* (Warsaw, 1727); and *De futura judaicorum conversione* (Warsaw, 1738); Guadenty Pikulski, *Zlość Żydowska przeciwko Boga i bliźniemu prawdzie i sumieniu na objaśnienie Talmudystów . . .* (Lwów, 1758). See also the summary of the disputation, Balaban, *Letoldoth*, pp. 139–64.

28 See Emden, *Sepher Shimush*, pp. 88–89.

29 Balaban assumes *(Letoldoth*, pp. 195–98) that, among others, two Polish clergymen who had been active a few years earlier (1753, 1756) in staging blood libels in Zhitomir and Jampol had endeavored to obtain from the king this privilege for the Frankists. In 1758 the papacy, through its nuncio in Poland, was investigating irregularities in the behavior of these clergymen. For this purpose the latter attempted to recall the Frankists who would testify that Jews really used blood, which would help the clergymen to justify their past actions. This assumption may perhaps be refuted by the fact that after the disputation in Lwów a few Frankists told the Lwów rabbi, Hayim Cohen Rapport: "Hayim, you have here blood for blood; you wanted our blood, so you have blood for blood"; *Divrey Binah*, reprinted in Braver, *Galitzia*, p. 249. This might indicate that the Frankists' later blood libel testimony was, for the most part, their own revenge against the Jews.

30 A number of sects in the Ukraine, Russia, and Walachia (Doukhobors, Khlysty, Skoptsy, and others) regarded Danilo Philipov (mid-seventeenth-century "prophet") as their spiritual ancestor. Like him, they used only their own oral tradition, repudiating the Bible and other scriptures and rejecting churches and priesthoods. Some of these or similar sects were apparently popularly known as Philipowcy. Some information culled from Jewish sources seems to indicate that the term may have meant

various groups. Frank talks about Philipowcy as being lowly peasants, while Emden —on the basis of a letter from Poland—identifies them with rich businessmen (Emden wrongly tries to derive the name "Philipowcy" from a supposed Christian apostle Philip); Kraushar, *Frank i Frankiści*, 2: 45; Emden, *Sepher Shimush*, p. 84b; Woodcock and Avakumovic, *The Doukhobors*, passim; Grass, *Die Russischen Sekten*, 2: passim.

31 In Ber Birkenthal's opinion the postponement was requested with a view to the large gifts to be expected from the nobles who would attend the fair opening on January 6. (Important noblemen customarily served as godfathers at conversions and later heaped gifts upon the new Christian.)

32 This becomes a certainty for Scholem; see Balaban, *Letoldoth*, p. 210; Scholem, *Hatenua*, p. 65; see also Kraushar, *Frank i Frankiści*, 1: 143). One may be inclined to doubt the soundness of this assumption; certainly, had the theses really been formulated by the Lwów clergymen, there would have been no reason for them to avoid mentioning Christ or Jesus—especially since they, having apparently arranged the disputation on their own initiative, would have been anxious to avoid any suspicion among the high church dignitaries as to the sincerity of the Frankists' intentions.

33 The sudden summons of the Lwów rabbi to appear at the meeting of the disputation within a day or so, at a time when other rabbis had all returned home and the Jewish syndic (shtadlan) was away on business, may have been a cause for anxiety. But judging from Ber's own story, average Lwów Jews may not have been greatly involved or interested in the whole matter. Ber, who hailed from Bolechów, was at that time actually staying mostly in Lwów, where he had his wine business. Nevertheless, when he happened to be talking about his native community (Bolechów) with the Lwów clergyman Wieniawski, who was then the leaseholder of Bolechów and with whom he was on good terms, it did not occur to him to touch on the matter of the disputation until another Jew on the premises induced him to do so. On the other hand, Jacob Emden reprints a letter from Abraham Hakohen of Zamość (September–October 1759), which points out that because the Jews in Lwów feared pogroms at the time of the disputation in Lwów, they requested and received a detachment of guards to protect them during that time (Emden, *Sepher Shimush*, p. 79b; see also p. 82b).

34 Emden, *Sepher Shimush*, pp. 3a–b, 8a–b, 9b, 15a–b, 62b; *PVAA*, no. 768. Emden also published parts of these letters elsewhere. Meetings of the council were held on September 3 and 26, 1759, in Konstantinow; *PVAA*, nos. 780, 784, 785, and pp. 416, 424.

35 This tactic is also mentioned in another source. The tradition of Besht's regret about the conversion may reflect the approaches of another Jewish faction.

36 A later story *(Maaseh Nora be-podolia,* told to Emden in 1769, reprinted in Balaban, *Letoldoth*, pp. 297–305) says that Besht was one of the three rabbis who participated in the Lwów disputation. This information was apparently taken from there and reprinted in Hassidic literature. Balaban proved conclusively that Besht was not present.

37 M. Balaban, *Letoldoth*, parts 1 and 2, passim; Pikulski, *Złość Żydowska*, 2d ed. (1760); Kraushar, *Frank i Frankiści*, vols. 1 and 2; Braver, *Galitzia*, part 3, "Letoldot Frank vasiato," pp. 197–275 dealing with Ber Birkenthal's *Divrey Binah* (first published in *Ha-Shiloach* 33 and 38); Jeske-Choinski, *Neofici Polscy*; Mateusz Mieses, *Polacy*

chrześcianie pochodzenia Żydowskiego (Lwów, 1939); Scholem, *Hatenua*, pp. 64–76; Graetz, *Frank und die Frankisten* (1868).

38 Rabbi Abraham Hakohen of Zamość, in the letter to Jacob Emden dated October 23, 1759, tells about two thousand ducats (a considerable amount of money for those times) that the regional Jewish Community Council allocated to hasten the conversion of the Frankists (Emden, *Sepher Shimush*, p. 82; Balaban, *Letoldoth*, pp. 269, 266; Braver, *Galitzia*, pp. 249–50). The extant accounts of the Lwów regional council, however, mention a smaller amount for expenses for the disputation, which may include all manner of items.

39 Emden, *Sepher Shimush*, pp. 84b, 86a-b, 89a. Emden printed pictures of the supposedly new converts Abraham and Isaac dressed in the stereotypical Jewish clothing of the time.

40 According to Ber Birkenthal, the Frankists, desiring to extort a large sum from the Jews, staged the blood libel. Other stories give a different rendering of the blood libel, assigning the Frankists either a lesser role or none at all (Kraushar, *Frank i Frankiści*, 1: 201 ff.; Balaban, *Letoldoth*, pp. 286–90; Braver, *Galitzia*, pp. 267–69).

41 The figures are given by Kraushar and other sources on the basis of entries in the church registers. Lwów clergymen mention a general figure of 1,000. There are larger —apparently highly exaggerated—estimates. Mieses surely exaggerates in putting the figure at 12,000. Others range from 1,000 to a few thousand (see Abraham Duker, "Polish Frankism's Duration," *JSS* 25 [1963]: 301–2 and note 90). Shlomo Yitzhak Heilpern, a rabbi from Podolia who was an eyewitness, wrote: "The sectarians, numbering a few hundred, stood up brazenly against us . . . and they left . . . they, their wives, and the big and little sons and daughters were persuaded to convert against their will . . . as my own eyes saw" (Dubnow, *Toledoth Hachasidut* quotes from the rabbi's manuscript). Also Abraham Hakohen of Zamość, a leader of the Four-Land Council, says in his letter to Jacob Emden in the fall of 1760: "All of them converted and they are encamped near our community—a few hundred" (Emden, *Sepher Shimush*, p. 84b). In truth, if a large number had converted this would not have been regarded lightly by Jewish contemporaries as a good way to be rid of them (see above). The same is indicated by the fact that the small number of actual conversions constituted an issue at Frank's hearing (at the end of January 1760) by the ecclesiastical court of investigation. He was charged with having falsely promised that 10,000 Jews would convert. He made the excuse that he had not promised 10,000 converts but had just estimated such a number, taking into account the large population of the region. Nor would there be any reason to assume a large-scale conversion took place later after Frank's arrest and the ensuing investigation and banishment to Częstochowa by the church authorities—especially since rumors spread among Jews said that Frank and some of his cronies were badly mistreated while under arrest, at the hearings, or in Częstochowa. See also Jeske-Choinski, *Neofici Polscy*, and Balaban's review in *KH* 19 (1905): 296–300; Emden, *Sepher Shimush*, pp. 84a, 85a-b, 86b.

42 Kraushar, *Frank i Frankiści*, 1: 157–60 and passim.

43 Emden, *Sepher Shimush*, pp. 83a–b, 84b.

44 Ibid.

45 Emden, *Torath Hakanaut* (1762).

46 Quoted in I. Tishbi, *Zion* 32 (1967): 10; Emden, *Sepher Shimush*, pp. 79b, 84b, 85a, 86a-b.

47 With his customary lies Frank supposedly promised to bring in twenty thousand converts. The letter reprinted Kraushar, *Frank i Frankiści*, 1: (Hebrew translation) 250–64.

48 It is conceivable that the beatings and incarceration in the cellar in Offenbach inflicted by Frank's daughter Eva in the years following his death (Gelber, *HS* 1) may have been practiced earlier, too.

49 Kraushar, *Frank i Frankiści*, 2: 233, 68–70, 114–116; 1 (Hebrew): 217. The following figures indicate the numbers as given in Frank's *Words* and reprinted by Kraushar: 1762: 1140, 1141, 1147, 1152, 1169, 1171, 1191, 1222, 1435, 1756, 1811, 1116, 1126, 1144, 1158, 1161, 1167, 1356, 1369, 1856, 2076.

50 Frank's ideas have never been developed in any systematic way. They appear rather as a jumble of varied attitudes and approaches. They are noted in the preserved *Book of the Words of the Lord* and in the *Chronik*, which were written or edited much later (see above). These are at best rationalizations of each current change of mood, attitude, or situation. Thus in one place he praises Poland and Catholicism, esteeming them highly, but in another place Russia ("Esau") becomes highly evaluated. In one instance he orders his followers "to keep their mouths shut" about their intentions, while elsewhere he maintains that he always insisted that everything be done openly. He forbids marriage to non-Jews and then again issues orders to unite with the nations and promises to marry their children to daughters and sons of nobles. The same is true with general goals. He wants to lead to perfection and to help the whole world but at the same time to go into the abyss and corrupt the world. Being aware of his own contradictions he warns: "If I say yes today and no tomorrow you should not raise any questions nor wonder" *(Words,* nos. 123, 227, 90, 251, 263, 202, 1784, 1324, 1487, 1613, 1816, 2097, 2153, 159, 2043, 1446, 1312, 883, 889, 1013, 238, 1494, 2152, 1767); Kraushar, *Frank i Frankiści*, 2: 74, 76–77, 40.

51 The information on one thousand "Polacks" in Offenbach (Kraushar, *Frank i Frankiści*, 2: 154; Scholem, *Hatenua*, p. 75) is no more than a wild exaggeration. It is based mainly on information from Offenbach about "800 *Polen*" or so. But apparently the people of Offenbach considered each Frankist—even those who came from Moravia and other countries—as a "Polack" or as a "Częstochauer," (named for the site of Frank's former imprisonment). In addition, these figures are also exaggerated. Porges, who lived in Frank's court for some time, maintains "there were in the house about 80 persons; about a hundred more lived outside of the house" (Gelber, *HS* 1: 272, 279–80, 296). This would mean that the Frankist group in Offenbach numbered some two hundred persons. Moreover, economic policies in Poland in those years inclined the state to limit emigration or travel abroad (the far smaller emigration of the Hassidim to Palestine in 1777 led to such limitations). Large-scale travels on the part of the Frankists to Offenbach would undoubtedly have had such legal results, especially since in that period a literary anti-Frankist (or anti–New Christian) campaign was running in Poland (see below).

52 Kraushar, *Frank i Frankiści* (Hebrew), 1: 159. The same fact may be indicated by the figures of the converted in Lwów. Against 156 men stand 119 women and 239 children (ibid., p. 191). Assuming that the number of men roughly signifies the heads of families, it may show that about one-third of the wives and a number of children were

missing. (An average of about two children per head of family would be low for those times.)

53 Kraushar, *Frank i Frankiści*, 2: 77, 97, nos. 169, 1762, 1121, 1122, 1124, 1127, 1137, 1177, 1246, 1252, 2131.
54 Kraushar, *Frank i Frankiści*, 2: 68, 78, nos. 807, 885, 1013.
55 *Vol. Leg.*, 7: 74; R. Mahler, "Statistik fun Yidn in der Lubliner woyevudztve 1764–5," in *Yunger Historiker* (Warsaw, 1929), 2: 107–8; Balaban, *Letoldoth*, 281.
56 Quoted in Duker, "Polish Frankism's Duration," p. 313, note 150.
57 Kraushar, *Frank i Frankiści*, 2: 24, 90, 165; Ringelblum, *Żydzi w powstaniu*, pp. 117 ff., 164 ff.
58 A love of Jewish food is not generally a sign of belonging to the Frankists or even of being a Jew. On the menus of the important pre-World War II Polish restaurants one could mostly find Jewish dishes (for example, "Jewish fish"—*Ryba po Żydowsku*). In the 1950s a non-Jew opened a restaurant in Warsaw specializing in "Jewish dishes" but did not draw enough customers. This had nothing to do with Frankists or other converts from Judaism.
59 Duker, "Polish Frankism's Duration," pp. 287–333 and esp. pp. 290, 292 ff., 296, 312 ff.; Ringelblum, *Żydzi w powstaniu*, pp. 113–20, 161–65; G. Scholem, "A Sabbatian Will from New York," in *Miscellanies of the Jewish Historical Society of England* (London, 1948), 5: 193–211; Shazar (Rubashov), *Al Tiley Beyt Frank*. About Mickiewicz see also Wladyslaw Wielhorski, "The Nationality of Mickiewicz in the Light of Modern Sociological and Ethnological Studies," *Antemurale* 11 (Rome, 1967).

While on the subject of Polish Frankism's duration it might be appropriate to dispel the fallacious belief held by some scholars that the high rank achieved by a descendant or two of converted Frankists in an army in Western Europe has something to do with Frank's having "played soldiers"; (they even appear to hint that this may, as it were, be an upshot of Frankist messianism). The historical truth is that after the end of the fifteenth century some converts and their descendants in Poland-Lithuania played a role as military leaders. This was facilitated by the fact that many had been adopted into noble families. The descendants of Abraham Józefowicz of Lithuania, who converted in 1495, and those of Stefan Fischel of Cracow (an uncle by marriage of R. Jacob Polak) converted at the end of the fifteenth century; the Abrahamowicze and Powidzki families included voivodes, a general of the Lithuanian artillery, and other military commanders. Also the families Zawojski, Dziekanski, Jakubuwski, and other descendants of converts in the sixteenth to the eighteenth centuries produced military men who attained high positions in Poland. On the lower rungs of the ladder were Jewish converts who joined the cossacks among whom some of them played a role (see also Stanislaw Didier, *Rola Neofitów w dziejach Polski* [Warsaw, 1934]; although this is an anti-Semitic pamphlet intended to show how pseudo-Catholics dominated Poland some of the facts about the families seem to be true).

Chapter 12

1 The expression Hassid (pious man) is found in the Bible and has been used in many connotations throughout the centuries. In the eighteenth century there were in Poland some ascetics who fasted and otherwise mortified their bodies, known as "Hassidim." Ber Birkenthal in southern Poland as well as Solomon Maimon in Lithuania mention this fact and their own attempts at imitation. It seems that Ber of Mezeritch (1714–

72), who became the leader of the Hassidic movement following Besht's death in 1760, was originally such an ascetic until converted by Besht, who had earlier also fasted on weekdays. The latter began, around 1740, to develop an antiascetic Hassidism, which started the Hassidic movement. Subsequently "Hassid" came to mean a definite type of pious man and a follower of the movement.

2   In *Shivchey Habesht*, the main work in which Besht's story is told, about fifty places are mentioned in connection with his travels and pupils; of these about sixteen were in Podolia and seventeen in Volhynia (Dinur, *Ba-mifneh ha-doroth*, p. 83, note 2). Besht was born around 1700 and began his activity apparently about 1736 (according to tradition he "revealed himself" at the age of thirty-six).

3   The figures for artisans are from Weinryb, *Neueste Wirtschaftsgeschichte*, p. 220; Mahler, *Yidn in Zifern*, p. 169. Some Christian sects in seventeenth- to eighteenth-century Ukraine and the neighborhood had time and again absolutely repudiated all the Scripture, accepting only oral legends, stories, and songs.

4   According to an estimate made at the end of the century, by one of the movement's opponents, Besht had 10,000 followers after ten years, 40,000 after fifteen years (Israel Liebel, *Sulamith* [1807], 2: 307; Dinur, *Ba-mifneh ha-doroth*, p. 84, note 4. Leibel's figures are none too reliable). For the end of the eighteenth century the number of followers is estimated at 100,000. Martin Buber maintains (as usual without indicating any source) that by the turn of the eighteenth century Hassidism "has taken possession of the Jewry of the whole Polish Kingdom as well as important parts of Northeast Hungary and the Moldau" (M. Buber, *The Origin and Meaning of Hasidism*, ed. M. Friedman [New York, 1960], p. 116). Although all these estimates may be highly exaggerated, the fact of large growth generally is not to be denied.

5   See Weiss, "Reyshit," pp. 70 ff.

6   Varied interpretations of Hassidism exist. These range from a view of the movement as a sort of Sabbatianism (Graetz), to one regarding it as a reaction to Sabbatianism and thus minimizing or neutralizing messianism (Dubnow, Scholem), to the reverse, viewing it as a pronounced messianic trend (Dinur, Mahler, and others).

7   Hassidic legend, however, notes at times that insubordination to the "rabbi" (meaning Besht), digression from a religious law, joking about Hassidism, or the desire to inform upon Besht may have brought severe punishment or even death from God's hands (*Shivchey Habesht*, pp. 19, 23, 25, 35–36, 53, 56, 91).

8   Israel Besht left nothing in writing except a few letters. Some of his sayings are mentioned by several of his followers or pupils. Legends and stories about his life and deeds were passed on by word of mouth. *Shivchey Habesht* constitutes a mixture of truth and fiction apparently fashioned upon the ideas of his followers at the time they were written down or printed (1815). The value of this work may be characterized by the story (page 97) that "one has written down Besht's teachings as he heard them from him." When Besht got wind of this writing he wanted to see it. Looking through the work he said, "There is not a single phrase here as spoken by me."

The arrangement and some of the content may be an imitation of *Shivchey Haari* (about Isaac Luria). Some stories resemble legends about Jesus. See Horodetski's introduction to his edition of *Shivchey Habesht* in 1922. See also the controversy between Gershom Scholem and Martin Buber in *Commentary*, October 1961 and September 1963.

9   Isaac (Seckel) Loeb Wormser, the Baal Shem of Michelstadt in Germany (born in 1767, some years after Besht's death) seems to have followed Besht's and his pupils'

ways in the traditions of Polish Hassidism. He was a pupil of Nathan Adler (1741–1800), rabbi in Frankfurt on the Main, founder of Frankfurter Hassidim. Isaac Wormser left two diaries, covering two years, in which he noted the services he rendered to his "clients." There *shiurim* (study of portions of the Torah) requested by individuals play a big role. Other "remedies" recommended were reading of certain chapters of Psalms, secret acts of charity, placing a mezuzah in a box on the body of a sick person, the wearing of white linen clothes, and so on. One may guess that similar "cures" were used by Besht. See Raphael Straus in *Historia Judaica* 8, no. 1 (1946): 135–44.

9a See Scholem, *Zion* 20 (1955): 80. The first Joel Baal Shem signs his name Joel ben Moshe Besht in his book *Kney Bina* (Prague, 1611) Another, eighteenth-century, author also calls himself Besht: Benjamin Beinish Hakohen ben Jehuda Leib, *Shem Tob Katan* (1706) and *Amtachat Benjamin* (1716).

10 *Shivchey Habesht,* pp. 18, 25, 45, 67–73, 83–84, 87, 89, 97, 99; Dubnow, *Toledot Hachasidut,* 1: 48–49; Weiss, "Reyshit," p. 103.

11 See also Weiss, "Reyshit," pp. 103–5.

12 *Shivchey Habesht,* pp. 29–30, 37, 47, 50, 53–54, 69, 75, 83, 103–5. Of course it is possible that the depiction of Besht's sedentary life is a later projection made on the basis of the then widespread practice of the Hassidic leaders of the time.

13 *Shivchey Habesht,* p. 25. Jacob Joseph of Polonnoe may have tried to indicate (by quoting or adding a few words to a passus from *Sifri*) in a sermon of 1761 that *baal shem* and "zaddik" were by then synonymous (*Ketonet Passim* 22b). Weiss, "Reyshit," pp. 54–55, tries to present this sermon as an attempt by Jacob Joseph to upgrade the *baal shem.*

14 *Shivchey Habesht,* pp. 76–78, 93; in writings ascribed to Besht (*Keter Shem Tov,* first published in 1784, p. 2a) remaining in one place (not needing to travel around) is highly valued—being projected back to the patriarchs.

15 The lack of documents "enabled" the late historian I. Schipper to construe a theory that Israel Besht's "deeds" had actually been accomplished by one Joel Baal Shem (taking a clue from Solomon Maimon's *Autobiography,* which confused Israel with Joel) and attributed later to Israel (*Hadoar* 1960, *Hajnt* Jubilee Issue [Warsaw, 1938]).

16 A. Kahane, *Sepher Hahasidut* 1 (Warsaw, 1922): 105. The English version is from Samuel H. Dresner, *The Zaddik* (New York, 1960), pp. 38–39.

17 Adam as a first name is seldom found among Jews. Zunz mentions one or two cases; Zunz, *Synagogale Poesie,* p. 704; idem, *Nachstrag* (Berlin, 1867), p. 38. In Lublin in 1564 we find two Jews named Adam and one other elsewhere in 1794 (Wojciechowski, "Yidn in Lublin," p. 128; *RIN* no. 2428). Two little Yiddish books of stories about an Adam Baal Shem have been preserved. The content of the story told about Adam in *Shivchey Habesht* (pp. 14–15) is in part identical with some of the printed story. Scholem maintains that by Adam in *Shivchey Habesht* is meant Heshel Zoref, an esoteric Sabbatian whose writings are known to have been circulated among Hassidic leaders. See Shmeruk, "Hasippurim al R. Adam Baal Shem," pp. 86–105; Scholem, *Zion,* 7: 28.

18 This image of Besht is largely based on *Shivchey Habesht* and *Toledoth Yaakov Josef.*

19 Margaliot, *Meir Netivim* (1791–92), and *Sod Yekhin uboaz* (1794), which contains the statement about Besht.

20 For the negative images see: Maimon, *Autobiography,* p. 170; Jacques Calmanson, *Essai sur l'état actuel des Juifs de Pologne et leur perfectibilité* (Warsaw, 1796); Leibel,

Sepher Havikuach, introduction, p. 1; idem, in *Sulamith*, 1807, pp. 308 ff.; Dubnow, *Toledoth Hachasidut*, pp. 70–75.

21 Nineteenth-century rationalists saw the Hassidim as a bunch of obscurantists or drunkards. The romantics searched for the "light" to be found among them. Religionists and nationalists considered Hassidism the most important Jewish movement for unification and regeneration of the Jewish people. Other writers and historians held views ranging between Hassidism as an "aftergrowth of Sabbatianism" or "revolt of the *Am ha-arez* [illiterate]," to regarding the Hassidim as popularizers of cabalistic thought, "endowing" them with a sort of super-Zionism, or formulating a neo-Hassidism (Buber).

22 G. Scholem, "Martin Buber's Hasidism," *Commentary*, October 1961, p. 312; see also Weiss, "Reyshit," pp. 46–47.

23 This is known to have affected medieval Latin sources. Those who wrote the documents usually translated them from their respective vernaculars into Latin, often using the same expression for different concepts or situations and vice versa.

24 Scholem, "Martin Buber's Hasidism," p. 310; see also Tishbi, *Zion* 32: 32, about the use of certain concepts.

25 In mentioning the Lurianic terms of "limitation," "breaking" the vessels, and *tikkun* (reparation) Jacob Joseph begins with the phrase "although we have no interest in esoteric matters" (*Toledoth*, p. 47). About the terms, see Scholem, *Major Trends*, index; cf. also Tishbi-Dan, *Enc. Hebraica*, 17: 772–73, about the changed meaning of these terms in Hassidism.

26 Baumgardt, *Great Western Mystics*, p. 9.

27 *Keter Shem Tov*, pp. 1b, 2a; *Degel Machne Efraim*, pp. 55, 58, 62.

28 *Shivchey Habesht*, p. 97; the statement is found in Dubnow, *Toledoth Hachasidut*, 1: 53; see also the introduction of the editor of *Maggid devarav Leyaakov* by Ber of Mezeritch on the merits of various versions.

29 See I. Tishbi, "Agnostic Doctrines in 16th Century Jewish Mysticism," *JJS* 6 (1955): 146–52; see also Scholem, *Major Trends*, p. 268, and his controversy with Buber in *Commentary*, October 1961. Scholem seems to hold fast to the doctrine and its literal meaning of "uplifting of the sparks" as transcending reality. In fact, however, Hassidism used it among other things to fulfill a more concrete function. Also, Tishbi (*Zion* 32: 32) doubts whether certain terms of cabala used in Hassidism retained their original meaning (*sitra ahara*—forces of evil).

30 The English wording from Scholem, "Martin Buber's Hasidim," p. 312; *Keter Shem Tov*, p. 24b.

31 E.R.Briggs, "Mysticism and Rationalism in the Debate upon Eternal Punishment," *Studies on Voltaire and the Eighteenth Century* 24: (1963), 247.

32 Amman, *Abriss*, pp. 294, 334; Grass, *Die Russischen Sekten*, 1: 6–39, 99, 155 ff., 264, 272 ff., 508 ff., 513, 591, 593, 611 ff.; 2: 357, 362 ff., 383 ff.; Bolshakoff, *Russian Nonconformity*, pp. 72, 86, 90, 91, 105.

33 See also Woodcock and Avakumovic, *The Doukhobors*, pp. 19, 20–22; Grass, *Die Russischen Sekten*, 1: 503, 658; Bolshakoff, *Russian Nonconformity*, pp. 81, 86.

34 The story about Besht's having refused to remarry after the death of his wife and his maintaining that for the preceding fourteen years he had abstained from intercourse with his wife (*Shivchey Habesht*, p. 113) may also show some parallel with those Christian sects that demanded abstinence from sexual relations. See also the preceding

chapter (11), note 4, about possible contacts of Frankists and Hassidim with the nonconformist Russian sects.

35 Hassidim were able to communicate with their neighbors in one or more of the Slavic languages (not necessarily using them correctly). Jacob Joseph of Polonnoe quotes a Jewish woman who expressed herself in Russian or Ukrainian about a theological theme. There are preserved a number of bilingual Jewish folk songs (Hebrew or Yiddish mixed with Russian or Ukrainian or Polish), some of which are apparently of a Hassidic origin. If we assume that they stem from the eighteenth century or are based on eighteenth-century models, this may indicate some closeness between the groups. See also U. Weinreich in *YIVO Bleter* 34: 282–88; J. Goldberg, "Di Idishe mishsh-prachike un fremdshprachige folkslieder," *Zeitschrift* 2–3 (Minsk, 1929): 589–600. In the 1930s an attempt was made to compare Hassidism with the religion in Russia. While the part dealing with the similarity of Hassidic and Greek Orthodox piety is valueless, the chapter dealing with the Russian sects indicates some parallels between them and Hassidism; see Ysander, *Studien zum Beschtschen*. A more recent attempt to connect Besht with Adam Zernikov, a Russian clergyman *(PAAJR* 36 [1968]: 57–83) through Besht's father, Eliezer, who is supposed to have lived in Russia, is based on a number of fallacies and on unfamiliarity with Russian history and is even worthless as a speculation. (A more comprehensive appraisal is found in an appendix to this writer's "Reappraisals in Jewish History" in the Salo Baron *Festschrift).*

36 Martin Buber denies that Hassidism was a revivalist movement, arguing that it lasted too long to be such a trend. His reasoning, however, seems to be very weak; some of the revivalist trends (Quakers, Methodists) went on for long periods, changing, of course, with the times just as Hassidism, too, changed. See M. Buber, "Interpreting Hassidism," *Commentary*, September 1963, p. 221.

37 In medieval Christianity, too, "individual and social life in all their manifestations were imbued with the conceptions of faith, so that people might lose sight of the distinction between things spiritual and things temporal." The result was that "details of ordinary life could be raised to a sacred level" but also that "all that is holy could sink to the commonplace" (Huizinga, *The Waning of the Middle Ages*, pp. 151–56).

38 Some also raised the problem of reward or interpreted it as an act of grace. This idea of passivity is connected with admonitions against pride and mystical self-denial, to consider oneself as naught, as demanded by Hassidic leaders. See, about the whole matter (and the quotations), J. G. Weiss, "Viva Passiva in Early Hassidism," *JJS* 11, nos. 3–4 (1960): 137–55; *Keter Shem Tov*, p. 11b.

39 They maintained "that the soul absorbed in God and therefore having no will, can no longer sin, even in following its carnal appetites" (Huizinga, *The Waning of the Middle Ages*, pp. 196–97. See *Or Haemeth*, p. 20; Uffenheimer, *Hachasidut ka-mistika*, especially chapters 1–2. The author, however, seems to attach too much importance to the quietist tendencies by attempting to derive from them almost all Hassidic doctrine.

40 *Toledoth*, p. 34; *Keter Shem Tov*, pp. 5b, 7b.

41 See *Toledoth*, pp. 85, 90.

42 See *Degel Machne Efraim*, pp. 150, 187; *Keter Shem Tov*, pp. 4b, 6b.

43 See Dresner, *The Zaddik*, pp. 275–76 about the confusion in the use of the term "zaddik" by Jacob Joseph of Polonnoe.

44 *Zofnath Paaneach*, pp. 86d, 30b, 64b; Dresner, *The Zaddik*, pp. 124, 127–30; *Zavaat Haribash*, pp. 7a, 9a, 11a; *Keter Shem Tov*, pp. 1b, 5a, 8b, 10a, 16a, 25a; Weiss, *Zion*, 16: 74–76, 82, 84; *Noam Elimelech*, pp. 3, 8–9, 13–16, 18.

45 *Meor Eynayim*, Brayshit; Abraham Hamalach, *Hesed Leabraham* (Czernowitz, 1851): Bamidbar, Bereyshit, Haazinu, Vaeyra, Miketz; Menachem of Nesvizh, *Rishpey Aysh Hashalom*: Noah; Bereyshit; Jacob Itzchak Halevi Horowitz, *Zot Zikaron;* Israel of Kożenice *Avodat Israel Hashalem* Teruma; Lashabat Hagadol (I. Raphael, *Sepher ha-Hasidut*, pp. 81–82; 101–2, 177–78, 212–13, 227); *Noam Elimelech*, pp. 19, 22, 36; *Keter Shem Tov*, pp. 156, 166a.

46 See also, Weiss, *Zion* 16: 70 ff.; *Toledoth*, p. 145. A tendency to defend the zaddik against criticism also became discernible early. His "littleness" and idleness is pictured as a necessary temporary situation; cases in which his prayers remain unanswered are rationalized by "God loves the zaddik's prayers and therefore he wants the zaddik to pray again"; *Zavaat Haribash*, p. 7a; Menachem Nachum of Czernobyl, *Yismach Leyv*, Yona; (Raphael, *Sepher ha-Hasidut*, pp. 39–40); *Noam Elimelech*, pp. 20, 25; *Keter Shem Tov*, pp. 8b, 13b, 15a; *Or Haemeth*, p. 32; *Degel Machne Efraim*, pp. 81, 109, 119.

47 *Shivchey Habesht*, pp. 33–34, 64–66, 69, 86, 89, 93, 95, 100; Baruch of Medzhibozh, *Bozina Dinhora Hashalem* (Lwów, 1880), p. 84.

48 *Kedushat Levi* (Slavuta, 1798) Peyrushey Agadot, Shoftim, Bo; Mordkhai of Nesvizh *Rishpey Aysh Hashalom* Mishpatim. Isaiah; Abraham Yehoshua Heshel *Torat Emet* Hayej Sarah; Jacob Isaak of Prysucha, *Tiferet Hayehudi* (Raphael, *Sepher ha-Hasidut*, pp. 166–67, 176–77, 237, 246). A number of Hassidic leaders, including Besht, were opposed to preachers who chastized Jews too much *(Shivchey Habesht*, p. 97).

49 Bernard Berelson and Gary A. Steiner, *Human Behavior* (New York, 1964), p. 386.

50 An outline of Hassidic doctrine is found below in "Aspects of Hassidic Doctrine" (Appendix 4).

51 It should be mentioned that a large number of Hassidic "innovations"—kavvanah (concentration) and joy in prayer, praying according to the Sephardic way *(nusach)*, use of the Lurianic prayer book, putting on two pairs of tefillin (phylacteries), plus some other "Hassidic ideas" were found in southern Poland at the end of the seventeenth or the beginning of the eighteenth century (before Hassidism arose). This is attested to by the anonymous book *Taharot Hakodesh* (pp. 28b, 30a, 32a, 12b, 15a, 17–25). There, too, are to be found some rudiments of social criticism of rabbis and community leaders somewhat similar to the social criticism of the Hassidic writers.

52 It was hardly a full-fledged philosophical system, but rather fragments of older writings picked up or reinterpreted and retaining inconsistencies and even contradictions.

53 Thus *Zavaat Haribash*, pp. 2b, 6b; *Keter Shem Tov*, p. 4b. Some traces of this sort of approach are also found in the stories about Besht.

54 As we shall see later, this playing down of sin and evil was attacked by the anti-Hassidic traditionalists.

55 *Keter Shem Tov*, p. 5a; *Degel Machne Efraim*, pp. 79, 159.

56 Yehuda Leib Puchowitser, *Diwrey Hakhamim* (1692), pp. 10a, 13b, 15–16, 18a, 20 f., 23b, 29–34; Aron Shmuel Kaidanover, *Kav Hayashar* (Lublin, 1912), p. 6. "There exists a group of evil spirits . . . who are in charge of people who gather to talk useless talk . . . and these demons . . . write down all their words in a book . . . and after these people die . . . the demons take their souls to the wilderness and swamps and inflict upon them heavy suffering" (ibid., p. 11, passim).

57 Many erotic or obscene expressions and metaphors appear in Hassidic writings. These may be seen as an attempt at sublimation or as Freudian slips. They may, however, reflect the way the average Jew in those times used obscene language, mainly of an erotic character, in his conversation. It is simply a translation into Hebrew of the customary day-to-day way in which he expressed himself in Yiddish, as spoken by the unlearned and little learned Jews in Eastern Europe (used in shtetl until a generation ago).

58 Abraham Hurewitz, *Brit Abraham; Taharot Hakodesh* (Amsterdam, 1733); this book was written either during the last half of the seventeenth or at the beginning of the eighteenth century—before 1713. See I. Halperin, *KS* 34 (1959); D. Tamar, *Areshet* 3 (1961): 166–72.

59 *Midrash Pinchas* 52; *Tiferet Maharal* 99.

60 " . . . the abuse of piety . . . of the so-called penitents. . . . Instead of aspiring after likeness of God and striving to escape from the bondage of sensual passions . . . they seek to annihilate their passions by annihilating their powers of activity" (Maimon, *Autobiography*, p. 171).

61 Solomon Maimon, writing about his youthful interest in Hassidism, points out that it spread widely "since it declared that fasts and vigils and the constant study of the Talmud are not only useless but even prejudicial to that cheerfulness of spirit which is essential to genuine piety" (ibid., p. 167).

62 One can also find differences between teachings and behavior in the other direction. Besht and Hassidic thought frowned on fasting, but Hassidim emphasized some fast days (six Fridays in winter, and in part on the eve of the new moon). Similarly, Besht, Jacob Joseph, and some others show concern about shechita (ritual slaughter) and kashruth. The latter may have had some relationship to the introduction of the sharp shechita knives by the Hassidim. The attempt by Professor Shmeruk to find a social reason for the introduction of the sharp shechita knives by the Hassidim, namely, as a means of controlling the "concerned communities," seems not to be applicable to the first decades. The first time those knives are mentioned is in the ban of Brody in 1772. At that time the Hassidim were concerned rather with "separatism" to organize their own congregations or *shtiblach* than to control community finances (see C. Shmeruk "Mashmauta ha-hevratit shel ha-Shehita ha-hasidith," *Zion* 20: 47–72.

63 Solomon Maimon, who around 1770 was interested in Hassidism and stayed for a while in the court of Ber of Mezeritch, emphasizes the "moderate enjoyment of all kinds of pleasures [which Hassidism recommended] as necessary for the attainment of a cheerful disposition." He was "displeased not a little by their cynical spirit and the excess of their merriment" in the house of Rabbi Ber. He tells further that "the elevation above the body" demanded at the prayers, with implied "self-annihilation before God," led to various excesses. One of these was that "people sauntered around idly the whole day, pipe in mouth" with the excuse that they were "thinking about God" *(Autobiography, pp. 171–72, 176).*

64 *Tanya*, ch. 1; *Degel Machne Efraim*, p. 150; cf. also p. 58; *Keter Shem Tov*, pp. 8b, 14b.

65 Besht told that he had seen in heaven how the angel Michael—the patron of the Jews —was defending the Jews because all their irregularities were committed for good purposes *(Keter Shem Tov, p. 10b).*

66 Solomon Maimon ascribes the spread of Hassidism to "the dryness and unfruitfulness of rabbinical studies, the great burden of the ceremonial law which the new doctrine

promises to lighten" in addition to "the tendency of fanaticism and the love of the marvelous which are nourished by the doctrine" *(Autobiography,* p. 172).

67 Most writers about Hassidism tried to find various reasons for its rise and development. These range from (mental) escapism from oppression or poverty and superstition, "revolt of the *Am ha-arez"* (illiterate), to the view that it was an outcome of Sabbatianism and a reaction to two big crises—the collapse of the Sabbatian movement and denigration of Jewish autonomy in Poland (Dinur) and others. But most of those writers fail to explain the relationships between the supposed cause and its effect. Dinur, for instance, must even admit that "Hassidism did not solve even one of the grave problems which precipitated these crises" (so how is the connection to the crisis proven?); Dinur, *Ba-mifneh ha-doroth,* pp. 84, 86.

68 *Shivchey Habesht* (pp. 25, 39, 45, 54–55, 58, 67, 76–77, 84, 87, 90, 93, 105, 107, 123) contains signs of Besht's struggle for recognition. Some of these may indicate a kind of "natural" opposition of Lithuanian Jews to Hassidism (provided this is not a "presentism" of the editors).

69 *Toledoth,* pp. 265–66.

70 Solomon of Chelm, *Mirkevet hamishne* (Frankfurt on the Oder, 1751), foreword; Emden, *Mitpachat sepharim* (published in 1768 but written mostly around 1758), p. 31. See also Dubnow, *Toledoth Hachasidut,* p. 77.

71 Some opponents of Hassidism, writing three or four decades later, give high figures for the 1760s and 1770s (Maimon—"the sect had almost acquired dominion over the whole nation"; Israel Leibel mentions sixty thousand adherents). They apparently exaggerated either in view of the later developments or (Leibel) for lack of familiarity with the history of the movement (Dubnow, *Toledoth Hachasidut,* p. 76).

72 *Shivchey Habesht,* pp. 38–39; Dubnow, *Toledoth Hachasidut,* pp. 82, 478–79; Halperin, *Yehudim,* pp. 333–39; Maimon, *Autobiography,* pp. 173, 185, 169, 177, 179.

73 Apparently attempts were made as early as the seventeenth or the beginning of the eighteenth century to use Sephardic or the Lurianic siddur (prayer book) in Poland. But these were sporadic attempts by individuals. The above-mentioned siddur of Besht —if the story about it is authentic—seems to have been according to the Ashkenazic *nusach* and thus not Lurianic. The first Lurianic prayer book printed in Poland (according to Ben-Yacob, *Otzar Hasepharim,* p. 664) was the one printed in Żólkiew in 1781. But they were used earlier in Poland, sporadically. The *Taharot Hakodesh* —written before 1713—mentions that some people wish to pray according to the Sephardic *nusach* or from the Lurianic prayer book, or both (p. 15a). The account seems to indicate that those were just a few individuals.

74 Efraim of Sadilkow tries to assure those who do not understand the zaddik's Torah (or the *Zohar)* that they nevertheless "absorb a good scent"; *Degel Machne Efraim,* p. 188.

75 Maimon emphasizes this point, possibly in an exaggerated form. "Excesses of some of its members . . . laid bare many weak spots. . . . Some of them . . . violated all laws of decency, wandered about naked in the public streets. . . . By their practice of extemporizing . . . they introduced into their sermons all sorts of foolish unintelligible, confused stuff. Some of them became insane" *(Autobiography,* p. 179). Maimon may reflect the opinion of many contemporaries about Hassidim. This would apparently allude to the early 1770s. Maimon's remark at the end of the paragraph about the

persecution of the Hassidim by the authority of Eliyahu Wilno "that scarcely any traces of the society [of Hassidim] can now be found" would apparently indicate that crucial time. At the time of the later attacks upon Hassidism (1781, the 1790s) it was far too strongly embedded to leave the impression upon observers that "scarcely anything remained."

76 Deuteronomy 14: 1; Talmud Babbi *Jebamot* 13b; see also Mahler, *Divrey yemei Yisrael*, vol. 1, book 3, pp. 256–60, 4: p. 244; Klausner, *Vilna batekufat hagaon.*

77 *Mirkevet Hamishne* (1751); *Lev Simcha* (1757); *Netia shel Mitzva* (1763); *Nezed Hadema* (1773); G. Scholem, "Shtay ha-eiduyot harishonot al havurot hahasidim va-Habesht," *Tarbiz* 20 (1950): 228–40; idem, *Zion* 20 (1955): 73–81; see also H. Liberman in *Bitzaron* 17 (1955): 113–20.

78 *Beyt midot* (Dyhernfurth, 1777; Prague, 1778), p. 42 ab.

79 The notes are published by Dubnow in *Toledoth Hachasidut*, pp. 484–86. It should be mentioned that the same rabbi (Halperin) expresses himself very positively about Besht. He calls him a "famous rabbi and erudite in cabala" who was shown in heaven the origin of Rabbi Halperin's father's soul.

80 *Divrey Binah*, reprinted in Braver, *Galitzia*, p. 204.

81 The community leadership in Lithuania seems to have been more authoritarian than in other regions. As early as the 1670s the leaders requested and received from the king the right to "punish like criminals" and expel recalcitrant individuals. The minutes of the Lithuanian Community Council have many entries dealing with the "conspiracies." By the beginning of the eighteenth century the Wilno kehilla already had an agreement depriving the newly appointed rabbi of all standing or any voice in the kehilla's affairs. When this rabbi, Baruch Katz Rapport, left three years later for a community in Germany his successor, Yoshua Heshel, found himself forced to turn to the king for help in 1712. The latter fined the kahal and ordered them to leave the man alone to pursue his duties as rabbi of Wilno *(RIN* 2, nos. 1139, 1163; *PML,* nos. 56, 373, 389, 446, 656, 754, 813, 816, 830, 859, 983; Bershadski, *Litovskie evrei,* pp. 21–22.

82 Klausner, *Vilna batekufat hagaon; Akty Archeograficheskoy Komisii dla razbora drevnich aktov* 29: (Wilno, 1902), 463–80; Zinberg, "Milchemet hakahal," pp. 45–74; idem, *HS* 2: 291–321; Eisenbach, "Do kwestii," *Biuletyn*, no. 17–18, pp. 129–70; no. 19–20, pp. 60–113; Israel Klausner in *Yahadut Lita* 1: 60; P. Kon in *HS* 2: 608–14; Mahler, *Polin*, pp. 395–410; P. Marek, "The Internal Struggle in Jewry in the 18th Century," *ES* 12 (1928): 102–78.

83 The usual idealistic-romantic attitude toward Eliyahu Wilno has made historians overlook the fact that Rabbi Eliyahu's livelihood was mainly dependent on the goodwill of the kehilla oligarchy. His income, paid by the kehilla, was about the same as the rabbi's but without any obligations, function, or official appointment. One may wonder to what extent this fact contributed to the oligarchy's manipulation of Eliyahu Wilno and their exploitation of the fact that the cultural symbols of kehilla leaders and Eliyahu Wilno were identical and they shared the official values. It is at least conceivable that the intimation in the 1790s (see below) that the Hassidim were maintaining that Eliyahu Wilno had ceased to oppose Hassidism, to which the kehilla leaders and Eliyahu Wilno himself reacted forcefully, was trumped up. (The "information" was discovered in Breslau by one of the notables of the kehilla.) This speculation

may be supported by the letter (published below) about Eliyahu Wilno's seeking reconciliation (provided this is not a fabrication of the Hassidim, as some believe). Also, the report that the Hassidim celebrated Eliyahu Wilno's death with a feast, which led to a renewed sharp attack upon the Hassidim, apparently lacks confirmation from any neutral source.

It should be mentioned that the opposition to Eliyahu Wilno by the leaders of the "ordinary people" went even beyond the attempt to deny him funds from the community chest. When the son of Abba ben Wolf, the head of the community who stood in the forefront of the struggle against the rabbi (he became a kind of acting rabbi when the latter was fired in 1785) and against the "ordinary people," converted to Christianity in January 1788 and was kidnapped by Jews and transported abroad, the opposition attempted to get Rabbi Eliyahu indicted by the Polish authorities. When in February 1788, Eliyahu Wilno was to be interrogated by the authorities, three or four of the leaders of the representatives of the "ordinary people" went to jail of their own free will in order to be able to appear as witnesses against Eliyahu Wilno. (In fact, however, their statements seem only indirectly to indict Rabbi Eliyahu.) See Klausner, *Vilna batekufat hagaon*, pp. 234–37.

84 Heilman, *Beth Rabbi*, p. 43. See also Mordecai Wilensky, *Hasidim*, 1: 23, 29, 63–64. According to a letter sent from Wilno to Brody, the discovery of the existence of the Hassidic group was made in the process of seeking sinners in Wilno because of a children's epidemic that had broken out in Wilno a year before (Wilensky, 1: 41); in Jewish communities in Eastern Europe it was usual to search for sinners whose sins allegedly caused children's epidemics; see also Rabinovitsch, *Lithuanian Hasidism*, p. 15 and passim.

85 This may have been a result of Eliyahu Wilno's displeasure with the "light" punishment, and his demand for stronger measures.

86 Maimon, *Autobiography*, p. 179.

87 Dubnow, *Toledoth Hachasidut*, pp. 107–25; 417–19. The letters and documents about this first attack on Hassidism were reprinted in a pamphlet, *Zemir Aritzim va-Harbot Zurim* (Aleksinetz, 1772), edited by Loeb Sofer (scribe) of Brody, who added a few items of his own. The little book was reprinted by Dubnow, "Hasidiana," *Haavar* 2: 1–28, and, more recently, by Wilensky, in *Hasidim*, 1: 27–69.

88 Literally, "opponents." It is unclear when the opponents of Hassidim began to be called mitnagdim. *Shivchey Habesht* uses the term (pp. 52 and 107). It is, however, impossible to know whether the term was used in Besht's time (before 1760) or only around the time in which the edition in question appeared (1815).

89 The accusation of Sabbatianism is to be found in scarcely any of the documents with the exception of Rabbi Avigdor's denunciation of 1800. A few hints are given in secondary writings, which may be regarded as stereotypes (Wilensky, *Hasidim*, 1: 18, 45–46, 116; Rubinstein, "Zimrat am haaretz," pp. 210–11). Such a stereotype is also used later in quarrels among Hassidic leaders themselves. (Thus in the 1830s Rabbi Bunem of Przysucha was labeled a Sabbatian by the Hassidic leaders who opposed him.) The charge of using the sharp knives for slaughtering appears mainly in the south (Brody) and only very selectively in the north; Abraham Katzenellenbogen of Brześć (or Brisk) complains in 1781 that the mitnagdim did not forbid the use of the sharp knives, and mentions it again in 1784. In 1787 this is mentioned in documents from

Mogilev and Shklov but only in connection with a slaughterer from Volhynia who came to the region. It is not mentioned by the big opponents of Hassidism, Israel Leibel and David of Makov. Possibly this kind of slaughtering did not really exist in Lithuania–White Russia until the nineteenth century or the last years of the eighteenth (Wilensky, 1: 18, 117, 127).

90 The letters reprinted now in Wilensky, *Hasidim*, 1: 89–100.

91 In the preserved materials there are found various differences in content between one community and another, which may make it appear that one community may have been more or less strict in its attitudes than another one. One would hardly be justified in drawing such conclusions, however. The original texts, written by different scribes in the flowery rabbinic style of the times, may have contained "additions" and "detractions" introduced by the respective writer or copyist. In addition, many of these documents are preserved in later copies only, and these may contain considerable changes introduced in the chain of copying.

   According to some information there were also bodily attacks on Hassidim; Heilman, *Beth Rabbi*, 1: 18; Wilensky, *Hasidim*, 1: 101–31.

92 *HZK* 2: 454 ff., 497–500; Wilensky, *Hasidim*, 1: 137–41. Gershom Bader in memoiristic notes tells how the Hassidic rabbi Kalman Neistetter (identical with Kalman Epstein) organized a minyan in Cracow for Rosh Hashanah and Yom Kippur in 1785. On the eve of Yom Kippur the community sent out two beadles with sticks to drive away the participants. They found there seven Hassidim and the rabbi, plus two poor Jews who had been hired to make up the required ten males (*YIVO Bleter* 34 (1950): 278).

93 This letter is in the Jewish National and University Library, Jerusalem, in a copy prepared by Solomon Dubno. It is undated. Most of it was published by the late Simcha Asaf in *KS* 1 (1924–25): 68–69. This writer is grateful to Dr. N. Nadav of the manuscript section of the Jewish National and University Library for sending him a Xerox copy. The assistant rabbi, the Rabbi David mentioned in the letter, was one of the two rabbis sent from Wilno in 1781 to Lithuanian communities to induce them to excommunicate the Hassidim. See S. Dubnow, "Hassidiana (II)," *Devir* 1 (1923): 291, 297–98, 302–3; Wilensky, *Hasidim*, 1: 332–33.

94 Weinryb, "East European Jewry since Polish Partitions," pp. 358–59.

95 The rationale was that Hassidim did not mourn Eliyahu Wilno's death but arranged a celebration instead. Another version is that just before his death Eliyahu Wilno bid his followers to continue—or complete—the destruction of Hassidism (the latter is related by Israel Leibel in his German pamphlet [1799] and by the Russian governor-general, Mikhail Kutuzov, in accordance with the information he received from Jews); Wilensky, *Hasidim*, 2: 327; Dubnow in *ES* 2 (1910): 259–60.

96 The document has not been preserved, so the full content of this denunciation remains unknown.

97 Dubnow, *Toledoth Hachasidut*, pp. 242–63; Klausner, *Vilna batekufat hagaon*, p. 32.

98 He became famous twelve years later as the defender of Moscow against Napoleon in 1812, and as the one who defeated Napoleon in Russia.

99 Document no. 10. Also, the Minsk governor, when sending Shneur Zalman to Petersburg, wrote a very positive account both of the Hassidim and of Shneur Zalman (document no. 14). (The documents about Shneur Zalman's second arrest have been

published by S. Dubnow in *ES* 2 [1910]: 84–109, 253–82; a full Hebrew translation is given by Wilensky, *Hasidim*, 1: 230–95).

100 Only at the time of the anti-Hassidic attack of 1772 was the hope raised that the Hassidim would return to traditional Judaism, and that was given as a motivation for the demand that the movement be repressed. This hope may have partially waned later. The 1797 announcement in Wilno points both ways: a Hassid or one who supports them "should not be considered as a Jew at all, but regarded as a gentile in everything," but at the end it promises "to pardon those people for their past offenses if they will forsake their habits."

101 It was not unusual for anti-Hassidic critics to misquote passages from Hassidic writings or to quote only parts of sentences in order to distort the meaning (see also Rubinstein, "Zimrat am haaretz," pp. 202, 218 ff.; Dubnow, "Hassidiana," II: 140, 157.

102 Solomon Maimon, too, ascribes the success of Besht and his followers to faking: "They employed the common means of medicine in their cures," but then ascribed their success to "their cabalistic hocuspocus." The robberies (which they detected) they either brought about themselves or discovered by means of their detectives who were spread all over the country." About the later times he tells that the Hassidic leaders "by means of correspondence and spies and a certain knowledge of men and . . . skillful questions . . . were able . . . to elicit secrets so . . . they succeeded in obtaining the reputation of being inspired prophets" (*Autobiography*, pp. 170, 171).

103 Dubnow, *Toledoth Hachasidut*, pp. 151, 154, 247, 254–56, 258, 287–88, 356–58, 360, 366, 369, 451, 453–55, 460, 471, 474–75; Rubinstein, "Zimrat am haaretz," pp. 201–5, 208–9, 213–14, 216–18 ff.; Wilensky, "The Polemic of Rabbi David of Makow against Hasidim," pp. 147–56; idem, *Tarbiz* 30 (1961): 396–404; idem, *Hasidim*, 2, passim.

104 Heilman, *Beth Rabbi*, 1: 8; Dubnow, *Toledoth Hachasidut*, p. 127, note 1.

105 Mitnagdim undoubtedly give exaggerated accounts of physical attacks by Hassidim upon their adversaries, of persecutions, violence, and burning of anti-Hassidic writings. Mention has already been made of cases in which Hassidim used non-Jewish authorities against their adversaries. But possibly this was done by local Hassidim without the consent or even against the will of the leaders. In one case we have the testimony of Shneur Zalman—written some years later—that in 1798/99 he forbade the head of a local Habad group (apparently meaning Meir ben Raphael in Wilno) to take revenge on the adversaries by informing upon them. "At that time their chief was a supercilious man, did not listen to me, saying that he is more astute than I" (Heilman, *Beth Rabbi*, 1: 79–81; Wilensky, *Hasidim*, 1: 313; Dubnow, *Toledoth Hachasidut*, p. 334).

106 *Noam Elimelech*, pp. 166–67. He blames them for sending out anti-Hassidic epistles in the 1780s. The lack of unity among Jews, he thinks, may have made possible "the issuance [by the government] of a decree forbidding early marriages" (199). Another Hassidic zaddik, however (Meshulam Fayvish Heller of Zbarazh), clearly accuses the mitnagdim "in this generation" who are wicked; out of jealousy they oppose those known sages in our time who have many followers, while nobody comes to them (*Derech Emet*, p. 10; quoted in Raphael, *Sepher ha-Hasidut*, p. 164).

107 *Noam Elimelech*, pp. 10, 16, 30–32, 36–37, 39, 41, 58–60, 68, 74, 76, 87, 90, 105, 116, 128, 130, 138–40, 147, 168, 174–76; *Tanya*, (English translation), pp. 41 ff., 48, 51, 60, 68 ff., 90 ff., 107, 108 ff., 136 ff., 137, 140 ff., 169 ff., 179 ff., 223–25, 337.

The content of Shneur Zalman's library would seem to afford a good illustration of his makeup and interests. In connection with his arrest in 1800 a list was made of the books found at his home (published in S. Dubnow, *ES* 2: 270). These books could be classified into the following categories:

Prayer books and commentaries			4
Bible	"	"	5
Midrash	"	"	3
Talmud	"	"	8
Codes and responsa			43
Jewish philosophy and mathematics			7
Grammar, dictionaries			3
Cabala			11
Morals, popular ethics			5
			89

This seems to have been a typical library for a rabbi of that period. Works of talmudic lore predominate, constituting here almost two-thirds of the total, with cabala taking up some 12 percent. There is nothing here of Hassidic writings—not even Shneur Zalman's own book *Tanya*—which could indicate that they had been removed earlier because of fear. (By 1800 about a dozen Hassidic books were in print.)

108 An acronym formed from the initial letters of the Hebrew words *hokhma* (wisdom), *binah* (understanding), and *daat* (knowledge) that form the divine intellect. This apparently does not mean wisdom or rational examination, of which some adversaries accused Shneur Zalman. Generally *daat* in Hassidism—and also in Jacob Frank's ideas —was credited with a number of meanings and allotted supernatural powers. Abraham of Kalisk and others criticized Shneur Zalman and his *Tanya* for having left Besht's way and concentrated too much on "ratio." These differences became much sharper in the first years of the nineteenth century (Abraham Yaakov Braver, in *KS* 1: (1924–25): 142–50, 226–38).

109 *Tanya*, pp. 20–26, 38 ff., 54, 59 ff., 136 ff., 140 ff., 144 ff., 159, 186, 188.

110 *Noam Elimelech*, p. 173. He even puts in "and mainly one should avoid drinking alcoholic beverages since this is a bad sickness" (p. 176); pp. 146, 167, 173–74, 175; Weiss, *JJS* 10, nos. 3–4, pp. 177, note 38, 184–87; *Tanya*, pp. 161 ff., 163.

111 Warsaw may have been chosen as a site for anti-Hassidic activity because in those parts of Poland, Hassidism was only just beginning to penetrate and possibly also because anti-Hassidic tendencies were to be found among some of the first Jewish Enlighteners; thus Mendel Levin-Lepin (1749–1826) in his pamphlet of 1792 and Jacques Calmanson in 1796 (see below). Solomon Maimon regarded the rabbis as "far more useful" than the Hassidim (*Autobiography*, p. 179). See also Dubnow, *Toledoth Hachasidut*, pp. 107 ff., 444 ff.; idem, *ES* (1910): 84–109, 253–82; Wolf Zeev Rabinovitsch, "Karlin Hasidism," *YIVO Annual of Jewish Social Science* 5 (1950): 123–51; Wilensky, "The Polemic of Rabbi David of Makow against Hasidism," pp. 137–56; idem, *Tarbiz* 30 (1960–61): 396–404; idem, *Hasidim*, vol. 2; Rubinstein, "Zimrat am haaretz," pp. 193–230.

112 *Glaubwürdige Nachricht von einer neuen und Zahlreichen Sekte unter den Juden die sich Chasidim nennt und ihren die Menschheit empörenden Grundsätzen und Lehren* (Frankfurt on the Oder, 1799). The text was reprinted later in *Sulamith* (Dessau, 1807), pp. 308–33. Until recently Israel Leibel's pamphlet was known only from the

Sulamith reprint. A. Rubinstein found a copy of the first edition of 1799 which contains besides the text a long introduction that was not reprinted in *Sulamith* (Rubinstein in *KS* 47 [1972]: 363).

113 See the whole title in Dubnow, *Toledoth Hachasidut*, pp. 420–24; see ibid. about the other writings. David of Makov's *Zemir Aritzim* and Leibel's *Sepher Havikuach* are now reprinted in Wilensky, *Hasidim*, vol. 2.

114 About the manuscripts see Dubnow, *Toledoth Hachasidut*, pp. 420–24, 459–65; Rubinstein, *KS* 35: 240–49; Wilensky, *PAAJR* 25 (1956): 137–56; idem, *Hasidim*, vol. 2.

115 *Even Bochen* (Frankfurt on the Oder, 1799); see also A.R. Malachi in *Sepher Hayobel shel Hadoar* (New York, 1952), 288 ff.

The first anti-Hassidic writings had already been published by the 1790s. Mendel Levin (or Lepin) in 1792 and Jacques Calmanson in 1796 picture the Hassidic leaders as being money-hungry and the Hassidim as either deceptive and mistaken zealots or a bunch of fools led by swindlers. They also accused them of unethical practices and spreading esoteric teachings; M. Levin, *Essai d'un plan de reforme ayant pour l'objet d'éclairer la nation juive en Pologne et de redresser par la ses moeurs* (1792); Calmanson, *Essai sur l'etat actuel des Juifs* (1796).

116 Shneur Zalman of Liady now (some time after 1803) had to assure non-Hassidic Jews that they would not be denied the possibility of obtaining meat slaughtered without the sharp knives (Heilman, *Beth Rabbi*, 1: 79–80).

117 See also Ashkoli, "Hachasidut ba-Polin," *Beyt Yisrael* 2: 86–141.

Appendix 3

1 Louis Chevalier, "Towards a History of Population," in D.V.Glass and D.E.D. Eversley, eds., *Population in History: Essays in Historical Demography* (Chicago, 1965), p. 71; David Landes, "The Treatment of Population in History Textbooks," *Daedalus* 97 (Spring 1968): 379.

2 See John Demos, "Families in Colonial Bristol, Rhode Island: An Exercise in Historical Demography," in *William and Mary Quarterly* (January 1968); J.C. Russell, "A Quantitative Approach to Medieval Population Change," *Journal of Economic History* 24 (March 1964)—both republished in Rowney and Graham, eds., *Quantitative History*, pp. 275–307; see also Russell, *Late Ancient and Medieval Population*.

3 See, for instance, the controversy about the Jews in the world around 1500. While Arthur Ruppin mentioned a figure of about 2.5 million, A. Kaminka estimated the number to have been only 500–600,000. But he also counts 60,000 for Poland whereas probably no more than 10,000–12,000 Jews lived there at that time (A. Kaminka in *Der Jude* 2 (1917): 503–4; see also ibid., 2: 140; *Hashiloach* 25 (1912): 611–18.

4 See M.M. Fryde, "The Population in Medieval Poland," in *Transactions of the American Philosophical Society*, new series 48, part 3 (Philadelphia, 1958): 146–48; Tadeusz Ladogórski, *Studia nad zaludnieniem Polski XIV wieku* (Wroclaw, 1958).

5 Russell, *Late Ancient and Medieval Population*, p. 12.

6 Brann, *Geschichte der Juden*, pp. 52, 56, and Appendixes II–III. For 1349 Brann estimates sixty-six to sixty-eight family heads in Breslau.

7 E. Mueller, *Zydzi w Krakowie w drugiej polowie XIV stulecia* (Cracow, 1906), pp. 12–13.

8   I. Schipper in *IEN* 11: 107 ff., 116 ff.; idem, *Toledoth ha-Kalkala*, pp. 489–93; idem, *ZPO* 1: 26–32; Elazar Feldman, "Do statystyki Żydów w dawnej Polsce," *Miesiecznik Żydowski* 3, no. 1 (1933): 130–35; *AYZR* 7, part 2, pp. 208–9, nos. 8, 10–13, 19, 20; 8, part 1, no. 121.

9   These include authors who themselves maintain that Jewish settlement in Polish villages dates only from the second half of the sixteenth century "while being very rare in earlier times." This, of course, contradicts Dr. Schipper's assumption that village Jews in the fifteenth century constituted one-fifth of the urban population (see Mahler, *Polin*, p. 94).

10   Feldman, "Do statystyki"; *AYZR* 7, part 2, nos. 11–13; Gelber in *Pinkas Hrubieszov*, p. 29.

11   Feldman, who also regarded Schipper's computations as exaggerated, suggests 6,300 Jews for the urban population.

12   Jews were expelled from Lithuania in 1495 and returned there from Poland, where they had lived temporarily, in 1503. In those years Volhynia and Kiev were also under Lithuanian suzerainty and suffered the same fate. The Volhynian communities are included in the above computation of 61 or 63 communities, respectively. Of Lithuania proper we know mainly about three or four communities (Grodno, Brest, Troki, Wilno) where Jews lived before the expulsion. The extant documents connected with the expulsion and dealing with the transfer of their property to non-Jews and, upon the Jews' return to Lithuania, the restoration of their property to them, give the impression that we deal here with very small numbers (some Jewish tax farmers, mostly wealthy ones, converted to Christianity and were not expelled). King Alexander's demand that Lithuanian (and Volhynian) Jewry be obliged to equip one thousand horsemen in case of war (later canceled) apparently has no relation to their size, even though the obligation to supply soldiers for the war was generally reckoned according to the number of houses, one soldier for every eight houses (*REA* 1, nos. 27–62).

13   See Isserles, *Darkey Moshe*, no. 116, par. 10; *YS* Babba Kama 6, no. 26; Weinryb, *HS* 2: 43 ff.; Halperin, *Yehudim*, p. 253.

14   Hurewitz, *Shnei Luchot Habrith*, p. 63a.

15   Seraphine Guerchberg, "The Controversy over the Alleged Sowers of the Black Death in Contemporary Treatises on Plague," reprinted in Sylvia L. Thrupp, *Change in Medieval Society* (New York, 1964), pp. 208–23 (originally appeared in *REJ* 108 (1948); see also Shelomo Eidelberg in *Tarbiz* 37 (October 1967): 97–98.

16   Stanislaw Wazak, "Ludność i zabudowa mieszkaniowa miasta Poznania w 16 i 17w.," *Przeglad Zachodni*, 1953, nos. 9/10, p. 113 (apparently Perles attributes the 1619 situation to 1641, see *MGWJ* 13:420); Avron, *Pinkas*, nos. 108, 678, 1063, 1226; see also *HZK* 1: 408 ff. Sources tell about the existence of body lice, mice, and rats, which were the carriers of diseases, and about afflictions of boils and similar infections caused by uncleanliness.

17   It should be mentioned that non-Jewish statements often point out the more rapid growth of the Jewish population but some at the same time list a number of disabilities of the Jews which would, by implication, indicate that the growth was slow. Thus Tadeusz Czacki tells about the rapid growth and computes a Jewish population in Poland for the 1780s as high as 900,000, but at the same time he quotes the investigations of the then existing Committee on Jewish Matters that: (1) infant mortality

among Jews is 40–50 percent higher than among the general population; (2) the young generation of Jews suffer from a number of illnesses, which are a result of early marriages among them; and (3) Jewesses often die in childbirth or become infertile, because in the whole country there is not to be found even one knowledgeable Jewish midwife (Czacki, *Rozprawa*, pp. 200–1).

18 Solomon Luria (sixteenth century) complains that young people transgress the Jewish norm and remain unmarried after eighteen or even twenty years of age. He rationalizes this as a result of the large dowries which became fashionable. An author of the end of the seventeenth or the beginning of the eighteenth century warns that one should not delay marrying after reaching the age of eighteen (the tone seems to indicate that such delay was not unusual). In "abnormal times," when a real or imagined prohibition against early marriages loomed, Jews hastened to marry off their small children—in Poland the first time c. 1764 or 1775 (see also Halperin, *Yehudim*, pp. 289–309; *YS* Yebamot 6, no. 40; *Taharot Hakodesh*, 1b).

19 See, for instance, F. Wettstein, "Letoldot Yisrael Vechachamav Bapolin," *Haeshkol* 7 (Cracow, 1913): 147–48, 151–52, 154, 159, 160–63, 172, 176, 182; Balaban, *HZK* 1, 2: passim; Dembitzer, *Kelilath Yofi* (reprint New York, 1960), pp. 59–60, 85–86, 99–100, 114–15; *ES* 5 (1913): 401–7, 526–36; Wurm, *Z dziejów*, pp. 92, 97. An author of the seventeenth to eighteenth centuries depicts the sufferings of the tenants, telling that they often lacked even the possibility of washing their hands; *Taharot Hakodesh*, 2: 3b, 5b.

20 Weinryb, *Texts*, pp. 39–40 and documents no. 48, 52–58; Balaban, *JJLG* 10 (1895): 329.

21 Some Hassidic stories (second half of the eighteenth century) indicate that purchasing firewood was a problem for the poor. Incidental mention in responsa of cases in which the baby was smothered inadvertently when the mother took it into her bed for the night may also have been connected with an attempt to keep it warm.

22 This is documented for Poland by letters of the sixteenth century from Cracow, and for Germany—which in this connection did not differ greatly from Poland—by the tale of Glückel of Hameln about the suspicion of sickness of her four-year-old daughter (c. 1664), which necessitated keeping her, together with a maid, in a village and hiring at considerable cost a Polish Jewish couple to take care of her. This is also illustrated by a responsum about a very rich man (Worms, 1636) who in the time of an epidemic was forced to promise a lowly butcher's assistant the hand of his daughter if he would take care of her during her sickness (this case came before the Jewish court because the rich man later wanted to retreat from his agreement) (Weinryb, in *HS* 2: 43–44; *The Life of Glückel of Hamelin*, pp. 48–52; Responsa *Havat Yair* of Yair Hayim Bachrach, no. 60).

23 *HZK* 1: 187–209; *Responsa Mas'at Benyamin*, no. 4; *Rishmey Shealah*, no. 1.

24 Bersohn, nos. 129, 522.

25 Schipper tried to reconstruct an alleged census of 1676 on the basis of the poll tax figures of 1717, but apparently no such census was ever taken. See also Halperin, *Yehudim*, p. 295.

26 Bershadski, *Litovskie evrei*, p. 335, assumes that the poll tax of 8,000 zloty paid by Lithuanian Jewry in 1566 was near the true number of the Jewish population; S. Ettinger thinks along the same lines in relation to the Ukraine, most of which

belonged to Lithuania until 1569 (S. Ettinger in *Zion* 21 [1956]: 120). Elsewhere, however, the same author (together with a coauthor) computes, for 1578, one zloty per family head in a Volhynian town (see *Pinkas Kremeniec*, ed. A.S. Stein [Tel Aviv, 1954], p. 11.)

27 Schipper, *IEN* 11: 116–17; idem, *ZPO* 1: 204 ff.; Halperin, *PVAA*, passim. Roman Rybarski, *Skarb i pieniądz za Jana Kazimierza, Michala Korybuta i Jana III* (Warsaw, 1939), pp. 214 ff.

28 Baranovich, *Magnatskoe*, pp. 13–16.

29 The year 1569 is when most of the Ukraine passed administratively from Lithuania to Poland proper.

30 See particulars and sources in Ettinger, *Zion* 21 (1956): 120–24.

31 It is estimated that the population of the Ukraine generally grew ten times during 1550–1600 (see Herbert Moller, ed., *Population Movements in Modern European History* [New York, 1964], p. 28).

32 Ibid., pp. 3–4.

33 Figures from Ettinger, *Zion* 21: 124; Mahler, *Yidn in Zifern*, pp. 29, 43.

34 Schipper's calculation of 120,000 Jews in Poland in 1578, 200,000 in 1598, and 450,000 in 1648 (in Poland and Lithuania) is a chimera. He bases his reckoning on statements in the anti-Semitic literature of the time. But anti-Semitic authors in most periods and countries are known to have exaggerated the number of Jews beyond any reality. One such author maintains in 1624, for instance, "that in Poznań alone were 100,000 Jews, in Cracow still more" at a time when both together may have housed 3,600–4,000 Jews (*Kruk w Złotej Klatce . . .* [1624], quoted in Bartoszewicz; Schipper, *ZPO*, 1: 31). As a curiosity it should be mentioned that a non-Jewish traveler of the sixteenth century maintained that there were 2 million (sic) Jews in Poland, and some believed him (see L. Lewin, *JJLG* 5 (1907): 143).

35 Zofia Lubiszowska, in *KH* 52, no. 3 (1955): 167; O. Górka, "Nieznana Kronika Tatarska z lat 1644–50," ibid., pp. 114, 118, 120.

36 *Yeveyn metzulah*, ed. Halperin, pp. 54, 80; *Zok Haitim* 7a, 10b.

37 Israel Halperin, in his detailed study on the prisoners (*Zion* 25: 17–56), rightly points out that Hanover "writes in an exaggerated form and his figures are rather pictorial numbers," while other figures in this sort of writing are exaggerated (pp. 44, 54); see also the contrasts in the figures about the Jewish dead from epidemics in Lwów, which range from 10,000 (Hanover, *Yeveyn metzulah*) and 6,000 (Abraham Ashkenazi, *Zaar bath rabim*) to "a few thousand" (Sabbatai Kohen) and "almost five hundred." In a chronicle of Lwów the total number of all dead (non-Jews and Jews together) is given as 7,000 (quoted I. Halperin "Ezrah va-Siyua la-Kehiloth Polin ba-ikvoth gzeyroth Tach vaTat," *Sepher Yobel La-Yitzchak Baer*, p. 338). See also Nadav, "Kehillat Pinsk," pp. 154–55, 157, 171–72. (This writer is grateful to Dr. Nadav for having made available copies of a few other chapters of his study of Pinsk.)

38 Thus Dubno: 1650 Jews owned one-quarter of all the houses; 1710, about two-thirds. Pinsk: 1648, 100 Jewish houses, 1710, 600 houses. Żólkiew: synagogue becomes too small for the increased population. Brody: considerable growth of Jewish population 1660s and 1670s. Similarly in Lissa and other places (Nadav, "Kehillat Pinsk," pp. 182–83; *RIN* 2, nos. 1498, 1563; see also Dinur, *Ba-mifneh ha-doroth*, pp. 114–15).

Information from some other towns shows the same trend of considerable growth in Jewish population.

Jewish Population Growth

Town	Date	No. of Jews
Kraśnik	beginning of 17th century	30 families
	1647	68 families
	1764	over 900 Jews
Biala	1621	about 30 families
	1742	about 1,000 Jews
Drohobycz	1663	15 houses (30–40 families)
	1685	70–80 families
	1765	about 1,000 Jews

The number of Jews in neighboring villages also increased a great deal. At the beginning of the eighteenth century about a dozen villages around Drohobycz had Jews living in them; by 1765 there were 86 villages in which the number of Jews exceeded 1,000; J. Morgensztern, *Biuletyn*, no. 36 (1960): 12; M. Hendel, "Hayehudim ba-Biala," *Sepher Biala Podlaska*, (Tel Aviv, 1961), pp. 10–12; Jakub Winkler, *Biuletyn*, no. 71–72 (1969): 42–43.

39 For instance, of the 38 smaller communities in the Krzemieniec region which existed in 1765, 25 or about two-thirds were newly settled by Jews sometime after 1648 (*Pinkas Kremenitz*, pp. 21–22).

40 Wettstein, "Letoldot Yisrael Vechachamav Bapolin," *Haeshkol* 7: 190–94. A comparison of the printed statistics with a copy of the same statistical materials in Wettstein's own handwriting shows almost no differences (some Cracow documents in copies made by Wettstein came to this writer in the 1930s from offices of the *Monatschrift für Geschichte und Wissenschaft des Judentum*, where Wettstein had left them many years earlier).

41 Ruppin's lower estimates of the birth rate and higher death rates (Arthur Ruppin, *The Jewish Fate and Future* [London, 1940], pp. 75–76) and consequently a very low rate of growth of Jews in the world during the seventeenth and eighteenth centuries are entirely arbitrary. Our estimates, or "guesstimates," appear realistic in comparison with situations among underdeveloped societies during the nineteenth and twentieth centuries (Egypt since 1800, India), which more or less resembled conditions in Europe a century or two earlier, and in light of actual population history in Poland. Some Italian cities show a death rate in the sixteenth and seventeenth centuries of 2.6–3.6 (see Russell, *Late Ancient and Medieval Population*, p. 34). Also for America of the eighteenth century (colonial and early national periods) a birth rate of 50–55 per thousand is estimated (*New York Times*, December 31, 1961, p. 36). It is also assumed that during the colonial times population in North America doubled every twenty-five years.

Appendix 4

1 G. Scholem, "Devekuth or Communion with God," *The Review of Religion*, January 1950, p. 123; see also *Toledoth*, p. 56; *Keter Shem Tov*, pp. 2b, 10a.

2 Weiss, "Reyshit," pp. 60 ff., 64 ff.; idem, "Talmud Torah leshitath R. Israel Besht,"

Sepher ha-yovel Tipheret Yisrael likhvod Israel Brodie (London, 1967), pp. 152 ff.; *Shivchey Habesht*, p. 110.

3   *Toledoth*, pp. 7, 14, 56, 60; see also *Zavaat Haribash*, pp. 1b, 2b, 3a, 5b, 7b, 10b; *Keter Shem Tov*, pp. 2b, 4b, 6a, 9a, 10b, 11b, 13a.

4   *Tanya*, ch. 2 (English trans. pp. 28–29).

5   Scholem, "Devekuth," pp. 131 ff.; Jacob Joseph, *Zofnath Paaneach*, p. 30b; English translation from Dresner, *The Zaddik*, p. 129; see also ibid., pp. 128–32; *Toledoth*, pp. 10, 111.

6   See J.G. Weiss, "R. Abraham Kalisker's Concept of Communion with God and Men," *JJS* 6 (1955): 92–99. Another version of the same idea of the role of a group is indicated by Efraim of Sadilkow (*Degel Machne Efraim*, p. 122): see also *Keter Shem Tov*, pp. 2b, 4b, 11b.

7   *Zavaat Haribash*, p. 8b; see also Jacob Joseph, *Ben Porat Joseph* (Korzec, 1781), p. 3, and G. Scholem, "Der Begriff der Kawwanah in der alten Kabbalah," *MGWJ* 78 (1934): 492–518. See J.G. Weiss, "The Kavanoth of Prayer in Early Hasidism," *JJS* 9, nos. 3–4 (1958): 163–92. While Dr. Weiss is surely right about kavvanah in Hassidism differing from that of Lurianic cabala, one may doubt how much sophisticated categorization is appropriate for this sort of writing; at least a part of the differences may result from the authors' confusion of terms; see also Uffenheimer, *Hachasidut ka-mistika*, pp. 129–47.

8   *Tanya*, chapters 30, 38.

9   Even Solomon of Karlin, who adhered to the Lithuanian brand of Hassidism, motivates the need of studying Talmud as a preparation for prayer. Only seldom does a Hassidic leader in the eighteenth century emphasize study of Talmud and codes for the purpose of knowing the halakha. Thus Meshulam Feivish Heller of Zbaraż (died 1795). *Shema Shelomo* (Piotrków), passim (quoted in Raphael, *Sepher ha-Hasidut*, pp. 158, 165).

10   *Keter Shem Tov*, pp. 9b, 11b; *Zavaat Haribash*, pp. 1b, 2b, 3a, 4a, 8b, 9b. Dr. Weiss assumes that the facts of life—Hassidic leaders not necessarily being great talmudic scholars—led to a de-emphasis of this sort of study (Weiss, "Talmud torah," pp. 151–52).

11   Weiss, "Talmud Torah," pp. 154 ff., 160 ff.; and the sources quoted there; *Shivchey Habesht*, pp. 59, 79, 84–5; *Likkutey Yakarim* (Lwów, 1792), quoted in Weiss, ibid., pp. 161, 168.

12   See particulars in J. Weiss, "Talmud Tora Bereyshit Hachasidut," *Hadoar* 45, no. 33 (August 6, 1965); see also *Keter Shem Tov*, p. 126.

13   Also the *Zohar* ascribes to prayer an important position.

14   *Keter Shem Tov*, pp. 5a, 7b, 11b, 13b; *Degel Machne Efraim*, p. 183.

15   *Zavaat Haribash*, pp. 1b, 2b, 3a, 4a, 6a, 7a; *Toledoth*, pp. 28, 72.

16   *Zavaat Haribash*, p. 6a; *Keter Shem Tov*, p. 12b.

17   *Keter Shem Tov*, p. 13b.

18   Buber, *The Origin and Meaning of Hasidism*, ed. M. Friedman, pp. 54–55; *Toledoth*, p. 417.

19   *Zavaat Haribash*, pp. 1–2, 6a–6b; *Keter Shem Tov*, p. 13a; *Toledoth*, p. 16. Many

variations of these themes are found in the writings of the Hassidic leaders. See also *Tanya*, ch. 28.

20   Weiss, "The Kavanoth of Prayer," note 47, pp. 186–87.

21   This stands in contradiction to some ideas of the eighteenth century which stressed weeping *(Shaar Hamelech)*. It should be mentioned that Hassidic tradition tells also about Besht and some other zaddikim who sometimes wept *(Shivchey Habesht*, pp. 41, 90, 92).

22   *Zavaat Haribash*, pp. 2, 3b, 7b, 8a, 10b; *Toledoth* 3, 40; (Raphael, *Sepher ha-Hasidut*, p. 111); see also M.M. of Vitebsk, *Peri Eytz* (Zhitomir, 1874), p. 18.

23   Pinchas Shapira of Koretz, *Midrash Pinchas* 59; Moses of Sasov, *Hiddushey Haramal*, Vayeyzey, Bereyshit; (Raphael, *Sepher ha-Hasidut*, pp. 27, 188).

24   *Tanya*, ch. 33, English translation by Mindel, pp. 193, 195; see also A. Shochat, "Al ha-Simcha ba-Hasidut," *Zion* 16 (1951): 30–43.

25   Buber and Scholem, each in his own way, try to explain the alleged decline in acuity of messianism in Hassidism as a result of messianism's collapse with Sabbatai Zevi, while Dinur (and some others) try to demonstrate heightened acuity in Hassidism (see also the summary of I. Tishbi, *Zion* 32 (1967): 1–3).

26   *Shaar Hamelech*, part 2, *shaar* 6, chapt. 4; *Beyt Perez* (Żólkiew, 1759), *derush* 9, p. 17b; *Yeriat Haohel* (1794) *Petach haohel* 6; *Mishmeret hakodesh*, Kedushat hadibur, quoted in Dinur, *Ba-mifneh ha-doroth*, pp. 175–76; see also ibid., pp. 179 ff. (Dinur uses these quotations to show the "promessianic trend of the generation"; in truth, if anything, they show the reverse, even though a few preachers were upset about the attitudes of the people.)

27   Emden, *Sepher Shimush*, p. 62b.

28   A. Kahane, in *Festschrift . . . A. Harkavy* (Petersburg, 1908), p. 447.

29   The letter was to be taken by Jacob Joseph to the addressee in Palestine, and it was written while he was preparing for the trip around 1751. But it remained with him because he himself stayed in Poland. Jacob Joseph published it at the end of his book *Ben Porat Josef* and from there it was reprinted elsewhere in full or in part (among others in *Maggid Devarav Leyaakov*). See Dubnow, *Toledoth Hachasidut*, 1:60–62; S. Horodetzki, *Hahasidim Va-Hahasidut* (Tel Aviv, 1928), 1:54–56; Dinur, *Ba-mifneh ha-doroth*, pp. 181–84, 192–206; Tishbi, *Zion* 32: 29–32 (Tishbi concludes rightly that very little about Besht's messianism can be deduced from this story); see also D. Frankel, ed., *Mikhtavim ma-ha-Besht ve-talmidav* (Lwów, 1923). It should be mentioned that there exists a tradition that, according to Besht, the sound of the shofar asks Elijah: "When will our Messiah come?" *(Keter Shem Tov*, p. 23a).

30   *Shivchey Habesht*, pp. 18, 30, 120.

31   Benjamin of Zalozhic, *Turey Zahav* (Mogilev, 1816), Behaalotcha; *Mayim Rabim*, Shemot; Samson Shlomo Schwartz, *Saraf, Pri Etz Hayim* (Czernowitz, 1864) (quoting his grandfather Moshe Shoham from Dolina) Raphael, *Sepher ha-Hasidut*, pp. 72, 76, 60; *Keter Shem Tov*, pp. 2b, 3b, 5b, 10a, 18, 19a, 22b, 24b, 25b; *Noam Elimelech*, p. 32; also Ber of Mezeritch expressed the same idea.

32   See also *Keter Shem Tov*, p. 26a; *Zavaat Haribash*, pp. 8b, 9a.

33   *Toledoth*, pp. 20–21, 28, 53, 57, 64, 66, 72, 80, 92, 153, 175, 277, 296, 350, 356, 394.

34   The first quotation, English translation, taken from Scholem, *Commentary*, Oct. 1961; *Maggid Devarav Leyaakov*, pp. 6a, 24b.

35 Shneur Zalman's statement is quoted in Werfel, *Hachasidut, Ve-Eretz Yisrael* (Jerusalem, 1940), p. 14; Yaakov Itzhak Halevi Horwitz, *Zikhron Zot,* Behar; David from Lilow in *Niflaot Hayehudi,* Hiddushey Tora; Abraham David of Buczacz, *Choze David,* Sukka (Raphael, *Sepher ha-Hasidut,* pp. 214, 239, 316).

36 *Toledoth,* pp. 243–44, 375, 288; *Maor Aynayim,* pp. 10, 55; *Degel Machne Efraim,* pp. 61, 118, 158, 178; *Noam Elimelech,* pp. 8–11, 16, 25, 32, 40, 62, 100, 149, 154. Similar ideas and variations thereof are found among a number of other Hassidic leaders (see the quotations in Raphael, *Sepher ha-Hasidut,* pp. 72–73, 76, 214, 231, 316); see also Uffenheimer, *Hachasidut ka-mistika,* pp. 168–77, and the quotations there from Hassidic literature.

37 *Degel Machne Efraim,* passim; quotations in Tishbi, *Zion* 32: 33–34. These quotations may very well serve Tishbi's purpose of showing that messianism was not intentionally "neutralized," but at the same time they do not attest to messianic tension. Generally many other passuses show the contrary.

38 Menachem Nachum of Czernobyl, *Meor Eynayim* (Slavuta, 1798); Elimelekh of Liżajsk, *Noam Elimelech* (Slavuta, 1794); Schneur Zalman, *Tanya* (1839); see the quotations in Tishbi, *Zion* 32: 35–39; see also Raphael, *Sepher ha-Hasidut,* p. 38.

39 Baruch of Medzhibozh, *Botzina;* see also Raphael, *Sepher ha-Hasidut,* pp. 49, 76–77, 231, 316.

40 Tishbi, *Zion* 32: 39–45; generally the term messianism is used very loosely among authors dealing with the subject, so that it is almost impossible to differentiate between expressions denoting acute messianism and those which belong to the category of mere metaphors. The prediction of the coming of the Messiah in 1840 by Arye Leib of Shpola (died 1812) may belong to that category. See Raphael, *Sepher ha-Hasidut,* p. 62.

41 Scholem, "Shtey Igrot Meeretz Yisrael," *Tarbiz* 25 (1956): 434, 436.

42 Menachem Mendel of Premyślan may have been in Palestine before that and have returned to Poland. *Shivchey Habesht,* pp. 29, 58, 120; Halperin, *Haaliyot,* pp. 16–17, 20; Simha ben Benjamin, *Ahavat Zion,* 9, 15.

43 The endless trips of the emigrants through Poland, and the echo about the emigration of Jews abroad, induced the Polish government to promulgate a law limiting travel to Palestine.

44 Halperin, *Haaliyot,* pp. 20–37, and the sources quoted there.

45 During the Middle Ages in Christian Europe importance was attached to being buried in the soil of one's own country (Huizinga, *The Waning of the Middle Ages,* p. 143). It is unclear if there was any connection between this and the Jewish tendency to be buried in Palestine.

46 Halperin, *Haaliyoth,* p. 18; G. Scholem, "Shtey Igrot," pp. 429–31.

47 Legend tells how two Hassidim, one of whom was Nachman of Horodenka, wanted to meet in Palestine so that together they could bring the Messiah, but they missed each other (*Shivchey Habesht,* p. 46); Halperin, *Haaliyoth,* pp. 20 (note 4) 49.

48 *Likkutey Amarim* (Lwów, 1911), letter 4 (Raphael, *Sepher ha-Hasidut,* p. 124).

Selected Bibliography

Abraham Hamalach. *Hesed Leabraham*. Czernowitz, 1851.

Aronius, Julius. *Regesten zur Geschichte der Juden im Fränkischen und Deutschen Reich bis zum Jahre 1273*. Berlin, 1887–1902.

Ashkenzi, Gershon. *Avodat Hagershuni*. Vol. 1. Frankfurt on the Main, 1699; Lwów, 1861.

Ashkenazi, Tzevi b. Jacob, Responsa *Chacham Zevi*. Fürth, 1767.

Ashkoli, A. "Hachasidut ba-Polin." In *Beyt Yisrael Bapolin*. Edited by I. Halperin. Vol. 2. Jerusalem, 1954.

————. *Hatenuot Hameshichiot Bayisrael*. Jerusalem, 1956.

Avron, Dov, ed. *Pinkas ha-Kesherim shel Kehilat Pozna*. Jerusalem, 1967.

Baechtold, Rudolf. *Südwestrussland im Spätmittelalter (Baseler Beiträge zur Geschichtswissenschaft, vol. 38)*. Basel, 1951.

Balaban, Meir. *Bibliografia Historii Żydów w Polsce i w krajach ościennych za lata 1900–1930*. Warsaw, 1939.

————. "Kiedy i skąd przybyli Żydzi do Polski." *MZ* 1 (Warsaw, 1930).

————. *Letoldoth ha-tenua ha-frankit*. Tel Aviv, 1934.

————. "Sabataizm w Polsce." In *Księga Jubileuszowa ku czci Prof. Dra. Mojżesza Schorra*. Warsaw, 1935.

————. *Yidn in Poylen*. Wilno, 1930.

Balzer, Oswald. *Sądownictwo Ormiańskie w Średniowiecznym Lwowie*. Lwów, 1909.

Baranovich, A.I. *Magnatskoe khozyaistvo na juge Volyni v XVIII v*. Moscow, 1955.

Bardach, Juliusz. *Historia państwa i prawa Polski do polowy XV wielku*. Vols. 1 and 2. Warsaw, 1957.

Baron, Salo W. *The Jewish Community*. New York, 1942.

————. *A Social and Religious History of the Jews*. Vols. 2, 3, 8. Philadelphia, 1957 et seq.

Bartoszewicz, Kazimierz. *Antysemityzm w literaturze Polskiej XV-XVII w*. Warsaw, 1914.

Baumgardt, David. *Great Western Mystics*. New York, 1961.

Ben-Sason, Haim Hilel. *Hagut va-Hanhaga*. Jerusalem, 1959.

Berlin, I. *Istoricheskiya sud'by Evreyskago naroda na territorii Russkogo gosudarstva.* Petrograd, 1919.

Bernfeld, Shimon. *Sepher ha-demaot.* Vol. 3. Berlin, 1926.

Ber of Mezeritch. *Maggid devarov le-Yaakov.* Korzec, 1784; Berditshev, 1808.

———. *Or Haemeth.* Zitomir, 1900.

Bershadski, S.A. *Litovskie evrei 1388–1569.* Petersburg, 1883.

Bersohn, Mathias. *Dyplomatariusz dotyczący Żydów w dawnej Polsce.* Warsaw, 1911.

Beth Hillel, Eben Haezer, by Hillel of Wilno. Dyhernfurth, 1691.

Beth Yacob, Responsa by Yaakov b. Shmuel. Dyhernfurth, 1696.

Bloch, Philipp. *Die General Privilegien der polnischen Judenschaft.* Poznań, 1892.

Bolshakoff, Serge. *Russian Nonconformity.* Philadelphia, 1950.

Borovoy, S. Y. "Natzionalno-osvoboditelnaya voina Ukrainskogo naroda protiv polskogo vladichestva i evreiskoye naseleniye Ukrainy." *Istoricheskie Zapiski* 9 (1940).

Brann, Marcus. *Geschichte der Juden in Schlesien (Jahresbericht des Jüdisch-Theologischen Seminars).* Vols. 1–5. Breslau, 1896–1910.

Braver, A.Y. *Galitzia vi-Yehudeha.* Jerusalem, 1956.

Breger, Marcus. *Zur Handelsgeschichte der Juden in Polen im 17. Jahrhundert.* Berlin, 1932.

Bruna, Israel. *Responsa.* Stettin, 1860; Jerusalem, 1960.

Buber, Solomon. *Kirya nisgava.* Cracow, 1903 (reprint Israel, 1968).

Cambridge History of Poland, The. Vols. 1 and 2. Cambridge, 1950–51.

Cohen, Gerson D. *Messianic Postures of Ashkenazim and Sephardim.* New York, 1967.

Cohn, Norman. *The Pursuit of the Millennium.* New York, 1961.

Czacki, Tadeusz. *Rozprawa o Żydach.* Warsaw, 1860.

Dembitzer, Haim Nathan. *Kelilath Yofi.* Vols. 1 and 2. Cracow, 1888–93 (reprint New York, 1960).

Dinur, Ben Zion. *Ba-mifneh ha-doroth.* Jerusalem, 1955.

Dokumenty ob osvoboditelnoi voinye Ukrainskogo naroda 1648–1654. Kiev, 1965.

Dubnow, S. *History of the Jews in Russia and Poland.* Vols. 1–3. Philadelphia, 1916 et seq.

———. *Toledoth Hachasidut.* Tel Aviv, 1930–31.

Efraim of Sadilkow. *Degel Machne Efraim.* Zhitomir, 1850.

Eisenbach, A. "Do kwestii walki klasowej w społeczeństwie Żydowskim w Polsce w drugiej połowie XVIII w." *Biuletyn,* nos. 17–18, 19–20 (1956).

Eisenstein, Aron. *Die Stellung der Juden in Polen im XIII und XIV Jahrhundert.* Cieszyn, 1934.

Eliade, Mircea. *Cosmos and History: The Myth of Eternal Return.* New York, 1969.

Emden, Jacob. *Mitpachat sepharim.* Altona, 1768.

———. *Sefat Emeth va-Lashon zehorit.* Altona, 1752.

———. *Sepher Shimush.* Altona, 1762.

————. *Torath Hakanaut.* Amsterdam, 1752.

Ettinger, S. "Helkam shel Hayehudim bakolonizacya shel Ukraina." *Zion* 21 (1956).

————. "Maamadam ha-mishpati ve-hahevrati shel Yehudey Ukraina ba-meot hatetvav-hayudzayin." *Zion* 20 (1955).

Even Hashocham u-meirath einayim, Responsa by Eliakim Getz b. Meir. Dyhernfurth, 1733.

Eytan Haezrachi, Responsa by Abraham Rapaport. Ostrog, 1796.

Feldman, Elazar. "Di eltste yedies wegn Yidn in Poylishe shteyt in XIV-XVI Yurhundert." *Bleter* 1 (Warsaw, 1939).

Freiman, Aron. *Inyaney Shabtai Zevi.* Berlin, 1913.

Gelber, N.M. *Toledoth Yehudey Brody.* Jerusalem, 1956.

Gevuroth Anashim, Responsa by Sabbatai b. Meir Hakohen. Desau, 1697; Sudzilkow, 1819.

Graetz, H. *Frank und die Frankisten—eine Sekten Geschichte.* Breslau, 1868.

Grass, Karl Konrad. *Die Russischen Sekten.* Vols. 1 and 2, 1905 (reprint Leipzig, 1966).

Grayzel, Solomon. *The Church and the Jews in the XIII Century.* Philadelphia, 1933.

Gumowski, Marian. "Monety Hebraiskie za Piastów." *Biuletyn,* nos. 41, 42 (1962).

Gumplowicz, Ludwig. *Prawodawstwo Polskie względem Żydów.* Cracow, 1867.

Gurland, H.J. *Lekorot ha-Gezeyrot al Yisrael.* Przemyśl, 1847.

Halecki, Oscar. *Borderlands of Western Civilization: A History of East Central Europe.* New York, 1952.

Halperin, I. *Yehudim Viyehadut Bamizrach Europa.* Jerusalem, 1969.

Hanover, N. *Yeveyn metzulah.* Edited by I. Halperin. Tel Aviv, 1945 (English translation: Abraham J. Mesch. *Abyss of Despair*).

Heilman, H.M. *Beth Rabbi.* Berditshev, 1903.

Historia Polski. Edited by Tadeusz Manteufel. Vols. 1–3. Warsaw, 1958 et seq.

Huberbrand, Szymon. "Żródla do historii Żydów w krajach slowiańskich." *Biuletyn,* no. 2 (1951).

Huizinga, J. *The Waning of the Middle Ages.* New York, 1956.

Hurewitz, Abraham. *Brit Abraham.* Lublin, 1577.

Hurewitz, Isaiah. *Shnei Luchot Habrith.* Amsterdam, 1698.

Hurwitz, Simon. *The Responsa of Solomon Luria.* New York, 1938.

Isserles, Moses. *Darkey Moshe.* Sultzbach, 1691.

————. *Sheeloth u-teshuvoth.* Hanau, 1710.

————. *Torath haoleh.* Lemberg, 1858.

Jacob, Conrad. *Hiltebrandt's dreifache Schwedische Gesandschaftsreise nach Siebenbuergen, der Ukraine und Constantinopel 1665–1668.* Edited by Franz Babinger. Leiden, 1937.

Jeske-Choinski, Teodor. *Neofici Polscy, Materjaly historyczne.* Warsaw, 1904.

Joel b. Shmuel Sirkis. Responsa *Bach (Beyt Hadash).* Frankfurt on the Main, 1697.

————. Responsa *Bach (Beyt Hadash) he-chadashot.* Korzec, 1795.

————. Responsa *Bach (Beyt Hadash) ha-yeshanoth*. Ostrog, 1834.

Kahane, Abraham. *R. Israel Baal Shem Tov*. Zhitomir, 1900.

Kaidanower, Zevi Hirsch. *Kav Hayashar*. Sulzbach, 1795; Lublin, 1912.

Katz, Ben-Zion. *Lekoroth ha-Yehudim ba-Rusia, Polin, ve-Lita*. Berlin, 1899.

Katz, Jacob. *Exclusiveness and Tolerance*. Oxford, 1961.

Kedushat Levi by Levi Itzhak of Berditcher. Slavuta, 1798.

Kellenbenz, Herman. *Sephardim an der Untern Elbe*. Wiesbaden, 1958.

Keter Kehunah by Ichaq Abraham b. Dov Berish. N. p., 1805.

Keter Shem Tov. Korzec, 1797; Lwów, 1865.

Kirdan, B.P. *Ukrainskii narodnyi epos*. Moscow, 1965.

Kisch, Guido. *The Jews in Medieval Germany*. Chicago, 1949.

Klausner, Israel. *Vilna batekufat hagaon*. Jerusalem, 1942.

Kolon, Joseph. *Responsa*. Warsaw, 1884.

Kraushar, Alexander. *Frank i Frankiści Polscy*. Vols. 1 and 2. Cracow, 1895.

Kutrzeba, Stanislaw. "Stanowisko prawne Żydów w Polsce w XV stuleciu." *Przewod-nik naukowy i literacki* 29, no. 7 (Lwów 1901).

Leibel, Israel. *Sepher Havikuach*. Warsaw, 1798.

Lewin, Isaac. "The Protection of Jewish Religious Rights by Royal Edicts in Ancient Poland." *The Quarterly Bulletin of the Polish Institute of Arts and Sciences in America* (April 1943).

Lewin, Louis. *Geschichte der Juden in Lissa*. Pinne, 1904.

————. *Die Landessynode der grosspolnischen Judenschaft*. Frankfurt on the Main, 1926.

Lipinski, Waclaw. *Z dziejów Ukrainy*. Kiev, 1912.

Luria, Solomon. *Responsa*. Fürth, 1718.

Maciejowski, Waclaw Alexander. *Żydzi w Polsce, na Rusi i Litwe*. Warsaw, 1878.

Mahler, Raphael. *Divrey yemei Yisrael; doroth achronim*. Vol. 1, book 3. Merchavia, Israel, 1955.

Maimon, Solomon. *Autobiography of Solomon Maimon*. London, 1954.

Mann, Jacob. *Texts and Studies in Jewish History and Literature*. Vol. 2. Philadelphia, 1935.

Margaliot, Meir. *Meir Netivim* 1. Polonnoe, 1795; Brooklyn, 1960.

Mark, Berl. *Di geschichte fun Yidn in Poilen*. Warsaw, 1957.

Mas'at Benyamin by Benjamin Slonik. Sudzilkow, 1833.

Megilat Eifa by Shabtai b. Meir Cohen. Reprinted in M. Wiener, *Das Buch Shevet Jehuda von R. Salomo Aben Verga*. Hanover, 1924.

Meir ben Baruch me-Rothenberg. *Responsa*. Prague, 1608.

Menachem Nachum of Czernobyl. *Maor Einayim*. Warsaw, 1889.

Mesch, Abraham J., trans. *Abyss of Despair* [Yeveyn metzulah by N. Hanover]. New York, 1950.

Meyer, Peter, Bernard D. Weinryb et al. *The Jews in the Soviet Satellites*. Syracuse, 1953.

Mintz, Moses. *Responsa*. Cracow, 1557; Prague, 1827; Lwów, 1851.

Morgensztern, Janina. "Regesty z metryki Koronnej do historii Żydów w Polsce." *Biuletyn*, no. 58 (1966); no. 67 (1968).

Nadav, M. "Kehillat Pinsk ba-tekufa she-mi-gezeroth Tach-Tat ad Shalom Andrusov (1648–1667)." *Zion* 31 (1966).

Noam Elimelech by Elimelekh of Lizhajsk (or Lizensk). Warsaw, 1901.

Olloth Ephraim by Efraim Luntshitz. Wilno, 1877.

Or Zarua, Responsa by Isaac b. Moses of Vienna. Vol. 2. Zhitomir, 1862.

Pazdro, Zhigniew. *Organizacja i praktyka Żydowskich Sądów podwojewodzinskich.* Lwów, 1903.

Peri ha-aretz by Menachem Mendel b. Moshe. Lemberg, 1862.

Perles, J. "Geschichte der Juden in Posen." *MGWJ* 13 (1864); 14 (1865).

Petach Teshuva by Gavriel b. Yehoshua (Shusberg). Amsterdam, 1651; Hayim Polack edition: Budapest-Cracow, 1903.

Pney Yehoshua, Responsa by Yehoshua b. Joseph. Amsterdam, 1715; Lemberg, 1860.

Pounds, Norman J.G. *Eastern Europe.* Chicago, 1969.

Ptaśnik, Jan. *Kultura wieków średnich.* Warsaw, 1959.

———. *Miasta i Mieszczaństwo w dawnej Polsce.* Warsaw, 1934, 1949.

Rabinovitsch, Wolf Zeev. *Lithuanian Hasidism.* New York, 1971.

Rabinowicz, Oskar K. "Jacob Frank in Brno." *The Seventy-fifth Anniversary Volume of the Jewish Quarterly Review.* Philadelphia, 1967.

Rabinowitz, L. *The Herem Hayishub: A Contribution to the Medieval Economic History of the Jews.* London, 1945.

Raphael, Ichaq. *Sepher ha-Hasidut.* Tel Aviv, 1955.

Rawita-Gawronski, F. *Żydzi w historii i literaturze ludowej na Rusi.* Warsaw, n.d.

Ringelblum, Emanuel. *Żydzi w powstaniu Kościuszkowskim.* Warsaw, n.d.

———. *Żydzi w Warszawie.* Warsaw, 1932.

Rosanes, S. *Divrei Yemei Yisrael ba-Togarmah.* Vols. 1–5. Tel Aviv, 1931–38.

Rosenthal, F. "Najstarsze osiedla Żydowskie na Śląsku." *Biuletyn*, no. 34 (1960).

Rowney, D.K. and J.Q. Graham, eds. *Quantitative History.* New York, 1969.

Rubinstein, Abraham. "Hakunteres Zimrat am haaretz biktav yad." *Areshet* 3 (Jerusalem, 1961).

Rutkowski, Jan. *Historia gospodarcza Polski.* Warsaw, 1953.

Samsonowicz, Henryk. "Badania nad dziejami miast w Polsce." *Kwartalnik Historyczny* 72, no. 1 (1965).

Sasportas, Yaakov. *Sheelot u-Teshuvot, Ohel Yaakov.* Amsterdam, 1737.

Schipper, Ignacy. *Dzieje handlu Żydowskiego na ziemiach Polskich.* Warsaw, 1937.

———. *Kulturgeschichte fun di Yidn in Poilin be-eisn Mitelalter.* Warsaw, 1926.

———. *Toledoth ha-Kalkalah ha-Yehudith.* Warsaw, 1935.

———. *Di wirtshaftsgeschichte fun di Yidn in Poilen beeisn Mittalter.* Warsaw, 1926. (Polish original: *Studia nad Stosunkami gospodarczymi Żydów w Polsce podczas średniowiecza.* Lwów, 1911.)

Scholem, Gershom. "Hatenua ha-Shabatait ba-Polin." In *Beyt Yisrael ba-Polin.* Edited by Israel Halperin. Vol. 2. Jerusalem, 1954.

———. *Major Trends in Jewish Mysticism.* New York, 1946, 1967.

———. "Mitzva habaah ba-aveira." *Knesset* 2, (Tel Aviv, 1937).

———. *Sabbatai Zevi va-Hatenua hashabtait bimei hayav.* Vols. 1 and 2, Tel Aviv, 1957.

Schorr, Moses. *Organizacja Żydów w Polsce.* Lwów, 1889.

———. *Rechtstellung und innere Verfassung d. Juden in Polen.* Berlin-Vienna, 1917.

———. "Zasadnicze prawa Żydóv w Polsce pszedrozbiorowej." *ZPO* 1 (Warsaw).

———. *Żydzi w Przemyślu do końca XVIII wieku.* Lwów, 1903.

Sepher Luck. Tel Aviv, 1961.

Serczyk, Wladyslaw A. *Koliszczyzna.* Cracow, 1968.

Shaar Hamelekh by Mordekhai b. Shmuel. Dyhernfurth, 1797.

Shazar (Rubashov), Zalman. *Al Tiley Beyt Frank.* Leipzig, 1923.

Shchepanski, Israel. *Eretz Yisrael basifrut hateshuvot.* Jerusalem, 1966.

Sheerit Joseph, Responsa by Josef b. Mordekhai Katz. Altdorf, 1760.

Shivchey Habesht. Edited by S.A. Horodetski. Berlin, 1922.

Shmeruk, C. "Hasippurim al R. Adam Baal Shem ve-gilgulahem ba-nuschaoth sepher 'Shivchey Habesht.'" *Zion* 28 (1963).

Shoshan Sodoth by Moses ben Jacob. Koretz, 1784.

Silnicki, Tadeusz. *Ustrój kościola Katolickiego na Śląsku do końca wieku XIV.* Warsaw, 1953.

Sternberg, H. *Geschichte der Juden in Polen unter den Piasten und den Jagiellonen.* Leipzig, 1878.

Taharot Hakodesh. Amsterdam, 1733.

Tishbi, Isaiah. *Netivey amuna u-minut.* Tel Aviv, 1964.

Tit ha-Yeveyn by Samuel Feivish b. Natan Feitel. Venice, 1650.

Trunk, Isaiah. *Geshichte fun Yidn in Plock.* Warsaw, 1939.

———. *Shtudies in yidisher Geshichte in Poilen.* Buenos Aires, 1963.

Uffenheimer, Rivka Schatz. *Hachasidut ka-mistika.* Jerusalem, 1968.

Weil, Jacob. *Responsa.* Hanau, 1680; Sudzilkow, 1835.

Weinryb, Bernard D. "East European Jewry since Polish Partitions." In *The Jews: Their History,* Edited by Louis Finkelstein. 4th ed. New York, 1970.

———. *Mechkarim ba-toledoth ha-kalkalah vaha-ḥevrah shel Yehudey Polin.* Jerusalem, 1939.

———. "The Myth of Samuel of Russia, 12th Century Author of a Bible Commentary." *The Seventy-fifth Anniversary Volume of the Jewish Quarterly Review.* 1967.

———. *Neueste Wirtschaftsgeschichte der Juden in Russland und Polen.* 2d ed. Hildesheim–New York, 1972.

———. "Private Letters in Yiddish of 1588." *HS* 2 (Wilno, 1938).

―――. *Texts and Studies in the Communal History of Polish Jewry.* New York, 1950.

―――. "Yehudey Polin michutz lapolin." *Beit Yisrael Ba-Polin.* Vol. 2. Jerusalem, 1954.

Weiss, J. "Reyshit zmiḥata shel haderekh Hahasidit." *Zion* 16 (1951).

Wettstein, F. *Mipinkasey Hakahal Bakrakau.* Vols. 1 and 2. Breslau, 1901.

Wilensky, Mordecai. *Hasidim u-Mitnagdim.* Vols. 1 and 2. Jerusalem, 1970.

―――. "The Polemic of Rabbi David of Makow against Hasidim." *PAAJR* 25 (1956).

Wojciechowski, Stefan. "Yidn in Lublin im sechzenten Jurhundert." *Bleter* 7, no. 1 (1954).

Wojciechowski, Zygmunt, ed. *Poland's Place in Europe.* Poznań, 1947.

Woodcock, George and Ivan Avakumovic. *The Doukhobors.* Toronto–New York, 1968.

Wurm, D. *Z dziejów Żydowstwa Brodzkiego za czasów dawnej rzeczypospolity.* Brody, 1935.

Yesh Nochlin by Abraham Halevi Hurevitz. Sadzilkov, 1835.

Ysander, Torsten. *Studien zum Bestschen Hasidismus.* Upsala, 1933.

Zaar bath rabim by Abraham b. Shmuel Ashkenazi. Edited by B. Friedberg. Lwów, 1905.

Zavaat Haribash, Lemberg, 1865.

Zeitschrift 1–5 (beginning with vol. 2, title changed to *Zeitschrift für Yidishe Geschichte, Demografie und Ekonomik*) (Minsk, 1926 et seq.).

Zemach Zedek, Responsa by Menachem Mendel b. Abraham. Krochmal, Amsterdam, 1675; Fürth, 1766; Wilno, 1874.

Zimmels, H.J. *Ashkenazim and Sephardim.* London, 1958.

―――. "Erez Israel in der Responsenliteratur des späten Mittelalters." *MGWJ* 74 (1930).

Zinberg, I. "Milchemet hakahal ba-harav ha-achron ba-Vilna." *Haavar* 2 (Petrograd, 1918).

Zofnath Paaneach by Jacob Joseph of Polonnoe. Korzec, 1782.

Index

Baltic Se̶

EAST PRUSSIA

LITH̶
Wilno R̶
Wil̶

Niemen River

Grodno

PRUSSIA

Danzig

GREAT POLAND

Vistula R.

Toruń

Plock

Tykocin

V. TYKOCIN

Brest Litovsk̶

Warta R. Gniezno

Leczyca

Warsaw

Wegrow

V. WEGROW

Poznań

Kalish

V. LUBLIN

Radom

Lublin

Kowe̶

Weisse R.

Oder R.

Chelm

Belz

Breslau

Opatow

Sandomierz

Żółk̶

SILESIA

Pinczów

Cracow

Rzeszów

Lw̶

LITTLE POLAND

Jaroslaw

(Lemb̶

Przemyśl

HAPSBURG EMPIRE

R̶

POLISH JEWRY
1667 – 1764
MAP ADAPTED FROM ISRAEL HALPERIN

KILOMETERS

0   100   200   300   400   500

LEGEND

V= VOIVODSHIP OR PROVINCE